Conventional Arms Control and East-West Security

Conventional Arms Control and East-West Security

Edited by Robert D. Blackwill and F. Stephen Larrabee

A research volume from the Institute for East-West Security Studies

Clarendon Press • Oxford

1989

Oxford University Press, Walton Street, Oxford OX2 6DP

Oxford New York Toronto
Delhi Bombay Calcutta Madras Karachi
Petaling Jaya Singapore Hong Kong Tokyo
Nairobi Dar es Salaam Cape Town
Melbourne Auckland

and associated companies in
Berlin Ibadan

Oxford is a trade mark of Oxford University Press

© 1989 Institute for East-West Security Studies

ISBN 0–19–827834–9

CONTENTS

LIST OF ACRONYMS

ABM	anti-ballistic missile
AFV	armored fighting vehicle
APC	armored personnel carrier
AS	aerial surveillance
ASM	air-to-surface missile
ASMP	long-range air-to-surface missile (French)
ASW	anti-submarine warfare
ATACMS	U.S. Army Tactical Missile System
ATBM	anti-tactical ballistic missile
ATGM	anti-tank guided missile
ATTU	Atlantic-to-the-Urals
AWACS	Airborne Warning and Command System
CDE	Conference on Disarmament in Europe
CDI	Conventional Defense Improvement
CDU	Christian Democratic Union (FRG)
CFE	Conventional Forces in Europe
CMEA	Council for Mutual Economic Assistance
CPSU	Communist Party of the Soviet Union
CSBM	confidence- and security-building measure
CSCE	Conference on Security and Cooperation in Europe
CSU	Christian Social Union
C^3I	command, control, communications and intelligence
CWC	chemical weapons convention
EC	European Community
ECM	electronic countermeasures
EEP	exit/entry post

EMS	European Monetary System
END	extended nuclear deterrence
EW	early warning
FBIS	Foreign Broadcast Information Service
FEBA	forward edge of the battle area
FOFA	Follow-on Forces Attack
FOTL	Follow-on-to-Lance
FRG	Federal Republic of Germany
GATT	General Agreement on Tariffs and Trade
GDP	gross domestic product
GDR	German Democratic Republic
GIUK gap	waters between Greenland, Iceland and the United Kingdom
GLCM	ground-launched cruise missile
GNP	gross national product
GOSPLAN	USSR State Planning Commission
IAEA	International Atomic Energy Agency
ICBM	intercontinental ballistic missile
IFV	infantry fighting vehicle
IGB	inter-German border
IMEMO	Institute of World Economy and International Relations (Moscow)
INF	intermediate-range nuclear forces
ISKAN	Institute of the USA and Canada (Moscow)
I&W	indications and warning
JSTARS	Joint Surveillance/Target Attack Radar Systems
LRSLBM	long-range sea-launched ballistic missile
LRTNF	long-range theater nuclear forces
MBFR	Mutual and Balanced Force Reductions
MBT	main battle tank
MLRS	Multiple Launch Rocket System
MRL	multiple rocket-launcher
NADE	NATO armored division equivalent
NATO	North Atlantic Treaty Organization
NGA	NATO Guidelines Area
NNA	neutral and nonaligned
NPA	National People's Army
NPT	Non-Proliferation Treaty
NTM	national technical means

NWFZ	nuclear-weapons-free zone
O&M	operating & maintenance
OECD	Organization for Economic Cooperation and Development
OSI	on-site inspection
PEEP	permanent entry/exit post
POL	petroleum, oils and lubricants
POMCUS	pre-positioned overseas material configured in unit sets
PRC	People's Republic of China
PVO	Air-Defense Forces (Soviet)
PUWP	Polish United Workers' Party
RMA	Restricted Military Area
SACEUR	Supreme Allied Commander Europe
SALT	Strategic Arms Limitations Talks
SAM	surface-to-air missile
SED	Socialist Unity Party (GDR)
SDI	Strategic Defense Initiative
SLBM	submarine-launched ballistic missile
SLCM	sea-launched cruise missile
SLOC	sea lines of communication
SPD	Social Democratic Party (FRG)
SRAM	short-range attack missile
SSM	surface-to-surface missile
START	Strategic Arms Reduction Talks
TEEP	temporary entry/exit post
TSA	tactical strike aviation
TVD	theater of military operations (Soviet)
V/STOL	Vertical/Short Takeoff Landing
WEI/WUV	weapons effectiveness indices/weighted unit values
WEU	Western European Union
WTO	Warsaw Treaty Organization

ABOUT THE AUTHORS

Oleg Amirov is a Senior Researcher in the Department on Problems of Disarmament in the Institute of World Economy and International Relations, Moscow. Dr. Amirov is the author of several articles and studies on the problems of disarmament and arms control.

Alexei Arbatov is the Head of the Department on Problems of Disarmament in the Institute of World Economy and International Relations, Moscow. Dr. Arbatov is the author of several books on international security, stability and disarmament, including *Lethal Frontiers: A Soviet View of Nuclear Arms Strategy, Programs and Negotiations* (Praeger, 1988).

Robert D. Blackwill, since completing the editorial process on this book, has become Special Assistant to the President and Senior Director for European and Soviet Affairs on the National Security Council staff. From 1985 to 1987 Ambassador Blackwill was the head of the U.S. delegation to the Mutual and Balanced Force Reduction talks. He has also served as Associate Dean and faculty member (1983–1985) and lecturer in public policy (1987–1989) at the John F. Kennedy School of Government at Harvard University.

Ian M. Cuthbertson is a Research Associate at the Institute for East-West Security Studies. He was previously at the Institute as a 1986–1987 Resident Fellow. From 1981 to 1987 Mr. Cuthbertson was a Senior Research Officer in the Arms Control and Disarmament Research Unit of the Foreign and Commonwealth Office in London.

Richard E. Darilek is the Director of the Policy and Strategy Program of the Arroyo Center/Army Research Division at the RAND Corporation in

Santa Monica. Dr. Darilek has also served as Associate Head of the Behavioral Sciences Department at RAND (1983–1985). From 1979 to 1981 he served as the Director of the U.S. Defense Department Task Force on Mutual and Balanced Force Reductions and as a Special Assistant in the Office of the Under Secretary of Defense for Policy.

Jonathan Dean is the Arms Control Advisor to the Union of Concerned Scientists. From 1949 to 1984, Ambassador Dean served with the U.S. State Department. He was the head of the U.S. delegation to the Mutual and Balanced Force Reductions talks between 1978 and 1981, having previously served as deputy head of the U.S. delegation since the inception of the talks in 1973. From 1968 to 1971 Ambassador Dean was Deputy U.S. Negotiator for the 1971 Four Power Berlin Agreement.

François Heisbourg is the Director of the International Institute for Strategic Studies in London. Previously he was Vice President of Thomson International in charge of cooperative ventures with European and U.S. defense industries between 1984 and 1987. From 1981 to 1984 Mr. Heisbourg served as the International Security Adviser to the French Minister of Defense; from 1979 to 1981 he was the First Secretary at the French Mission to the United Nations in charge of international security issues and outer space affairs; and from 1978 to 1979 he was a member of the Policy Planning Staff of the French Foreign Ministry.

Arnold Kanter, since writing this essay, has become Senior Director for Arms Control and Defense Policy on the National Security Council staff. Previously Dr. Kanter was a Senior Research Associate at the RAND Corporation, where he also served as Director of the National Security Strategies Program and as Associate Director of the International Security and Defense Program. From 1977 to 1985 Dr. Kanter served in the U.S. State Department, holding the posts of Deputy Assistant Secretary of State for Politico-Military Affairs, Deputy to the Under Secretary of State for Political Affairs and Director of the Office of Policy Analysis in the Bureau of Politico-Military Affairs.

Andrzej Karkoszka is a 1988–1989 Krupp Foundation Senior Associate at the Institute for East-West Security Studies. Since 1969 Dr. Karkoszka has been a Research Fellow at the Polish Institute of International Affairs specializing in conventional weapons, chemical and biological weapons, verification and the military balance. Dr. Karkoszka was also a 1986–1987 Resident Fellow at the Institute for East-West Security Studies.

Nikolai Kishilov is a Head of Section in the Department on Problems of Disarmament in the Institute of World Economy and International Relations, Moscow. Dr. Kishilov took part in the U.S.-Soviet strategic arms reduction negotiations and served as the general secretary of the Soviet delegation to the SALT I negotiations.

Andrei A. Kokoshin is Deputy Director of the Institute of the USA and Canada, Moscow. A specialist in conventional forces and arms control, Dr. Kokoshin has been with the Institute for the Study of the USA and Canada since 1969, and has previously served as a scientific secretary there.

Alexander A. Konovalov is the Head of Section on General Purpose Forces and Conventional Arms at the Institute of the USA and Canada, Moscow. Dr. Konovalov is also an expert member of the Soviet Committee For Peace, Against the Nuclear Threat.

Richard L. Kugler is Associate Head of the Political Science Department at the RAND Corporation, Santa Monica, specializing in NATO military issues and U.S. defense planning. From 1984 to 1988 he was the Director of the Strategic Concepts Development Center of the National Defense University. Dr. Kugler also served from 1980 to 1984 as the Director of the NATO/European Forces Division of Program Analysis and Evaluation in the Office of the Secretary of Defense, where he was a Senior Analyst from 1975 to 1980.

László Lábody is a staff member in the Department of Foreign Affairs of the Central Committee of the Hungarian Socialist Workers' Party. He is the author of a number of publications on East-West relations, Hungarian foreign policy and security issues.

Peer H. Lange is a 1988–1989 Krupp Foundation Senior Associate at the Institute for East-West Security Studies. Since 1971 Dr. Lange has been a Research Associate at the Foundation for Science and Policy in Ebenhausen, FRG. Dr. Lange has published extensively on Soviet foreign policy and Soviet military power and doctrine.

F. Stephen Larrabee is Vice President and Director of Studies at the Institute for East-West Security Studies. From 1978 to 1981 Dr. Larrabee served on the staff of the National Security Council. He has also served as Co-Director of the Soviet and East European Research Program of the

Johns Hopkins School of Advanced International Studies and as a Visiting Professor in the Department of Government at Cornell University.

Manfred Mueller is the Head of the International Relations Department of the Institute for International Relations in the GDR Academy for Political Science. Dr. Mueller is a member of the Advisory Board on Disarmament Matters of the UN Secretary General.

David A. Ochmanek is a Defense Analyst with the RAND Corporation in Washington, DC, specializing in arms control, strategic forces and tactical air forces. Prior to joining RAND he was a foreign service officer, serving as a political-military policy analyst at the Department of State. Mr. Ochmanek has also served as an intelligence officer in the U.S. Air Force.

Adam-Daniel Rotfeld is Head of the European Security Department of the Polish Institute of International Affairs. He has also served as the Deputy Head of the Polish delegation to the CSCE follow-up meeting in Vienna (1986–1988); as a member of the Polish delegation to the CSCE meeting in Geneva (1973–1975) and the CSCE follow-up meetings in Belgrade (1977–1978) and Madrid (1980–1983); and as a member of the Board of Public Advisors to the Polish Minister of Foreign Affairs. Dr. Rotfeld was also a 1984–1985 Resident Fellow at the Institute for East-West Security Studies.

John K. Setear is a Policy Analyst at the RAND Corporation, Santa Monica, specializing in conventional forces in Central and Eastern Europe.

K.-Peter Stratmann has been a Staff Associate in the Research Institute for International Affairs of the Foundation for Science and Policy in Ebenhausen, FRG, since 1967. He specializes in military options for NATO and the Warsaw Pact in Central Europe.

Janusz Symonides is the 1987–1989 Distinguished Scholar-in-Residence at the Institute for East-West Security Studies. From 1980 to 1987 Dr. Symonides served as Director of the Polish Institute of International Affairs. A specialist on disarmament, international relations and security, he also served from 1985 to 1987 as a member of the Board of Directors of the Institute for East-West Security Studies.

Alexei A. Vasiliev is the Head of the Military-Political Department of the Institute of the USA and Canada, Moscow. He also serves as a special advisor to the talks on Conventional Forces in Europe held in Vienna.

Edward L. Warner III is a Senior Defense Analyst at the RAND Corporation in Washington, DC, where he conducts studies on Soviet defense and foreign policy, arms control and U.S. military policy. Dr. Warner is also an adjunct professor at Columbia University's W. Averell Harriman Institute for Advanced Study of the Soviet Union and at George Washington University.

Timothy E. Wirth is a United States Senator (Democrat) representing Colorado. Senator Wirth serves on the Subcommittee for Conventional Forces and Alliance Defense of the Senate Armed Services Committee and on the Commission on Security and Cooperation in Europe. From 1975 to 1987 he was a U.S. Representative from Colorado.

FOREWORD

With the signing of the 1987 INF Treaty and important progress being made in the Strategic Arms Reduction Talks to reduce American and Soviet nuclear arsenals, conventional arms control has risen to the top of the East-West policy agenda. The talks on Conventional Forces in Europe (CFE), which opened in Vienna in March 1989, have broadened the scope of their predecessor, the Mutual and Balanced Force Reduction (MBFR) talks, to encompass an expanded geographical region covering all of Europe from the Atlantic to the Urals. Soviet General Secretary Gorbachev's December 1988 proposal for unilateral reductions of Soviet forces and the positions taken by the two sides in the opening round of the CFE carry the hope that the two alliances can create greater stability in Europe at significantly lower levels of armaments.

This volume, which analyzes ten key issues concerning conventional arms control, represents a significant and timely contribution to the East-West debate. The distinctive character of the volume lies not only in the quality of the individual contributions but in its East-West nature. The volume is a true "joint venture" on conventional arms reduction—the first of its kind. Soviet, American and European specialists have participated in an intensive process to produce this volume in a very short period of time. The political climate appears propitious for progress in the CFE negotiations and it is our hope that this book will make a positive and practical contribution toward that end.

The volume is part of a larger effort at the Institute for East-West Security Studies devoted to examining the prospects for conventional arms control. This effort includes the Institute's Task Force Working Group on Conventional Arms Reduction and Stability chaired by Professor

Karl Kaiser, Director of the Research Institute of the German Society for Foreign Policy in Bonn. This group brings together high-ranking government officials, military officers and civilian experts from NATO and Warsaw Pact countries to discuss critical issues related to conventional arms control. The Working Group's first meeting, held in Budapest in August 1988 and co-sponsored by the Hungarian Institute of International Relations, attracted wide attention and made an important contribution to clarifying many of the conceptual issues currently under discussion in Vienna. In addition, half of the members of the Institute's 1988–1989 Resident Fellows team are engaged in research on various aspects of conventional arms control, and several of them, including Janusz Symonides and Andrzej Karkoszka of the Polish Institute of International Affairs and Peer H. Lange of the Foundation for Science and Policy, Ebenhausen, have contributed pieces to this volume.

The unusual interactive process involved in shaping and assembling this book has made it a particularly useful guide to the key issues at this stage in the conventional arms control process as seen by both East and West. A direct exchange among the contributors was made possible at an authors' review conference in Moscow hosted by the Soviet Committee on European Security and Cooperation. The timing of the Moscow meeting was propitious—one day after General Secretary Gorbachev's announcement of unilateral cuts in Soviet conventional forces—allowing the authors an opportunity to reassess the outlook for conventional arms control in Europe in light of the new proposals. But more important, the authors' review conference offered the chance for frank debate among leading experts and a valuable opportunity for both Eastern and Western specialists to increase their understanding of the thinking, approaches and concerns of the their counterparts in the other alliance.

Because of the topicality of conventional arms control, every effort was made to publish this volume expeditiously. Many people and organizations helped to make this book possible. We would like to thank in particular the Carnegie Corporation of New York and the Ford Foundation for their generous financial support. The dedication of the authors, editors and the Institute's staff ensured the quality and timeliness of the volume. F. Stephen Larrabee, the Institute's Vice President and Director of Studies, and Robert D. Blackwill, Special Assistant to the President and Senior Director for European and Soviet Affairs on the National Security Council staff and formerly a faculty member of the John F. Kennedy School of Government at Harvard University, did an excellent job of guiding the authors in their writing as well as pulling together the many strands of the subject in their introduction and providing valuable insight for the future in their concluding chapter. I would especially like to thank Yevgeni Silin, Head of the Soviet Committee for European Security and Cooperation, which hosted the authors' review conference in Moscow, for the warm and gracious hospitality he and his colleagues extended to our contributors. Special appreciation is paid to Peter B. Kaufman, Director of Publications at the Institute, who managed the book's production process smoothly, despite the intense pressure of time and longer-standing publication commitments. He and Institute Publications Editor Mary Albon spent many long hours editing and revising the manuscript to ready it for publication. Institute Research Analyst Kent D. Lee assisted in the editing process and translated many of the Soviet contributions. Deputy Director of Studies Allen Lynch assisted in the translation. Institute Research Associate Ian Cuthbertson and Richard Haass, a lecturer at the John F. Kennedy School of Government and currently a member of the National Security Council staff, contributed many helpful comments on various parts of the manuscript. Amy Lew, Jennifer Lee, Elizabeth Cristancho, Lydia Herbert and Jan Zamoyta worked overtime on many occasions to process the manuscript through its seemingly endless revisions.

The Institute for East-West Security Studies is pleased to sponsor this publication. We believe that it will be widely read in East and West and will constitute an important milestone for future cooperative undertakings in the security field. The extent of change in East-West relations over the last three years is readily apparent from the quality of analysis, the seriousness and the low level of polemics found in these chapters. This volume is a significant contribution to the debate on conventional arms control and the future of East-West relations.

John Edwin Mroz
President
March 1989

EDITORS' PREFACE

After years of being overshadowed by nuclear arms control, conventional arms control has moved to the forefront of the East-West agenda. Both Soviet leader Mikhail Gorbachev and U.S. President George Bush are giving it high priority. The talks on Conventional Forces in Europe (CFE), which opened in Vienna on March 9, 1989, also ensure that the issue will receive high-level policy attention. This book therefore appears at a propitious moment. Its purpose is to clarify the key conceptual issues of the Vienna talks at an early stage of the negotiations.

The volume began when the two co-editors met over coffee in New York in the late spring of 1988. Both felt the need for a book that addressed the critical issues of conventional arms control in a dispassionate and objective manner. We also agreed that one of the prime values of the book would be its East-West nature. The initial ideas for the volume were developed in greater detail during several further meetings at conferences of the Institute for East-West Security Studies in Potsdam and Budapest over the course of the summer. We decided to address ten important topics of debate at the CFE, and invited leading experts from Eastern and Western Europe, the Soviet Union and the United States to contribute their views. Chapters were commissioned at the start of September, with first drafts due in early November.

The chapters were subjected to a detailed critical review at an authors' review conference held in Moscow, December 8–11, 1988. The Moscow meeting was an extremely important aspect of the whole project. It not only gave the authors a greater sense of group cohesion, but also sensitized each side to the other's positions. While there were many issues of disagreement, the discussions were remarkably frank and free of polemics—a tribute on the Soviet side to the new spirit of *glasnost'* under Gorbachev—and most authors left Moscow with the feeling that they had gained important insights into the thinking and approach of their colleagues on the other side.

During the discussions in Moscow, each chapter was reviewed in light of Gorbachev's December 7, 1988, UN initiative announcing a unilateral withdrawal of Soviet troops and arms from Eastern Europe. We asked authors to revise their chapters with the initiative in mind. We also sought to ensure as much parallelism in each chapter as possible without infringing upon each author's freedom to focus on the issues he felt most important.

In editing the volume we have tried to be as evenhanded as possible, reserving our own views for the concluding chapter. Where differences between authors exist, we have encouraged the authors not to blur them but to sharpen them. The structure of the book is intended to highlight these differences: Part 1 of each chapter is a Western contribution, Part 2 is an Eastern contribution on the same topic.

As the editing process was being completed one of the co-editors, Robert D. Blackwill, joined the National Security Council staff as Special Assistant to the President and Senior Director of European and Soviet Affairs. The views expressed here are his own and should not be interpreted as reflecting those of the U.S. government or any of its agencies.

Robert D. Blackwill
F. Stephen Larrabee

INTRODUCTION

Robert D. Blackwill and F. Stephen Larrabee

For many years conventional arms control was regarded with indifference within the scholarly and diplomatic community. The negotiations on Mutual and Balanced Force Reductions (MBFR), which began in 1973, droned on for nearly 16 years without any visible result. For most of that period the talks were largely a sideshow. High-level policy attention was focused on other issues, particularly nuclear arms control.

The lack of results in MBFR largely reflected the fact that neither superpower accorded conventional arms control a high priority. The U.S. government and its West European allies initially saw the MBFR negotiations primarily as a way to stave off congressional pressure for unilateral troop withdrawals from Europe (the Mansfield Amendment). Once the pressure for unilateral withdrawals subsided, active Western interest in MBFR plummeted. The talks soon became bogged down in a dispute over "data"—i.e., the number of troops on each side—and remained deadlocked for the next decade.[1]

Western indifference to conventional arms control was matched by Soviet disinterest. Like that of the U.S., the main Soviet preoccupation at this time was nuclear arms control. Moreover, in the late 1960s the Soviet Union embarked upon a major buildup and modernization of its conventional forces, and thus had little incentive to consider serious conventional reductions. In addition, the Brezhnev leadership, shaken by the trauma of the Prague Spring in 1968, feared that any major troop withdrawals might accentuate political instability within the bloc.

This period of benign neglect, however, is clearly over. Over the last year or two conventional arms control has emerged as a major focal point of attention in think tanks and government circles. Indeed, hardly a month goes by without a new proposal being put forward by a major political leader or an analyst in one of the top research institutes in East or West.

In the East, Soviet leader Mikhail Gorbachev has led the way with a series of far-reaching proposals, the most significant of which was the offer he made at the UN on December 7, 1988, to unilaterally pull six Soviet divisions and 5,000 tanks out of Eastern Europe and reduce the overall size of Soviet forces by 500,000 troops by 1991. Polish leader Wojciech Jaruzelski,[2] East German leader Erich Honecker and Czechoslovak leader Milos Jakes have also launched their own conventional arms control initiatives.

The West has also begun to focus greater attention on conventional arms control. In its meeting at Halifax in June 1986[3] NATO called for "bold new ideas" in the conventional area, and the High-Level Group within NATO is currently at work on a "comprehensive concept" for arms control, which will deal in large part with conventional arms. In addition, President Bush has said he intends to give the issue high priority. Several U.S. Congressmen, most notably Senator Sam Nunn (D-Georgia) and Representative Les Aspin (D-Wisconsin), have also put forward their own proposals for conventional reductions.[4]

The Changing East-West Context

At the same time changes in the East-West political context have enhanced the interest of both sides in lowering the level of military confrontation in Europe.

The Reykjavik summit and the INF Treaty—especially the latter—have played a critical role in this process. On the one hand, the INF Treaty raised fears of "denuclearization" within parts of Western Europe. On the other, it made Eastern advantages at the conventional level all the more glaring and militarily significant in the eyes of many Western—especially West European—leaders.

Another key factor has been the new approach adopted by Soviet leader Mikhail Gorbachev. In contrast to his predecessors, Gorbachev has been willing to address Western concerns more forthrightly. Among the most important indications of this new, more flexible approach have been Gorbachev's willingness to extend the negotiating zone to include Soviet territory up to the Urals;[5] his acknowledgement of conventional asymmetries and his expressed commitment to eliminating them; his radically more flexible position toward verification, particularly on-site inspection; and a more forthcoming attitude toward the release of data on the composition of Warsaw Pact forces.

Gorbachev has also announced publicly a shift in Soviet military doctrine toward a greater emphasis on defense. Soviet military doctrine is now said to be solely "defensive" and oriented toward the prevention rather than the conduct of war (see Andrei Kokoshin's contribution in this volume). And according to Soviet officials, the Soviet armed forces are now being trained to fight defensively in the initial period of any conflict.[6] Soviet civilian analysts, some of them with apparent high-level political support, have also begun to examine ways to reduce the potential for conventional conflict by restructuring the forces of both sides in a defensive manner.[7]

Moreover, this public commitment to a defensive doctrine has now been officially adopted by the Warsaw Treaty Organization as a whole. The communiqué issued at the end of the meeting of the Political Consultative Committee in East Berlin in May 1987 explicitly asserted that the military doctrine of the WTO is purely defensive.[8] It also stated that the goals of the Vienna negotiations on Conventional Forces in Europe (CFE) should be guided by the principle of "reasonable sufficiency" and designed to eliminate the capability for surprise attack and large-scale offensive action. Finally, in it the WTO offered to open a dialogue on military doctrine with the West.

Many of these moves remain largely declaratory and it will be some time until their true significance can be judged. However, Gorbachev's speech to the UN General Assembly in December 1988 strongly suggests that the Soviet leader is indeed serious. In his speech Gorbachev promised to unilaterally

–withdraw 50,000 Soviet troops and 5,000 Soviet tanks from Hungary, Czechoslovakia and the GDR;
–reduce the Soviet armed forces by 500,000 men by 1990;
–withdraw from Eastern Europe assault-landing troops and other offensively oriented accessories such as bridge-crossing equipment;
–cut Soviet forces in the Atlantic-to-the-Urals area by 10,000 tanks, 8,500 artillery systems and 800 combat aircraft; and
–restructure Soviet forces in Eastern Europe along "clearly defensive" lines.

While the initiative still leaves the Soviet Union with substantial advantages in key conventional areas, it will significantly undercut the Soviet capability to launch a short-warning attack—a long-standing Western concern.

The withdrawal of 5,000 tanks from Eastern Europe is particularly important. This is nearly half of the Soviet tanks in Eastern Europe. To be sure, many uncertainties still remain—for instance, whether the cuts will come entirely from combat units and whether these tanks will be destroyed. Nevertheless, the Gorbachev initiative will increase the pres·sure on Western governments to come up with a more substantial proposal of their own as well as complicate any effort to modernize NATO's short-range Lance missile.

At the same time, the Gorbachev initiative highlights the importance of a detailed exchange of data, discussed by Jonathan Dean and Andrzej Karkoszka in their chapter on verification. Unless NATO has a detailed layout of Soviet forces before the unilateral reductions begin and a subsequent presentation two years later of updated data covering the situation after the completion of reductions, it will have difficulty monitoring the withdrawals and be faced with a confusing turbulence in its own picture of Soviet forces. Neither the aggregate figures put forward by NATO nor the figures presented by the WTO in January 1989 are sufficient in this regard.

Economic considerations, moreover, seem likely to give both sides an added incentive to reduce and restructure their conventional forces in the future. This is particularly true in the Soviet case. Gorbachev will face increasing economic pressures if he is to carry out his program of *perestroika*. If he wants to save money and divert scarce resources from the military to the civilian sector, it is in the conventional area that he can best do it, since nuclear weapons make up a much smaller portion of the defense budget than conventional forces. Indeed, the unilateral withdrawals announced by Gorbachev at the UN in December 1988 appear in part to have been motivated by economic considerations.

Technological developments may provide an additional incentive for Moscow to consider conventional reductions. Western advances in high-tech conventional weapons, especially precision-guided missiles, may eventually erode some of the current Soviet advantages in manpower and equipment.[9] As Alexander Konovalov's contribution to this volume makes clear, the ability of these weapons to strike deep into the WTO rear is a major Soviet concern. Finally, demographic factors may create incentives for reductions. Due to the declining birth rate among the

Russian, Ukrainian and Baltic populations, the Soviets may find it increasingly difficult to maintain the current 5.7 million men under arms, especially at a time when qualitative changes in weaponry require highly skilled and better educated manpower to operate them.

Economic pressures are also likely to increase the interest of Moscow's East European allies in conventional arms control. All the East European members of the WTO face major economic problems, and, like the Soviet Union, they indicate that they would like to reduce the size of their armed forces and transfer resources from the military to the civilian sector. The first tentative steps in this direction have already begun. At the end of 1988 Hungary announced a 17-percent cut in defense spending for the coming year. Poland also announced a shift in resources from the military to the civilian sphere and plans to make major cuts in its military personnel. In January 1989, Bulgaria, Czechoslovakia and the GDR announced they would make similar reductions in manpower and tanks.

Some of these same pressures may provide the West with incentives for reductions as well. As François Heisbourg points out in the opening essay of this volume, the need to address the U.S. budget deficit and trade imbalance will put strong pressure on President Bush to make cuts in the defense budget. As a result, congressional pressure to reduce U.S. forces in Europe could grow. Some leading former U.S. officials such as Zbigniew Brzezinski have called for withdrawals of up to 100,000 men.[10] These financial and political pressures could increase the administration's interest in conventional arms reductions.

The West European governments also have a strong economic interest in reductions. Despite their desire to raise the nuclear threshold, few seem willing to spend the money to strengthen conventional forces. With the exception of Greece and Turkey, none have been able to meet the commitment to increase defense spending by 3 percent per year which was put forward as a goal for NATO's Long Term Defense Program.

Demographic pressures are likely to reinforce economic incentives. Nowhere is this more true than in the Federal Republic of Germany. As a result of the decline in the West German birthrate, Bonn will have a hard time manning the Bundeswehr at its current levels. This is likely to increase the FRG's already strong political interest in reducing conventional forces.

Finally, there are also strong political incentives. Many Western governments feel that the West should respond more positively to Gorbachev's initiatives, particularly those in the military area. At the same time public opinion in many Western countries, especially West Germany, no longer perceives the Soviet Union as a major military threat. If Gorbachev's policy of *perestroika* continues along current lines, public pressure for tangible progress in conventional arms control is likely to grow.

At the same time achieving a Western consensus on the nature and scope of any future reductions will not be easy. As Ian Cuthbertson's essay in this volume points out, the perspectives of the various NATO governments differ on a number of key issues, including the nature and utility of the talks themselves. France, for instance, has strong reservations about the usefulness of conventional reductions, fearing that they could be destabilizing and accelerate American disengagement from Europe. The U.K. shares many of these concerns, although London has been less vocal in expressing them.

The Conventional Force Negotiations: Issues and Dilemmas

It is against this background that the current talks on Conventional Forces in Europe, which opened in Vienna on March 9, 1989, should be viewed. These talks will supercede the MBFR negotiations and are designed to achieve greater stability at lower levels of forces. Unlike the MBFR talks, however, they will focus on reductions and constraints on equipment rather than manpower. Moreover, the negotiating zone has been expanded to include all territory "from the Atlantic to the Urals" (ATTU). Finally, France, which refused to participate in MBFR, has agreed to take part in the new CFE talks.

The CFE negotiations will be parallelled by a continuation of the 35-member Stockholm talks on confidence-building measures, officially termed the Conference on Confidence- and Security-Building Measures and Disarmament in Europe (CDE). CDE II will continue to focus on confidence-building measures. In contrast to CFE, however, CDE II will include the neutral and nonaligned (NNA) countries as well as the 23 members of NATO and the WTO.

There is a broad consensus on both sides regarding the general objectives and principles that should guide the CFE negotiations. Both sides have declared their desire to achieve stability at a lower level of weapons. They also agree that the negotiations should be aimed at eliminating the capacity for launching a surprise attack and conducting large-scale offensive operations. Finally, they agree that the talks should eliminate current asymmetries and imbalances in force structures.

The Soviet proposal presented at the opening of the CFE talks in Vienna, moreover, contains a number of points of agreement or near-agreement with the NATO approach made public in December 1988. The Soviet plan, like the Western one, calls for an elimination of asymmetries as part of a first phase of reductions over two or three years. In ground equipment such as main battle tanks, where the Soviet Union has a substantial advantage, Moscow would eliminate tens of thousands more tanks than NATO. The Soviet plan also calls for equal ceilings that would be 10–15 percent lower than the lowest level currently possessed by either alliance; NATO's plan calls for equal ceilings 5–10 percent below current Western levels. Finally, both proposals call for extensive verification measures including on-site inspection.

However, while East and West agree on a number of broad objectives, they still remain far apart on many substantive issues. Among the most important are:

–*The nature of the conventional balance*. The East argues that there is approximate parity, whereas the West says that the East has superiority in most militarily significant categories.

–*Which weapons to reduce*. The West wants to focus on forward-deployed armor—main battle tanks, artillery and armored personnel carriers—while the East argues that aircraft should be included and naval forces taken into account.

–*How to treat combat aircraft*. The WTO insists that these aircraft must be included in the negotiations and reduced. NATO, however, has been reluctant to see its fighter-bomber force reduced, given the increased importance of nuclear-capable aircraft in the wake of the INF Treaty. The problem is complicated, moreover, by serious definitional problems and by the fact that aircraft withdrawn from the reductions zone can easily return.

–*Data exchange*. The East has proposed an exchange of data on troop and equipment levels. Although the West had argued for such an exchange for years, its reaction to the Soviet proposal has been hesitant, in part because of intra-alliance divergences and in part because it fears a repeat of the MBFR experience, where differences over data deadlocked the talks for years. The preliminary release of data on force levels by each side, moreover, revealed wide discrepancies in many areas, partly because of different counting rules.

–*How deep the cuts should be*. NATO wants deep cuts in Soviet forward-deployed armor, which it sees as the most important threat. However, deep cuts in NATO's own forces, many Western analysts argue, would render its strategy of forward defense impossible.[11]

–*Verification*. Both sides agree that verification is important. But verifying an agreement will be much more complex than in previous, nuclear agreements and will require intensive, intrusive on-site inspections as well as an agreed data base.

–*Short-range nuclear weapons*. The East wants parallel negotiations on these systems. The West, however, is divided: France, Britain and the United States argue that these systems should be treated in separate negotiations after an agreement on conventional weapons has been achieved, whereas West Germany favors parallel negotiations.

The difficulties of obtaining an agreement are further complicated by the lack of consensus within NATO on many of these issues. France, for instance, views the conventional balance as relatively stable and sees little need for rushing forward in the negotiations. In contrast, for reasons related to *Deutschland-* and *Ostpolitik*, the Federal Republic would like to see rapid progress. A number of countries, such as France and Turkey, also are opposed to a large-scale disaggregation of data. Finally, there are differences between flank countries like Norway and Turkey, which are interested in constraining Soviet amphibious forces, and the countries located in Central Europe, which are primarily concerned about the problem of land-invasion capability posed by WTO forward-deployed armor.

The Political Dimension

These military-technical questions are reinforced by larger political issues. The current disposition of forces in Europe both reflects and reinforces the current political division of Europe. Any major alteration of the size and disposition of these forces could have a significant impact on the postwar political order in Europe.[12] A radical reduction of U.S. and Soviet forces, for instance, could revive the German question. Thus the Vienna talks raise in submerged form the issue of the future of Europe. What kind of Europe do the various sides want? And can it be achieved without unleashing destabilizing forces that might prove difficult to control?

At present neither side seems ready to face this dilemma squarely. Yet the long-term result of any agreement could be a fundamental alteration of the postwar status quo. This is all the more true, as François Heisbourg points out in his opening essay, because of the dynamic and potentially destabilizing impact of Gorbachev's policy of *perestroika*, the outcome of which is highly uncertain. Hence military objectives in the Vienna talks must be reconciled with the long-term political objectives —a topic addressed in particular by Ian Cuthbertson and László Lábody in their chapter.

The Need for Conceptual Clarity

The foregoing discussion highlights the complexity and importance of the issues being negotiated in Vienna. As East and West enter what promise to be protracted negotiations on these issues, there is a need for greater conceptual clarity about the issues and greater understanding of their military and political implications. It was with this goal in mind that the present volume, in which both Eastern and Western views on the same topic are represented, was conceived.

The book is divided into ten chapters which address the key issues to be discussed in the CFE talks. In each chapter, two specialists—one from the West (in Part 1) and one from the East (in Part 2)—analyze one topic. The intention is to identify and highlight the differing points of view of each side. Where do the sides agree? Where do they disagree? What is the nature of their disagreement? How, if at all, could their views be reconciled?

In the first chapter, François Heisbourg, Director of the International Institute of Strategic Studies in London, and Janusz Symonides, former Director of the Polish Institute of International Affairs and now Distinguished Scholar-in-Residence at the Institute for East-West Security Studies in New York, examine the changing context of European security and the economic, political and military factors that are likely to affect the general security environment in which the negotiations on conventional arms control will take place. It is, after all, these larger political and economic issues that will influence arms control choices in the future.

In his essay, Heisbourg suggests that the question of change must be viewed on two levels: the military-strategic and the economic and social. On the military-strategic level, he argues, the postwar European system exhibits a great deal of stability and continuity. However, if one takes into account forces of economic and social change, especially within the Eastern bloc, there is, Heisbourg maintains, a "significant degree of geopolitical fragility with a potential for evolution unprecedented since the emergence of the postwar order in Europe."

Looking ahead, Heisbourg predicts a growing debate over "burden-sharing" within NATO. However, he argues that NATO should be able to manage the issue, provided the United States does not fall prey to perceptions of decline. In addition, he argues that nuclear deterrence will remain an important and necessary component of stability, albeit at reduced levels. Indeed, it is precisely the existence of nuclear deterrence, in Heisbourg's view, that has alleviated the potentially destabilizing consequences of conventional asymmetries.

Looking at the Eastern alliance, however, Heisbourg sees the potential for significant change as a result in particular of the impact of Gorbachev's policy of *perestroika*. While he acknowledges that recent developments in the East are historic in scope, their outcome, he argues, is highly uncertain. Hence statesmen, Heisbourg warns, should be careful not to lock themselves into diplomatic options prematurely.

In his companion essay Janusz Symonides argues that the most important source of change at work today in Europe is the improvement in U.S.-Soviet relations and the signing of the INF agreement. These developments, he suggests, have changed the context in which the negotiations on conventional arms control will take place and increased their prospects for success. Indeed, Symonides believes that, for the first time in postwar history, Europe is confronted with a real chance to enhance military detente. This results, in his view, from the fact that the current European agenda is broad enough to address not only the central problem—reduction of conventional forces—but at the same time to deal with the psychological dimension of military confrontation through negotiations on confidence-building measures and discussions on the evolution of military doctrines.

In Chapter 2, Richard Kugler, a former Pentagon analyst and now a senior staff member of the RAND Corporation, and three senior researchers at the Institute of World Economy and International Relations (IMEMO) in Moscow, Alexei Arbatov, Nikolai Kishilov and Oleg Amirov, examine one of the key issues dividing East and West in the CFE talks in Vienna—the conventional balance in Europe. The two pieces neatly summarize the essence of these differences. Kugler emphasizes force-to-space ratios, particularly the advantages that would accrue to the Warsaw Pact in a conflict due to its numerical superiority in key categories, such as tanks and armored vehicles, and its more rapid mobilization capability. The unilateral troop withdrawals announced by Gorbachev at the UN in December 1988, he asserts, would reduce the threat of a short-warning surprise attack. However, the cuts would not significantly constrain the WTO's capability to carry out a large-scale invasion through a buildup over weeks. Moreover, Kugler warns that some quantitative reductions could be offset by qualitative improvements and restructuring.

In their essay Arbatov, Kishilov and Amirov, while acknowledging that asymmetries exist, argue that the problem is not the specific number of forces on each side but the counting method. In addition, whereas Kugler emphasizes the importance of ground forces in any conflict, Arbatov, Kishilov and Amirov underscore the importance of tactical aircraft and air superiority, especially in the initial period of conflict—a point Arbatov addresses more fully in Chapter 6. Also interesting for the Western reader is their discussion of the impact of technological change on the nature of war. They argue that technological change has increased the unpredictability and intensity of conventional combat as well as the unprecedented scale of destruction likely to occur.

Chapter 3 focuses on the political objectives of arms control. Ian Cuthbertson, Research Associate at the Institute for East-West Security Studies, highlights the problem of defining long-term objectives within the Western alliance because of varying national perspectives and the differing nature of the two alliances touched upon earlier. These divergent viewpoints severely complicate the negotiating process and will make it difficult to achieve consensus on an evolving common negotiating strategy. Although these problems are by no means as great within the East, differing national priorities, as Cuthbertson notes, are beginning to emerge within the Eastern alliance as well. This fact is well illustrated by the companion piece by László Lábody, a staff member of the Hungarian Socialist Workers' Party. Lábody stresses the *political* nature of the arms control process and argues forcefully that political considerations should take precedence over military factors. He raises the basic question at the very heart of the negotiations: what type of Europe do we ultimately want and how can conventional arms control contribute to achieving this goal? Particularly interesting in light of Gorbachev's UN initiative is Lábody's suggestion that Hungary would be ready to serve as "experimental terrain" for the process of disarmament.

In Chapter 4, K.-Peter Stratmann of the Foundation for Science and Policy in Ebenhausen, FRG, and Alexander Konovalov of the Institute for the Study of the USA and Canada in Moscow examine the military objectives of conventional arms control. Stratmann begins by sounding a cautionary note, pointing out that the WTO's current offensive strategy, for reasons of force structure, weapons-procurement patterns and bureaucratic inertia, is likely to continue to confront NATO for some time. Hence, he argues that it is the WTO that must do more to reorient its forces towards a greater reliance on defensive capabilities. The ultimate goal, Stratmann asserts, should be a comprehensive and jointly agreed model of what constitutes military stability, a model which allows for a smooth transition from the current military status quo. The first phase should be designed to restructure the general military configuration so as to eliminate the capacity for large-scale, strategic offensive operations. The second phase, Stratmann suggests, could concentrate on eliminating offensive capability at the operational level as well, through creating a posture of "non-offensive defense."

Konovalov reinforces the idea that the objective of the two alliances should be stability at a level and structure of forces which would make strategic offensives impossible. To achieve this, he argues, the two alliances must first identify common elements in their approaches and establish a single methodological basis for determining threat perceptions and force capabilities. Only then will it be possible to work out practical recommendations for decreasing military confrontation in Europe.

The prime task, Konovalov argues, is to reduce the offensive capabilities of the armed forces of both sides. This can be done, he suggests, by: (1) selectively reducing armed forces and weapons that possess offensive capabilities; (2) refraining from procuring systems with clearly offensive characteristics; and (3) creating conditions that hinder—and, ideally, eliminate—the capability of using arms for offensive purposes. Konovalov advocates not only quantitative reductions, but also a restructuring of units and formations having high mobility and firepower and the withdrawal of key "strike formations" from the immediate line of contact.

Chapter 5 is devoted to a discussion of military doctrine by Peer Lange, a Senior Researcher at the Foundation for Science and Policy in

Ebenhausen and a Krupp Foundation Senior Associate at the Institute for East-West Security Studies in 1988–1989, and Andrei Kokoshin, Deputy Director of the Institute for the Study of the USA and Canada in Moscow. In his contribution, Lange stresses the conceptual and methodological problems related to any discussion on doctrine. He points out that these arise because both sides mean different things when they refer to doctrine. To illustrate his point, Lange traces the origins and developments of Soviet doctrine. His juxtaposition of socialist military principles and axioms with those of NATO is particularly useful in pointing out the differences between the two approaches and the difficulties of conducting a dialogue on doctrines between the two alliances.

In Part 2 of the chapter, Andrei Kokoshin underscores the importance of the "dialectic of development" of the means and modes of offense and defense. Changes in the correlation of offense and defense, he suggests, have had a highly significant impact on the security policies of a number of states. Particularly interesting is Kokoshin's discussion of the role of defense in Soviet strategic thinking. He argues that in the Soviet case the necessities and possibilities of strategic defense were underestimated in the early part of World War II, largely because the advocates of strategic defense in the USSR such as Alexander A. Svechin had been crushed or silenced by Stalin. As a result, the USSR incurred heavy, and in many cases unnecessary, losses which could have been avoided had strategic defense been taken more seriously.

Kokoshin also points out that in recent years greater emphasis has been placed on defense in Soviet doctrine. He argues that the WTO countries have considerable grounds for doubting NATO's statements that its doctrine (to the extent it can really be said to have a "doctrine") is entirely defensive. In this regard he cites NATO's adoption of Follow-on Forces Attack (FOFA), which he argues is aimed not at defending the West German border but "at launching large-scale strikes in depth against the territory of the WTO countries." Similarly, Kokoshin is critical of current U.S. naval strategy, especially the "New Maritime Strategy," which he argues is clearly offensive. (Compare his discussion of U.S. naval strategy, for instance, with that of Kugler in Chapter 2.) Thus Kokoshin sees a clear gap between "doctrinal" statements about NATO's defensive orientation and some of its operational concepts.

Chapter 6 examines approaches to conventional reductions. David Ochmanek and Edward Warner of the RAND Corporation discuss key elements of a conventional arms reduction regime in Europe. They focus in particular on the difficulty of categorizing various weapons systems and underscore the complications that large-scale reductions pose for NATO. The main problem, Ochmanek and Warner argue, is the difference in the operational strategies of the two alliances and the force structures needed to implement these strategies. For political reasons NATO is forced to plan a forward, relatively static defensive strategy at the inter-German border. By contrast, the Warsaw Pact, they argue, has an offensive operational strategy designed to seize and hold territory. It can mass its forces in an area of its choice in order to achieve a breakthrough in NATO's defense. As a result, modest reductions, they maintain, could cripple NATO's defense capability, whereas even sizeable reductions might not significantly reduce the combat power that the Warsaw Pact is able to direct against NATO in the opening days and weeks of a war. With this in mind, Ochmanek and Warner propose that reductions should be focused on those forces that are best suited for seizing and holding territory: main battle tanks, artillery and armored vehicles. Aircraft, in their view, should be excluded from the negotiations, at least in the first phase, because reductions in airpower could hobble NATO's ability to defend.

In his companion piece Alexei Arbatov addresses the question of what to count—that is, which forces are the most critical in terms of reductions. He advocates focusing on combat-ready divisions because only these forces, he argues, can be used for conducting military operations, including surprise attack, without additional mobilization. An effort to capture everything at once, he warns, would entail numerous complications and could derail the negotiations.

Arbatov also argues that aircraft—"tactical strike aircraft," to use his term—should be included in the negotiations because they can be used for important offensive missions. The Western approaches, he maintains, fail to consider the important differences between the situation today and that which existed on the eve of World War II. The main difference is the deployment of tactical nuclear weapons. The attacker today must reckon with the possibility of the use of tactical nuclear weapons by the other side and rapid escalation to the nuclear level. This gives the attacker a major incentive to destroy nuclear depots and launchers with conventional weapons in order to eliminate the other side's capacity to "cross the nuclear threshold" or at least delay that decision as long as possible.

Another key issue raised by Arbatov is the relationship between the offense and the defense. Particularly interesting from the Western point of view is his discussion of the problem of the "counteroffensive": that is, whether simply to expel the aggressor from the defender's territory after an attack or to seek the total defeat of the aggressor by developing a counteroffensive and carrying it over to the opponent's territory until he ceases combat operations. Soviet operational strategy, influenced by the experience in World War II, has traditionally been based on the second path. But, Arbatov points out, such a strategy

> assumes the prior development and maintenance of the kind of military potential that the other side would most likely perceive as a potential for attacking and conducting extended large-scale offensive operations.

This statement goes to the heart of Western concerns raised by Warner and Ochmanek.

Chapter 7 deals with verification. As Jonathan Dean, former head of the U.S. delegation to the MBFR talks in Vienna and now Senior Arms Control Advisor to the Union of Concerned Scientists, points out, the problem of verifying a conventional arms control agreement for a zone extending from the Atlantic to the Urals will be considerably more difficult than was the case in previous nuclear negotiations. He argues that a verification system should not be expected on its own to do the entire job of detecting possible moves toward attack; it can be a valuable supplement to, but not a substitute for, alliance intelligence efforts. Moreover, given the number of armaments, activities and the large geographic area to be covered by any agreement, there will be limits to the degree of simultaneous coverage that will be possible. Thus, Dean states, the difference between the ideal and the possible will inevitably create some uncertainty.

The companion piece by Andrzej Karkoszka, Senior Researcher at the Polish Institute of International Relations and a 1988–1989 Krupp Senior Associate at the Institute for East-West Security Studies in New York, examines the requirements that a broad range of possible reduction and restriction measures would pose for verification. Karkoszka also discusses in detail a number of the prerequisites for effective verification, such as data exchange, organizational and financial issues, intrusiveness of verification and the influence of the political context.

The essays by Dean and Karkoszka underscore the enormous complexity of the verification tasks in any future agreement, the importance of on-site inspection as one of the indispensible methods of verification and the wisdom of reductions by unit holdings instead of reductions on an individual basis. Both authors also agree that manpower limitations are less important than limitations on weapons and equipment. They disagree, however, on the importance of a detailed exchange of data. Dean argues that a preliminary exchange of detailed data at the outset of the talks is essential in order to establish a baseline against which information provided after reductions can be compared. Karkoszka, however, believes that a preliminary exchange is not so important since such an exchange would have to be followed by much more detailed data at the time when the agreement enters into force and during subsequent limitations.

In Chapter 8 U.S. Senator Timothy Wirth (D-Colorado) and Adam-Daniel Rotfeld of the Polish Institute of International Affairs examine the prospects for developing a third generation of confidence- and security-building measures (CSBMs). Unlike arms control, which seeks to limit force levels, CSBMs are designed to improve trust and confidence through increasing transparency and predictability. Given the current differences over reductions, CSBMs, Wirth argues, offer the best opportunity for early progress in Vienna. Agreement on CSBMs, moreover, could help improve the political climate and give the talks on force levels greater momentum.

Wirth suggests a number of possible follow-on CSBMs such as notification of alert exercises and mobilization exercises, as well as increasing the number of inspections from the current level of three per year. In contrast to many Western observers, moreover, he favors giving serious thought to naval CSBMs. To date, NATO has been reluctant to consider naval CSBMs, fearing that they would constrain its ability to maintain critical sea lines of communication. Yet, as Wirth points out, if the talks in Vienna make progress on reducing land forces, NATO is likely to face increasing pressure to discuss naval forces.

In the companion essay Rotfeld argues that a follow-on regime to the Stockholm CDE measures needs to include constraints on military activities such as reductions in the scale and number of simultaneous exercises as well as limits on troop transfers and their equipment. Rotfeld also advocates expanding the zone of application of CSBMs to independent naval and air activity—a proposal which the West has repeatedly rejected in the past. While the idea of widening the zone to include naval forces is likely to continue to provoke Western opposition, both Wirth and Rotfeld agree that there may be some utility in considering more modest measures designed to contribute to the prevention of incidents on the seas, inadvertent conflict and escalation as long as they do not impinge on the principle of freedom of navigation.

In Chapter 9, Richard Darilek and John Setear, two staff members at the RAND Corporation, and Manfred Mueller of the Institute for International Relations in Potsdam/Babelsberg, GDR, examine the likely impact of various forms of military force and weapons constraints on both conventional stability and the disarmament process. Darilek and Setear define constraints as measures intended to directly limit or prohibit current or future operations by conventional military forces. This ambitious objective, they believe, can be achieved through a focus on military operations and force deployments, not, in the first instance, by attempting to reduce numbers. They put forward three criteria—defensive asymmetry, clarity and economy—as a basis for assessing the usefulness of the various constraint measures now being discussed. Darilek and Setear emphasize that even the most effective constraints, in the event of conflict, buy the defender only hours, days or weeks—not months—of additional warning with regard to the intentions of the attacker. They share with Mueller the view that constraints can form a useful middle stage between CSBMs and a full-scale reduction agreement. Despite the considerable overlap in the types of measures discussed in the two parts of the chapter, Mueller takes strong issue with the idea put forward by Darilek and Setear that the constraint process would require much more from the WTO than from NATO. He disputes the NATO view that only the WTO has offensive forces which need to be constrained. Mueller outlines the areas, such as the introduction of new technologies, in which he believes NATO will also have to make changes.

Chapter 10 examines the relationship between nuclear weapons and conventional stability. In Part 1 Arnold Kanter, a senior staff member at the RAND Corporation,* analyzes the role of and requirement for nuclear weapons in NATO's strategy of defense as well as the conditions that could lead to their reduction and possible elimination. He underscores the important political as well as military function provided by nuclear weapons in NATO strategy. These weapons, Kanter points out, are designed as much to reassure America's West European allies of the continued strong U.S. commitment to Western Europe as they are to

---

* Editors' note: Since completing this essay, Arnold Kanter has been appointed Special Assistant to the President and Senior Director for Defense and Arms Control on the National Security Council staff.

deter WTO attack. Consequently, even if the WTO were to agree to reductions that left both sides with equal conventional capabilities, NATO would still have a strong interest in maintaining and modernizing its nuclear forces. Moreover, based on the historical record, Kanter expresses strong skepticism that conventional forces alone are inadequate to guarantee deterrence. Hence NATO, he argues, will have a requirement for *some* nuclear weapons—and the need to modernize them—for the foreseeable future.

Alexei Vasiliev, head of the Disarmament Affairs section at the Institute for the Study of the USA and Canada in Moscow and special advisor to the Soviet delegation to the CFE talks in Vienna, takes a diametrically opposite point of view. He argues that nuclear weapons are destabilizing and fulfill no real military function in deterring attack. The U.S. nuclear guarantee, in his view, is irrational and cannot serve as a significant means of ensuring NATO unity. The unity of an alliance based on the willingness to take a suicidal step, he asserts, is inherently incredible and cannot provide genuine security. Similarly, Vasiliev rejects the idea of escalation control, which forms the basis of NATO's strategy of flexible response. Instead he calls for a gradual transition to a nuclear-free world along the lines outlined by Gorbachev in his Comprehensive Proposal of January 15, 1986.

The concluding chapter, written by the two co-editors, Robert D. Blackwill and F. Stephen Larrabee, examines the prospects for the CFE talks. While acknowledging the significance of Gorbachev's UN initiative, we discuss the possibilities for and obstacles to any early agreement. As the chapters in this volume underscore, the technical problems associated with calculating the balance are enormous, as are the problems related to verification of any eventual agreement. In addition, the difficulties of achieving consensus within the Western alliance are considerable.

In our view, reductions in and of themselves will not necessarily lead to enhanced stability. What really matters is the impact of these reductions on military capabilities, especially the ability to carry out a surprise attack and large-scale offensive. Genuine security will not be enhanced unless reductions significantly diminish both these capabilities.

Notes

1 Many Western analysts have, only half in jest, claimed that the talks were a success, since they achieved their main initial objective—keeping U.S. troops in Europe.
2 The Polish plan is by far the most extensive and detailed of the East European proposals.

For details see Andrzej Karkoszka, "The Merits of the Jarurzelski Plan," *Bulletin of the Atomic Scientists* 44, No. 7 (September 1988), pp. 32–34.

3　For the text of the Halifax statement see *Europa Archiv*, Folge 14 (1986), pp. D379–381.

4　In the Spring of 1987 Senator Nunn suggested that the U.S. consider a trade of 13-plus Soviet divisions for at least two U.S. divisions in Central Europe. For an analysis of the strengths and weaknesses of Nunn's proposal, see Robert D. Blackwill, "Specific Approaches to Conventional Arms Control in Europe," *Survival* 30, No. 5 (September/October 1988), pp. 436–437.

5　The MBFR negotiating area had included only the territory of East Germany, Czechoslovakia, Poland, the Federal Republic of Germany and the Benelux countries.

6　See Marshal Sergei F. Akhromeev, "Arms Control and Arms Reduction—The Agenda Ahead," Olof Palme Memorial Lecture 1988, Stockholm International Peace Research Institute (unpublished). For two good Western discussions see William Odom, "Soviet Military Doctrine," *Foreign Affairs* 67, No. 1 (Fall 1988), pp. 114–134 and Edward L. Warner III, "Soviet Military Doctrine: New Thinking and Old Realities in Soviet Defense Policy," *Survival* 30, No. 1 (January/February 1989), pp. 13–33.

7　Andrei A. Kokoshin and Valentin V. Larionov, "Protivostoianie sil obshchego naznacheniia v kontekste obespecheniia strategicheskoi stabil'nosti" (The Confrontation of General-purpose Forces in the Context of Guaranteeing Strategic Stability), *MEMO* No. 6 (June 1988), pp. 23–31. See also the contributions by Kokoshin, Konovalov and Arbatov in this volume.

8　*Pravda*, May 30, 1987.

9　For a good discussion of Soviet concerns in this regard see Lt. Col. Michael J. Sterling, *Soviet Reactions to NATO's Emerging Technologies* (Santa Monica, CA: The RAND Corporation, N-2299-AF, August 1985).

10　Zbigniew Brzezinski, *Game Plan. A Geostrategic Framework for the Conduct of the US-Soviet Contest* (Boston: Atlantic Monthly Press, 1986), p. 181.

11　On this point see the essay by David Ochmanek and Edward Warner in this volume.

12　For a detailed discussion of this point and its political implications, see Robert D. Blackwill, "Conceptual Problems of Conventional Arms Control," *International Security* 12, No. 4 (Spring 1988), pp. 28–47.

PART ONE

The General State of European Security

François Heisbourg, France

The state of European security at the end of the 1980s is a perplexing combination of immobility and change. A description of the existing security situation based on military and strategic criteria leads one to conclude that the present is still much like the past—not necessarily pleasant, certainly not optimal, but eminently stable. If one takes into account the forces of economic and societal change, however, a rather different picture emerges, that of a significant degree of geopolitical fragility with a potential for evolution unprecedented since the emergence of the postwar order in Europe. It is thus important not only to recall the elements of continuity in European security, but to assess the potential of the forces of change. Clearly, a discussion of European security has to include an analysis of economic trends. Policy options in the area of conventional arms control need to be examined with regard to the factors of transformation of the European security scene; indeed, choices in arms control can have a significant influence, positive and negative, on both strategic change and stability. Therefore, and in view of the likelihood of lengthy, complex conventional arms control negotiations, European security must be analyzed not only in the present context but also in light of the potential impact of the ongoing changes affecting Europe.

"Déjà Vu" and "Plus Ça Change . . ."

The use of military and strategic indicators to describe the general state of European security produces an image of basic continuity. Briefly summarized, the postwar geostrategic scene in Europe is characterized by a combination of overlapping factors, five of which stand out particularly prominently:

–the division of Europe;
–the permanence of the postwar alliances;
–the superpowers' military presence and involvement on the continent;
–the deployment of massive and asymmetrical conventional forces, concentrated most notably in Central Europe; and
–the central role of nuclear deterrence.

These five factors are not equally acceptable or stabilizing: it is now generally admitted, for example, that major conventional force imbalances are undesirable, whereas the legitimacy of nuclear deterrence in Europe is not universally accepted. Nor is their moral, political or military content identical in the East and the West. This truism has fundamental implications for defining the objectives of conventional arms control, and for the difficult choices that may have to be made between ethical, political and military goals on both sides. Nor are these elements immutable: Soviet General Secretary Gorbachev's announcement at the United Nations on December 7, 1988, of major conventional force reductions[1] may indeed herald significant movement in the bases of European security. However, these factors have been, and currently remain, the foundations of the current order, and the fact that they mean different things to the two sides bears recalling.

The Division of Europe

The political division of Europe remains a physical reality, embodied by the 'Iron Curtain'[2] not only in Berlin and between the two German states. Beyond the existence of a steel and concrete *cordon sanitaire* from the beaches of the Barents Sea southward, division is also deeply rooted in sharply differing economic and political regimes on both sides of the divide. Setting aside all other considerations, the strategically most relevant political difference in the current situation between the members of the Council of Europe,[3] on the one hand, and the states affiliated with the Warsaw Pact, on the other, may well be the absence of a reasonably transparent and stable process of political legitimization and succession in the latter group of countries. This creates basic uncertainties as to the stability of incumbent regimes, with a corresponding risk for the future of the arms control process and the security situation more generally. The specific situation of Germany, as a divided nation in a divided Europe, remains as topical as ever and imposes its particular political and strategic constraints on both alliances, as discussed further below.

The Permanence of the Postwar Alliances

The postwar alliances have been remarkably durable by any historical peacetime standards: NATO, a 40-year-old alliance primarily composed of multi-party,[4] economically liberal states with a modicum of agreement on the bases of joint defense vis-à-vis the Warsaw Pact's military threat (and, in the case of the members of the integrated commands, a common military organization and strategic concept, of which extended nuclear deterrence is an essential component); and the Warsaw Pact, the military and political grouping of states governed by communist parties, with any real or potential departures from the single-party monopoly being forestalled, in the past, by military intervention.

The Superpowers' Military Presence and Involvement

The superpowers structure the security order in Europe through their respective alliances, as well as through the presence of their military forces.[5] These roles and this presence are not equivalent. This is clear in moral as well as in political terms. The United States has refrained from using its military forces to deal with domestic political contingencies in Europe; and when U.S. forces have been requested to leave, they have agreed to do so (France, 1966; Torrejón, Spain, 1988).

This absence of equivalence also holds true in strictly military terms, whether on the central front or in the whole European theater. U.S. ground and air forces (245,800) represent 27 percent of total allied (stationed and West German) manpower in the FRG (926,200). The U.S. Army in the FRG has 204,700 permanently stationed troops versus 332,100 for the West German Bundeswehr. Conversely, Soviet ground forces in the GDR account for some three-fourths of such forces present in East Germany; the Group of Soviet Forces in the GDR has 380,000 troops, versus 120,000 for the East German Nationale Volksarmee. The contrast is just as remarkable when one looks at the much broader Atlantic-to-the-Urals region: Soviet ground forces west of the Urals represent 53 percent of all Warsaw Pact forces in Europe (some 2,143,000 soldiers) and more than two-thirds of all battle tanks. Out of 776,400 U.S. Army troops, a total of some 212,000 are stationed in Europe, representing some 10 percent of allied forces in Europe (2,102,000). A further 65,000 are assigned for the reinforcement of Europe.

The priority assigned to the European theater by each of the superpowers is also marked by a disparity which is particularly stark if only in-place forces are taken into account. The Soviet Union permanently deploys 69 percent (more than 1,300,000) of its active ground forces west of the Urals. In contrast, 22 percent of U.S. active ground forces (975,000— Army plus Marine Corps) are stationed in Europe. The number rises to 42 percent if all U.S. Army and Marine Corps forces assigned to (65,000) or earmarked for possible use in (137,000) Europe are taken into account.

This set of figures results from the high contribution of non-U.S. NATO forces to the total number of allied active ground forces in the Atlantic-to-the-Urals area, in comparison to the relatively low share of non-Soviet Warsaw Pact forces in the Warsaw Pact total. Ninety percent of NATO forces in Europe are non-American; under 50 percent of Warsaw Pact forces west of the Urals are non-Soviet. These figures reflect—but only in part—the disparate demographic weight of the non-superpower contributions. Non-NATO Europe has a total population of 376 million (and the United States 245 million). The non-Soviet Warsaw Pact countries have a population of 114 million (and the USSR 285 million)—28 percent of the Warsaw Pact's total population—which is, on average, richer in per capita terms than the Soviet population.

This situation will be altered by the Soviet unilateral reductions announced by Gorbachev on December 7, 1988, although less significantly in the broad European area than in Central Europe. Once these cuts are effected, Soviet tanks will represent more than 50 percent of Warsaw Pact battle tanks west of the Urals (instead of 71 percent). Sixty-three percent (instead of 70 percent) of all Soviet tanks will be deployed west of the Urals.

These changes will have a deeper impact in the central area: in the "Jaruzelski zone" (encompassing Poland, Hungary, the GDR and Czechoslovakia on the Warsaw Pact side), Soviet tank forces will drop sharply, from 9,790 to 4,790 battle tanks, thus representing less than 30 percent of the Warsaw Pact's total in the area (instead of 46 percent).

*The Deployment of Massive and Asymmetrical Concentrations
of Conventional Forces*

The balance of forces is further explored in Chapter 2 of this book. However, several general observations can be made here concerning the relationship between the concentration of conventional forces and European security. First, one of the dominant features of the European strategic landscape is the existence of Warsaw Pact forces sufficiently numerous, well equipped and adequately deployed for the conduct of large-scale, sustained and deep offensive operations into Western Europe. Such an offensive option is not available to NATO.

Second, the nature and relevance of asymmetries differ widely between the central front and the northern and southern flanks. The central front is precisely that: an uninterrupted zone of contact, from Bohemia to the Baltic, bounded by a geographically homogeneous hinterland on both sides. It is separated from the flanks by the neutral Alpine states to the south and by the Baltic Sea to the north. Therefore, it is logical to establish numerical force comparisons between the two alliances, encompassing frontline forces and the rear echelons. The term "asymmetry" applied to numerical disparities does have a demonstrable significance as regards the central front.

The situation on the flanks is rather different. In the north, there is a limited zone of contact (less than 200 kilometers of the Soviet-Norwegian border lying between Kirkenes and Pechenga) and a longish north-south array of buffer states—Sweden and Finland—which are themselves partially separated by the Baltic Sea. There is no contiguous hinterland zone for the northern flank. The southern flank for its part is fractioned into four subtheaters: Portugal-Spain, Italy, Greece-Thrace and eastern Turkey. Each of the last two areas, which are contiguous to the Warsaw Pact, can lend themselves to local frontline force comparisons. However, rear-echelon force comparisons are far from simple. For example, Turkish forces in Anatolia can reinforce a variety of sectors. Some of these countries also have to take into account potential non-Warsaw Pact threats in their immediate vicinity: e.g., the Middle East and Cyprus for Turkey and Morocco for Spain. A comparable discontinuity applies to Warsaw Pact forces, with large distances separating forces available for operations against Slovenia and northern Italy, on the one hand, and Macedonia and Thrace, on the other, not to mention Transcaucasia. "Bean-counting" for arms control purposes is an exercise that covers only part of the overall military reality in the best of cases; on the southern flank its relevance becomes highly questionable, notably vis-à-vis ground forces. Lastly, the concentration of armed forces in Europe is awesome by any standard: a total of close to 1,800,000 active ground forces in Central Europe (NATO Guidelines Area) with more than 31,000 main battle tanks; and a total of close to 4,500,000 active troops from the Atlantic to the Urals, with close to 80,000 main battle tanks—and still more than 65,000 after the "Gorbachev cuts" and the ensuing reductions by the non-Soviet Warsaw Pact countries will have been implemented. Europe thus plays host to the world's greatest concentration of forces, both conventional and tactical nuclear.

The Central Role of Nuclear Deterrence

Last but not least, the iron law of the nuclear age remains a linchpin of strategic stability in Europe: any confrontation between the alliances in Europe carries with it the possibility of drawing in the strategic forces of the nuclear powers. Even if the use of these strategic weapons is extremely improbable, such a risk makes aggression an unappealing policy option. True, the nuclear threshold may be perceived as uncomfortably low, nuclear deterrence may be considered increasingly unpalatable, and some analysts may indeed consider that nuclear deterrence (and particularly extended nuclear deterrence [END]) has ceased to exist except against the use of other nuclear weapons.[6] Furthermore, there certainly is a degree of "deterrence fatigue" among publics and leaderships[7] in the West, with, as a corollary, a correspondingly greater emphasis on conventional forces and options. Nonetheless, the fact remains that it would be an extraordinarily foolhardy aggressor who would choose to exploit his conventional advantage at the risk of escalating to the nuclear level. Indeed, it is the existence of extended nuclear deterrence that has alleviated the potentially destabilizing consequences of the conventional force asymmetries. Further, many would argue that nuclear deterrence will still be desirable even if approximate parity of restructured, smaller and defensive conventional forces emerges: a Europe with purely conventional forces is not necessarily stable or peaceful, at least from the perspective of history. In short, the "end of END"[8] is not in sight, despite certain trends in that direction. Important as they may be in various respects, the INF Treaty and the prospective success of the START negotiations will not, in and of themselves, basically alter this situation.

The net effect of these structural factors of the postwar order is not continuity but inherent stability. This stability not only applies to the relationship between the two alliances, with its absence of open military conflict in Europe since the end of World War II. Continuity has also held within the two coalitions: by choice in the West (not necessarily unreservedly, e.g., France, Spain) and by coercion in the East (although not without some difficulties, notably in 1956, 1968 and 1981). This raises the question of the relationship between inter-alliance and intra-alliance stability. The experiences of Budapest in 1956 and Prague in 1968 tend to indicate that inter-alliance stability is relatively insensitive to intra-alliance instability. However, these precedents may not necessarily be relevant guides any more, for several reasons:

–Human, cultural, economic and political exchanges between Eastern and Western Europe were considerably less developed 20 and 30 years ago than is the case today; the stakes are much higher at present, making intervention a less appealing option, and thus providing greater leeway for internal change, which may in turn become uncontrollable, in Eastern Europe and the USSR.

–The breakdown of intra-Warsaw Pact stability would pose a new challenge, if such fragmentation did not simply pit the Soviet Union against one of its proteges, but involved several of the latter simultaneously. Tension between member-states (e.g., Hungary vs. Romania) or within strategically located European countries themselves (e.g., Yugoslavia) would further complicate an already complex picture in Eastern Europe and the USSR.

The Forces of Change

Along with the new political reality in the USSR, it is the pressure of economic factors that has provided new fuel for change in Europe. The economic parameters at play could be encapsulated as follows:

–The relative role of the superpowers in structuring European security is, to a certain extent, dependent upon their economic weight, both vis-à-vis each other and vis-à-vis their allies; economic weight will in turn be a function of the new criteria characterizing economic performance in the "information age."

–The third industrial revolution, driven by information technology, is changing the currency of economic performance and imposes a dual logic of societal change (information technology prospers in open and decentralized societies) and growing interdependence (to be a player in an information-driven world economy, you need to cooperate internationally).

However broad these generalizations may seem, they have concrete implications for the future of European security and provide useful tools for analyzing strategic trends within the two alliances, between each superpower and its allies, as well as within the West and East European states themselves.

The United States and Transatlantic Coupling

The Euro-American agenda for 1989 onward may well be dominated by a vivid resurgence of that hardy perennial, the burden-sharing debate within NATO. For some, this will be a sign of the United States' relative decline, a theme which Paul Kennedy's recent book[9] has done much to popularize—i.e., the recognition of "imperial overstretch" leads the United States to substantially reduce its overseas commitments. Such a drastic scenario is, however, based on a premise—relative decline—which is far from proven (unless one were to consider the abnormally high American share of world production in the wake of World War II as the sole appropriate yardstick). Among the many arguments that have been put forward by the "anti-declinists,"[10] there is one which is particularly relevant since it relies on Paul Kennedy's own basic yardsticks for assessing relative decline, i.e., shares of world gross product and defense spending. In these respects the United States is in no worse a position than it was in the early 1970s: then as now, the U.S. economy represented approximately 41 percent of the combined gross national product (GNP) of the Organization for Economic Cooperation and Development and somewhat less than one-fourth of the world's production. Defense spending in 1989 stands at slightly more than 6 percent of American gross domestic product (GDP), somewhat below the postwar peacetime average.

The burden-sharing debate will more probably flare up in the context of U.S. efforts to reduce a relatively modest budget deficit (3.5 percent of GNP) without raising taxes, a course which would reinforce current constraints on the U.S. defense budget. As a result it may become necessary to envisage some reduction of the U.S. force structure. If such were the case, the burden-sharing issue would remain controllable and its effect limited, since this would be a question of degree rather than kind. The American commitment within the alliance would not be fundamentally altered. NATO should be able to weather such burden-sharing turbulence provided the United States does not allow itself to become overwhelmed by an excessive perception of decline, and provided also that the burden-sharing discussion is broadened to include the related issues of roles and responsibilities and that the West Europeans keep their cool, presenting their case effectively on Capitol Hill.[11] By historical standards these are conditions with which the U.S. and West European political systems can ultimately cope, albeit painfully. As in the past, therefore, it seems unlikely that the general state of European security will be seriously threatened by disagreements on financial contributions. It is unlikely but not impossible that the discussion might get out of hand if several negative developments occurred simultaneously, e.g., a trade war breaking out with a collapse of the General Agreement on Tariffs and Trade, the unilateral elimination by Bonn of all short-range nuclear forces in the FRG, or other drastic changes of a political nature such as the emergence of an anti-NATO administration in one of the major NATO countries.

Barring such catastrophes, transatlantic coupling will continue to be questioned, as it has been in the past, but there is no reason to believe that the bottom-line answer will change.

The West European Enigma

Trends within Western Europe itself are more likely to produce significant changes in European security over the next few years. These are essentially linked to the process initiated in 1985 with the signing and subsequent ratification of the Single European Act, which aims at the creation of a homogeneous marketplace within the European Community (EC) by 1992. The success or failure of this process is by no means guaranteed. There is, however, one outcome which is unlikely, and that is the preservation, in case of the failure of the "1992 process," of the pre-1985 status quo, i.e., the EC remaining essentially a useful free-trade zone, albeit with a costly agricultural policy, plus a number of its core members belonging to an efficient European monetary system (EMS) and enjoying a loose coordination of foreign policy through European Political Cooperation.

Starker outcomes (positive or negative) are more likely, with potentially significant effects on European security. If the European Community's process of economic unification succeeds, the creation of a single market will more or less inevitably lead to a degree of fiscal harmonization and, for the EMS countries, to further limits on national sovereignty, possibly including the creation of a central bank. Even setting aside such ulterior developments, the effects of the single market on growth could be spectacular, adding more than a percentage point to the annual growth rate,[12] producing a positive spinoff in terms of resources made available for defense spending. However, the qualitative effects may be even more important: (1) a commercially unified Europe will exercise a strong economic and societal pull on the East European countries, going well beyond the current, already significant, examples of the European Community's "gravitational attraction" in the Warsaw Pact; and (2) an economically more coherent and successful Western Europe would, in all likelihood, feel encouraged to increase its own role within NATO, albeit not necessarily through EC institutions. European identity in the field of security, the lineaments of which have been emerging during the past few years, could then evolve towards the oft-evoked "second-pillar" type of structure within the alliance. All in all, a more prosperous, open and assertive Western Europe would be a factor of strength within NATO. However, if post-1992 Western Europe were to turn into a closed regional trading bloc, the potential damage to alliance cohesion could be tremendous. This is, however, an entirely avoidable outcome.

If the process of economic unification fails, possibly as a consequence of a global economic recession, then several scenarios appear plausible. In a "best-case" situation Franco-German rapprochement could become a substitute for broader European unification; such a Franco-German core would exercise a good deal of attraction in Central Europe and could possibly do so without adverse effects on NATO. In the "worst case," encouraged by disappointment with European unification, a more general Balkanization of Western Europe would coincide with widespread nationally-based protectionism, causing significant tension with the United States and between the European countries.

At present, the jury is still out, although a non-protectionist outcome is more likely given the EC's vulnerability to trade wars. The 1992 process is presently on track (if not necessarily on time), notwithstanding the different "Europanschauungen" between the continental countries, on the one hand, and the British political leadership, on the other.

The USSR: Uncertainty and Volatility

Important as trends within the Atlantic alliance and the European Community may be, their potential repercussions on security remain unrealized. There may be uncertainties about the future makeup of Western Europe and the alliance, but the current situation is one of relative continuity, at least in comparison to the numerous crises which NATO and the EC have lived through in recent decades. The Warsaw Pact countries, in contrast, are entering a period of uncertainty in which the stakes exceed even those of the years of de-Stalinization, with the Soviet Union being the pivotal actor in an unusually dynamic and changing scene.

Several variables are of prime importance here in terms of their impact on the state of European security. The manner in which they evolve and, just as important, the degree of uncertainty which is attached to the nature of their evolution, need to be factored into the West's own calculations.

First, the breadth and speed of the implementation of *perestroika* are central variables which affect all of the others. A failure of the Soviet economy to "deliver the goods" could not only affect the fate of the Soviet political leadership; more significantly it would confirm the impossibility of moving away in a gradual and controlled fashion from a centralized single-party state to one capable of holding its own in high technology. The alternatives in such a case would probably be stark: either a *fuite en avant* of the sort already apparent in the Baltic republics, with the toleration of non-communist, politically active organizations and economic decentralization; or, conversely, an attempt to implement modernization through authoritarian and centralizing policies, with a strong Great Russian component—a belated adoption of the Catherine the Great approach to reform. The former course would create new uncertainties not necessarily acceptable to the single-party state and its *apparat*; the latter policy would generate its own problems and could lead to the temptation of seeking "quick fixes" by using the assets it has at its disposal, notably the armed forces, domestically and abroad. Such an extreme choice will hopefully remain purely hypothetical, but cannot be considered as being outside the scope of uncertainties surrounding the progress of *perestroika*.

Second, the success of *perestroika* is linked to the relationship between defense spending and *perestroika*. A liberal democracy suffering from deep economic woes without being under an acute military threat[13] would as a matter of course transfer resources from defense to the general economy in one way or another. This would *a fortiori* be the case if such a country were devoting more than one-sixth of its national revenue to defense. Until Gorbachev's UN speech of December 7, 1988, there was no sign that any such transfers of resources had been decided upon, let alone implemented. It remains to be seen to what extent the announced unilateral arms reductions will translate into diminished defense expenditure. One can only speculate as to why no significant reductions had occurred during the first four years of Gorbachev's stewardship. It may be argued that it makes little sense to transfer resources from a relatively efficient military sector towards an as yet unrestructured civilian economy. One can also make the case that reductions in military expenditure would normally occur in the Soviet centrally planned economy as an integral part of the next five-year plan (1991–1995), rather than of the current one, which was elaborated before Gorbachev came to power. Therefore nothing much could happen before the first half of the 1990s.

There may be a more political reason for holding off on reductions in Soviet defense spending. Gorbachev's control on the *apparat* remains subject to resistance and inertia. The Soviet high command under Marshal Sergei Akhromeev had been broadly supportive of Gorbachev's economic and foreign policies,[14] but this probably had its price. This clearly is a constituency which Gorbachev cannot antagonize lightly.

In any case, basic choices for the next five-year plan will need to be made sometime during 1989. At present there is simply no way that we can forecast the precise content of the decisions that will be made, the effects of which will be valid until the latter half of the next decade. Nor is it clear whether these decisions and the reasoning behind them will be elaborated upon in public.

Third, in the political arena, the policy of *glasnost'* has uncorked nationalism in the peripheral republics of the USSR, most spectacularly in the Baltic and Transcaucasian regions. A backlash in Russia proper against such events cannot be discounted, particularly if other republics were to follow the same road. A convergence of traditional Great Russian nationalism, on one side, with disaffected planners, technocrats and party hard-liners, on the other, would create an entirely new and highly unstable situation. Such an admittedly extreme scenario would be reminiscent of the events leading to World War I: the combination of decline and nationalism in the Ottoman and Austro-Hungarian empires was not a happy moment for European security.

Such a train of events simply cannot be ruled out as long as another key variable remains in flux, i.e., the future of the Soviet political process. Political legitimization and succession in the Soviet Union remains uncertain despite the remarkable elections held in March 1989. There is no obvious, proven and transparent mechanism for the orderly transfer of power, and as long as that is the case, sharply contrasting scenarios cannot be excluded, generating corresponding uncertainty in the field of security policy.

There are obviously many other major variables; but on the basis of those which have been enumerated, two general consequences for strategic stability in Europe can be noted: .

–In the current circumstances and in view of the great uncertainties concerning the Soviet Union's future, the instruments which have prevented war in Europe over the past 40 years continue to be relevant; from a Western perspective, this entails the continued existence of the Atlantic alliance, nuclear deterrence and a robust conventional defense, including a significant American force presence.

–Although events in the Soviet Union make it possible to further the cause of human rights and introduce greater economic and political pluralism in Eastern Europe, there would be grave dangers were the West to raise expectations it could not fulfill in the face of a possible Soviet backlash, as the precedents of 1956 and 1968 demonstrate.

"The Other Europe": Drift Toward Mitteleuropa?

Many of the questions raised by events in the USSR naturally pose themselves in the states of Eastern Europe (including Yugoslavia), albeit with some differences. One fundamental contrast resides in the effect of the contradictory aims of Soviet policy in Eastern Europe. The imperative for keeping the western flank politically and militarily secure runs counter to the exigencies of *glasnost'* and *perestroika*. The virtues of a Jakeš or a Zhivkov or a Honecker are compatible with the former imperative rather than the latter. Moscow may therefore find it preferable to tolerate the leaders in East Berlin who restrict or ban Soviet publications,[15] rather than run the risk of compromising its vested security interests in a critical part of Europe. Reconciling security and economic goals is not simplified by the existence in several East European countries of vocal and autonomous bodies politic. These factors could, as in 1956, lead to severe challenges to the Soviet leadership.

The difference between a "Sovietized society" in the USSR and the "non-Sovietized" East European states is sometimes overstated: after all, Bulgaria has probably been more successfully "Sovietized" than some of the peripheral Soviet republics. The fact remains that in Poland and Hungary, and, less overtly, in the GDR and Czechoslovakia, the "civil society" has remained basically impervious to Sovietization and is ready to fill in whatever cracks can be found or created in the single-party state. Similarly, these states have remained fundamentally European in nature. Indeed, the appellation "Eastern Europe" may no longer be the most relevant one. The concept of *Mitteleuropa* is, for better or worse, fast becoming once again a more apt characterization for societies and even governments which are rediscovering historical and geographical affinities[16] torn asunder by World War II. This highly visible trend is exemplified by the flow of travel between East and West Germany[17] or between Austria and Hungary. Such an evolution could in theory have a stabilizing effect: after all, "reverse Austrianization" of Eastern Europe is not necessarily incompatible with the Soviet Union's security interests. However, Moscow does not at the moment appear to see it that way. Nor is it certain that aspirations fueled by rising expectations in the non-Soviet Warsaw Pact countries can be satisfied within the existing order or kept in check without resort to force.

Last but not least, much as in the Soviet Union, *glasnost'* has been accompanied by a "decompression effect,"[18] revealing or exacerbating previously latent ethnic conflicts, most notably between Hungary and Romania over the treatment of the Hungarian minority residing in Romania. At the same time, tensions within Yugoslavia have risen to a point where some of the more dramatic scenarios concerning the future of the Federation, which were bandied about before Tito's death, no longer seem entirely implausible. "Balkanization," with its concurrent risks of involvement by outside powers, could once again become a descriptive rather than an abstract term.

Uncertainties about the future of Eastern Europe interact with those concerning the Soviet Union. In this situation, there is only one certainty which we can surmise with any degree of confidence: no analyst or policy-maker can, at this stage, rule out either a positive or a negative course of events, although the latter is far from inevitable. Impatience with the status quo may well be tempered by geopolitical realism, by the civil societies of Eastern Europe, while at the same time the Soviet Union forgoes overt intervention.

The Specific Weight of the German Question

The observations concerning the non-Soviet Warsaw Pact countries also apply to the German Democratic Republic, although in the GDR there is a greater degree of latent tension between the nature of the state and society at large, which remains German in a way that Austria has ceased to be. The East German state is essentially ideological in character, particularly since the policy of *Abgrenzung* (delimitation) led the GDR to renounce its initial pretension to represent the German nation as a whole. The division of Germany into two states has practical implications in the field of security which may gain greater relevance at a time when East-West relations appear to be undergoing deep changes: most notably, the Federal Republic cannot avoid giving great prominence to its relationship with the Soviet Union and the GDR in order to alleviate some of the consequences of division for the German nation. An equivalent situation also applies, although in a less overt manner, to the GDR itself: the refusal of the East German government to take countermeasures[19] relating to inter-German relations after the deployment of Pershing 2 missiles in the FRG was an example of this underlying tension between the Warsaw Pact's broader security policy and East Germany's de facto recognition of the importance of *Deutschlandpolitik*.

The division of Germany accompanied by direct contact between the concentrated might of the armed forces of the two alliances has specific strategic consequences which continue to prevail, including, for example:

–the non-possession of nuclear weapons by the two German states, and the resultant dependence of the FRG on the U.S. nuclear security guarantee;
–the forward defense of the FRG has been a political imperative from the West German point of view. In the framework of NATO's current doctrine, a forward posture is sustainable only through the presence of

large numbers of stationed forces. This may constrain NATO's capability to reduce its own conventional forces significantly, if force-to-space ratios adequate for forward defense are to be preserved; and

–the West German refusal to accept measures which would be seen as further deepening the physical division of the German nation: hence, permanent and visible fortifications and obstacles along the inter-German border are not part of NATO's defensive measures.

With "new detente," another factor gains prominence: the strong reticence evinced by West German public opinion against short-range nuclear weapons which are perceived as being destined for use primarily against targets on German soil, East or West. This trend has been reinforced by the INF Treaty—and notably the provisions eliminating short-range intermediate nuclear forces having a range of 500 to 1,000 kilometers—which has in turn eliminated an element of risk-sharing among the allies.

The convergence of *Deutschlandpolitik*—and therefore of *Ostpolitik*— as an essential and legitimate part of the FRG's foreign policy, with opposition to short-range nuclear weapons and their modernization, could be a powerful factor of division within the Atlantic alliance. The particular constraints under which the FRG operates are of prime importance for the future of conventional force negotiations. This is the case not only because the FRG and the GDR are the deployment zone of such a large proportion of armed forces in Europe and the states most vulnerable in the first stages of a military conflict, with a correspondingly high degree of West German interest in the disarmament process, but also because *Ostpolitik* figures so prominently on the FRG's political agenda, leading strictly military imperatives to enter into conflict with broader political considerations in the course of the negotiations—and the temptation will be strong to more or less systematically subordinate the former to the latter. NATO's Councils, West European bodies such as the Western European Union (WEU) and the budding institutions of the special relationship between France and West Germany are among the fora in which the relevant compromises will need to be struck.

The State of European Security and Conventional Arms Control

In attempting to assess the forces of stability and change, the analyst is confronted with a straightforward, albeit difficult, question. The policy-maker has the considerably more onerous task of defining what is desirable and what is not. Strategic stability is not good in itself—the division of Europe is an extravagant anomaly from a moral, political and economic point of view—but the danger of war in the nuclear age gives stability a more positive value than it has had in the past. Similarly, change on its own is not a positive value either if it leads to a situation worse than the *status quo ante,* if its costs outweigh its benefits or if its risks are inordinately high. However, change does occur, and, if it is associated with an extraordinarily broad range of possible but uncertain outcomes, then the prudent policy-maker will avoid locking himself prematurely into definitive options. Positive as it may be and however great the opportunities it offers, change in the Warsaw Pact gives the impression of being in a "controlled skid," but the difference between control and lack of control when skidding on an icy road is a narrow one. Similarly, in presenting guidelines linking conventional disarmament to European security, it will therefore be assumed that policy-makers will assign greater priority to war-avoidance—i.e., limiting international instability—than to favoring change at any cost.

Precise policy options for conventional arms control are discussed in the following chapters. On the basis of the preceding analysis and its conclusions, however, a number of guidelines can be drawn, against which various approaches to the future of European security, not least in relation to the conventional arms control process, can be evaluated. First, there will be no reward for following policies which will make one country deliberately hostage to the turn of events in another. From a Western perspective, this could mean, for example, that policies should not be a function of Gorbachev's ensured success or, conversely, of his guaranteed failure. Second, when there is such extraordinary uncertainty surrounding the capability of the Soviet Union to effect changes in areas over which it has at least some control, it would be presumptuous for other countries to assume that they can deliberately secure the success or failure of change in the Soviet Union. This does not mean that the outside world's actions are irrelevant, but simply that experience—notably that of East-West relations in the 1970s—along with prudence and awareness of the limits of external power should normally lead a country and its alliance to conduct a policy centered on its own interests, rather than on its purported capability to influence events on the other side of the East-West divide. Acting on the basis of one's underlying national interests may sound terribly passé. However, it remains the only guide for the *stable* and *predictable* conduct of one's international relations—qualities which are particularly important in a period of intense flux.

This should also apply in the area of arms control. If a unilateral disarmament measure is in one's own interest, then it should be taken. If such is not the case, then it should not. This should apply to all states, in West and East alike. This was the case for NATO's short-range nuclear forces, which were reduced unilaterally from 7,000 to 4,500 over a period of some ten years. Gorbachev's announcement of major unilateral conventional force reductions is a recent and encouraging move which applies the same principle of self-interest. The Soviet Union has no reason to deprive itself of the possibility of reducing its armed forces or restructuring them along less costly and less offensive lines, if that can further the aims of *perestroika* while contributing to the overall security situation in Europe by providing a promising backdrop to the conventional arms negotiations.

Because unilateral measures can be the result of a sober calculation of what one's own interests are, they should not be excluded out of hand. This approach counsels against a process whereby negotiations on conventional forces cause all force components to be transformed into bargaining chips.[20] Indeed, such a process may be the preferred outcome for some military decision-makers who could thus resist changes in the status quo and reinforce their claim to budgetary resources by arguing for the need to avoid weakening one's own negotiating stance.

The complete removal of all short-range nuclear weapons from Central Europe would be a high-risk proposition in the best of times. The elimination of one of the key elements of strategic stability in postwar Europe should not even bear mentioning in the current situation of flux and uncertainty. Indeed, in a period of geopolitical change, the Soviet Union could make a major contribution in the field of arms control by publicly recognizing the positive role nuclear deterrence plays in ensuring strategic stability in Europe. In the absence of common ground between East and West on the role of nuclear weapons in Europe, there is little incentive for the West to negotiate on short-range nuclear forces, with a "third zero" lurking around every corner.

Similarly, as long as there is no tangible sign of reduced Soviet military spending and insofar as conventional force asymmetries persist, there is no strategic reason to significantly reduce defense spending in the vulnerable West European countries.

Given the possibility of a change of leadership in the USSR and the risks of adverse geostrategic developments in Europe, the conventional arms control process should focus on militarily and strategically significant results and not be made to bear the burden of broader political goals which would simply delay substantive results and incur the risk of irrelevance, if not worse. Arms control, and particularly conventional arms control, is sufficiently (some would say excessively) complex without having to be overloaded with political aims which are best pursued through the multiplicity of other means our countries have at their disposal in the framework of the East-West dialogue.

Similarly, the talks should not have as their prime objective the transformation of the geostrategic order in Europe and particularly in Central Europe. Such a transformation may ultimately be desirable. But the risks involved are great enough to warrant extreme caution.

Last but not least, the discussion between the United States and the European allies on the sharing of roles, burdens and responsibilities should not be allowed to weaken NATO's negotiating posture by leading to major unilateral U.S. force withdrawals in the face of the Warsaw Pact's conventional force overhang. Similarly, particular restraint would have to be exercised if negotiated U.S. troop reductions opened the prospect of a complete withdrawal of U.S. forces from Europe. The USSR (and its forces between Brest-Litovsk and the Urals) would not cease to be a part of Europe, whereas the United States would no longer share Western Europe's geostrategic fate.

In conclusion, given the possible instability that may occur within the Soviet realm, it would be appropriate for conventional arms control—as well as the broader security dialogue—to focus on those areas which are amenable to practical discussion early on and could lead to a situation not easily reversed if a less congenial Soviet leadership emerged. This consideration would normally lead one to insist on measures reducing the possibility of large-scale offensive operations and making the peace-time concentration and ambiguous movement of forces more difficult. In short, West European security would benefit first and foremost from a further drawdown of the Group of Soviet Forces in Germany, on the one hand, and from measures reducing the levels, constraining the movements and hampering the logistics of Warsaw Pact follow-on forces in the broader Atlantic-to-the-Urals zone, on the other.

In other words, in a time of geopolitical transformation, developments in the arms control arena should enhance strategic stability. As we are entering into a period of reordering the situation established after World

War II, such stability may help ensure that we harness the winds of societal change and international cooperation rather than unleash the storms of strategic disorder.

Notes

1 "In the next two years [the strength of Soviet armed forces] will be reduced by 500,000 men and substantial cuts will be made in conventional armaments. These cuts will be made unilaterally, regardless of the talks on the mandate of the Vienna meeting. . . . We have decided to withdraw from the GDR, Czechoslovakia and Hungary by 1991, six tank divisions and disband them. . . . [L]anding-assault and some other units, including landing-crossing units . . . will be withdrawn from Soviet forces . . . in these countries. The Soviet forces stationed [there] will be reduced by 50,000 men and 5,000 tanks. The Soviet divisions which still remain [there] will be restructured, a large number of tanks will be withdrawn and they will become strictly defensive . . . The total reductions of Soviet armed forces in the European regions of the USSR and on the territory of our European allies will amount to 10,000 tanks, 8,500 artillery systems and 800 combat aircraft." Speech by Mikhail Gorbachev at the UN General Assembly, December 7, 1988.

2 This expression now figures in official Soviet parlance. As Eduard Shevardnadze noted in his speech to the CSCE in Vienna on January 19, 1989, "The Vienna meeting has shaken up the 'Iron Curtain,' weakened its rusty supports, made new breaches in it and sped up its corrosion."

3 The Council of Europe's membership is limited to European states which "accept the principles of the rule of law and of the enjoyment by all persons within [their] jurisdiction of human rights and fundamental freedoms." In 1989, its members included all of the European NATO states, plus Austria, Cyprus, Finland, Ireland, Liechtenstein, Malta, Sweden and Switzerland. The significance of this otherwise essentially powerless body is that it has its own court of justice (the European Court of Human Rights) the obligatory jurisdiction of which has been recognized by 19 of its member-states in matters relating to the basic rights and freedoms of individuals.

4 Since the fall of the Portuguese and Greek dictatorships in the mid-1970s, the sole exception vis-à-vis this norm has been military rule in Turkey during the first half of the current decade.

5 All figures in this paragraph are derived from the International Institute for Strategic Studies, *The Military Balance 1988–1989* (London: IISS, 1988), except for those relating to U.S. forces assigned to or earmarked for Europe and for those drawing on Gorbachev's speech to the UN General Assembly on December 7, 1988 (see fn. 1).

6 See Edward N. Luttwak, "Nuclear Weapons, The Logic of Strategy and the Decline of Extended Deterrence," in "The Changing Strategic Landscape, Part II," *Adelphi Papers* 236 (London: IISS, 1989).

7 With France being the least affected by this shift.

8 See Lawrence Freedman, "Extended Nuclear Deterrence," in "The Changing Strategic Landscape, Part II," *Adelphi Papers* 236 (London: IISS, 1989).

9 Paul Kennedy, *The Rise and Fall of the Great Powers* (New York: Random House, 1987).

10 See Walt Rostow, "Beware of Historians Bearing False Analogies," *Foreign Affairs* 66,

No. 4 (Spring 1988), pp. 863–868; Richard Haass, "The Use (and Mainly Misuse) of History," *Orbis* 32, No. 3 (Summer 1988), pp. 411–419; and Samuel Huntington, "The United States: Decline or Renewal," in "The Changing Strategic Landscape, Part I," *Adelphi Papers* 235 (London: IISS, 1989).

11 See François Heisbourg, "Can the Atlantic Alliance Last Out the Century?" *International Affairs* (London) 63, No. 3 (Summer 1987), pp. 413–423.

12 See European Commission, "Economic Gains from the 1992 Programme Could Rise to 200 Billion ECU or More . . . ," *Information Note*, European Communities, Brussels, March 29, 1988.

13 The absence of an acute military threat is not systematically acknowledged in the USSR. Moreover, a number of Soviet analysts do state that the nature of the threat has changed qualitatively due to systemic change in the West, with economic competition as its main focus. See V. Zhurkin, S. Karaganov and A. Kortunov, "Vyzovy bezopasnosti —starye i novye," *Kommunist* No. 1 (1988), pp. 42–50.

14 See Dale R. Herspring, "The High Command Looks at Gorbachev," and Paul Dibb, "Changes in Soviet Strategy," in "The Changing Strategic Landscape, Part I," *Adelphi Papers* 235 (London: IISS, 1989).

15 For example, the ban on the sale of the Soviet periodical *Sputnik* in the GDR in November 1988.

16 Not necessarily for the better, as many students of pre-1945 history will no doubt readily admit. On this topic, see *Herodote—l'Europe mediane* (Paris: 1988).

17 Approximately 2 million East Germans—one person out of eight—traveled to the FRG in 1988.

18 The expression is borrowed from Jose Thiago Cintra in "Regional Conflicts: Trends in a Period of Transition," in "The Changing Strategic Landscape, Part III," *Adelphi Papers* 237 (London: IISS, 1989).

19 The deployment of Soviet operational-tactical missiles (SS-12 and SS-23) in the GDR as a countermeasure did not impinge on the human, economic and financial substance of inter-German relations.

20 The MBFR negotiations performed such a military "status quo" function for 15 years.

PART TWO

The General State of European Security

Janusz Symonides, Poland

Changes in the Political and Military Context of European Security

Although the present landscape of European security is still characterized by the division of the continent, the existence of two opposing military alliances, the presence of foreign troops on the territory of various nations, a steady qualitative military buildup and a high degree of military confrontation, the following analysis demonstrates that the situation is far from stagnating—indeed, that European security is in flux and potent forces of change are already making their impact felt.

1. Constructive Trends in East-West Relations

The Superpower Dialogue

Among various factors determining European security, relations between the Soviet Union and the United States occupy a high place. Europe echoes and mirrors the ups and downs, the warmer and colder periods in superpower relations. Both powers are organically linked with this continent, they are part of it—geographically in the case of the Soviet Union and functionally in the case of the United States. Europe also sits at the center of their relationship. Soviet-American interaction is thus followed with utmost interest by all European states.

What is the most visible characteristic of superpower relations in the second half of the 1980s? The answer is rather obvious—the development of a dialogue. After years of almost no contacts but full of ideologically motivated charges, the international community could observe the gradual intensification of contacts and the broadening of their agenda. The dialogue has been conducted on various levels. There were four summit meetings between General Secretary Gorbachev and President Reagan in Geneva, Reykjavik, Washington and Moscow.[1] Foreign Minister Shevardnadze and Secretary of State Shultz met about thirty times. There were numerous meetings of negotiating and working groups and officials.

The talks and discussions brought about a number of results, starting with the drastic improvements of the international climate. The beginning of a "new era" in superpower relations was proclaimed during the 1988 summit meeting in Moscow.

Among the most spectacular achievements of the bilateral negotiations in the field of nuclear disarmament one should list the INF Treaty. Cooperation in seeking solutions to regional conflicts helped to conclude the Geneva accords on a political settlement concerning Afghanistan, to bring about the cease-fire in the Iran-Iraq war and to reach in November 1988 an agreement at the Geneva talks on Namibia and Angola.

Why was such an improvement in superpower relations in such a relatively short time possible? The reasons are manifold—subjective and objective, impelled on both sides as much by domestic political factors as by dynamics of the international situation. The readiness to accept restraints on their military competition was caused in the case of the United States by the mounting budgetary deficit, the pressure of Western allies, as well as President Reagan's desire to go down in history as a peacemaker.[2] In the case of the Soviet Union, apart from economic considerations, *perestroika*, "new political thinking," the concept of "reasonable sufficiency" and the devotion to the idea of a denuclearized world played an important role.

In addition, both sides switched from ideologically motivated to more pragmatic foreign policies. As Soviet Foreign Minister Eduard Shevardnadze stated at the UN General Assembly:

> . . . the Soviet leadership has tried to reinterpret more profoundly the idea, originally inherent in Marxism, of the interrelationship between class and universal human value, according priority to the interests shared by all nations. In our vision of peaceful coexistence as the universal principle of international relations, it does not appear as a special form of class struggle.[3]

Credit for the results achieved, for the improvement of the international climate, should certainly be given to both superpowers and their leaders. However, the advancement of the dialogue does not mean that all problems and difficulties existing between the United States and the Soviet Union have been removed.

A New Detente in Europe?

The "new era" of cooperation between the superpowers, the general improvement in East-West relations, poses a question of how those developments influence the situation in Europe. Is this continent simply returning to the policy of detente of the 1970s, or is the present stage of relations qualitatively different and accordingly should be described with other terms? In the debate on this question some analysts stress, with a dose of oversimplification, that the detente of the 1970s collapsed mainly because of the introduction in Europe of medium-range nuclear missiles and the deterioration of the international climate caused by the superpower rivalry in the Third World and by Soviet involvement in Afghanistan. If this is true, then after the INF Treaty and the Geneva agreement concerning Afghanistan, as well as the improvement of relations between the Soviet Union and the United States, the *status quo ante* was restored. However, the situation in Europe in the second half of the 1980s cannot be seen as a simple replica of the former model. This justifies the search for a different term. As a new word has not yet been found, various qualifiers like "pragmatic," "genuine," "second," "broader," and "new" are affixed to "detente."[4]

As in the superpower relationship, so in the broader context of East-West relations in Europe important changes have occurred:

–In the period of old detente the East stressed that the relaxation of tensions, a political rapprochement, does not extend to the ideological sphere, and that struggle in this domain should be continued. Now common values are emphasized and given priority over class interests, and ideological differences are not hampering the development of economic cooperation with the West, for example, through joint ventures.

–The agreement on mutual recognition signed in Luxembourg on June 25, 1988, by the EEC and CMEA ended more than 30 years of official non-recognition of the political and economic integration of Europe by the states of Eastern Europe, which established diplomatic relations with the Common Market.

–Human rights and their implementation were recognized as an important element strengthening European security and a legitimate subject of discussion within the CSCE process. New approaches to this question were demonstrated, *inter alia*, by the Soviet proposal to organize an international conference on human rights in Moscow in 1991, by Hungarian accession to the facultative protocol to the International Covenant on Civil and Political Rights, as well as by discussions in the East regarding joining some of the human rights agreements adopted by the Council of Europe.

At the root of many European problems lies the artificial division of the continent that dates back to the Cold War. The need to reduce gradually and then overcome this division, expand cooperation and restore the unity of Europe is felt independently of the existing blocs and sociopolitical differences. It stems from the awareness of mutual responsibility for the future of the continent.

To meet these legitimate expectations the socialist states have put forward the concept of the "common European home." This concept, which still needs further elaboration, underlines the importance of the common historical and cultural heritage of Europe, and stresses the links that objectively continue to exist and preserve European identity. The concept assumes that in a longer-term perspective political-military blocs will be dissolved and the unity of Europe from the Atlantic Ocean to the Ural Mountains will be restored. The common home does not exclude the coexistence of sovereign but different states. Its goal is to achieve unity in plurality. This concept is not aimed at the separation of the United States from Western Europe, nor does it rule out the integration processes going on in both parts of Europe.[5]

2. Sources and Directions of Change in Europe

In the shaping of the European security system an important role is played by the Conference on Security and Cooperation in Europe (CSCE). The Final Act adopted in Helsinki in 1975 created a framework for the evolution of interstate relations, for thinking about security in all-European terms, for overcoming the division of the continent. From the adoption of the CSCE Final Act arose the hope that an all-European security system based on confidence and mutual cooperation would emerge, a system embracing a broadly conceived balance of interests.

What elements constituted the embryo of that informal system? First of all, note should be taken of the adoption of the declaration of principles governing mutual relations of the participating states. The adoption of rules of conduct by all states of Europe is a *sine qua non*, a point of departure for the building of any system of lasting security. A vital factor for shaping European peace should be seen in the acceptance of the territorial status quo, i.e., confirmation of the inviability of Europe's existing frontiers; in a broad system of bilateral political consultations between states belonging to different sociopolitical systems; in development of trade and industrial, scientific and technological cooperation; as well as in the development of cooperation in the humanitarian field.

Why did hopes pinned on the building of European security fail to materialize? Apart from already mentioned reasons, the main flaw of this informal security system resulted from the absence of any program or steps for European disarmament, for scaling down military confrontation in Europe. The Final Act took notice only of the military aspects of security. The decisions were, in practice, limited to a few modest recommendations on military confidence-building measures. However, certain principles were agreed upon which paved the way for the mandate of a conference on confidence- and security-building measures and disarmament in Europe that was agreed upon at the Madrid meeting of the CSCE. The informal all-European security system gained its desired comprehensiveness when, by the decision of the Vienna meeting, negotiations on conventional armed forces in Europe became a part of the CSCE process.

New Developments in Eastern and Western Europe

The new dynamism in Europe is twofold. On the one hand, the Soviet Union and a number of socialist countries are engaged in the implementation of far-reaching programs of domestic economic and political reforms, and, on the other hand, the European Economic Community is moving toward the elimination of internal trade barriers and the creation of a single European market by 1992.

The main objective of *perestroika* in the Soviet Union is to reject command administrative methods of management and incorporate market mechanisms into the planned economy in order to increase its effectiveness. The socialist countries are in search of a new model of socialism appropriate to the times, based on democratization, openness and greater social and political pluralism.

What is the impact of *perestroika* on Soviet foreign policy? Soviet foreign policy is closely linked with domestic policy—in fact, it is even viewed in Moscow as an extension of the latter. Such a profound program of reforms as *perestroika* has to affect foreign policy. In order to concentrate on domestic concerns, a higher degree of cooperation with Western Europe and a reduction of military expenditures are necessary. These goals are achievable only through a change in Soviet foreign policy. A second set of factors that contributes to the modifications of foreign policy is linked with Soviet "new political thinking," which, in view of the unprecedented threats and opportunities confronting both the world and Europe, is urging a radical break with many conventional approaches to international relations and traditional views on problems of war and peace, defense and national and international security. Third, change has been needed in order to dismantle the hostile image of the Soviet Union and to put an end to anti-Soviet propaganda based on overblown perceptions of the Soviet threat.

What are the most important effects of combined changes in Soviet domestic and foreign policy? Probably the greatest effect has been the practical modification of traditional Soviet stances on arms control and defense policy. The Soviet Union is demonstrating a very flexible position and great determination to achieve deep reductions in the military forces and capabilities deployed in Europe. Recent decisions concerning unilateral cuts in conventional forces and armaments, the gradual elimination of chemical weapons, the pullback of not only conventional but also tactical nuclear weapons from Eastern Europe,[6] as well as the announcement that the USSR will reduce its military budget by 14.2 percent and cut production of weapons and military hardware by 19.5 percent[7] are the best evidence of new Soviet efforts to dismantle the East-West military confrontation on the continent.

The principles of *glasnost'*, democratization and legalism followed by the Soviet Union domestically are being transferred into its international relations. The best known manifestations of *glasnost'* in the military realm include the permission given to U.S. visitors to inspect the Krasnoyarsk radar in September 1987 and the opening in October 1987 of a chemical weapons facility at Shikany for a visit by diplomats and experts from 45 countries. Openness is also being demonstrated in the critical evaluation of the history of Soviet foreign policy now under way, and in particular the rejection of the long-standing official "presumption of infallibility." The new Soviet approach to international law, the recognition of the rule of law and the emphasis on the primacy of common human values in relations between all states strengthen the shift in Europe from bilateralism toward multilateralism, open the way toward future acceptance of an all-European system of the peaceful settlement of disputes and an all-European system of international protection of human rights.

Fundamental changes in relations between the Soviet Union and Eastern Europe are under way, including recognition of the principle of sovereign equality, rejection of the concept of one model of socialism, differences in the degree and direction of the reforms being implemented by socialist countries and stronger articulation of national interests. Naturally the question arises whether these developments present a danger to European stability. One may agree with the opinion that:

> The present period in socialist countries—where the new coexists with the old and the cumbersome but ingrained forms and methods of political and economic activity are still being overcome—is pregnant with crises. Even reforms as such, which aim at the eventual recovery of society and improvement of socialism, might become in the course of their implementation new sources of public discontent and conflict.[8]

However, possible unrest or crisis in Eastern Europe cannot be avoided by slowing down or halting reforms—this would only aggravate the existing situation. Thus the danger for European stability does not stem from reforms as such but from external reactions to possible unrest or conflict. No doubt interference in internal affairs, an attempt to treat them instrumentally as a means of damaging the interests of the other side, may destabilize all of Europe. Thus a recognition of the legitimate security interests of the other side; cooperation between the United States and the Soviet Union and in a broader sense between East and West; as well as the adoption of a new code of conduct in case of crisis in either part of Europe seem to be the only rational responses to situations which otherwise could greatly jeopardize European security.

The parallel development in Western Europe, the process of establishing a single market by 1992, also may not be free of tensions. Some analysts foresee that approximately 300 directives (e.g., eliminating internal barriers in trade and transport, harmonizing banking and financial systems, creating greater competitiveness in electronics and telecommunications) may lead to a temporary increase in unemployment, thus causing a certain social opposition.

What might the impact be of the single market on European security? There are two possible scenarios. The first is negative: the European Economic Community would be closely integrated and separated from the rest of Europe, thus deepening the division of Europe and hindering East-West economic cooperation. The second, more probable scenario is positive, namely that a stronger Common Market will be interested in the expansion of trade and credit relations and in technology transfer with the Soviet Union and Eastern Europe, which would create new possibilities for all-European cooperation.

Trends Toward Closer Cooperation

In overcoming the division of Europe and creating a new climate of confidence and understanding, the role of all-European cooperation cannot be overestimated. The pressure for cooperation springs from growing interdependence, which is felt not only globally but regionally. A push toward closer cooperation in Europe stems from common dangers and challenges, interests and obligations.

Probably the area in which the existence of threats endangering the whole continent is the most obvious is the environment. From an ecological point of view, European divisions and existing frontiers are of secondary importance. The protection of the natural environment demands bilateral, subregional and regional cooperation independent of any differences in sociopolitical systems. The struggle against river pollution will not bring many results without close cooperation between the two German states in the case of the Elbe, or without subregional cooperation among all Eastern and Western states bordering the Danube. The same may be said about the protection of the marine environment of the Baltic Sea and the Mediterranean Sea. The elimination of acid rains devastating Central European forests and endangering the quality of human life in this subregion cannot be achieved without broad, all-European efforts in fighting long-range trans-boundary air pollution. The dangers of radioactive pollution were dramatically illustrated by the Chernobyl catastrophe. The need for intensifying all-European environmental cooperation and a new sense of common responsibility for the environment are growing.

Regional cooperation is greatly needed to combat problems such as terrorism, drug abuse and increasingly widespread diseases. In the final document of the Vienna meeting of the CSCE, the participating states agreed to reinforce and develop bilateral and multilateral cooperation in order to prevent and combat terrorism. They will develop cooperation in medicine and related sciences by intensifying research and the exchange of information on drug abuse. They will cooperate in particular in combating the spread of AIDS.[9]

From the European security perspective, the developments and steady increase in East-West economic cooperation are of paramount importance. But which factors are prevailing—positive or negative? Among those hampering increased cooperation are limitations on the transfer of technology as well as the growing indebtedness of the socialist states. Nevertheless, the list of positive factors is longer. Europe is still characterized by a large degree of economic complementarity. In both East and West there is a pronounced awareness of the persistence of negative phenomena, above all technological restrictions, that can lead to a serious technological and economic division of the continent as well as negative consequences for broader inter-system contacts. A clear example of this is the cooperation between the two German states, which see the necessity of promoting their economic ties in as wide a range of areas as possible.

A number of positive impulses to greater progress in economic cooperation stem from the CSCE process. The present roadblocks to East-West cooperation are largely non-economic. The opportunity presented by the CSCE process boils down to the possibility of doing away with those unfavorable external factors. The Vienna final document, for example, imposes on participating states the obligation to facilitate direct contacts between business people, including on-site contacts relevant to the business being transacted.

Perestroika and reforms in the socialist countries have also stimulated the development of cooperation with the West. The socialist states are now more interested in intensifying trade and economic relations with other countries.[10] This has already been demonstrated by their access to a number of international economic organizations and the establishment of relations between the European Community and the Council for Mutual Economic Assistance. The removal of various bureaucratic obstacles is evident in new laws regulating joint ventures as well as the dismantling of the state foreign-trade monopoly. Improvements in the international political climate, as well as the economic reforms in most

Eastern countries, have led to a flurry of contracts, negotiations and agreements among governments and business firms. After several years of stagnation, East European exports to the West rose in the first half of 1988, increasing by 6 percent.[11] Despite the recent upturn, however, prospects for a continued expansion of East European exports are uncertain. Although the profit motive is of primary importance for the development of sound economic relations between East and West, the political importance of economic relations should not be neglected.

New Ideas and Concepts

Among various vehicles of present and potential change in Europe, a prominent place should be given to new thinking about security problems. Broad debate and the emergence of alternative security concepts is the best evidence that, for broad segments of public opinion and different social and political forces, many of the existing axioms that were worked out in the past no longer form an adequate or a sufficient basis for European security.

Although *perestroika* provides a natural impetus toward new thinking, as proven by the emergence in the Soviet Union of the principle of "military sufficiency" and the concept of "comprehensive" security, many new ideas—e.g., common security and non-offensive defense (structural incapability for attack)—were born in the West.

The security debate has numerous ramifications and raises questions concerning the role of nuclear arms in Europe. No first use, flexible response and minimum deterrence are in question not because of the Soviet campaign for denuclearization of Europe but because of basic doubts concerning the implications of the present NATO nuclear strategy. Nuclear deterrence is challenged in the West not only by peace movements but also by churches, mainly on moral grounds. The military, political and psychological implications of deterrence are debated by political parties and social movements.

Is the discussion of alternative security concepts an example of an "academic," i.e., purely theoretical, exercise without any practical implications? As is already evident in the case of "non-offensive defense," new concepts have more than just a chance to bring about far-reaching change. Occasionally discussed over the years, non-offensive defense has become an object of intensive and broad debate in Western Europe in the 1980s.

A detailed enumeration of all the elements of non-offensive defense is difficult since the whole concept is more theoretical than analytical. Nevertheless, it is sufficiently defined to be able to suggest the direction in which the present military postures and doctrines of both alliances might or should be changed.[12] The concept assumes at a minimum raising the nuclear threshold and accepting the principle of no first use. As far as conventional forces are concerned, a non-offensive posture signifies a need for "transarmament" (a switch from one type of arms to another) and restructuring as well as the acceptance of the new axiom, "the best defense is (not an attack but) a good, well prepared defense." These changes through, *inter alia*, the reduction of offensive weapons should bring about a structural incapability for attack on the strategic and operational levels.

Although none of the NATO countries officially come out in support of non-offensive defense, the concept is very much present in political debate, especially in the FRG, Denmark and the United Kingdom and to a lesser degree in other states. This is mainly due to the fact that the majority of European socialist and social-democratic parties are in search of an alternative security policy.

Among various changes brought about in the Soviet Union by *perestroika* may also be included the acceptance of this idea. In the updated proposal of armed forces and arms reduction in Europe put forward by the WTO in July 1988, the member-states suggested that the last of three stages foreseen for the implementation of their proposal should entail making the remaining forces strictly defensive. It is worthwhile to note that elements of the concept of non-offensiveness were also embodied in the Jaruzelski Plan of May 1987. The unilateral steps announced by Mikhail Gorbachev in December 1988 were prepared in full accord with this concept. The Soviet Union is withdrawing six tank divisions and assault-landing and assault-bridging units from the GDR, Czechoslovakia and Hungary, reducing offensive weapons and reorganizing the Soviet forces remaining outside Soviet territory to make them strictly defensive.

An important and welcome step toward acceptance of the main tenets of the concept of non-offensive defense was recently taken by NATO, which declared in its Statement on Conventional Arms Control of December 1988: ". . . we would then be willing to contemplate further steps to enhance stability and security in Europe, for example . . . the restructuring of armed forces to enhance defensive capabilities and further reduce offensive capabilities."

3. Changes in the European Military Environment

The new climate in Europe is by no means limited exclusively to the political sphere; it also involves the military field. This is mainly due to the positive results of the INF Treaty, agreed upon by the two superpowers, and the CSCE Final Document agreed upon by the 35 participants in the CSCE process in Stockholm. A promising atmosphere and expectations are also created by hopes invested in the ongoing negotiations and by recent unilateral steps announced by the Soviet Union.

The INF Treaty requires the destruction of all ground-launched Soviet and American missiles with ranges between 500 and 5,000 km during the three years after it enters into force. The signing and the initial implementation of the treaty were welcomed in East and West as a practical step towards a world without nuclear weapons. Indeed, there are good reasons to call the INF Treaty a historic achievement, since for the first time an entire class of nuclear weapons is to be eliminated instead of only limited in growth. The agreement proves that when the security interests of both sides are adequately taken into account, far-reaching objectives may be arrived at and the traditional obstacles in the arms control process—asymmetries and verification problems—can be overcome. No doubt the INF Treaty has created a certain momentum facilitating further progress in disarmament and increasing hopes for a 50-percent reduction of strategic nuclear systems, which would strengthen the process from "above" as an agreement on limiting tactical nuclear weapons would strengthen it from "below."

Although the implications of the INF Treaty transcend the bounds of Europe, it is this continent which benefits most. Consequently it is in Europe that the basic security dilemma is gaining a new dimension and urgency. The success of the INF Treaty underlines the very pertinent question of whether both alliances should follow the traditional pattern of the development of their military potentials, which results in the arms race, or engage themselves in further lowering the level of military confrontation in Europe. An appealing precedent has been established.

Prospects for the Reduction of Armed Forces

The necessity to halt the arms race and reduce conventional forces in Europe rests on a number of arguments. The present level of armaments, far exceeding the security needs of both alliances, may actually be seen as an autonomous threat decreasing crisis stability in Europe. New weapons systems which present the possibility of a "technological war" cannot but change the military doctrine on conventional forces, inevitably heightening Europe's sense of jeopardy. The current arms momentum absorbs an excessive amount of human, technological and financial resources and hinders the political, economic, social and cultural development of Europe.

The improvement of conventional stability in Europe would not only have a positive impact on the political climate, it would also facilitate progress in making Europe less nuclear. Furthermore, conventional arms reduction has to be seen as an indispensable and important element in efforts to scale down the East-West military confrontation.

Despite the well known obstacles the CFE talks face (addressed elsewhere in this volume), there is general agreement on a number of important objectives. Informal talks between the two alliances held in Vienna have resulted in the acceptance of three goals for the talks:

–the establishment of a stable and secure balance of conventional forces at lower levels;
–the elimination of disparities prejudicial to stability and security; and
–the elimination of the capability for launching a surprise attack or initiating a large-scale offensive.

As the text of the CFE mandate mentions in several places that stability (and security) should be increased, this objective can also be seen as the overall purpose of the negotiations. The group of 23 did not define or explain any of the terms describing the goals of the talks. This may lead to future debates on terminology because even such notions as "surprise attack" or "stability" can be understood in different ways. However, the mandate enumerates the methods by which this objective can be achieved. The subject matter of the negotiations embraces conventional forces, including conventional armaments and equipment. Nuclear and chemical weapons as well as naval forces are beyond the scope of the talks. During informal discussions participants agreed that no conventional armament shall be excluded from the negotiations solely on the basis of the additional capabilities it may possess.

As far as reductions are concerned, attention should focus on weapons and equipment that are particularly well suited for offensive operations. Those weapons should be taken into account together with manpower in combat units. Units are easier to verify than weapons and firepower taken alone. The most frequently mentioned reduction units are battalions and divisions. Regiments and brigades are also listed.

Tactical nuclear weapons—to eliminate, reduce or modernize?

The exclusion of nuclear weapons from the CFE talks quite naturally poses the question of whether tactical land-based missiles and nuclear warheads for dual-mission systems can be left out of any disarmament negotiations in Europe. This issue has become more acute since the entry into force of the INF Treaty.

In the debate within NATO on this question two approaches have emerged. The first, represented by the United States, the United Kingdom and France, moves the possibility of reductions of tactical nuclear systems to the end of the whole disarmament process, suggesting that negotiations should be undertaken only after a conventional balance in Europe and a 50-percent reduction of strategic nuclear systems have been achieved. The second approach, advocated by the Federal Republic of Germany, foresees the possibility of parallel talks and reductions.

In the statement adopted at the July 1988 Warsaw session of its Political Consultative Committee, the WTO declared that a considerable reduction and subsequent elimination of tactical nuclear weapons, including warheads for dual-capable systems, would be an important measure toward reducing the risk of an outbreak of war and creating a more stable situation in Europe. The WTO proposed that talks on this issue be opened in the very near future.

Beginning separate talks to fill the existing gap in the European disarmament process could lead to reductions of land-based short-range nuclear systems through the establishment of common ceilings. There is even a chance to eliminate nuclear munitions because their combat usefulness is questioned by many specialists on the basis of command and control complexities and the risk involved for one's own or allied troops.

Modernization, like reduction or elimination, of short-range nuclear weapons is another issue hotly debated within NATO. A decision to upgrade some systems and to add new nuclear weaponry was undertaken at Montebello in October 1983, when prospects for an agreement on the elimination of two classes of land-based nuclear systems were rather bleak, and relations between the United States and the Soviet Union strained.

The WTO position concerning modernization, formulated in a communiqué of the July 1988 Warsaw session of its Political Consultative Committee, highlights the threat presented by "plans to 'compensate for' the intermediate-range and shorter-range missiles that are being eliminated by building up and extensively modernizing other weapons, the realization of which can lead to another spiral of the arms race."[13]

It goes without saying that an obligation not to undermine the INF Treaty "from below" is not a one-way street. Both alliances should refrain from modernizing their short-range nuclear systems. Existing imbalances should be eliminated through negotiations, either by establishment of common ceilings or through adaptation of a third zero option.

The Greater Military Confidence in Europe

The agreement signed on September 22, 1986, by the 35 nations participating in the Stockholm Conference proved for the first time that far-reaching measures of verification, including on-site inspection, can be agreed upon and implemented in East-West arms control agreements, that building confidence may precede disarmament agreements, and that greater openness and predictability in military activities strengthen European security. The agreement provides prior notification of certain military activities, an observation of military activities above a threshold of 17,000 troops, an exchange among participating states of annual calendars of their military activities and challenge inspections up to three times each year on the territory of the participating states to resolve doubts about compliance. It is worth noting that implementation of the Stockholm agreement is another confidence-building measure in itself as (up through early 1989, in any case) a breach of its provisions has not been invoked.

Unilateral Steps. In his December 1988 UN speech Mikhail Gorbachev announced that in 1989–1990 the strength of the Soviet armed forces will be reduced by 500,000 troops, 10,000 tanks, 8,500 artillery systems and 800 combat aircraft. The Soviet Union decided to withdraw from the GDR, Czechoslovakia and Hungary six tank divisions as well as landing-assault and landing-crossing units with their arms and combat material by 1991. The Soviet forces stationed in these countries will be reduced by 50,000 troops and 5,000 tanks. Moreover, the remaining divisions will be restructured and will become strictly defensive. The declared cuts are militarily significant. Suffice it to note that the estimated 500,000 troops are comparable to the numerical strength of the entire FRG Bundeswehr.

The unilateral cuts can be interpreted as proof that the Soviet Union is following the principle of military sufficiency not only in words but in deeds. For the first time the concept of non-offensiveness and structural incapability for attack will be tested in practice. The Soviet leadership has again demonstrated its willingness to encourage the process of building a new model for European security through the reduction of armaments rather than their buildup.

The reduction and restructuring of the Soviet forces are to be carried out unilaterally, unconditionally and are not connected with the negotiations of the 23. Nevertheless, they are addressing the negotiations' main objectives: the elimination of disparities in conventional forces and the elimination of the capabilities for launching a surprise attack. No doubt the withdrawal and disbandment of six tank divisions from the line of direct contact between the WTO and NATO, the withdrawal of assault and bridging equipment and defensive restructuring of the remaining troops in Central Europe has to be interpreted as depriving the Soviet forces of much of the offensive capabilities attributed to them by many in Western Europe. The announced cuts will also bring about a significant reduction in existing imbalances.

As Soviet commentators have noted, the implementation of reductions will take place in conditions of the greatest possible openness, including dissemination of the necessary information about the timetable for conducting these measures and invitations to foreign observers and representatives of the media to witness that all reductions and withdrawals really do take place.[14]

It is worth mentioning that the planned reduction of Soviet forces will bring about positive economic effects. It is assumed that part of the military hardware (e.g., vehicles, cranes, mobile generators, diesel engines) and military specialists involved may be transferred into the civilian economy.[15]

Economic considerations have determined the nature of the unilateral steps undertaken by other WTO countries. On December 8, 1988, during the session of the Defense Committee of the Hungarian National Assembly, Minister of Defense Ferenc Karpati stated that reductions in Hungary's economic and social situation justify a 17-percent cut in the real value of the military budget for 1989. He also underlined that the unilateral withdrawal of Soviet troops has made it obvious that their presence on the territories of other socialist countries is based exclusively on military considerations; thus their withdrawal and disbandment depends not so much on political considerations, but on change in the European military situation.[16] Polish Defense Minister General Florian Siwicki, commenting on information that Polish military spending in 1989 will be cut by 4 percent in real terms, announced that savings will be arrived at by cuts in personnel—not replacing some retiring officers and cutting the number of reservists called up for military training. He also stated that in 1987–1988 the Polish army had already been cut by 15,000 troops. Similar cuts were announced by the GDR (10,000 men and a 10-percent reduction of military spending in two years), Czechoslovakia (12,000 men and a 17-percent reduction of the military budget by 1991) and Bulgaria (10,000 men and a 12-percent reduction of military spending in 1989). Romania had declared a unilateral reduction of 5 percent in defense spending in 1986.[17]

4. Changes in Threat Perception

Improvements in East-West relations challenge many preconceptions concerning the danger and the nature of war in Europe and the Soviet threat. At present neither public opinion nor a majority of analysts, in East or West, believes that there is any immediate danger of war in Europe. This is a step forward in comparison with the early 1980s, when emotions linked with the deployment of medium-range missiles, the deterioration of superpower relations and the exchange of accusations and sharp rhetoric undercut a feeling of stability in Europe.

Although there is a remote danger that military conflict may begin in Europe through escalation of a European or Third World crisis involving the two alliances or by an accident linked with misperception or miscommunication,[18] the possibilities of war by design, by a preplanned attack, are close to none. There are good reasons for this.

Military force cannot be effectively utilized either for political or military goals between the WTO and NATO in Europe. A conventional war on this continent, not to mention a nuclear one, is unimaginable because of its disastrous consequences. Extremely potent new conventional systems such as area weapons and precision-guided munitions, the existence of nuclear power plants, major chemical works, magazines of dangerous materials, reservoirs, and the delicate infrastructure of modern societies and densely populated towns together may bring about an unforeseeable degree of destruction. Besides, any conventional conflict can easily be turned into a nuclear one. Thus Europe is already in a "post-Clausewitzian" period.

If this assumption is true, it also excludes the possibility of a Soviet attack. However, the existence of a Soviet threat has played an important role in both bringing NATO into existence and maintaining its cohesion. For this very reason Western military officials continue to speak about the existence of a Soviet threat. Former U.S. Defense Secretary Frank Carlucci stated: "We are still facing a very substantial military threat."[19] A British defense official observed: "The key problem for NATO right now is convincing our publics that there is still a threat from the East in raw military power."[20]

Despite these efforts, the Soviet threat is declining in public perception as few West Europeans see a real danger of Soviet invasion.[21] This is confirmed by recent polls. In the United States, the "Americans Talk Security" project conducted a series of polls on this subject and it found a dramatic turnaround on the following question: "Do you believe the military threat from the Soviet Union is constantly growing and presents a real, immediate danger to the United States?" In February 1986, 69 percent of respondents answered affirmatively. In October 1987 the figures were reversed—67 percent answered in the negative.[22] Surveys on international security were conducted by the Canadian Institute for International Peace and Security in July 1988 in Canada, the United Kingdom and the Federal Republic of Germany on the question, "In the next ten years, how likely is it that the Soviet Union would attack Western Europe?" Answers "very likely" and "likely" received 22 percent in Canada, 10 percent in the United Kingdom, and 4 percent in the FRG, whereas responses "unlikely" and "very unlikely" reached 78 percent, 90 percent and 96 percent, respectively.[23]

What brought about such changes in the evaluation of the Soviet threat? The reasons are manifold, but limiting the answer to the military sphere one can observe that Western publics are now convinced that NATO is stronger than a few years ago, that it has a technological edge over the WTO. No doubt the evolution of Soviet military doctrine, the Soviet flexibility and desire to reach arms control agreements, as well as greater openness generally have also played a role.

The disappearance of the danger of war and the profound shifts in threat perceptions will most probably strengthen important new trends already felt in both parts of Europe. Public support for high military expenditure will be on the decrease, whereas the pressure to lower the level of military potential will be on the rise. Alternative security concepts, more responsive to the demands and needs of the present period, will fall on more fertile ground. Last but not least, the security agenda will be gradually changed, giving more attention to new non-military threats linked with the economy, the environment, drugs and terrorism.[24]

Toward a Comprehensive, Common Security System in Europe

"Security" can be taken to mean a lot of things: freedom from the threat of external attack or the ability to repulse it, but also freedom from outside intervention or pressures. There is also no doubt that the security of a state can be taken to mean the absence of threats and the ability to preserve its fundamental values and to pursue fully its own development.

Not all threats to state security are of a military character. Not all threats can be removed through recourse to military force. Concepts of security may stress national unilateral action or multilateral cooperative approaches. International security requires a balance between military and non-military elements and between national and international interests.

In today's world, international security can be achieved mainly through political means. A nation's security involves many elements (one can speak about economic or ecological security), and it cannot be assured by the accumulation of weapons. The concepts of national and international security have become "indivisible." The present system of security based on the balance of forces and deterrence has failed to address the fundamental dilemma of security in the nuclear age, i.e., the assurance of mutual security. The means used to strengthen the military security of one side invariably have worked (or could work) towards weakening the sense of security of the other. Today, for the first time in the history of mankind, states are forced to consider—for the sake of survival—the security of the potential enemy. The security of one side cannot be assured at the expense of the other side's.

It would be naive, even erroneous, to think that creating a new system of security would be a matter of a single act, such as, for example, an agreement. The elements of deterrence will persist for a long time even if we concede that a new security system based on elements of cooperation and confidence has begun to emerge. The search for an alternative system of security cannot be reduced to the substitution of cooperation for deterrence. In practical terms the issue boils down to the following question: whether and by what means we could downplay the traditional elements of deterrence and enhance the role of cooperation and confidence among states.

The military security of states no longer is the sole issue of international security. The newly emerging security system will bind into an organic whole military, political, economic, environmental and humanitarian aspects of security. A new relationship between the military sphere and the other, non-military spheres will be the most distinguishing feature of the future system as compared with the present one. This is, however, *a long-term prospect*—regardless of how desirable it is at present to place state security on more stable foundations.

In order to establish a comprehensive common security system in Europe, political detente should be supplemented by military detente. Military detente in Europe includes not only reductions but a change of doctrines, dismantling of the enemy image, confidence-building measures and openness, self-restraint and, last but not least, a halt to the arms race. In other words, military detente is a process leading to the reduced role of military force in East-West relations. Through unilateral acts and recognition of the other side's legitimate military interests, states can convince one another about their intentions and prove that their doctrines are evolving. Perhaps, for the first time in postwar history, Europe is confronted with the real chance to enhance military detente. Now, as never before, thanks to numerous initiatives and profound change in the political landscape, a European agenda has been reached that is broad enough to address not only the central problem—the reduction of conventional forces—but at the same time the psychological dimension of the military confrontation through negotiations on confidence-building measures and discussions of military doctrines.

Does this mean that Europe is moving toward the end of the arms race, toward military detente, in an irreversible way? A positive answer would be premature. Europe is still at a crossroads.

Notes

1   Their next meeting (with the participation of President-elect Bush), although not having the rank of a summit, took place on December 7, 1988, in New York.
2   Canadian Institute for International Peace and Security, "International Security and Canadian Interests," Report of a Working Group, June 1988, pp. 11–12.

3 *Pravda*, September 28, 1988, p. 4.

4 Charlotte Saikowski, "A New 'Detente' for the 1980s," *Christian Science Monitor*, May 24, 1988; Joseph C. Harsch, "New Detente Waxes as East-West Empire-Building Wanes," *Christian Science Monitor*, June 10, 1988; Don Oberdorfer, "Woerner Urges New Era in East-West Relations," *The Washington Post*, September 14, 1988.

5 *Disarmament and Security: 1987 Yearbook* (Moscow: Novosti Press Agency Publishing House, 1988), p. 332. As Mikhail Gorbachev writes: "Integrative processes are developing intensively in both parts of Europe. It is time to think what will come next. Will the split in Europe be further aggravated or can a blend be found to the benefit of both the Eastern and the Western parts in the interests of Europe and indeed the rest of world? The requirements of economic development in both parts, as well as scientific and technological progress, prompt the need for a search for some form of mutually advantageous cooperation." Mikhail Gorbachev, *Perestroika: New Thinking for Our Country and the World* (New York: Harper & Row, 1987), p. 196.

6 Gordon McKibben, "USSR Announces Missile Pullback," *The Boston Globe*, January 20, 1989.

7 Bill Keller, "Gorbachev Promises Big Cut in Military Spending," *The New York Times*, January 19, 1989.

8 Institute of the Economics of the World Socialist System, "East-West Relations and Eastern Europe (An American-Soviet Dialogue) . . . The Soviet Perspective," *Problems of Communism* (May–August 1988), p. 66.

9 Text in *The New York Times*, January 17, 1989.

10 The Soviet Union and Eastern Europe produce 20 percent of the world's GNP, yet East-West trade is only 2 percent of total world trade.

11 See the review of 1988 developments in East-West trade and financial relations in the *Economic Bulletin for Europe*, United Nations Press Release, ECE/446, November 25, 1988, p. 3.

12 See Anders Boserup, "Non-Offensive Defense in Europe," in Derek Paul, ed., *Defending Europe: Options for Security* (London and Philadelphia: Taylor & Francis, 1986); Albrecht A. C. von Mueller, "Conventional Stability in Europe. Outlines of the Military Hardware for Second Detente" (Starnberg: 1987), p. 14; Janusz Symonides, "Toward Non-Offensive Defense in Central Europe" (Warsaw: Polish Institute of International Affairs, Occasional Papers 5, 1988).

13 *Pravda*, July 17, 1988.

14 See briefing by Viktor P. Karpov, Deputy Foreign Minister, *Pravda*, December 16, 1988; also interview with Major General V. Kuklev, *Krasnaia zvezda*, December 28, 1988.

15 Major General Iu. Lebedev, deputy chief of an Armed Forces General Staff directorate, has stated that the economic effect of the planned reduction of the armed forces will be considerable and will be felt fully in two to three years (*Sovetskaia Rossiia*, December 23, 1988).

16 Attila Balint's conversation with Defense Minister Ferenc Karpati, Budapest Domestic Service in Hungarian, Foreign Broadcast Information Service, *Daily Report-Eastern Europe* 88–237, December 9, 1988, p. 23.

17 Christopher Bobinski, "Poland to Cut Forces by 'Tens of Thousands,'" *The Financial Times*, January 4, 1989; *Jane's Defence Weekly*, February 11, 1989, p. 207.

18 Consultancy Document, "Common Security in Europe," Vol. I, "Defense of Europe, A Conceptual Framework," Foundation for International Security, May 1987, pp. 4–5.

19 Quoted in Fred Hiatt, "Britain and U.S. Say Soviet Military Is Still a Threat," *The Guardian*, June 8, 1988.

20 Quoted in Tim Aeppel, "NATO Seeks 'Harmonious' Image on Eve of Moscow Summit," *Christian Science Monitor*, May 27, 1988.

21 F. Stephen Larrabee, "East-West Security in the 1990s: Challenges and Prospects," paper prepared for the Institute for East-West Security Studies, Seventh Annual Conference, Potsdam, GDR, June 9–11, 1988, pp. 8–9.

22 See William Schneider, "Evil Empire Vanishes as GOP Issue," *National Journal*, June 4, 1988.

23 Canadian Institute for International Peace and Security, "Canada-United Kingdom-Federal Republic of Germany, Survey on International Security," August 22, 1988. The Canadian survey was carried out by the Longwoods Research Group, the British poll was carried out by Social Surveys (Gallup Poll) Ltd and the German poll was carried out by the Institut fuer Angewandte Sozialwissenschaft.

24 Walter S. Mossberg and John Walcott, "U.S. Redefines Policy on Security to Place Less Stress on Soviets," *The Wall Street Journal*, August 11, 1988.

PART ONE

The Conventional Military Balance in Europe: Strategy, Forces and the Dynamics of War

Richard L. Kugler,* United States

Introduction

In Central Europe today thousands of heavily armed NATO and Warsaw Pact soldiers confront each other across the border that has divided Germany since 1945. Notwithstanding the changes now taking place in European security affairs, this dangerous confrontation of conventional forces is no historical anachronism. It is a product of a lengthy East-West struggle over Europe's destiny that continues today, albeit in more muted terms than in earlier years. Notwithstanding the unilateral Soviet troop cuts announced by Gorbachev in December 1988, it does not show signs of dying a natural death anytime soon. In fact, in purely qualitative terms, it continues to grow daily as each side slowly but steadily improves its forces with new weapons. As it grows, it continues to complicate any attempt to bring enduring stability to Europe.

The upcoming talks on Conventional Forces in Europe (CFE), like the long and fruitless MBFR negotiations that preceded them, will aim at resolving this confrontation. While their prospects are as unclear as their agenda is ambitious, one thing seems certain: the exact nature of the military balance in Europe will be a key issue at these talks. If the MBFR experience is a prologue, technical discussions are likely to dwell heavily on each side's views. Reduction proposals are likely to be made, and accepted or rejected, on the basis of contending theories about the

*   The views expressed in this essay are solely those of the author, and do not necessarily represent those of the RAND Corporation or any of its research sponsors.

balance. Ultimately, success or failure might hinge on whether the two sides can reach a common understanding of it.

Despite its critical importance, the military balance is a topic that, while hotly debated, is poorly understood. Part of this owes to the complexity of the balance and the classified nature of much of the data. But even so, it is not beyond comprehension. The purpose of this chapter is to shed some clarifying light on this subject. In particular, it focuses on the controversial issue of whether an imbalance of forces exists in Central Europe, as NATO claims and the Warsaw Pact denies. Unavoidably this chapter presents a Western perspective on this issue. But its goal is not to win this argument on NATO's behalf or to underscore any negotiating position. By treating the issues as fairly as possible, while also making clear NATO's main concerns, it aims at establishing a better basis for a profitable dialogue between the two sides.

The following pages begin with an appraisal of an all-important facet of the balance: the military strategies on both sides, including how each alliance sees itself and perceives the other. The analysis then focuses on NATO and Warsaw Pact forces themselves. While it briefly discusses the peacetime balance, it particularly addresses the wartime balance and how an actual war might unfold. This is necessary to bring into sharp focus the sources of instability in Central Europe. It then briefly examines future trends in the balance, including both Warsaw Pact and NATO improvements.

Soviet Military Strategy in Europe

Someone wise once said that truth, like beauty, is relative and is a function of one's angle of vision. To the uninitiated observer, this dictum certainly would seem to apply to the current East-West debate over the military balance in Europe. He quickly would discover that each alliance claims innocence in its own strategy and forces. Meanwhile each regularly condemns the other for allegedly sinister intent.

NATO, of course, has long proclaimed that its military strategy is purely defensive whereas Warsaw Pact strategy is offensive in nature. What is less commonly appreciated is that ever since the Cold War began, the Soviets have been making the same claim, only in reverse. They have accused NATO of plotting aggression against them, while asserting that their strategy and forces are intended exclusively for deterrence and defense. Over the years their military exercises evidently have acted out this interpretation. Warsaw Pact spokesmen assert that these exercises always have begun with a NATO-initiated crisis and a postulated NATO assault into Eastern Europe. Through 1986, they ended with a Warsaw Pact counteroffensive into Western Europe. But beginning in 1987, Eastern spokesmen say, they apparently were revised to conclude with a counterattack only to the inter-German border.

Against this historical background, Soviet General Secretary Gorbachev's recent proclamation of a defensive military doctrine of "reasonable sufficiency" can be seen more as a reassertion of a traditional position rather than any new departure. Its newness lies in its greater sensitivity to Western fears and its stated willingness to scale back specific aspects of Soviet forces that appear threatening. But in its core message, it reaffirms Moscow's long-standing theme rather than proclaiming any newly found virtue.

Why then are some in NATO skeptical of Moscow's claims to defensive intent, including Gorbachev's new doctrine? Are the fears that NATO expresses nothing more than politically motivated complaints? Are they the products of misperception or an excessively conservative "worst-case" mentality that divines a threat where none exists? And how can NATO, which spends well over $200 billion each year to train and equip its forces, claim defensive intent for itself? Is this stance not hypocritical or at least insensitive to the threatening signals that NATO's military preparations emit?

NATO's answers to these questions are worth exploring for they provide important insights into the inner workings of its military planning. In its view, NATO's long-standing distrust of the Soviet Union is neither a ploy nor an erroneous judgment. On the contrary, it stems from a combination of reasons that are regarded as being valid. Purely military factors play a large role in this appraisal, as discussed below. But underlying and reinforcing them lie worrisome judgments about Moscow's political goals in Europe.

Nearly all Western experts today would grant that the Soviet Union's severe setbacks early in World War II provide some basis for understanding how the fear of an external threat could linger long after the reality has disappeared. Most also would agree that this experience can help explain why the Soviets still might prefer ample margins of insurance in forces and a geographical buffer zone to hedge against invasion ever happening again. But in equally strong terms, most would not be prepared to accept this rationale as a fully adequate explanation for the USSR's behavior in Europe since 1945, much less an acceptable justification for it.

Indeed, since the Cold War's onset NATO consistently has concluded that the Soviets have been pursuing not only defensive goals in Europe, but distinctly offensive ones as well. These aims include both absolute control in Eastern Europe and the ability to exert improper influence over Western Europe by intimidation or force, if necessary. Nor has this appraisal been appreciably affected by Gorbachev's activist diplomacy over the past three years. The primary reason for continued skepticism is that although Gorbachev's lofty rhetoric about better East-West relations strikes responsive chords, his specific vision of the future European security order is less reassuring. It seems anchored on closer Soviet–West European ties against a background of a militarily weakened NATO and a less influential U.S. presence in Europe. To many NATO experts, this sounds suspiciously like old wine in new bottles.

In NATO's eyes, the forward positioning of large Soviet forces in Eastern Europe, backed up by massive reserves in the western USSR, has long played an integral role in supporting these traditional goals. Particularly since these forces have been employed three times to squash rebellion in Eastern Europe, NATO officials look askance at the proposition that they are not an instrument of offensive policy. Indeed NATO believes that the absence of war in Europe since 1945 can be ascribed not to Moscow's pacific intent but rather to the fact that NATO always has been prudent enough to maintain a powerful deterrent.

The skeptical conclusions suggested by this political appraisal are reinforced by NATO's technical analysis of the Warsaw Pact's military posture. Influencing this analysis is the fact that the size of any alliance's military forces often is a key measure of its political goals. Defensive aims can be signalled clearly and offensive intent often is rendered equally transparent by the character of military forces. This phenomenon is well known to defense analysts, whose awareness of military capabilities often enables them to see clearly through the fog of confusing rhetoric about political intentions.

The methodology employed by military analysts begins with the use of simple but powerful building blocks based on force-to-space relationships. Western military professionals commonly credit a modern NATO/ Warsaw Pact division (armored or mechanized) as being able initially to defend a frontage of about 20–30 kilometers on the Central European terrain. Based on this and related calculations, a defending army needs at least 45 to 60 divisions, along with appropriate tactical air support, to defend the front line of 750 kilometers there against a major invasion. Some 30–40 divisions are needed to establish an adequately dense, contiguous front line astride the roughly 14 invasion corridors that lie along the inter-German border. The remaining units are required to form "operational reserves" that can be employed to replace casualties on the front line and to contain localized enemy penetrations into the rear areas.

By contrast an attacking army ideally needs well over this amount to prosecute an offensive campaign to completion. One reason is that attacking divisions need to narrow their frontages to about 10-15 kilometers in order to concentrate their combat power enough to overpower defending units that bar their advance. The need to achieve these narrow attack frontages in several sectors along the front significantly increases the number of units that initially must be deployed on the forward line. In addition, the attacker needs large operational reserves of its own in order to replace losses, maintain momentum and prosecute breakthroughs against the defense.

When these requirements are added up, an attacking army in Central Europe preferably should number between 80 and 100 divisions. An attack with fewer forces of course is possible. This especially is the case if the defender's forces are too small to populate the front in adequate density or are surprised and caught off guard. But against a prepared defense of 45–60 divisions, an attacking posture of 80–100 divisions is highly desirable for confidence of a sustained advance.

Since these force requirements are dictated by the terrain and standard military planning factors, they are fairly universal. For example, in World War II the Western allies, fighting on the same terrain, eventually amassed about 90 divisions after the Normandy invasion to conduct their march to the Rhine River and beyond. The Germans, despite their eastern front travails, always tried to maintain at least a defensively sized force against the advancing allies. They also tried to deploy a similar posture in the east against the advancing Russian army, which was amply sized to conduct a steady offensive. These force levels, on all sides, were no accident.

For this reason, NATO believes, its posture cannot be confused with offensive intent. Starting with only about 30 divisions in peacetime, it would build to somewhere between 45 and 60 divisions only after French forces are committed and U.S. reinforcements fully arrive: a process that would take several months. These ground forces would be supported by about 3,600 tactical combat aircraft: a level that also is derived from NATO's defensive planning factors based on the multiple air missions that must be performed in a war.

By contrast, the Warsaw Pact's posture begins with about 60 similarly armed divisions in Eastern Europe and quickly would build to about 90 divisions and 4,200 aircraft upon reinforcement from the western USSR (comparative buildup rates are discussed later). As far as NATO is concerned, this posture cannot be mistaken as defensive. It is far too large to serve this purpose alone, even taking into account Soviet desires for a margin of safety and different planning factors. Nor can a skeptical interpretation of it be labelled "overly conservative." It is a posture that reflects conscious planning by military professionals. As a matter of mathematics, irrefutably it has been sized to execute an offensive strategy aimed at decisive victory in a war.

This NATO appraisal is reinforced by the internal composition of Warsaw Pact forces, which are equipped with the large numbers of armor and artillery that normally are associated with fast-moving offensive campaigns. Like NATO, the Soviets entered the 1960s with a largely nuclear-oriented strategy and a military posture to match. Also like NATO, they altered their strategy during the 1960s to place greater emphasis on conventional war as well. Without downgrading their nuclear programs, they promptly embarked on a systematic buildup of their conventional posture.

This buildup did not take the form of an overall expansion. The number of Warsaw Pact divisions arrayed against Central Europe, which already numbered about 90, remained roughly constant. The posture increased only with the Soviet deployment of several divisions in Czechoslovakia following the 1968 invasion. Instead the buildup was implemented by a dramatic increase in the size and armaments of each division. For example, Warsaw Pact divisions grew from about 8,500 men in the early 1960s to about 12,000 now. In the process, they received more tanks, artillery, armored personnel carriers, infantry and other weapons to the point where they now rival NATO's largest divisions in armaments. They also have been given the improved doctrine and tactics, command and control, logistic support and tactical aircraft needed to execute the complicated combined-arms operations of the modern battlefield.

For the past 25 years, the Soviets have been spending billions of rubles to equip these units not only with more weapons, but with the most modern models possible. For example, Soviet tank production since the early 1960s has seen the introduction of the T-62, T-64, T-72 and T-80: an impressive rate of innovation in technology development. Due to this costly effort in both modernization and internal expansion, Warsaw Pact forces have grown significantly stronger in recent years. In terms of static weapons scores, a technique often employed by Western analysts to gauge trends, their total firepower has at least doubled since the early 1960s: an increase that exceeds NATO's growth by a wide margin. In actual battlefield capability, the Warsaw Pact's increase probably has been greater than twofold. Whatever the case, one trend stands out in recent history. In NATO's view, Soviet/Warsaw Pact forces steadily have been brought into alignment with the requirements of an offensive military strategy in Central Europe.

To NATO, this ambitious effort exceeds even a generous interpretation of legitimate defense needs. It is difficult to interpret as having been undertaken for any purpose other than to intimidate Western Europe. As a result of it, Warsaw Pact forces today, as in years past, resemble a dagger pointing at Western Europe's heart. An expression of the Soviet Union's willingness to pursue its interests to the point of threatening the security of others, as far as NATO is concerned, they lie at the core of Europe's security problems.

The Evolution of NATO's Military Strategy

NATO's perception of imbalance and instability in Central Europe thus derives from a more sophisticated calculus than a simple numerical count of manpower and weapons. It is based on an appraisal of how Soviet strategy and forces work together to pose a direct offensive threat to the alliance's vital interests. NATO has responded to this Soviet dual nuclear and conventional threat by crafting a complex but defensive military strategy of its own, one aimed at deterring aggression rather than prevailing in an actual war.

At the Cold War's onset in the late 1940s, the Western allies found themselves with only about ten understrength divisions facing a Soviet Union perceived as hostile and armed with huge land forces. As a temporary expedient, they relied on the threat of a U.S. strategic air bombardment, including conventional weapons and the nuclear bombs then existing, to deter an attack. Even so, their defense plans envisaged a major loss of territory in the event of a Soviet invasion. Any effort to recapture this territory, they believed, could be launched only many months later: after the bombing campaign had taken effect and large U.S. ground forces had been mobilized.

The Korean War galvanized NATO, which had been officially formed in 1949, into an effort to bolster its continental defenses. This led to the deployment of larger U.S. combat forces to Europe and efforts to increase the forces of the United Kingdom, France and other members. It also led to the landmark decision in 1954 to rearm Germany and to integrate its forces into NATO's command structure.

Although NATO's plans originally stressed conventional defense, this ambitious goal soon proved beyond immediate reach. A contributing factor in this regard was West Germany's entrance into the alliance, which appropriately led NATO to move its front defense line forward from the Rhine River to the inter-German border. By denying NATO the flexibility to trade space for time and defend in depth, this change tended to elevate force needs. Also, the terrain in the forward areas lacks many natural defensive features, such as the rivers to the west or the mountains and forests to the east. As a result, the force requirements for forward defense grew to be well above what NATO then was capable of providing.

As a direct result of this constraint, NATO in the mid-1950s adopted MC-14/2, a largely nuclear strategy that envisioned only a brief period of conventional defense. It acknowledged that NATO's thin defenses quickly would be overwhelmed by a steamroller Warsaw Pact attack. Accordingly it placed primary emphasis on the threat of nuclear retaliation to provide the missing ingredient of deterrence and defense against nearly all forms of provocation.

As the 1960s unfolded, NATO began to feel that due to its growing economic and military power, it was now becoming better able to field larger conventional forces. The FRG's rearmament effort, which came to fruition then, played a key role in this upward appraisal of NATO's military potential. Equally important, NATO became increasingly concerned that a nuclear strategy no longer could deter a nuclear-armed aggressor. It feared that under the mantle of mutual nuclear stalemate, the Warsaw Pact might discount NATO's threat to escalate in the face of conventional defeat. Therefore it concluded that an improved conventional posture had become a necessary addition to its deterrent strategy.

As a result, in 1967 NATO adopted MC-14/3, the strategy of "flexibility in response." The main effect of this strategy was to place greater emphasis on conventional forces, while not wholly abandoning reliance on nuclear deterrence as a backstop. MC-14/3 called for deterrence and defense along the entire spectrum of possible aggression, with NATO's response to be calibrated to the provocation. It established a defense concept based on three mutually reinforcing tiers within the framework of forward defense: direct defense, deliberate escalation and general nuclear response. To execute this concept, it called for a triad military posture of strong conventional defenses, nuclear forces for theater operations and strategic nuclear forces. The goal of this triad was to provide NATO with a broad range of military options and particularly to ensure that NATO would not be driven into inappropriate decisions due to inadequate forces in any area.

When it established this strategy, NATO addressed the critical question of how large its conventional forces should be. It called ideally for an impregnable defense capable of halting an attack in the forward areas. But recognizing that this posture could be built only over an extended period, if at all, it resolved to aim immediately for an "initial" defense. By this it meant a posture capable of defending forward, with confidence, for a reasonably long period of time—at least long enough to make aggression costly and uncertain. A related purpose was to remove all uncertainty about the need to escalate should the conventional defense eventually collapse.

In adopting this planning goal, NATO also established strict upper limits on its conventional forces. It wanted to ensure that its posture, in the process of steadily improving over the years, would clearly signal defensive intent and could not be misconstrued as offensive. It resolved to maintain its combined peacetime forces at unambiguously defensive levels: to include about 30–45 divisions in Central Europe, comparable forces on the flanks, and a modest mobilization capability. These force goals, and the military strategy that they support, have been in effect for the past two decades and remain so today.

NATO's naval strategy reflects similar defensive goals in operational concepts and force design. The dominant factor driving NATO's naval planning is the need to preserve control of the North Atlantic sea lines of communication (SLOCs) to allow for resupply and reinforcement from the United States. While Central Europe is an obvious focal point, it is important to note that NATO's naval plans cannot be limited to this region. NATO's naval forces also must protect the SLOCs to member nations on the northern and southern flanks, especially such exposed countries as Norway, Greece and Turkey. This strategic need requires

NATO to conduct peacetime and wartime naval operations not only in the Atlantic Ocean but also in the Norwegian Sea and the Mediterranean.

This need for "forward" naval operations is reinforced by NATO's perceptions of the growing threat posed by Soviet naval forces. For some years after World War II, the Soviet navy primarily was a coastal defense force and did not possess major power projection capabilities. Over the past two decades, however, its configuration has changed dramatically. Its Northern, Baltic and Black Sea fleets have steadily acquired a "bluewater" dimension. To be sure, they still lack the carrier forces and replenishment capability of the U.S. Navy. Warsaw Pact assertions that NATO still enjoys a naval edge thus are technically accurate. But, as far as NATO is concerned, these claims miss the central point deriving from the two sides' quite different maritime requirements.

In particular, Soviet naval forces have acquired the submarine, naval air and surface combatant forces needed to conduct major offensive operations intended to interdict NATO convoys sailing the SLOCs. Evidence that the Soviet navy is now constructing sizable carriers capable of providing air cover far beyond the USSR's borders reinforces NATO's concern that these fleets aggressively would be used in this role.[1]

Western studies have shown that these forces, especially Soviet attack submarines and medium bombers, could inflict devastating destruction on NATO's shipping if it is left unprotected. Accordingly NATO's defense plans require major efforts to safeguard the SLOCs. These plans primarily center on establishing local escort of convoys, port protection and defensive screens along the GIUK gap (waters between Greenland, Iceland and the U.K.) and the SLOCs to Norway and Greece/ Turkey. They also call for supplementary area defense in the northern waters to help thin out and disperse enemy forces transiting these areas on their way to the SLOCs. The West's extensive experience with antisubmarine warfare operations in World War II showed that such area defense operations are an essential adjunct to local escort efforts.

Operations of this sort, it is important to point out, would be conducted for strategically defensive purposes. Although some in the West have advocated a shift in maritime goals, NATO's naval strategy has remained defensive, not offensive. Its goal is to protect NATO, not to erect an offensive threat to the Soviet Union. NATO's naval forces, including U.S. and allied units, are designed to implement this defensive strategy. NATO studies have shown that given the many missions that must be performed simultaneously in several different waters, the

Table 1 Current Force Deployments in Central Europe[3]

	NATO		Warsaw Pact		
	France/UK/ Lowlands	FRG	GDR W. Czech	Poland E. Czech	USSR WMDs*
Divisions	10	32	34	23	33

* (western military districts)

alliance's forces are somewhat deficient in relation to their requirements.[2] This shortage is responsible for the naval buildup being undertaken by the United States and other NATO nations in recent years. For example, the U.S. concepts of the "600-ship" navy and the maritime strategy reflect this thinking as applied to both NATO and the U.S. Navy's global missions. But this buildup falls far short of what is needed to conduct a major campaign of naval bombardment and amphibious assaults against the Soviet landmass, especially given the USSR's strong coastal defenses.

Military Dynamics of the Force Balance in Central Europe

The NATO-Warsaw Pact military confrontation in Central Europe thus is one of forces and strategy, rather than forces alone. What form would this confrontation take in an actual war, and how would it play itself out? And what can be said about whether an imbalance exists to the point of threatening stability?

The extent to which Europe resembles an armed camp does not become apparent by a simple numerical count of the peacetime balance in the immediate vicinity of the inter-German border. But when force deployments are examined throughout the depth of Europe, the true picture emerges. As Table 1 shows, no military imbalance seems evident if we compare only Warsaw Pact forces deployed in the GDR and western Czechoslovakia with NATO's forces in the FRG. But when forces deployed further back are included, a definite imbalance emerges. The key point is that the Warsaw Pact enjoys large reserves, while NATO lacks comparable strength in the rear. This chart displays current forces; the impact of Gorbachev's unilateral cuts, which are to be implemented over the next two years, will be discussed later.

A similar appearance of peacetime imbalance emerges when data are examined for a broader category of weapons and for the entire

Table 2 Current Force Data for the Atlantic-to-the-Urals Region (in-place or rapidly deployable/fully reinforced)

	Warsaw Pact	NATO	WP:N Ratio
Division equivalents	132/229	104/134	1.27:1.71
Tanks (MBTs*)	32,400/53,100	23,400/28,200	1.38:1.88
Artillery	23,800/44,000	19,000/22,200	1.25:1.98
ATGW launchers	20,100/30,800	14,900/24,600	1.35:1.25
IFV/APCs**	42,000/60,000	34,300/39,800	1.22:1.50
Attack helicopters	1,050/1,250	780/1,480	1.35:.84
Combat aircraft	6,150/7,120	410/6,200	1.40:1.15

* main battle tanks
** infantry fighting vehicles/armored personnel carriers

"Atlantic-to-the-Urals" area. Table 2, drawn from the U.S. Defense Department's *Soviet Military Power*, displays force data in two categories: forces that are "in-place or readily deployable" and "fully reinforced." It includes French and Spanish units for NATO. The first category includes forces on both sides that readily could participate in contingencies in the center region or along the flanks. The second category is composed of these forces plus strategic reserves for both sides, including Soviet forces in the more distant military districts and U.S. reinforcements that are not prepositioned and would deploy by sea. Similar data can be derived from the International Institute for Strategic Studies' *Military Balance* and other publications.

The table shows that the Warsaw Pact has amassed sizable superiorities in virtually all categories. As a result, its forces pose a serious military threat not only in Central Europe, but also to NATO's nations in the northern and southern regions. Moreover, the United States provides only about 25–33 percent of NATO's combat power in each category whereas the Soviet Union provides 60–80 percent of the Warsaw Pact's forces. Hence the Warsaw Pact's posture is dominated by its superpower while NATO's posture represents a more evenly balanced collection of many nations. This provides the Warsaw Pact considerably greater flexibility in allocating its forces among Europe's different regions.

While these data illustrate why NATO is concerned for its military security, we can best gauge the balance by focusing not on aggregate levels but rather on the forces that would deploy to specific regions over time in an actual war. This particularly is the case for the center region. The "wartime balance" there would include the forces normally based nearby, but it also would be influenced heavily by each side's relative ability to introduce reinforcements from the outside. For example, Soviet forces in the USSR's western military districts would move to the forward areas to participate in combat. NATO's forces in Europe also would move forward. In addition, sizable U.S. ground and tactical air forces based across the Atlantic would be deployed to Europe, albeit at a rate constrained by NATO's strategic airlift and sealift capabilities.

In theory, either side might be able to amass a huge but temporary advantage if it were to mobilize and reinforce fully while the other side did nothing. Between these two highly improbable extremes lies a broad range of more plausible scenarios. While this entire subject is beset with enormous uncertainty, Table 3 depicts likely NATO and Warsaw Pact buildup rates in the scenario that seems most likely to transpire. This scenario assumes that a war would grow out of an extended, slowly building crisis in which both sides steadily intensify training of their forces to make them proficient for combat, while not moving them forward. As this training reaches completion, the Soviets are presumed to make a decision to go to war, whereupon they initiate the process of rapidly moving their forces to the forward areas by road and rail in order to attack as soon as possible. NATO, in turn, is assumed to react to the forward movement of Soviet forces by promptly initiating its own reinforcement effort.[4]

This scenario partially has a historical basis. It is modelled after the Soviet invasions of Hungary and Czechoslovakia, in which Soviet reserve units were called to duty, trained as the crises built, and then attacked. In addition, it has the advantage of being a reasonably unbiased basis for assessment: it accords neither side a large lead in its decision to proceed up the mobilization ladder. For this reason, it is the scenario commonly used in Western quarters for weighing the balance. But it does not have to be employed on the assumption that the Soviets are attacking Western Europe. It is neutral in this regard: it just as easily could be used to analyze a hypothetical NATO attack on Eastern Europe. Table 3 displays illustrative buildup rates in this scenario.

The table shows that by $M+5$, when forces in the vicinity have arrived at the border, the Soviets could amass a 1.6:1 lead in maneuver units. By between $M+15$ and $M+30$, this lead increases to 2:1. The primary reason is that the Soviets by then are able to deploy their forces from the western military districts, whereas NATO's buildup rate is slowed by the need to deploy U.S. forces from across the Atlantic Ocean.

Table 3 Illustrative Buildup Rates in Central Europe: Current Forces (division-equivalents at days after mobilization)[5]

	M+5	M+10	M+15	M+30	M+45	M+90
Warsaw Pact	40	60	80–90	90	90	90
NATO	24	37	43	46	50	60
WP:N Ratio	1.66:1	1.62:1	1.9–2.1:1	1.9:1	1.8:1	1.5:1

The ratio drops to 1.5:1 only by M+90. During the entire intervening period, the Soviets enjoy an advantage that, most Western analysts believe, is uncomfortably high. Equally important, NATO's posture during the entire first month is at the lower end of the desirable 45–60 division range specified earlier. As a result, it lacks reserves, depth and staying power.

Some analysts believe that the Soviets might attack as early as M+5 in order to catch NATO unprepared. While this tactic cannot be ruled out, the Warsaw Pact temporarily would lack enough maneuver units to sustain a full offensive, and therefore might wait until as late as M+15-M+30, when its posture had reached the planned 80–90 division level. By this time, NATO's posture would have built to 43–46 divisions: a level below the ideal but considerably better, given the terrain and frontage requirements, than the M+5 posture.

Especially since numbers are often deceptive, what exactly are the implications of the 2:1 advantage that the Soviets would enjoy at M+30? Does this ratio truly measure combat power on both sides? Or is it illusory? Does NATO, as some claim, enjoy hidden advantages in such areas as technology, air power and support structures? Or would the Warsaw Pact's advantage in sheer mass prevail? To help answer these questions, Table 4 illustratively displays the M+30 balance in more detail.

The table shows that the Warsaw Pact's advantage in tanks and artillery, the major weapons that determine offensive combat power, would be greater than the ratio of maneuver units. This disparity derives from the fact that virtually all Warsaw Pact divisions are structured as tank or motorized rifle divisions: highly mobile units that can attack at high speed. By contrast, NATO's forces include a more balanced combination of infantry and armor typically associated with defensive tactics. This large Warsaw Pact advantage in tanks and artillery is a source of major worry on the part of NATO defense officials.

When other elements of this table are examined, the balance appears

Table 4   NATO/Warsaw Pact Force Balance At M + 30 (Current Forces) (illustrative)[6]

	Warsaw Pact	NATO	WP:N Ratio
Division equivalents	90	46	2.0:1
Tanks	29,400	13,000	2.3:1
Artillery	22,300	8,100	2.8:1
Static scores (NADEs)*	79	41	1.9:1
Combat manpower	1,350,000	850,000	1.6:1
Total manpower	2,100,000	1,575,000	1.3:1
Tactical combat aircraft	4200	3600	1.2:1

* NATO armored division equivalents

to narrow somewhat. But it never reaches the point where NATO seems equal to the Warsaw Pact, much less superior to it. For example, the data on static firepower scores show that when all weapons in Warsaw Pact and NATO divisions are counted—not just tanks and artillery—the Warsaw Pact's advantage falls only to about 1.9:1, or roughly the ratio of maneuver units. This is a smaller drop than might seem likely, given the common belief that NATO enjoys a large lead in weapons quality as well as larger inventories of such infantry-associated weapons as armored fighting vehicles, helicopters, mortars, anti-tank weapons and small arms. Indeed, 20 years ago, the ratio would have dropped to about 1.5:1. But in the interim, the Soviet Union has so expanded its inventories and improved its weapons quality that NATO's traditional advantages in these areas have all but been wiped out.

In combat manpower, the Warsaw Pact's advantage drops to 1.6:1; the advantage declines to 1.3:1 when all manpower is counted, including soldiers performing corps-level functions for NATO and their counterparts on the Warsaw Pact side. The reason is that NATO's divisions and non-divisional units typically have more soldiers than do those of the Warsaw Pact performing such support functions as maintenance, engineering, command and control, intelligence, communications and medicine.

This extra support doubtless would help NATO's units perform well on the battlefield. However, it would tend to manifest itself largely over a sustained period rather than in the critical early stages of the short, violent war that Soviet doctrine apparently envisions. Also, NATO's heavy manpower allocation to support functions reflects the redundancy that inevitably occurs in a military coalition of sovereign nations with different practices. The Warsaw Pact, by contrast, enjoys the advantage of more complete integration and thus can afford to fight with a leaner support posture. In any event, the Warsaw Pact has significantly beefed up its support forces in recent years and now possesses adequate capabilities to execute its own strategy.

Finally, Table 4 shows that the numerical air balance is fairly close: about 1.2:1 in the Warsaw Pact's favor. Although the Warsaw Pact air forces have improved dramatically in recent years, NATO's air forces still hold quality advantages in such areas as pilot training, tactical doctrine, command and control, electronic warfare, avionics and munitions. As a result, the air balance is at least equal, and NATO possibly enjoys an overall lead. Any NATO air edge, however, is not nearly large enough to compensate for the Warsaw Pact's lead in ground forces. For example, if air forces somehow could be incorporated into the data on ground static firepower scores, the Warsaw Pact still would enjoy a combined lead of about 1.6-1.75:1.[7]

Analysis of the air balance, moreover, must take into account the air strategies likely to be employed by both sides and the resulting dynamics of the air battle. NATO intends to employ its air forces not only to defend its airspace, but also to provide support to its outnumbered ground forces in the form of close air support and interdiction missions. As a result, most of its air wings are trained to perform multiple missions; during an actual war, anywhere from 50 to 70 percent of its wings might be performing in the ground attack role at any one time. By contrast, the Warsaw Pact's air strategy is aimed primarily at neutralizing NATO's air forces. As a result, its air campaign might initially focus on strikes against NATO's rear areas, but then it probably would revert to a campaign of air defense, supplemented by only limited offensive missions.

The relative strengths of each side's air forces should be evaluated in the context of these competing strategies. While NATO is strong in the ground attack mission, the Warsaw Pact possesses parallel strengths in performing its primary air-defense mission. To the extent that NATO is capable of asserting sufficient localized control of the battlefield airspace to permit unhampered ground attack operations, it would win the air battle. But to the extent that the Warsaw Pact can deny NATO this tough mission, it would prevail.

Given the complexity of modern combat and the differences in force structures on both sides, the outcome of a NATO-Warsaw Pact conventional war is impossible to predict. Nonetheless, four themes commonly stand out in Western analyses employing dynamic wargaming systems.

First, a NATO/Warsaw Pact war inevitably would be an exceedingly intense, bloody affair in which there would be hard fighting and major losses on both sides. In light of the major uncertainties, neither alliance possesses enough confidence of victory to justify a decision to attack.

Second, NATO clearly falls far short of the capacity to conduct a serious offensive advance into Eastern Europe. Any such attempt doubtless would be repulsed by Warsaw Pact forces in a major defeat. Indeed, Warsaw Pact forces could be reduced by significant margins and still possess ample insurance for blunting decisively a NATO attack.

Third, in the event of a Warsaw Pact attack on Western Europe, NATO would enjoy many of the classical advantages of fighting on the defensive. These include the ability to prepare positions and the terrain, to establish a cohesive front line capable of generating highly lethal firepower, and to conduct a coordinated effort. As a result, NATO's forces would not be easily defeated. They likely would do particularly well in a classical war of attrition. In this case, the Soviets would attack in a traditional "broad-front" array with their forces deployed across the front in uniform fashion. NATO then would be able to conduct the linear defense anchored on firepower that its forces are best prepared to fight. The outcome cannot be predicted, but NATO might well succeed in stalemating the attack in the forward areas.

Fourth, NATO's prospects would be less positive if the Warsaw Pact was successfully able to foster the warfare of breakthrough and maneuver that its forces and doctrine are oriented to fighting. In this war, Warsaw Pact forces evidently would concentrate at selected points along NATO's front line and would advance in successive waves of echeloned formations. They would attempt to gain localized penetrations through highly synchronized combined-arms assaults employing massed artillery, infantry and armor. Once beyond NATO's forward defenses, they would advance quickly into the rear areas and attempt to destroy NATO's forces by employing classical maneuver tactics, including encirclements and envelopments.

Western experts typically are pessimistic about NATO's ability to contain this type of attack. This particularly has been true for professional military officers; for example, former SACEUR General Bernard Rogers has estimated that NATO's forward defenses might break down within two weeks.[8] This negative judgment derives partially from recognition that the Warsaw Pact forces have acquired powerful combat capabilities for executing this type of attack. It also derives, however, from the belief that NATO's posture lacks enough depth and staying power, especially operational ground reserves that are critically needed for containing breakthroughs. In any event, this judgment plays a critical role in NATO's assertion that a military imbalance exists in Central Europe.

Future Improvements in Soviet/Warsaw Pact Forces

Present trends suggest that the Warsaw Pact intends to continue modernizing its forces with more and better weapons. As this effort proceeds, Warsaw Pact forces increasingly will develop improved capabilities to execute the offensive warfare by breakthrough and maneuver that historically has been the goal of Soviet military strategy. As far as NATO is concerned, this improvement effort continues to pose a serious threat to stability in Central Europe as well as the flanks.

The size of the overall Warsaw Pact threat to Western Europe evidently will be reduced somewhat as a result of the unilateral cutbacks that Gorbachev announced in his speech to the United Nations in December 1988. Gorbachev outlined a plan to withdraw six divisions, 5,000 tanks, specialized assault formations and 50,000 personnel from Soviet forces in East Germany, Czechoslovakia and Hungary. In addition, 5,000 tanks and several hundred artillery tubes are to be removed from Soviet forces elsewhere in the Atlantic-to-the-Urals area, while a total of 500,000 personnel are to be dropped from the active posture. Several hundred combat aircraft also are to be deactivated.

Judged in absolute terms, this cutback will be a sizable one and will reverse the Soviet Union's pattern of steadily expanding its forces since the 1950s, when Khrushchev imposed large reductions as part of his reforms. In total, about 15 percent of the Warsaw Pact's combat power in Central Europe (including the western USSR) will be eliminated. As Western analysts evaluate this cutback, a key issue will be its "relative" impact: the extent to which it reduces the Soviet offensive capacity against the West, taking into account the size of the Warsaw Pact's remaining forces in relation to the requirements for an offensive strategy against NATO.

In this regard, some preliminary observations can be offered. First, the removal of six divisions from Eastern Europe will leave the Soviets with 24 divisions there—still a large force. Taking into account available East European forces, the Warsaw Pact still will have available about 35 divisions (versus 40 previously) to conduct a short-warning attack against

NATO after only five days of preparation. This might still be enough to launch such an attack, provided the basic precondition for it is valid: a lack of advance preparation by NATO. At the same time, this attack would depend more heavily on East European troops and would lack the options of a 40-division posture. Moreover, residual Soviet and GDR units would have 30 percent fewer tanks than they now possess. All in all, the threat of a "surprise" attack thus will be reduced, but not entirely eliminated.

With respect to an attack launched after a period of training and mobilization, the Warsaw Pact still will have available some 48 divisions in Eastern Europe versus 57 now (taking into account reductions also planned in East European forces). Soviet reinforcement divisions in the USSR's western military districts evidently will be pared back by several divisions. But the Soviets, counting all remaining units, still will have about 70–80 divisions to commit to Central Europe—enough for an imposing attack. Beyond this, the Soviets will still be able to draw on other strategic reserves to the south or east of the Baltic, Byelorussian and Carpathian military districts. Thus the cutback of forces in these districts might help constrain the Soviets from waging simultaneous conflicts along NATO's flanks. But it will not physically hamstring Moscow from assembling, over a period of some weeks, the 80–100 divisions that (in the Western view) the Soviets have regarded as necessary for an invasion.

Beyond this, Western analysts will be closely watching steps that the Soviet military might take to offset these quantitative cuts by making qualitative improvements and achieving greater efficiency. A number of options are available to the Soviet Union in this regard. For example, the loss of tanks and artillery can be counterbalanced by increases in infantry, other elements of the combined-arms team, and even better command and control, intelligence and communications, and logistics. Similarly, the loss of maneuver units can be partly offset by structural reorganization: replacement of divisions with large brigades and tank armies with corp formations. Better doctrine, enhanced air-ground cooperation and improved training also can be employed to this end. Almost inevitably, the Soviet military will pursue one or more of these options. This is not to imply that Gorbachev's cuts will not change things at all, or that they should be discounted as militarily and diplomatically meaningless. Nonetheless, when the dust has settled, the actual reduction in Soviet combat capability is likely to be less than what meets the eye.

Trends in NATO Forces

NATO's foreign ministers officially reacted to Gorbachev's cutbacks by pointing out that a larger drawdown would be needed before the Soviet offensive threat could be regarded as eliminated. They called for NATO's own force-improvement efforts to continue apace. In this regard, NATO has crafted a set of improvement plans that are intended to remedy critical deficiencies in its posture. These measures are expressed in NATO's Resource Guidance, which calls for annual real increases in defense spending, official force goals, and the ongoing "Conventional Defense Improvement" (CDI) plan. These plans call for a balanced combination of measures in readiness, modernization and sustainability. They do not envision any significant expansion of NATO's ground and tactical air forces for forward defense.

NATO's measures particularly are concentrated in three broad areas: Follow-on Forces Attack (FOFA) systems for striking at the enemy's second-echelon forces as they approach the battle area; new weapons, doctrine and support systems for bolstering NATO's frontline defenses; and reserve mobilization and sustainability measures for adding depth and staying power, especially to NATO's rear-area forces. The goal of this combined effort is to erect a more robust and stalwart posture: one that will be able to withstand the shocks and pressures of a Warsaw Pact armored attack. Present indications suggest that these measures, if fully implemented, will improve NATO's defense prospects in whatever form of warfare might occur. But they will not provide NATO with a theater-wide capability for offensive actions. Nor will they remedy the major force imbalance that, NATO believes, will continue to exist in Europe.

Conclusion

In summary, NATO and the Warsaw Pact perceive the European military balance in quite different terms. According to its spokesmen, the Warsaw Pact argues that an overall "balance" of forces exists, within which there are some specific asymmetries that are an appropriate subject for negotiations. The Warsaw Pact contends that while it might enjoy numerical advantages in ground combat forces and associated weaponry, NATO enjoys an offsetting lead in air and naval forces and other areas. NATO perceives the balance in considerably less sanguine terms. Believing that the two sides have been pursuing quite distinct military strategies, it contends that the ground imbalance is a central factor that is not offset by any NATO edge in air and naval power, real or imagined. The upcoming CFE talks will aim at resolving whatever imbalances actually do exist. But more fundamentally, they will focus on whether the two sides can find common ground in these quite different perceptions and evaluations.

Notes

1   The U.S. Defense Department's *Soviet Military Power* has portrayed the NATO-Warsaw Pact naval balance in the following terms:

	NATO	Warsaw Pact
Aircraft Carriers/V/STOL	11	0
Helicopter Carriers/Kiev-class Ships	8	4
Cruisers	16	22
Destroyers/Frigates/Corvettes	310	201
Coastal Escorts/Patrol Boats	267	586
Attack Submarines	171	214
Oceangoing Amphibious Ships	57	25
Mine Warfare Ships/Craft	270	330
Sea-based Tactical Aircraft	832	210
Land-based Tactical Aircraft	389	530
Land-based ASW Aircraft	462	210

This chart excludes some 100 French and Spanish warships.

2   As an estimate, Western studies typically conclude that NATO's naval forces should be enlarged by 10–30 percent to meet defensive requirements.

3   In these and related charts, the term "division equivalent" includes divisional units and independent brigades (three of these are assumed to form one division equivalent). "Tank" data include main battle tanks; "artillery" data include artillery tubes over 100 mm plus multiple rocket-launchers and heavy mortars.

4   A key point here is that both sides maintain their combat and support forces in a "staggered" readiness profile. Typically, combat units deployed in the forward areas are maintained at high peacetime manning levels and conduct extensive training regimens that leave them well prepared for combat. Forces in the rear areas, by contrast, generally are manned by an active cadre (25–75 percent of manning requirements) and do not train as extensively. These forces particularly would require rounding out by reservists and refresher training before they are committed to battle. As a result, a period of training, lasting days and perhaps weeks, would be necessary before both sides could enter combat with confidence in their proficiency. The simplifying assumption is made here that both sides would undergo this training at similar schedules, and only then would the forward movement process be initiated. Hence neither side is granted any major lead over the other.

5   Based on a variety of U.S. Defense Department official publications and unclassified studies of buildup rates in Europe. These data are unofficial and are merely illustrative.

6   These data also are unofficial and illustrative estimates. The category "NADE" signifies a NATO "armored division equivalent." This refers to the static weapons score amassed by a typical NATO armored or mechanized division (e.g., FRG or U.S.), based on the U.S. "WEI/WUV" (weapons effectiveness indices/weighted unit values) system. To determine the NADE score for the entire posture, the combined static score is divided by the NADE score. Thus each Warsaw Pact division, on average, is about 85-90 percent as strong as a heavy NATO division. The difference lies not in the number of major firepower weapons, but rather in a small NATO quality lead and larger infantry forces and small arms inventories in each unit.

7   This estimate is based on the highly simplified basis of comparing air and ground units on the basis of costs and total payload in ground-attack missions (excluding Soviet medium bombers). In an operational sense, air and ground units cannot easily be compared. They perform quite different missions and their combat values, relative to each other, are not constant. In some situations, ground forces are worth more than air forces, and vice versa. Given their respective force structures, NATO seems to place a higher value on air forces than does the Warsaw Pact by virtue of investing a larger portion of its resources in them.

8   The present SACEUR General John Galvin has not disputed Rogers's estimate. In testifying before the Senate Armed Services Committee, I broadly agreed with Rogers' appraisal of the risks by estimating that the probability of an early major breakthrough would be at least 50 percent and perhaps higher. The exact timing of a breakthrough, in days and weeks, is highly sensitive to combat dynamics on both sides and therefore is a matter of conjecture. This means that a breakthrough could occur later than Rogers has estimated or, if things go very poorly for NATO, even earlier. Some academic experts, testifying at the same time, offered a more optimistic appraisal, but generally agreed that the risk of a breakthrough still could be as high as 30 percent.

PART TWO

Assessing the NATO-WTO Military Balance in Europe

Alexei Arbatov, Oleg Amirov and Nikolai Kishilov, USSR

The European-based armed forces of the two military alliances differ significantly in their geographic deployment, composition and structure. A consequence of historical, strategic and other factors, the asymmetry of the two sides' armed forces and their corresponding arms seriously complicates a quantitative (and to an even greater degree, a qualitative) aggregate assessment of their military potentials. More important, the asymmetry frequently leads to directly contradictory conclusions by both sides on the state of the military balance and, in turn, on the combat capabilities of NATO and WTO armed forces and on the strategic and operational concepts for their use.

A Static Approach to Assessing the Military Balance

The military balance has its own political-strategic, operational and tactical logic. There are two basic methods of assessing it—static and dynamic.

Under the static method, when the armed forces of the two sides are compared for purposes of highlighting existing asymmetries, the basic indices are data on the composition and the structure of the forces, specific types of weapons and combat supplies, material reserves, etc. In the most general way, this approach may be depicted in the following way:

$$R_{x,y} = \sum_{i=1} (K_{xi} - K_{yi}), (_i = 1, 2..., n)$$

Where R = value of the forces of sides "x" and "y" defined as the sum of the asymmetries;

and K_x, K_y = quantitative values of the indices being compared.

Quite substantial discrepancies are the norm for existing assessments of the NATO-WTO conventional balance in Europe. Such assessments differ (even in the most basic indices[1]) by dozens of divisions, thousands of tanks and hundreds of aircraft. With modern national technical means of verification, it is impossible to hide troop formations and their corresponding arms on such a scale. Thus the main problem here, it seems, is not the specific numbers (which, by the way, even according to Western publications differ substantially) or the verification technology, but the counting method.

In developing criteria for assessing the balance of both sides' forces on the basis of the static method, one must first of all determine what to count, i.e., which index of East-West military potentials should be considered most important in a comparison. The first but most superficial index is a comparison of the number of existing combat-ready divisions along with their organic equipment, i.e., those divisions that are prepared to fight without additional mobilization measures. In this comparison one must consider the following factors.

In the first place, in the countries of the WTO there are divisions of three categories, depending on the degree of their readiness to engage in combat actions. Category I divisions (approximately one-fourth of the total number of divisions) are divisions found in total combat readiness in peacetime. Category II divisions (also about one-fourth of the total number) are divisions requiring one month to become combat-ready. Finally, Category III divisions (more than half of the total number) need up to several months in order to become combat-ready. In order for divisions of the latter two categories (which comprise the significant majority) to become operational, around 2 million men must be mobilized.

The NATO countries possess analogous reserve formations. Thus, in 1986 the total number of organized reserves, which are considered the basis for the accelerated buildup of U.S. general-purpose forces, comprised 1.1 million men. Here are included both the organized reserves of those armed forces which make up their own integral unit (11 "heavy" and nine "light" Army brigades, and one Marine Corps division), as well as troops of the National Guard (ten divisions).[2] An attempt to capture all the combat and non-combat formations at once would lead to numerous difficulties, since agreement would be required on the specific scenarios of the outbreak of military actions (in particular, how much time may be available to each side for mobilization), and also the development and duration of combat (and in particular, how many major units may be mobilized, equipped and trained, and sent to combat regions in the course of the war).

Secondly, it is also necessary to determine in detail which types of combat-ready divisions should be compared. In the combat structure of NATO and WTO ground forces are 12 basic types of divisions: infantry; motorized infantry; mechanized infantry; mechanized; tank; armored; armored cavalry; artillery; airborne; air-assault; mountain infantry (alpine); and special forces. Furthermore, in the armed forces of NATO and the WTO there are as well independent operational-tactical units (brigades, regiments, battalions and other groups) which are not directly included in the divisional formations but closely interact with them. For example, according to existing data, in U.S. ground forces deployed in the FRG, besides the two armored and two mechanized divisions there are also an armored and mechanized brigade, two armored cavalry regiments, seven field artillery brigades, four independent artillery groups, 30 air-defense batteries and nine surface-to-surface missile battalions.[3] No doubt, consideration of such combat-ready troop formations is necessary in the balance of forces.

Thirdly, besides the organic equipment of combat-ready divisions there also exist significant reserves of arms and combat supplies in warehouses for equipping reserve components, as well as for contingents which may be quickly transferred by air to combat regions.

In analyzing the correlation of armed forces and conventional arms it is most useful, in our opinion, to consider and compare the following data:

–the number of combat-ready divisions (Category I and II WTO divisions and fully deployed and equipped NATO divisions);

–the total number of divisions grouped according to three basic types: tank, motorized (mechanized) rifle and other divisions;

–the aggregate levels of arms and equipment falling into the two basic types of divisions: tank and motorized (mechanized) rifle; and

–the aggregate levels of all basic types of arms and equipment found in combat-ready units.

Such an approach, it would seem, would permit shifting the emphasis from an endless manipulation of numerical data to the main problem— an analysis of the correlation of the armed forces and conventional arms on an agreed basis.

In assessing the European conventional balance one must also take into consideration the geostrategic factor. In contrast to the United States, which, due to geography, may provide for the defense of its own national borders with relatively few general-purpose forces and transfer all combat-ready divisions from its Atlantic coast to Europe, the USSR must spread its forces throughout many regions of its territory and within many sectors of its border for its reliable defense. However, the WTO countries have greater operational depth than NATO for structuring their forces and weapons in Europe. They have much greater capabilities for rein-forcing their troops in Central Europe via the transfer of forces from the European portion of the USSR in the prewar period. As for reinforcements at the beginning of combat actions, the traffic capacity of WTO railroad and highway communications is of course greater than NATO's sea and air communications, but their comparative vulnerability to forces capable of destroying their communications is a highly controversial issue. In our judgment, the greater vulnerability of ground-based communications (especially railroad terminals, bridges and tunnels) largely balances the less traversable conditions of sea and air communications.

Another question is whose forces are to be considered, i.e., which states' armed forces must be taken into account in assessing the NATO-WTO military balance. In assessing the conventional balance in the zone from the Atlantic to the Urals it would seem to be useful to take into account the following forces and weapons:

–the conventional forces and weapons of the 14 European military and political members of NATO;

–U.S. and Canadian troop formations in Europe, as well as forces deployed in certain units within their own territories;

–the forces and weapons of the six Soviet allies in the WTO, as well as all Soviet units and formations deployed in these countries; and

–the armed forces and conventional arms of the USSR deployed in the European military districts of the Soviet Union.

Finally, the last question is how to count. One of the difficulties is that on both sides there are great differences in the numerical composition and organic makeup of divisions in terms of arms and equipment. U.S. combat-ready divisions number 16–19,000 men, FRG divisions number 17–23,000 men, French divisions number 7–9,000 men, while fully equipped divisions of the WTO number 11–12,000 men. Therefore, for the sake of comparing the number of armed forces personnel we may introduce a numerical coefficient based on the number of men in Soviet divisions:

–motorized rifle divisions—12,000; and
–tank divisions—9,500.

The data cited in Tables 2 and 3 (see end of chapter) are based on these coefficients.

In assessing the balance of forces, it is also necessary to consider air forces, especially tactical strike aviation. The results of ground forces' combat operations in modern conditions largely depend on air superiority, which allows the attacker to strike the opponent's defensive lines in order to create favorable conditions for a ground force offensive, the defender to strike the attacker's second echelons and rear targets, and both to render direct support at the forward edge of the battle area (FEBA), and so on.

For the European continent air superiority in certain conditions can be a decisive factor in combat operations. And in achieving air superiority the role of a preventive air strike by the attacking side on airbases, command points and air-defense missile systems is significantly growing. For the defending side the best chance to prevent rapid destruction may be a preemptive strike on enemy airbases in order to capture air superiority at the very outset of the conflict. The threat of aggression or the perception of such a threat may push one side to attack. Consequently, modern tactical aviation, their technical capabilities, operational plans, and especially their enormous destructive power—combined at the same time with their great vulnerability at airbases (as well as the vulnerability of the airbases themselves)—are an extremely destabilizing element of the existing conventional balance of forces in Europe. Any assessment of the balance of forces in the area of tactical aviation cannot be considered complete and objective if it does not consider all types of aircraft possessed by one side or the other. For example, the WTO lags behind NATO in the number of fighter-bombers and close-air-support aircraft, but has a significant superiority in air-defense fighters. At the same time, there are great difficulties in determining the criteria for assigning aircraft into this category (fighters) due to the fact that a number of systems are modified to perform both fighter and close-air-support functions (F-4, F-15, F-16, F/A-18, MiG-21, MiG-29 and others.). Many fighters can with some degree of effectiveness strike ground-based targets and may frequently be reconfigured for these tasks. Therefore, in assessing the balance of forces, in addition to strike aircraft it is obviously necessary to include in this category the corresponding new types of frontal aviation and air-defense (PVO) aircraft (which in and of itself does not mean that arms reduction agreements should treat all types of aircraft the same way).

The static approach examined above for assessing the balance of forces is to a certain degree inadequate and one-dimensional. Based on only this approach, it is difficult to make judgments about the true capabilities of both sides in any concrete armed conflict, since such an approach fails to consider the probable scenarios, objectives and tasks of a war, as well as the form and means of conducting combat operations. For example, whereas the WTO is superior to NATO in tanks by 70 percent, and the latter, in turn, is superior to the WTO by 50 percent in tactical strike aviation, it is not at all clear from this which advantage is more important for the combat capabilities of armed forces as a whole, which side is superior overall, whether there is an inequality, and if so, in which capabilities.

Yet another inadequacy of the static method is the difficulty of considering qualitative indices, which may substantially change the final analysis. For example, the data cited in Tables 1 and 3 on the significant WTO superiority in tanks hides the fact that a significant portion of this arsenal (nearly 80 percent) is made up of obsolete combat equipment, whose analogues in the West have already been retired from the arsenal. The same picture is found in a qualitative comparison of tactical aviation and anti-tank guided missiles (ATGMs).[4]

Since the uncertainty of the hypothetical conditions for the belligerents and their armed forces is quite great, a multi-variable assessment of the possible outbreak and course of the conflict is necessary for modeling and predicting in this area. In this connection an important role is played by both sides' military doctrines, strategic concepts and operational plans, which reflect the objectives and methods for using armed forces in the event of war. These concepts and plans do not at all mean that a possible war would proceed in the way that is stipulated in the official guiding documents. On the contrary, these outlooks may determine the very probability of the outbreak and escalation of a conflict. In other words, it depends on the extent to which the objective proclaimed by both sides to prevent or deter war is realized in practice with respect to the operational plans, structure of the armed forces and their preparation.

Strategic Concepts and Operational Plans

At the basis of Soviet military doctrine in the 1950s and 1960s lay the concept of the notion of the character of a nuclear-missile war, in accordance with which conventional and nuclear weapons were to be deployed in coordination with each other all the way down to relatively low-level echelons for inflicting strikes on the opponent.[5] This approach was reflected not only in military doctrine, but also in combat field manuals and in the combat preparation of the armed forces of that period.

As a result of the gradual revolution of strategic views in the second half of the 1960s and the early 1970s substantial changes took place in the outlooks of the Soviet military leadership: along with the tasks of "preparing to conduct a world nuclear-missile war," the possibility was stipulated ". . . to conduct combat operations . . . even without the use of nuclear weapons, i.e., with conventional forces."[6] Thus the main feature of Soviet military doctrine was its orientation toward retaliatory (i.e., in the broad military-political sense, defensive) actions, and in the most general way was formulated as follows: "predatory wars are foreign . . . to the Soviet state."[7]

But the main task of Soviet strategy and operational planning was the "development of means for repulsing an aggressor's attack and subsequently destroying him by way of conducting decisive actions."[8] Therefore, the offensive was considered the main type of military action in this period. As for defense, it was considered " . . . as only a temporary phenomenon for repulsing an opponent's strategic offensive, inflicting major losses on him, holding important regions, and creating the conditions for shifting to a strategic offensive."[9] It was also observed that in certain instances such a defense could be "used intentionally."[10]

Meanwhile, the content of these principles of Soviet military doctrine and strategy has led to a distorted understanding by the West of the military-political policy of the Soviet Union.

From the current standpoint, the ambiguous nature of the role of ground forces in this period is clearly apparent, the basic tasks of which were "the destruction of the enemy's operational-tactical means of nuclear attack, the destruction of his forces in the continental TVD [theaters of military operations], the seizing of enemy territory and the holding of the most important regions and frontiers, and so on."[11] The possibility that the opposing side would create a stable and deep defense demanded in turn a deep operational structure for attacking forces. Motorized infantry formations, interacting with tank formations, were to "complete the destruction of the remaining enemy groups." It was also recommended to widely use "forward detachments" and in so doing to overcome the defensive frontiers in the enemy's operational depth, using for this "primarily tank formations operating in close interaction with missile troops [tactical and operational-tactical] and aviation."[12]

Along with the experience of the Great Patriotic War, the specifics of the East-West correlation of nuclear forces have also exerted enormous influence on the strategic and operational concepts for the combat use of Soviet ground forces. According to Soviet military views, tactical nuclear weapons help facilitate offense in the TVD, not defense (as NATO considers). In the conditions of NATO's manifest superiority in nuclear weapons up through the mid-1970s, and with its strong intention to initiate their use, a purely defensive strategy, deployment and structure of WTO ground forces would have meant an inevitable catastrophe in the event of a NATO preemptive nuclear attack, which in the initial hours could have completely changed the correlation of forces in the theater of war.

In the mid-1980s the Soviet Union and the other socialist countries publicly advanced the fundamental principles of their new military doctrine, which now lie at the basis of the activities of the Warsaw Treaty Organization and reflect the commonality of the defensive military-political objectives of its member-states and their national military doctrines. A great role in this is played by the formation of a much broader military-strategic parity between the USSR and the United States, the WTO and NATO, the adoption of a policy for the deep reduction of the quantitative levels of parity, and the strengthening of strategic stability. All of this has allowed the WTO to look in a new way at both the military balance and the military requirements in the regional theaters of military operations. At this level the main assumption was the unattainability of victory either in a nuclear or large-scale conventional war between the two principal alliances. Therefore, the new WTO military doctrine is subordinate, as is observed in official documents, ". . . to the task of the inadmissability of war, both nuclear as well as conventional."[13]

The defensive character of doctrine presupposes a corresponding defensive strategy and operations. Applying this to general-purpose forces,[14] the defensive character of strategy implies operational plans which are based on the corresponding force structure and which stipulate repulsing an attack on any member-state of the WTO. A defensive doctrine and strategy rule out beginning military actions against anyone with the first use of either nuclear or conventional weapons.

Among the important political features of "new thinking," the principle of reasonable sufficiency, which henceforth is the basis for the development of the armed forces of the USSR and the countries of the WTO, has special significance. The implementation of this principle could include radical qualitative limitations, structural and organic changes in the armed forces, and equally the deep reduction of conventional arms. The limits of sufficiency in this sense must be determined based on the levels and capabilities of the other side's armed forces and arms, which in turn influence the criteria for the sufficiency of the forces and means necessary for defense. By 1991 six tank divisions from the Soviet forces stationed in the GDR, Czechoslovakia and Hungary will be withdrawn and disbanded. Assault-landing formations and units and some others, including assault-crossing support units with their armaments and combat equipment, will also be withdrawn from the forces stationed in these countries. The Soviet forces there will be reduced by 50,000 troops and 5,000 tanks. The Soviet divisions which still remain on the territory of our allies will be reorganized. Their structure will be changed, and they will become strictly defensive.

At the same time the Soviet armed forces in the European and the Asian parts of the USSR will be reduced by 500,000 men. The total reductions of the Soviet armed forces in the European regions of the USSR and on the territory of our European allies will amount to 10,000 tanks, 8,500 artillery systems and 800 combat aircraft.[15]

An agreement on the reduction of the two sides' military potentials, a dialogue on their military doctrines and an elaboration, comparison and agreement of strategic and operational concepts would lower the demands for the reliable defense of either side.

The further application of the principle of reasonable sufficiency in the course of the mutual reduction and restructuring of conventional forces and weapons may logically lead to a position whereby each side would be incapable of conducting major offensive operations, but at the same time would possess a capability for the effective defense of its own territory. In turn, both the military doctrine as well as the military strategy and operational plans of each side would in such a way have a purely defensive character.[16]

For its part, in the West in the 1960s and 1970s the opinion was widespread that, given the existing superiority of the USSR and its allies in conventional armaments and the enormous nuclear potentials of both sides, a war in Europe could only be a brief one (several days or at most a week) and would quickly lead to NATO's defeat or to the use of nuclear weapons at an early stage with a high probability of escalation to a global nuclear war. Just as throughout the entire postwar period, in the Reagan administration the concept of "nuclear deterrence" remained dominant. But whereas earlier the U.S. and NATO military-political leadership in the framework of the "flexible response" concept planned to use nuclear weapons first, and as a rule, even in the early stage of an armed conflict (especially with operational-tactical weapons), during U.S. Secretary of Defense Casper Weinberger's tenure (in 1982) the concept of "general conventional war" or, as it is also called, "general war" came into use.

In the postwar years increasing attention has been given to the conduct—including in the framework of developing NATO's strategy of "flexible response"—of protracted combat actions with the use of conventional weapons. Such an approach is justified by Western military experts by the fact that, in the conditions of U.S.-Soviet nuclear parity at the global level and in the absence of clear Western advantages in tactical nuclear weapons in Europe, the United States and its NATO allies must substantially increase the combat capabilities of their general-purpose forces. This must be achieved, in their view, primarily through procuring new, qualitatively more effective (and at the same time, significantly more expensive) conventional weapons systems developed on the basis of recent technology, as well as through broad measures for preparing to conduct a "conventional war."

Paradoxes of the Strategy of Protracted "Conventional War"

It seems that the strategic concepts and operational plans that stipulate the conduct of a protracted conventional war between the USSR and the

United States, between the WTO and NATO, are totally detached from reality—from whomever such concepts may originate. Accordingly, the practice of maintaining enormous reserves of arms and combat supplies, fuel and ammunition, retaining large reserve (along with large combat-ready) formations, and preserving an enormous mechanism for the mobilization of defense industry and armed forces is an anachronism.

A large-scale conventional war, even if it would not quickly boil over into a nuclear war, would have numerous unpredictable features that would make it quite dissimilar to World War II, the experience of which continues to be used even now as the point of departure for the strategic and operational planning of combat operations for NATO and WTO ground forces, air forces and naval forces. The fact that during the past 40 years incomparably greater changes have taken place in technology than those that took place in the earlier interwar periods of 1870-1914 and 1918-1939 supports such a conclusion.

Therefore, war in the modern era is even less similar to World War II than that war was to War World I, and the latter in turn to the Franco-Prussian war. It is exceptionally difficult, if it is possible at all, to predict its course. But there is every justification to say that the numerous contradictions and paradoxes of a hypothetical new war would in practice have the most unexpected consequences, consequences most likely incompatible with the concept of "protracted" conventional combat on the European continent or on a global scale.

This concerns, for example, the fact that the sharply increased interdependence of different types of armed forces and troops, individual formations and units and various weapons systems is a distinguishing feature of the functioning of enormous and highly complex organizations, which is what modern armed forces are. A great spacial scope of operations (on the scale of entire TVDs), the rapidity and intensity of combat actions, and the multinational structure of opposing coalitions of states will characterize their actions. All of this poses unprecedently high demands for coordinating the actions of all elements of military potentials and for carefully planning operations, their priority, sequence of interaction and so on.

At the same time, the character of modern warfare makes inevitable the constant and rapid change of the combat situation on the fronts, deep breakthroughs and envelopments, and the intermixing of one's own and others' formations, units and subunits. In view of the high maneuverability of troops even the traditional FEBA may no longer exist.

In place of it zones of combat contact of a depth of dozens of kilometers will arise and rapidly change and shift. The unpredictability, mutability and intensity of probable combat actions would so overload the capabilities of a centralized command and control in the theater of war and the separate TVDs that they would most likely rapidly lead to total chaos.

The intensity of the anticipated combat also renders inevitable exceptionally great losses in arms and equipment. At the same time, because of the rapid increase in the cost of weapons systems, the quantitative levels of armed forces and arms on the whole have a tendency to decrease. Fewer but much improved and more powerful arms have a much lesser chance than in World War II of being used repeatedly in several battles. Their longevity will entirely depend on how successfully they may outstrip the opponent and destroy his forces and capabilities earlier than they will be destroyed by him. Therefore, combat actions will in any event most likely have a short-term character, if not for both, then at least for one of the sides. And this is not to mention the enormous losses among the civilian population and the damage to the economic infrastructure in the region of combat, which may now envelop the greatest and most densely populated portion of the European continent. Neither the population, economy nor ecology of Europe can withstand a large-scale conventional war for any amount of time—even in the improbable event that nuclear power stations, chemical enterprises and nuclear and chemical weapons depots are not destroyed.

The limited capabilities of the "human factor" in conditions of modern battle are clearly demonstrated by the experience of the local wars of the 1970s and the 1980s. Thus, for maintaining the combat capability of troops at a "sufficiently high level" during the Falklands conflict (1982), the British command was forced to replace forward units every two days. Furthermore, the high sortie rate of Great Britain's air force and naval aviation in this period was guaranteed largely thanks to the use of special medicinal preparations.

Naturally, it is impossible to compare and carry over the experience of individual local conflicts to potential large-scale combat operations on the European continent, where their character would be quite different both in terms of intensity and scope. This concerns the anticipated transient "fire contacts" with the rapid change of the tactical and operational situation, the threat of using nuclear weapons at any moment, the swift advance of enemy troops, the simultaneous envelopment of large territories with combat actions, the premeditated violation of lines of communication and C³I, and the conduct of combat operations at any time of the day (including at night) and under any weather conditions—all of which maximally increase the physical and psychological stress on a person, and cannot be compared with what took place in the years of World War II, in the Middle East in 1973 or in the Falkland Islands in 1982.

It is also necessary to observe that the replacement of the leading units by their withdrawal to the rear for rest and replenishment, as was done in the past, becomes practically impossible in the conditions of large-scale combat operations. Where to withdraw the units for rest, and at what time, if just 30-50 kilometers from the front there would be a zone of combat operations just as intense as at the forward line?

Any assessments of the losses of the sides participating in the conflict can only be highly abstract. Only one thing is clear—the human and material losses in the event of a "general conventional war" will be characterized, undoubtedly, by a scale many hundreds of times greater than that in analogous conflicts of the past, and, what is especially important, by a significantly higher "attrition rate" of people and equipment, of the share of irreplaceable losses.

The infrastructure for medical assistance and treatment is not prepared for the anticipated losses in personnel. The replenishment of the combat structure through returning the wounded to the ranks, as in the years of World War II, is practically impossible. The same relates in significant measure as well to the capabilities for repairing damaged combat equipment, considering the complexity of new weapons systems.

The following calculated data to a certain degree testifies to the enormous leap in the characteristics of the scale of the destruction of modern weapons systems, and in the sizes and rates of losses of combat equipment. Whereas during World War II (on the western front) 100 aircraft destroyed 100 enemy aircraft in air battles on average over six months, in modern war such results may be achieved on average after two days. Whereas 40 years ago 100 aircraft could destroy 1,000 ground combat vehicles on average over 35 days, today the same task may be resolved in 1.5 days. Other data as well are cited in the scientific literature which confirm the sharp—one to two orders of magnitude—increase in the destructive capabilities of modern weapons. This tendency continues.

In the course of the Arab-Israeli wars in the Middle East the correlation of losses in aircraft was in 1967 20:1; in 1973 40:1; and in the course of only a single air battle in Lebanon in 1982, 80:1 in favor of Israel.[17] During just the 18 days of the 1973 Arab-Israeli war 600 aircraft, 3,000 tanks, and 16 naval ships were destroyed. It is indicative that 50 percent of the aircraft and 70 percent of the tanks were destroyed by new weapons systems (ATGMs and air-defense missiles) that did not exist in World War II.

All of the examples cited above are on the whole characteristic of local conflicts in which the participants were opponents generally possessing relatively identical combat equipment, but with different professional preparation and a different level of operational thinking and art. Furthermore, these examples testify more to the intensity of conflicts than to their duration.

A large-scale conflict in Europe in which the participants may be opponents who have approximately equal technical capabilities and professional skills would probably be even more intense. Even assuming the same intensity of combat operations in the European TVD (but again, it probably would be much greater) and with a greater territorial scope of combat (obviously, it would be much broader), all the basic NATO and WTO combat equipment now deployed in the European theater and oriented towards it (50,000 tanks, 7,000 tactical strike aircraft, 30,000 artillery weapons, etc.) would be practically "used up" in the course of two to three weeks.

The attrition time for initial combat equipment in a large-scale conventional war as well is much shorter than the period for mobilizing military production (which itself would be subject to continual strikes even in the deep rear), or the time necessary for mobilizing reservists, training them in the handling of complex new technologies and preparing for modern combat operations. No single military officer and no single military expert can with a sufficient degree of confidence determine how all of these contradictions and all of these absolutely unpredictable circumstances may be resolved in practice.

A Dynamic Analysis of the Military Balance in Europe

Recognizing all the difficulties inherent in predicting a military conflict on the European continent, one still cannot completely reject a prediction methodology that increasingly relies on computer-based mathematical modeling, which permits the manipulation and integration of enormous factual material. It is precisely the modeling of different versions of combat operations that permits one to fill the concept of a "military balance" with real content, and to explain not "how much" of something one or the other side has, but how capable their armed forces are in the event of a conflict, and what kind of threat they can pose to each other in peacetime. This approach helps to create a well justified characterization of the military balance, and of the importance and influence of this or that asymmetry.

But a dynamic analysis has serious shortcomings as well. The main one is the arbitrariness and subjectivity of the enormous number of qualitative parameters introduced, of the assumptions concerning the conditions of the outbreak and course of a probable conflict, and of the strategy and tactics of both sides. Changing even a small number of these assumptions allows one to decisively influence the result of the "course" of the entire programmed model of military operations and the final conclusions concerning the correlation of forces. In essence, mathematical modeling replaces intuition and general unsubstantiated judgments only to the extent that it formulates and strongly links assumptions and conclusions on the basis of a chosen logic. But modeling does not replace the subjectivity of determining assumptions and qualitative parameters, and for that reason is often unscrupulously used to give an appearance of "objectivity" to politically and ideologically determined assessments.

There can only be one way to develop objective assessments of the military balance (excluding the hardly acceptable "applied experiment" of conducting a real war), and that is in making transparent all assumptions, main qualitative parameters and logic, and in comparing and mutually enriching different models and methodologies, in order that experts of various countries can judge and agree on each position of a program and, in such a way, come to an opinion. A dynamic analysis presupposes the use of various combat scenarios of and models for the opposing sides, as well as the revelation of the role and significance of existing differences and asymmetries between NATO and WTO armed forces and their organic arms. The balance of forces in this case is a criterion determining the sides' combat capabilities in individual operations, engagements and the war as a whole. Thus, the dynamic approach to assessing the force balance helps predict the ability to resolve set tasks—depending on the underlying factors and conditions in which countries and their armed forces operate or will operate.

This may be expressed by the following formula:

$R_{xy} = F(E_f, T, t, \Delta t, N)$.

where R_{xy} = balance of forces determining the capabilities of sides x
and y
F = model of armed conflict
E_f = both sides' objectives in the conflict
T = duration of combat
t = mobilization time
Δt = delay in the other side's mobilization
N = both sides' forces and weaponry

In IMEMO's Department on Problems of Disarmament, along with other Soviet research centers, a methodology for the dynamic analysis of the NATO-WTO balance of forces from the Atlantic to the Urals is being developed. In particular, the MODUS-2 model[18] permits us to make certain preliminary observations regarding the strategic and operational nature of the military balance in Europe.

First of all, it seems useful to examine three hypothetical combat scenarios:

–a surprise attack by one side after a relatively brief (three-to-four-day) mobilization;
–an offensive by one side after the mobilization of existing forces and the bringing up of reserves over the course of 10–14 days;
–an attack by one side after a 30-day mobilization.

In each of these versions it is anticipated that there will be some differences in the structure of the sides' forces for combat actions. The greatest threat for one side or the other is an attack in which there is minimal time for preparation. In these conditions, the significance of the combat-ready forces found in peacetime directly in the region of the outbreak of the conflict maximally increases.

The first zone (a "surprise attack" zone) may conditionally be designated as "M+4" and include for hypothetical opponents A and B the national and foreign combat-ready forces found immediately in the central region of the conflict.

The second zone, or "M+14," includes in addition to the first zone both the combat-ready divisions of the reserve formations within the greater territory, as well as reinforcement divisions (which during this time will be transferred into the central region).

Finally, in the third zone, or "M+30," may be included (in addition to the second zone) the armed forces of all the states of sides A and B found within the bounds of the theater of war and able to be transferred in part before and in part after the beginning of combat operations in the central region, as well as able to directly enter into combat on the flanks of the theater of war. The summarized data according to the number of combat-ready divisions and basic types of arms taking part in the hypothetical modeled conflict are found in Tables 4 and 5.

Considering the conditions outlined above, two factors will have decisive significance in a dynamic analysis of the balance of forces (assuming that the main combat operations arise in the zone of the confrontation):

–each side begins combat operations and shifts to the offensive; and
–each lag in one side's mobilization allows the other to create the superiority necessary for an offensive.

All of these assumptions were used for a dynamic analysis of the balance of forces with the help of the model and informal methods in the given scenarios. Accordingly, the dynamic analysis of combat operations of groundorces and tactical air forces directly focuses on the consequences of a conflict under the following conditions:

–each side is within range of the other's means of destruction; and
–strikes are inflicted on forces and capabilities directly taking part in combat.

The research conducted has shown that in the event of a surprise attack (Scenario 1—four days of mobilization for the attacking side and one day for the defending), side A, were it to initiate offensive actions, would hypothetically be able to penetrate after seven days to a depth of 100–120 kilometers[19] along the axes of the main strikes, while side B, if it were the attacker, during the same time would penetrate 60–80 kilometers into the territory of its opponent. During these seven days the defending side would conduct the necessary preparatory measures, and the war would most likely have a "quasi-positional" character similar to World War I, but with an enormous spatial scope, high tactical mobility in the zone of combat, enormous losses in equipment and troops, and the creation of a region of total destruction for the population, economy and infrastructure to a depth of 200–300 kilometers on both sides of the zone of contact. At this stage, all the factors of unpredictability noted in the previous section would come into play. It is obvious that the relatively small size of seized territory and the doubtful political significance of such an "acquisition" cannot compare at all with the scale of the losses and the risk of the unpredictable development of events.

To guarantee the ability to penetrate much more deeply into the opponent's territory requires a much longer period of preparation for attack. An alternative, purely hypothetical extreme scenario (Scenario 2) includes a 30-day mobilization by the attacking side, and by the defending side only at the beginning of combat actions (i.e., preparation time equals zero). Under such assumptions, side A could penetrate side B's territory to a depth of some 300–400 kilometers over 14 days. If side B attacked under the same conditions, it would be able to penetrate some 200–250 kilometers into the opponent's territory during the same period. After this, the conflict would enter into the same phase of uncertainty that it did in Scenario 1, but with an even larger zone of total destruction (400–500 kilometers) from the final line of contact. It is obvious, however, that the probability that one side could mobilize over the course of 30 days with the other side completely inactive is, in practice, excluded. This scenario is only important as an extreme endpoint on the spectrum of potential outcomes.

More complex and ambiguous are the intermediate scenarios. Under one of them (Scenario 3) the attacking side mobilizes over a 14-day period, while the defending side lags by four days. In the other (Scenario 4) the attack takes place after a 30-day mobilization, while the defending side delays its mobilization by four days. Finally, in yet another version (Scenario 5), the attacking side conducts a 30-day mobilization, while the defending side lags by 14 days.

In Scenario 3, if side A attacks, its advance is 90–110 kilometers. In Scenario 4 side A advances 30–50 kilometers. In Scenario 5 side A penetrates into the enemy's territory some 80-100 kilometers.

If side B would be the initiator of the war, then in Scenario 3 it would penetrate to a depth of 70–80 kilometers; in Scenario 4, 20–30 kilometers; and in Scenario 5, 40–60 kilometers. In all cases, purposeful combat actions continue no more than 14 days, after which the war most probably enters a stage of uncertainty.

In all instances, the main influence on the spread of the estimates is exerted by the assumed level of attrition that forces one side to retreat and in which the other, despite a maximum level of attrition, will nonetheless continue the offensive. There is also the effectiveness of one side's air power for capturing air superiority. And finally, the results may seriously change depending on the character of the attacker's operations (for example, the number of main axes of attack, and the share of forces covering other sectors of the front against counteroffensives), as well as on the defender's ability to identify the attacker's intentions in time.

If the mobilization of both sides lasts more than two weeks, then it seems improbable that either will decide to attack. In this case, both sides will have mobilized such powerful forces and capabilities that any offensive operation would entail unacceptable damage and extremely high combat losses. Furthermore, the political stakes of the war, the consequences of the destruction and the price of victory would altogether be so high that it would be almost impossible to avoid the use of tactical nuclear weapons by the side that found itself at the brink of destruction or faced failure in implementing its intended strategic plans. This probability is intensified by a number of additional factors. The use of tactical nuclear weapons—against ground forces units; naval groups; aircraft on the ground (and in the air, if massed); C^3I centers; ports and major communications junctions; rear logistics and supply targets; and nuclear weapons depots and means of delivery—may instantaneously and radically change the local correlation of forces and the course of combat, and ultimately lead to a global nuclear catastrophe.

It is necessary to say that the cited results of the model have a purely conditional and preliminary character. In contrast to the authors of other similar models, including in the West, we ourselves recognize that the MODUS-2 model cannot predict the picture of real combat actions in Europe, but is only one of several analytic instruments for assessing the essence of the military balance and its key asymmetries. Furthermore, as with any other such model, its results only formalize the subjectively chosen assumptions and logic; it cannot correct assumed mistakes, but rather intensify their significance.

Conclusion

Even this conditional method of assessment, as one tool of analysis, permits one to come to the justified conclusion that in the sphere of the correlation of conventional forces and weapons in Europe, where the opposing alliances possess asymmetrical but on the whole largely comparable forces, the unleashing of war under any more or less probable scenarios cannot bring the aggressor results (in particular, as expressed in the capture of the other side's territory) that would in any degree be commensurate with the losses and risk of the conflict's escalation to a global nuclear catastrophe.

At the same time, to an even lesser degree than in any other areas of the military balance can attempts to insure defense through the buildup and modernization of one's own capabilities lead to any kind of positive results. They would inevitably be perceived by the other side as a threat requiring countermeasures to prevent aggression. Neither equality, nor even numerical superiority in individual parameters will ever be sufficient for defense, especially when including the unfavorable scenarios of the prewar period, the outbreak of combat and the course of combat actions in military plans and forecasts.

The threat presented by the outbreak of war is directly proportional to the time that the attacker's mobilization outstrips that of the defender. However, this is not a linear relationship, for the absolute duration of the mobilization for attack also influences it. The peak threat for the outbreak of war comes after a two-week mobilization period for offense with a lag by the defending side of ten or more days. In that case, the attacker has the greatest incentive to begin combat actions before the defender is sufficiently strengthened, while the defender will have the greatest incentive to launch a preemptive strike before the attacker has undertaken active offensive operations.

A mutual reduction of NATO and WTO conventional forces and weapons (especially through the reduction of their offensive elements and their withdrawal, disbandment, redeployment and restructuring with the objective of relatively strengthening the capabilities of defense) as well as a comprehensive system of permanent observation, verification and third-generation confidence-building measures (designed to increase the warning time of attack and make preparation for it noticeable and unambiguous) may effectively eliminate the probability of war and guarantee the stability of the military balance on the European continent.

Table 1 Discrepancies in WTO and NATO Evaluations of the Military Balance in Europe

Indices	WTO Data			U.S. Defense Department Data			IISS Data		
	WTO	NATO	WTO:NATO	WTO	NATO	WTO:NATO	WTO	NATO	WTO:NATO
Divisions	78	94[A,B]	1:1.2	229[C]	121[D]	1:0.5	107⅓	101⅓	1:0.9
Tanks	>50,000	>30,000[E]	1:0.6	53,100	25,900[D]	1:0.5	52,200	22,200	1:0.4
Tactical-strike aircraft	2800	4200	1:1.5	3,450[C]	3,850[D]	1:1.1	2,594	2,393	1:1.1

[A] Including French and Spanish Divisions.
[B] Division-equivalents.
[C] Including forces and equipment in the eight military districts of the USSR's European territory.
[D] Does not include the 13 divisions, 2,300 tanks, and 400 aircraft belonging to France and Spain.
[E] Including French and Spanish tanks, as well as U.S. and West European tanks stored in Europe.

SOURCES: *Otkuda iskhodit ugroza miru* (Moscow: Voenizdat, 1987), pp. 85–86; *Pravda*, February 8, 1988 and October 10, 1988; *Soviet Military Power* (Washington, DC: U.S. Government Printing Office, 1988), p. 114; *The Military Balance 1987–1988* (London: IISS, 1987), pp. 231–232.

Europe From the Atlantic to the Urals

Table 2[A] WTO-NATO: Number of Combat-Ready Divisions

Division Type	WTO		NATO	
	In Soviet Division-equivalents	Total		In Soviet Division-equivalents
Tank	40	28⅔		38⅓
Motorized rifle	56	74⅓		88⅔
Other	7⅔	8⅓		11
Total	103⅔	111⅓		138

Table 3[A]   Tank and Motorized Rifle Divisions and Main Types of Armaments

Main Indices	WTO	NATO
Comparable tank and motorized rifle divisions	96	127
Tanks[B]	27,700	18,000
Heavy artillery (>100mm), mortars and multiple rocket-launchers	18,300	14,150
Tactical strike aircraft	2,800	4,200

[A] The following sources were used for calculating the initial data base in Tables 2 and 3: *Otkuda iskhodit ugroza miru*, pp. 85–86; Jonathan Dean, *Watershed in Europe* (Lexington, MA: Union of Concerned Scientists, 1987), pp. 39–41; *Soviet Military Power 1987* (Washington, DC: U.S. Government Printing Office, 1987), pp. 89–91; *The Military Balance 1986– 1987*, pp. 226–229; Karsten Voigt, *Draft General Report on Alliance Security: NATO-Warsaw Pact Military Balance—Nuclear Arms Control After Reykjavik* (Brussels: North Atlantic Assembly, September 1987), pp. 2–6.

The figures contained in the tables may not coincide with official Soviet data.

In the future, in the event of an exchange of data on quantitative levels of armed forces and equipment, certain amendments will have to be made to the initial data base which, naturally, will lead to changes in the correlation of both combat-ready divisions and basic arms.

[B] Calculations of the balance of tanks, heavy artillery, mortars, and multiple rocket-launchers vary widely depending on the methodology employed. For example, under other assumptions (reserves in storage, incompletely equipped divisional formations) the ratio of NATO and WTO tanks and artillery could be seen as follows: 50,000:30,000 tanks; and 60,000:57,000 heavy artillery guns, mortars and multiple rocket-launchers, respectively.

Table 4   Number of Combat-ready Divisions in Division-equivalents by Zones

Divisions Types	M + 4		M + 14		M + 30	
	A	B	A	B	A	B
Tank	27	23⅓	33	30⅔	40	38⅓
Motorized Rifle	27	17⅓	33	29	56	88⅔
Other	2⅔	1	4⅔	4⅓	8⅔[A]	18[A]
Total	56⅔	41⅓	70⅔	64	104⅔	145

[A] Including amphibious or marine divisions.

Table 5 Balance of Combat-ready Tank and Motorized Rifle Divisions and Their Organic Arms, Including Tactical Aircraft, by Zones

Main Indices	M+4		M+14		M+30	
	A	B	A	B	A	B
Divisions	54	40⅔	66	59⅔	96	127
Tanks	15,900	9,400	19,400	11,400	27,700	18,800
Heavy artillery (>100mm), mortars and multiple rocket-launchers	10,200	4,000	11,300	500	18,300	14,150
Tactical Aircraft	6,500	7,000	6,500	7,000	6,500	7,000
Of which, strike aircraft[A]	2,800	4,200	2,800	4,200	2,800	4,200

[A] Including carrier-based aircraft.

Table 6 Results of Various MODUS-2 Model Scenarios

Scenarios[A]	Penetration in km, Side A attacking	Penetration in km, Side B attacking
Scenario One: Four days mobilization for attacker; one day for defender	100–120km	60–80km
Scenario Two: 30 days mobilization for attacker; zero days for defender	300–400km	200–250km
Scenario Three: 14 days mobilization for attacker; 10 days for defender	90–110km	70–80km
Scenario Four: 30 days mobilization for attacker; 26 days for defender	30–50km	20–30km
Scenario Five: 30 days mobilization for attacker; 16 days for defender	80–100km	40–60km

[A] Scenario One assumes seven days of fighting. All other scenarios assume 14 days of fighting.

Notes

1 See Table 1 as well as the other tables, above.
2 Caspar W. Weinberger, *Annual Report to the Congress, Fiscal Year 1988* (Washington, DC: U.S. Government Printing Office, 1987), p. 153.

3 International Institute for Strategic Studies, *The Military Balance 1987–1988* (London: IISS, 1987), p. 24.

4 *Pravda*, October 13, 1988.

5 N. Ia. Sushko and T. R. Kondratkov, eds., *Metodologicheskie problemy voennoi teorii i praktiki* [Methodological Problems of Military Theory and Practice] (Moscow: Voenizdat, 1966), p. 88.

6 S. N. Kozlov, ed., *Spravochnik ofitsera* [The Officer's Handbook] (Moscow: Voenizdat, 1971), p. 75.

7 Nikolai V. Ogarkov, ed., *Voennyi entsiklopedicheskii slovar'* [Military Encyclopedic Dictionary] (Moscow: Voenizdat, 1st ed., 1983), p. 240.

8 Ibid., p. 712.

9 M. M. Kirian, ed., *Voenno-tekhnicheskii progress i Vooruzhennye Sily SSSR* [Military-Technical Progress and the Armed Forces of the USSR] (Moscow: Voenizdat, 1982), p. 315.

10 Ibid.

11 Ibid., p. 316.

12 Ibid., p. 317.

13 *Pravda*, May 30, 1987.

14 WTO general-purpose forces include ground forces, air-defense forces, tactical aviation and naval forces. See A. A. Babakov, *Vooruzhennye Sily SSSR posle voiny* [The Armed Forces of the USSR After the War] (Moscow: Voenizdat, 1987), p. 249.

15 Address by Mikhail Gorbachev at the United Nations, December 7, 1988 (Moscow: Novosti Press Agency Publishing House, 1988), p. 26.

16 *Krasnaia zvezda*, July 28, 1987.

17 Joshua M. Epstein, *The 1987 Defense Budget* (Washington, DC: The Brookings Institution, 1986), p. 34.

18 MODUS—*modelirovanie otsenok dinamicheskoi ustoichivosti (sootnosheniia) sil* [modeling of assessments of the dynamic stability (of the correlation) of forces].

19 Averaged data are cited here and below in the first five scenarios. One must take into account that the unilateral reduction of the armed forces in the central region of a possible military conflict (the first zone) not only diminishes the threat of a surprise attack but also reduces the mobilization time lag in other zones.

PART ONE

The Political Objectives of Conventional Arms Control

Ian Cuthbertson, United Kingdom

Conventional arms control seeks to deal with the most dangerous manifestation of the central question of European security—the long-standing adversarial relationship between two massively armed military alliances which face each other across a political fault line that divides the continent in half. However, the military confrontation between NATO and the Warsaw Treaty Organization (WTO) is only the most tangible expression of the political, economic and social competition between the countries of the two alliances. It is therefore important to remember that even though conventional arms control would represent an important achievement, it would still only be treating a symptom of the disease and not striking at the roots of the problem itself. It is this conundrum which lies at the heart of the issue of setting priorities and objectives for conventional arms control.

There can be a contradiction between the types of measures pursued in the conventional arms control process. On the one hand, there are agreements which seek largely to codify the existing situation in Europe, through ringing political declarations and treaties of non-aggression or non-interference. While such agreements have little military impact, they can have some political significance as modest confidence-building measures.

On the other hand, there is a second group of measures, such as limitations on logistical infrastructures or on the introduction of new military technologies, which are both militarily desirable and achievable but which might have relatively little impact in the wider political and economic sphere because of their limited scope and technical nature. Soviet General Secretary Gorbachev's decision to withdraw assault crossing units with their weapons and combat equipment is a unilateral measure which falls into this second category.[1] However, there still seems to be a lack of political will in both East and West to seriously interfere in the constant process of technological improvement of military systems, despite the threat which some of these innovations may pose to either stability or the disarmament process.

Finally, there are agreements which have as their objective enhanced security at the lowest practicable level of military force—the core security concern for both alliances. These include large reductions and redeployments of troops which would change more or less dramatically force levels, deployments and hence military strategies. While there may be some instability inherent in making large-scale changes—for example, force-to-space ratios could radically change, making the job of defense harder—such changes promise the most significant long-term political benefits. It is this last set of measures, the most risky but also the one with the greatest potential military and political benefits, which both alliances need to pursue.

If progress is going to be made in the field of conventional arms control, then both alliances must accept that there is an element of risk which will attend every step of the process. Not to accept such risks, to adopt an approach of taking small, balanced and incremental steps, is to condemn the negotiating process to an endless round of small-scale tradeoffs, with both sides seeking cast-iron guarantees at every stage that their security will not be compromised in any way. There is no doubt that such an approach is militarily desireable, but politically it would probably condemn the Conventional Forces in Europe (CFE) negotiations to the same fate as the Mutual and Balanced Force Reduction (MBFR) talks: endless negotiation, with no major change in the current level of armaments and forces.

Mikhail Gorbachev, in his December 1988 speech to the United Nations, set out the WTO's priorities for immediate changes in the East-West military balance: reductions in forces but also restructuring in order to make residual forces more combat effective. NATO's ideas seem to be evolving in a similar direction. Gorbachev began the process with his restructuring of Soviet forces in Eastern Europe. While a great deal still needs to be done on the WTO side, NATO must also begin to focus on critical elements in its own forces and strategy, mainly those air- and land-based systems dedicated to deep strike on putative WTO second-echelon forces, and address what measures it can take, either unilaterally or as part of the negotiating process, to reorient these forces towards a more defensive use.

In addition, conventional arms control must also carry the burden of being the key to any future nuclear disarmament on the continent. A number of Western countries, after the successful implementation of the INF Treaty, have made any further reductions in the number of nuclear weapons deployed in Europe contingent upon dramatic changes in both the nature and the level of the conventional balance in Europe.[2] This is a great weight to throw onto a negotiating process with a previous track record—from the Washington naval treaties of the 1920s, through the Geneva Surprise Attack Conference, up to the long-running stalemate of the Vienna MBFR negotiations—that is hardly auspicious.[3] A number of critical questions should be at the forefront of the thinking of governments as they engage in conventional arms control negotiations. What should be the agreed criteria for a successful negotiation and a worthwhile treaty? What is the optimum time-scale for reaching such an agreement? What, in the short term, could a successful negotiation ending in an agreement acceptable to all the parties, involving, for example, changes in the level and nature of military competition, contribute towards reducing the military confrontation in Europe? And beyond this relatively modest contribution towards improving European security, what impact on the wider adversarial relationship between the two alliances would this type of agreement have? The corollary when reviewing these questions is what changes in the overall relationships between East and West are also required to enable significant changes in the military confrontation to take place?

Of course, these types of assessments mean that both NATO and the WTO should have well thought-out and coherent military and political objectives for the talks. To establish such objectives requires a clear idea of the level and nature of the residual military forces which should remain deployed at the conclusion of not only every stage of the negotiating process, but also at its ultimate conclusion. It also presupposes that some attention be devoted to defining the future European political and economic framework into which such residual military forces would fit, and their roles within this wider framework. This model of rational decision-making is, however, largely missing from the councils of both alliances. Both NATO and the WTO collectively, and their constituent member-states individually, have shied away from carrying out this type of strategic planning. There is no agreed objective, military or political, on an intra-alliance (let alone on an inter-alliance) basis for the outcome of conventional arms control, beyond the somewhat selective and circumspect aims set out in the mandate of the CFE negotiations.

The recent thaw in relations between East and West should make some form of conventional arms control agreement, even if it is cosmetic in nature, easier to obtain. After the windup of the MBFR talks, both sides will be unwilling to see another set of conventional arms negotiations fail completely. However, to get beyond limited measures, such as CSBMs or small-scale reductions in military forces, requires a fundamental rethinking of the nature of the political, economic and social relationships which have characterized Europe for the past 40 years. It is this type of rethinking which is only now getting under way in both East and West.

Only recently have thoughts begun to turn beyond short-term concerns to the wider political objectives embodied in the CFE process. The lack of forethought in the past was understandable. The MBFR process hardly gave hope for significant changes either in the military balance or any more general change in the European political scene as a result of a conventional arms agreement.[4] MBFR was always a sideshow for both NATO and the WTO. Even at its inception few held out much hope for any significant agreement emerging from MBFR, but this is not the case for the CFE negotiations. Since the signing of the INF Treaty, the talks have been invested with a great deal of political symbolism. The withdrawal of INF missiles means, at least according to many NATO governments, that the state of the conventional balance in Europe is more critical than it has been in years. The elimination of conventional asymmetries between the two alliances is no longer an academic issue but a burning political and military concern.

For the first time in years, public opinion in both East and West has been sensitized to the issue of conventional disarmament. While there continues to be a lack of widespread understanding of all the complex and interrelated issues involved in the process, there is a growing desire to see tangible and worthwhile results. Public opinion, which, at least in the West, does much to fuel disarmament policy, will not readily accept failure or even stalemate. In the East, expectations of improved physical well-being, which to a large extent is seen as contingent upon redirection of resources presently consumed by the military, affect public attitudes even more directly than do the more abstract political and security concerns of the West. The genuine activism which motivated much of the opposition to INF missile deployment in both halves of Europe was a genie which cannot be forced back into its bottle. While conventional disarmament may not provide the tangible excitement of removing nuclear missiles, it is a topic which the press, aided by a series of WTO proposals, has kept in the public eye.

It would be a mistake in the Europe of the 1980s to identify too high a level of patriotic fervor attached to national military institutions. There are more immediate manifestations of national sovereignty, ones which impact more directly on the daily lives of citizens. However, it would also be a mistake to dismiss out of hand the symbolism that continues to be invested in military forces. Today this finds its expression less in positive support for indigenous military forces than in a growing neuralgia towards the stationing of foreign troops on the territory of one's own state, a phenomenon not restricted to Europe. Regardless of security considerations or even economic benefits, the tolerance level of the general public for military maneuvers, low-flying military aircraft or visits to ports by naval ships has dropped precipitously in recent years.[5] In Western Europe, this neuralgia is the result of a number of interrelated developments.

First, there is a growing sense, among a number of governments and more especially among their general publics, that military and political relationships which were developed in the postwar period have increasingly less significance in today's world. In the FRG in particular, the sense that West Germans are shouldering an unfair and increasingly insuperable burden, with more than half a million foreign troops on their soil in addition to their own large military commitments, is widespread.[6] This change in outlook has come about largely as a result of a recent and dramatic change in the threat perception among the West German public with regard to the possibility and likelihood of the Soviet Union launching an offensive into Western Europe. If there is no real danger of war, why put up with tanks ripping up roads and fighter aircraft plowing into buildings? For West Germans, these points are particularly pointed because the soldiers doing the damage are often not their own and they are practicing to meet a danger which the population as a whole can no longer clearly perceive. Those in the West who claim that NATO has no significant pressure on it to rapidly pursue reductions in conventional forces would do well to remember this type of resurgent nationalism, as well as its corollary, the desire on the part of countries with forces stationed abroad to "bring the boys home." NATO, an alliance which for decades has represented not only the bedrock of Western defense, but also the major defining element of the West's political identity, now seems more and more mutable. If threat perceptions of the Soviet Union and its WTO allies within some West European NATO countries continue to diminish at anything like the present rate, there are likely to be a number of future fracases surrounding burden-sharing issues within the alliance.[7]

In addition, different countries in NATO bring different philosophies to bear on the arms control process. The nuclear-weapons states tend to view conventional arms control not as a means of eliminating the military confrontation in Europe but rather as a useful tool for managing the slow transition from one type of force structure to another, a transition which must inevitably take place for economic and demographic reasons, regardless of whether there are arms control agreements or not. While this view is also shared to some extent by the non-nuclear-weapons states in the alliance, there is also present among them a much stronger belief in the usefulness of weapons and force reductions for their own sake.

A somewhat different situation exists in the WTO countries. While they share the same problems caused by rapid increase in costs connected with military preparedness, the Soviet Union, Poland and Hungary have in addition all made direct connections between lowering military spending and transferring resources, both scientific and industrial, from military to civilian production. As part of Gorbachev's conventional disarmament plan and his announced reductions in the Soviet military budget, the Soviet Union will cut back its production of new military equipment. All of the East European WTO countries, except maverick Romania, have also announced reductions in their military forces and defense budgets. Whereas the Soviet Union took the dramatic step of advertising the conversion of the SS-20 production facility into a factory producing prams, the East Europeans have been more prosaic.[8] However, they have also announced that parts of their military industries are to be converted to civilian production. All of this, furthermore, before the CFE negotiations had even officially begun.

In the past, in their relationships with the Soviet Union and Eastern Europe, most NATO governments placed a higher premium and devoted more of their political and bureaucratic attention to ensuring their immediate political and military security than to the many long-term economic or environmental problems which unite the two halves of Europe. This focus was even more central to WTO policy because the constituent economies were much less able to absorb the burden of supporting the military structure thought necessary to face NATO. A new willingness to address these issues, to see beyond the immediate adversarial relationship, characterizes the situation which now exists between East and West. However, in the desire to solve many of the deep-rooted problems facing all European states, it is also possible to go to the other extreme and overlook the immediate security problems which continue to confront the two alliances. The way in which these continuing problems are solved will do much to determine the future course of the overall relationship between East and West.

The Role of the Soviet Union and the United States

Much has been written about Mikhail Gorbachev's concept of a "common European house."[9] Some have seized upon the idea as the blueprint for the future course and nature of the relationship to be built between East and West in a Europe which is economically united but continues to have two competing social and political systems. The idea has gained great currency because it launched into a vacuum in which few others have dared to delve. Not that the concept outlined by Gorbachev is radically new. It merely seeks to extrapolate outward from the CSCE process and envisages a Europe where the original Helsinki and later Vienna accords function in the manner in which they were designed to, rather than the haphazard and partial adherence they enjoy at the moment.

The major advantage of Gorbachev's concept is that it at least provides a starting point for a discussion of the future nature of relations between East and West. Such intellectual leadership has been conspicuously absent from the other superpower, the United States. Dazzled by discussion of the "Pacific century," concerned about its economic performance, the United States government has given little thought to the future of Europe. In its recent relations with its Western allies, the United States has tended to focus either on micro-issues of alliance management, such as burden-sharing, or on the overall economic competition between the West European market economies and that of the United States. The debate in the United States has focused not on the future of Europe but on how the U.S. should react to *glasnost'* and *perestroika* in the Soviet

Union. Three competing approaches have found expression. The first is that the United States has no interest in helping the Soviet Union to reform itself because it will simply produce a leaner, meaner opponent. The second is that some modest encouragement of *perestroika* and support for Gorbachev is desireable, because success will produce a less aggressive Soviet Union, albeit without fundamentally altering the nature of the Soviet system. The last is that the successful implementation of economic pluralism must inevitably bring with it political pluralism which will produce the gradual eclipse of the one-party state. For now, option two enjoys the widest support because it asks least of the U.S. policy-making community.[10] It does not ask the United States to oppose the more positive attitudes of its European allies towards Gorbachev and *perestroika*, nor does it require the U.S. to do much to aid the Soviet Union in the process of reform. Despite originally sounding hawkish on East-West relations, President Bush and his administration carry a more positive attitude into the conventional arms control negotiations.

The CFE is seen as one of the three crucial political pillars in the forging of a new relationship between the United States and the Soviet Union. The other two consist of the Strategic Arms Reduction Talks (START) and the human rights dialogue between the two superpowers. There is likely to be relatively little interplay between CFE and START, however. While the Bush administration is likely to prove more flexible on issues such as SDI, the negotiations for a START treaty are already well advanced. They deal with weapons systems with no direct connection to the conventional balance in Europe. Any conceivable change in the strategic balance between the two superpowers is highly unlikely to do anything to alter, in any practical sense, the conventional balance in Europe. But beyond tangible implications, the START talks do exercise a strong political imperative on the CFE negotiations: success in Geneva will increase pressure on both alliances for an agreement in Vienna. In the same way, stalemate or a breakdown in the START negotiations could cast a pall over the CFE which could make forging the necessary compromises even more difficult. The same is true of the human rights issue. Beyond the direct linkage which France has sought to make between the two issues, there is a strong implicit relationship between Western perceptions of WTO behavior on human rights and the sincerity with which the Soviets and East Europeans approach the issue of conventional disarmament.

On a more prosaic level, the need for a more positive attitude on the part of NATO was highlighted by U.S. Secretary of State James Baker's February 1989 trip to all of the NATO capitals. During his trip the West European allies repeatedly expressed their concern that after Gorbachev's UN speech and the various force and budget reductions promised by the USSR's East European allies, NATO needed a more forthright arms control approach if the initiative on conventional disarmament was not to be ceded to the WTO. This concern was triggered by a growing recognition in West European capitals that if pressure for unilateral action by the West, both within NATO's councils and from the public, is to be avoided, the West must undertake serious negotiations in Vienna aimed at making substantial reductions in the number of troops stationed in Central Europe. As part of this process, many American politicians, especially in the Congress, seem more willing to consider redeploying some American units from Western Europe to the United States, and perhaps even following the Soviet lead and not only withdrawing but also disbanding such units. Here the precedent set by the INF Treaty, which required the destruction of weapons, looms large.

There remains, however, a widespread perception in the United States that the Soviet Union and its Eastern allies need large-scale conventional disarmament if they are to achieve even modest economic restructuring, a perception reinforced by recent statements by some WTO governments. While the problems the West is experiencing in maintaining its military posture are acknowledged, they are regarded as minor compared to the enormous economic burden being shouldered by the Soviet Union in maintaining its military forces. While Western estimates of Soviet military spending have placed the burden at between 15 percent and 17 percent of the Soviet Union's gross national product (GNP), the real figure may be even higher.[11] The Soviet Union has admitted that the resources necessary for the major restructuring of the Soviet economy can only come from the bloated Soviet military budget.[12] There remains a view that in the conventional arms negotiations the Soviet Union should be made to pay as high a political price as possible for achieving its economic objectives through the signing of an agreement (as illustrated by Western reaction to the Soviet Union's desire to host a CSCE follow-up meeting on human rights in Moscow). Dramatic reductions in the Soviet armed forces are seen as a possible Soviet concession, especially in those forces stationed in Eastern Europe. Asymmetrical reductions on the order of 5 to 1 have been viewed as a militarily necessary rate of exchange for NATO to pursue in conventional arms control.[13] The

December 1988 NATO proposal for the CFE negotiations, by contrast, would require NATO to reduce its forces by only 5 to 10 percent, to around 90 percent of their current levels.[14] NATO also sees little need for any major restructuring of its military forces.

However desireable these objectives are for NATO, they fail to take into account the political realities which underpin the relationship between the Soviet Union and its East European allies or indeed the realities of political power within the Soviet Union itself. The Soviet military have repeatedly made clear that they are not interested in making unilateral reductions in their forces.[15] There is little doubt that Gorbachev fought a hard battle with the Soviet General Staff to table the dramatic cuts laid out in his UN speech in December 1988. It cannot be a struggle he will be anxious to revive in pursuit of further unilateral cuts. The Soviet military's own thinking appears to be much more closely reflected in the WTO's three-stage conventional disarmament proposal put forward in July 1988; Gorbachev's unilateral reductions went considerably beyond this gradualist approach which has as its centerpiece significant reductions by both alliances and the restructuring of both sides' military forces, with the objective of making them incapable of launching any large-scale offensive.[16] The proposals put forward in Vienna in March 1989 by the WTO build on the July 1988 ideas, but the two-to-three-year timetable anticipated for each stage of the process appears to require much more rapid reductions than those envisaged in the original WTO plan.

Finally, there is the underlying issue of the future role of the two superpowers in their respective alliances, and in the world in general. There is little doubt that a trauma is beginning to seize both the American and Soviet political psyche. The two superpowers are now beginning their decline from their preeminence of the past 40 years. It will not be an easy descent for either superpower—old habits die hard. The United States increasingly faces being overhauled in economic terms by its allies.[17] If arms control is successful, where does the Soviet Union, a country with a backward economy, stand in the community of nations when it no longer has the crutch of outstanding military capabilities to support its stature? What is the likely course of its future relations with its current clients when it can no longer wave the big stick, and as those same countries use their own political and economic solutions to overtake it economically as their economies become more efficient? The question of the future role of the two superpowers in Europe is one of the critical determinants in mapping out the prospects for conventional disarmament.

These are roles which neither superpower has yet sought to clearly define, but they must entail a considerable loss of power and influence. Accepting this situation will not be easy for either state.

West European Attitudes

The other NATO nuclear-weapons states, France and the United Kingdom, find themselves somewhat isolated in the conventional disarmament field. Lacking a clearly defined objective regarding the shape of the residual force structures which might be produced for both alliances by the conventional arms control process, these two countries have tended instead to define their approach more in terms of the traditional arms control negotiating strategy of reducing and restructuring the opponent's armed forces while seeking to make minimal changes in one's own military structures. Increasing American willingness to consider reductions in U.S. stationed forces as the necessary price of an agreement does not sit well with them.

The United Kingdom, as befits the most Atlanticist power in NATO, continues to have the most adversarial view of the Soviet Union. Despite a relatively warm personal relationship between Margaret Thatcher and Mikhail Gorbachev, characterized by her description of him as "a man we can do business with,"[18] the British have tended to give less credit in the military field to the rhetoric and expectations of *glasnost'* and *perestroika*. Instead, the British government continues to dwell on the evolution of Soviet conventional capabilities that render the WTO an increasingly impressive military machine. The British watchword continues to be capabilities, not intentions. The 1988 British Defence Ministry White Paper emphasizes the continuing Soviet conventional buildup which, in its view, has been largely unhindered by talk of "reasonable sufficiency" or any putative change from an offensively to a defensively based military strategy.[19] In the immediate aftermath of Gorbachev's December 1988 UN speech, U.K. Foreign Secretary Geoffrey Howe was still unwilling to specify any cuts NATO could make in its forces, either as a unilateral gesture in response to Gorbachev, or even at the negotiating table. He was also at pains to point out that the case for the modernization of NATO's existing nuclear forces in Europe was just as compelling after Gorbachev's speech as before.[20]

In the field of conventional arms control, it is the United Kingdom which may well be the most formidable brake on the negotiating process.

A Conservative government in London, more concerned with ensuring continued U.S. support for NATO's West European allies than changing the political and economic complexion of Europe, is unlikely to countenance any arms control solution which would involve significant reductions in the number of U.S. troops deployed in Europe. On this issue, the British may well be more Catholic than the Pope. The Bush administration may be willing to accept withdrawal of some of the 350,000 U.S. troops deployed in Western Europe. As the CFE negotiations proceed, based on the projected U.S. defense budget, the U.S. armed forces are likely to be shrinking in overall numbers because of financial constraints caused by the need to pay off the U.S. budgetary deficit. The U.S. Congress is more xenophobic and isolationist than it has been in decades— it would be dangerous for West European governments to ignore this trend in American politics. The electoral failure of Michael Dukakis and fading memories of the presidential campaign should not blind America's West European allies to the widespread appeal of the message that he was promulgating at the end of the race—that foreign influences are weakening America. The thrust of Dukakis's message was economic— but there are a number of other prominent American politicians who are only too anxious to apply the same rationale to the security field. They dwell on both the cost, claimed to be $1,527 billion, or 64.8 percent of the U.S. defense budget, for the years 1982–1989 to maintain and support the United States' foreign bases and commitments, with $849 billion, or 38.8 percent, spent on Europe alone, and the increasing unpopularity of the U.S. presence in many of the countries which the U.S. taxpayer is spending hard-earned money to defend.[21]

Perhaps the most successful change in rhetoric on the future of Europe has taken place in France. Once solidly Gaullist, recently the French government has rediscovered its enthusiasm for NATO. With typical panache, it has done so at a time when some other NATO countries are beginning to question the fundamental *raison d'être* of the alliance. A country with long-standing ties to Eastern Europe and a special relationship of its own with the Soviet Union, France has begun to take a new interest in the restructuring of Eastern economies and societies. Yet far from being an ardent supporter of change in the relationship between East and West, France, despite its Socialist government and president, is as least as conservative in its outlook as the United Kingdom. The British have traditionally seen their role as a struggle to bridge the Atlantic and keep the Americans fully engaged in NATO. The

French have long viewed their function as being that of the anchor which keeps the Federal Republic of Germany firmly in the Western camp.

For most of the past 40 years this has not been too arduous a task. The West Germans have long been among NATO's most enthusiastic and forebearing members. However, recent years have seen a change in the attitude of the West German public towards its obligations to NATO, symbolized by the strong resurgence of antipathy towards NATO nuclear weapons stationed in the FRG and strong local opposition to military maneuvers being carried out. With the exception of the nuclear modernization debate, these are still relatively minor issues. However, even the somewhat ambiguous symptoms of disaffection have sparked a new French approach to Franco-German relations. Even on the issue of the early modernization of NATO's short-range nuclear weapons, a cause which had received the vociferous support of the French government, there is a new flexibility. Long before the alliance agreed to postpone its decision, the French minister of defense had suggested that NATO need not reach any quick conclusions on modernization, but should instead postpone any decision for a couple of years to see whether the Soviet Union will agree to large-scale reductions in its nuclear forces.[22] The clear intention of this proposal was to remove some of the considerable pressure on the West German government to make up its mind on the subject of modernization, in the hope that with the passage of time the subject will either become moot, or at least some of the political tensions and public attention which now surround the issue will dissipate. Whatever the merits of the French proposal, and regardless of the decision which NATO finally takes on modernization, the French government deserves credit for recognizing that on this issue, as in much of the topic of conventional disarmament, it is the FRG whose attitude and approach is critical.

The fiasco over the neutron bomb, the political debates engendered by cruise and Pershing deployments and the rise of Mikhail Gorbachev and the changing threat perception of the Soviet Union have all served to make West Germans increasingly restless with an alliance which a growing number of them seem to believe places great burdens upon them but which does not fully value their contribution. The French have watched this evolution of West German attitudes towards NATO with increasing alarm. This was coupled with French concern over American behavior at the Reykavik summit, which gave rise to strong perceptions that the Reagan administration was insensitive to West European interests in its pursuit of improving superpower relations. There were also strong misgivings about the impact of the INF Treaty on the long-term viability of flexible response. The Mitterrand-Kohl relationship, the joint brigade and military staff talks, the vocal support for INF deployments and the acceptance that France's first line of defense stands on the inter-German border, not at the French frontier, were all designed to reassure the West Germans of the value which Paris places on their contribution to the defense of the West. The growing frustration among some sections of the West German public with the FRG's role and position within NATO, as well as with the alliance itself, and the widespread neuralgia towards all nuclear weapons which is an increasing factor in the West German security debate have come as a profound shock to France—the only country in Western Europe which had managed to maintain its domestic consensus on defense issues and a largely unchanged military threat perception toward the Soviet Union. As a result, even the French domestic consensus has begun to erode. Despite these changes, however, French willingness to participate in the CFE talks should not be seen as a dramatic shift in French policy. The attitude is strong within the French government that if France is to have a hand in guiding and to some extent controlling a process, which, unlike MBFR, promises to lie at the center of the political dialogue between East and West for the next decade, then France must be fully involved in the negotiations and the talks must be held between 23 sovereign states, not between two alliances. In addition, the talks must be carried out within the CSCE process, not as independent negotiations.

The prospect of a Europe in which West German attention is not firmly fixed on the West, Moscow becomes part of the equation and the Paris-Bonn axis is not the dominant political reality foretells an inevitable diminishment of France's voice. If this is any part of the vision the West Germans want the French to embrace, then the clear benefits of a Europe without military competition, and with economic cooperation, need to be clearly spelled out. It is by no means clear yet what these benefits could actually be. The savings in military spending in the West, while substantial, could easily be soaked up in increased social welfare, domestic and international development assistance, even reduced levels of domestic taxation. The economic benefits of converting military to civilian production need to be clarified. Hard data, not wishful thinking, are needed to convince the skeptics in London and Paris, not to mention Washington. The political and to some extent economic benefits for the FRG of greater

European integration between East and West have been endlessly discussed. In addition, the political and economic rewards for most WTO countries are increasingly clear. But the wider political and economic implications of a less divided Europe must be addressed if the FRG's NATO partners are to enter wholeheartedly into greater integration.

The CFE negotiations appear to offer the best hope of both changing and controlling the future course of East-West relations—as long as the military confrontation continues, the scope for political, social and economic rapprochement must continue to be limited. A negotiating process which ends up as a super-MBFR, vastly complicated and largely incapable of achieving quick solutions, could stall any dramatic reorientation of the current order in Europe almost indefinitely. The wider implications of the CFE negotiations have evoked a clear response. For example, France has long indicated that it wants to include the question of human rights and economic matters in a broader discussion of European security. While it may be that the French motive in this linkage is an attempt to further complicate the negotiations, it is also possible that France wants to see a closer link between the CFE and CSCE to ensure that artificial progress is not made in one area to the detriment of others.

Fathoming the motivations of the two European nuclear-weapons states is relatively straightforward when it comes to arms control. Both depend to a large extent on their military power to provide at least a vestige of their former international stature. Other states in Western Europe, in particular the constellation of smaller states both within and outside of NATO, have no such pretensions. Their vision of the future of Europe is driven largely by a desire to perpetuate and stabilize the long postwar period of peace that Europe has enjoyed. As long as NATO continues to meet this critical criterion for viability it offers the best assurance to its member-states of both national security and international stability. As long as its ideological underpinnings remain coherent and intact and it provides the most effective ideological framework for Western economic cooperation and development, then NATO will continue to enjoy widespread support. However, it is these same smaller, and in some cases not so small, countries which have taken the lead in questioning the continued utility of the alliance in its present form. All of the non-nuclear members of NATO have changed their political and military threat perceptions of the WTO. They do not view Mikhail Gorbachev as the likely instigator of an invasion of Western Europe. Nor are Eastern countries in the midst of a debilitating economic crisis seen as a plausible launching pad for military adventurism. The suggestion that crises at home breed a wish for military aggression to divert attention from pressing problems is simply not regarded as credible in most West European capitals. While the danger of an August 1914 situation remains (that is, an unexpected political event which triggers a process of escalation into war), there is increasing confidence that the web of relationships between East and West, coupled with the well-known risks inherent in this type of escalatory situation, act as a sufficient brake to any real danger of military confrontation. The experience of the West's muted response to the Solidarity crisis in Poland and the threat of Soviet military intervention in the early 1980s tends to bear out an analysis which dismisses the possibility of military confrontation in essentially political crises between the two alliances.

All of the West European states, including the two nuclear powers, are highly conscious of the perception that their own military postures represent an increasingly onerous burden. They are unable, due to domestic political pressures, even to consider the levels of expansion in defense budgets which would be necessary to sustain their current military postures. The fact that defense spending in NATO countries represents only a small percentage of GNP, and a percentage which has steadily shrunk over the past few decades, makes little impact on publics and legislators appalled at the high cash figures and opportunity costs which these expenditures represent. Added to these resource constraints, a number of countries, especially in northern Europe, are faced with a demographic crisis which has severely reduced the number of young men available for conscription. For these reasons a significant number of these countries would welcome an arms control agreement that would reduce their military burdens, as well as pave the way for increased economic, social and political cooperation between the two halves of Europe.

East European Attitudes

Among international political issues, conventional disarmament offers perhaps the greatest scope for the East Europeans to make independent proposals that give them clearly identifiable opinions, but which at the same time do not challenge the current Soviet dominance of the structure and objectives of the WTO. Disarmament measures and proposals put forward by the East Europeans fall into two relatively distinct categories.

The implications of military force and budget reductions in Hungary and Poland, as well as the Soviet Union, relate essentially to their domestic economies. Although these were vigorously advertised as measures developed to contribute to the conventional disarmament process, they are largely divorced from the actual negotiations, except for the fact that they place pressure on NATO states, indirectly through public opinion, to match these positive steps. The GDR's decision to cut its armed forces by 10,000 men, disband six tank regiments and an air force squadron and cut 600 tanks and 50 aircraft—reducing its military budget by 10 percent—was motivated only in part by economic necessity. It was taken more to keep the GDR in step with the reductions in the Group of Soviet Forces in Germany (GSFG) that already had been announced by the Soviet Union, as well as to influence West German opinion and increase pressure on NATO to make reciprocal unilateral gestures.[23]

Poland has made the greatest impact with the Jaruzelski Plan, which sought to perpetuate the tradition of Polish initiatives in conventional disarmament dating back to the Rapacki Plan in 1958.[24] The Jaruzeski Plan was intended to be a flexible, open-ended contribution to the disarmament debate.[25] It sought to encompass all the issues covered by the European security debate, embracing proposals for a gradual with-drawal of all types of nuclear weapons, including theater and tactical nuclear missiles, nuclear-capable artillery and aircraft and nuclear dem-olition charges. The first step was to be a freeze at current levels of nuclear forces in Europe. In parallel there was to be a thinning out of conventional weapons, particularly those of great destructive power or most useful for either surprise attack or full-scale offensives (i.e., tanks, attack aircraft and helicopters, long-range artillery and rocket artillery). Changes were also proposed in each alliance's doctrine to eliminate any offensive elements and stress strictly defensive concepts. Although somewhat overtaken by subsequent events, many of the ideas contained in the plan find an echo both in the mandate of the Vienna talks, which emphasize the need to shift away from offensively based forces, and in later Soviet proposals to reduce offensive military equipment. Certainly, in 1987–1988 when the Poles were formulating their ideas and promoting the plan most vigorously, they were given credit for some innovative ideas, particularly in the field of non-offensive defense, which placed their thinking ahead of the Soviet Union and the rest of the WTO.

The GDR has also been active in the conventional weapons field. In concert with Czechoslovakia, the GDR has proposed the creation of a nuclear-weapons-free corridor in Central Europe, a proposal which has obvious implications for NATO's policy of flexible response. In a somewhat parallel proposal, the GDR's ruling party, the SED, signed with the FRG's opposition party, the SPD, a draft agreement on eliminating chemical weapons from a corridor in Central Europe which would embrace the territory of the two German states.[26] The joint SED-SPD working group on questions of security policy in Europe also has as one of its stated objectives bringing about a mutual non-offensive capability based on a simultaneous adequate defense capability.[27]

The southern-tier WTO states also have been active in the field of conventional disarmament. Bulgaria and Romania have continued to press the idea of a Balkan nuclear-weapons-free zone, enjoying some success in convincing the Greek government of the potential attractiveness of the idea. Hungary, while not putting forward any proposals for continent-wide solutions for conventional disarmament, has been anxious not to be overshadowed by the northern-tier East Europeans and has been actively reducing its own military forces, and in particular its military budget. The need to reduce the military burden and facilitate the transfer of resources from the military to the civilian sector of the domestic economy has been a major impetus. The decision by the Soviet Union to withdraw an armored division stationed in Hungary, as well as a small air-assault unit, can only strengthen Hungarian resolve to act as an "experiment" for conventional reductions in both local and stationed forces.[28]

It is hard to say what the payoff is for all of this activity. All the East Europeans have been disappointed by the lack of interest and seriousness with which most NATO countries, and in particular the big four, have greeted their proposals. The GDR's agreement with the SPD was to some extent pilloried as interference in West German domestic politics. The 1985 election showed that its discussions with the GDR did the SPD little good at the polls. However, there is little doubt that conventional disarmament and even nuclear disarmament remain areas in which the East Europeans can independently flex their muscles, allowing them to derive some international credit for changes in their military forces imposed on them by largely domestic economic considerations, and to emphasize, in a way not always possible in nuclear disarmament, their own direct interest in making progress. In the majority of cases the East Europeans are entering the CFE process with considerable hopes that rapid and successful negotiations will allow them to shift substantial resources from the military to the civilian sectors of their economies. If their expectations are to be realized, then their hopes must focus primarily on the one country with the political and economic muscle, as well as the emotional incentive, to radically change the previously rather lackadaisical attitudes and outlook of the West towards both the immediate and wider implications of conventional disarmament. Thus, if a real change is to come about in the nature of the relationship between East and West through conventional disarmament, it will happen because the Federal Republic of Germany considers such a change to be in its own long-term interest, particularly in regard to its relationship with the German Democratic Republic.

The Role of the Two German States

For the past 20 years, since Willy Brandt began his brand of *Ostpolitik*, the FRG has walked a tightrope between its relations with its Western partners and the relationship it pursues with the GDR and the Soviet Union. In recent years, however, the nature of this balancing act has altered dramatically. Instead of precariously trying to balance competing demands for loyalty and attention, the Federal Republic now finds itself in the pivotal position, able to do more than any other power (with the exception of the two superpowers) to influence the nature of the future relationship between East and West.

West German attitudes towards a more cooperative relationship between East and West are very positive. While the United Kingdom and France seem determined to preserve the status quo—and with it the adversarial relationship with the Soviet Union—and the United States strives to identify long-term objectives for its East-West policy, the FRG so far is alone among the major Western states in pursuing the clear military and political objective of a more cooperative security system which would make it impossible for any state to start or successfully wage a war in Europe. The reason is not hard to identify. A more cooperative military security system would be a major step towards overcoming the political division of Europe, which is a prerequisite for overcoming the division of Germany. Without clear objectives of their own, the three nuclear powers find the FRG's clarity of purpose, and the energy with which it pursues it, a source of considerable discomfort. Yet they can hardly be surprised by relatively positive West German attitudes towards the idea of radical reductions in conventional forces in

Central Europe, the restructuring of residual troops into wholly defensive units incapable of launching short-warning attacks and a more cooperative system of military security which is not heavily dependent upon nuclear weapons systems, the major effect of the use of which would be to kill Germans. It is the FRG which finds itself firmly planted on the front line of any putative European conflict. Between them, the two German states have tolerated on their soil for 40 years the largest concentration of military forces the world has ever seen. It should come as no surprise that the goodwill of both West German politicians and public opinion is wearing thin regarding a NATO military posture based on a threat perception that an overwhelming majority of West Germans no longer find credible.[29] This impatience has found expression across the entire political spectrum in the FRG. There exists strong opposition to the further modernization of the remaining nuclear weapons stationed in the FRG. Some leading CDU politicians regard existing NATO proposals for cuts in conventional weapons in Europe as too limited and have proposed cuts in land forces, especially armored forces, which go well beyond NATO's currently agreed upon stance.[30] The critical question for NATO in all of these rumblings is where, in terms of the FRG's vision for the future of Europe, the bottom line actually lies.

To a great extent it is because of West German opposition to further nuclear weapons modernization in Europe and West German desires to see substantial cuts in military forces in Europe that all 16 members of NATO are now sitting as an alliance at the CFE talks in Vienna. The United Kingdom and France, concerned that West German opposition to nuclear force modernization may be the first step towards active FRG support for the "triple zero"—i.e., elimination of all short-range nuclear weapons—have made it clear that before any further nuclear disarmament is contemplated the WTO numerical advantages in key categories of conventional weapons must be eliminated. With this approach in mind, both countries expect the process of negotiation between the two alliances to be long and complicated. The process of change would therefore be slow enough to manage much more thoughtfully. The major flaw with this approach is that the WTO, newly galvanized with a different approach than it brought to MBFR, seems unlikely to go along with this game plan.

It is also doubtful whether the FRG would play along with such a gradualist scenario. For the first time, what unites East and West may be greater than the divisions between them. This conjunction of interests may well prove to be an even more powerful stimulus to the intra-alliance debate in NATO than was originally anticipated. Gorbachev's troop reductions in Europe and his cuts in the Soviet military budget and weapons procurement programs highlight once and for all that the Soviets are serious about conventional disarmament. Most of the East Europeans believe that progress in conventional disarmament is critical. The West Germans are certainly serious, and they have the active or tacit support of the majority of NATO states. The United States does not wish the transition to be distorted or flawed because of the widespread euphoria that surrounds Gorbachev, whose long-term political survival is uncertain. But the Americans, driven by their own budgetary concerns and also by a growing awareness of the emergence of a multipolar world, are no longer prepared to bear the heaviest burden in underwriting the security of a rich and increasingly united Western Europe. Trade wars, not shooting wars, loom larger in the mind of the American body politic. And the United Kingdom and France are not, at base, opposed even to sweeping conventional disarmament. Their foot-dragging is motivated more by a wish to see a well-managed transition from one type of East-West relationship to another. The British and French know that they have little choice but to embrace conventional disarmament and fight to ensure that NATO gets the best deal possible from the negotiations.

Outside the field of military security, it is the FRG which leads the West in economic, political and social rapprochement with the East. West Germans are ready to consider the possibility of making real changes in the European security environment. They are at the forefront of arranging the loans and credits that the East European and Soviet economies require to bring about the restructuring of their economies. Although these efforts are relatively modest judged by the standards of what these economies require, they still far outstrip the combined contribution of all other Western states. While it would be wrong to overestimate the dangers of the FRG leaving NATO and slipping into neutralism in the foreseeable future, there is a real risk that the FRG will increasingly regard its NATO allies as less relevant for maintaining its security. In such a situation, the type of structural changes in Western defense strategy which currently appear radical and almost unthinkable could come about as a result of a unilateral West German decision to tell its allies that their support and assistance were no longer required. It is a distant danger, but it is one which lurks in the background as a possible consequence of outright failure of the CFE talks. It is an issue which

NATO as an alliance would prefer not to address, and NATO will do all in its power to avoid having to.

Conclusion

NATO has barely begun to explore the military ramifications of conventional arms control, let alone carry out a serious investigation of the political implications of a process in which it has become involved almost by default. In many ways it has fallen victim to the success of its own propaganda on the Soviet military threat over the last 30 years. The alliance and its member-states have long been telling the world about their concerns over the huge Soviet military presence in Eastern Europe, the offensive cast of WTO military strategy and the large number of numerical advantages enjoyed by the WTO over NATO's forces stationed in Europe. With these perceptions of the military balance in mind, NATO should be anxious to address the issue of conventional arms control and disarmament and seeking radical reductions and restructuring of the two alliances' military forces. However, this is not the case.

That large asymmetries between the force levels of the WTO and NATO exist in Europe is undeniable. NATO believes that in nearly all categories of weapons the WTO holds a numerical advantage. Similarly, despite signs it is evolving towards a more defensive cast, the WTO's military strategy remains based on launching a rapid offensive into the heart of Western Europe to paralyze the West's ability to defend itself, and thus prevent a protracted conflict from taking place. However, NATO has long understated its ability to offset the WTO's numerical advantages by its qualitative advantages in both weapons and personnel. This military balance is treated in detail in Chapter 2 of this volume. The essential point, however, is that NATO's military leadership remains relatively confident about its ability to deal with any WTO aggression in Europe. While that confidence is far from 100 percent, it is high enough for most of NATO's military leadership not to wish to tamper with the current military equation in Europe. Coupled with the innate conservatism of all military structures, such a perception of the military balance hardly translates into support for a process of conventional arms control which could radically alter NATO's current force posture.

A lack of enthusiasm among the alliance's military leadership does not, of course, preclude a serious approach on the part of NATO's political elites. But in some countries, military skepticism was coalescing with a lack of political foresight to form a substantial obstacle to real progress in the field of conventional arms control. This risk, in part due to West German activism, but also due to Gorbachev's sweeping unilateral reductions, has made the issue of conventional disarmament one of the key litmus tests for the seriousness with which governments approach the transformation of the East-West relationship—military, political and economic—from confrontation to cooperation. The final result of this process of transition is almost impossible to predict. But it would take a serious roadblock to derail it. The challenge for the WTO and NATO is to ensure that conventional disarmament, difficult and complex though it may be, does not become such a roadblock.

This will not be an easy task. The topic of conventional disarmament has long existed in limbo, typified by the long and moribund MBFR talks. It was the success of the INF negotiations, coupled with the refusal of the United Kingdom and France to countenance any further negotiations on nuclear weapons in Europe, that forced conventional arms control to the center of the international arena. The pattern of negotiation that led to the INF Treaty convinced the West Europeans that arms control negotiations affecting Europe could no longer be left to the two super-powers. The West Europeans realize that they have no place at the START talks. Once again, the two states that might be able to claim seats at strategic nuclear arms reduction talks, the U.K. and France, are determined to keep their distance from the entire subject.

A great deal of hyperbole has been expounded on the INF Treaty. Of course, the provisions of the treaty are important in themselves. The elimination of an entire class of nuclear missiles and agreement by the Soviet Union to allow on-site inspection to verify compliance with the treaty can hardly be dismissed as minor steps forward for disarmament. However, the West Europeans have attached equal importance to the fact that the successful conclusion of the treaty marks the inauguration of a long-term process of arms control and disarmament negotiations designed to reduce the military competition between the two alliances in Europe to its lowest possible level. The problem lies in the fact that this is an objective the content and implications of which are still not fully understood in either East or West. Neither alliance seems to have asked itself what actually constitutes the lowest practical level of military force that can still guarantee the security of its members. The West has many ideas on how it would like to see WTO forces restructured, but fewer on how NATO forces should evolve. WTO thinking seems to be further advanced. While anxious to highlight the threat it sees in NATO's force structures and levels, it has also begun to accept that parts of its own doctrine and force structure are threatening. In NATO there is also a growing willingness to admit that WTO concerns regarding FOFA and AirLand Battle, not to mention naval and tactical air forces, may have some legitimacy. It will be interesting to see, as the negotiations proceed, what the tangible results of this embryonic soul-searching will be.

The current negotiating position of NATO as a whole on the issue of conventional arms control is based on a belief that competition between the two alliances in Europe will continue indefinitely. Arms control is intended to manage that competition, not to end it—an assumption which is not in accord with the national approaches of all NATO member-states. Some assign a much greater importance to arms control, seeing it as a vehicle which, if utilized with skill and imagination, can serve to fundamentally alter the relationship between East and West and pave the way for much greater cooperation between the two halves of Europe. NATO must resolve the fundamental differences in outlook which underline these two approaches to conventional arms control if it is to set realistic political objectives for the process. That is why, outside of an extremely limited discussion on purely military issues, the attitude, approach, expectations and objectives of the WTO as an alliance, and of its individual members, can no longer be ignored in NATO's consideration of conventional arms control. For NATO the issue cannot simply be one of alliance management rather than arms control. There is a growing realization that, because of the rapidly evolving nature of the Soviet approach to conventional disarmament, NATO no longer has the luxury of time. The conventional balance which has existed for 40 years is not likely to survive much longer. The task has become, for both alliances, to manage military change cooperatively, to allow the two halves of Europe to reap the maximum political and economic benefits.

Notes

1 "The Problem of Mankind's Survival," *The New York Times*, December 8, 1988, p. A16.
2 See the statements by French Defense Minister Jean Pierre Cheverement: "France Puts Priority as Conventional Arms Curbs at Talks," *The Washington Post*, September 27, 1988, p. A15; and "Prime Minister Margaret Thatcher Blows Cool on Early N-Arms Talks," *Financial Times*, February 18, 1988, p. 2.
3 Chilaty Dariush, *Disarmament: A Historical Review of Negotiations and Treaties* (Iran National University: 1978).

4 See Phil Williams, *The Senate and U.S. Troops in Europe* (London: Macmillan, 1985), pp. 157–159.

5 There has been a rash of press reports and public opinion surveys that highlight the increasing intolerance of the general public, especially in the FRG, to putting up with the noise and inconvenience and, in the case of combat aircraft crashes, dangers which arise as a result of military activities. See "Green Hammer," *The Economist*, November 26, 1988, p. 53. However, the first tangible result of this underlying current is the American decision to cancel the 1989 "Reforger" reinforcement exercises. See *Jane's Defence Weekly*, February 11, 1989, p. 206. In a similar move, the West German government has also decided to cut all corps and divisional exercise by half beginning in 1990.

6 The critical changes which are taking place in West German attitudes is discussed by Arnulf Baring in *Unser Neuer Groessenwahn: Deutschland Zwischen Ost and West* (Stuttgart: Deutsche Verlags-Anstalt, 1988).

7 The dimensions of the issue are best discussed in Samuel P. Huntington, "Coping with the Lippmann Gap," *Foreign Affairs* 66, No. 3 (America and the World, 1987/88), pp. 453–477.

8 Edgar Cheporov, "Changing Public Opinion and the Summitry Process," unpublished paper for the Institute for East-West Security Studies, New York, 1988.

9 Since Gorbachev launched his ideas on the "common European house" there has been a good deal of discussion of the issue. I have attended three five-day conferences sponsored by the Aspen Institute (Berlin) in various European capitals to examine different aspects of the idea; the Working Group of which I am a member has not yet reached any firm conclusions on the exact nature of any long-term pan-European interests, but there is no doubt that such interests exist and are growing stronger.

10 Robert D. Blackwill, "Conceptual Problems of Conventional Arms Control," *International Security* 12, No. 4 (Spring 1988), pp. 28–47.

11 The U.S. Department of Defense, in *Soviet Military Power: An Assessment of the Threat*, gives estimates of between 15 and 17 percent of the Soviet Union's GNP. However, in private conversations, some leading Soviet economists have speculated that, when the Soviets are able to properly identify and calculated their military budget, the real figure may be as high as 25 percent of GNP. See "Statement as Military Expenditures Urged" *Izvestiia*, Moscow, January 4, 1989, Foreign Broadcast Information Service, *Daily Report-Soviet Union*, SN 89003, January 5, 1989, pp. 58–60.

12 Much of the discussion on conversion in the Soviet Union is anecdotal, focusing on the switch in particular industrial plants from military to civil production. Another favorite theme is the huge expenditures on arms by the West. Academician Boris Ponomarev, "The Way Out of the Impasse," *Pravda*, August 9, 1989, p. 4. But a more serious discussion of the Soviet situation is now getting underway: see Vladimir Konorseyen, "Benefits of Converting Arms Production," *International Affairs* (Moscow) No. 2 (February 1988) pp. 33–40, 58. While not giving figures, the article provides a good discussion on the possible scope and impact of the convergence of military industries for the Soviet Union. See also Graham Thompson, "Converting the Soviet Defence Industry," *Jane's Defence Weekly*, March 4, 1989, p. 355.

13 See James A. Thomson and Nanette C. Gantz, *Conventional Arms Control Revisited: Objectives in the New Phase* (Santa Monica, CA: The RAND Corporation, N-2697-AF, 1987).

14 "Conventional Arms Control: The Way Ahead. Statement Issued Under the Authority of the Heads of State and Governments Participating in the Meeting of the North Atlantic Council in Brussels, March 2–3, 1988," *Atlantic News* No. 1998 (March 4, 1988), pp. 5–9.

15 See the interview with General I. M. Tretiak (Commander-in-Chief of the Soviet Air Defense Forces), *Moscow News*, February 21, 1988.

16 See *Pravda*, July 16, 1988, pp. 1–2, translated in FBIS, *Daily Report-Soviet Union* 88-137, July 18, 1988, pp. 13–14.

17 Paul Kennedy, *The Rise and Fall of The Great Powers* (New York: Random House, 1987).

18 It is important to remember that Thatcher made the observation before Gorbachev became general secretary and launched his reform program. It is a view the British prime minister has stuck to ever since.

19 *Statement on the Defence Estimates* (London: Ministry of Defence, Her Majesty's Stationary Office, 1988), pp. 5–6.

20 Sir Geoffrey Howe, *"On the Record,"* British Broadcasting Corporation, London, December 4, 1988.

21 *The Reagan Military Legacy: Haste Made Waste* (Washington, DC: Center for Defense Information, 1989), p. 3.

22 "That Was a Fat Lot of Help," *The Economist*, November 26, 1988, p. 16.

23 "East Germany Cuts its Armed Forces by 10,000," *The New York Times*, January 24, 1989, p. A9.

24 *A Documentary History of Arms Control and Disarmament* (New York: Bowker, 1973), pp. 436–437.

25 See Andrzej Karkoszka, "Merits of the Jaruzelski Plan," *Bulletin of the Atomic Scientists* 44, No. 7 (September 1988), pp. 32–34.

26 "The SED/SPD European Chemical Weapon-Free Zone Proposal," in Rolf Trapp, ed., *Chemical Weapon Free Zones?* (Oxford: Oxford University Press, 1987), pp. 198–201.

27 "SED-SPD Working Group in Favor of Continuing Process of Disarmament," *Foreign Affairs Bulletin*, Ministry of Foreign Affairs of the GDR, Vol. 28, February 7, 1987, p. 105.

28 See László Lábody's companion piece in this chapter.

29 Lucy Komisar, "In Working Eastward, Germans See Profit," *The Los Angeles Times*, October 28, 1988, p. 7.

30 Volker Ruehe, "NATO muss Offensive ergreifen," *Frankfurter Allgemeine Zeitung*, September 6, 1988, p. 2.

PART TWO

The Political Objectives
of Conventional Disarmament

László Lábody, Hungary

Practically all politicians and experts agree that the negotiations on
Conventional Forces in Europe (CFE) promise to be complicated to a
degree virtually without precedent in the history of diplomacy. The
"bean-counting" experience at the MBFR talks is not the only indication
of this. The complexity of the new talks is immediately obvious because
the negotiations must cover hundreds of complex arms systems that
serve several purposes, thousands of instruments, and the effective
strength and structure of armed forces. CFE must also take into consideration such barely quantifiable factors as geographical situations and the
economic abilities of individual states and military alliances or the
adaptability of entire societies to the extraordinary conditions of war.[1]
Nevertheless, these factors must somehow be quantified.

Conventional Disarmament and Politics

The situation is further complicated by the fact that conventional forces
have extremely deep roots in societies. They play a role in both domestic
politics and foreign policy of the individual states, and there is a wide
range of particular interests linked to their development and eventual
application. Economic interests have always been the most important
factor behind the perceived need for conventional forces, from the
acquisition of slaves and territories essential for the functioning of the
ancient empires through the Nazi cynicism of fighting "not for ideas but
for steel, wheat and oil," to contemporary wars over territories rich in

natural resources. Furthermore, the significant role of military industry in economic development should not be underestimated. Armies have always had weapons reflecting the highest level of technical development of a given age.

The means and organization necessary for employing force are in themselves an important factor in society. Force is more than the internal and external deterrence necessary to preserve given power: in numerous societies, the army is a very important political and social force; moreover, in certain countries it is the most important cohesive and integrating force, one destined to preserve society's operability. The reason for military takeovers—from the Praetorian guards' toppling of Roman emperors to the coups d'etat of today—is that in many cases the army is better organized than society at large, an intellectual force not to be underestimated and experienced in operating a vast organization. The most developed states are practically the only ones able to renounce this role of the military; Poland and Turkey in the past ten years have no longer been able to do so. The military also plays an important role in the political socialization process by integrating young generations into society, educating, transmitting values, creating jobs and so on.

Only the political sphere is capable of holding together, integrating and representing as a unified whole the almost inextricable tangle of interests linked to armies. One of the many functions of politics is just to make conflicting interests—unmanageable in themselves—manageable by transforming them politically. Only politics can assist in harmonizing and integrating the disparate interests intrinsic to the various sectors of society.[2] Clausewitz's oft-quoted dictum that war is the continuation of politics by other means is the embodiment of precisely this idea.

Politics will assume an important role at the CFE talks not only because the negotiations can only be held by making their subject a political issue, but also because the structure of interests originating from the social function of conventional forces and armaments is inherently political. It emphasizes the importance and responsibility of politics, that the consequences of a *failure* of the negotiations are difficult to foresee and may in the most extreme case result in the destruction of humanity. Negotiations held in other spheres (such as economy and culture) do not imply similar risks.

Consequently, whereas the subject of the negotiations is military power, it cannot be held to the rationality of the military sphere alone. To do so would guarantee that the talks would to come to an impasse.

In the first place political considerations should prevail. In contrast, if political interests do not head in the direction of arms limitation, then it is *political will*—the involvement of the highest political echelon—that may provide the impetus indispensable for a breakthrough. At the same time it is precisely those interests that are organically held together in politics which make these negotiations particularly complicated.

Examining politics and the structures of interests appearing within the East-West context, one can conclude that there no longer exist economic constraints on states that might necessarily prompt them to expand geographically, that is, to use conventional forces for offensive purposes.[3] In the West this process took place between the two world wars, when the lack of new territories for colonization put a limit on external markets and the economy's attention turned towards the internal market. Karl Polanyi called this phenomenon "reform capitalism."[4] In the East there had never been any such constraints, and there is still a considerable contradiction between the present level of economic productivity and market demands, the main concern being the lack of capital rather than the search for external markets. Hence, beside the direct interest of military industry, the primary engine for armament must be sought in the sphere of politics: in ideological motivation—i.e., the evaluation of threat and of the possibilities for asserting one's interests. (The "expansion" of the Soviet Union in the developing world can also primarily be explained by security policy and ideological reasons rather than by economic constraints.) The internal dynamics of the armaments process are significantly influenced by the demands of politics—that is, by the position of violence, of armed forces, within the political arsenal.

The prominent role of military power in the international system is becoming increasingly difficult to maintain, above all because there is no harmony between political aims and disposable military power. Whereas there is no objective pressure for territorial expansion, military power has—on the basis of the particular laws of confrontation—increased many times. As Johan Huizinga wrote in 1935: "The expedience of war is diminishing in proportion as the effect of the means of war grows and as the vital interest of the belligerents require a mutual peaceful relationship."[5] The fact that nowadays war has—in the East-West context—no expedience at all has also been recognized by the two superpowers in Gorbachev and Reagan's joint statement adopted at the Geneva summit in 1985.[6]

On the basis of present political and military thinking it is increasingly difficult to create the necessary military power for maintaining the expedience of war. The budgetary problems of the United States and the Soviet Union's economic difficulties, as well as the attitudes and situations of their allies, are well known. It is in vain that military industries create jobs, that the "by-products" of military research and development usable for civilian purposes represent a significant economic driving force, that arms exports bring considerable profits, since the final products of military industry are not being returned to economic circulation. In this respect, the armaments process is a "use of resources." It is more difficult to maintain the level of conventional forces because of population decreases in most of the developed countries, especially in age groups eligible for military service.[7] The fact that a considerable part of the public in various countries does not consider war a "legitimate" continuation of politics at all and hardly tolerates the present levels of defense expenditures can also be considered in the East-West context. Another factor contributing to the difficulty of maintaining conventional forces may be the contradiction that is tightening between the claim for national sovereignty and the inevitable supremacy of the most influential power within a military alliance system (which should not be confused with the voluntary renunciation of a part of national sovereignty within international economic and political organizations).[8] To sum up, it stands to reason that in the East-West context, military confrontation has to be reduced to a minimum in order to maintain a stable balance. Thus the political strategy of confrontation has to be replaced with one of cooperation. (There already exists a vast bibliography on this, from the "prisoners' dilemma" to sophisticated theoretical analyses.)[9]

The basis of the global military balance is, all things considered, constituted by strategic nuclear means—although there are intense debates over whether nuclear weapons make military sense at all and whether they are therefore applicable for political aims. This, however, is only true in the case of the two superpowers, which have global interests, and their three "main front lines" of confrontation, of which Europe—according to Brzezinski—makes up only one.[10] The presence of short-range nuclear forces in Europe, however, is justified by NATO through references to a conventional threat coming from the Soviet Union. Thus, if negotiations on conventional matters prove successful and the conventional offensive capabilities of the Warsaw Treaty diminish substantially, the reason for the existence of the former will also disappear. The significance of the WTO's conventional capacity is further underlined by the INF Treaty since, of the three "main front lines," only a conflict in Europe would inevitably lead to a global nuclear war. The INF Treaty, however, eliminated precisely that link in the chain of escalation which is most capable of involving the two superpowers in a nuclear conflict. A comprehensive agreement on conventional arms limitation in Europe, however, would eliminate offensive capacities—that is, the means of military conflict itself—in Europe, thus eradicating—at least in the military sense of the word—the potential starting point of nuclear escalation. Such an arrangement would most certainly put the whole complex problem of nuclear disarmament in a new light, and on a global level. Thus the beginning of conventional disarmament in Europe is a crucial element in the reduction of East-West military confrontation worldwide. Its objective is to radically limit offensive capacities and to stabilize balance on a low level.

The Future Role of the Superpowers in East-West Relations

The basic structure of the East-West relationship, the roles of the superpowers and the alliance systems, developed after World War II. Having examined the potentials of the Soviet Union and the United States, one may say in a slightly simplified manner that neither could afford *not* to be a superpower.

The United States could not afford to renounce its position as a superpower because it was supplier of 40 percent of world production and in possession of a monopoly on the atomic bomb. If only for domestic political considerations (because of the "greatness of the nation") was this true, especially with no notable external constraints or rivals. Any administration that would reject the superpower role was destined to fail. Another factor not to be neglected in the U.S. case was ideological motivation, the stimulating force of anti-communist hysteria.

The Soviet Union could not afford to renounce its role as a superpower either, if only because of the United States. After the experience of foreign intervention in the Civil War and especially after World War II, the USSR was forced to concentrate the greatest part of its resources in the area it felt most threatened: defense. The communists' belief in a world revolutionary mission also played a role in intensifying confrontation. In addition, there was a need for strengthening the feeling of both external and internal threats in order to spread and maintain the Stalinist dictatorship. All this, however, was considered a challenge by the United States. The aggressive and expansionist ideological missionary belief is only now beginning to gradually disappear in the USSR; the latest to speak about the necessity of exempting international relations from ideology was Soviet Foreign Minister Shevardnadze at the UN General Assembly in December 1988.

During the period of U.S.-Soviet rivalry, which increased quite rapidly in the wake of their wartime cooperation, both parties were striving to build their own "security zone." This took place in a decisive manner in Europe: it was from here that the Soviet Union had been attacked, and precisely for that reason the USSR attempted to push its defense lines further west.[11] The United States tried to contain this movement and wanted to extend its influence further east and set up its own alliance system. The situation which was thus created in Europe proved to be so stable that the East-West rivalry was shifted to the developing world. Detente and the development of East-West cooperation have produced many changes but the structures that evolved during the Cold War have remained basically intact.

To date the most important shift has taken place on two levels: in the relationship between the superpowers, and in the relations between their respective European allies. The question, however, is to what extent conditions exist for permanent change on the part of the two superpowers and their respective allies, on the one hand, and how the roles and structures developed after World War II might be modified, on the other.

As far as U.S.-Soviet relations are concerned, experts who view permanent coexistence with skepticism raise two problems the solution of which fundamentally concerns progress in conventional arms limitation. First, the Soviet Union is a "one-dimensional giant,"[12] whose global role is provided by its military power: if the USSR renounced its military might, with what could it be replaced? The *horror vacui* applies not only to nature, but to the international system as well. The second dilemma is how the West should view transformations taking place in the Soviet Union: what is the guarantee that the Soviet Union, strengthened by the support of Western Europe, will not return to its former policy?[13]

The answers to the two questions are identical. One must not call the relative rectitude of the former Soviet leadership into question, but the inappropriate evaluation of situations, the false theoretical-political basic position and the stereotyped structures and decision-making mechanism of Soviet society almost inevitably led to inappropriate policies.

The essence of the present Soviet reforms is a fundamental reconsideration of theoretical-ideological bases and a radical change of social structures. It was said that the intervention in Afghanistan had been a decision of a narrow circle: such a step would hardly be possible in an open and democratic Soviet Union. The significance of the "new political thinking" should in no way be underestimated. When the leadership of one country propagates the forthcoming failure of another country's system on the basis of its internal contradictions, it is, in its practical policy, not necessarily strengthening elements of cooperation and compromise. But if a leadership starts, like that of Gorbachev, from the necessity of making preparations for long-term coexistence,[14] the general interests of humanity are of primary importance; and if it recognizes the determining tendencies of internationalization, then it may assure a realistic, practical, cooperative foreign policy.[15] A reformed Soviet Union linked to the West through close ties of cooperation cannot become the old enemy again.

Within the new political thinking, the perception of security policy enjoys outstanding importance. The pragmatic West, which almost exclusively evaluates steps of a practical nature, has scarcely taken notice of the fact that at the 27th Congress of the CPSU Gorbachev's speech approached the question of security in a totally new manner, attributing equal importance to political, military, economic and humanitarian components alike—but with the political factor in the first place. The practical consequences of this way of thinking have already become tangible and have led to a significant shift in the field of security policy as well:

–It is beyond question that Soviet military doctrine, and in particular its political component, has changed.[16] The transformation of the military-technical aspect, however, naturally needs more time. In this context it is worth noting that, whereas it was easy to trace the increasing influence of military considerations on foreign-policy decisions in the last years of the Brezhnev era, Gorbachev is attempting to restore the primacy of politics.[17]

–The Soviet Union is no doubt one step ahead by having a comprehensive disarmament concept that ranges from space warfare to conventional forces, even though it is primarily a political conception and each of the problem areas are not elaborated alike. Nevertheless, the USSR handles its position in a flexible manner and is ready to modify and make it more precise, if necessary.

–A quite significant change has taken place in the entire approach to conventional arms limitation in Europe. This is already evidenced by the fact that the issue is now being included in the arms control agenda: previously the Soviet Union mainly concentrated on nuclear matters. The present position, which recognizes asymmetries—including Soviet superiority in certain fields—and defines the elaboration of exclusively defensive strategic capacities as the ultimate goal, takes into account the Western perception of threat and offers opportunities for a shift. Furthermore, Gorbachev's December 1988 speech at the UN announcing the 10-percent reduction of the Soviet army, the withdrawal of six tank divisions from the GDR, Czechoslovakia and Hungary, as well as other unilateral disarmament measures unprecedented in their size and significance, gives a clear indication of Soviet readiness to reach an important large-scale agreement with NATO.

–As a global power the Soviet Union cannot neglect rethinking the whole of its engagement in the Third World as a function of Soviet economic capacity. This forces ideological and military motives into the background. Soviet readiness to cooperate in the political settlement of local crises has grown, which has, through the superpower relationship, repercussions on the prospects for conventional arms limitation in Europe.

Regarding Europe, a new Soviet position is beginning to take shape. In the USSR's previous behavior the traces of a war-winning superpower's attitude are evident, such as the dismissal of West European integration schemes and campaigns against West German "revanchism." The overemphasis on quantitative factors in Soviet security perceptions is indicated by the dimensions and deployment of Soviet forces in Europe. It is difficult to assess whether the deployment of the SS-20s was motivated only by military considerations or by the intention to exert military pressure on Western Europe to decouple it from the United States. In any case, the effect proved how inappropriate military means are *in general* to achieve political aims in Europe.

One of the key motives of present Soviet foreign policy seems to be the goal of its inclusion in the international system on a global basis, and within that, on a European basis. This is not only because of the necessity for capital and technology for economic modernization, but also because of the need to overcome more general lags in Soviet society. The path that has been chosen by Moscow for this purpose is the opposite of its predecessors: persuasion and partnership instead of pressure.[18] The collective expression of these ambitions is the so-called "common European house," inside of which the thickest division is the conventional forces confronting each other on the borderline between the Warsaw Treaty and NATO.

In the cooperative European system of the "common European house," an important role could also be assumed by the United States (this would argue against past attempts to push it out). If European armed forces are drastically reduced and their strategic offensive capacities eliminated in the course of conventional arms limitation in Europe, the security-policy coupling of the United States and Western Europe will also appear in a new light.

This cannot be achieved overnight, however, nor against the will or without the active participation of the United States. The limitation process itself must, as a matter of course, include U.S. armed forces, if only because NATO does not possess a genuine offensive potential in Europe without the United States. (NATO reproaches the Warsaw Treaty with the same question: political declarations are one thing, capacity another. The trustworthiness of political statements on readiness to cooperate is provided by the genuine lack of offensive military capacity.) In the course of the limitation process, U.S. forces within the alliance will also have to obviously decrease in both absolute and relative numbers, and in such a way that the socialist countries do not feel threatened by their presence or, in particular, their armaments. Thus the real question is not the presence in Europe of U.S. forces, but rather the nature of this presence.[19] In a totally defensive West European military structure— lacking any kind of offensive capacity—there could hardly be any objection to a U.S. presence.

This is all the more true because the concept of total European "security independence" is illusory. While the basis of global balance is strategic nuclear forces (namely between the U.S. and the USSR), with Europe being one of the subsystems of that global balance, Soviet nuclear forces are *objectively* creating a feeling of threat in Western Europe, whether or not it has such weapons at its disposal. The respective counterbalance will (hopefully) not be the creation of an independent European strategic nuclear force and/or the further development of British and French nuclear capacities, but a linkage to the United States, including the presence of U.S. troops in Europe.

The existence of non-numerical asymmetries, particularly geostrategic factors, also makes the presence of U.S. troops in Europe acceptable. It would scarcely be possible for the West to counterbalance its disadvantaged position in this respect, especially the lack of strategic depth and the distance of the main forces, by making a certain superiority of NATO forces acceptable. It seems more efficient to maintain a linkage, all the more because on the part of the WTO this is a logical consequence deriving from its geographical position, even without the direct presence of Soviet troops in Eastern and Central Europe.

Thus one may conclude that in the course of the CFE negotiations and in the resulting defensive structures the outstanding role of the two superpowers will be dominant but its nature will change. The United States and the Soviet Union will prevail because the European security system constitutes one of the subsystems of their global balance, which has to be stabilized in such a way as to avoid the danger of being drawn into a conflict. An indispensable condition of agreement, however, is the political readiness of the superpowers. Yet their role will change because the balance within Europe is assured not by the deterrent effect of their conventional and nuclear offensive capacities but by their organic integration into a military system serving defensive purposes alone.

The Future of the Two German States[20]

The CFE talks throw new light on and once again put on the agenda the German—or rather, inter-German—question. Along the borderline between the two German states vast forces of the Warsaw Treaty and NATO face each other, and here, too, geographical circumstances make it possible to launch larger-scale conventional offensive operations.[21] The existence and the still formally limited sovereignty of the two German states[22] are among the most striking realities that have taken shape since World War II. For a long time the European question was practically identical with the German question. Its significance from the point of view of security policy is indicated by the fact that the foundation of the Warsaw Treaty was directly prompted by the FRG's admission to NATO. One of the most indispensable components of European detente was the West German *Ostpolitik*, through which—and for lack of a peace treaty in force—the FRG normalized its relationship with the GDR, Poland and all socialist countries.[23] On the other side, however, the GDR was given notice of its statehood through diplomatic recognition. This process, the "reintegration" of the two German states into Europe, was made complete through the signing of the Helsinki Final Act and their admission to the United Nations.

The relationship between the two German states shows, on one hand, a unique unity of uncompromising confrontation and separation and, on the other hand, a close intertwining.

–Besides the different social systems, there is a considerable asymmetry between the two German states as far as territory, population, economic performance and so forth are concerned. These objectively result in a certain "need for separation" (*Abgrenzungszwang*), especially on the part of the GDR. In order to defend its independent statehood and the identity of its system the GDR even found it necessary to elaborate a document together with the FRG Social Democrat Party on ideological separation.[24] The FRG is barely sensitive to such pressures, owing to its economic power and democratic achievements.

–As mentioned above, the main line of East-West military confrontation in Europe lies along the border of the two German states. The concentration of armed forces—national and allied—on their territories is probably the highest in the world. *Any* kind of armed conflict between them—including West Berlin—would almost inevitably escalate. (It is no mere coincidence that most of the "worst-case scenarios," such as the film *The Day After*, take this as a starting point.)

–The force of separation and military confrontation require the maintenance of sharp-featured hostile images. (It is enough to consider the two states' reports on each other in their respective mass media.)[25]

–Both states became an integral part of their own systems of not only military but also economic and political cooperation. Their neighbors' historic experiences and fear of a reunified Germany also contribute to the maintenance of the division. Relations with "the Germany of the other side" increase the scope of foreign policy towards the allied German state (see, for instance, relations between France and the GDR, or Poland and the FRG).

At the same time, however,

–There is, the realities of independent statehood aside, a quite strong "attraction" between the FRG and the GDR. This is made asymmetrical by the difference in basic positions evident between, on the one hand, the phrase appearing in the constitution of the FRG regarding unification (*Wiedervereinigungsgebot*) and, on the other hand, the GDR emphasis on state sovereignty.

–There is a mutually strong interest in economic cooperation, in intra-German trade, and a demand for humanitarian and cultural relations which is becoming increasingly reciprocal.

–Last but not least, the military danger put upon the two German states is, as a consequence of their geostrategic position, extraordinarily great. The perception and awareness of this is shown by the debates on Pershing-2 missiles and the French nuclear deterrent; and by the GDR's foreign policy activities in the East-West context, which has increased considerably beginning during the U.S.-Soviet "ice age" of the early 1980s.

The last factor—the extraordinary military danger put upon the two German states—has led to a peculiar kind of inter-German security-policy cooperation through inter-party channels between the East German Socialist Unity Party (SED) and the opposition West German SPD. The aim of their proposals—a nuclear-weapons-free corridor, a chemical-weapons-free zone, a zone of disengagement and so on—is, without exception, to diminish the danger put upon the German territories "in a European guise," that is, through linkage to the European processes. Another particular feature of these plans is that the means intended to be included do not always fall under national competence and the measures also go beyond the borders of state sovereignty. Their territorial validity, however, includes only the countries of the parties submitting this proposal (thus differing from the Jaruzelski or the Jakeš Plans). It is an important development that the CDU/CSU parties which replaced the SPD in government in Bonn are continuing their predecessor's *Ostpolitik*; moreover, they are an increasingly determined and constructive force as far as arms limitation issues are concerned. The latest proof of this was the proposal submitted by the CDU in the Bundestag on September 5, 1988,[26] on conventional arms limitation. It appears as if in certain questions a new kind of security-policy consensus is beginning to take shape in the Federal Republic.

The effect of the factors connecting and separating the two German states will also be long-term in nature. However, their basic interest in the European conventional arms limitation process and in diminishing the danger put upon them is most important. Since there is no longer any need to maintain an external threat to safeguard the legitimacy and strengthen the internal cohesion of either German state, such considerations do not set limits on their interests either. The two states are not expected to oppose the military forces deployed on their territories—as one of the ultimate goals of the limitation process, of course—having purely defensive capacities; moreover, it is in their own direct interest to promote this.[27] At the same time, new light will be thrown on the old concern of the allies, the so-called neutralist ambitions of the FRG, since the reduction of offensive capacities will take place *not against* the alliance's will but in accordance with it. Moreover, it will be a common endeavor.

Nevertheless, it is hard to imagine that in "cooperative Europe" the establishment of any kind of unified German state will be put on the agenda. First of all, the European balance-of-power system was based upon the existence of *two* German states, and this is hardly likely to change. Reunification, which would upset that balance, would be unacceptable for East and West alike. There is also the fear of the power of a reunified Germany, even if it possessed military capacities of a strictly defensive character; because of its economic power, both East and West are interested in the maintenance of this division. It is also unlikely that the schemes for economic integration will become so close to each other that a reunified Germany would belong to both of them—nor is it probable that such a state would abandon either of them.

Finally, one very essential condition for the creation of a Europe based upon stability at a low level of conventional armaments and upon comprehensive cooperation is the preservation of the identity of social systems. If the identity of one system is questioned in any country, the latter will inevitably cease to cooperate with the representatives of the other system. From this perspective a different attitude cannot be expected from the leaderships of the two German states either. However, the question of German reunification—in any form—would raise the issue of system identity.

Progress in the conventional arms limitation process, however, is the most important precondition for inter-German cooperation to fully exert its beneficial impact on the East-West relationship since this is the crucial field of division and confrontation. Progress would make it possible to eliminate hostile images and to ease sometimes almost absurd rules of separation. The two German states, strengthened in statehood, identity and confidence, in the long run could become one of the broadest bridges of East-West relations.

The Role of Alliance Systems

The two military alliances play a decisive role in conventional arms limitation. Neutral and nonaligned countries do not maintain armies capable of launching large-scale attacks; rather, they are prepared for territorial defense. This difference is also expressed by the separation of the negotiations of the 23 from those of the 35. The question is whether the positions of the two alliances promise some kind of step forward: what are the two alliances' interests in an agreement, or, what kind of changes may conventional limitations lead to within the Warsaw Treaty and NATO, and in their mutual relationship?

NATO's negotiating positions were formulated in the communiqué issued at the March 1987 Brussels summit.[28] The leaders of the Atlantic alliance saw the origin of the problems in the imbalance of the two alliances' armed forces, in the superiority of the Warsaw Treaty's forces and in the capacity to launch a large-scale conventional attack. Thus, in NATO's opinion, the avoidability of war is only safeguarded by deterrence, that is, by an appropriate mix of conventional and nuclear deterrence. Therefore their negotiating aims are as follows:

–to create a stable balance of conventional forces at lower levels;
–to eliminate asymmetries; and
–to eliminate capacities to launch surprise attacks or large-scale offensives.

The Warsaw Treaty's proposals were defined in the communiqués issued at the 1986 Budapest and 1988 Warsaw sessions of the Political Consultative Committee[29] and show a significant shift in the WTO position. Whereas in 1986 the WTO proposed a basically symmetrical procedure, the Warsaw declaration states that reductions may take place in three phases. First, a level of armed forces lower than the present one must be developed by eliminating asymmetries. Second, there should be a 25-percent reduction of the remaining force levels, that is, 500,000 troops. Finally, further reductions should be taken in which "both parties' armed forces would assume a strictly defensive character." In addition, the Warsaw Treaty also proposes concrete measures limiting the threat of surprise attacks.

Thus the positions of NATO and the Warsaw Pact are close to each other on the necessity of the removal of asymmetries and the establishment of a balance on a lower level. In a way, the political determination making it possible to take a first step is there. This, of course, does not diminish the expected difficulties of the CFE negotiations, which are also affected by the considerable differences that exist despite the similar will.

The point is, above all, that the Warsaw Treaty has long-term conceptions; in contrast, NATO's proposal is for a first phase, the final result of which is far from being purely defensive. The source of another problem is that at present NATO is aiming for reductions on the part of the Warsaw Treaty in fields where the latter enjoys superiority; as for itself, NATO is trying to withdraw from the negotiations those armaments in which NATO maintains a superior position. For the time being it is impossible to tell whether this is strictly a negotiating tactic or whether it indicates a lack of genuine readiness to come to an agreement. This is all the more important because the extent of interest in reaching an agreement is not necessarily identical in certain member-states of both the Warsaw Treaty and NATO.

As far as the Soviet Union and its allies are concerned, it seems that they are all without exception interested in conventional arms limitations. This is primarily because of their domestic political situations: their economies suffer from a lack of capital and are in need of every resource that may be freed. Within that framework, most of the allies either border NATO countries or are situated so close to the front line that, consequently, an armed conflict would eventually extend to their own territories as well. Also, it must not be overlooked that conventional arms limitation enjoys the unanimous support of public opinion in the East, and in the present situation the leadership of each of these countries is in need of any attainable increase in prestige and respect. Finally, because they have recognized that the greatest obstacle to the system of foreign relations—which is indispensable for domestic modernization—is military confrontation, and specifically conventional forces, there is a resulting lack of confidence.

This tendency is being strengthened by the development of security-policy relations within the East bloc.[30] While the Soviet political leadership is stimulating its allies to assume an independent international role—as evidenced by the SED's initiatives, the Jaruzelski and Jakeš Plans and increasing Hungarian activity—this will naturally have repercussions on the military alliance as well, which is, by its nature, more strictly organized. Taking into account the differences in the views of the individual socialist countries on their own internal tasks and international roles, it may be assumed that the elaboration of Warsaw Treaty documents reached by consensus will meet difficulties that should not be underestimated. The contents of joint positions—e.g., evaluations of situations—also prove that they are being reached through concessions made by countries that are more sensitive to internal problems and more open in the context of East-West relations. This includes the Soviet Union.

Studying the points of view of both NATO as a whole and its individual member-states, one can conclude that the structure of interests is in this case more complex. This situation has its origin first of all in the geographical distance from Europe of NATO's leading power, the territory of which is, contrary to that of the Soviet Union, not threatened by any kind of potential conventional attack.[31] The same also goes for Canada and Iceland. As for the FRG, Denmark and the Benelux countries, their geographical position and dimensions certainly underline their respective interest. France, however, though not a member of NATO's military organization, demands a leading role in Europe, an important component of which is its insistence on maintaining conventional and nuclear forces. The conventional threat to Spain, Portugal, Greece and the United Kingdom should not be considered notable. As for Norway and Turkey, the threat there is also limited in spite of their direct proximity to the USSR. Thus, beyond general connections and apart from certain countries, very little motivation can be perceived on NATO's part to strive for a further large-scale reduction of conventional forces and armaments after asymmetries are eliminated and a slightly lower level of confrontation is achieved. Another question for NATO is the dilemma hinted at in connection with Soviet *perestroika*.

Nevertheless, it is evident that even the completion of the first phase of conventional disarmament would considerably modify the internal state of the two alliances and their mutual relationship, since one of the most important factors of internal cohesion, the external threat, would considerably diminish. Mutual confidence would also increase as a consequence of related, but different, kinds of purposeful measures.

Reductions must also include troops stationed abroad. Their total withdrawal, however, is hardly to be expected. Possible justifications for the presence of U.S. troops in Europe—in considerably reduced numbers and armaments and integrated into defensive structures—has already been mentioned. The Soviet Union, on its own behalf, has already expressed its readiness to withdraw its troops stationed abroad.[32] It was a serious question, however, whether this might take place in the framework of negotiations and as a result of an agreement or whether certain steps may already be taken in advance, in order to build confidence, and on a unilateral basis.[33] However, Gorbachev's UN speech answered this question.

The Nature of Relations Between Eastern and Western Europe

Perhaps the most important achievement of the post-Cold War period is the change that took place in East-West relations within the structures established during the Cold War: a loosening of the strict hierarchy of the bipolar world system. With the economic boom in Japan and Western Europe, the economic order has become multipolar as a matter of course. In addition, instead of the former rigid mutual separation, a circulation of political, economic, cultural and humanitarian ideas and values has started. Bipolarity has basically remained only in the military field because of the overwhelming nuclear arsenals of the two superpowers and the existence of military alliances. The result of these changes is that Eastern and Western Europe are confronting each other not directly but primarily as parts of the race between the superpowers: their perception of threat derives less from each other than from the leading power of the other side. To this has been linked the particular situation that took shape in the early 1980s, when strains in U.S.-Soviet relations were not followed by a deterioration of relations between their respective allies. On the contrary, Western Europe and some smaller socialist countries have made serious efforts to avoid an irreversible rupture in East-West relations.[34] This shock-absorbing action proved to be successful and progressive— though it could be supposed that, had there been no change in the position of the Soviet Union or, consequently, in that of the United States, Eastern and Western Europe would eventually have been forced to yield to a certain extent to superpower pressure. It is no coincidence that the real focus of tensions between the Soviet Union and the United States was the arms race and military confrontation (Afghanistan, Grenada, SS-20s, Pershing 2s, SDI and so forth).

To return to the problem of the "one-dimensional giant," there is no doubt that nowadays one of the key issues for Western Europe is the perception of threat created by the military power of the Soviet Union. This threat perception is one of the driving forces behind West European efforts for cooperation with socialist countries. But what will happen if, at the end of a long negotiating process and the successful elimination of offensive military capacities, this factor ceases to exist? Will enough motivation remain to keep the West from retiring within itself (or turning elsewhere)?

It is obvious that this problem cannot be simplified to such an extent because, first of all, not only does the West feel threatened by the Soviet Union, but the opposite is also true. To remove this mutual perception of threat is in the interest of both the West and the East. Second, it is also true that conventional arms limitation is possible only in the broadest political context, which, considering its ultimate goal, is the development of a cooperative European system. Third, because of their present state and their attempts to change the structures and the model, the socialist countries are only to a limited extent attractive partners for cooperation. However, this may change considerably, partly as a result of the reform process under way and partly as a result of cooperation itself.

Strong ties between Eastern and Western Europe may be considered natural, not only because of their centuries-old economic relations and their common culture but also because historically Western Europe served as an example for Central and Eastern Europe, which usually lagged one phase behind. This organic relationship was cut short by the Cold War. Today, now that overcoming the Stalinist model is on the agenda in the socialist countries, it is again Western Europe that may offer, under particular circumstances, an example for effective methods of managing the economy, democratic techniques of government and social achievements. (The application of the latter, however, and this has to be duly emphasized, does *not* mean a "return to capitalism," as is expressed by anti-reformist forces, since these techniques are independent of social systems.) Besides, East European modernization also offers favorable opportunities for Western capital investment, thus serving direct and concrete economic interests.

Nevertheless, it would be a mistake to characterize the nature of relations between Eastern and Western Europe as in the interest of the East alone. This is especially true from the security and political perspectives. An insecure East, struggling with internal crises—and thus unpredictable—cannot be in the interest of the West. The opposite is also true.

This point is also proved by the spectacular boom of relations between Eastern and Western Europe. The structural root of the reversibility of cooperation, however, lies in the division, and especially in the traditional confrontation. If no step forward can be taken in this area, mistrust and hostile images linked to confrontation may reappear, like the swing of a pendulum, leading to yet another setback in East-West relations.

But the post-INF situation makes developing a security partnership urgent. If the West tries to fill the "deterrence vacuum" that it fears may appear through armament, large-scale modernization and development, this will cause a perception of danger on the other side which in turn might react in an equivalent manner. If the East's backwardness does not make equal quality possible, it might counterbalance quantitatively and by deploying troops close to the NATO-WTO border. The dangers lurking in this situation should not be underestimated. Nonetheless, this is a favorable moment for a breakthrough. Not only should the West "take Gorbachev at his word" but it could, in this situation, offer genuine proof of its strictly defensive intentions, especially after the announcement of the unilateral Soviet steps.

Progress is also urgent because, with the advancement of Western integration, a kind of economic-political unit is to take shape that can reasonably be considered a "superpower" on the basis of its population and economic capacities. It is quite important, however, that conventional arms limitation be started in parallel with this process. Thus, from the military point of view, this political-economic integration could be prevented from creating a feeling of threat in the East that would inevitably lead to an increase in the level of military confrontation. The way to go, however, can only be to reduce the constraints stimulating military solidarity; that is, the limitation of the socialist countries' conventional forces should result in a decrease of the West's perception of threat—this, in turn, can only be the result of negotiations and a process of mutual reduction.

As for the structure of East-West relations, various levels of cooperation have been developed. There is intensive motion going on at nongovernmental levels, between the most different organizations, institutions and economic units. The web of bilateral interstate relations is operating successfully, and on the all-European level there is the CSCE process which efficiently integrates Europe into the negotiating process of the superpowers. At the same time, little progress has been made in establishing contacts between integrational-cooperative bodies, the area in which the East-West division of Europe is most tangible. The establishment of relations between the EEC and the CMEA and between the EC and Hungary may set an example in that respect. It is an urgent task, however, to start a dialogue between NATO and the Warsaw Treaty beyond the negotiations of the 23.

Conclusion

Finally, one can raise the question of whether conventional arms control has political aims at all. The answer must be a definitive yes, if we accept as a premise that war cannot be a continuation of policy, at least not in the East-West context. The logical consequence of such a statement must be the practical elimination of warfighting capabilities. Having examined the roots of the arms race and military confrontation in the present political system and societies, it can be further stated that the present military situation does not correspond to political development, nor to the general tendency of internationalization of production and other economic activities. The elimination of European warfighting capabilities on both sides could proceed in two stages, formulated in the broadest political context: 1) stabilization of the European (NATO-WTO) military balance and termination of the destabilizing effects of the arms race; and 2) changing relations between states by replacing the military factor with economic, political and cultural factors of the system of balance, thus creating a cooperative European order. These aims seem to be realistic even under present conditions. Some basic points must not be questioned, and, in fact, they are not. The outstanding role of the two superpowers in the international order is a reality that will prevail. The existence of the alliances is also a given. Yet another iron law of stability is the maintenance of the territorial and social status quo in Europe. The political status quo is more fragile (and more difficult to define); a transition to a cooperative system of interstate relations would necessarily alter it, but it is hard to predict in what ways it would change. Within this framework, however, when the necessary political determination exists on both sides, it will be possible to make a historical step: to begin conventional disarmament in Europe.

Notes

1   Senator Carl Levin's report, *Beyond the Bean Count: Realistically Assessing the Conventional Military Balance in Europe* (Washington, DC: Office of Senator Carl Levin, January 20, 1988), specifies 13 components of a realistic assessment of the conventional military balance between NATO and the Warsaw Treaty.
2   The rationality of subspheres of modern society is dealt with in Kulcsár Kálmán, "Reform, modernizacio, politika," *Világosság* No. 10 (1987), pp. 606–607.
3   Speech by Géza Kótai, "Military Aspects of East-West Relations," Seventh Annual Conference of the Institute for East-West Security Studies on "New Approaches to East-West Security," Potsdam, German Democratic Republic, June 9–11, 1988.
4   Karl Polanyi, *Fasizmus, demokracia, ipari tarsadalom* [Fascism, Democracy and Industrial Society] (Budapest: Gondolat, 1986).
5   Johan Huizinga, *A holnap arnyekaban* [In Tomorrow's Shadow] (Budapest: Kmeny, 1938), p. 157.
6   "The Parties . . . declare that a nuclear war should never be unleashed and that it can have no winner. Recognizing that any conflict between the Soviet Union and the United States may have disastrous consequences, they stressed that it is important to

prevent any kind of war between the two of them, be it either nuclear or conventional. They will not strive to achieve military superiority." *A szovjet-amerikai csucstalalkozo* [The Soviet-American Summit Meeting] (Budapest: Kossuth Koenyvkiado, 1986), pp. 6–7.

7 Demography is also mentioned in Chapter 11 of Senator Levin's report. The problem also appears in Jeffrey Record, "Lighter American Units to a Denuclearized Europe," *Armed Forces Journal International* (October 1987), pp. 76–80; and Jeffrey Record and David B. Rivkin, Jr., "Defending Post-INF Europe," *Foreign Affairs* 66, No. 4 (Spring 1988), pp. 740–741.

8 National sovereignty and the problem of integration is also analyzed by Mátyás Szürös, "A nemzeti es a nemzetkoezi erdekek oesszefueggese a magyar kuelpolitikaban," [The Interrelation of National and International Interests in Hungarian Foreign Policy] *Kuelpolitika* No. 2 (1987), pp. 3–16.

9 A number of particularly thorough analyses of this matter have been published in *World Politics*. Just a few examples include: R. Harrison Wagner, "The Theory of Games and the Balance of Power," *World Politics* 38, No. 4 (July 1986), pp. 546–576; George W. Downs and David M. Rocke, "Tacit Bargaining and Arms Control," *World Politics* 39, No. 3 (April 1987), pp. 297–325; the entire issue of *World Politics* 38, No. 1 (October 1985).

10 Zbigniew Brzezinski, *Game Plan* (Boston: The Atlantic Monthly Press, 1986), pp. 41–52.

11 Today these questions are also being dealt with by historical science in certain East European socialist countries: ". . . the Soviet Union saw its own vital interests endangered. Its interpretation was that its former partners were intending to undermine the greater security the Soviet Union had developed at immense sacrifice of war. It made no concessions at all, moreover, it considered taking steps which would, in its opinion, increase the role of Central and southeastern Europe as a foreground of Soviet defense policy." Also: "The leaders of the Soviet Union . . . considered it extraordinarily important that . . . more homogenous, more uniform political systems emerge in this region with which the Soviet Union might build up closer cooperation." Károly Lipkovics, "Az SZKP tevekenysege es allasfoglalasa a nepi demokratikus atalakulas kerdeseiben (1944–1949)" [Activity and Positions of the CPSU on Questions of the Peoples' Democratic Transformation (1945-1949)], in *A nepi demokratikus forradalmak elmeleti es toerteneti kerdesei* [Theoretical and Historical Questions of the People's Democratic Revolutions] (Budapest: MSZMP Politikai Foeiskola, 1986), pp. 20, 22.

12 Zbigniew Brzezinski, *Game Plan*, pp. 99–135.

13 These dilemmas are reflected by such statements as this: " . . . though *perestroika* and *glasnost'* do show such a kind of change, the realization of the latter will not be easy. . . We do not deceive ourselves. The Western democracies cannot do very much to contribute to that process only by convincing the Soviets that they will not attack them" (Fred C. Ikle and Albert Wohlstetter, *Discriminate Deterrence: Report of the Commission on Integrated Long-Term Strategy* [Washington, DC: U.S. Government Printing Office, January 1988]). The problem is dealt with in a substantially more comprehensive approach in *How Should America Respond to Gorbachev's Challenge? A Report of the Task Force on Soviet New Thinking* (New York: Institute for East-West Security Studies, 1987). "Moscow could change its course abruptly as its domestic and international positions improved, and it could challenge the West with renewed vigor," writes Milan Svec in "Removing Gorbachev's Edge," *Foreign Policy* 69 (Winter 1987–1988), pp. 158–159.

14 Keeping in mind the 1961 Party Program which predicted capitalism's rapid downfall, Gorbachev's statement at the 27th Party Congress was indeed of great significance: "It is certain that the present phase of the general crisis does not mean a total stagnation of capitalism and is not excluding possibilities of economic growth and the introduction of new scientific-technical tendencies. It makes it possible furthermore to preserve concrete economic, military and other kinds of positions, moreover, in certain fields, even the chance of social revanche, and the recovery of positions lost in the past." *Az SZKP XXVII kongresszusa* [27th Congress of the CPSU] (Budapest: Kossuth Koenyvkiado, 1986), p. 24.

15 Soviet foreign policy is analyzed in detail by Csaba Tabajdi in "Az uj szovjet kuelpolitikai koncepcio" [The New Concept of Soviet Foreign Policy], *Kuelpolitika* No. 1 (1988), pp. 51–65.

16 "American military experts and scientists are both of the opinion that a fundamental change is taking place in the Soviet military doctrine and that the latter is turning from an offensive doctrine to a doctrine of defense. American experts following the tendencies and changes in Soviet military theory base their conclusion on Soviet declarations and specialized military literature. So far, however, doctrinal change has not changed the structure of the armed forces themselves yet." Bernard E. Trainor, "A Strategic Shift Observed in Moscow," *International Herald Tribune*, March 8, 1988, pp. 1, 6.

17 "*Role of the Military*—There has been a reduction in the Soviet military's role and influence in the highest policy-making councils, and Gorbachev has made clear to the military that they have to accept spending restraints and greater openness in the dissemination of military information" (*How Should America Respond to Gorbachev's Challenge?*, p. 25). A detailed explanation of this problem can be found in F. Stephen Larrabee, "Gorbachev and the Soviet Military," *Foreign Affairs* 66, No. 5 (Summer 1988), pp. 1002–1026.

18 This change is defined quite fittingly in Milan Svec, "Removing Gorbachev's Edge," pp. 149–150: "There is a common denominator underpinning most of Gorbachev's proposals. Rather than applying heavy-handed military and diplomatic pressure—the staple of past Soviet leaders—Gorbachev proclaims his flexibility and readiness to pay a previously 'unacceptable' price to achieve basic goals."

19 For the time being, however, the subject of the discussion is the presence itself, or rather, its extent (Jeffrey Record, "Lighter American Units to a Denuclearized Europe").

20 Although there is enough literature on this question to fill a library, Wolfgang Seiffert's *Das ganze Deutschland* (Munich: Piper, 1986) merits particular attention. Though its argumentation is not identical with the thoughts of the present study, its thoroughness and the sources used are noteworthy.

21 Nevertheless, there are authors who call one's attention to the character of this assumption and maintain that it is not exempt from problems. See, for example, Chapter 12 of Senator Levin's report *Beyond the Bean Count*; and Andreas von Buelow, "The Conventional Defense of Europe," *Europe-America* No. 5 (1986), pp. 112–151.

22 "The rights maintained of the Four Powers: The Four Powers' rights and responsibility for Berlin and Germany as a whole, as they derive from the victors' original rights and the Four-Power agreements. These remained untouched by the Eastern treaties and the admission of the two German states to the United Nations alike, and their priority in inter-German relations has been emphasized by the special exchange of letters on Article 9 of the Basic Treaty." Wolfgang Seiffert, *Das ganze Deutschland*, p. 234.

23 See the appraisal of *Ostpolitik* from the Eastern and Western points of view in Horst Ehmke, Karlheinz Koppe and Herbert Wehner, eds., *Zwanzig Jahre Ostpolitik, Bilanz und Perspektiven* (Bonn: Verlag Neue Gesellschaft, 1986).

24 "Der Streit der Ideologien und die gemeinsame Sicherheit," *Neues Deutschland*, August 28, 1987. It is noteworthy, however, that this document also argues for internal relations free of ideologies.

25 An extraordinarily expressive example of hostile images is presented in *Die Frage nach der deutschen Identitaet* (Bonn: Schriftenreihe der Bundeszentrale fuer politische Bildung, Band 221, 1985), pp. 107–111, which contrasts quotations taken from speeches held by the defense ministers of East and West Germany.

26 The essence of this proposal is a reduction of the number of tanks in Europe. The idea was first presented by Volker Ruehe at the Institute for East-West Security Studies Conference on Conventional Disarmament in Budapest (August 30–31, 1988).

27 Many researchers in the FRG are dealing with the possibilities of developing defensive defense. See, for instance, Dieter Senghaas, "Der wunde Punkt liegt zur Zeit im konventionellen Bereich," *Frankfurter Rundschau*, September 1, 1987; Andreas von Buelow, Helmut Funk and Albrecht von Mueller, *Sicherheit fuer Europa* (Koblenz: Bernard und Graefe, 1988).

28 *MTI Daily Bulletin*, March 4, 1988.

29 Communiqué of the Berlin session in *Népszabadság*, May 30, 1987; communiqué of the Warsaw session in *Népszabadság*, July 18, 1988.

30 A new approach to attitude and language of East-East security relations alike is given by Zdislaw Lachowski in "East-East Security Relations within a 'Common European House': a Polish Perspective," paper submitted to the Second Meeting of the Aspen Institute Berlin Study Group on Perspectives for a "European House" within the framework of the CSCE Process (September 21–25, 1988, Paris).

31 It is not only the different geographic situation but also the difference in world policy roles—the United States' global and Europe's regional interests—which result in different evaluations of the "Soviet threat" in the United States, on the one hand, and Western Europe, on the other. This also influences readiness to cooperate with the Soviet Union. See Cristopher Layne, "Atlanticism Without NATO," *Foreign Policy* 67 (Summer 1987), pp. 25–26.

32 At the Moscow forum entitled "For a Nuclear-Free World and the Survival of Mankind" Gorbachev declared on February 26, 1987: "It would be better to return to the ancient idea of abolishing military bases abroad. Troops should also be sent home. This applies to us as well. We have already taken the first practical steps. As you may know, we have, in accordance with our Mongolian friends, withdrawn a part of our troops from the Mongolian People's Republic." Mikhail Gorbachev, *Haboruk es fegyverek nelkueli vilagert* [For a World Without Arms] (Budapest: Kossuth Koenyvkiado, 1987), pp. 350–351. The latest to repeat the proposal that aims at abolishing foreign military presence on a worldwide basis by the year 2000 was P. Demichev, alternate member of the CPSU Politburo, at the international conference on nuclear-free zones held in Berlin (GDR) (*Népszabadság*, July 21, 1988).

33 What kind of discussions the question of an eventual withdrawal of Soviet troops may trigger can also be surveyed in the Hungarian press. The first declaration according to which the Hungarian political leadership considered the territory of Hungary suitable

for the Warsaw Treaty to take unilateral measures—which would obviously concern Soviet troops as well—was made by Géza Kótai, Head of the Hungarian Socialist Workers' Party's Department for Foreign Affairs, at the Seventh Annual Conference of the Institute for East-West Security Studies in Potsdam (see *Népszabadság*, July 13, 1988) and was confirmed by Mátyás Szürös, Secretary for Foreign Affairs at the Berlin conference on nuclear-free zones (see *Népszabadság*, July 22, 1988). Csaba Tabajdi, Deputy Head of the Department for Foreign Affairs, explained in detail in an interview that the withdrawal of Soviet troops is above all a bilateral Hungarian-Soviet question, under given circumstances of course (*Magyar Hirlap*, September 27, 1988). This was denied, also in an interview, by Minister of Defense Ferenc Kárpáti, who said that this withdrawal is conceivable only within the framework of a comprehensive East-West agreement (*Népszabadság*, September 29, 1988). Referring to the opinion of "the party and state leadership," a newspaper article repeated Kárpáti's point of view (András Kanyó, "Hiteluenk a vilagban," *Népszabadság*, October 8, 1988).

34 In 1984, West German Chancellor Helmut Kohl, British Prime Minister Margaret Thatcher and Italian Prime Minister Bettino Craxi visited Hungary one after the other— that is, the leaders of precisely those NATO countries in which the deployment of the U.S. missiles began.

IV

PART ONE

The Military Objectives of Conventional Arms Control

K.-Peter Stratmann, Federal Republic of Germany

The Negotiations on Conventional Forces in Europe: Professed Common Aims, Persisting Ambiguities

Both Warsaw Treaty Organization (WTO) and NATO governments seem to be in agreement on the general objectives and principles that should guide the course of the upcoming negotiations on conventional forces and armaments in Europe.[1] Both sides have declared their intention to strengthen stability and security in Europe by establishing a stable and secure balance of conventional armed forces at lower levels. More specifically, they have committed themselves to the goal of eliminating the capability for launching a surprise attack, large-scale offensive action and such disparities as may be prejudicial to stability and security.

Regarding the subject matter of the negotiations, both parties seem to concur in the goal of limiting the scope to land-based conventional forces and their armaments and equipment in the European area from the Atlantic to the Urals (ATTU). Proposed measures include force reductions, limitations, redeployment provisions, equal ceilings and collateral measures. These instruments could be applied to the ATTU area as a whole and on the basis of regional differentiation in order to cope with disparities and preclude circumvention. Both sides envisage a step-by-step approach that ought to ensure that the security of each participant is not adversely affected at any stage. In addition, they stress the importance of exchanging military data and of establishing a stringent and effective verification regime.

The progress made in formulating these common goals and principles as part of the mandate for the talks on Conventional Forces in Europe (CFE) is of major political significance. It may indicate a genuine political interest in transforming the existing military configuration in Europe into a more stable and less burdensome situation of defensive stability at a level of "reasonable sufficiency" for both the Warsaw Pact and NATO.

This positive evaluation is reinforced by the WTO's declared intent to eliminate disproportions and asymmetries and to restructure its conventional force posture in accordance with the defensive orientation of its new military doctrine. WTO spokesmen point out that the announced program of unilateral force reductions has to be understood in this light. It remains to be seen, however, to what extent the specified reductions, redeployments and restructuring measures, which are intended to demonstrate a build-down of the existing WTO potential for "surprise attack," will subsequently lead to the elimination of the general WTO capability for large-scale offensive action in Europe. So far it has remained unclear which of the previous strategic directives for restructuring and modernizing the Soviet (and WTO) force posture, which were worked out under the aegis of Marshal Nikolai Ogarkov, are going to be changed and which will be continued. The internal debate on this important and controversial issue has apparently not yet been concluded, and the evidence so far suggests caution and guarded optimism are in order for the time being.

The debate itself mainly stems from a group of primarily civilian analysts at the institutes of the USSR Academy of Sciences who have raised and articulated the pertinent questions and problems. In contrast, official Soviet and WTO political and military spokesmen, in presenting the emerging WTO negotiation stance for the conventional arms negotiations to the public, have followed a line of argument that glosses over the essential fact that it is the WTO, not NATO, that—at least until the mid-1980s—has espoused a military doctrine which embodies a military strategy for the European theater of war aimed at achieving victory in the traditional political-strategic meaning of the word, namely through rapid, decisive, large-scale "counter-offensive" operations, destroying and disarming the opposing armed forces as well as seizing and controlling key territory. These official spokesmen remain reluctant to admit that the Warsaw Pact conventional armed forces facing the strategically crucial Central European region were, and still are, sized, structured and deployed in accordance with this strategic mission—i.e., concentrated and echeloned in the direction of the main offensive strategic thrust.

They also fail to address the problem of the ongoing effort to restructure and modernize the Soviet and non-Soviet Warsaw Pact conventional ground and air forces in Europe, which was initiated and in part implemented during the tenure of Marshal Ogarkov, and designed on the basis of precisely this strategic concept. Given the powerful momentum of active arms production and procurement programs, the long active-service lifespan of major combat equipment, as well as the bureaucratic and institutional inertia inherent in operational doctrines and force structures, NATO will probably be confronted with this offensive posture for some time to come.

The character and scope of the military objectives that can realistically be aimed for in conventional arms negotiations in Europe depend on political motives, interests and objectives of both parties.

Concerning the political goals the Warsaw Pact countries pursue through arms control, the current stance adopted by these countries on the eve of the CFE talks is rather ambivalent. It is questionable to what extent the arms control strategy of the Soviet Union and its allies is at present 1) genuinely directed toward the goal of achieving "mutual security" on the basis of military stability in Europe or 2) an instrument of an offensive competitive strategy along the lines of Brezhnevian "peace offensives" designed to weaken the Western security system.

In particular, it remains unclear to date whether the Soviet leadership, within the framework of a European conventional arms control regime, is in principle prepared to forgo the present offensive strategic option vis-à-vis Western Europe, or would prefer to retain this option, albeit in a less conspicuous and burdensome variant. If indeed it is prepared to take the first route, the question arises as to the likely concessions it would demand in return from the NATO countries.

Thus far, the declared long-term goals of the Soviet Union for the arms control process in Europe still seem to imply the abolition of the Western security structure. The long-standing proposals of nuclear-weapons-free zones and banning the first use of nuclear weapons as steps on the way to a denuclearized Europe continue to challenge the foundation of NATO's strategic concept. In addition, the Warsaw Pact proposals of withdrawing foreign troops from European soil, closing foreign military bases and dissolving the military organizations of the two alliances are apparently still intended to reduce the American presence and influence in Western Europe.

One can, of course, deny the importance of the obvious continuity in the Soviet position by arguing that it is merely of a declaratory nature. The argument could perhaps be supported by the apparent Soviet willingness to accept terms of reference which will limit the CFE negotiations to land-based conventional forces in Europe and therefore *exclude* naval and air forces stationed outside Europe, as well as nuclear weapons. However, as was recently underlined by Marshal Sergei Akhromeev in his address at the Stockholm International Peace Research Institute,[2] American naval and air forces outside Europe are to be included in a *broader* conventional arms control context in Europe.

The suggestion by Soviet arms control specialists to connect the inclusion of Soviet forces in the western and central military districts of the USSR with the inclusion of American forces in the continental United States points in the same general direction.[3] Furthermore, there are indications that the Soviet Union wants to establish a political and conceptual linkage between progress in CFE and further nuclear disarmament. Such tendencies raise the crucial question of whether, from the Soviet leadership's point of view, the declared objectives for the CFE talks can in fact be attained within their terms of reference.

A broader negotiation approach would reflect the fact that the Soviet Union has always placed its capability to hold Western Europe hostage by means of its offensive option in the context of the global strategic situation.[4] Moscow has considered this capability the most important means with which to compensate first for the monopoly and subsequently the superiority of the United States in nuclear offensive strategic arsenals and theater nuclear forces. In addition, the capability to ensure military victory in Europe was designed to balance the global strategic advantages of the Western alliance, namely geostrategic encirclement of the Soviet Union, superior naval and offensive air forces and a larger economic, technological and demographic potential. Such advantages were particularly important in WTO scenarios of protracted world war.

A further complicating factor is that the Soviet leadership has in all likelihood constructed and maintained its offensive military option against Western Europe not only for military-strategic purposes but also for various political reasons. Soviet military preponderance in Central Europe, for instance, was probably intended to discourage any hope among the population of the allied Warsaw Pact countries that it might be possible to break away from the Soviet Union in a crisis or conflict. It was also most likely meant to cast a "shadow of power" over West European countries in order to prevent them from pursuing "anti-Soviet" aims in their foreign policy and to induce them to reorient their security interests away from transatlantic cooperation and into the direction of the "pan-European" collective security system proposed by the Warsaw Pact.

Preparing for the CFE:
The Controversial Military Baseline

To what extent the future military capabilities and options of the Soviet Union in Europe will be developed according to the regionally oriented principles of the "common European house" or pursuant to requirements of global strategic competition with the United States and its allies is one element of ambiguity in the Soviet approach to conventional arms control. But there are others: to date, as was indicated previously, it has only been a small group of Soviet civilian analysts who, if only in the form of tracing the evolution of Soviet military affairs, have acknowledged that the basic direction of Soviet strategy and the associated force posture in Europe until recently had been offensive.[5] It is encouraging that these specialists have advanced beyond the traditional Soviet habit of strictly separating the "social and political" content of Soviet military doctrine from its "military-technical" aspect, and have raised the problem of reconciling one with the other. One of them has stated that,

> Indeed, if a state or an alliance of states prepares armed forces for large-scale offensive operations and has corresponding plans, a system of training for its headquarters and armed forces, and maintains the necessary correlation of forces with its possible adversaries in terms of numbers, quality, structure, deployment of troops and weapons and logistical infrastructure, then the other countries will hardly feel secure.[6]

He also argues that, while Soviet

> military doctrine maintained its purely defensive nature, strategy and tactics, individual areas of the military buildup had an increasingly offensive orientation. A new way of thinking in security matters presupposes a revision of the previous requisites and view and a greater conformity between foreign policy and military doctrine, on the one hand, and the development of the art of war and military buildup on the other.[7]

Although such acknowledgements are laudable, a critical assessment is appropriate since they ignore important questions. They too follow the established line of explaining the development of the offensive Soviet military strategy for Europe in exclusively reactive and "defensive" terms, i.e., as a response to the policies and strategies of the United States and its allies. The explanations may be plausible for the late 1940s, 1950s and perhaps even for most of the 1960s. They are, however, much less plausible for the 1970s, during which the Soviet Union achieved full nuclear strategic parity with the United States and changed the regional nuclear "correlation of forces" in Europe to its own advantage. The "reactive" and "defensive" explanations are even more untenable when they are applied to the 1980s and the foreseeable future.

In this context it is legitimate to ask to what extent the preservation of the Soviet offensive option in Europe must also be regarded as an element of an offensive political strategy towards Western Europe, i.e., as an expression of hegemonic pretensions originating in the "period of stagnation."

At best, historical value can be attributed to the explanation of Soviet offensive strategy in Europe on the grounds that the Warsaw Pact would have had to counter a surprise and a massive strategic nuclear first strike by the United States and NATO.[8] However, for the past two decades the Soviet capability for assured nuclear response at the intercontinental and regional level and the degree of damage that would result from such an attack for the NATO countries make the rationale offered seem incredible.

The same conclusion applies to the proposed variant of a geographically limited although massive nuclear first strike by NATO on the battlefield or within the European theater. It is alleged that NATO, by destroying the forces of the Warsaw Pact first strategic echelon in Central and Eastern Europe and interdicting reinforcements brought up from the rear, would achieve a dramatic reversal of the balance of forces in favor of NATO that would enable it to carry out a large-scale offensive deep into Warsaw Pact territory.

Such scenarios are at variance with official Soviet assessments, also shared by NATO, of the inevitability of further escalation to general nuclear war that would result from large-scale nuclear employment in the European theater. They also fail to take into account NATO's documented assessment that in such an intensified "nuclear battle" the Western alliance would be at an even greater disadvantage due to the fact that the Warsaw Pact has larger, deeply echeloned forces and thus would be better able to replace massive losses.[9]

However one may evaluate the nuclear component of NATO's strategic concept of flexible response, it would be erroneous to portray it as giving the Western alliance the capability for a combined conventional and nuclear offensive on a strategic scale and as the means with which to achieve "victory." NATO's concept of terminating war through nuclear escalation has, on the contrary, enabled the alliance to forgo a strategy of military victory, settle for the goal of restoring the *status quo ante*, plan for a defensive concept of land operations on its own territory in the form of "forward defense" and limit its conventional forces in accordance with the principle of reasonable sufficiency.

For all of these reasons it is unconvincing that political and military spokesmen in the Warsaw Pact countries continue to portray the offensive strategic orientation of the WTO forces against the Central European region as a response to an allegedly equal or essentially equivalent strategic offensive capability of NATO in the same region. This mirror-imaging is strategic fiction, made even less credible when Western operational concepts such as AirLand Battle or Follow-on Forces Attack (FOFA) are used as "proof." Obviously, different levels of analysis get confused here.

Nor will NATO be able to establish an offensive strategic option in Europe as a result of the "scientific-technological revolution" in conventional warfare, i.e., the advent of more effective, "intelligent," long-range conventional weapons, delivery and target engagement systems. The fact remains that only the Warsaw Pact, currently and for the foreseeable future, possesses such an offensive option.[10]

In short, the numerous efforts of WTO military specialists and spokesmen to demonstrate the existence of a NATO offensive threat capability of strategic proportions in Europe remain questionable in both methodological and factual respects. They are based upon arguments that seem to be anachronistic, although in opposing directions: either they are connected to the past strategic context of massive American nuclear superiority and doctrines of general nuclear war, i.e., clearly outdated; or they are futuristic, crediting NATO with the possession of advanced conventional weapons capabilities that purportedly approximate the effectiveness of nuclear weapons and enable NATO's air and missile forces to mount a massive surprise conventional "fire strike," thus decisively crippling and paralyzing the WTO defense.

Without slighting the importance of the ongoing "revolution" in the enhancement of the performance of conventional capabilities (e.g., in terms of accuracy, range, depth of penetration, speed, destructiveness, autonomous homing capacity, mobility, observability of weapons systems), one should be very careful not to base strategic assessments— current or projected—on narrow extrapolations of technical performance parameters. Real-world restrictions in terms of, for example, costs and budget limits, manpower constraints, technical risks and limits, problems of systems integration and interaction, countermeasures or organizational and political impediments, should not be ignored. One would wish to see a higher degree of operational realism and discrimination in the writing of Soviet experts who address the issue of conventional "surprise attack" in Europe. Rather than mirroring the technological fixation and visionary tendency of some Western approaches to strategy (e.g., as displayed by the European Security Study Group or the more recent American project on "Discriminate Deterrence"), one ought to strive for a comprehensive "systems approach." In this connection it seems to be of particular importance to answer the following questions:

–To what extent does the ability to carry through a strategic offensive operation in Europe depend on the strength and readiness of mechanized ground forces?
–To what extent can this state of preparation be achieved through mobilization and movement of reinforcements without sacrificing the option of strategic surprise?
–To what extent would the effectiveness of a conventional precursory "fire strike" be impaired if the opposing side had warning indications and took the appropriate counter-surprise measures?
–To what extent could a "conventional fire strike," dealt out of the blue, be so effective in operational-strategic terms as to obviate the need for prior mobilization and reinforcement of those forces that would have to mount the large-scale offensive on the ground?
–Or should one assume that the initial success of a limited aggression would already disrupt the opposing alliance and assure a strategic victory? On the grounds of this political assumption it would, of course, be possible to construct a "standing-start" attack scenario in which a surprise air offensive operation would be conceivable.

It is certainly an exaggeration if the aforementioned Soviet analysts claim that there is a "phase difference" in the approach to "conventional war" between the Warsaw Pact and NATO.[11] In their view, NATO has proceeded to reorient its "conventional war" strategy towards more clearly defined offensive operations and weapons after the WTO had revised *its* military doctrine along defensive lines. From their perspective, this development may seriously impede negotiations on the mutual reduction of forces and armaments in Europe.

This portrayal ignores two important aspects.

First, it underrates—from NATO's point of view—the long-standing necessity to compensate for its inferiority in forward-deployed combat-ready ground forces in Central Europe and its inferior capacity for rapid force mobilization and reinforcement from the rear, primarily by means of interdiction and close air support with air forces. It has to be kept in mind that American tactical air units are the only reinforcement capability readily available to NATO in Europe. As regards army reinforcements that can be made rapidly available for NATO in Central Europe, they largely consist of U.S.-based units (Reforger or POMCUS) that must be transported to the European theater by air. This explains why NATO ascribes such great importance to the achievement of air superiority and, in particular, offensive air operations.

It is difficult to assess the possible effects of NATO's offensive air operations on the course of the battle. The air capabilities, however, do not provide NATO with the capacity for a combined land-air offensive on a strategic scale. Several factors testify to a limited impact on overall military operations. They include 1) the high rate of attrition that has to be expected due to the effectiveness of Warsaw Pact air defenses and 2) the great number, wide dispersal and varied characteristics of the Warsaw Pact target array that has to be covered. Offensive air operations could only have a decisive effect if they were carried out in conjunction with offensive operations by sufficiently strong mechanized ground forces.

Second, the need for a compensatory function of NATO's air forces in Europe has been enhanced by the buildup of a modern and effective Soviet offensive air capability. In Marshal Ogarkov's concept of a strategic conventional operation, the "air offensive" (i.e., the integrated employment of fighter-bombers, long-range rocket artillery, radioelectronic combat support and air-mobile combat units) plays an important role in implementing the Soviet objective of being able to attack NATO defenses in Europe in depth. In contrast to U.S. operational concepts, this Soviet version of an integrated land-air battle envisages the attainment of strategic objectives. The Soviet approach indicates a systematic effort to utilize the development of military technology and military science for an offensive strategy. The consequences of this policy will probably determine the military situation in Europe in the foreseeable future.

In view of this state of affairs, NATO considers problematical the Warsaw Pact proposals to trade off, in the first phase of the negotiations, reductions and limitations of NATO's tactical air capabilities in exchange for reductions and limitations of WTO ground forces. Of course, since tactical air forces have a significant impact on the course of battle, they ought to be included in the negotiating process. It is, however, necessary to recognize the mechanized ground forces as having the primary capability for a large-scale offensive and to phase and coordinate the different reduction measures accordingly.

As mentioned above, the ideas generated by the WTO thus far concerning comparisons of conventional forces and the tradeoff of military imbalances in certain categories of weapons display a consistent effort to conceal the fundamental strategic asymmetry that characterizes the military situation in Europe. This tendency can be observed when examining the following WTO ideas and suggestions for the CFE negotiations:

–To put the superiority of WTO mechanized ground forces on an equal footing with NATO's tactical air capabilities and to ascribe to the latter a particularly dangerous and destabilizing capability for surprise attack.
–To trade off the quantitative preponderance of the Warsaw Pact forces for the qualitative advantages that NATO allegedly has in most categories of weapons.
–To fragment geographically the integral zone of deployment where those Warsaw Pact forces of the first strategic echelon and reinforcements and reserves are located which are assigned to the strategically decisive Central European area. This conclusion would seem to follow from proposals to trade off Soviet forces that are deployed in the European part of the Soviet Union for NATO's total force potential in the whole European area of application or even against American forces stationed in the Atlantic or in the continental United States. In this way the Central European deployment area would be deprived of its depth. It would be reduced to the zone of "direct confrontation," and the relation of a major part of the Soviet reinforcement potential to this strategic *Schwerpunkt* (focal point) would be negated. It is obvious that such an approach would have grave consequences for the evaluation of the regional military balance in Central Europe.

–To make deep reductions in the forces deployed in this narrow zone of contact. This would bring down NATO's land forces in this area below the required operational minimum for a coherent forward defense. The Warsaw Pact could thereby preserve its capability to initiate large-scale offensive action even at a reduced level of forward-deployed forces. This would apply in particular if Soviet forces in the western military districts of the USSR, the mainstay of the WTO's capability for rapid reinforcement, were to remain exempt from *effective* limitations and constraints.

–To trade off the admitted partial superiority of Warsaw Pact land forces in Central Europe against the purported NATO superiority on the southern flank in air forces, armed forces personnel and numbers of divisions. There is, however, no basis for establishing a direct linkage between that area and the central front since NATO land and air forces in the Mediterranean do not possess a strategic offensive capability.

The underlying rationale of the WTO conventional arms control proposals thus far appears to be to convey the impression that the problems of security and stability in Europe originate primarily from NATO's military policy and strategy. Furthermore, they seem designed to constrain NATO's ongoing military programs while at the same time they aim to shield Soviet strategic preponderance from scrutiny and political pressure in the West.

If Warsaw Pact governments were to continue this approach in the CFE, the Western alliance would probably rule out the possibility of far-reaching negotiation results. It would, however, be premature for NATO to proceed from this pessimistic assumption. To date, maximalist opening positions in East-West arms control negotiations have been the rule rather than the exception. It is not surprising that WTO governments attempt to construe tactical positions against expected NATO demands that they regard as unbalanced. This may also be connected with the fact that, since the early 1980s, there have been developments in Western military policy, particularly in the United States, that could have and certainly did give rise to concerns in the Warsaw Pact countries. Such developments included the numerous concepts of a "new American global strategy" which espoused the importance of offensive operations. They also included the "competitive strategy" approach which aims at exploiting the United States' prowess in military technology and pointing the East-West arms competition in a high-technology direction.

The conventional arms control negotiations will most likely challenge established Soviet views and military solutions in areas of policy touching vital national security interests. Such changes will need time to become accepted.

This is primarily true for the question of how the Warsaw Pact will deal with the crucial task of war termination if it actually abandons its offensive strategy. Would the WTO, under such conditions of strategic defense, not have to prepare for the contingency of a war of attrition in Europe? How could the consequences of such a strategy in terms of military preparation be reconciled with the stated interest to use fewer resources for military purposes? Is it conceivable that these contradictions could, in fact, only be solved if the Soviet Union and its allies were to revise their long-standing rejection of the concept of nuclear escalation as a mechanism for war termination without military victory?

The Choice of Perspective

The task of translating the general objectives and principles for the CFE, as described in the first part of this paper, in the form of specific military objectives and requirements poses a difficult problem. Which method would seem to be most suitable? Should one start by analyzing the possible motives and interests, aims and options of the most important actors and assess on this basis such objectives as may be relevant and negotiable? Or should one disregard these elements of the "real world" in order to construct an ideal model of stability from which to derive individual military objectives? Such a prescriptive procedure would, however, elicit much skepticism among political practitioners. The reproach of naiveté certainly has to be expected since negotiations hardly ever follow their rationally constructed models. Furthermore, the preparations for the CFE within the Warsaw Pact and, above all, within NATO have indicated enough diverging political interests, anxieties, aims and qualifications to suggest the limits of negotiating on the basis of excessively ambitious analytical schemes.

Despite these observations, it appears to be desirable to attempt to arrive—in the first phase of the negotiations—at a common definition of the final shape of the military security structure envisaged for Europe as well as of intermediate negotiation results that would have to be reached on the way to this goal. Even if this were not to occur, and common views on the future long-term objectives and conditions for military security in Europe were not to develop, such an endeavor would still be a valuable test. It could clarify the current political ambiguities and delineate the probable latitude for agreement in the forthcoming negotiations.

In contrast, an arms control approach that remained fixed on the status quo would seem to be less promising. It would rule out the search for conceivable opportunities to improve the current situation. A pragmatic incrementalist variant of such a negotiation policy, while precluding major progress, would probably generate enough symbolic atmospheric effects to constrain prematurely the political latitude for defense efforts, at least in many NATO countries. An approach that would attempt to protect the military status quo against change by putting forward one-sided maximalist demands carries the same risk of losing domestic political support for defense policy.

For these reasons, it would be clearly preferable to advocate a policy that aims for substantive military results and to promote a correspondingly long-term, comprehensive and complex negotiating strategy. In this way, the current adherence to the asymmetrical starting point and its obvious impact on the definition of the next steps in the negotiation process could be superseded by a less narrow frame of reference. This would have the advantage that, rather than being called upon to justify and defend the details of the historically developed status quo, it would be possible to concentrate on designing a phased process for establishing an optimal alternative military structure. The required results of the individual negotiating phases could then be determined in relation to the objectives and criteria set for the final projected outcome.

The choice of a comprehensive approach for the negotiations would permit taking into consideration much broader parameters which define the freedom of maneuver for both sides. Above all, this approach would make it possible to clarify American and Soviet global strategic orientations and related arms programs that go beyond the CFE framework but probably are crucial for their progress.

The adoption of a comprehensive approach also facilitates a complex and integrated procedure. The readiness to include all relevant military factors and to apply all suitable arms control instruments will make it possible to exploit synergisms and multiple tradeoffs. It will also facilitate packages consisting of various linkages between different subjects and measures that may become effective at different times. This may make it easier to embark on a process of change that at the same time must be both reciprocal and asymmetrical.

Directing and Structuring the Process of Conventional Arms Control

There seems to be general agreement that the CFE negotiations should serve the purpose of establishing a more stable military situation in Europe by means of reducing offensive capabilities without impairing defensive capabilities. Ultimately, this process of defensive restructuring of the opposed force postures should result in a configuration that would physically assure the mutual superiority of defensive over offensive options and capabilities. It is, of course, conceivable that this situation of maximum military stability will remain a theoretical construct. Certainly, it would not be realized unless both alliances were to agree to embark on a cooperative venture of thoroughly redesigning their force structures and strategic concepts. While there are many good reasons to visualize this ultimate goal, political conditions and the enormous complexity of the problems involved rule out any attempt to achieve it in one single round of negotiations. Most likely, the NATO and WTO governments are about to engage in a long process that could lead to a number of interim agreements. In order to structure this negotiation process it seems useful to envisage two basic phases: the *first phase* would aim to restructure the military configuration at large so as to *eliminate any capability for large-scale, strategic offensive operations*. After this objective had been achieved, subsequent negotiations could be directed to eliminate *offensive capability also at the operational level*, thus creating a posture of "non-offensive defense."

The military situation at the end of the first major stage of the negotiations would be significantly more stable than the status quo. Despite the fact that the two sides still could carry out *limited* aggressions, these options would be fraught with discouraging political and military risks, since their possible success probably could not be developed into a decisive and conclusive strategic victory. This interim level of stability could be attained while preserving currently existing structures of mechanized and armored units as well as established tactics and operational concepts for combined arms and services combat. Consequently, it would remain impossible to draw a clear distinction between "offensive" and "defensive" categories of weapons systems or individual units and formations. Combat and combat-support troops could be employed flexibly for defensive and offensive operations. This distinction could, however, materialize through the restructuring of the overall configurations of the force postures, for example, with regard to the balance of forces in critical areas, force-buildup and reinforcement ratios or comparative logistic sustainability.

In contrast, the establishment of a situation of mutual dominance of the defense hinges on the construction of new types of non-mechanized combined arms units that have a high combat value in defensive terms but do not enjoy significant offensive potential. In a process of "transarmament," "offensive" mechanized units would have to be replaced accordingly by defensively oriented units yet to be developed. Numbers, strength, deployment patterns and states of readiness for the remaining mechanized units could then be regulated in such a way that they would constitute the indispensable elements for counterattack within a defensive framework that would not possess any significant offensive threat potential.

Without addressing the problems and prospects of a "defensive defense" concept in detail, it is worth pointing out that the process of "transarmament" could already be started during the first phase of the CFE negotiations. The incremental conversion of mechanized units on both sides could contribute to attenuating one of the predictable major problems: how troops could be reduced below current levels without falling short of the minimum of force capabilities required operationally for an effective defense against an attacker who is able to concentrate highly mobile, mechanized units in selected breakthrough sectors. In short, "transarmament" will probably become a key instrument in the effort to arrive at substantive force reductions without destabilizing the defense.

For this reason it seems prudent for political leaders in NATO and the WTO to direct their military staffs to design and test non-mechanized units which would have to make optimum use of advance barriers, indirect precision-guided fire, third-generation anti-tank guided missile (ATGM) systems and so forth. Since such "alternative" concepts so far run counter to prevailing modes of thinking on general staffs in both East and West, clear political instructions from the highest levels are necessary to get things done.

The problem of conventional instability that results from existing capabilities for large-scale ground-air offensive operations is today largely, if not exclusively, confined to Central Europe. In northern and southern Europe the military situation appears much more stable, partly because there are no large, combat-ready, mechanized ground forces stationed at the front, in part because quick and comprehensive reinforcements from other regions seem impossible, but also because accessability is made considerably more difficult due to geographical conditions. Attacks by airborne and amphibious forces might be possible, but such attacking forces could, at least initially, pursue only limited goals. Offensive operations with larger objectives would require prior large-scale mobilization measures and force movements. All of these considerations point to the conclusion that an already acceptable situation could be maintained without too much difficulty by way of non-increase commitments, limited asymmetrical reductions and some specific constraints. The following observations are intended to apply, therefore, mostly to the situation prevailing in Central Europe.

In order to achieve the essential interim CFE objective of establishing a situation of parity of military capabilities which would eliminate the option of carrying out large-scale offensive action in Central Europe or in other European regions, the two alliances have to adjust their current postures in significantly diverging measure. As NATO does not possess the necessary military capabilities for such a strategic option, its contribution to the conventional arms control process will remain limited at least in the initial phase, namely to preserve this condition by not undertaking any disproportionate arms buildup program. In contrast, the WTO countries, and in particular the USSR, must significantly reduce, redeploy and restructure their current military posture in Central and Eastern Europe. In short, the actions to be taken by the sides have to be very asymmetrical in order to create a force balance that is more symmetrical in terms of force levels, force mixes and force deployments.

The conditions of balance and symmetry at force levels that are adequate for effective defense while excluding large-scale attacks can be put into effect by restricting and regulating the following categories of conventional armed forces and armaments (Table 1).

The envisaged arms control regime must be designed to cope with various conventional attack scenarios, including:

–major unreinforced (or short-notice) attack;
–major attack after mobilization and partial reinforcement; and

Table 1

Categories of Armed Forces	Holdings of Weapons Systems, Major Equipment, Logistical Capacity
Mechanized ground forces (combined arms) –combat units	–tanks –MICVs/APCs –attack helicopters
–combat support units artillery	–tube artillery, rocket artillery (MRLs, SSM)
engineers	–bridge-laying equipment mine-clearing equipment
–combat service support/supply units	–ammunition, POL –war reserve and POMCUS-type stocks
Air-mechanized forces –airborne units –air assault units	–tanks –APCs –armed helicopters –transport aircraft
Air force units	–bomber aircraft –fighter-bomber aircraft –dual-role fighter aircraft
Operational-tactical missile units	–launchers –refire missiles

–major attack after full mobilization and forward deployment.

Consequently, the measures to be agreed upon must affect the capabilities of forward-deployed active forces, which, in conjunction with the potential of the air forces and of rapidly deployable rear-based active ground units, determine the capacity for attack after only short preparation. At the same time they have to assure an appropriate balance with regard to the relative force-generation and force-buildup/deployment capabilities of the sides. These ratios seem more relevant for the second and third classes of scenarios. However, they also bear upon the capability to exploit and expand surprise attack mounted with a limited force and thus critically dependent on timely reinforcement.

In general terms, conventional arms control efforts must be aimed at changing force postures so as to preclude the possibility of initiating major offensive action without undertaking major preparatory action in terms of mobilization and force movement, which would both be highly visible and time-consuming. Of greatest importance are such limitations and constraints that contribute to circumscribing the capability to plan and execute with confidence large-scale offensive combined-arms operations in a well coordinated and synchronized fashion. To the extent possible, such operations should entail foreseeable frictions with regard to the task of providing the required force mix with sufficient strength at the right time on the battlefield and subsequently sustain this force through the timely and continuous flow of reinforcements and supplies.

In more specific terms, NATO and WTO governments ought to resolve to achieve enhanced military stability in the extended Central European region by establishing a largely symmetrical regime which would be comprised of the following elements:

–Reductions to equal levels of capabilities required for a robust conventional defense. Such levels would be implemented primarily by means of common ceilings for major combat-essential equipment, and they would apply to active and equipment-holding mobilizable units.
–Calibrated ceilings and limitations on the deployment areas and readiness of units in accordance with their designation as frontline forces, operational reserves, reinforcements and strategic reserves.
–Constraints on critical activities of the armed forces in peacetime, especially for mobilization measures; movement of forces (forward deployment) and field exercises.
–Effective and reliable procedures and instruments for verification, monitoring and control.
–Other transparency-enhancing measures.

These arms control measures must be designed and connected so as to reflect the fact that the military capability to initiate and carry out large-scale offensive action in Europe hinges on the potential for combined arms and services operations. Consequently, all of the relevant branches of the armed forces ought to be included in the process of effecting limitations and reductions. In fact, such a comprehensive approach is envisaged in the CFE mandate. However, for the time being, the sequence and correlation of the various force elements and capabilities to be covered remain controversial. It will certainly be the most difficult task for the initial stage of the impending negotiations to agree on a road map of priorities, phases, linkages and tradeoffs.

From NATO's viewpoint, the single most important and urgent issue on the agenda is the elimination of the current WTO—and primarily Soviet—preponderance regarding forward-deployed active mechanized ground forces and rear forces that constitute the WTO's superior mobilization and reinforcement capacity. As long as this dominant combination of strategic factors continues to exist, NATO is in no position to accept reductions in or limitations on its own air forces. Nor can NATO commit itself to confidence-building measures and constraints which would preclude the possibility of taking early mobilization measures in a crisis, setting into motion the transatlantic reinforcements of air and ground forces and deploying them in Western Europe. Only through such measures can NATO hope to build up a level of forces sufficient for a successful initial defense against WTO armies already present in Eastern and Central Europe, and, in addition, for offsetting the WTO's force-buildup capacity.

WTO suggestions for trading off reductions in its ground forces against unspecified reductions of NATO air forces are complemented by a variety of proposals clearly designed to stifle or delay key programs in NATO's current Conventional Defense Improvement (CDI) initiative. In particular, weapons and supporting systems, the development and procurement of which are planned to provide NATO forces with a more effective capability to "strike deep" against WTO airbases, lines of communications, forward-moving follow-on echelons and so forth, are singled out as being particularly dangerous and destabilizing. The WTO includes them in the category of weapons and force units that possess the most distinct and important offensive characteristics. In order to contain the danger of increasing preemptive instability and escalatory pressure that are allegedly going to result from the deployment of conventional "reconnaissance-strike" complexes, two basic approaches are offered:

–the creation of disengagement zones in the area of direct confrontation from which "offensive" weapons systems such as strike aircraft, long-range heavy artillery and operational-tactical surface-to-surface missiles are to be withdrawn; and

–a freeze on the modernization of such systems and a ban on their development.[11]

These assessments and proposals do, of course, address legitimate and substantial problems and concerns. The ongoing increase in the capability of conventional fire support assets in terms of precision, target discrimination, destructive effect, range, speed, responsiveness and so forth may in the future add a new dimension to the concept of surprise attack. These trends, incidentally, pertain to the arms buildup programs of both alliances. It would, however, seem imprudent and impractical to choose a "freeze" approach in order to control this challenge. So far arms control theory and practice have not developed suitable definitions, measures and procedures that would enable negotiators to halt the progress of technology and its manifold qualitative applications for the modernization of weapons systems and systems components or elements.

Moreover, even if one were to disregard the insoluble problems of developing unequivocal treaty language and high-confidence verification methods and instruments, the consequences of a freeze on deployment of new conventional weapons systems in Europe would put NATO at a disadvantage. For the time being NATO must seek to protect and further develop its capabilities for "deep" target engagement and stand-off weapons delivery. NATO governments should, however, be in the position to accept quantitative limitations as well as additional specific constraints with regard to the deployment and readiness status of such weapons systems and associated troops in Europe, provided the WTO had already carried out a major build-down of its ground forces, thus establishing a more balanced situation. In addition, the WTO would, of course, also have to accept equal ceilings and constraints on the deployment of its strike aircraft and surface-to-surface missiles.

Success or failure of the CFE negotiations seems predicated upon the ability of the sides to work out a staged action program that would envisage, in its early phase, primarily Soviet troop reductions and redeployment, while meeting Soviet concern about the allegedly operational-strategic scope and objectives of arms buildup concepts and plans within NATO (see Appendix).

The phased inclusion of European-based air force capabilities and operational-tactical missile forces in the overall process of conventional force reductions and limitations seems to be prudent for the following reasons. As was pointed out above, even at a level of parity for ground forces in the Central European region, offensive actions of an operational scope would remain feasible as long as these forces consist almost exclusively of armored and mechanized combat formations. Defense against a mechanized opponent requires a fairly large minimum of active forces in order to maintain a sufficient force-to-space ratio for a coherent first-line defense which must be backed up by the necessary operational reserves. Any reduction below that level would result in insufficient force densities for the defender and thus would carry with it the risk of rapid breakthroughs and possible disintegration of the defense. The advantages accruing to the attacker would increase, since he could fully exploit the effects of operational surprise in concentrating his mobile forces against the defender's overextended frontages. In addition, in such a configuration the concentrated employment of strike aircraft and armed helicopters in breakthrough sectors would strongly enhance the attacker's option for surprise attack and subsequent exploitation.

For these reasons the desire for significant reductions of ground forces below the threshold of parity at a virtual current "operational minimum" level required for a robust defense can be realized only on the basis of a far-reaching restructuring of existing mechanized and armored units. By exchanging a large fraction of such units for non-mechanized units it would be possible to eliminate critical offensive capabilities more discretely without thereby weakening the defensive combat potential. In this way both alliances would be able to construct a situation of military stability that would be even less susceptible and sensitive to real or hypothetical threat parameters which are influenced by assumptions about crisis scenarios, conceivable enemy tactics, comparative performance of troops and weapons on the battlefield and so forth. Consequently, it could be much easier to mutually signal restraint and cooperative political intentions by means of structuring the force postures. Both sides would gain additional latitude for the reduction of peacetime force structures and total arms inventories, and for reducing resources spent on defense.

Appendix
Packages and Tradeoffs: An Illustrative Concept
for a Staged Negotiation Process

NATO	WTO

Stage 1[A]

No reduction of mechanized units;

No constraints on rapid reinforcement capacity.

Withdrawal of "n" Soviet mechanized divisions (including equipment) from the NATO Guidelines Area (NGA) to military districts in the European part of the Soviet Union adjacent to the Urals (e.g., one tank army), including:
–transformation to equipment holding units;
–equipment in secure storage;

Restrictions for forward-situated logistical sites (ammunition, POL);

Non-increase regarding active mechanized units and equipment holding units in European part of USSR;

Constraints on force-generation activities, redeployment of forces;

Limitations and constraints for Soviet offensive air in the extended Central Europe region.

Result: Superiority remains for WTO forward-deployed active mechanized units and reinforcements, although in a less asymmetrical ratio.

Stage 2[A]

Limited transformation of forward-deployed active NATO units (mechanized) to reduced manning level;

No constraints on rapid reinforcement capacity.

Withdrawal of additional Soviet mechanized divisions (including equipment) from the NGA to military districts in the European part of the Soviet Union adjacent to the Urals;

disbandment of "n" non-Soviet WTO forward-deployed active mechanized divisions, including:
–destruction of equipment;
–no POMCUS-type storage in NGA;

Reduced manning levels and storage of equipment of "n" active Soviet mechanized divisions in USSR west of the Urals.

Result: "Parity" would exist for combat-essential equipment of NATO and WTO mechanized forces in the extended "Jaruzelski" zone: WTO active holdings would equal NATO's total equipment holdings (active equipment holdings, POMCUS, plus war maintenance reserve). WTO edge in active forces (both forward-deployed and second-echelon) would be compensated by unimpeded NATO mobilization and reinforcement capability.

Stage 3

Constraints on NATO offensive air deployment;

Initiation of force restructuring (replacement of mechanized units by defense-oriented units).

Continuation of Stage 2 activities;

Initiation of force restructuring (replacement of mechanized units by defense-oriented units).

Result: Full parity/symmetry would exist for NATO and WTO active and reserve mechanized forces in the extended "Jaruzelski" zone at lower levels, reflecting progress of restructuring, while remaining Soviet advantages in force generation and reinforcement capability in the European part of the USSR would be compensated by U.S. POMCUS forces, which would be exempted from reductions in this phase.

Stage 4

Continuation of restructuring.

Continuation of restructuring;

Further Soviet reductions of mechanized capabilities in the extended Central Europe region.

Result: Symmetrical configuration of defense dominance would exist in the extended Central Europe region.

^A Optional reciprocal or identical measures for Stages 1 and 2 could include:
–Disaggregated data exchange plus verification;
–Transparency measures (e.g., mutual information on force-planning goals, major arms production and procurement programs; clarification of meaning and consequences of announced strategic and operational concepts);
–Improved confidence- and security-building measures;
–Enhanced constraints for out-of-garrison activities (movement of forces, field exercises) and mobilization exercises plus monitoring and verification;
–Withdrawal of forward-deployed bridge-laying and mine-clearing equipment (secure central storage);
–Low common ceilings on operational/tactical surface-to-surface missiles in the ATTU area of application;
–Common ceilings on attack helicopters in the ATTU area and the extended Central European zone.

Notes

1   See the text of the mandate for negotiations on conventional armed forces in Europe in *Neue Zuercher Zeitung*, January 18, 1989, p. 4; in addition, see the Declaration of the WTO Member States on the Reduction of Conventional Armed Forces and Armaments in Europe, July 16, 1988, as published by ADN (GDR news agency), July 16, 1988; "Conventional Arms Control: The Way Ahead. Statement Issued Under the Authority

of the Heads of State and Governments Participating in the Meeting of the North Atlantic Council in Brussels, March 2–3, 1988," *Atlantic News*, No. 1998 (March 4, 1988), pp. 5–9; "Draft General Report on Alliance Security: Towards Conventional Stability in Europe, North Atlantic Assembly," Karsten Voigt, General Rapporteur (International Secretariat, November 1988).

2 Marshal Sergei F. Akhromeev, "Arms Control and Arms Reduction—The Agenda Ahead," Olof Palme Memorial Lecture 1988, Stockholm International Peace Research Institute (unpublished).

3 *Disarmament and Security: 1987 IMEMO Yearbook* (Moscow: Novosti Press Agency Publishing House, 1988), pp. 396–99.

4 Ibid., pp. 356–58.

5 Ibid.

6 Alexei Arbatov, "On the Crossroads: Contemporary Trends in the Evolution of East and West Military Doctrines," unpublished paper prepared for the Institute for East-West Security Studies Seventh Annual Conference, Potsdam, GDR, June 9–11, 1988, p. 19.

7 Ibid., p. 18.

8 See Yuri A. Kostko, "Alternative Conceptions and Models of Security and Defense for Europe and the Soviet Military Doctrine," *Current Research on Peace and Violence* 11, No. 3 (1988), p. 29.

9 See the clear refutation of the long-standing justification for Soviet tank superiority on the basis of nuclear-war scenarios and the need to compensate for Western nuclear superiority by Vitaly Shlykov in "Strong Is the Armour . . . Tank Asymmetry and Real Security," *International Affairs* (Moscow) No. 12 (1988), pp. 37–48 (esp. 46–47): "These explanations seem to me no more convincing tha[n] the attempts of the Soviet military leaders of the 1960s and 1970s to justify an increase in tank production by the requirements of nuclear war. I am confident that the emergence and protracted maintenance of the post-war Soviet tank superiority is accounted for not by nuclear weapons but by [an] exclusively pre-nuclear way of thinking." Compare Andrei A. Kokoshin's positive or agnostic depiction of this argument in Chapter 5 of this book. He refers to "many military experts" who perceive "a threat of the surprise tactical-operational and tactical use of nuclear weapons in Europe for the achievement in the shortest possible time of a decisive imbalance over the WTO in general-purpose forces with the goal of executing successful strategic offensive operations." See also the contribution of Alexei Arbatov, Nikolai Kishilov and Oleg Amirov in Chapter 2.

10 As illustrations of Soviet authors' tendencies to credit NATO with offensive strategic concepts and options and to highlight the destabilizing potential of NATO's arms programs that are related to FOFA and offensive counter-air (OCA) missions, see Andrei A. Kokoshin's and Alexei Arbatov's contributions to this book; see also Andrzej Karkoszka, "Advanced Technology and European Security—Conceptual Considerations," in F. Stephen Larrabee, ed., *Technology and Change in East-West Relations* (New York: Institute for East-West Security Studies, 1988), pp. 85–111; for a competent treatment of the level of analysis problem, see Arbatov, "On the Crossroads," pp. 32–34.

11 *Disarmament and Security: 1987 Yearbook*, p. 369.

12 See, for example, the thrust of Alexander Konovalov's contribution to this book.

IV

PART TWO

The Military Objectives of Conventional Arms Control

Alexander Konovalov, USSR

It is obvious that the military objectives of the process of conventional arms control are significantly determined by those political issues that are intended to be resolved in the course of its realization.

The problem of reducing the level of military confrontation, strengthening military-strategic stability and limiting military rivalry in the area of general-purpose forces and conventional arms is presently one of the key issues. The signing and ratification of the Soviet-American INF Treaty have made this task all the more urgent. Thus it is quite apparent that a strong dialectical link exists between conventional and nuclear arms, and that successful progress in the area of nuclear arms reduction is impossible without resolving problems existing in the area of conventional arms.

The situation is also complicated by the fact that the sides have still not worked out any detailed concepts or models of the military-strategic balance which could be proposed as a mutually acceptable objective in the process of limiting the arms race, guaranteeing a more stable and secure peace under decreased levels of military confrontation.

In these conditions the task of defining the military objectives of the process of limiting and reducing conventional arms may be divided into several independent problems:

–the identification of existing common elements in the views and political positions of NATO and the WTO;
–the development of a single methodological basis for assessing the scale and character of existing threats and comparing the sides' forces; and

–the elaboration of practical recommendations for decreasing the levels of military confrontation in Europe in the area of conventional arms.

The positions of the USSR and the WTO in this area, and their assessments of the possible ways of resolving the problems at the general political level, have been developed and set forth in a much broader and more detailed way than those of the United States and NATO. As is known, at the meeting of the Political Consultative Committee of the WTO member-states in Berlin (May 1987) these countries proposed an application of the principle of military sufficiency in the structure and equipping of armed forces whereby the possibility of a surprise attack and the ability to undertake offensive operations would be excluded.[1]

Speaking at the UN General Assembly's Third Special Session on Disarmament on June 8, 1988, USSR Minister of Foreign Affairs Eduard Shevardnadze emphasized the necessity of "reorienting military postures exclusively for purposes of non-offensive defense." He observed that defensive strategy and sufficiency require not only a reduction of arms, "but also a deep restructuring of their postures and dislocations, and a change in the very character of the military activities and organizational development of armed forces."[2]

At this session of the UN General Assembly the USSR formulated a three-stage program for reducing conventional forces and armaments. At the first stage it proposed an exchange of reliable official numerical data and the beginning of the elimination of the sides' existing military asymmetries; at the second, the reduction of armed forces by each side by approximately 500,000 men; and at the third stage, along with the further reductions, a reorientation of forces toward a purely defensive character and dismantlement of their offensive core. More recently, Soviet General Secretary Mikhail S. Gorbachev has announced a series of unilateral Soviet initiatives in the area of conventional arms and force limitations in his speech to the UN General Assembly on December 7, 1988. The meaning and significance of these Soviet initiatives will be discussed in detail below.

NATO's position on reductions in conventional forces and armaments is still only beginning to be formulated. The concept of "non-provocative" (essentially non-offensive) defense has not yet officially reached the state level. As Director of the Stockholm International Peace Research Institute Walter Stuetzle observed in an interview with *Izvestiia*, "it is currently only a slogan."[3] The basic tone of the statement on conventional arms control at the NATO Council's Brussels session (March 1988) demonstrates that for its part NATO recognizes only the existence of quantitative imbalances in the conventional area in favor of the WTO. As was emphasized in this statement, "the imbalance in the area of conventional arms in Europe remains the main cause for concern regarding the security of Europe."

At the same time in the section of this document that formulates the objectives of the NATO allies there are positions consonant with the ideas advanced by the WTO states:

–the establishment of a reliable and stable balance of conventional forces at lower levels;
–the elimination of imbalances that hurt stability and security; and
–the elimination of the capability for a surprise attack and for conducting large-scale offensive operations as a first step.[4]

Thus, by isolating the common elements in the NATO and WTO military-political declarations, we may say that both sides have clearly stated their interest in the mutual elimination of imbalances and asymmetries in conventional forces and armaments and their desire to eliminate the capability for a surprise attack and the conduct of large-scale offensive operations. The commonality of these goals creates a real basis for searching for ways to resolve conventional arms issues.

In these conditions one of the central issues is the problem of comparing NATO and WTO forces, especially in Europe, and identifying and assessing the level and character of the imbalances and asymmetries. An analysis of published documents and materials shows that at the present time primarily two approaches to assessing the correlation of the sides' conventional forces prevail.

The first approach is based primarily on comparing the overall number of NATO and WTO armed forces and their basic arms categories (e.g., tanks, aircraft, artillery, armored personnel carriers). This purely quantitative method of assessing the balance of the sides' conventional forces is found in the publications of the London-based International Institute for Strategic Studies, the "Threat Assessment" report of the Western European Union, the Pentagon's *Soviet Military Power* series, NATO brochures and Bundestag reports devoted to comparing NATO and WTO forces and in the annual reports of the Joint Chiefs of Staff on U.S. force posture. It also prevails in the USSR Ministry of Defense publication *Whence the Threat to Peace*.[5] Many people think that such an approach does not fully represent the actual correlation of the sides' forces, since beyond the bounds of purely quantitative comparisons lie an assortment of factors and parameters that directly influence the combat capabilities of the opposing military alliances.

Along these very lines a number of works have recently appeared in which a comparison of NATO and WTO forces is made on the basis of a new approach that considers not only the state of the static quantitative situation, but also the array of integral and contextual factors of the sides' real combat capabilities, including those applying to the tasks of ensuring defense and offense. Attempts to go outside the framework of comparing only quantities of troops and arms are being undertaken in, for example, the 1988 edition of the IMEMO yearbook, *Disarmament and Security*.[6] In various works other factors, including the qualitative parameters of weapons systems, combat training and personnel readiness, soldiers' morale, the level of states' mobilization capacities, C^3I systems and the development of the material-technical supply system, are being taken into consideration. Such an overall approach is in part used by Senator Carl Levin in his report on the balance of arms and armed forces in Europe.[7]

Recognizing the necessity of eliminating imbalances and asymmetries in the conventional arms area, we are forced at the same time to state the enormous complexity of its objective assessment, of going beyond simple quantitative comparisons. One of the main concerns expressed by the NATO countries is the imbalances in tank forces in favor of the WTO. And in a highly publicized article USSR Minister of Defense and Army General Dmitrii Yazov acknowledged that the number of WTO tanks in Europe surpasses the number of NATO tanks by 20,000.[8]

But even in this apparently quite obvious case, when WTO superiority over NATO appears overwhelming, consideration of the weapons' qualitative characteristics radically changes the assessment of the balance of the sides' tank potentials.

Malcolm Chalmers and Lutz Unterseher have conducted such an analysis.[9] In particular, they examine the correlation of tank forces in the most important region—Central Europe. According to the authors' evaluation, on the tenth day from the beginning of mobilization the ratio of the number of both sides' tanks would appear to be 1.41:1 in favor of the WTO. But considering the relatively better logistics system and more developed infrastructure in the NATO countries as opposed to the WTO, according to the authors' estimates, 20 percent of WTO tanks sent to the front and 10 percent of NATO tanks would not arrive at the zone of combat by this time because of breakdowns. This factor would lower the WTO advantage to 1.25:1.

The authors of the report have determined that the combat potential of the "average" WTO tank is lower than that of the analogous NATO tank. Thus the majority of NATO tanks have significant advantages in target-acquisition capabilities, firepower, mobility and armor protection. This is true even when comparing the most modern WTO tanks.

Taking into consideration these qualitative parameters, the authors, on the basis of their own expert analysis and numerous discussions with FRG officers, propose that a reasonably conservative estimate would define the combat potential of the "average" NATO tank to be 1.5–2 times that of the "average" WTO tank. Even if one assumes that this qualitative advantage in combat potential of the "average" tank is estimated at 1.75:1, then the WTO 1.25:1 advantage, determined by its great number of vehicles, translates into a NATO advantage of 1.4:1.

If one considers the certain increase in tactical capabilities that is given to a greater number of albeit less modern tanks, then the ratio of tank force potentials in Central Europe is still 1.17:1 in NATO's favor. As we see, even in an example with typical kinds of military equipment, the consideration of qualitative factors can radically change the quantitative correlation.

At the same time, as historical experience also emphasizes, the complete consideration of the quantity of weapons and their qualitative characteristics cannot provide a true picture of the sides' force ratio. As an example we may cite a study recently published in the USSR which compares the Soviet and German tank forces on the eve of World War II (1941).[10]

In terms of tanks at the moment of the German invasion the USSR had some 21,000–23,000 vehicles. Germany, by contrast, allocated for the attack on the USSR 3,582 tanks and self-propelled guns from an overall total of the 5,639 that it possessed on May 1, 1941. That is, the USSR had 5–6 times as many tanks as Germany.

A comparison of qualitative parameters such as the caliber of the main armament, mobility and armor thickness convincingly shows that according to qualitative characteristics as well the Soviet tanks on average substantially surpassed the German. Nevertheless, in the first weeks of the war the Soviet Union suffered enormous losses in tanks. Analyzing the reasons for these gigantic losses, one can cite the absence of clear concepts for using armored units, organizational and command confusion, and much else.

As was observed in one American study, the great losses of Soviet tanks in the beginning of the war were explained primarily by the comparative "lack of experience of tank crews, the appalling shortage of officer cadres as a result of the purge in the army, and also the paralyzing lack of spare parts."[11] Thus there are other factors besides the quantity and quality of weapons and military equipment that may render impossible their effective use and must be considered in comparing the sides' forces and in formulating the military objectives of the arms control process and how to achieve them.

Thus one may conclude that to objectively assess the threat to security and stability posed by general-purpose forces and conventional arms, and to determine mutually acceptable military objectives in the reduction process in terms of quantity, structure, deployment, verification systems, as well as those tasks whose resolution may be entrusted to general-purpose forces and conventional arms, it is necessary to develop a shared methodological basis, a kind of "common language" for the conventional arms control process.

Such a common language would allow a clear definition of the elements of the current NATO-WTO military confrontation that arouse the greatest concern of both sides, as well as the prospects for change. It would also permit the systematization of a whole set of political and military instruments suitable for eliminating the causes that undermine military-strategic stability.

For the development of such a methodological basis it would be useful to more clearly define the subject of a comparative analysis and to introduce the concept of "both sides' combat potential." In this framework combat potential is understood to be the aggregate of quantitative and qualitative characteristics of the sides' armed forces and weapons in combination with the factors that define the capacities of their effective use relative to the tasks of defense and offense.

It would be helpful to systematize all the factors and relevant concepts of the combat potential of conventional forces and armaments according to three basic levels.

The first and simplest, but also least informative for objectively assessing the balance of forces, may be conditionally called the *quantitative level*. The number of personnel of each side's armed forces and the number of units of similar types of weapons (such as tanks, aircraft, APCs and artillery) are compared at this level.

At the second, *qualitative level*, primarily the qualitative characteristics of forces and armaments of both military alliances and individual states are analyzed and compared. Concerning personnel, indicators such as the number of combat-ready (Category 1 and 2) units and formations and the level of soldiers' and officers' education and combat training have to be considered.

In comparing various types of weapons, one must consider the criteria developed by experts which define the potential combat effectiveness of each weapons system. It would also be useful to develop weighted coefficients defining the degree of compensation for the quantity of a weapon by its qualitative superiority. It is especially important to distinguish the types of weapons and their characteristics that define and characterize the sides' offensive capabilities.

Finally, there is the third *level of capabilities* of the effective *use* of conventional forces and armaments, especially in conducting major offensive operations. Here such factors as the mobilization capabilities of states and military alliances, the characteristics of the economic-industrial base for ensuring combat operations, infrastructure, geographic features of the theater of military operations, the extent to which necessary communications are ensured, and capabilities for collecting and processing information may be considered.

The sides' combat potentials must be compared in corresponding categories and on all three levels (quantity, quality and capability of use). In my view, such a generalized and all-inclusive methodological approach permits not only the creation of a sufficiently objective picture of the correlation of conventional forces and the assessment of the true capabilities for conducting offensive operations, but also a broader approach to the problem of limiting and reducing conventional forces and armaments and strengthening stability in Europe.

Under such an approach a certain logical gap is excluded, a gap which currently exists between the scope of declared political objectives (the elimination of imbalances and the ruling out of the capability for surprise attack and conducting large offensive operations) and the limited means (the reduction of conventional forces and arms) essentially being proposed for their attainment. The reduction of conventional forces and armaments is, first of all, technically and politically one of the most complicated paths. Furthermore, there is no direct connection between quantitative reductions in conventional forces and armaments and a decrease in their offensive capabilities and a strengthening of military-strategic stability. One may examine many hypothetical situations whereby a simple quantitative reduction would lead to a destabilization of the political situation and an undermining of the balance. Therefore it is useful to emphasize that the reduction of weapons and armed forces is not an end, but a means to solving the common problem of "increas[ing] mutual security and stability by way of *reducing the offensive capabilities of the sides' combat potentials.*"

Guided by such an approach, it may be possible to identify the most destabilizing factors in the components of the sides' combat potentials and to determine the possible means of limiting or eliminating their negative influence, i.e., in practice the most important military objectives of the arms control process. This methodologically proposed approach is depicted clearly in Table 1. Of course, this table does not pretend to capture in their entirety all the factors that determine the characteristics and capabilities of combat potential. It could be supplemented and further refined. However, even in its present form the table illustrates the essence of a methodology for finding solutions to the problem of how to lower the offensive capabilities of the sides' combat potentials. The parameters of combat potential components which, in my opinion, play a key role in the ability to conduct offensive operations and should be focused upon from the very beginning in the conventional arms control process are in italics.

Perhaps one of the most notable factors that destabilizes the military-political situation in Europe is the glaring contradiction between the peaceful objectives declared by NATO and the WTO and the overall quantity of troops and arms in Europe. Analogous assessments can be made of the structures and deployments of formations and the types of combat weaponry, i.e., the discrepancy apparent on both sides between the military-political and military-technical components of military doctrine.

To summarize the basic claims concerning the contemporary state of the NATO-WTO conventional balance, for NATO, judging by its publications, there is anxiety over the WTO's superiority in the numbers of tanks, infantry fighting vehicles, artillery and mobile bridging equipment. For its part, the WTO is especially worried about NATO's advantages in tactical strike aviation, active means of electronic countermeasures,

Table 1 A Model for Comparing the Combat Capabilities of NATO and WTO Conventional Forces

	Quantitative variables	Qualitative variables	Variables characterizing the capabilities for the effective use of force components
Manpower	total active forces	*Number of combat-ready (Category 1 and 2) divisions* Number of division-equivalents Force readiness (education, training, exercises)	*Share of highly-mobile strike combat formations (mechanized, airmobile, airborne and amphibious units)* Share of highly-mobile combat formations deployed near NATO-WTO border Mobilization capabilities Availability, size and readiness level of reserves
Tanks	*total tanks*	Target acquisition capability Firepower Mobility Armor complement	*Share of tanks in strike formations Deployment of tank formations* Supply/logistics support capabilities for offensive actions
Artillery	total artillery	*Share of large-caliber (>120–150 mm) artillery* Range and accuracy Yield of single volley (for MLRs)	*Share of large-caliber self-propelled artillery grouped in independent strike formations Share of large-caliber self-propelled artillery*
Tactical surface-to-surface class missiles (non-nuclear)	*total launchers*	*Range Share of "smart" missiles able to detect and destroy designated targets*	*Deployment of missile units*
ATGMs	total launchers	Share of first-, second- and third-generation ATGMs	*Share of helicopter-borne ATGMs* Share of mobile ATGMs
Air-defense interceptors	total aircraft	Range of target acquisition Effectiveness of target-destruction systems	
Bombers	*total aircraft*	*Total bomb payload deliverable to ranges of 100 and 700 miles*	Difficulty of technical maintenance
Fighter-bombers and attack aircraft	*total aircraft*	*Air defense penetration capability (e.g., "stealth" technology, ECMs) Standoff capability (80–100 km or more)*	*Presence of bases near probable axes of attack* Deployment of aircraft units
Transport aircraft	total aircraft	Range Payload capacity	
Reconnaissance aircraft	total aircraft	Quality of detection Speed of data processing and transmission	
Attack helicopters	*total helicopters*	*Yield and effectiveness of on-board armaments* Range Vulnerability	*Share of attack helicopters deployed near NATO-WTO border*
Transport helicopters	total helicopters	Range Lift capacity	
Reconnaissance helicopters	total helicopters	Quality of detection Speed of data processing and transmission	

elements of offensive infrastructure (particularly C³I systems), as well as the obvious imbalance in naval forces, which in NATO have a pronounced offensive configuration and may in the most direct way influence the overall correlation of forces in Europe.

The overall correlation of naval forces, according to the estimate of Marshal Sergei Akhromeev, former chief of the General Staff of the Soviet Armed Forces, is as follows: NATO has 4.5 times as many naval personnel, 7.6 times as many oceangoing ships, 3 times as much total ship tonnage and 2.4 times as much naval combat aviation as the Warsaw Pact.[12] Considering, however, the complexity of assessments of the role and significance of naval forces in the overall balance of forces, we may for the time being, in formulating the military objectives of the conventional arms control process in the initial stage, concentrate on ground forces.

As for the quantitative state of tactical aviation, in Western sources these data are cited as reinforcements, that is, aircraft that must be flown from the United States. Thus, if one considers that in the course of two to three days after the outbreak of a conflict these aircraft would be in Europe, then even according to the data of the U.S. Department of Defense in the categories of tactical strike aviation (i.e., aircraft intended for attacking ground-based targets and playing a key role in the organization of offensive actions), the correlation would appear as follows: for NATO, 3,450 and for the WTO, 2,600 aircraft; i.e., a 1.3:1 ratio in favor of NATO.[13]

There is yet another characteristic that determines the offensive capabilities of tactical strike aviation. It is connected with the size of the bomb payload deliverable to targets at certain distances. According to the findings of a study conducted by the Carnegie Endowment for Peace and Security, in the most important region—Central Europe—the correlation appears as follows: at a radius of 100 miles NATO has a 3:1 advantage over the WTO, and at a radius of 700 miles, the ratio is 7:1.[14]

According to other Western sources, the overall correlation of "combat payloads" of aircraft based in Europe was, in 1985, the following: the U.S. air force, 4.5 million ton-miles; the Soviet air force, 1.8 million ton-miles; and the FRG air force, 1.5 million ton-miles.[15]

Of course, an objective balance of forces in tactical aviation requires an analysis of all types of aircraft possessed by both sides. Thus, for example, while inferior to NATO in tactical strike aircraft in Europe, the WTO surpasses it in air-defense fighter-interceptors. However, aircraft of this type cannot in and of themselves carry out major offensive missions, and such an imbalance therefore arouses significantly less concern.

The great mobility of tactical air forces and their large operational radius make the achievement of agreements on their limitations and verification especially difficult to reach. At the same time, one often encounters views in the West that tactical air forces are not by themselves capable of seizing and holding territory, and that therefore the issue of their reduction can be put off to a later date.

Such views are untenable. It is precisely their mobility and their capacity for deep and accurate strikes that make air forces one of the most destabilizing elements in the military balance. While airplanes cannot seize territory, their skillful employment can make seizure and control possible with smaller numbers of troops and with significantly fewer casualties.

Therefore, a reduction of offensive military capabilities should necessarily include significant reductions in tactical air forces, and possibly even limitations on the basing of certain types of airplanes in zones close to the NATO-WTO border. Here the approach that was worked out for a future 50-percent reduction in strategic offensive arms could be applied. In this instance a reduction in ICBMs and their throw-weight is envisaged. Regarding limits on tactical aviation, one might restrict both the overall number of planes and the total weapons-delivery capacity (over a certain distance per sortie).

In determining the basic mutual anxieties in the present character of the confrontation of general-purpose forces and conventional arms, we must at the same time consider the prospects for imminent change in the character of this confrontation, primarily as a consequence of the process of the modernization of conventional arms and the influence of scientific-technical advances on them. In order to assess the impact of scientific-technical progress on the military-strategic situation I will introduce a somewhat generalized qualitative notion of military-strategic stability at the level of general-purpose forces and conventional arms.

A situation will be considered hypothetically stable if, first, no side has real capabilities for military aggression for any rational practical results and, second, each side is confident that his opponent does not possess such a potential.

The second principle is connected not only—and in certain situations not so much—with the real combat capabilities of existing potentials, as it is with the psychological aspects of the perception of these potentials by the other side. Having adopted such a definition, we may now assess whether any particular step in constructing armed forces and developing military-strategic concepts will strengthen military-strategic stability or vice versa. It should be emphasized that any actions that enhance the offensive capabilities of one side or are perceived by the other side as doing so will destabilize the situation. From this point of view it is important to assess the potential influence of prospective technologies in the military sphere.

The plans for modernizing conventional arms, widely discussed in NATO, emphasize the utilization of scientific-technical achievements to make a qualitative leap in this area. An example of this approach is the U.S. use of "competitive strategies" in choosing the directions of military development, particularly in the second half of the 1980s. The essence of these strategies lies in the choice of directions for military construction that permits the maximum use of American technological leadership, renders more difficult the maintenance of Soviet military parity and seriously devalues Soviet investments already made in the military sphere.

In his final annual report as U.S. Secretary of Defense, Caspar Weinberger stated that "Our competitive strategies thereby enhance deterrence, by making significant components of the Soviet force structure and their operational plans obsolete."[16] In the first annual report prepared by Secretary of Defense Frank Carlucci, the strong emphasis on economically exhausting the USSR in a race of military technologies was somewhat softened, although competitive strategies remained "the main element of military strategy and planning." Carlucci's report emphasized that the United States is "not attempting to bankrupt the Soviet Union or undermine its economy"[17] with the help of competitive strategies. However, the task advanced in the Weinberger report of using "pronounced American advantages against pronounced Soviet weaknesses" was preserved unchanged.

The important role of conventional arms and the prospects for their technological improvement is also emphasized by the adoption of the statement on conventional arms control at the NATO Council's Brussels session in March 1988. There is every reason to assume that the significance of these arms and the influence of scientific-technical progress in this area on military-strategic stability will grow before the end of the current century. As the *Discriminate Deterrence* report on long-term U.S. strategy prepared by a select commission at the request of the Department of Defense observed, "dramatic developments in military technology appear feasible over the next twenty years. . . . These developments could require major revisions in military doctrines and force structures. . . . The precision associated with the new technologies will enable us to use conventional weapons for many of the missions once assigned to nuclear weapons."[18] The same report maintains that "revolutionary changes in the nature of war will result. The much greater precision, range, and destructiveness of weapons could extend war across a much wider geographic area, make war much more rapid and intense, and require entirely new modes of operation."

Scientific advances and the prospects of their further development feed the hopes for revolutionary achievements in resolving an extremely important (from the point of view of military application) class of military missions—automated control over a wide variety of objectives in real time. Such a broad formulation covers various types of military technologies, including the new generation of anti-tank weapons; tactical air-to-air, air-to-surface, surface-to-surface and surface-to-ship missiles; and systems for gathering, storing, processing and transmitting information for managing combat operations.

For the creation of these types of new-generation military technologies it is necessary to solve a number of problems in basic technologies, with particular regard to microelectronics and the development of computer systems. It is first of all anticipated that successes in microelectronics and computer technology will allow small tactical missiles of various classes to be equipped with such features as real-time sensors and computers in order to give them the capability to seek and destroy stationary and mobile targets (e.g., tanks, aircraft, ships, airfields) at ranges previously considered unattainable (up to 400 km). As a result it is assumed that the ability to launch missiles from such distances will significantly increase the security of both the launch platform (such as an ATGM launcher, aircraft or ship), as well as the platform operator.

This prospect promises to be exceptionally dangerous since, on the one hand, it creates the illusion that combat actions do not differ fundamentally from any other involvement with complex technologies and, on the other, it facilitates the avoidance of any moral problems, since it dehumanizes the enemy. The problem of a soldier's attitudes toward the enemy degenerate into the problem of the soldier's attitudes toward a machine that he must only target on a distant foe. As the American specialists Leonard Siegel and John Markoff have observed,

Microelectronics technology has not only made global nuclear war possible; it has thoroughly transformed the way conventional wars are fought. Modern-day electronic warriors frequently do not even consider themselves to be soldiers. They have become technicians, controlling a complex machine of which few can see all the parts.[19]

Such a tendency is reinforced even more by the fact that by virtue of the growing complexity of military technology, an increasingly small number of people are engaged in its direct application and increasingly more are involved in ensuring its functioning.

It is obvious that this tendency will be strengthened, and that in turn it will simplify overcoming the threshold that defines the transition to the use of military force as an instrument of policy. One must therefore recognize that the prospects of technological improvements in conventional arms, long before such weapons became reality, had influenced in the most serious way the character of military-strategic concepts being developed in NATO for their use.

The adoption of the "Follow-on Forces Attack" (FOFA) concept by NATO in November 1984 reflected the new views on the role and capabilities of conventional forces and armaments. This concept calls for inflicting deep strikes against the WTO's combat order from a distance of up to 300–400 km—into regions of troop concentrations and deployments, military command and control points, airbases and troops advancing to marshalling points before entering into battle. NATO assumes that, in theory, such strikes will prevent the WTO from bringing the fresh units into battle that are necessary for developing the offensive actions undertaken. One must observe, however, that conceptually, deep strikes are not fundamentally new for NATO. In particular, the "active defense" concept adopted in 1976 also called for carrying out strikes to a sufficient depth. Previous concepts, however, did differ fundamentally in the character of the weapons required for their realization.

Thus a characteristic feature of the new military-strategic concepts adopted by the United States and NATO in the 1980s was the fact that the weapons for implementing them largely remained to be developed. As in the United States itself, in the framework of NATO a whole array of projects are planned for developing the various weapons systems and military technologies necessary for the practical application of these concepts.

To turn to the controversial issue of the feasibility of such weapons systems and concepts for their use in actual combat conditions, one can only agree with the assessment provided in the journal *The Nation*:

"The push to develop so-called 'intelligent' weapons," as the Computer Professionals for Social Responsibility notes, is only another "futile attempt to find a solution for what is, and will remain, a profoundly human political problem." The idea of an artificial intelligence more logical and reliable than our own is a seductive one, especially if we believe it could protect us from a nuclear Armageddon. Sadly, it cannot.[20]

The prospect of the appearance of improved conventional weapons systems along with new concepts for using them will lead to an extremely dangerous reduction in the level of military-strategic stability. Even assuming that the developers of such a concept as FOFA sincerely consider it defensive, it is impossible not to consider how changes in technical capabilities and the character of their use are perceived by the other side. And if NATO is planning to bring into its arsenal systems able to detect and destroy targets at a depth of tens or even hundreds of kilometers, then it will inevitably enhance the alliance's offensive capabilities as well and will be perceived accordingly by the other side.

In these conditions it is extremely important to halt the process of the qualitative modernization of weapons systems and to develop some alternative approach to the issues of military posture that will allow us to move in the direction of strengthening military-strategic stability at the level of general-purpose forces and conventional arms.

Thus, in the most general view, the military objectives of the process of limiting conventional forces and armaments can be formulated in the following way: to reduce the levels of the military confrontation to the limits of reasonable sufficiency along with the strengthening of military-strategic stability. Accordingly, a general understanding of stability may be based upon the conditions formulated by Andrei A. Kokoshin:

Stability presupposes that neither side can conduct major offensive (strategic) operations or mount a surprise attack (on a strategic scale, chiefly) following a secret concentration of forces for the unexpected massive use of aviation and missiles, seaborne included.

–Tight restrictions are to be imposed on possibilities for a rapid buildup of forces deployed in peacetime by mobilization and transferring troop contingents and combat-ready reserves from other areas.

–Military activities outside the zones within which measures are being taken to ensure strategic stability at lower levels of confrontation should not lead to the upsetting of the overall equilibrium.

–A regime is to be established making it impossible to change the balance of forces to favor either side through the development (modernization) of weapons systems, both those covered and not covered by restricting agreements.

–The sides' observation (intelligence), control and communication systems, as well as the structure and facilities of their forces should be such as to enable heads of state and the supreme army command of both sides to obtain, in the event of a conflict, essential and sufficient information, in good time, on the state of the conflict, so as to terminate it at the lowest possible level.

–The mechanism for interaction between the sides should contain "built-in" elements which would localize an armed conflict if political and diplomatic "safeguards" failed to work. Paradoxical as it sounds, the effort to prevent a war should not be restricted to the period immediately preceding actual combat action.

In other words, WTO's defence potential should considerably exceed NATO's attack capability, and vice versa. The result would be a shift of emphasis from the offensive to the defensive in the military doctrines of both sides.

The military-political objectives and strategic concepts of the two sides are to be formulated in exclusively defensive terms.[21]

Of course, a structural reconfiguration of armed forces on the basis of defensive sufficiency also requires a definition of the permissible scale of remaining counteroffensive capabilities and a reevaluation of strategic and operational concepts as well as the very concept of military victory. The most acceptable model for a future NATO-WTO military structure in Europe able to serve as a realistic goal for short-term reductions in conventional forces and armaments might be that advanced by Andrei Kokoshin and Valentin Larionov,[22] which envisages a joint capability only for defeating an invasion on one's own territory, without a transition to counteroffensive operations beyond one's own border.

The essence of such a defense lies in the fact that military operations will not carry over into the territory of the side that launched the invasion.

Through active defensive actions, the defenders will only reestablish the *status quo ante*. Capabilities for launching active (offensive) operations are limited to the operational level, while the capacity for launching a counteroffensive (army group, army) as well as the concept of victory are admissable only on the operational and tactical, not strategic, scale.

The basic instrument for guaranteeing these goals would be the reduction of the sides' conventional weapons and armed forces; the disengagement and redeployment of forces and armaments; the restructuring of armed forces and the dismantling of infrastructure that supports offensive operations (e.g., forward-based ammunition depots and POL supply systems); and the organization of verification systems and confidence-building measures at a substantially higher level than those presently existing.

The primary task, in my view, now consists of such reductions of conventional forces which bring about a decrease in their offensive capabilities. This may be achieved, first, through a selective reduction of those categories of armed forces and arms that possess increased offensive capabilities; second, by refraining from procuring systems with clearly expressed offensive characteristics (e.g., increased range, accuracy and yield); and third, by creating conditions that hinder—and ideally, exclude—the capability of using arms for offensive purposes. The first stage may be achieved not only through major quantitative reductions, but also through the restructuring and disbanding of units and formations having high mobility and firepower, the withdrawal from the line of contact of strike formations and the creation of a zone of reduced troop concentration with the establishment of a strict regime of mutual verification and so on.

To achieve the goal of strengthening stability, the optimal combination of actions on all three of the above-mentioned levels must be investigated in each specific instance. In the structure of armed forces the number of combat-ready formations, the share of highly mobile units and the regions of their deployment and concentration are critical parameters. Therefore the reduction of offensive capabilities would be greatly facilitated by the reduction of the total number of troops along with the disbanding of units of highly mobile formations and their withdrawal from the zone close to the NATO-WTO border.

It may be observed that although the total number of tanks also may arouse certain anxieties, it is significantly more important to identify which tanks are positioned in tank strike formations. An effective measure would be to dismantle the greater portion of tank strike units and prohibit the deployment of large (above battalion- or regiment-size) tank formations closer than 100 kilometers to the NATO-WTO border. The same may be applied to units of large-caliber self-propelled artillery and mobile multiple-rocket-launcher systems. Within a zone somewhat closer to the border (for example, 30–50 km), it would be necessary to remove all large-caliber artillery systems.

As for tactical non-nuclear missiles, the prospect of "smart" weapons systems being developed within the framework of AirLand Battle and FOFA represents a special threat. The appearance of such systems is absolutely impermissible because of their destabilizing consequences and incompatibility with the concept of non-offensive defense and military sufficiency. Accordingly, the deployment of tactical missiles equipped with artificial intelligence systems is impermissible if it is agreed that combat potential should exclude the capability of surprise attack and large-scale offensive operations.

Furthermore, the appearance of such systems forces the other side to resort to measures of special camouflage and to the concealment of military activities in close proximity to the NATO-WTO border, while it is precisely in these border corridors that the greatest level of openness is necessary.

As for tactical aviation, special attention must be paid to aircraft with strike capabilities. If the number of interceptors is of no serious concern to either side, then it is necessary to reduce first of all aircraft intended for attacking ground targets; along with this it would be useful to prohibit their deployment at bases from which they could pose a real threat to the other side's territory. In addition, it is obvious that it would be useful to remove or at least significantly reduce the number of attack helicopters from border zones.

These points allow a number of steps to be outlined for the reduction of offensive capabilities of both sides' combat potentials. It appears that from the practical point of view the following measures could be agreed upon and implemented:

–a complete withdrawal from the WTO-NATO zone of contact (the width of the corridor for each component of combat potential and for each side from the border may be stipulated separately) and gradual dismantling of highly mobile strike units;

–a mutual withdrawal of tank formations from the NATO-WTO border with an agreed upon number of tanks spread among infantry units remaining in each side's corridor;

–a complete mutual withdrawal from the NATO-WTO zone of contact of large-caliber (greater than 120-mm) artillery and multiple-rocket-launcher systems;

–a ban on the basing of strike aviation at airbases located closer than several hundred kilometers to NATO-WTO borders. Special efforts to reduce the numbers of aircraft of these categories, or to mothball them by way of a partial dismantling, must be explored;

–a ban on the deployment of tactical non-nuclear missiles with artificial intelligence elements intended for attacking ground targets at distances permitting the destruction of targets on the other side's territory. Since such a point is quite complicated to verify from the point of view of assessing the range of deployed missiles, it would generally be more advantageous to limit their range to 50 km, along with analogous air-based missiles that allow strike aircraft to attack surface targets from great distances;

–an agreed reduction of the number of combat helicopters in the NATO-WTO zone of contact;

–a ban on concentrations of troops and arms above a certain level and on the conduct of large-scale exercises in the NATO-WTO zone of contact; and

–a ban on the warehousing of military supplies and ammunition in quantities sufficient for maintaining offensive operations closer than 150 kilometers to the NATO-WTO border.

To be sure, the creation of such a border zone would require the establishment in it of a fundamentally new level of openness, of additional confidence-building measures by permanent and challenge on-site inspections and the opportunity for regular air observations.

As we see, most of these proposed measures do not include immediate quantitative reductions and may be psychologically easier to implement. They also do not require a preliminary detailed comparison of the balance of forces. At the same time, it is obvious that the implementation of such measures would truly lead to a reduction of the threat of surprise attack and would create a fundamentally new political and psychological environment in Europe. An important catalyst for moving toward a higher level of military-strategic stability in Europe was the previously cited unilateral Soviet initiatives spelled out in General Secretary Gorbachev's December 1988 speech to the UN. It is important to note that these initiatives are of interest not only for the scale of the intended reductions—although they are indeed impressive—but for the methodological principles which, if we can abstract them for purposes of analysis, lie at their foundation.

It is obvious that the USSR is not simply reducing its troops and weapons, but in the most serious possible way it is limiting their offensive capabilities. Six tank divisions (nearly 2,000 tanks) based in the GDR, Czechoslovakia and Hungary are being disbanded. But in all the number of Soviet tanks in these three countries will be reduced by 5,000. This means that tanks will be withdrawn from other infantry units, which will also reduce their capacity to launch large-scale offensives.

In all, the European territory of the USSR and its WTO allies will witness a reduction of 10,000 tanks, 8,500 artillery systems and 800 tactical airplanes. It is important that these forces cannot be redeployed, especially by basing them east of the Urals since, as Gorbachev declared, the armed forces based in the Asian USSR will be significantly reduced. This Soviet approach to the issue of reducing armed forces and conventional arms convincingly demonstrates that these reductions are seen, not as an end in themselves, but as a means of strengthening military-strategic stability by reducing the offensive capabilities of military potential.

Tank divisions will be removed and disbanded from the territory of the GDR, Czechoslovakia and Hungary, from where (especially from the first two countries) they are theoretically capable of a highly effective large-scale offense. Other heavy weapons also will be withdrawn from these countries. And highly mobile landing-assault components, which are designed for lightning attack, will be withdrawn too. This signifies the dismantling (still unilateral) of units with the most negative potential impact upon stability.

It is very important that the withdrawal of heavy armaments from forward-based divisions be accompanied by their reconfiguration, so as to impart to them a purely defensive structure. This means that the divisions with the most significant impact upon stability will begin to undergo a defensive-oriented structural reconfiguration.

If we speak of the infrastructure of the offensive, then one of the most important qualities determining success is unquestionably the capability to overcome water barriers by offensive units. The West has often emphasized that Soviet mobile bridging units deployed in the GDR and Czechoslovakia clearly are prepared for a *blitzkrieg* and the breakthrough of Soviet tank forces deep into the territory of the United States' European allies. And although the effectiveness of contemporary anti-tank systems and the number of these systems in NATO countries renders the very idea of such an offense absurd, the concern of non-specialists, which can be especially heated, is understandable. The recent Soviet initiatives envisage a step which will largely remove this alarm: landing-assault and river-bridging forces, with their equipment and weapons, will also be withdrawn.

The implementation of these steps will undoubtedly play an important role in one more process already under way. This is the dismantling of the enemy image and the perception of a military threat. Soviet policy in recent years has already achieved something in this direction. Simply by announcing the foundations of future large-scale reductions of troops and armed forces, the Western perception of a Soviet military threat has radically changed. With practical steps in this direction it will change even further; it is very important that the long-term and serious character of the Soviet approach is confirmed by its intention to develop on a nationwide scale a plan for the conversion of military production and to begin the first experiments in this field, i.e., to make the retraining of specialists from military industry a state concern.

The Soviet initiatives are also important in that they effectively entail the elimination of imbalances and asymmetries in military power by dismantling their offensive core, i.e., to creatively develop the concept of the three-step proposal advanced by Soviet Foreign Minister Shevard-nadze in his UN speech in the summer of 1988. In these conditions further progress would be substantially facilitated toward the elimination of military imbalances and asymmetries and the radical reduction of conventional forces and armaments in Europe, with the overall objective of reducing and eliminating the offensive capabilities of both sides' combat potentials.

Notes

1   *Pravda*, May 30, 1987.
2   *Pravda*, June 9, 1988.
3   *Izvestiia*, March 28, 1988.
4   "Conventional Arms Control: The Way Ahead. Statement Issued under the Authority of the Heads of State and Governments Participating in the Meeting of the North Atlantic Council in Brussels, March 2–3, 1988," *Atlantic News* No. 1998 (March 4, 1988), pp. 5–9.
5   *Otkuda iskhodit ugroza miru* [Whence the Threat to Peace] (Moscow: Voenizdat, 1987).

6 *Razoruzhenie i bezopasnost': ezhegodnik IMEMO, 1987* [Disarmament and Security: IMEMO Yearbook, 1987](Moscow: Novosti Press Agency, 1988).

7 *Beyond the Bean Count: Realistically Assessing the Conventional Military Balance in Europe* (Washington, DC: Office of Senator Carl Levin, January 20, 1988). Senator Levin chairs the Subcommittee on Conventional Forces and Alliance Defense of the Senate Committee on Armed Services.

8 *Pravda*, February 9, 1988.

9 Malcolm Chalmers and Lutz Unterseher, "Is There a Tank Gap? Comparing NATO and Warsaw Pact Tank Fleets," *International Security* 13, No. 1 (Summer 1988), pp. 5–49.

10 V. Shlykov, "I tanki nashi bystry" [And Our Tanks Are Fast] *Mezhdunarodnaia zhizn'* No. 9 (September 1988), pp. 117–129.

11 S. Zaloga and J. Grandsen, *Military Modeling*, February 1982, pp. 125–126, as cited in Ibid., fn. 25.

12 *Pravda*, September 5, 1988.

13 *Razoruzhenie i bezopasnost'*, p. 439.

14 See Carnegie Panel on U.S. Security, *Challenges for U.S. National Security, Part II, Assessing the Balance: Defense Spending and Conventional Forces* (Washington, DC: Carnegie Endowment for International Peace, 1981), p. 71.

15 Assembly of the Western European Union, 33rd Ordinary Session, *Threat Assessment, part II*, p. 24.

16 Caspar Weinberger, *Annual Report to the Congress, FY 1988* (Washington, DC: U.S. Government Printing Office, 1987), p. 66.

17 Frank Carlucci, *Annual Report to the Congress, FY 1989* (Washington, DC: U.S. Government Printing Office, 1988), p. 115.

18 Fred C. Ikle and Albert Wohlstetter, *Discriminate Deterrence: Report on the Commission of Integrated Long-Term Strategy* (Washington, DC: U.S. Government Printing Office, January 1988), p. 8.

19 Leonard M. Siegel and John Markoff, *The High Cost of High Tech* (New York: Harper & Row, 1985), p. 23.

20 Paul N. Edwards, "Are 'Intelligent Weapons' Feasible?" *The Nation*, February 2, 1985, p. 112.

21 Andrei A. Kokoshin, "Defence is Best for Stability," *New Times* 33 (August 12, 1988), p. 19.

22 Andrei A. Kokoshin and Valentin V. Larionov, "Protivostoianie sil obshchego naznacheniia v kontekste obespecheniia strategicheskoi stabil'nosti" [The Balance of General-purpose Forces in the Context of Preserving Strategic Stability], *Mirovaia ekonomika i mezhdunarodnye otnosheniia* No. 6 (June 1988), p. 27.

V

PART ONE

NATO and WTO "Military Doctrines" in East-West Consultations

Peer H. Lange, Federal Republic of Germany

The idea of including consultations on military and security precepts in the framework of European conventional arms control efforts was mentioned in the July 1987 Jaruzelski Plan,[1] and previously officially proposed in the Warsaw Treaty Organization's (WTO's) declaration of doctrine in May of that year.[2] This idea was endorsed in the West by Foreign Minister Hans-Dietrich Genscher of the Federal Republic of Germany as early as January 1986[3] and explored by leading figures of the West German Social Democratic Party and within the Palme Commission since the early 1980s.

This essay outlines the methodological and procedural problems inherent in East-West consultations on this issue in the talks on Conventional Forces in Europe (CFE). The first part critically examines the Soviet term "military doctrine" and its specific qualities that are relevant for East-West consultations. It purposely does not address the issue now in vogue of the changes Mikhail Gorbachev has implemented in Soviet military thinking ("reasonable sufficiency," "non-offensive defense" and others). Also purposely, it will not add to the innumerable and mostly uncritical descriptions of how the various components of military thought allegedly fit—according to Soviet understanding—into a monolithically and hierarchically structured "military doctrine." The second part describes each side's current perceptions of military and security precepts and the consequences of these perceptions for developing appropriate methods within an arms control context. The third part deals briefly with the emerging subject of national military doctrines in the East. The fourth and last part analyzes the layers of problems that any consultations will face and proposes a broad but tightly structured agenda for dealing with them.

The Limited Value of the Soviet Term "Military Doctrine"

If the main goal of initiatives to hold East-West consultations on military and security precepts is to promote security and stability by enabling the two sides to agree upon desirable and undesirable structures, postures, capabilities and developments, then at the outset it is necessary to determine an adequate theoretical approach to the subject.

The Soviet ideological culture has offered a theoretical setting that seems to promise the best approach because it includes the whole range of relevant ideas, from political principles down to tactical military rules—all covered by the specific term "military doctrine." The official Soviet definition is as follows:

> Military doctrine is the system of views on the essence, aims and character of a possible future war, on the preparation of the country and its armed forces for it and on the ways to fight it, which are adopted in a state at a given time.[4]

Because of the widespread use of the term military doctrine today, one must question whether its nature and intended purpose are appropriate to the goals of the forthcoming consultations. What limitations or built-in "blind spots" may obstruct the desired outcome? Might the very nature of the term "military doctrine" ultimately be misleading rather than helpful, and if so, what are the characteristics which may lead officials and analysts astray?

The most important aspects of the Soviet understanding of the term military doctrine appeared in Mikhail Frunze's article "The Unified Military Doctrine and the Red Army," formulated in close cooperation with Lenin and published in 1921[5]. Frunze described the leading imperialist powers' military doctrines as being predetermined by their class interests: colonial and maritime, in the case of the United Kingdom; preservational-defensive for France; and expansionist-offensive for Germany. He used the same underlying rationale of class struggle to characterize the military doctrine of the Red Army as being determined by the historical revolutionary function of the proletariat: offensive, maneuver-oriented and decisive.

Frunze's analysis suggests two points of primary importance for our discussion here:

–a specific ideological approach, based on historical materialism, that determines the political orientation of a state. The same then is applied to the orientation of the buildup of the armed forces of that state. Both should be interrelated by an ends-means rationale. Consequently, the "military doctrine" of a state should be identical with the content of the policy of a state, determined by criteria of class struggle.

–the definition of the term "military doctrine" as being a "system of assumptions generally accepted at a given time in a state, about the essence, goals and character of a future war and about the necessary preparations . . . ," makes the extrapolation of the content and the interpretation of its sources dependent upon the two terms "system" and "generally accepted." What belongs to this "system" and what doesn't? What can be counted as "generally accepted" and what cannot?

Adherence to Ideological Axioms

Regarding the first point, the Soviet perception of the rationale of imperialist ends and means has remained basically unchanged since Frunze and Lenin. Despite "new thinking," this approach was still apparent in the first waves of Soviet statements (predominantly by the Soviet military) on military doctrine after the WTO's declaration on doctrine in May 1987.[6] It is also inherent in the proposal "to compare the character" of military doctrines.[7] If, in consultations on doctrine, East and West are to debate the ends and means of differing social systems and the place of class interests, there is every reason to anticipate fruitless propagandistic battling.

The "new thinking" under Gorbachev has changed basic assumptions about "class struggle" and has subordinated this to the higher goal of avoiding war—a goal shared by all humanity. However, as far as the perception of threats stemming from other powers is concerned, the general Soviet understanding as formulated by Frunze and Lenin is still valid in Soviet thinking today. More important changes have occurred in the Soviet rationale of socialist ends and means. The revolutionary impetus concerning the military power of the first socialist state as conceived by Trotsky was quickly and fundamentally transformed under Stalin into a rather traditional rationale for state military power. But the inclination toward an "offensive" attitude remained untouched. For decades Soviet military thinking was oriented more toward what was perceived as the "laws of military art," expressed primarily by the development of weapons technology to increase speed, mobility and range and to shorten reaction time. Only the new thinking of the Gorbachev leadership has introduced political axioms designed to determine military thought—although their real effect is as yet unknown.

The original intention attached to military doctrine, however—namely, the ideologically oriented characterization of a military theoretical superstructure by yardsticks of historical materialism or international class struggle—is outdated and of little use for present conventional arms control efforts because it focuses on divisive categories rather than on the areas most important in present-day arms control: mutually perceived dangers and stability.

The Primacy of Policy—How Determining Is "Military Doctrine"?

Given the basic aims of the upcoming consultations on military and security precepts, will the term "military doctrine" properly cover the items: military structures, options and capabilities? The two criteria for making this determination are hierarchical dominance and durability. "Hierarchical dominance" assumes that the functional effect moves from top to bottom—i.e., from the highest political spheres and ideas down to military production, structures and training. However, in the Soviet case such movement must be seriously questioned in light of Soviet historical experience. Soviet military and security precepts and military buildups have often not been in harmony with one another. For example:

–The offensive orientation of the structure and training of the Red Army in the late 1930s did not correspond with the political assumptions about the war the USSR would eventually be forced to fight: a defensive war against German attack;
–The military buildup against China during the period of tensions in the late 1960s continued without any mention in the military literature, especially the part dealing with the "character of a future war," of the possibility of a "war among socialist states";
–Brezhnev's 1976 Tula speech, which renounced any intention of trying to achieve military superiority, was delivered at a time when a major

conventional buildup was well under way. The central purpose of this buildup was the enhancement of firepower to suppress anti-tank defense and the rapid enhancement of air mobility by the introduction of helicopters into the first-echelon forces and the deployment of inter-mediate-range missiles (SS-20s) designed to achieve escalation domi-nance in the theater.

The problem is directly connected with the Soviet teaching of the "two sides" of military doctrine, namely, its so-called political and military-technical sides—the former, in a hierarchical sense, supposedly the decisive one. The definitions and descriptions of the military-technical side are nearly identical to those of strategy, the top level of "military art," which in itself should constitute a component of this part of doctrine. Strategy and military doctrine are said to interact—which seems rather logical. But on the other hand, military doctrine is said to determine strategy. In the Soviet case, however, it is questionable whether in fact the political component of military doctrine determines the military-technical part (or even strategy). The question may be put into arms control terms: Which side is the most important one to deal with?

In some historical cases, the obvious motivations behind important decisions in the Soviet armaments process were military ones, and thus followed a bottom-to-top functional direction instead:

–this is true for the buildup of the armed forces during Stalin's forced industrialization, beginning with the implementation of the first five-year plan along lines designed by the military (Tuchachevskii, Shaposh-nikov); and
–the same is true for the restructuring of the Soviet army during the late 1970s and early 1980s, designed and promoted by Marshal Ogarkov.

One then must ask whether the military or the political leadership plays the decisive role in the design of the armed forces and the pace and purposes of armaments. From its very beginning until the early 1980s, the Soviet military maintained almost exclusive responsibility for developing the ideas and concepts of military doctrine—although, ac-cording to the various definitions and descriptions of doctrine, the political elites ought to have been its authoritative architects. In the 1970s only a few civilian authors contributed to the basic military-theoretical discus-sion, the journalist Aleksandr Bovin being the best known. Only later were the *institutchiki*, as representatives of the political elite, able to join the debate. By defining the political component of threat perceptions and Western strategies they developed a set of political rationales for military power. Beginning with the Soviet reaction to the U.S. Strategic Defense Initiative (SDI) and then with Gorbachev's new leadership, these Soviet "strategists" became more closely involved in the development of concepts, thus legitimizing ex post facto previous statements that the political side of military doctrine determines the military-technical side.

But it is precisely here that doubts arise whether the alleged primacy of the political side in relation to the military-technical side will in fact always be the case in the near future, and therefore whether the term "military doctrine" is a useful subject for East-West consultations. The decisive factor is the willingness of the professional Soviet military to subordinate itself to new security precepts instead of insisting on their traditional prerogative of formulating military doctrine on the basis of military-operational considerations. Despite a few declaratory statements and preliminary organizational steps, a certain reluctance among the military to cede this task to the political leadership is still evident.

At the United Nations in December 1988, Gorbachev announced deep cuts in the Soviet Union's military capability to conduct sudden and maneuverable combined strategic operations by armored and air-mobile formations ("deep battle")—in short, in its capability to carry out an invasion, especially a short-warning attack. This move was obviously designed to demonstrate a determination to give greater weight to political criteria in deciding military matters. Marshal Sergei F. Akhromeev's simultaneous resignation as Soviet chief of staff, as well as Marshal Victor Kulikov's removal as commander in chief of the WTO several months later, suggests that influential military men still support differing doctrinal rationales.

Given the purpose of the envisaged consultations, the problem arises whether military and security precepts actually can be found under the rubric of "military doctrine" which are capable of determining military structures, options and capabilities on a long-term basis and thus can serve as worthwhile subjects for East-West consultations. Doctrinal changes declared to be oriented toward "defense" and "sufficiency," such as the ones presently under discussion, remain entirely dependent on volatile political preconditions—namely, the possible reversibility of some of the basic tenets of the "new political thinking" and their dominance over military thought.

Furthermore, the supposed durability, according to the Soviet understanding, as guaranteed by hierarchical dominance is conceivable only insofar as political dominance is interpreted as the dominance of class interests in a historical-materialist sense. In an ideology-free understanding, political dominance does not guarantee the durability of this or that doctrinal concept; in fact it is subject to change, as exemplified in the abrupt "doctrinal" reforms and political decisions in the Soviet world today. This suggests that for security and military precepts to be durable over time, the "primacy of politics," promised by the Soviet definition of "military doctrine," is inconsequential. Rather, durability can be achieved by a continuous effort to adapt precepts to inevitable change. The envisaged consultations about military and security precepts therefore must be thought of as a continuous effort, rather than a single act.

Qualities and Sources of Military Doctrine

The second aspect of the traditional Soviet understanding of military doctrine, its characteristic as a "system of commonly agreed upon views," distinguishes the term from the normal Western understanding of doctrines as specific declarations by governments. It also provides great room for interpretation of what can be included in this "system" and what should be perceived as "commonly agreed upon." Even the WTO's and USSR's first declaration of its military doctrine on May 29, 1987, did not alter this major weakness because it was extremely imprecise.

The various definitions of military doctrine following Frunze's initial formulation are still plagued by the need to find sources for the components out of which a mosaic-like "system of commonly agreed upon views" can be constructed—or at least discussed. This difficulty was not resolved in the 1960s when the sources for the doctrine of a given state— particularly the Soviet Union—were defined as "statements from the leading figures of the government or the party, the military high command, orders of the day and other military statements."[8] What was described as Soviet military doctrine was never substantiated by the citation of sources of that kind! The consequence is not only that detailed subjects for the prospective consultations have to be extrapolated, but also that methodological criteria for reliable, mutually accepted sources have to be elaborated.

Furthermore, certain difficulties arise regarding the military content of military doctrine. According to most Soviet definitions, military doctrine should describe "the essence, ends and character of a future war [nowadays its avoidance], . . . the preparation of the nation and its armed forces for war and the patterns of waging it. . . ." Yet the above-mentioned sources of military doctrine rarely deal with these items, and there has never been anything like a definitive publication or statement on these issues. Thus the military content of military doctrine is rather vague and completely dependent on interpretation—and so is its utility as a subject of consultations.

Monolithism vs. Pluralism

The last point to be mentioned here is that from the beginning the characteristic Soviet perception of the term "military doctrine" centered around the *state*, even if the original perception related Soviet military doctrine to the Red Army (Frunze). Traditionally, there were no political-ideological concepts for the creation of socialist military alliances and, accordingly, no concepts for a military doctrine for an alliance of socialist states. When the WTO was created, in 1955, a military doctrine was neither formulated nor announced. Rather, by force of the Soviet Union's actual dominance within the WTO, its military thought and concepts were tacitly imposed upon the alliance. Thus, from the WTO's foundation through 1987 Soviet national doctrine was identical with that of WTO doctrine—and the WTO's doctrine was imposed upon its member-states, which, according to the original definition of "military doctrine," should have had their own individual doctrines.

Several historical examples underscore that geostrategic necessities and national security prerogatives create strong rationales for national doctrines, and there is good reason to believe that national and regional doctrines and strategic concerns played a certain role here, but they had no chance to be integrated into or even to influence the military doctrine of the Warsaw Pact as a whole. Thus, the WTO's May 1987 declaration, which noted the existence of other "national military doctrines," signaled a major change.

General Conclusion

The only possible useful feature of the term "military doctrine" lies not in the very specific Soviet understanding of it, but rather in its lack of precision and its all-embracing character. This allows the most important principles of security policy—on which military-strategic, operational and tactical concepts (as components of "military art") have to be based—to be included and treated in any East-West consultations. As was stated even by the Soviet side, "official materials published in the West on military strategy focusing on operational, organizational and military-technical questions lack a parallel in the Soviet Union."[9] The problem then is to agree upon the arrangement of themes and issues and to prevent the lack of clarity embodied in the term "military doctrine" from leading to ideological confusion or complicating the consultations to the point where they become unresolvable.

Eastern and Western Military and Security Precepts and Perceptions

The following tables summarize the key points of the current Eastern and Western military and security precepts and the perception of them by the other side. Their purpose is not comparison, but to find a point of departure for determining the most important issues to be dealt with in East-West consultations on military precepts. The tables have been extrapolated from related sources which cannot be explored in detail here.

Continuity and Change

The dominant impression one gets from the synopsis below is of doctrinal change in the East and lack of change in the West.

Gorbachev's reforms have affected the military and security sphere as much as they have affected the economic and social ones. The developments that have caused the most confusion in the West[10] have been Eastern statements and publications concerning the counterproductive overreliance on military power and the shift toward the principles of defense and "sufficiency." Gorbachev's December 1988 announcement of unilateral deep cuts in the USSR's conventional force posture (followed by similar steps on the part of its European allies) was presumably driven by the desire to establish a "non-provocative" posture, which would be a more ambitious and politically far-reaching goal than one aimed simply at "defensiveness" and "sufficiency."[11] However, in our context, those statements of intent point first to the problem of rather frequent discrepancies between what is declared and what is perceived. Consequently, the problem is less an issue of erroneous perception than one of reliability.

Table 1 Soviet (WTO) and Western Security Precepts

Category	Soviet	Western
1. Main goal of military power	To guarantee against blackmail and avoid war by possessing military capability to deny a potential enemy military success. This implies: 1. Rejection of deterrence as a principle for guaranteeing security; instead, political means are emphasized. However, deterrence on lower levels (minimal deterrence) is considered 2. Warfighting capability aimed at "destructive defeat" *[Western perception: Still unclear whether the past socialist aim of gaining political advantages from the arms race, perceived as a political process of competition between socialism and imperialism, remains valid among, for example, the military. Also, the West views this as a means of exerting control over the socialist camp (extended "internal function" of armed forces)]* 3. Formation of new principles: "defensive" posture and structure and "sufficient" strength only *[Western perception: Still in the making; announced arms reductions seen as oriented toward decreasing "provocativeness"; skepticism about "defensiveness"; differing Soviet treatment of "sufficiency" does not yet allow for reliable assessment]*	To avoid war, forceful subjugation, the spread of revolution and being outarmed. This implies: 1. Deterring opponents from war or use of military power as blackmail is the main means of guaranteeing security *[Eastern perception: Deterrence is aimed at intimidation or blackmail]* 2. Desire to eventually restore troubled political order or stability in local conflicts. (However, strong legislative restrictions on and/or a general renunciation of the use of force for political aims, except defensive ones, exist) 3. Arms races are perceived as a competition of options (including anticipated ones); no ultimate zero-sum goals *[Eastern perception: Arms races are aimed at economically exhausting the opponent]*
2. Origins of all-out intersystemic war and threats	Imperialism Accident Local motives Internal instabilities	Undeterred rival superpower Uncontrolled local tensions Terrorism
3. Extent of danger	Destruction of human civilization, or at least European civilization in the case of even a conventional war on the continent, because of collateral damage	Destruction of human civilization, even in a conventional battle zone
4. Values to be secured	–Existence of humanity –Existence of socialism and its achievements –Parity with the West in nuclear and conventional strength –Territorial and systemic integrity of the Soviet Union and the socialist camp *[Western perception: The option of further expansion is included and the option of shrinkage is denied (Brezhnev Doctrine) despite declared "sovereignty to choose the way" and "mutual interdependence."]*	–Existence of humanity and civilization –Social order based on freedom, democracy and human rights –Sufficiency in military strength –Systemic and territorial integrity of allied nations

Table 2 Soviet (WTO) and Western Military Axioms

Category	Soviet	Western
1. Ultimate goals	Destruction of the "aggressor"	To stop warfighting at the earliest possible point, but not under unfavorable conditions. Nuclear deterrence, despite shortcomings (stalemate, self-deterrence paradox), is the most reliable and non-substitutable means of preventing, controlling or stopping warfighting (escalation, intrawar deterrence) because of its unique potential for an unacceptable cost-benefit ratio
2. Modes of military and armament options, and strategic imperatives	Declaratory orientation toward "defensiveness" in the sense of reaction only, not to originate hostile or escalatory actions (no first use of nuclear weapons, no first use of military means for political ends)	Belief in qualitative modes and *innovation* as the primary mode for preventing (as well as anticipating) the possibility of being cheated or outdone
	No nuclear first strike, but heavy reliance on "counterforce" option, potential and related efforts (from damage limitation to capacity suppression)	*[Eastern perception: Aimed at qualitative superiority]*
	[Western perception: Also includes preemptive strike options on all levels and aimed at preserving military parity to achieve and maintain a nuclear stalemate on all rungs of the ladder of escalation for the purpose of devaluing the opponent's reliance on nuclear options and enhancing the value of conventional preponderance]	Strong reliance on technical means and quantifiable dissuasion
		Preservation of nuclear first-use (not to be equated with first-strike) option, including controlled counterforce strikes
		[Eastern perception: In contradiction to other Soviet assessments of options considered a capability for disarming strikes]
	Preserving the option of tactical nuclear warfighting	Fixation on strategic doctrine of "flexible response," meaning voluntary choice of response to degree of military descent
	Controversial declaratory vs. professional treatment of the problem of escalation and limitation	*[Eastern perception: Allows unlimited attack options]*
	Preponderance not sought on any level; instead, oriented toward "military sufficiency" (in quality and quantity related to the degree of threat and taking into consideration one's own aims) and "reasonable sufficiency" (related to cost-benefit optimization)	Guarantee of reliability of deterrence through ability to control escalation (escalation dominance) and by determined coupling
		[Eastern perception: Related to intimidation]
	[Western perception: Other elements in this declaratory policy also evident, including:	Nuclear escalation as a means to *stop* conventional warfighting by the *political quality* of nuclear battlefield weapons rather than their military-tactical qualities (e.g., lack of tactical nuclear warfighting training and concept-building; complex release procedures).
	1. Not being followed by actual constraints in arms production	
	2. Preservation of partial preponderance with the precondition of overall compensatory balance of potential	
	3. Preservation of the option to modernize weapons technology, force structure and command structure	
	4. Quantitative preponderance tentatively substitutable for by qualitative options and capabilities (higher maneuverability, massing by maneuver of force and fire in all three dimensions, penetration by dispersal)]	

Table 2 *(Continued)*

Category	Soviet	Western
3. Main orientation on "defense" in conventional options	Defense by modern, maneuver-oriented options No shift toward an understanding of defense as static Strategic conventional defense without border crossing only for an intermediate period *[Western perception: as previously, offensive and counteroffensive operations based on structures and organization tailored for "deep operations" with strong reinforcement, with the goal of defeating the enemy on his territory (i.e., invasion). This is evident in reliance on maneuverable, massable, interchangeable and substitutable diverse conventional firepower as a means of defense; this sort of firepower can act as a "can opener," leaving the "exploitation of success" to the armored forces, traditionally tailored for deep intrusion, wedging action and quick paralysis of the enemy's warfighting options.]*	Conventional defense concept is oriented toward *Verneverteidigung* (in contrast to border-crossing *Vorwaertsverteidigung*) in a (non-static) maneuvering mode (FM100-5/AirLand Battle). Deployment, structures, training and logistics are all tailored to this task. Since the early 1960s the underlying political rationale has been for non-provocative structure and behavior, especially in respect to training and indicative logistical peculiarities. The recent West German *Heeresstruktur 2000*, despite enhanced mobility, is structurally unmistakably defense-oriented *[Eastern perception: NATO posture permits the option of invasion on a limited scale of non-Soviet WTO countries (e.g., the GDR, Czechoslovakia). Exercises include provocative behavior]* Reinforcement interdiction: because of the growing importance of the WTO's and USSR's reinforcement capability, growing reliance on the modernization of firepower based on emerging weapons technology (FOFA/Rogers Plan) *[Eastern perception: Main indicator of "offensiveness"]* Firepower including airpower, not limited to the forward edge of battle area (FEBA) Air force concept is *interdiction-oriented*, in contrast to "can opener" tasks.
	Conventional naval options subordinated and integrated in strategic operations, ASW (anti-submarine warfare) capabilities directed against SSBN/SLBN options of adversary *[Western perception: Western sea lanes of reinforcement under considerable threat]*	*[Eastern perception: "Offensive"]* Naval concepts aimed at defending reinforcement sea lanes by exit-blocking tactics *[Eastern perception: Indicative of "offensive-mindedness"]*

The forthcoming consultations will already be burdened at the outset with the traditional problem of "verifying" declaratory doctrinal statements, thus mixing or unfortunately complicating doctrinal and intelligence matters.

Even more important is the subsequent problem of understanding the role and function of the deceptive use of declaratory doctrinal pronouncements and the inclination to secrecy, in adherence with an understanding of doctrines as a means of gauging warfighting capabilities which in general have to be kept secret to assure surprise. The alternative approach is to announce potentials, capabilities and the underlying rationales, concepts or doctrines, the function of which amounts to "dissuading" the opponent from taking risks or engaging in conflict (this basic Western rationale is now being gradually adopted in the East).

In contrast, in the West no comparable shift in military and security theory occurred at the authorative government level, whereas unofficial, "alternative" thinking on concepts such as defensive defense had long ago been developed rather broadly. The INF Treaty did not weaken adherence to the principle of nuclear deterrence, despite its effects on the rationale of escalation control. Regarding conventional military concepts, the basic Western adherence to maneuverable armored defense and the obsession with the fundamental problems stemming from the quantitative superiority of the WTO[12] generally did not lead to the development of alternative arms control-related models of military postures based on a changed threat perception. Even financial and demographic constraints, forcing reconsideration of, for example, the structure and size of the Bundeswehr or of the U.S. military presence in Europe, have not yet been translated into new concepts for conventional military stability in Europe.

Some justification exists for this continued conservative thinking, and such conservatism can be anticipated in the upcoming East-West consultations. The basic Western orientation, directed less at warfighting than at war prevention by deterrence and denial, is much closer to the principles under discussion in early 1989 than is the traditional Eastern orientation toward warfighting capability, even if motivated by "deterrence credibility." The validity of traditional Western claims of Eastern military superiority, and the consequent demand for deep unilateral reductions, has been confirmed by recent Soviet figures and announcements. Furthermore, there remains no reliable alternative to nuclear deterrence. But this Western thinking about security is less responsive to the new perceptions of challenges to security and stability, especially in Europe. These focus on different dangers, such as the inability to cope with mounting defense burdens and military redundancy.

Gorbachev's new thinking about security matters seems to be better adapted to this kind of political current, which will exert its influence even if it is not directly represented in the forthcoming consultations. The different approaches of the participants in the upcoming consultations will develop in response to this influence and their predisposition. To be sure, the most active proponents of the reform-oriented strategic thinking in the Soviet Union interact strongly with serious, critical peace researchers in the West. The alignment of these sides' new principles and concepts for "nonoffensive defense" is obvious.

Military Doctrine and Coercion

The second important conclusion arising from the above synopsis is the coincidence of perceptions concerning the use of military power in the nuclear age. Both sides emphasize the threat of coercion rather than that of an all-out war between the two sociopolitical systems.

Military concepts, or doctrines, however, are concerned predominantly with the art of warfighting. There is a reason for this—the need for credible deterrence, which demands that military means be perceived as usable in warfare. But it is still unusual in military or strategic thinking to measure military capabilities by their usefulness for coercion. All the strategies, doctrines and concepts presently in force or under discussion are vague in respect to their coercive qualities. But given that coercion is the main purpose of military power under present conditions, the military and security precepts discussed in the forthcoming consultations will have to be addressed in terms of their effectiveness for coercion.

Limitations apparently exist, however. The same preconditions that determine the credibility of deterrence and the improbability of a major war are likely to stimulate assumptions about the greater probability of the limited use of military power. This is valid not only because the Soviet Union has repeatedly used military force to quell political dissension in various East European states, but also because of Israeli surgical strikes against Iraq and U.S. consideration of using force to prevent the dangerous proliferation of chemical weapons to unreliable governments. Limited military options as an objective of military and security precepts will inevitably be tabled at the consultations because of their close relationship to disabling (decapitating, blinding) strikes and their great significance for Eastern Europe.

Invasion vs. Destruction: Incomparable Threat Characteristics

A third item of importance is the different definition of the main threat in East and West. After several years of debate the West has finally arrived at a consensus that the most dangerous threat in terms of both military capability and political coercion arises from the capability to launch a large-scale conventional invasion, especially in an era of reduced reliance on nuclear deterrence. The East, however, focuses on the threat posed by means by destruction, including limited options; it considers firepower of enhanced range and accuracy, capable of striking deep in the rear and conducting disabling strikes, the most dangerous threat.

Three problems inherent in this Eastern thinking are important to note. First, the upcoming consultations will have to overcome a considerable degree of ignorance, on the Eastern side, of the rationale lying behind the Western understanding of nuclear deterrence at lower levels of escalation. Strategic thought in the East still seems to be influenced by scenarios alien to current or prospective deterrence rationales, and to be still closely related to the limited-nuclear-warfighting concepts of the 1970s. Second, the West will face a rather uniform perception in the WTO's "northern tier" that the highly centralized political leaderships in the East are put at risk by the decapitating capability of the West's emerging technologies. Third, these political assumptions cause Eastern thinking—especially in Poland—to correlate "offensiveness" with the criterion of "border-crossing"—regardless of the capability to seize territory—thus vastly blurring the differences between deterrence- and warfighting-related capabilities. Interestingly, the two states located beyond the perceived limited-invasion capability of NATO, the USSR and Poland, are the most active ones in opposing NATO's modernization efforts by pointing to NATO's allegedly dangerous capability for "limited invasion" (depths of up to 150 km) or "political decapitation."

Another factor leading to different conclusions in East and West is the quantitative calculation of military superiority or inferiority. In the Eastern view, the qualitative superiority of quantitatively inferior advanced weapons systems allows for militarily limited, but politically successful, invasion even by inferior conventional armed forces. The West, however, has considered numerical superiority in conventional forces, even obsolescent ones, the main factor creating instability and action-reaction functions within the arms race, and has viewed quantitative inferiority and the structural incapacity of conventional armed forces to conduct large-scale seizure and occupation of politically important objectives as guarantees of non-provocativeness. These divergent evaluations are predetermined by the differing underlying rationales for the purposes of military force (deterrence vs. defeat). The upcoming consultations on military and security precepts will be challenged to find objective criteria to correct invalid assumptions in both sides' rationales and concepts.

Threat Assessment: The Most Promising Item on the Agenda

The desired criteria for stable security structures can best be deduced from Eastern and Western threat perceptions. Talks on this issue should not be a simple exchange or comparison of intelligence data; rather, the validity or invalidity of military rationales concerning military capability has to be proved critically. There seems to be enough evidence to support the assumption that these rationales are often invalid (e.g., the rationale for redundant outmoded weapons in the armies of socialist countries) and could be improved in order to develop military and security precepts.

This is especially true for modern computer-based evaluations of military options, where, it is common knowledge, seemingly minor changes in the logic of order or in the input of primary data produce huge changes in the results. Of no minor importance is the degree of complexity a given model is capable of working on.

But threat assessment is a promising approach, given that it allows discussion of the political logic (or illogic) of threat assumptions in addition to the military logic. Thus in threat assessment the desired connection between military and political issues can be kept alive.

"National Military Doctrines" and Subregional Security Concepts

"National Military Doctrines" in the East

A detailed discussion of subregional security concepts or national military doctrines is beyond the scope of this chapter. However, this issue is bound to arise in any East-West consultations on military and security precepts. One of the most important innovations of the WTO doctrinal declaration of May 29, 1987, was the notion of "national military doctrines" in an authoritative statement.[13] If serious, it could produce major qualitative changes in the European security structure. By offering more leeway for innovative doctrinal developments within the framework of national military and security policy, the elaboration of national military doctrines may open the way for a greater contribution by the non-Soviet members of the WTO to a future non-provocative WTO military posture.

Taking into account and integrating various national security interests based on different geostrategic preconditions, defense policy parameters and sociopolitical necessities—as the Western alliance has done since its creation—is without a doubt a difficult and complicated task. But the more individual interests are taken into consideration, the greater the chance of replacing subordination in the alliance with true integration, and thus enhancing stability.

In this context the most urgent problem is the offensive tendency inherent in the Soviet and WTO military reforms of the last decade: Whereas the main tendency in the 1960s was to equalize and standardize as many of the WTO's efforts as possible, the military reforms of the late 1970s and 1980s undertaken by Marshal Ogarkov displayed a strong inclination toward qualitative improvements and, consequently, differentiation in qualities and tasks. Intensive Soviet and Polish experiments with various air-mobile and air-assault brigades, with different kinds and sizes of armored units and formations, is one example. These developments had the potential of changing the character of the WTO warfighting capability and the tasks of and interrelationships among the various national armies. The tendency to enhance the range, speed and mobility of military actions inevitably left an imprint on the national security situation of the non-Soviet WTO countries and strengthened the importance and self-reliance of the Soviet army.

It is not yet clear how military thinking within the East European states reacted to this development. Eastern Europe has no tradition of discussing the narrower matters of defense policy openly or publicly (the Polish military press being to a certain degree an exception). To what extent the notion of the existence of national military doctrines is indicative of a stronger contribution from the non-Soviet WTO member-states to the overall military doctrine based on their own assessment of the changes in the European military and security environment remains an open question. Nevertheless, it seems useful to mention a few objective conditions that might be taken into consideration in east Central Europe.

The GDR was greatly affected by the INF Treaty (as it had been by INF deployments a decade ago), which enhanced the importance of conventional forces and tactical nuclear weapons. The emphasis on increased readiness within the Soviet army makes a mission-based integration of the National People's Army (NVA) formations in the first echelon a problem of integrated warfare strategy. The same is true of a possible reorientation toward a defensive structure, in which case the role and function of NVA formations may have a different importance than they do under an offensive orientation. The functions of different national components and their structures will also change accordingly if forces in Central Europe are thinned out. Furthermore, the potential importance of the GDR's militia (*Kampfgruppen der Arbeiterklasse*), which up to now has been perceived in the West mainly as reserve forces, will have to be reconsidered if the capability for rapid mobilization grows in importance under a conventional arms control regime of reduced stand-by readiness in Central Europe.

Czechoslovakia's geostrategic situation was characterized by the grave change that took place in 1968 as a result of the Soviet military inter-vention—a change not motivated by Czechoslovakia's national security interests. The continuing presence of five Soviet divisions stationed in Czechoslovakia and their specific deployment was primarily due to the "enhanced internal function of the army"—in other words, to the Brezhnev Doctrine. Strategic considerations were secondary: given the local geography in relation to the deployment of these five divisions, their structure and lines of communication, they represented a potential threat to Austria. Thus the problems posed by these divisions were unusual. The cuts announced in December 1988, particularly the with-drawal of one division from Czechoslovakia, will diminish the invasion capability of the Soviet forces stationed in Czechoslovakia, although not drastically; the cuts will have an even smaller impact on the "enhanced internal function" (intervention capability) of Soviet troops stationed abroad.

Poland's geostrategic situation is characterized, first of all, by its importance as a transit area, creating specific targets and vulnerabilities to specific threats such as deep interdiction. The related threat perceptions contributed to the famous Rapacki Plans, as well as to the Jaruzelski Plan of 1987. Furthermore, Poland's situation is influenced by the importance of its army, which is the second largest in the WTO and the social role which this army plays in Polish society. The Polish army cultivated a very strong tradition of close professional ties to the Soviet army, culminating in the Polish contributions to the development of offensive operational concepts in the late 1970s, thus leaving the development of concepts of non-provocative postures mainly to the civilian analysts. The importance of Poland's role might grow in the future because of a possible change in the WTO's focus from forward-based forces to defensive deployment or rapid redeployment. The more the redeployment problem is at stake, the more Polish interests will be involved. The same is true for the reinforcement problem. Both topics are increasingly important not only for reinforcement by land but also by air.

Tasks assigned to Polish naval and assault forces in the Baltic were given a high priority in the past, but they may become less important if the current offensive orientation is reconsidered. Under these circumstances the restructuring of the Polish air defense could be as important as a change in the ratio of heavy armored formations (which are earmarked for shock armies) to the troops designated for territorial defense.

Hungary claims a specific geostrategic situation: it shares no border with "imperialist" nations or NATO, and faces no direct military threat from the West. Leading Hungarian officials and analysts have therefore maintained that the country is in a prime position to contribute to conventional disarmament, especially through the withdrawal of stationed (i.e., Soviet) forces on its territory. This position is in accordance with the traditional Hungarian policy of putting a low priority on defense and maintaining a high interest in disarmament. However, this tendency has never been translated into specific defense concepts (such as the territorial defense models worked out by Romania, Yugoslavia or by the Central European neutrals, Austria and Switzerland).

National or Subregional Defense Concepts in the Western Alliance—A Specter of Instability?

The first efforts toward closer military cooperation between France and West Germany, not yet integrated into NATO's doctrinal framework, present a certain conceptual challenge. Nevertheless, their immediate condemnation as dangerous by officials and specialists from socialist countries seems to have been motivated more by political concerns than sober military analysis. This reaction, if taken seriously and not as mere propaganda, points to a rather important misunderstanding of the stabilizing effect of close international integration. This stabilizing effect has not yet been adequately taken into account in the threat assessments by the socialist countries. In particular, in making threat assessments the WTO countries fail to consider the extent to which the organizational arrangements within the Western alliance—particularly the high degree of interdependence and the complex structure of alliance decision-making—act as a barrier to the alliance's ability to carry out a surprise attack.

As far as Franco-German military cooperation is concerned, it is obvious that there cannot be anything even resembling a "French shield" and "West German sword" because of the small military potential of both nations relative to that of the WTO and the degree of West German integration in NATO. In particular, this cooperation cannot be seen as an enhancement of the "German threat"—the Federal Republic can have no better watchdog than France.

A detailed discussion of this issue is beyond the scope of this chapter. However, inasmuch as threats and their perceptions are an integral part of military precepts, these problems should also constitute a subject of East-West consultations. Clearly, national interests and security concerns are more highly developed and closely integrated in the West than in the East, and this difference cannot be ignored.

Methodological Challenges and Organizational Approaches

The Upcoming Agenda

Given the historical experience in discussing precepts of security and defense policies, the need for some kind of ordering of the questions and problems is obvious. Three levels of problems can be differentiated: 1) general, abstract problems of the theories of security; 2) practical security-policy problems on the national and international levels; and 3) military-professional problems.

The general, abstract problems of security policy and military strategy are interrelated and are basic for the other levels of problems as well. Typical are the problems of deterrence, war aims and the related general assumptions of threat perceptions. Faulty threat assessments can easily derail the consultations if they do not take into account political phenomena such as the constraints on NATO's structure that hinder the capability for surprise attack. In contrast, war aims inevitably leave their imprint on the development of force structures. Thus, for example, one repeatedly hears in Western discussions that the Soviet experience in World War II—only victory on the enemy's territory ended the war—led to the Soviet emphasis on warfighting and the need to deliver a "decisive crushing blow." Indeed, there is little evidence in Soviet doctrinal thinking on ultimate warfighting purposes based on concepts other than defeat.

Conventional arms control and the related question of military and security precepts cannot be addressed if the concept of nuclear deterrence is ignored. In this area a specific culture of strategic thinking has developed, particularly in the United States, accounting for a rather important share of the work done on strategic thinking. Now, however, a group of experts has appeared in the USSR, whose contribution, for example to the question of minimum nuclear deterrence, seems to be rather ingenious. Conventional stability and the related scenarios can be dealt with only if the rationales of comprehensive nuclear deterrence are dealt with as well. (With this in mind, the Soviet program for total global denuclearization announced in January 1986 is at best a gesture of goodwill.) This issue also belongs to a specific strategic sphere, as does the almost philosophical question of the interrelationship between fire-power and seizure of territory as a criterion for military "offensiveness" or "defensiveness."

A further example of this high level of abstraction is the problem of the obvious trend in East and West toward modernization of weapons technology and the consequent shortened time of action, enhanced interdependence of support subsystems for sophisticated weapons complexes (e.g., all real-time-related weapons complexes), range, yield and interoperability. This trend calls for a new understanding of stability. Soviet theoretical thinking must be given credit for having helped to raise consciousness regarding the significance of this problem for arms control. But theoretical thinking in Western Europe has yet to develop a conceptual framework for arms control purposes.

These few examples show that the qualities of expertise needed for this level are the capability for abstraction and generalization and a high degree of knowledge of international interaction.

The second layer of problems demands primarily skills of a different type: the ability to translate concepts of defense or stability into political arrangements or agreements and to establish an appropriate institutional base and relevant interactions in order to develop interrelated military and security precepts.

The modes of harmonizing hierarchically national security interests with the ones of alliances constitute another kind of problem belonging to this level. Closely related to this are security precepts of special regions, subregions, areas or zones —all of them growing in importance in terms of arms control and disarmament.

A further set of problems in this category is that of the modes of arms control behavior. One example is the role of determining weaknesses in armaments and in anticipated armaments developments that are based mainly on different national political (rather than military) perspectives (e.g., German—and Polish—sensitivity concerning tactical nuclear weapons and force density) but influence the military capability and entice competing parties to misuse arms control to gain one-sided advantages.

A further set of conceptual problems that strongly influences security arrangements, especially in the conventional field, is the relationship between supreme (hegemonic) powers and their smaller allies structurally determined, e.g., by armament monopolies, out-of-area interests and the scope of goals. Thus, for example, the Soviet Union's armament monopoly is no less important in determining the character of alliance doctrines than the geostrategic factor of short reinforcement routes is in determining the WTO's force posture.

The third level of problems related to specific qualities of expertise is the most basic stratum. Without this category criteria for more stable conventional structures cannot be identified, especially if the sophisticated demands of "dynamic stability"—a progressive development of stability—are the goal.

An urgent need exists in arms control, for example, for criteria and categories that allow for more precise measurement of various military threats, instability and the characteristics of military potential creating specific options. The military rarely use their expertise and their knowledge of the art of war to extrapolate clear-cut categories and criteria for anticipated, reasonably reduced threat scenarios that would allow for the reduction of their own armament efforts. The need for this can be exemplified by the problem of a threat emphasizing rapid actions necessary for preemption and surprise, and the enhanced target value of fewer key elements in the case of massive reduction and thinning out of conventional forces in Europe. The related threat scenarios and their underlying criteria and rationales have not yet entered the ongoing arms control debate as a model either of a changed and thus enhanced threat or of a mutually acceptable threat reduced beyond the famous 95 percent of existing NATO levels.

A seemingly very simple, yet actually sophisticated, problem that is unavoidable in the conceptualization of stable security conditions is understanding what degree of military preponderance should be considered dangerous and destabilizing on the tactical, operational and strategic levels. For example, the famous 3:1 ratio allegedly needed by the attacker for a successful offensive clearly means nothing in military reality if it is not related to specifics. Furthermore, historical experience shows that strategic inferiority can go hand in hand with political risk-taking—e.g., Hitler's Germany. Military expertise must be able to extrapolate such relevant criteria; otherwise its threat assessments and related demands are baseless, and so too are the military concepts and doctrines depending on those very criteria.

Only through discussions of the doctrinal rationales for military *options* stemming from military capabilities, potentials and structures will arms control progress from bean-counting to conceptualizing stability. Without complex reconsiderations of options, consultations will be in vain and be mere eyewash.

The Consequence: A Complex Structure for the Consultations on Military and Security Precepts

The levels of problems described above require the search for adequate levels for handling the various facets of military and security precepts. Three well-established levels of expertise ought to be available for dealing with the three strata of problems. The first would be "strategic culture," based on the academic research institutions, which could rely not only on an established national apparatus but also on strong international contacts. The second level would be the political-diplomatic, the relevance of which is obvious. But even in this sphere, interaction between the political and government levels is rather unusual, and the resulting difficulties must be envisaged and planned for. The third level would be the military, where the most important organizational demands point to a need for institutions specially designed to formulate arms-control-related concepts and doctrines.

Merely to activate these three levels, however, would not be enough. They need proper and adequate interaction, and that means a specific organizational setting and management. If either this or the appropriate choice and integration of different levels of expertise is ignored, an adequate solution of the problems will be jeopardized. The same will be true if one of these layers of expertise is allowed to claim primacy over the others.

The effort to elaborate criteria for commonly agreed security structures can also be derailed because of other weaknesses. One such error would be to choose the wrong terms or topics for approaching the task—as was mentioned in the first part of this essay. The experience since the proposal to hold consultations on "doctrine" was tabled suggests that the main problem will be fleshing out such attractive and enticing themes as "defensive defense," "non-provocative postures" and "common security." The actual challenge will be to move from abstract declarations to a mutual understanding of the criteria for what constitutes dangerous, destabilizing capabilities and options—or "threats." Only on the basis of criteria for what is not desired can comparable perceptions and then agreeable non-provocative structures be developed. The challenge is to select the most promising method for moving from the past (mutual deterring threats) and present into the future: precepts for further development of one's own security that take into account security of the other side.

Another way the talks could be derailed is if the handling of this issue were limited to a single, short conference. Such a meeting would result in little more than an exchange of well-known, one-sided arguments. It would not stimulate the ongoing broad political discussion on this subject, and it would be absolutely insufficient to meet the demanding requirements described above. The only sound reason for such an approach would be to stimulate further action to work out a more structured mandate for future consultations.

Rather, it seems that a bottom-to-top process is more promising at the beginning. Such a process would entail a heavy reliance on the preparatory stages at the national level, paralleled by international coordination at various levels of expertise. This would guarantee that the needed expertise would be drawn into the process, which would be refined through cross-checking (e.g., political-diplomatic checking of military concepts and vice versa).

The complexity of this theoretical—and seemingly unrealistic—setting has its origin not in analytical thinking, as many would believe, but in reality itself, as a brief glance at activities in the last year or so alone reveals. Awareness of this issue's complexity and its dependence on political currents and institutions should have made clear that it cannot be "resolved" quickly. Consultations on military and security precepts need to be seen and planned as a long-term process.

Long-term processes require not only specific approaches to organize coordination, but also cooperation—especially where a lack of it has obviously caused damage in the past. This may be the most demanding challenge for keeping the task of cultivating mutual development of security concepts on track in the long run.

Notes

1   Press Release No. 7/87 of the Polish embassy in Bonn. See explanations given at a press conference in Warsaw, May 5, 1987, by Jerzy Nowak, Stefan Staniewski and Wlodzimierz Konarski as reported by Radio Warszawa, May 8, 1988. The texts of both announcements were published in English in *Polish Plan to Decrease Armaments and Increase Confidence in Europe* (Warsaw: Interpress, 1987).

2   "O voennoi doktrine gosudarstv-uchastnikov Varshavskogo dogovora," *Krasnaia zvezda*, May 30, 1987.

3   *Bulletin des Presse und Informationsamts der Bundesregierung* 10 (1986), pp. 68ff.

4   *Voennyi entsiklopedicheskii slovar'*, (Moscow: 1986), p. 240.

5   Mikhail V. Frunze, "Edinaia voennaia doktrina i krasnaia armiia," in *Izbrannye proizvedeniia* (Moscow: 1977), pp. 29–46.

6   See, for example, Mikhail Kirian, "Soviet Military Doctrine," *Soviet Military Review*, No. 6 (1987), pp. 2–3, 6; "Voennye doktriny imperializma," *Krasnaia zvezda*, June 5, 1987, p. 3; "Edinstvo bor'by za predotvrashchenie voiny i gotovnost' 'zashchishchat'' sotsialisticheskie zavoevaniia," *Krasnaia zvezda*, June 18, 1987, p. 2; Manki Ponomarev, "Pod gruzom imperskikh ambitsii," *Krasnaia zvezda*, June 12, 1987, p. 3; V. Markusin, "Dve politiki—dve doktriny," *Krasnaia zvezda*, July 14, 1987, p. 3; Radio Moskau, "Ein Vergleich der Militaerdoktrinen der NATO und des Warschauer Vertrages zeigt, wer mit Gespraechen ueber die Sicherheit das Streben nach Hegemonie zu bemaenteln sucht," in BPA, *Ostinformationen* No. 134, July 20, 1987, pp. 17–18; L. Levadov, "Stavka na agressiiu," *Krasnaia zvezda*, August 4, 1987, p. 2; P. Lusev, "Na strazhe zavoevanii revoliutsii," *Mezhdunarodnaia zhizn'* No. 8, pp. 60–70; Alexei Slobodenko, "The U.S. Military Doctrine: Reliance on Force," *International Affairs* No. 9 (September 1987), pp. 38–46; General A. I. Gribkov, "Doktrina sokhraneniia mira," *Krasnaia zvezda*, September 25, 1987, pp. 2–3; Rear Admiral G. Kostev, "Dve politiki—dve doktriny," *Krasnaia zvezda*, November 11, 1987, p. 3.

7   This was given particular emphasis in the WTO's declaration on doctrine of May 29, 1987, and less stress in the Jaruzelski Plan.

8   A. A. Grechko, *Vooruzhennye sily sovetskogo gosudarstva*, 2nd ed. (Moscow: Voenizdat, 1975), pp. 344ff.

9   Alexei Arbatov, "Voennyie doktriny" (Ch. 11) in *Disarmament and Security:1987 IMEMO Yearbook* (Moscow: Novosti Press Agency Publishing House, 1988), pp. 233–58, esp. p. 235.

10 In the U.S. discussion, perhaps the two best-known positions are those of Raymond L. Garthoff, "New Thinking in Soviet Military Doctrine," *The Washington Quarterly* (Summer 1988) pp. 131–158 (compare this to the subsequent articles in the same journal); and Phillip A. Peterson and Notra Trulock III, "A 'New' Soviet Military Doctrine: Its Origins and Implications," *Strategic Review* (Summer 1988) pp. 9–33. In West Germany the controversy seems to be much more intense. On the political side, doubts were obvious in a series of articles by State Secretary Lothar Ruehl, the most telling of them being "Eine offensive Strategie der Niederwerfung," *Frankfurter Allgemeine Zeitung*, October 16, 1987, p. 12. In the West German research community the "disbelievers" are led by Gerhard Wettig, who has written numerous articles on this theme, including, "Die gegenwaertige Entwicklung der sowjetischen Militaerdoktrin,"

Aussenpolitik (February 1988), pp. 172–185; this article in particular was criticized by Christoph Royen in his book *Osteuropa: Reformen und Wandel* (Baden-Baden: Nomos, 1988), in which he emphasized the importance of reevaluating the sources. The most intriguing contradictions are showing up in two publications of the same institution, the BIOST in Cologne: Gebhard Weiss, "Suffizienz als sicherheitspolitische Leitvorstellung," *Berichte des Bundesinstituts fuer ostwissenschaftliche und internationale Studien* 29 (1988); and Anton Krakau, "'Kriegsverhinderung' und 'Verteidigung' in der militaerischen Doktrin und Strategie der UdSSR," *Berichte des Bundesinstituts fuer ostwissenschaftliche und internationale Studien* 30 (1988).

11 Consequently, in this particular case, Western evaluations were conflicting and inconsistent. Philip Karber, a distinguished American expert on Soviet military affairs, in a remarkably cautious examination of Gorbachev's announcement, stated that "He is doing it exactly the way we would have wanted him to do it!" (*The New York Times*, January 26, 1989). In contrast, NATO officials denounced the move as a "PR ploy" (*International Herald Tribune*, January 25, 1989). The latter understanding does not take into consideration that a "PR ploy" would necessarily have been aimed at precisely that orthodox inflexibility to adapt Western security policy to the foreseeable changes showing up in such statements.

12 The preponderance of WTO conventional forces is of particular concern in the West German threat assessment. See, for example, Lothar Ruehl, "Seit Lenin und Trotzky heisst die Sowjet-Strategie Angriff und Sieg," *Die Welt*, February 3, 1988, p. 8.

13 Notions of "national military doctrines" have appeared in the open military literature from time to time, showing no specifics. In Poland in the mid-1950s and in Czechoslovakia in 1968 steps were undertaken to achieve more responsibility or an independent assessment of national security interests. In the 1960s and 1970s the Polish army established its own doctrine concerning the territorial army and then influenced heavily the promotion of offensive concepts in the alliance. The Hungarian doctrinal thinking remained rudimentary—except a few cases of mentioning specific national-geostrategic defense problems and a rather general treatment of the national defense doctrine in the framework of the WTO. The NVA, being totally integrated into the WTO structure was for a long time not in a position to promote sovereign concepts, but developed a few national peculiarities in tactical and operational terms. Only after disarmament considerations approached the sphere of geostrategic and theater-related postures were the GDR's elites able to introduce considerations and initiatives of their own.

V

PART TWO

On the Military Doctrines of the Warsaw Pact and NATO

Andrei A. Kokoshin, USSR

The comparison of military doctrines and concepts and the process of giving them a purely defensive character could play a most important role in arms control and disarmament and in the stregthening of strategic stability. This would clearly contribute to the elimination of the mutual suspicion and mistrust that has built up over the years. An open and substantive discussion of military doctrines and concepts would also facilitate mutually agreed bans on the most dangerous dogmas of military thinking. The evolution of military-doctrinal views in a clearly defensive direction, together with reductions and corresponding force restructuring of Soviet and U.S., WTO and NATO forces (by composition, as well as deployment), would create the necessary conjunction of conditions that could radically lower political-military tension in Europe and in the world at large.

One of the key issues here is the analysis of the dialectic of development of the means of offense and defense in both the nuclear and the conventional spheres. Changes in the correlation of offense and defense in turn have exercised a highly significant impact on states' policies, and on the evaluations and conclusions of governmental and political figures as well as the military high command on the character and scale of the use of armed force.

In World War I the large-scale use of heavy automatic weapons,[1] artillery and engineering methods dominated the forms and means of military conflicts and showed that the defense was stronger than the offense. Time and again, large-scale strategic offensive operations failed in the military theaters of both Western and Eastern Europe. Troop actions on the whole assumed a positional-defense character.[2]

In the interwar period a number of countries actively sought ways to overcome the situation that had arisen in World War I. At one point—from the late 1920s until the early 1930s—a relatively stable balance between offense and defense developed.

In the following years military thinking in many countries began to recognize the possibility of overcoming the superiority of the defense over the offense. This had an enormous impact on the development of military doctrine and on strategic and operational thinking in many countries.

The widespread use in World War II of means of breakthrough and exploitation of success (tanks, artillery, aviation, submarines and aircraft carriers) from the very outset added an active offensive character to military operations on land, air and sea. Tactical breakthroughs immediately developed into operational ones. Large-scale mobile units, especially tank groups and tank armies, played a decisive role in this respect.[3]

If we look at history, it turns out that the Franco-Prussian War overwhelmingly demonstrates the superiority of the offense over the defense, while the Crimean War demonstrates just the opposite. (The latter was also the first historical example of a positional war). If we go back even further in history, it then becomes clear that the Napoleonic wars were primarily a triumph of an offensive, active strategy. They were conducted with decisive objectives and were oriented toward the annihilation of the opponent's armed forces and large territorial acquisitions. In contrast, the Seven Years' War showed no clear superiority of offense over defense, and in many cases the defense was generally superior to the offense and there were no decisive objectives like those characterizing the Napoleonic wars.

World War I presented several examples of successful strategic operations—the offensive on the Russian southwest front in July-August 1916 (Brusilov's breakthrough), as well as the series of allied offensives on the Western front in 1918 (the Marne victory and the Amiens and St. Mihiel operations).

World War II, in turn, showed that a previously prepared defense-in-depth, which takes into account the thinking of an adversary—even one prepared for the offensive—can be highly successful and lead to the defeat of the most powerful offensive combinations. Such was the lesson of the battle of Kursk, one of the major battles of World War II.[4]

In spite of the generally defensive character of Soviet military doctrine, the necessity and possibilities for strategic defense on the eve of the Nazi invasion in 1941 were clearly underestimated. The possibility of conducting a defensive campaign was admitted only on the operational and tactical levels.

In the beginning of the war strategic defense was organized, as a rule, in the course of the active offensive operations of the enemy in conditions of incomplete defensive deployments and in the absence of defensive lines prepared well in advance. By the summer of 1942 the failure of defensive operations in the Voronezh sector and in the Donbass led to a breakthrough on the southern flank of the strategic front. All of these fundamental errors led to heavy defeats for the Red Army, to enormous human losses and the loss of large amounts of territory.

The sources for these miscalculations in the development of the Red Army's prewar doctrine had emerged at least by the late 1920s, when, under the guise of criticism, an entire school of military and military-political thinking associated primarily with the name of Professor Aleksandr A. Svechin was effectively crushed and silenced. His works were not free of shortcomings. However, on the basis of a multifaceted analysis of the relationship between means of attack and defense, of the offensive and the defensive, of profound historical tendencies and the history of warfare—including World War I and its results—they contained exceptionally important prophetic conclusions as to how a second world war might come about, about the nature of the threat to the USSR's western borders and so on.[5]

The allies also failed to exploit the opportunities for strategic defense on the western front in May 1940. The armed forces of the United Kingdom, France, Belgium and the Netherlands suffered a devastating defeat due in large measure to tragic errors in the deployment of the allied armies.

Considering the cyclical development of offense-dominance and defense-dominance in Europe, including during World War II, there is one stable, long-term tendency which cannot be ignored, and which runs through all of these phases of development: the consistent increase in the destructive capabilities of weapons used, the intensity of military operations, and the depth of theaters of operations and square territory involved in military operations. There has also been an increase in the demand for resources needed to conduct war, in the level of mobilization, and in the military-economic strain that every state experiences in time of war.

The appearance of nuclear weapons, in spite of the revolution they have produced in military affairs, has not led to a renunciation of the development of general-purpose and conventional forces. Moreover, many specialists emphasize the necessity of possessing even in peacetime extensive and concentrated general-purpose forces, perhaps even in larger numbers than were demanded before the appearance of nuclear weapons. This is based on the assumption that in the event of the use of weapons of mass destruction, communications and the system for mobilizing reserves would inevitably be destroyed. Consequently, it would be exceptionally difficult to quickly make up the losses exacted by a U.S. nuclear strike. From this the conclusion is drawn that it is necessary to field in peacetime, on a consistent basis, very large general-purpose forces. As a result, in time of peace and in Europe alone, two large-scale groupings of troops confront each other in the guise of NATO and the WTO. This premise encourages a high level of military confrontation as well as a conventional arms race.

Considering the development of the means of offense and defense in the area of conventional and general-purpose forces after World War II, one can observe a very important factor. Even during the course of the war, and later in the postwar period, the means of defense were being created at an accelerated pace—anti-tank artillery, anti-tank mines, various missile systems, anti-tank guided missiles (ATGMs), fighter aircraft, anti-ship missiles and so on. New possibilities for using such weapons were demonstrated on various occasions in the local wars of the 1970s and 1980s.

According to the views of many experts, the sharply increased capabilities of infantry and the uninterrupted development of mobile ATGMs lead to the conclusion that tanks and fighter-bombers, dominant on the battlefield since 1940, have lost their primacy as a decisive tactical element. Today it is necessary to add helicopters armed with ATGMs as well as the opponent's anti-ATGM forces to tanks and fighter-bombers.[6]

Thus the newly arisen correlation of offense and defense must be taken fully into account in the elaboration of practical approaches to the limitation and reduction of armed forces and conventional arms, in the elaboration of new elements of military doctrines, and in strategic and operational concepts.

Approaches to conventional arms control and reduction need to take account of the actual developmental dynamics of new weapons, particularly highly accurate, long-range weapons and the latest methods of radioelectronic combat. Their appearance is in large part capable of transforming the traditional axioms of military art, but not entirely in the direction demanded by "new thinking" on international security, which is based on the recognition that security, like strategic stability, can only be mutual. High-accuracy, long-range weapons, used on a large scale against conventional armed forces and weapons, would add an additional element of instability. Their deployment will stimulate the development of new weapons and types of armed combat and will make the arms race even more expensive.

In a number of indices, strategic stability on the conventional level should be radically distinguished from the situation prevailing on the nuclear level. The basis of stability in the latter instance is the threat of retaliation, particularly the infliction of unacceptable damage in a retaliatory strike. The main element in the field of strategic stability in conventional forces is the creation of a network of conditions that would insure the superiority of one side's defense (both strategic and operational) over the other side's offense, and vice versa.

As we develop the issue of providing for a stable military-strategic balance and define the limits of the reasonable sufficiency of military capabilities, it should be kept in mind that the search for alternative military concepts and force structures that would yield a clearly defensive nature has a long tradition in Europe.

In arguing that defense is the stronger form of warfare, Clausewitz made the following exceptionally important observation from the viewpoint of developing, on a mutual basis, approaches to strengthening strategic stability and to creating conditions for preventing a war involving general-purpose forces and conventional weapons: "Absolute defense is in total contradiction to the concept of warfare. . . ."[7] It follows from this view that with the two sides' shift to purely defensive force structures, concepts and strategic and operational forms, the physical possibility of waging any large-scale war could disappear. Here it is once again necessary to stress that this applies only to general-purpose forces and conventional weapons and does not extend to the strategic nuclear sphere.

The foundations of Soviet military doctrine were laid in the 1920s, in the first instance through the efforts of the representative of the Revolutionary Military Council and People's Commissariat for Defense of Soviet Russia Mikhail V. Frunze. In particular, he defined the two major groups of questions which encompass military doctrine: the technical and the political. In the technical category, Frunze included the organizational basis for building the Red Army, the nature of preparing troops for war and methods of broadening combat tasks. In the political category lay questions of the dependence of the technical side of building the armed forces on the general state order, which defines the social environment in which military work should be perfected as well as the very nature of the military tasks to be solved. On this basis, Frunze gave the following definition of a "unified military doctrine":

> A "unified military doctrine" is the teaching, accepted in the army of a given state, that establishes the nature of the development of the country's armed forces, the methods for the military preparation of the troops and their leadership on the basis of the views prevailing in the state on the character of key military problems and ways of resolving them, which derive from the class nature of the state and define the level of development of the country's productive forces.[8]

Later, the question of the nature and content of military doctrine, of its incorporation of political and military (military-technical) elements was developed in detail by Soviet military theorists and commanders.

Marshal Nikolai V. Ogarkov provided an extensive definition of military doctrine. According to Ogarkov, military doctrine as understood today is the accepted system of views in a given state at a given time on the goals and nature of a possible future war, on the country's and armed forces' preparation for it and on the capabilities for its conduct. Military doctrine usually defines: 1) how probable a future war is and who the opponent will be; 2) what form the war might take; 3) what aims and tasks might be given to the armed forces in anticipation of such a war; and 4) what kinds of armed forces are needed to attain these goals.

It appears that there is no direct analogue to the Soviet and WTO understanding of the "unified military doctrine" in the United States and NATO. The term "doctrine" is often used in the United States for strategic operational or operational-tactical concepts without reference to the political side of the issue.[9]

In solving its practical challenges, military strategy, as the highest form of military art, is to be fully guided by the fundamental political directives of military doctrine; in turn, the main postulates of military strategy, considering the developing views and new tendencies in military affairs, should be used for refining doctrinal views and provisions. That is, strategy and operational methods should be fully adequate for military doctrine, in its political as well as in its military-technical aspects. The defensive character of doctrine, focused on its political aspect, should dictate a corresponding character in strategy and operational methods.

The analysis of a series of specific historical situations which I have undertaken demonstrates that in the real world such a correspondence is incomplete or absent altogether. Strategic thinking can begin to develop relatively independently of political thinking, but operational thinking must begin from strategic concepts. The Soviet military theorist Aleksandr A. Svechin turned his attention to this dichotomy in the 1920s.

With the advent of nuclear weapons we have seen an increasingly greater politicization of many traditionally "military" issues. The U.S.-Soviet strategic arms limitations talks, which culminated in the SALT I and SALT II agreements, clearly facilitated this trend. The scale of the politicization of military affairs widened in the 1980s, due to the negotiations on nuclear and space weapons and the signing of the INF Treaty. This tendency receives further impulse from the growing attention of political leaders, scholars and public opinion to the problem of reducing armed forces and conventional arms in Europe from the Atlantic to the Urals.

In this light, the content of military doctrine may be divided into its constituent political and military (military-technical) aspects. Among the basic military-political doctrinal issues in this area, we should include:

–views regarding the possibility of victory in one or another form of war;
–the issue of the conditions for using nuclear weapons (no first use); and
–views on the idea of a limited nuclear war.

These issues may be considered on the basis of official political and military documents (including military directives), as well as publications of authoritative military officials and civilian experts working in the military-political area. All three of these themes are of great importance for the evolution of major elements of political-military thinking, military doctrines (and their equivalents), in relation to both strategic nuclear forces and to general-purpose forces.

The road to understanding the realities of the nuclear age was not an easy one for either side. Ogarkov, for instance, looking at this issue from the military point of view, writes that in the 1950s and 1960s, when there were relatively few nuclear weapons, they were only considered a means of providing the possibility of qualitatively higher firepower for troops. In a variety of ways nuclear weapons were adapted to the prevailing forms and methods of conducting military operations, in the first instance for solving strategic tasks. In the 1970s and 1980s, however, the rapid quantitative growth of nuclear weapons of various destructive powers and the development of multiple, long-range and highly accurate delivery vehicles and their widespread introduction into the armed forces (including the navy) "led to a radical reevaluation of the role of these weapons, to a break with previous views on their role and significance in war, their use on the battlefield and even on *the possibility of their use at all in war*"[10] (emphasis added).

It is noteworthy that at the outset of the 1980s, during a period of significant worsening of U.S.-Soviet relations and the international atmosphere, both the Soviet political and military leaderships issued a whole series of declarations on the impossibility of victory in a nuclear war. Thus, in June 1982 Former Defense Minister Dmitrii Ustinov wrote that the understanding of the impossibility of gaining the upper hand in a nuclear war had reached the point where the USSR "is not counting on victory in a nuclear war."[11]

"In contemporary conditions," Soviet Defense Minister General Dmitrii Yazov emphasized in a July 1987 *Pravda* article, "when the accumulation of enormous arsenals of nuclear weapons threaten the fate of mankind itself, nuclear war cannot be a means for achieving political objectives."[12]

At the same time, right up to the mid-1980s, the word "victory" figured in the works of Soviet military commanders; it was applied to military actions, without a clarification of their scale and character. Usually, such statements bear a kind of ritualistic nature, as they were above all aimed at "reinforcing the lofty moral spirit" of the troops. In this respect the fact that the concept of "victory" (a key concept in the military-political sphere) may be applied not only on a strategic but also on an operational and tactical scale, i.e., on levels which cannot signify victory in war as a whole, was often overlooked.

A similar formula appeared in the report of President Reagan, "U.S. National Security Strategy," published on January 28, 1987. This report in particular noted that

The United States, in cooperation with its allies, must seek to deter any aggression that could threaten that security and, should deterrence fail, must be prepared to repel or defeat any military attack and end the conflict on terms favorable to the United States, its interests and its allies.

The exact same phrasing is contained in Reagan's 1988 address as well.[13]

In the view of the USSR and its allies, this appears as a camouflaged call for the attainment of military superiority over the USSR, for preserving the option of victory in war by practically any means.

Conditions for the Use of Nuclear Weapons

In the summer of 1982 the USSR made a number of declarations to the effect that it assumed a strict obligation not to use nuclear weapons first. These declarations are directly related to the understanding that there cannot be a victor in a nuclear war.[14] Ustinov observed that the USSR "soberly considers as adventuristic the Pentagon's thinking, as well as the state of military preparedness and the potentials of U.S. strategic offensive forces." He also emphasized that,

> if the aggressor uses nuclear weapons first, he will cause our people incalculable suffering. However, the aggressor should know that an advantage from the preemptive use of nuclear weapons will not lead him to victory. Having committed this crime against humanity, he will not obtain tangible gains. With the current state of reconnaissance systems, the military preparedness of the USSR's strategic nuclear forces will not permit a disarming strike by the United States against the socialist countries. The aggressor will not escape from a crushing retaliatory strike. He who devises a "flawless prescription" for conducting a victorious nuclear war, calculating, as it were, to "decapitate" the opponent through one knockout blow, pronounces sentence upon himself.[15]

Previously, the USSR had expressed its willingness not to use nuclear weapons against those states which refuse to produce or acquire such weapons and do not have them on their territory. After the assumption of this obligation, the principle of no first use was applied to all states, without exception.

The Soviet commitment to no first use has not had merely a politically and psychologically stabilizing effect. As Defense Minister Ustinov explained,

> This means that now in the military training of the Armed Forces all the more attention will be given to the tasks of preventing a military

conflict from becoming a nuclear one; these tasks in all of their multifaceted aspects will become a central part of our military activities .... This requires even stricter measures in training troops and officers, in the determination of available weapons, in the organization of even tighter control to rule out the unauthorized release of nuclear weapons, from tactical to strategic.[16]

The United States, as well as its NATO allies France and the United Kingdom, rejects the strict and straightforward obligation not to use nuclear weapons first. The possibility of using nuclear weapons first is laid out in official NATO strategy. It is justified by the putative superiority of the WTO in conventional forces and equipment. As many Soviet military specialists have observed, the WTO does not have sufficient grounds to believe NATO's assurances that it would use nuclear weapons in Europe only "in case of an aggression by the WTO," i.e., only in the second phase of the development of an armed conflict, when NATO's "non-nuclear defensive" forces would be crushed.[17]

The fact that the United States and NATO have kept the principle of first use in their arsenal for some decades now must necessarily have had an impact on Soviet and WTO military thinking. It has been viewed, and continues to be viewed, by many military experts in the USSR and in other European socialist states as a threat of the surprise tactical-operational and tactical use of nuclear weapons in Europe for the achievement in the shortest possible time of a decisive imbalance over the WTO in general-purpose forces with the goal of executing successful strategic offensive operations. The threat of the first use of nuclear weapons in the theater of war in conditions of a U.S. advantage in tactical nuclear weapons spurred the development of ideas aimed at rapidly shifting military activities to NATO territory in order to remove its forces from the threat these weapons posed.

The adoption by the United States, France and the United Kingdom of no first use (after the USSR and the People's Republic of China) would permit the beginning of a serious dialogue on the adoption of mutually agreed measures aimed at reinforcing this obligation to the maximum extent by organizational and material measures.

On Attitudes Toward the Idea of "Limited" Nuclear War

For several decades, especially in the early 1980s, certain political, military and industrial-finance circles in the United States stimulated the elaboration and adoption of various types of concepts and plans for a "limited" nuclear war. Special emphasis has been given to the possibility of fighting a "limited" nuclear war based on an exchange of strikes only in the theater of military operations, so as to avoid a retaliatory strike on U.S. territory.

The elaboration of theories, concepts and operational plans for a "limited" nuclear war and the corresponding means of fighting it have been based by U.S. politicians, military leaders and theorists on the need to make "deterrence by means of intimidation more credible." The central element in enhancing the credibility of deterrence is seen as demonstrating the capability and readiness to strike in the first instance military targets. This is motivated by the recognition that basing deterrence only on the threat of a massive strike (i.e., against cities and industrial facilities) would be incredible and exceptionally dangerous, insofar as the launching of such a strike would be an act of suicide. Therefore, the U.S. elaboration of "limited" nuclear war maintains the need for intermediate options and means for using nuclear weapons, including strategic weapons, on the lowest levels of escalation.

One should immediately note that there is also a reverse dependence as far the relationship between new weapons and new concepts is concerned. That is, as much in postwar U.S. history bears witness, military concepts in significant measure have been developed to justify the deployment of new weapons systems at exactly the moment when the previous cycle of weapons development was coming to a close.

Even if we accept the argument that the development of the theory and means for waging a "limited" nuclear war are aimed only at "increasing the credibility of deterrence," in and of themselves developments in this direction clearly lead to an increasingly less stable military-strategic balance. They make all the more vulnerable 1) governmental and military command posts, and 2) a significant fraction of strategic nuclear forces, and they decrease, at least hypothetically, the invulnerability, reliability and credibility of the means of retaliation and the organizational structure for their use.

Soviet political thinking and military doctrine rejects the very idea of "limited" nuclear war. As former Chief of the General Staff Sergei F. Akhromeev observed:

In contemporary conditions, with the presence on both sides of many thousands of nuclear warheads, a limited war is impossible. If nuclear war breaks out, it will inevitably assume a general character, with all of the resulting consequences. The theory of "limited" nuclear war proceeds from a false understanding of the essence of the matter and from the effort to make the very idea of nuclear war acceptable for public opinion, to convince people that a nuclear conflict can be waged according to previously elaborated "rules."[18]

And as Ogarkov wrote, "the calculations of overseas strategists on the possibility of waging a 'limited' nuclear war can have no basis in contemporary circumstances. This is a kind of utopia: any such 'limited' use of nuclear weapons will inevitably lead to the immediate use of the entire nuclear arsenals of both sides. Such is the bitter logic of war."[19]

The Soviet military command, which rejects in principle the notion of "limited" nuclear war, at the same time underscores that it is compelled to take account of the other side's activity along these lines. In order to guarantee a reliable and credible deterrent on all basic levels of a potential conflict, Soviet military art—including strategy, operational art and tactics—in turn considers the presence of nuclear weapons as deterring the other side from using armed force, including especially nuclear weapons. One can find in a whole number of Soviet military publications a consideration of the kind of role that nuclear weapons play in general-purpose forces, i.e., how they can be used on not only a strategic, but also an operational and tactical scale. One can detect here a certain dualism in Soviet military thinking as well.[20]

Recent Developments

The USSR and its allies took an important step toward strengthening strategic stability with the adoption at the May 1987 Berlin meeting of the WTO's Political Consultative Committee of the document "On the Military Doctrine of the WTO States." This document contains a proposal to NATO

> to conduct consultations with the aim of identifying the military doctrines of both alliances, analyzing their nature and jointly evaluating their further evolution; to overcome years of accumulated suspicion and mistrust and achieve a better understanding of each other's intentions; and to insure that military concepts and alliance doctrines are based on a defensive orientation.[21]

This document, as well as a number of subsequent declarations by governmental and political officials and WTO military commanders, creates the basis for the constructive discussion of issues of military doctrines and strategic concepts with the NATO countries.

The chief distinguishing feature of current WTO military doctrine, as with the military doctrines of each of its constituent states, is, according to the declaration of Soviet Defense Minister Yazov, that it is subordinated to the resolution of those fundamental challenges facing mankind, such as the prevention of war, both nuclear and conventional.[22]

Previously, strategy and military doctrine did not concern themselves to such a degree with the prevention of war. Now, however, essential changes and additions have been introduced into the very essence of "military doctrine."

Soviet and WTO military doctrine is aimed at providing for sufficiency in defense in accordance with the principle of reasonable (defense) sufficiency of the military capabilities of states advanced at the 27th Party Congress. The WTO states, proceeding from the principle of sufficiency, propose to mutually reduce military capabilities to such a level that neither side, while remaining able to defend itself, would be capable of launching offensive operations. In Yazov's works, the concept of sufficiency, together with the defensive orientation of military doctrine, entails parity and equal security; changes in the nature of military activities and the structure of military forces, including their deployment; as well as the mandatory reduction (and verification) of arms and armed forces.[23] One may compare this new interpretation of the main orientation of Soviet and WTO military doctrine with the classical definitions of Frunze and Ogarkov.

According to Yazov, sufficiency in strategic nuclear forces is defined today by the capability to exclude a retaliation-free nuclear attack on the USSR in any, even the most unfavorable, circumstances. "For conventional weapons, sufficiency presumes a minimal necessary number and quality of armed forces and arms capable of reliably defending the country."[24]

The current Soviet military leadership has been assigned the task of rapidly developing the priority directions of military thinking, above all "new concepts of military art in conjunction with the defensive nature of our military doctrine."[25] As noted above, a most important issue in the context of strengthening strategic stability is the establishment of complete correspondence between the political and military (military-technical) aspects of military doctrine.

The postulates of WTO military doctrine are an authoritative guide for the theory and practice of developing the Soviet Armed Forces, as well as the allied armies, including the issues of planning for the defensive, training of leadership and troops, development of the conceptual postulates of military art and, in particular, the choice of means for waging war in the event that war occurs. As Deputy Chief of the Soviet General Staff Colonel-General Makhmut A. Gareev noted in his statement of June 22, 1987, the chief means of action for the Soviet Armed Forces in repelling aggression will not be offensive but defensive operations and battlefield actions. In this way, complete accord is being established between the political and military-technical aspects of Soviet and WTO military doctrine; they are closely interrelated and assume a consistently defensive character as far as both the goals and means of solving defensive challenges are concerned.[26] "Our country," Chief of Administration of the General Staff Nikolai F. Chervov has declared, "is in favor of limiting its military capabilities to the bounds of reasonable sufficiency. By this we mean that the armed forces should, by their very structure, be intended to conduct only defensive operations."[27] The thesis that from now on the main lines of action for the Soviet armed forces will be defensive operations and tactics is one of the most important changes in Soviet military doctrine, not only in the postwar period but since the 1920s.

The last very important postulate of the military-technical aspect of current Soviet and WTO military doctrines is the conceptual response to the issue often raised in the West about the offensive nature of Soviet military strategy.

For the sake of comparison, one could look at what was said in this respect in the Soviet *Military Encyclopedic Dictionary*: "The strategic offensive is the main kind of action of armed forces used to achieve strategic goals."[28]

There are certainly several ways in which this new operational-strategic orientation of the Soviet and WTO military doctrine could be implemented. One option is the adaptation of the "Battle of Kursk model" (summer of 1943 in central Russia), with emphasis on defensive operations in the first phase and on a strong strategic-scale counteroffensive with "decisive goals" in the second phase. Another option is the use of the "Khalkin-Gol model" (summer 1939 in Mongolia), with counterattack capabilities only for restoring the *status quo ante bellum* without crossing the border.[29] Concepts similar to the second model are now becoming increasingly prominent among Soviet and WTO defense analysts.

Of course, a great deal of work needs to be done in order to realize the above changes in strategic directives in terms of the nature of the combat and operational training of troops, their deployment, structure and composition. A number of measures could be adopted here on a unilateral basis, while others require mutual agreement between the WTO and NATO.

A substantial unilateral step on the side of the USSR and the WTO according to the new military doctrine and the principle of reasonable sufficiency was announced by Soviet General Secretary Mikhail Gorbachev in his speech to the UN General Assembly on December 7, 1988. This step includes not only cuts of 500,000 Soviet troops, 10,000 tanks and 800 aircraft in Europe, but the restructuring of the remaining forces in a way that will give them a definitely defensive character.

If we consider the interrelationship between the political and military-technical (military) components of the U.S. and NATO equivalent of military doctrine, we can observe the following. The WTO countries have considerable grounds for adopting a negative attitude toward NATO's strategic-operational concept, Follow-on Forces Attack (FOFA), a close cousin to the openly offensive, destabilizing U.S. operational (in the opinion of many Soviet specialists, strategic-operational) concept AirLand Battle, officially adopted by the United States in 1982. With the adoption of the concept of FOFA in NATO strategy, the issue is no longer one of defending intermediate lines up to the Rhine, but of launching large-scale strikes in depth against the territory of WTO countries.

Current U.S. naval strategy also bears a clearly aggressive and dangerous (in the final analysis, dangerous for both sides) nature. This strategy, linked with the names of former U.S. Chief of Naval Operations Admiral James Watkins and former Navy Secretary John Lehman, calls for U.S. naval forces to inflict preemptive strikes against the opponent's fleet, shore installations and strategic submarines even during the non-nuclear phase of a conflict, and not anywhere in general but directly in NATO's zone of responsibility.

Such U.S. and NATO strategic and operational concepts are incompatible with declarations of the defensive nature of NATO's military doctrine, which are contained in its political side as formulated above all in the 1967 Harmel Report on "The Future Tasks of the Alliance." According to the report, "The Atlantic alliance has two main functions. *First*, to maintain adequate military strength and political cohesion so as to deter aggression and defend the territory of alliance members in case of aggression. . . ." The second NATO function in the Harmel Report is the search for progress toward more stable relations, capable of solving fundamental political problems. Military security and detente do not contradict, but mutually reinforce each other.[30]

The postulates of the Harmel Report are contained in many subsequent NATO documents, including the declaration of the heads of state and government participating in the session of the NATO Council in Brussels March 2–3, 1988, in the section "Arms and Principles of the Alliance." This declaration contains no clear-cut military-doctrinal clauses analogous to the Berlin Declaration of the WTO's Political Consultative Committee, "On the Military Doctrine of the WTO States." Currently, NATO leaders have not been able to reach consensus on these issues. Therefore, this NATO document contains only individual elements which, to a certain extent, could be considered equivalent to the political aspect of NATO military doctrine. The document reflects the position of those who support the preservation of the existing nature of WTO-NATO political-military relations; it also contains, if only in muted form, the traditional accusations of the NATO leadership against the USSR and its allies about the scale and nature of WTO military activities. At the same time the declaration recognizes that "arms control is an intrinsic part of our security policy," as well as the need "to provide for security and stability at lower levels of arms."

The adaptation of U.S. and NATO strategic and operational concepts to the numerous U.S. and NATO statements about the defensive orientation of their activity in the political-military spheres, to the postulates of the political aspect of the "flexible response" strategy, would permit an advance in the level of trust and a strengthening of mutual security and strategic stability.

The growth of interdependence among states—especially in the military-strategic sphere, due to the nuclear factor—demands a qualitatively new attitude toward military doctrines and concepts, their own as well as those of the other side. In the pre-nuclear era, the adoption by this or that state of unrealistic plans for waging war was in significant measure advantageous to its opponent. But today the situation is entirely different. A state leadership that adopts military concepts without taking due account of the actual nature of war, and which believes in the "manageability" or "limited nature" of a nuclear or even conventional conflict, would, in the case of war, bring upon its country and people utter catastrophe; it is even capable of condemning the human race to extinction.

An open consideration of both sides' military doctrines and concepts, the elaboration of a general approach to the issue of their future directions of development, is an extremely difficult and in many respects unprecedented enterprise. But the nature of the threat facing Europe and all of civilization in the event of war is also unprecedented.

The successful solution of the problem of preventing surprise attack, of adjusting offensive operations, will require an evaluation of the total military capacities of all sides as far as offensive and defensive tasks are concerned. By a number of criteria this demands more complex calculations, especially research including "hard" and "semi-hard" computer models, rather than a quantitative comparison of opposing forces in the traditional sense—by means of counting divisions, tanks, artillery, aircraft, missile-launchers and so on.

The conditions for verifying agreements today vastly surpass those of 30 or 40 years ago. Already, this very fact is borne out by the possibilities for establishing stability in a non-nuclear world, for raising the stability of the strategic-military balance on various levels of reduced nuclear arsenals. Strategic stability at lower levels of military confrontation can be achieved by the creation on each side of clearly defensive groupings, structures and kinds of equipment, which would not be utilized for offensive, surprise-attack operations. The most destabilizing types of weapons should be limited and banned.

Both sides' entire force structure and capabilities, as well as their reconnaissance, battle management and communications systems, should be of such a character that, in the event of armed conflict, they would not only preclude escalation but provide the political and military leaderships with adequate information at any moment on the course of the conflict in order to manage it and end it at the earliest possible stage.

One of the main principles in the creation of an essentially new strategic-military balance in general-purpose and conventional forces may be put as follows: WTO defensive capabilities should decisively exceed NATO's offensive capabilities, while NATO's defensive capabilities should decisively exceed WTO offensive capabilities, and at the lowest possible levels of military confrontation.

Notes

1   Machine guns sharply increased the capabilities of the defense, which became obvious toward the middle of World War I. The appearance toward the end of the war on the Western front of light, hand-held machine guns markedly strengthened the hand of offensive infantry. The further development of these weapons dramatically reinforced this tendency by the beginning of World War II.

2   See Nikolai V. Ogarkov, *Istoriia uchit bditel'nosti* [History Teaches Vigilance] (Moscow: Voenizdat, 1985), pp. 48–49.

3   See A. Radzievskii, *Tankovyi udar* [Tank Strike] (Moscow: Voenizdat, 1977); M. Katukov, *Na ostrie glavnogo udara* [On the Cutting Edge of the Main Strike] (Moscow: Voenizdat, 1976), pp. 242–243; V. Semenov, *Kratkii ocherk razvitiia sovetskogo operativnogo iskusstva* [A Brief Study of the Development of the Soviet Operative Art] (Moscow: Voenizdat, 1979), pp. 199–250.

4   For more detail, see Andrei A. Kokoshin and Valentin V. Larionov, "Kurskaia bitva v svete sovremennoi oboronitel'noi doktriny" [The Battle of Kursk in the Light of Contemporary Defense Doctrine], *Mirovaia ekonomika i mezhdunarodnye otnosheniia (MEMO)* No. 8 (August 1987), pp. 32–40.

5   See Andrei A. Kokoshin, "A. A. Svechin. O voine i politike" [A. A. Svechin. On War and Policy], *Mezhdunarodnaia zhizn'* No. 10 (October 1988), p. 129.

6   V. P. Shipovalov, "Bor'ba s tankami" [Battle with Tanks], *Voenno-istoricheskii zhurnal* No. 9 (September 1986), pp. 77; I. E. Shavrov, *Lokalnye voiny; istoriia i sovremennost'* [Local Wars: History and the Present] (Moscow: 1981), pp. 161, 163.

7   Karl von Clausewitz, *O voine* [On War], Vol. 2, (Moscow: Voenizdat, 1937), p. 5.

8   Mikhail V. Frunze, *Edinaia voennaia doktrina i Krasnaia Armiia* [The Single Military Doctrine and the Red Army], in *Izbrannye proizvedeniia* [Collected Works] (Moscow: Voenizdat, 1957), Vol. 2, p. 8.

9   The difference between the Soviet and U.S. interpretation and use of the term "doctrine" was analyzed, for example, in M. A. Milshtein and A. K. Slobodenko, *O burzhuaznoi voennoi nauke* [On Bourgeois Military Science] (Moscow: Voenizdat, 1961), pp. 160–163.

10 Ogarkov, *Istoriia uchit bditel'nosti*, p. 67.

11 Dmitrii F. Ustinov, *Otvesti ugrozu iadernoi voiny* [To Reject the Threat of Nuclear War] (Moscow: Voenizdat, 1982), p. 2.

12 Dmitrii T. Iazov, "Voennaia doktrina Varshavskogo Dogovora—doktrina zashchity mira i sotsializma" [The Military Doctrine of the Warsaw Pact—the Doctrine of Defense of Peace and Socialism], *Pravda*, July 27, 1987.

13 "National Security Strategy of the United States" (Washington, DC: The White House, January 1987), p. 4.

14 See Ustinov, *Otvesti ugrozu iadernoi voiny*, p. 6.

15 Ibid., p. 11.

16 Ibid., p. 6.

17 See, *Vseob'emliushchee issledovanie, kasaiushcheesia iadernogo oruzhia. Issledovanie I* [Comprehensive Research Related to Nuclear-Weapons. Study I] (New York: United Nations, 1980), p. 219.

18 *Vestnik Akademii Nauk SSSR* No. 9, 1983, p. 48.

19 See *Krasnaia zvezda*, May 9, 1984.

20 A detailed critique of the concept of "limited" nuclear war has been presented in Soviet political-military literature by Alexei G. Arbatov in *Bezopasnost' v iadernyi vek i politika Vashingtona* [Security in the Nuclear Age and the Policy of Washington] (Moscow: Politizdat, 1980), pp. 186–188.

21 *Soveshchanie Politicheskogo konsul'tativnogo komiteta gosudarstv-uchastnikov Varshavskogo Dogovora. Berlin: mai 28–29, 1987. Dokumenty i materialy* [Meeting of the Political Consultative Committee of the Member-States of the Warsaw Pact. Berlin: May 28–29, 1987. Documents and Materials] (Moscow: Politizdat, 1987), p. 11.

22 *Pravda*, July 27, 1987.

23 See *Izvestiia*, March 18, 1988.

24 Dmitrii T. Iazov, "O voennom balanse sil i raketno-iadernom paritete" [On the Military Balance of Forces and Nuclear Missile Parity], *Pravda*, February 8, 1988.

25 Dmitrii T. Iazov, "Kachestvennye parametry oboronnogo stroitel'stva" [Qualitative Parameters of a Defensive Structure], *Krasnaia zvezda*, August 9, 1988.

26 *Vestnik Ministerstva inostrannykh del SSSR* No. 1 (1987) p. 52.

27 Ibid., pp. 56–57.

28 *Voennyi entsiklopedicheskii slovar'* [Military Encyclopedic Dictionary] (Moscow: Voenizdat, 1983), p. 711.

29 See Andrei A. Kokoshin and Valentin V. Larionov, "Protivostoianie sil obshchego naznacheniia v kontekste strategicheskoi stabil'nosti" [The Confrontation of General-purpose Forces in the Context of Strategic Stability], *MEMO* No. 6 (June 1988), pp. 6–8.

30 *Future Tasks of the Alliance. Report of the Council* (Brussels: NATO Information Service, 1978), pp. 67–68.

VI

PART ONE

Approaches to Conventional Arms Reductions

David A. Ochmanek and Edward L. Warner III,*
United States

Introduction

It is widely agreed that the fundamental objectives of the Conventional Forces in Europe (CFE) talks should be to reduce substantially conventional forces in Europe, eliminating in particular glaring imbalances in selected weapons types; to contribute to a durable detente; to allow the participants to direct resources away from military expenditures; and to reduce (or at least not increase) the risk of war.[1] It seems intuitively reasonable that the nations of NATO and the Warsaw Pact should be able to find ways to reduce and disengage the massive military forces that have been deployed in Europe during the past four decades. Yet, as this chapter and others in this volume demonstrate, defining a concrete approach to conventional arms reductions that meets these objectives and proves acceptable to both sides is exceedingly complex. In particular, it is difficult to identify what, if anything, NATO should be prepared to give up in return for the Warsaw Pact's eliminating or reducing its substantial numerical superiority in virtually every category of weapon examined.

This chapter attempts to provide a broad conceptual framework with which to analyze the conventional force balance in Europe. It discusses key elements of a possible conventional arms reduction regime in Europe, examining what types of forces might be reduced, how reductions could

* The views expressed in this essay are solely those of the authors, and do not necessarily represent those of the RAND Corporation or any of its research sponsors.

be implemented, the possible extent of any cuts, and potential reconfigurations of the forces that would remain following reductions.

While the geographic scope of the Vienna talks—"from the Atlantic to the Urals"—encompasses all of Europe, including NATO's northern (Scandinavian) and southern (Mediterranean/Turkish) regions, the primary focus of the negotiations should be on Central Europe, where the largest concentrations of NATO and Warsaw Pact military forces are deployed.

Assessing the Balance

Before proceeding with an examination of the alternative approaches to conventional arms control, it is necessary to describe the numerical balance in somewhat more detail than do the discussions in Chapters 3 and 4.

Static Measures

It is fashionable among defense analysts these days to deride "bean counts"—comparisons of total weapons or combat units deployed by two opposing forces—as inadequate measures of relative combat power. (The cognoscenti among defense analysts refer to such accountings as static measures of the balance. The use of an explicit model to simulate warfare yields dynamic measures.) Obviously, bean counts alone are inadequate, given the important role played by many of the intangible factors mentioned above in determining the outcome of battles. But bean counts are not irrelevant and they are relatively unambiguous: both absolute and relative numbers of combat units and weapons available to opposing forces are major determinants of the outcome of warfare.[2]

Perhaps equally significant, static measures play an important role in the development of perceptions of the political-military balance. The purpose of military forces is not to fight wars, except *in extremis*. Nations deploy military forces above all to deter attack, and secondarily to help ensure that they cannot be coerced by the threat of attack by an adversary. Military forces can also be used to underwrite implicit or explicit coercive threats aimed at altering the behavior of other states. Precisely because dynamic assessments of the military balance are so complex and so rife with uncertainties, a clear-cut degree of Western inferiority as seen in static measures can undermine Western willingness to resist Soviet coercion *regardless of the actual relative combat capabilities of NATO and Warsaw Pact forces.*[3]

For all of these reasons, the numerical balance of forces matters. This balance is unfavorable to NATO more or less across the board. Figures 1 through 4 and Table 1 below show the levels of some selected elements of NATO and Warsaw Pact forces. As Figure 1 shows, when forces available today (early 1989) for combat in Central Europe are compared (that is, forces deployed in the "Central Europe extended" region), Warsaw Pact divisions outnumber NATO's in the central region by a margin of approximately 1.6:1 in peacetime. Under mobilized conditions, when both sides would have approximately two weeks to bring reserve units up to full strength, the divisional balance remains roughly the same (1.7:1).[4]

Also shown are the force balances that would most likely pertain in 1991, assuming that the Soviet Union fully implements the two-year program of unilateral force reductions announced by Soviet General Secretary Mikhail Gorbachev in December 1988.[5] Impressive though these cuts are, they would reduce the disparity between Warsaw Pact and NATO divisions only from 1.6:1 to 1.5:1 in peacetime and from 1.7:1 to 1.6:1 under mobilized conditions.

Individual Warsaw Pact divisions are generally smaller than those of NATO nations. A typical American or West German division, for instance, is comprised of approximately 16,000 troops, whereas a Soviet division is comprised of 11,000–12,000. Despite this difference, the firepower associated with Pact divisions tends to be comparable or, in some cases, superior to that of NATO's larger divisions. This is because NATO divisions allocate more manpower to logistical support activities, such as supply and maintenance, than Warsaw Pact divisions. Thus, military manpower in Central Europe is somewhat more balanced than combat units and firepower.

As Figure 2 shows, larger asymmetries appear to exist in the levels of weapons deployed by the two sides. Today, the Warsaw Pact enjoys numerical superiorities of 2.4:1 in main battle tanks, 3.8:1 in artillery and multiple rocket-launchers, and 1.1:1 in armed helicopters. By 1991, the disparity in tanks might be reduced to 1.8:1 and in artillery to 3.1:1.

Table 1 below shows numbers of combat aircraft deployed in the Central Europe extended region. Overall, the Pact enjoys a superiority of 1.4:1 over NATO in tactical aircraft. When disaggregated into ground-attack and air-to-air aircraft, however, NATO shows a small advantage

Table 1 The Air Balance in Europe

Reduction Area		Warsaw Pact (current)	NATO
Atlantic to the Urals	Ground-attack	2570 (+ 400)[a]	2881 (+1034)[b] (+ 18)[e]
	Fighter-interceptor	2620 (+ 970)[c]	1245 (+ 216)[b]
		5190 (+1370)	4126 (+1268)
Central Europe Extended	Ground-attack	1445 (+ 180)[d] (+ 400)[a]	1655 (+1034)[b] (+ 18)[e]
	Fighter-interceptor	1975 (+ 970)[c]	787 (+ 216)[b]
		3420 (+1550)	2442 (+1268)

SOURCES: International Institute for Strategic Studies, *The Military Balance, 1987–1988* (London: IISS, 1987), and *U.S. Ground Forces and the Conventional Balance in Europe*, Congressional Budget Office, June 1988, pp. 97–98.

[a] Soviet medium bombers of the Smolensk Air Army based in the European USSR.

[b] U.S.-based aircraft earmarked for reinforcement deployment to Europe according to the 1988 CBO study cited above.

[c] Soviet fighter-interceptors of the Air Defense Forces for homeland defense based in the European USSR.

[d] Fencer fighter-bombers of the Vinnitsa air army based in the Kiev military district.

[e] French Mirage-IVP strategic bombers based in France.

of 1.1:1 over the Pact in the former category, while the Pact has a sizable lead of 2.5:1 in the latter.[6] Figures 3 and 4 provide a detailed breakdown of NATO and Warsaw Pact air power in the Central Europe extended region.

Comparing the size of Warsaw Pact and NATO forces ("counting the beans") is not as straightforward a task as one might expect. Many types of weapons defy easy categorization. For example, Soviet Mi-8 Hip helicopters are used primarily for transporting assault troops. Some of them have been armed with missiles and rockets for ground attack. Should they be considered as "attack helicopters" even though they are generally used in roles different from those assigned to smaller, anti-tank helicopters, such as NATO's Cobra and Apache and the Soviet-built Mi-24 Hind?

There are many other examples of such ambiguous cases. Thus, even if the two sides can quickly agree on an overall count of weapons and equipment deployed by both sides, it seems certain that an important (and time-consuming) element of the Vienna talks will be the determination of which weapons to put into which categories. In some areas,

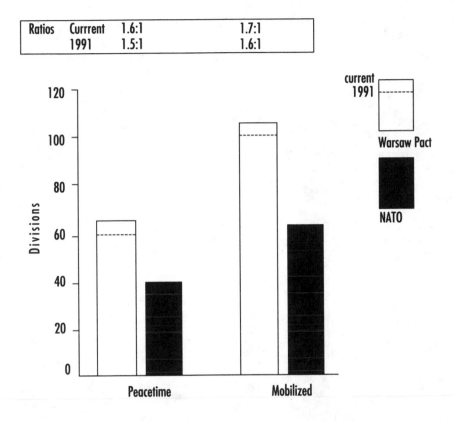

Figure 1 Warsaw Pact and NATO Forces (and Ratios) in Central Europe Extended. Based on information in International Institute for Strategic Studies, *The Military Balance, 1988–1989* (London: IISS, 1988).

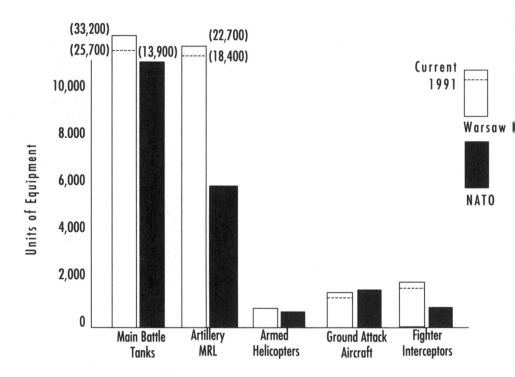

Ratios	Current 1991	2.4:1 1.8:1	3.8:1 3.1:1	1.1:1 1.1:1	1:1.1 1:1.3	2.4:1 2.2:1

Figure 2 Comparative Deployments of Warsaw Pact and NATO Equipment in Central Europe Extended. Based on information in International Institute for Strategic Studies, *The Military Balance, 1988–1989* (London: IISS, 1988).

Table 2 NATO Tactical Aircraft in Central Europe Extended

	Fighter-Bombers		Fighter-Interceptors	
	Aircraft (Location)	#	Aircraft (Location)	#
United States	F-111E/F (UK)	140	F-5E (UK)	19
	A-10A (UK)	108	F-15C/D (FRG/Ne)	96
	F-16C/D (FRG)	96[a]	F-16C/D (FRG)	60[a]
	F-4G (FRG)	36		
Total		380		175
Belgium	F-16A/B	36[a]	F-16A/B	36[a]
	Mirage 5 BA/BD	50		
Total		86		
Canada	CF-18 (FRG)	18[a]	CF-18 (FRG)	18[a]
Denmark	F-16A/B	26[a]	F-16A/B	26[a]
	Draken/F-35	15[a]	Draken/F-35	10
	Draken/RF-35	18		
Total		59		36
France	Mirage IIIE	80[b]	Mirage F-1C	135
	Mirage 5F	30	Mirage IIIE	26
	Jaguar A	127[b]	Mirage 2000B/C	45
	Mirage 2000N	13[b]		
Total		250		206
Federal Republic of Germany	Tornado (FRG/UK)	190	F-4F	71[a]
	F-4F	71[a]		
	Alpha Jet	153		
Total		414		
Netherlands	F-16A/B	86[a]	F-16A/B	61[a]
	NF-5	47		
Total		133		
United Kingdom	Tornado (FRG/UK)	149	Tornado	36
	Harrier (FRG/UK)	51	F-4 (FRG/UK)	114
	Jaguar	63	Hawk	72
	Buccaneer	34		
Total		297		222
TOTAL		1637[c]		825[c]

SOURCE: International Institute for Strategic Studies, *The Military Balance, 1988–1989* (London: IISS, 1988)

[a] Multirole Belgian, Danish, and Dutch F-16s and Danish Draken F-35s are split between the ground-attack and air-defense categories in accordance with mission specialization data from *The Military Balance*. The multirole U.S. F-16s, Canadian CF-18s, and German F-4Fs, whose pilots are trained for both air-to-air and air-to-ground combat, have been split evenly between the two mission areas.

[b] Includes French 15 Mirage-IIIE, 45 Jaguar, and 13 Mirage 2000N fighter-bombers that are identified by IISS as "prestrategic" nuclear delivery systems. Does not include the 18 French Mirage-IVP "strategic" bombers that are configured solely for nuclear delivery.

[c] Includes combat-capable aircraft used in training and conversion units.

Table 3 Warsaw Pact Tactical Aircraft in Central Europe Extended

	Fighter-Bombers		Fighter-Interceptors	
	Aircraft	Number	Aircraft	Number
Soviet Union				
In GDR, Poland	MiG-27	135	MiG-21	90
Czechoslovakia	Su-17	225	MiG-23	315
& Hungary	Su-24	90	MiG-25	45
	Su-25	45	MiG-29	90
Total		495		540
In Legnica Air Army	Su-24	225	n.a.	
In Baltic,	MiG-27	180	MiG-21	90
Belorussian &	Su-17	45	MiG-23	135
Carpathian MDs	Su-25	45	MiG-29	135
Total		270		360
Poland	Su-17	125	MiG-21	360
	Su-7	30	MiG-23	40
	LIM-6	70		
Total		225		400
GDR	MiG-27	25	MiG-21	225
	Su-17	35	MiG-23	45
Total		60		270
Czechoslovakia	MiG-27	40	MiG-21	225
	MiG-21	45	MiG-23	45
	Su-25	40		
	Su-7	45		
Total		170		270
Hungary	n.a.		MiG-21	45
			MiG-23	90
Total				135
TOTAL		1445[a]		1975[b]

SOURCE: International Institute for Strategic Studies, *The Military Balance, 1988–1989* (London: IISS, 1988)

[a] Does not include the 120 Backfire, 120 Blinder, and 160 Badger bombers of the Strategic Air Army headquartered in Smolensk in Belorussia, although many of these bombers are based in the "Central Europe extended" area and would very likely be employed to deliver conventionally armed bombs and missiles against NATO targets in Central Europe during a conventional war. A portion or all of the 180 Fencer fighter-bombers of the air army headquartered at Vinnitsa in the Ukraine might also be deployed forward to carry out conventional bombing missions in Central Europe.

[b] Does not include the 135 fighter-interceptors of the Air Defense Forces based in the Baltic, Belorussian and Carpathian military districts that protect the Soviet homeland.

such a categorization will be crucial to determining both the existing static balance of forces and the scale of reductions necessary to achieve compliance with any negotiated ceilings.

Of course, disparities in the quality and capabilities of individual items of equipment (sustainable rates of fire for artillery pieces, mobility and survivability of armored vehicles, range and accuracy of missiles and so forth) can have significant effects on the balance. Alexander Konovalov, for instance, claims in Chapter 4 of this volume that even in the case of tanks, where the Pact clearly enjoys a massive degree of quantitative superiority, consideration of the weapons' qualitative characteristics radically changes the assessment of the balance of the sides' tank potentials.

It is beyond the scope of this essay to assess such qualitative differences on the NATO-Warsaw Pact balance. However, the conventional wisdom among Western observers today is that the "qualitative edge" NATO forces were said to enjoy in the 1960s and early 1970s is being lost, at least in some areas. The new MiG-29 Fulcrum and Su-27 Flanker fighters, for example, are considered by most Western analysts to be the equal of NATO's best comparable aircraft. And the deployment by Warsaw Pact countries of explosive "reactive armor" on their most capable tanks may have effectively negated many of NATO's anti-tank weapons. On the other hand, NATO is on the threshold of developing and deploying new guided weapons, surveillance systems and information correlation and display capabilities that could greatly enhance the effectiveness of its conventional forces.

The net effect of these and many other qualitative factors on the actual combat capabilities of the two sides' forces is, to say the least, unclear. But it seems unrealistic to expect an arms control agreement to take much account of qualitative disparities in any case. For arms control is meant to place constraints only on the gross dimensions of military forces. Any effort to denominate military capabilities in detailed, qualitative terms and to enforce a balance on them through a treaty is bound to fail if only because the forces of the signatories will constantly evolve. Each new weapon or support system introduced into the forces of the two sides would alter the balance, necessitating negotiated adjustments in the terms of the agreement. Thus, in our view, the CFE talks should seek to identify numerical asymmetries in a few key categories of weapons and to eliminate those asymmetries over time. But NATO must be extremely careful in choosing what it might give up in exchange for reductions in Pact forces. It is necessary to examine the operational strategies of the two alliances in order to understand why this is so.

Operational Strategies in Europe

"Operational strategy" describes the ways in which theater-level military commanders plan to employ the forces available to them. Recent claims of the Warsaw Pact's commitment to a "strictly defensive doctrine" notwithstanding, the Pact's operational strategy has long been offensive in nature. Soviet military writings of the 1970s and early 1980s make it clear that, however war might be initiated, Warsaw Pact commanders intended ultimately to seize the initiative and conduct a *blitzkrieg*-style "decisive offensive" that would allow them to determine the time and place of major thrusts.[7] This approach would permit the Pact to concentrate its forces at narrow sectors of the front to make breakthrough assaults. NATO, meanwhile, has long been compelled for political and geographic reasons to plan for a forward, relatively static defensive strategy. Because NATO cannot plan to cede large portions of the Federal Republic of Germany to Pact forces during an early phase of a war, allied forces must man a "thin blue line" stretched across the front from the Baltic to Austria.[8]

Tanks, infantry fighting vehicles, artillery and attack helicopters have played a central role in the Pact's plans for offensive operations. Armored forces, operating in concert with massive fire support, are to pierce NATO's forward defenses in order to permit the attacker to insert exploitation forces of division size or larger through the resulting gaps. The purpose of these exploitation forces—operational maneuver groups and other second-echelon formations—is to cripple NATO's capability to respond to breakthroughs by driving deep into NATO's rear area to interfere with Western reinforcement activities and command and control capabilities. In so doing, these forces would pave the way for larger units to come into NATO's rear areas, encircling the West's forward corps, neutralizing remaining operational reserves, and seizing theater objectives at or beyond the Rhine.[9]

For these reasons, many in the West have favored deep reductions in NATO and Warsaw Pact armored vehicles, artillery and attack helicopters as a means of hobbling Soviet offensive capabilities. But the same types of weapons play a key role in NATO's operational strategy for defending its territory. Because NATO must spread its initial echelon of defending forces more or less evenly across the entire front, the only way it can cope with breakthroughs is to have operational reserve forces available with adequate firepower and mobility to engage and defeat exploitation forces soon after they breach NATO's forward defenses. The mobility, survivability and firepower offered by armored vehicles, self-propelled artillery, anti-tank helicopters and fixed-wing aircraft used in close air support make them ideal weapons for these operational reserve forces.

Likewise, aircraft used for ground attacks in rear areas can contribute to the Warsaw Pact offensive by damaging NATO's airbases, reserve forces, command and control posts, weapons storage depots, airports and seaports of debarkation, and other rear-area assets. The so-called air operation employing a combination of Soviet medium bombers, fighter-bombers, jamming aircraft, escort fighters and conventionally armed tactical ballistic missiles might attack such targets repeatedly in a series of massed raids during the opening week of the war. Yet NATO also relies heavily on such aircraft to attack Pact airbases as well as follow-on forces, supplies and the roads and rail lines over which they move in order to suppress Pact sortie generation and to prevent follow-on forces from being brought forward in a timely, organized fashion and to reduce their strength before they reach the battle area. In summary, the very types of weapons that pose threats to NATO are those most needed to defend against the threat.

In wartime, the Pact's breakthrough assaults would likely be mounted simultaneously at several points along NATO's forward defense line. As Richard Kugler notes in Chapter 2 above, so many of NATO's forces are needed to cover the lengthy forward line that allied commanders find it difficult to constitute operational reserve forces adequate to cope with breakthroughs that might occur. Thus, substantial cuts in NATO's forces could reduce NATO's ability to implement its operational strategy for coping with a Warsaw Pact invasion.

In contrast, Warsaw Pact forces, which are already considerably larger than NATO's, can concentrate in areas of their choice, while manning other sectors of the front more thinly. Because terrain limitations allow only a limited number of forces to be deployed opposite NATO's line in support of a breakthrough assault, the Warsaw Pact commander would "stack" his divisions behind one another in successive echelons in his rear area. Thus, while modest reductions could cripple NATO's defense capability, even sizable reductions in Pact forces might not significantly diminish the combat power the Pact is able to direct against NATO in the opening days and weeks of a war.

Two major implications emerge from this brief analysis of numbers and strategies. First, singling out specific types of weapons and equipment for reductions on the basis of their supposedly inherently offensive nature can be risky, because it could weaken NATO's defensive capabilities as much as or even more than it reduces the Pact's offensive punch.

Second, if NATO forces are to be reduced by a CFE agreement, such reductions ought to be accompanied by much larger reductions in Pact forces, such that the Pact's combat power available to mount and exploit multiple breakthrough assaults in the opening days of a war would be significantly diminished.

Options for Conventional Arms Reductions

In framing a conventional force reductions regime, one must specify *where* reductions are to take place, *what* is to be reduced, *how* reductions are to be implemented and *how much* to reduce forces from existing levels.

Where to Reduce?

Many have suggested that forces found throughout the Atlantic-to-the-Urals area should be reduced from the very outset by a CFE agreement. Others propose that reductions be focused on selected subregions, in most cases in Central Europe where the heaviest concentrations of air and ground forces on both sides are found.[10] If such focused reductions are to have maximal impact on the combat capabilities of the two alliances, they should be accompanied by a commitment not to increase the holdings of the selected armaments and military manpower in the remainder of the Atlantic-to-the-Urals area. The bulk of the remaining discussion in this chapter will address issues associated with reductions in the Central Europe extended region described earlier.

Such an emphasis is not wholly arbitrary. It captures not only the forces based in the center of Europe (that is, in the FRG, Belgium, the Netherlands and possibly Denmark on the Western side; the German Democratic Republic, Poland, Czechoslovakia and possibly Hungary from the East),[11] but also forces stationed in France on the NATO side and the Baltic, Byelorussian and Carpathian military districts in the western USSR on the part of the Warsaw Pact. (This zone corresponds to the "intermediate zone" described by Alexei Arbatov in the Eastern counterpart piece in this chapter, minus forces in the United Kingdom and Italy, which would be available for combat in Central Europe only after a lengthy period, if at all.)

Should aircraft ultimately be included for limitation (a subject discussed below), the Western side of an extended Central European subregion might properly be further expanded (for purposes of counting aircraft only) beyond the area just described to include the United Kingdom. In this case, expanding the Eastern portion of the subregion to include the Kiev military district in the USSR in order to capture additional bombers and fighter-bombers of the Smolensk and Vinnitsa air armies might also be warranted. Some Soviet commentators have suggested that large numbers of U.S. tactical fighter-bombers based in the United States and earmarked for possible deployment to Western Europe in the event of a European crisis or war should be included within the portion of NATO's forces subject to reduction.[12] We see no reason why American aircraft in the United States should be counted against a European ceiling, particularly when equally mobile Soviet aircraft stationed east of the Urals are excluded.

The discussion above assumes that over the next few years the negotiations on conventional force reductions in Europe will be focused on reaching a CFE agreement that involves collective cuts by the member-states of NATO and the Warsaw Pact. In the spring of 1986, U.S. Senator Sam Nunn proposed a different approach. He suggested instead a bilateral agreement between the superpowers that would result in the withdrawal of 50 percent of their ground forces stationed in the center of Europe.[13] The Soviets, who would be required to withdraw 13-plus divisions from the GDR, Poland and Czechoslovakia in return for the departure of at least two U.S. divisions from the FRG under this approach, have shown little interest in such an agreement. They, like the NATO allies, prefer to seek a broader accord that would involve greater reductions from a larger number of states. We also believe that the West should take advantage of the current opportunity to seek a more comprehensive reduction of the type discussed in the CFE mandate talks.

What to Reduce?

There seems now to be a consensus in both East and West that individual weapons and items of equipment along with their associated manpower represent the most useful metric for denominating a conventional arms reduction agreement. Ceilings on active-duty military manpower alone—the basic approach taken in the abortive MBFR negotiations—would be difficult to verify and easy to circumvent. Put simply, it is far easier to conceal or to return to the theater a division's worth of personnel than a division's worth of equipment.

Having settled on hardware as the basic element for denominating reductions, one must next determine what types of hardware to reduce and what types to leave unconstrained. The conventional wisdom in both East and West has it that reductions should be focused on those weapons that can play the most important roles in the conduct of offensive operations. Tanks, infantry fighting vehicles, artillery, ground-attack aircraft, attack helicopters and surface-to-surface missiles are the most commonly cited candidates for reductions according to this criterion.[14] Other items important to Warsaw Pact offensive operations but less often mentioned as candidates for reductions are tactical bridging equipment and vehicles for clearing mines and other obstacles. By implication, other weapons, including fighter-interceptors, surface-to-air missiles and infantry weapons, would be left unconstrained, as would certain support systems, such as reconnaissance platforms, radars and electronic jamming devices.

As we explained earlier, a simple bifurcation of weapons into "offensive" and "defensive" categories is potentially dangerous, since NATO relies on all of these weapons to support its defensive operational strategy. In light of these considerations, it would seem better to think of all of the weapon types mentioned above as contributing to both sides' combat capabilities, whether applied to offensive or defensive operations. Thus, NATO must be wary of an agreement that would allow the Warsaw Pact to retain sizable advantages in some important categories of weapons while both sides reduce in other areas. NATO must also avoid giving up too much in return for too little, a subject we shall turn to in a moment.

In our view, conventional force reductions should be focused on forces that best lend themselves to seizing and holding ground. This focus points to cuts in main battle tanks, the linchpin of modern mobile maneuver warfare; artillery, their most crucial supporting element; and possibly armored vehicles that carry the infantry into battle. These are the weapons deployed in the greatest numbers by both sides in the central region. NATO's primary negotiating objective should be to eliminate or sharply reduce Warsaw Pact superiority in these weapons in Central Europe extended, while retaining a sufficient number of them to support its own defensive operational strategy.

By any accounting, Pact numerical advantages in these areas are sizable. Are there other types of weapons that NATO might be able to agree to reduce bilaterally with the Pact as a way of making highly asymmetrical cuts in armor and artillery more palatable to Moscow?

We have already noted that the Soviets have placed NATO ground-attack aircraft (or, in their parlance, "strike aviation") along with tanks at the top of their agenda for cuts. Soviet officials and analysts have arranged their accounting scheme for strike aviation available for combat in Central Europe so as to show a higher total for NATO than for the Pact. Consequently, Soviet spokesmen have repeatedly asserted that NATO will be required to take deep cuts to eliminate this imbalance as the price for far heavier Pact reductions in main battle tanks, where they admit to a very sizable superiority.[15] Our accounting, however, like those of most Western analysts, shows at most a small Western advantage when truly comparable ground-attack aircraft are counted. Thus, it is not clear that including ground-attack aircraft in the talks would, in fact, be terribly favorable to Moscow, at least on the basis of numbers alone. Nevertheless, Soviet military writers have long credited NATO's tactical strike aviation with making a potentially decisive contribution to the West's military capabilities. Therefore, if the Warsaw Pact and NATO are nearly equal in ground-attack aircraft, or even if the Pact was found to enjoy a modest degree of numerical superiority in this area, the Soviets might be prepared to accept marginally greater cuts in their own tactical aviation in order to get reductions in what they perceive to be NATO's higher-quality ground-attack capabilities.

Of course, when both ground-attack aircraft and fighter-interceptors are included, as Table 1 indicates, the Pact enjoys a superiority over NATO regardless of the scope of the basing area. Analysts from Warsaw Pact states (along with some from the West) argue, at least implicitly, that fighter-interceptors (or "air defense" aircraft, as they like to call them) are defensive in nature and therefore should not be subject to reductions. As is so often the case, however, an examination of operational strategy makes it clear that such a clear demarcation between "offensive" and "defensive" systems is not warranted. Fighter-interceptors can contribute to an offensive both by protecting troops, supplies and lines of communication in friendly rear areas from air attack, and by accompanying attack aircraft over enemy territory to protect them from the enemy's air-defense fighters. On conceptual grounds, therefore, NATO would seem justified in resisting attempts by the Warsaw Pact to single out ground-attack aircraft for reductions while fighter-interceptors are left unconstrained.

NATO will be reluctant to consider reductions in ground-attack aviation in any case during the initial phase of the CFE negotiations because such cuts would reduce NATO's theater nuclear delivery potential along with its conventional defense capabilities. As the Pershing 2 and ground-launched cruise missiles are withdrawn from Europe in the wake of the INF Treaty, land-based "dual-capable" tactical fighter-bombers (those that can deliver both conventional and nuclear weapons) will shoulder an increasing share of the alliance's long-range, theater-based nuclear delivery capability.

So substantial reductions in NATO's tactical aviation capabilities might be risky. But reductions taken by redeploying some aircraft to bases outside of the Atlantic-to-the-Urals region need not result in a serious diminution of NATO's wartime air capabilities. Aircraft and air crews withdrawn to the United States but retained in active service, for instance, could be returned to Europe in a day or two if the basing and support infrastructure necessary for operating the aircraft were maintained in the theater. The Warsaw Pact might resist such an approach as yielding only token reductions, but short of imposing global limits on the two alliances' tactical aviation (something the Soviets tried and failed to do through the INF talks), it is unclear how one might achieve more militarily significant reductions.

On balance, then, it would seem best to leave tactical aviation out of the CFE negotiations, at least during the initial round of reductions. If aircraft are included, we see no reason why fighter-interceptors should not be considered along with ground-attack aircraft. Finally, given the wide range of potential reinforcement options available to both alliances, it appears most useful to limit the reductions to in-place aircraft in the extended Central Europe zone.

How to Reduce?

In addition to the question of what to reduce, the question of how to reduce will have far-reaching ramifications for any agreement's impact on stability and security. What should constitute elimination of a piece of equipment such that it would no longer be counted against an agreed-upon ceiling?

The most obvious approach to eliminating weapons is to destroy or dismantle them.[16] This has been the approach taken in the SALT and INF treaties: broadly speaking, a missile or launcher is no longer counted against a treaty ceiling when it ceases to exist. Using similar dismantlement and destruction criteria in a conventional reductions regime would necessitate the cutting up or melting down of large numbers of weapons— an approach that is quite irreversible, even if symbolically appealing to many. Since the Soviet Union could still maintain a vast reserve of such unlimited weapons east of the Urals, such an approach might be risky for NATO if employed on a large scale.

This brings us to a second approach: removing the items in question from the reductions zone. Because the SALT and INF treaties are of global scope, this option was not available in those cases. But given the more narrow geographic scope of the Atlantic-to-the-Urals talks, the Soviet Union, the United States and Canada will have the option of achieving compliance by moving equipment out of the region altogether, while other participants could have this option with regard to any subregions created within Europe.

This approach has disadvantages of its own, however. On its face, it would appear to favor the Soviet Union, since moving equipment the 3,000 or so miles overland from the Urals to Central Europe appears to be less problematic than moving it across the Atlantic Ocean to vulnerable seaports and airports. It would also be difficult for other members of the alliances to take advantage of this provision, since (with the exception of Denmark, which could, theoretically, use Greenland for these purposes) their own national territories lie wholly within the overall reductions zone.[17] Perhaps most important, however, simply removing large numbers of forces from the reductions zone as a means of complying with ceilings would allow the Soviets to redirect their existing military capabilities to other regions around their borders, with unfavorable consequences for their neighbors and for U.S. security interests in those regions.

Thus, a third approach to implementing reductions has been suggested.[18] Both sides could agree not to count equipment placed in "secured storage" against treaty ceilings, even if the storage areas were within the reductions zone. These secured storage areas would consist of fenced compounds equipped with a variety of sensors and seals to prevent the covert withdrawal of stored equipment. Compounds would be subjected to periodic and short-notice on-site inspections. The treaty would specify that equipment could be withdrawn from secured storage areas only following a notification period.

This approach seems promising for several reasons. First, it would allow any U.S. weapons in Europe that were subjected to treaty ceilings to remain in Europe. Once heavy U.S. ground-forces equipment was removed from the continent (much less destroyed), it would be difficult, both logistically and, in some circumstances, politically, to return it there. Secured storage would also provide countries whose entire territory lies within the reductions zone with an option less draconian than dismantling and destruction to comply with treaty limits.

Of course, reductions implemented by consigning weapons to secured storage could be reversed if a party to the treaty chose to cease compliance overtly. In order to extend the period needed to break out of treaty restrictions and to reduce incentives for surprise attack, therefore, equipment in secured storage would need to be partially dismantled. For example, turrets, treads and gun barrels could be removed from tanks and self-propelled artillery and stored in warehouses far removed from those housing their chassis.

Finally, if both sides agree to impose ceilings on weapons between the Atlantic and the Urals, facilities producing these weapons within the reductions zone would have to be monitored in order to ensure continued compliance with the ceilings. Monitoring measures agreed to within the INF Treaty may provide a useful model here.

How Deep Should We Cut?

"How far to go?" is perhaps the single most critical question in contemplating reductions in conventional forces. Space does not permit a detailed examination of this issue here. Clearly, however, the most salient factor in this regard is the pervasive presence of numerical superiorities in Warsaw Pact equipment over that of NATO: NATO simply has little it can safely afford to give up in compensation for necessarily massive reductions in Pact forces.

As noted earlier, NATO has indicated its readiness to cut its own tank force by approximately 10 percent if the Warsaw Pact will reduce its tanks to that level. A CFE agreement that resulted in common ceilings in tanks, artillery and armored fighting vehicles (AFVs) at a level around

10 percent below that of current NATO forces in the extended central region would strip Pact forces of approximately 70 percent of their tanks and artillery. The Pact would give up more than 20,000 tanks to NATO's 1,400 (a ratio of 14:1) and 17,000 artillery pieces compared with 600 from NATO (a 28:1 ratio!). Figure 5 illustrates these ratios as well as those resulting from cuts in smaller Pact forces projected for 1991. Were the cuts to be taken, as suggested by Robert Blackwill, throughout the entire Atlantic-to-the-Urals area, the absolute magnitude of the Pact's reduction would be even more daunting—some 30,000 tanks and 25,000 artillery pieces as opposed to 4,000 and 2,000, respectively, for NATO.[19]

Of course, by accepting heavier cuts, NATO could reduce these enormously disparate ratios. A 50-percent reduction in NATO's tanks in the central region, for example, would require a reduction of "only" 3.8 Warsaw Pact tanks for each of NATO's. But reductions by NATO of this magnitude, even if accompanied by reductions in Warsaw Pact forces to equal levels, might undermine stability in Central Europe. Put simply, it is not clear that NATO would retain sufficient forces to man its forward defense positions adequately and to back these forces with the operational reserves required to cope with breakthroughs, were it reduced to such a small number of tanks and artillery.[20] In our judgment, then, such deep reductions in NATO's forces should not be contemplated unless and until evolving political-military circumstances and detailed analysis of alternative military balances convince the political and military leaders of the alliance that the residual forces would be adequate to deter aggression and prevent intimidation by the Warsaw Pact.

If Pact negotiators balk at reduction ratios of 10:1 or greater, yet NATO cannot safely accommodate cuts in its own forces deeper than 10–15 percent, it might be desirable for the allies to propose, as an interim solution,[21] an outcome that resulted in something less than the full elimination of the current imbalances in these weapons. An agreement that imposed a 10-percent reduction on NATO's tank force in the central region and a 40-percent cut in the Pact's tanks, for example, would leave an imbalance of around 1.6:1 (20,000 versus 12,500 tanks)—a substantial improvement, from NATO's perspective, over today's imbalance of 2.4:1 (33,200 versus 13,900). Even this partial redressing of the imbalance yields a reduction ratio of approximately 9.5:1.

Considerations of negotiability aside, such "interim" or phased approaches fall short of an ideal outcome. In particular, they might be perceived as codifying for the indefinite future Warsaw Pact numerical

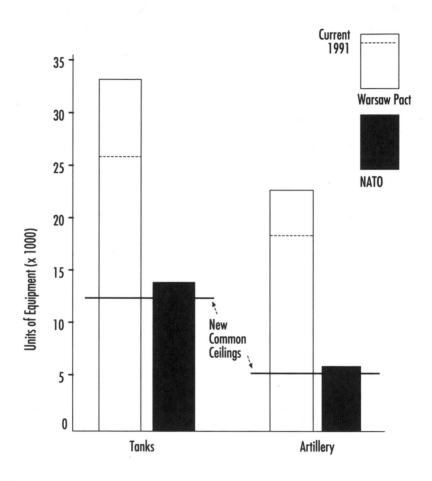

Figure 3 Potential Reductions in NATO and Warsaw Pact Tank and Artillery Forces in Central Europe Extended

superiorities in weapons covered by the agreement. In addition, an agreement along these lines risks placing NATO at a greater disadvantage than today because the Pact forces have so much "reserve" equipment to draw on in implementing reductions. For example, Pact forces could take a sizable portion of their cuts by eliminating obsolescent tanks, such as the T-54 and others, while NATO would be hard-pressed to find many tanks that it could easily do without. Having completed an initial phase of reductions, the Pact would presumably have little incentive to negotiate in good faith toward an eventual elimination of remaining asymmetries.

Reductions and Restructuring

Proponents of "non-offensive defense" schemes (first in Western Europe and now among some civilian defense specialists in Moscow) have called for revisions to the military balance in Europe that go beyond merely reducing the number of combat units there. They advocate the abandonment of traditional force structures in favor of forces equipped and deployed in radically different ways. They insist, with some justification, that reductions in conventional forces in Central Europe will not increase stability unless they are accompanied by measures to restructure the forces that remain in ways that would reduce their capabilities for offensive action.[22]

While there seems to be some merit to these arguments, they tend to overlook the fact that, considerations of negotiability aside, simply reducing substantially or eliminating the Warsaw Pact's numerical advantages in key categories of weapons would, in and of itself, significantly improve NATO's ability to defend itself. Further, those who advocate the radical restructuring of conventional forces tend also to classify particular types of equipment (typically, tanks, infantry fighting vehicles, artillery, and ground-attack fighter-bombers) as being inherently offensive in nature. As we have argued, such a distinction can be dangerously misleading.

It should be noted that virtually any agreement to reduce substantially conventional forces on the basis of specific classes of equipment and their directly associated manpower (as opposed to entire large combat units) will almost certainly result in some restructuring of the forces to which they are applied. For example, a reduction in Warsaw Pact tanks and artillery in Central Europe to a level 15 percent below NATO's currently deployed level would result in the loss by an average Pact armored division of more than 40 percent of its total firepower, assuming the Pact retained its current number of divisions.[23] Thus, a conventional reduction agreement that substantially reduced or eliminated numerical asymmetries in the forces of NATO and the Warsaw Pact might, in itself, bring about a rather fundamental restructuring of at least Warsaw Pact forces.

If sizable portions of both sides' tanks and artillery were eliminated from the extended European zone posited above, the remaining forces would consist largely of motorized infantry. If these forces were well armed with modern anti-tank weapons and prepared to use minefields and other barriers, they might indeed possess only a limited offensive capability, but be well suited to carrying out an effective defense of their own territory. Forces of this character, then, might possess characteristics closely resembling those that have been sought by some advocates of "non-offensive defense."

Unilateral Reductions

The conceptual complexities, uncertainties and political sensitivities surrounding conventional arms control in Europe, combined with the paucity of bargaining chips available to NATO, justify a rather pessimistic assessment of the prospects for rapid progress toward a negotiated CFE agreement. Yet participants on both sides seem to be facing heavy economic and demographic pressures to reduce the resources they devote to defense in Europe. Most important, Gorbachev's announcement of sizable unilateral reductions in Soviet forces may signal a recognition by the top Soviet leadership that military forces have only very limited utility in European political affairs. The Soviet military buildup in the 1970s by all evidence failed to intimidate the nations of the Western alliance into a more concessionary posture toward the Soviet Union. On the contrary, the steady growth of Soviet military power under Brezhnev helped stimulate increases in the military budgets of the United States and other Western countries.

If this perspective has taken hold in the Kremlin (it already seems to be well established in the West), a basis might exist for a series of East-West unilateral reductions "by mutual example." Such a mechanism would be tacit and approximate: states would determine for themselves what forces to reduce on the basis of their cost, their contribution to military capabilities, and the "appearance" of the reduction in terms of its comparability to those of the other side. As such, unilateral reductions and voluntary verification measures could cut through many of the time-consuming complexities of intra- and inter-alliance negotiations.

To further dramatize these reductions and to convince the opposing side that they have, in fact, been fully implemented, the sides could voluntarily provide one another with opportunities to observe the reductions via on-site inspection and to verify that they were not subsequently being reversed.

Of course, there is no guarantee that reductions imposed as a result of such a process would increase or maintain stability in Central Europe. But it is far from clear that a negotiated outcome from Vienna would meet this criterion anyway. Surely, analysts of the problem have yet to present impressive evidence to substantiate their theories of stability and conventional arms control. Besides, we agree with the overall thrust of Arnold Kanter's contribution to this volume that the presence of viable theater-based nuclear forces in Central Europe provides a decisive contribution to stability there. Thus, as long as these forces are maintained and modernized, there appears to be considerable room for error in the balance of conventional forces.

Should a dynamic of mutual unilateral reductions commence, the CFE negotiators might most usefully focus their efforts on devising modalities for data exchange, verification and long-term monitoring of force levels on both sides.

Summary

The Soviet Union's apparent willingness to consider radical revisions in conventional force deployments in Europe provides the West with an unprecedented opportunity to redress chronic and sizable imbalances in conventional forces in Europe. Nevertheless, NATO faces some risks in contemplating reductions in its forces in Central Europe.

We believe that NATO today faces an unfavorable imbalance of conventional military capability in the central region and thus would probably be incapable of conducting a sustained defense of its territory in the face of a determined Warsaw Pact invasion. Two major implications emerge from this assessment:

–NATO must insist on highly asymmetrical reductions in the much larger Warsaw Pact forces in order to offset any reductions in its own defense capabilities. In particular, NATO must retain sufficient ground and air forces to maintain a coherent forward defense line and to provide mobile reserves to cope with breakthroughs.

–NATO should eschew further major reductions in its theater-based nuclear forces for the time being. These forces are needed in order to ensure that the Soviet leaders understand that war in Europe could very likely result in nuclear escalation and thus an outcome that would be totally unacceptable to them. It would therefore be inadvisable to accept significant reductions in the aircraft, missiles and artillery pieces used to deliver these nuclear weapons.[24]

Within the context of these broad guidelines, the two sides' approach to the CFE negotiations should embody the following basic elements:

–Reductions in conventional forces should be denominated in terms of weapons and equipment and their associated personnel, rather than directly in manpower, as was the case in MBFR.

–Reductions should be focused on weapons most conducive to seizing and holding territory in modern maneuver warfare: tanks, artillery and possibly armored troop carriers.

–NATO might consider a modest reduction in tactical aviation so long as the aircraft eliminated could be redeployed outside of Europe and the in-theater basing structure for them maintained. Fighter-interceptors should be counted along with ground-attack aircraft.

–The lion's share of reductions in NATO's ground equipment should be implemented by placing weapons in secured storage within the area from the Atlantic to the Urals. Equipment stored within these compounds would have to be partially dismantled and stored separately in order to prevent rapid breakout.

Notes

1 Robert D. Blackwill, "Specific Approaches to Conventional Arms Control in Europe," *Survival* 30, No. 5 (September/October 1988), p. 429.

2 Force ratios, of course, are not always decisive determinants of the outcome of battles or wars. History is replete with cases in which numerically inferior forces have emerged victorious.

3 We say that numerical inferiority *can* undermine Western resolve because it seems for the most part not to have had such an effect to date. This can be accounted for largely by the existence of a sizable arsenal of nuclear weapons, in both Western Europe and the United States. As long as the prospects for large-scale nuclear use in response to a Warsaw Pact attack are not wholly incredible (a perception grounded in part on the

state of the conventional balance), Moscow will find it difficult to actualize, vis-à-vis NATO, the coercive potential of its numerically superior conventional forces.

4 NATO ground forces included in these counts are those of Belgium, Denmark, Luxembourg, the Netherlands, France and the FRG, as well as those actually deployed in Central Europe from Britain, Canada and the United States. For the Warsaw Pact, forces of Czechoslovakia, the GDR, Poland and Hungary are counted, as well as Soviet forces deployed in those countries and forces in the Baltic, Byelorussian and Carpathian military districts of the western Soviet Union. Many of these latter units would be brought forward into Poland, the GDR and western Czechoslovakia during mobilization and reinforcement.

5 In calculating 1991 Warsaw Pact forces, we assume that only Soviet forces are reduced from 1988 levels and that the reductions, made in accordance with Gorbachev's UN speech, will involve the withdrawal and dismantlement of 5,000 tanks from Soviet forces stationed in Eastern Europe and assume that 50 percent of the remaining 5,000 tanks, 8,500 artillery systems and 800 combat aircraft that are to be eliminated from the European USSR will be removed from the western military districts and thus from "Central Europe extended."

6 NATO's advantage in ground-attack aircraft disappears if the 400 medium bombers of the Smolensk air army are counted against Warsaw Pact totals. Such an accounting yields a Warsaw Pact superiority of 1.1:1.

7 For a comprehensive description of this "theater strategic offensive" based on a wide range of Soviet sources, see Phillip A. Petersen and John G. Hines, *The Soviet Conventional Offensive in Europe* (Washington, DC: Defense Intelligence Agency, DDB-2611-4-83, 1983).

8 NATO plans to erect additional forward defense positions should the Soviets attack in northern Norway, northern Italy (through Yugoslavia or Austria) or Turkish and Greek Thrace.

9 Since 1987, military and political leaders of Warsaw Pact nations, led by Gorbachev himself, have asserted that they have fundamentally revised their "military technical doctrine" (which, for our purposes, is analogous to operational strategy) for warfare. In the main, these revisions are said to have downplayed the role of offensive operations in favor of defensive ones. Substantial evidence is accumulating that Warsaw Pact leaders are serious about implementing innovations in military exercising and other areas to bring about these revisions. Nevertheless, absent substantial and lasting changes in the structure and posture of Warsaw Pact forces, as well as their training, prudent Western planners will have to assume that these forces retain considerable capabilities for offensive military operations. For a discussion of these trends, see Edward L. Warner III, "New Thinking and Old Realities in Soviet Defense Policy," *Survival* 31, No. 1 (January–February 1989), pp. 13–33.

10 See, for example, Jonathan Dean, "The New NATO-Pact Force Reduction Talks—An Optimal Outcome," paper prepared for the American Academy of Arts and Sciences, Washington, DC, May 18, 1988, pp. 9–19.

11 This collection of states has been singled out as a potential reduction area in the recent proposals of General Wojciech Jaruzelski and thus has become known as the "Jaruzelski zone." See Andrzej Karkoszka, "Merits of the Jaruzelski Plan," *Bulletin of the Atomic Scientists* 44, No. 7 (September 1988), pp. 32–34.

12 This suggestion appears in an intriguing exploration of several alternative reduction

approaches by members of Alexei Arbatov's Arms Control Department of the Institute of World Economy and International Relations in Moscow, in *Disarmament and Security: 1987 IMEMO Yearbook* (Moscow: Novosti Press Agency Publishing House, 1988), pp. 371–399.

13   For an analysis of this approach see Phillip A. Karber, "Conventional Arms Control Options or Why 'Nunn' is Better than None," in Uwe Nerlich and James A. Thomson, eds., *Conventional Arms Control and the Security of Europe* (Boulder, CO: Westview Press, 1988), pp. 158–181.

14   See, for example, Jonathan Dean, "The New NATO-Pact Force Reduction Talks," pp. 4–5.

15   See, for example, Army General Dmitri Yazov, "The Soviet Proposal for European Security," *Bulletin of the Atomic Scientists* 44, No. 7 (September 1988), p. 9, in which the Soviet defense minister acknowledges that, throughout the Atlantic-to-the-Urals zone, the Pact deploys approximately 20,000 more tanks than NATO.

16   Richard Darilek and John Setear argue in Chapter 9 of this volume that the complete dismantlement or destruction of weapons represents the only true form of force "reduction." In their view, various forms of redeployment or storage of weapons systems represent "constraints" on but not "reductions" in military capabilities. We believe the wider range of measures discussed here would all "reduce" military capabilities in useful ways.

17   It is not inconceivable that continental NATO nations could elect to locate some of their military equipment in the United States. Rebasing a few wings of allied aircraft in the United States, for instance, might be a particularly attractive option if the Vienna talks result in ceilings on ground-attack aircraft. Air crews from the nation that owned the aircraft could rotate to the United States periodically for training, taking advantage of the generally superior flying weather of the American southwest.

18   See Dean, "The New NATO-Pact Force Reduction Talks," pp. 16–17.

19   Blackwill, "Specific Approaches to Arms Control in Europe."

20   For a fuller exploration of this problem, see James A. Thomson and Nanette C. Gantz, *Conventional Arms Control Revisited: Objectives in the New Phase* (Santa Monica, CA: The RAND Corporation, N-2697-AF, December 1987), pp. 6–12.

21   "Interim solution" is proposed here as a term of art that would allow NATO to avoid the appearance of accepting, as a matter of principle, a continuing (albeit greatly reduced) Warsaw Pact superiority in armor and artillery in the central region.

22   See, for example, Andreas von Buelow, "Defensive Entanglement: An Alternative Strategy for NATO," in Andrew J. Pierre, ed., *The Conventional Defense of Europe: New Technologies and New Strategies* (New York: Council on Foreign Relations, 1986), pp. 112–151; and Lutz Unterseher, *Towards a Feasible Defence of Central Europe: A German Perspective* (Bonn: Studiengruppe Alternative Sicherheitspolitik, 1983).

23   For a listing of equipment types in NATO and Warsaw Pact divisions, and the contribution of each type to a division's firepower, see William P. Mako, *U.S. Ground Forces and the Defense of Central Europe* (Washington, DC: The Brookings Institution, 1983), Appendix A, pp. 105–125.

24   It may be that NATO governments will find political pressure for further reductions

in theater-based nuclear forces irresistible, in which case the best approach might be to implement cuts unilaterally in nuclear artillery (shells, not tubes), while modernizing remaining forces. Enhancements should be focused on the deployment of a follow-on missile to the Lance that would have greater range and accuracy, and a standoff missile for delivery by theater-based aircraft.

VI

PART TWO

Problems of Reducing the Military Confrontation
Alexei Arbatov, USSR

The two military alliances significantly differ from each other in the specific structure and composition of their armed forces, especially of those kinds that can be used in the event of a military conflict in Europe. Such an asymmetry, the product of historical, geographical and other factors, substantially complicates an assessment of the real correlation of military forces and conventional arms of the WTO and NATO in Europe. This assessment must be the starting point for future negotiations on the deep reductions of conventional forces and weapons from the Atlantic to the Urals (ATTU).

An even more important and difficult question is the way in which to move toward the objective of the negotiations: to strengthen stability and security in Europe by way of establishing a balance of armed forces and conventional arms at decreased levels. In other words, how to change the existing military balance in quantitative, structural and spacial parameters in order to implement the Vienna mandate formula; how to eliminate inequality and the potential for a surprise attack and for initiating large-scale offensive actions?

At the same time, along with the political will of the participants, the success of the negotiations may be facilitated by the fact that the military balance has its own political, strategic, operational and technical logic that may serve as the basis for fair and mutually acceptable solutions in this area.

Methods for Comparing Ground Forces in Europe

In developing common criteria for assessing the aggregate military power of the East and the West it is necessary to determine what to count, i.e., which indices of military potential to consider most important in a comparison and, in turn, in an anticipated reduction. One aspect of the correlation of both sides' ground forces may be a comparison of their existing combat-ready divisions. And it is precisely combat-ready divisions in which we are interested, since it is only they that may be used for conducting military actions, including a surprise attack, without additional mobilization measures. An attempt to capture everything at once in the reductions—including the non-combat-ready formations as well—would entail numerous complications, since agreement would be required on specific scenarios for the beginning of military actions (in particular, how much time may be required by both sides for mobilization), as well as for the development and duration of combat operations (such as how many major reinforcements would have to be formed, trained and sent to the front during the course of the war). However, reserves may be captured by certain limitations on, for example, the number of their active and warehoused weapons and combat equipment, especially of offensive kinds.

Besides the equipment organic to combat-ready divisions there also exist significant warehoused reserves of arms and combat materiel. These supplies are intended mainly for replenishing combat losses, equipping reserve units and for troop contingents that are rapidly moved by air to the region of combat.

A determination of the specific zone of reductions goes beyond the bounds of this study. A political decision and a mutually acceptable compromise are necessary for such a solution. However, an analysis of this problem may help to find logical relationships in developing this or that approach. For example, if one poses the question of including in the zone of reductions the entire territory of Turkey, then on the Soviet side it would obviously be necessary to consider those districts that relate to the corresponding TVD, even if they lie beyond the geographical limits of Europe (as does most of the territory of Turkey itself). Furthermore, from the point of view of strategic logic the inclusion in the zone of reductions of central Soviet military districts (the Urals and Volga)— significantly removed from the NATO-WTO line of contact and not oriented solely toward the European theater of war—raises the question of including in this zone certain units deployed on the territory of the United States itself. The Pentagon, as is known, plans to significantly reinforce American armed forces deployed in Europe by way of transferring forces and weapons from the United States. For these purposes, reserves of heavy arms for four U.S. Army divisions are warehoused in

Europe. The creation of such reserves for yet another two American divisions is under way. Other U.S. divisions are to be sent by sea together with their respective arms and combat supplies. Therefore, it may be possible in this interpretation to consider as the region of reductions "from the Atlantic to the Urals" a zone that captures not only the European continent but also a certain portion of U.S. territory on its Atlantic coast, or in any event to consider the forces deployed there. By the same logic, in including the northern (Leningrad) and southern (Kiev and Odessa) districts in the region of the USSR's European territory, for the West's part it would be reasonable to consider if not the entire NATO navy, then at least the marine forces and carrier-based aviation intended for operations on NATO's northern and southern flanks. Here one can see military logic contradicting political and diplomatic considerations reflected in the Vienna CFE mandate. This has to be kept in mind when discussing military aspects of reductions in the ATTU area.

On the whole, quite substantial differences are observed in Western assessments of the correlation of NATO and WTO conventional forces and weapons in Europe, but they all come down to a significant "WTO superiority" in both combat-ready divisions and in basic types of arms (in a number of instances even through underestimating the quantitative composition of their own divisions and arms). In analyzing the correlation of conventional forces and weapons in the zone of the Atlantic to the Urals, we may take into consideration, it would seem, the following forces and weapons:

–all forces and weapons of the 14 European members of both the military and political organization of NATO;
–U.S. and Canadian troops deployed in Europe and prepositioned arms and equipment of units deployed outside the ATTU and on the American continent and designated for rapid reinforcement;
–the forces and weapons of Soviet allies in the WTO, and also all Soviet units and formations deployed in these countries; and
–the forces and weapons of the USSR deployed in its European military districts.

And lastly, the final question: how to count. One complication is that great differences exist on both sides in the quantitative structure and related equipping of divisions with combat supplies and arms. Quantitative and qualitative comparisons play a most important role in assessing the correlation of strategic nuclear forces (although here as well the problem hardly boils down only to this) by virtue of the unambiguous nature of their combat tasks and the relatively few hypothetical scenarios for their use. As for general-purpose armed forces, non-quantitative factors and, most importantly, assumptions concerning the conditions of the outbreak of war, the political motives and objectives of the two military-political alliances in such a war, and their strategy and tactics, have much greater significance than partial quantitative disproportions. Thus, the Western conclusion of "WTO superiority" usually proceeds from the most pessimistic assumptions from the NATO point of view, while all advantages and favorable features, including initiative and the resolve to "attack," are ascribed to the other side.

Tactical Aviation

An integral element of the European military balance is the correlation of the forces and capabilities of airpower, in view of its great range of operation, ability to be quickly moved, and the significance of its interaction with friendly and hostile ground forces in the operational plans of both alliances.

Certain Western specialists (in particular James Thomson of RAND) contend that tactical strike aviation (TSA)—i.e., fighter-bombers and close-air-support aircraft armed with weapons for destroying ground targets—is needed more in defense than in offense or is at least neutral in defense/offense interaction. TSA are equated with "flying artillery" that provide the delivery of explosive power to a given region, but at several times greater cost per unit of time, area and payload than conventional artillery. In such a way it is assumed that whereas an offensive can concentrate artillery beforehand on the main axes of strikes, the defense will have no such opportunity. From this follows the conclusion that aircraft, possessing the ability to concentrate strikes on any sector of the forward edge of the battle area (FEBA), independent of where they are based, are much more necessary to defense. This is one of the Western arguments against considering and reducing tactical aviation in general and in particular TSA in the framework of a future agreement on conventional weapons in Europe.

It seems, however, that such an approach does not consider the number of radical differences separating the current strategic situation from that of an earlier time (although even earlier, beginning with 1939, aviation has played a great role in an offensive). The main difference is that troops are saturated with tactical nuclear weapons. A potential aggressor cannot help but reckon with the possibility of their use by the other side and of the threat of rapid escalation to a total nuclear war. The first task of an aggressor who wishes to prevent such a turn must therefore be to strike with conventional weapons the nuclear warhead depots and the positions of their launchers (aircraft, missiles and artillery) in order to reduce to the extent possible the other side's physical capability to cross the nuclear threshold, or to maximally delay this moment. Another most serious difference of modern armed forces and operations is their enormous complexity, scope and rapid pace of combat which requires an immeasurably more improved C³I system for coordinating the actions of troops, arms and logistical services, without which combat operations would quickly degenerate into total chaos. A second task of an aggressor, thus, will be to rapidly disorganize the defender's C³I system, a move that will have a far greater effect, especially in the first hours and days of the war, than destroying from the air some portions of his vital forces and supplies.

Finally, yet another difference of modern troops with their colossal firepower and mobility is the sharply increased requirement for ammunition and fuel. If one follows the logic of James Thomson, an aggressor will concentrate in advance not only artillery and tanks, but also ammunition and fuel on the axes of the main strikes—something which the defense itself will be unable to do. This means that the effective destruction of the defender's logistics infrastructure in order to hinder the supply of fuel and ammunition as well as the transfer of reinforcements for closing off breakthroughs is yet another primary task of an attack.

In all three functions, whose importance in modern war clearly surpasses the tasks of close-air support (especially in the initial period of military actions), tactical strike aviation is the most important, if not the only weapon. This in turn means that in this sense it is relatively more important for the offense than for the defense and must surely be captured by a future agreement.

In modern conditions the results of ground combat actions largely depend on the achievement of air superiority, which allows one to carry out reconnaissance from the air without interference, to launch strikes on the opponent's command and control system and defensive positions with the objective of creating conditions for a ground force offensive, as well as on second echelons, rear targets of attacking forces, and depots and launch sites of tactical nuclear forces, and to directly support combat actions at the FEBA. Air superiority is achieved in battles between the two sides' fighters throughout the entire theater of war, between fighters and the opponent's close-air-support aircraft in his own airspace, between strike aviation and the opponent's ground-based air-defense systems (including missiles) in the other side's airspace, and so on. The technical and operational interaction of opposing forces and weapons in competition for air superiority has reached an extreme degree of sophistication and complexity. But the main Achilles' heel of modern aviation, however capable it may be, remains airfields. Therefore the task of striking airfields, runways and shelters is considered a primary function for tactical aviation.

However, striking airfields with the use of aircraft and missile weapons is clearly an offensive operation, independent of whether the armed forces as a whole are fulfilling a defensive or offensive strategic task. And, according to commonly understood notions, a first strike on airfields before the opponent's aircraft have taken off is the most decisive. Due to the inadequate effectiveness of conventional munitions, for these purposes a great incentive arises to use tactical nuclear weapons, which will fully guarantee the fulfillment of the task.

For the attacking side a classic operation before the beginning of a ground-force offensive would be a massive air raid (and missile strike), the effectiveness of which has been shown by the historical examples of the German attack on the USSR on June 22, 1941, the Japanese air attack on the American navy in Pearl Harbor on December 7, 1941, and the Middle Eastern wars of 1956 and 1967. And for the defender, the best chance to prevent his own rapid defeat may be connected with a preemptive strike on the enemy's airfields in order to capture air superiority at an early stage. The threat of aggression or the perception of such a threat may provoke an attack. Modern tactical air forces, their technical capabilities and operational plans are therefore an extremely, perhaps even the most, destabilizing element of the contemporary conventional balance.

It is quite obvious that radical measures for reducing the conventional confrontation in Europe are inseparably linked with the problem of the substantial reduction of tactical aviation and ground forces. Deep reductions of ground forces and aviation would facilitate reducing the possibility and probability of attack with the use of conventional means of destruction. And conversely, the reduction and restructuring of ground forces in order to fulfill primarily defensive strategic and operational missions, while preserving one side's superiority in offensive types of air forces, could give it overall superiority and destabilize the military balance.

There are, however, great internal complexities of the very problem of reducing aviation. Questions arise, for example, over the kind of correlation between reductions of aviation relative to reductions of the numbers of ground forces, over how to designate the geographical region of reductions, and in what way to prevent (or hinder) the rapid redeployment of aviation from other theaters in the event of a crisis situation. There are complications as well with criteria for counting aircraft in a given category, since a number of systems are modified to function as both combat, trainer and reconnaissance aircraft, while others are modified to function as air-defense interceptors, frontal fighters as well as ground-attack aircraft (F-4, F-15, F-16, F/A-18, Mirage F-3E, Tornado, MiG-21, MiG-23, etc.).

And there are other problems as well. Western assessments as a rule cite data on the quantitative structure of tactical aviation prior to reinforcement, i.e., before over 1,000 aircraft arrive from the United States. According to our assessments, such a NATO-WTO ratio (considering the ground-attack aircraft of France and Spain as well as both sides' medium-range bombers) is 2,400:1,800, i.e., 1.3:1 in favor of the West. But the high mobility of aircraft permits a sharp increase of air forces on the continent after only several days (i.e., the minimum amount of time for bringing the ground forces into combat readiness). In this case the NATO-WTO ratio, according to official American data, may become 3,500:2,700.[1] According to data of the U.S. Congress the NATO-WTO tactical strike aviation ratio on the European continent in the expanded central region before reinforcements is 1,500:1,250.[2] Official Soviet estimates give the West an advantage on the order of 1.5:1 (more precisely, 4,200:2,800).[3] According to certain West European sources, the correlation of forces directly in Europe is 2,400:2,600, respectively (considering medium-range bombers), and in combat helicopters is 800:1,600 in favor of the East.[4]

Such a significant scattering of estimates undoubtedly reflects not so much the differences in factual data as much as discrepancies in the counting methodology: i.e., which aircraft, which units and formations, which territories and which states are being considered and compared. Only an exchange of official data between NATO and the WTO and agreement on a common way of counting may resolve this problem. Nevertheless, the capability for rapid reinforcement should be considered in the negotiations either in coefficients to the initial level for reductions or at the very heart of the reductions—in classifying the tactical aircraft being reduced and in verification methods for preventing the return to the zone of reduced aircraft.

It is obvious that any assessment of the balance of forces in the area of tactical aviation cannot be considered complete and objective if it does not consider all types of aircraft possessed by one side or the other. For example, the WTO lags behind NATO in number of fighter-bombers and close-air-support aircraft but has a significant superiority in fighter-interceptors. Many fighters with some degree of effectiveness can strike ground targets and may be quickly reconfigured for such missions. However, reducing ground-attack aircraft, fighters and air-defense interceptors in the framework of tactical aviation would mean reducing offensive along with defensive forces as well, without relatively strengthening defense. Applying to aviation the same analytic "force-to-space ratio" method used in connection with ground forces, one may conclude that the mutual reduction of all types of tactical aviation may relatively strengthen the offense (as long as the number of strike aircraft is not reduced to a very small number). In such a case fighters and interceptors would have to defend an airspace just as extensive as before with fewer resources. But the offense will have the ability to concentrate the necessary forces of strike aircraft and escort fighters for strikes on selected targets, even starting with a smaller total number of aircraft.

Therefore, in solving the problem of reducing strike aviation, it will be necessary to come to an agreement on the precise technical differentiation (for example, according to the principle of functionally related observable differences) between offensive and defensive types of aircraft.

The Offense-Defense Correlation in Reducing Conventional Weapons

Recently substantial interest has been aroused by alternative concepts advanced at the level of nongovernmental, but quite competent, academic and public organizations as a counterweight to the official military-strategic concepts. These concepts are consonant with the general thrust of the WTO initiatives at the Budapest (1986) and Berlin (1987) meetings of the Political Consultative Commitee for radical quantitative and qualitative changes of WTO and NATO armed forces on principles of reasonable sufficiency, and for the elaboration of military doctrines built on the principles of non-offensive defense. There are quite a few such concepts ("non-provocative defense," "defensive defense," "alternative defense," and "territorial defense"[5]), and they form a distinctive spectrum of ideas in the area of defense. They are united by the fact that all these concepts exclude from the arsenal of defensive means both nuclear and conventional offensive weapons. These ideas pose objectives for the distant future, and generally aim toward moving to purely defensive minimum forces for both sides. In the foreseeable future, however, it will be possible to advance in this direction, to be sure, by changing the correlation of offensive and defensive potentials of the armed forces of the two sides in favor of the latter.

New conventional weapons systems have practically erased the dividing line between offensive and defensive weapons, between the principles of deploying and equipping armed forces for offense and defense. Any modern offensive force contains elements that are intended for defense, just as any modern defensive force has units and formations intended for counterattacks and counterstrikes. Tanks, artillery weapons, missile systems and aircraft alike may be used both in offense and in defense. Everything ultimately depends on the operational and tactical missions given to troops, on their deployment, and on how effectively they may use objective conditions (overall and local force ratios, terrain, logistics, etc.).

In developing an approach to zones, means and methods of reductions it is necessary, obviously, to take into account a whole number of fundamental considerations. If one side intended to retain for itself the capability for carrying out a large-scale attack on the other with the use of conventional forces and arms, then any negotiations on their substantial reduction in accordance with the goals of the Vienna mandate would be condemned to failure from the outset. The basis for the CFE negotiations is in fact the obvious lack of such political intentions and plans on the part of both East and West. But in and of itself, the lack of aggressive intentions still does not mean that a military conflict in Europe is totally impossible and that reductions may be carried out sweepingly and at will.

By analogy with the reduction of Soviet and U.S. strategic offensive arms, the objective of the negotiations on conventional arms in Europe, one must suppose, is the comprehensive reduction and elimination of those elements of the military balance that in a hypothetical crisis situation would present the NATO and WTO leadership with a dangerous dilemma: either to decide on launching a preemptive attack or to assume the high risk of catastrophic damage in the event of aggression by the other side. Such a danger is intensified by the fact that while many measures for bringing troops into increased combat readiness, for moving them into forward regions, and for building up strength through mobilizing reserves and transferring reinforcements may be implemented with the goals of increasing the capability for defense, for the other side such measures would be indistinguishable from preparations for an attack. The colossal destructive power, flexibility and range of modern conventional weapons combined with high troop mobility aggravate even more the danger of such a dilemma arising in a crisis situation.

The prevention of the inadvertent escalation of a crisis and armed conflict as a result of a political miscalculation may thus be considered the main objective of negotiations on this problem. Just as with the reduction of strategic offensive arms, the priority task here is the strengthening of stability (the elimination of the fear of a counterforce attack and the incentive for a preemptive strike) on the basis of a military equilibrium at decreased levels of the military balance. Only on this basis is the resolution of other problems possible—in particular, the reduction of military expenditures through the reduction of troops and arms.

It is exceptionally important, however, to emphasize that the restructuring of the military potentials of both alliances must proceed primarily by way of reducing their offensive elements, not by building up their defensive. Otherwise, an increase of "defensive" capabilities by one side may appear quite threatening for the other (such as the systems of AirLand Battle and FOFA), which will in turn provoke a retaliatory reaction and lead to a destabilization of the balance, not to mention enormous additional economic costs. Increasing "stability" unilaterally, just as in the sphere of strategic arms, may undermine the overall, total stability. Negotiations open a more reliable path toward this objective.

On the technological level, the resolution of this main task is complicated by the circumstance that the correlation of quantitative indices has relatively lesser significance in the conventional area then in strategic nuclear arms reductions. For conventional forces a much more important role is played by the structure of units and formations, deployment, capabilities for increasing strength through second and third echelons, interaction between different types of armed forces (in particular, ground forces and naval and air forces), material-technical supply, and many other factors (including the effectiveness and durability of C³I, the level of troop training, morale, the art of command, etc.).

On the tactical and operational levels (at the scale of divisions, corps and armies) the complexity of the problem grows even more because of the fact that the strategy of defense includes not only purely defensive, but clearly offensive operations and combat actions as well. In connection with the high mobility and firepower of modern conventional armed forces the main emphasis in both NATO and WTO military planning is made, as far as can be judged, on the concept of mobile, not positional defense. That is, defense for ground forces includes principles of meeting engagements, flank attacks on an attacking enemy, active counteroffensive actions against invading troops of the aggressor (and possibly holding captured territory). As for tactical aviation, similar actions for it, like close air support of ground forces, achieving air superiority, and inflicting strikes on enemy airfields, second echelons and rear infrastructure and communications are in practice indistinguishable in both defense and offense by armed forces on the whole.

Finally, at the strategic level (within the framework of theaters of military operations and the theater of war) the main issue for defense is what to do after an aggressor is expelled from the territory that he has captured: to stop and wait while he regroups his forces, moves up his reserves, and inflicts new, possibly more effective strikes; or, to develop a counteroffensive to the depth of the aggressor's territory until his total defeat or agreement to cease combat actions. The experience of World War II and of local conflicts in the postwar period suggests a choice of the second path. But it assumes the prior development and maintenance of the kind of military potential that the other side would most likely perceive as a potential for attacking and conducting extended large-scale offensive actions. If the other side is not deliberately preparing for an attack, then it would inevitably consider such a defensive potential of the opponent as a threat to its own security and would hardly agree to legitimize it by way of an agreement on a mutual reduction and restructuring of armed forces "on purely defensive principles."

In this respect it is necessary to emphasize that the political realities of Europe, the catastrophic consequences for it of a large-scale war even with the use of only conventional forces and weapons, the saturation of troops with tactical nuclear weapons and the inevitability of escalation of such a conflict to a global nuclear war—all raise the question of the applicability of the experience of the war of 1939–1945 and subsequent local conflicts to the modern situation on the European continent.

However, the above-mentioned considerations place before the negotiations a number of most difficult tasks. How, through quantitative reductions, to reduce both sides' offensive capabilities, which are determined in no lesser measure by qualitative characteristics, structure, deployment, training character, rear supply, reinforcement capabilities and the interaction of various elements of the armed forces? How, through a mutual reduction of forces and weapons, to avoid changing the correlation of the capabilities of defense and offense in favor of the latter when as a result of the reductions it will be necessary to cover the same length and depth of defended territory with fewer forces, while at the same time the offense will retain the capability to concentrate forces for a strike at the time and place of his choosing? How to preserve for the defense the capability for mobile defensive actions, for shifting reserves to cover breakthroughs in the defended territory, and for a counteroffensive for expelling an invading enemy—while not creating simultaneously the threat of a first strike for the other side? And how to retain the capability of deep air and missile strikes on the rear for disorganizing and weakening an offensive without increasing the threat of those same actions for disorganizing and undermining defensive operations?

In other words, it is necessary to resolve the most complex problem of such a reduction of conventional forces and weapons whereby the capabilities of attack would be radically decreased and the relative capabilities for repelling aggression would not be simultaneously decreased.

It seems that in solving this problem it is necessary to proceed from several basic principles. In the first place, although all arms, troop units and formations without exception may be used both for defensive as well as offensive actions, the massed deployment and especially concentration on separate axes of certain types of arms facilitates an offensive much more than the repulsing of aggression. This relates in the first place to tanks, self-propelled artillery and long-range artillery weapons, combat helicopters, tactical surface-to-surface missiles and tactical strike aviation. Certain auxiliary equipment is also included: movement to forward regions of mobile bridging equipment, means for rapidly clearing mines, and large reserves of fuel and ammunition.

Second, correctly chosen zones for the reductions and withdrawal of offensive arms and supplies in the framework of the entire "Atlantic-to-the-Urals" area will facilitate reducing the concentration of these forces and weapons close to the NATO-WTO line of contact and "separating" the sides' military potentials. This will substantially decrease the capability for a surprise attack, and will give to the defense a much greater warning time for the threat of aggression, but will not hinder the adoption, in the event it becomes necessary, of corresponding measures for repulsing a first strike.

Third, reducing the capability for surprise attack weakens the requirements for the size of offensive groups of forces for a mobile defense, a counteroffensive on the tactical and operational levels, and means for deep counterstrikes (in particular, tactical strike aviation), which may be perceived by the other side as a potential for a first strike.

Fourth, reserves for a strategic counteroffensive may in these conditions be deployed in the deep rear, where they do not create the threat of an attack, and their size may be limited by the bounds of reasonable sufficiency, so as not to arouse anxieties with respect to the capability for developing a broad offensive after a surprise strike deep into the other side's territory in the course of a protracted conventional war. The latter in any event is extremely unlikely in modern political and military-strategic conditions on the European continent.

Fifth, the introduction of broad confidence-building measures and measures for limiting military activities, of war risk-reduction centers, and of a comprehensive system of verification (including on-site inspection, permanent land- and air-based observation, and verification of communications, airfields, ports and large garrisons) would practically eliminate the capability for a secret violation of the agreement, for moving and concentrating forces and weapons for a surprise attack.

Possible Options for Reducing the Military Confrontation

The proposals advanced by the socialist countries on the issue of reducing armed forces and arms were first formulated at the Budapest (1986) meeting of the Political Consultative Committee of the member-states of the Warsaw Treaty. (In 1987 these proposals received further development at the meeting in Berlin.) In the 1987 Berlin communiqué it was proposed to reduce the inequalities that arose in certain elements of the balance of forces, ". . . by way of corresponding reductions for whomever is ahead."[6]

Thus the issue is how, while lowering the level of the military confrontation, to implement such measures that would permit reducing, and in the future completely exclude, the capability for a surprise attack and large-scale offensive operations. The latter WTO proposals call for a three-stage reduction: at the first stage, an elimination of asymmetries through reductions by the side that is ahead; at the second stage, mutual reductions of the number of NATO and WTO troops by 500,000 men on each side; and at the third, a final restructuring of armed forces on defensive principles at minimum levels of defensive sufficiency. Even before the beginning of negotiations it is proposed to exchange the whole range of numerical data with the opportunity for demand verification via on-site inspection.

It would seem that the following general principles could form the basis of the negotiations. First of all, in reducing conventional forces and weapons in Europe, independent of the scale of the reductions it is necessary to solve a number of most complex technical problems. This will require a maximum of good will, flexibility and foresight on both sides, as well as consent to refrain from many traditional military and political views. Readiness to sacrifice many customary and established practices of both sides' armed forces for the sake of the more important new objectives will be required as well. Similarly, the physical size of the reductions must be as great as possible so as to "make the game worth it," and to insure that the situation will be radically changed for the better in the military-political respect and will confer significant savings through the reduction of military expenditures. In this connection, the principle of eliminating imbalances at the first stage of the reductions has great importance. In such a way whichever types and kinds of arms and troops were affected, the reductions would have an even greater strategic and political significance were they to be carried out not simply to the existing level of the side that is behind, but to even lower equal levels. In such a way, the bloc that had fewer forces and weapons of a given category would from the very beginning take part in the reductions, even if this would mean an even deeper reduction by the superior alliance. It is gratifying that such authoritative specialists in the United States and the USSR as, for example, Ambassador Jonathan Dean and General G. Batenin are thinking in this very direction.[7]

Second, even with significant reductions at the first stage, both sides will still possess in historical terms an enormous number of offensive arms. But in such a case the relative balance between the offensive and defensive elements of the armed forces should be noticeably changed in favor of the latter. The offensive elements will to a lesser degree be sufficient for a strategic offensive, but will remain for conducting, if necessary, counteroffensive actions in the context of mobile defense at the operational and tactical levels. In order to strengthen this situation it would be useful to introduce, in addition to the reductions, a carefully developed set of subzones (defined in both longitudinal as well as latitudinal terms) in which to deploy the remaining troops and arms, and strict measures for permanent verification in order to exclude the possibility of moving offensive forces both in the direction of the main strike as well as parallel to it—i.e., not to permit the concentration of forces for creating groups for breaking through the defense on individual axes.

Furthermore, so that the reductions will weaken offensive potential, but not defensive capabilities, it is hardly possible to avoid the most complex but necessary questions of differentiating offensive and defensive weapons not only by kinds but also by types of weapons. This involves differentiating—for example by useful lift capacity (total payload)—between strike aviation (bombers, fighter-bombers and close-air-support aircraft) and defensive aircraft (fighters and air-defense interceptors). It requires differentiating between such offensive systems as tanks and armored combat vehicles (for example, by weight, gun caliber, frontal armor thickness) and armored personnel carriers (equipped with anti-tank missiles, light howitzers and machine guns) which are necessary for defense. The same applies to artillery (especially self-propelled), helicopters (for example, according to their bottom armor thickness) and surface-to-surface missiles (as opposed to air-defense missiles). With mutual desire it would be quite possible for the sides to reach agreement on these issues as well.

Finally, an important question is how to deal with the equipment being reduced. Simply destroying the newest weapons, while at the same time continuing their production in order to equip remaining troops, is hardly rational and too expensive. Rather, the arms being reduced should be withdrawn from the NATO-WTO zone of immediate contact and may be in part given to reserve formations, and also warehoused. So that these weapons could not be quickly reconstituted and given to combat-ready units, it would obviously be useful to reach an agreement on their partial dismantling and separate warehousing under strict verification (tanks separate from turrets, helicopters from rotors, self-propelled guns from their barrels, aircraft from their engines, missile launchers from transport vehicles, etc.). For reserve formations verifiable differences could be stipulated that distinguish them from combat-ready units. (For example, 20–30 percent of the given arms of the total complement of a given unit could be maintained for active use and training, while the remainder would be kept separately in a partially dismantled state in warehouses with the right of verification by the other side.)

Obviously, in connection with the stored arms of reserve units, it will be necessary to reach agreement on the permitted quantities of offensive arms in both combat-ready units and reserve formations, as well as in warehouses, in storehouses near weapons-manufacturing enterprises, in transit and so on. All these reserves must be subject to verification, including permanent monitoring, regular on-site inspection and challenge inspection with minimal warning time. The regulated withdrawal of arms from warehouses and their transferral to troops for the replacement of equipment in the framework of the established limits should be implemented with the corresponding notification of the other side. The great stored supplies of arms and equipment (including brand new models) formed in such a way will permit a sharp reduction of the annual volume of production of new combat arms and provide a significant saving of resources.

Finally, in order to facilitate verification it would be useful to carry out the reduction of offensive arms together with that of armed forces personnel, who would be subject to demobilization or be partially transferred to a reserve status. The question of how to reduce armed forces and arms is not simply a technical question, but a fundamental problem. A reduction through the removal of individual weapons from units and formations and reducing the number of their personnel will hardly facilitate reliable verification. A reduction of large formations—for example, corps, divisions, air wings, and air armies—would be easier to verify (after, of course, having agreed upon their relevant complement of arms and combat supplies), but it could contradict the idea of restructuring military potentials on defensive principles. In fact, these major formations have a heterogeneous structure of troops and arms, and are intended for offensive and defensive combat actions. The indiscriminate reduction of both offensive and defensive elements of armed forces (for example, tanks and ATGMs, tactical strike aircraft along with air-defense interceptors and air-defense missiles) would simply lower the level of the military balance without restructuring it on defensive principles, which—considering the immutability of geographic factors and the possibility of intensified qualitative modernization—could even relatively strengthen the offense.

Accordingly, it would be useful to carry out reductions of maximally large (for the facilitation of verification) but homogeneous formations, (i.e., those having uniform, offensive types of basic weapons). For example, tanks and armored personnel carriers can be reduced by battalions, artillery by regiments or by divisions, aviation by air regiments or wings, etc. Corresponding premises in garrisons (barracks, garages, storehouses) would be subjected to closure, mothballing or dismantling. Then, along with the reduction of arms would proceed a significant demobilization of personnel, which would entail substantial savings of military expenditures and eliminate the danger of a rapid buildup of forces in the zones of the reductions by way of transferring their weapons and supplies to combat-ready garrisons with all the facilities and infra-structure.

It is obvious that such a complex and multifaceted problem as the reduction of conventional forces and weapons in the face of the continual modernization of the means of defense and offense does not permit simple formulas. Here is required a complete and comprehensive ap-proach the various elements of which would supplement and complement each other.

On the whole, in generalizing the experience of consultative meetings, bilateral and multilateral negotiations, the initiatives of the Soviet Union and the other WTO member-states, and also the proposals and statements of official representatives and non-governmental research organizations, it is possible to consider, as an illustration, the following parameters of an agreement on eliminating asymmetries in the first stage of the negotiations.

Geographically, the entire territory from the Atlantic to the Urals may be subdivided into three zones. The measures for reducing the military confrontation in these zones would be differentiated according to scale, depth and form, though reductions would be undertaken simultaneously. Proposed reductions may constitute the first stage of the CFE talks—elimination of asymmetries—though they may be spaced into several consecutive phases spanning a period of five to seven years.

The first zone may be conditionally designated the "Jaruzelski zone" and include, from the West, the territory of the FRG, Belgium, the

Table 1 *"Jaruzelski Zone."* Correlation of WTO and NATO Combat-ready Tank
and Motorized Rifle Divisions in Basic Types of Weapons[8]

	WTO	NATO
Tanks	15,900	9,400
Artillery (100-mm and above), mortars and multiple rocket-launchers	10,200	4,000

Netherlands, Luxembourg and Denmark, and from the East, the GDR,
Czechoslovakia, Poland and Hungary. (The estimated data on the number
of WTO and NATO combat-ready divisions' basic types of arms deployed
in this zone are listed in Table 1). Here are concentrated more than 50
percent of the tanks and more than 40 percent of the artillery of the total
number of NATO and WTO forces in the European theater.

The most radical steps may be implemented in this zone, including:

–the withdrawal from the "corridor" of direct contact of the two military
alliances' armed forces of the most maneuverable and powerful ("offensive") types of arms and combat supplies (tanks, tactical strike aviation,
long-range artillery, combat helicopters and tactical missiles) to a distance
of, for example, 50 kilometers from the border;

–a reduction of offensive arms in the entire zone by 50 percent on
average, to equal levels, taking as a starting point the lowest level of
one side in view of the cited data in the table. With a 50-percent
reduction of the basic types of combat supplies and armaments to equal
levels for both sides, the number of tanks would be 4,700 apiece, and
artillery, mortars and multiple rocket-launchers 2,000 units apiece. Thus,
the WTO would have to reduce 11,200 tanks[9] and NATO 4,700 tanks;
and artillery, mortars and multiple rocket-launchers—8,200 and 2,000
units, respectively;[10]

–arms and combat supplies may be partially destroyed and partially
warehoused in sites that along with existing warehouses would be
under permanent observation by international observers;

–with the agreement of both sides, not more than 30 percent of the
remaining offensive arms and corresponding troops could be deployed
in the subzone 50–100 kilometers from the border and not more than
30 percent in the next strip 150 kilometers from the border;

–also by agreement of both sides a subzone 50-100 kilometers from the
border would be divided along latitudinal lines into five to six sectors,

Table 2 *Intermediate Zone.* Correlation of NATO and WTO Combat-ready Tank and Motorized Rifle Divisions in Basic Types of Weapons

	WTO	NATO
Tanks	3,500	3,700
Artillery (100-mm or greater), mortars and multiple rocket-launchers	1,100	2,100

in each of which it would be permitted to have not more than a certain portion of the troops of those that are deployed in this subzone (i.e., of the 30 percent of the forces and weapons in the "Jaruzelski zone"); and

—since the greatest foreign military presence of the two sides is stationed in this zone and with consideration of a number of delicate political issues, it may be possible in addition to agree that in certain arms categories foreign forces should not surpass 50 percent of the remaining forces, and that any single state also should not possess more than 50 percent of the deployed weapons of particular types.

A second zone (conditionally called "the intermediate zone") could include, for the West, those ground forces and combat arms on the territory of the United Kingdom, France and Italy, as well as stored arms and equipment of the six U.S. divisions of reinforcements on American territory, and for the East, the border districts of the USSR—the Baltic, Byelorussian and Carpathian. (Estimated data on the number of basic arms in combat-ready divisions located in this zone are cited in Table 2.) In the combat-ready units in this zone are concentrated a relatively small portion of the overall NATO and WTO forces (15 percent of the tanks and 7 percent of the artillery), but these forces may be quickly moved into the Central European TVD for reinforcing groups already deployed there.

Here would be implemented measures of the second stage of the reductions, including:

—the reduction of offensive arms and combat supplies by 30 percent in the same conditions. Considering the data cited in the table, in the event of a 30-percent reduction of the arms and combat supplies to equal levels for both sides (tanks to 2,500 units apiece and artillery, mortars and multiple rocket-launchers to 800 units apiece), the WTO

Table 3 *ATTU Zone.* Correlation of NATO and WTO Combat-ready Tank and
Motorized Rifle Divisions in Basic Types of Weapons and Tactical Aviation

	WTO	NATO
Tanks	8,300	5,700
Artillery (100-mm and above), mortars and multiple rocket-launchers	7,000	8,100
Tactical strike aviation	2,800	4,200

would have to eliminate 1,000 tanks and NATO 1,200; artillery, mortars
and multiple rocket-launchers, 300 and 1,300 units, respectively; and
–also in this zone would be established limitations on reserve formations
and the number of offensive types of warehoused combat supplies and
arms contained in them.

Finally, in the third zone may be included, from the West, all the
remaining countries of NATO in Europe (including Turkey), and from
the East, Romania, Bulgaria and the remaining eight military districts in
the European section of the USSR's territory. (The estimated data on the
number of combat-ready divisions' basic types of arms located here are
listed in Table 3.)

This zone is significantly removed from the Central European TVD,
but in it are deployed significant combat-ready forces (around 30 percent
of the tanks and 50 percent of the artillery of both alliances) and major
reserve formations. In the event of an extended prewar period, as well
as after the beginning of combat actions, these forces could be fully
mobilized and transferred to the central front. On the flanks some of
them could enter into battle almost simultaneously with the groups in
Central Europe. In the same zone are conditionally considered tactical
strike aviation which, due to their high mobility and systems of dual
basing, are difficult to count according to internal subzones. Here the
reductions may be undertaken along the same lines as they are in the
two other zones, including;

–the reduction by 20 percent of ground forces' offensive arms to equal
 levels for both sides: tanks to 4,600 apiece; artillery, mortars and multiple
 rocket-launcher systems to 5,600 apiece;
–in all three zones, tactical strike aviation would be reduced by 30 percent,
 i.e., to 2,000 units for each side (that is, 30 percent of the WTO level).

Not more than 20 percent of the remaining aviation would be permitted at a given time to be in the first zone, and not more than 30 percent in the intermediate zone. Both sides would also undertake an obligation to prohibit the redeployment to Europe of strike aircraft from other locations. Verification would be implemented by way of permanent observers at the main military airfields, inspections on command at the secondary military and civilian airfields, and also by means of airborne systems of verification and satellite observation;

–with consideration of the data cited in Table 3, the WTO in this option would have to eliminate 3,700 tanks and NATO 1,100; and artillery, mortars and multiple rocket-launchers, 1,400 and 2,500 units, respectively. WTO and NATO tactical strike aircraft would have to be reduced by 800 and 2,200 units, respectively, and in the first and second zones the reductions would be more than 30 percent, considering that around 35 percent of NATO tactical strike aircraft and up to 40 percent of WTO tactical strike aircraft are deployed there; and

–similar to the second zone, maximum limits on the number of units and combat supplies of reserve formations and warehoused equipment would be established here as well.

In sum, in the whole ATTU area in this first stage of CFE the WTO would thus reduce its holdings by 15,900 tanks and 9,900 artillery pieces. Holdings in low-readiness and reserve units may be limited in quantity at existing or reduced levels, provided there are verifiable and hard-to-break distinctions between weapons holdings of combat-ready and non-combat-ready formations. Depending on the concrete method in which the Soviet unilaterally announced (December 1988) reductions are undertaken (10,000 tanks, 8,500 artillery pieces, 800 aircraft), the proposed cuts by the WTO in the context of a treaty may be smaller: i.e., 5,000 tanks, 1,900 artillery pieces and no reduction in aircraft.

Parallel with the reductions should proceed a joint discussion and review of the military doctrines of both alliances with the objective of giving them an exclusively defensive character. In the framework of the structure of all 35 CSCE participants, it would be useful to continue to elaborate "third-generation" confidence-building measures and the "openness" of military potentials and military activities.

The scheme that has been outlined here, to be sure, is purely illustrative. More than anything else, it demonstrates the logic of and details the possible approaches to the resolution of problems, but in no measure pretends to serve as a basis for an anticipated agreement. The actual negotiations of the states on these issues, the political solutions and compromises of both sides, will most likely bring substantial amendments both to the initial estimates of the correlation of forces as well as to the concrete parameters of an agreement on the reduction of armed forces and arms. At the same time, it is obvious that consideration of a maximally wide circle of estimates and opinions, including those of an informal character, may facilitate constructive discussion on this most important problem.

Notes

1   U.S. Department of Defense, *Soviet Military Power 1986* (Washington, DC: U.S. Government Printing Office, 1986), p. 89.
2   Congressional Budget Office, *U.S. Ground Forces and the Conventional Balance in Europe* (Washington, DC: U.S. Government Printing Office, June 1988), pp. 97–98.
3   Dmitrii Yazov, *Pravda*, February 8, 1988; G. Batenin, *Pravda*, October 10, 1988.
4   Joachim Krause, *Prospects for Conventional Arms Control in Europe* (New York: Institute for East-West Security Studies, Occasional Paper No. 8, 1988), p. 12.
5   For more information see: *Razoruzhenie i bezopasnost', 1986 g.* [Disarmament and Security, 1986], Vol. 1 (Moscow: Novosti Press Agency, 1987), pp. 230–232.
6   *Pravda*, May 30, 1987.
7   Union of Concerned Scientists, *Presidential Priorities: A National Security Agenda for the 1990s* (Boston: Union of Concerned Scientists, 1988), p. 32; G. Batenin, *Pravda*, October 10, 1988.
8   The data cited here and in the following tables are based on calculations from the IMEMO yearbook *Razoruzhenie i bezopasnost', 1987 g.* [Disarmament and Security, 1987] (Moscow: Novosti Press Agency Publishing House, 1988), pp. 451–453. Differences in these data are due to a different methodology of conceptualizing them and to differing concepts in the levels and order of the reductions.
9   After the unilateral Soviet reductions are carried out, these numbers will change correspondingly (i.e., instead of reducing 11,200 WTO tanks, 6,200). The same would apply to artillery and other weapons.
10 Aircraft, in view of their high mobility within the theater are considered completely in the third zone ("Europe from the Atlantic to the Urals"). But should the sides agree, they could of course be directly considered in the first and second zones.

VII

PART ONE

Verifying Conventional Force Reductions
and Limitations

Jonathan Dean, United States

Introduction

It is evident from negotiation of the INF Treaty and of strategic nuclear reductions that reaching agreement on verification procedures and measures is for both practical and political reasons often more difficult than agreeing on reductions themselves. As this chapter seeks to make clear, the difficulty of verifying reduction of conventional force armaments may be considerably greater in the new NATO-WTO Atlantic-to-the-Urals force reduction talks, here called "ATTU" talks, than in either of the U.S.-Soviet nuclear armaments negotiations.

Despite the acute difficulties facing these new East-West talks, mounting political and economic pressures in both alliances argue for some at least modest success within the next five to six years. Even a limited first ATTU agreement would probably comprise three types of obligations: 1) force reductions and residual ceilings on remaining equipment and units of the type reduced; 2) stability measures—sometimes called "constraints" or "operational arms control," namely, agreed restrictions on force activities and deployments; and 3) measures of various types, including temporary and permanent observation, designed to increase transparency and to reduce the possibility of attack without warning. Continuing compliance with these obligations will have to be verified by measures which will apply to both sides reciprocally.

The Gorbachev leadership has accelerated a development toward decreasing Soviet and Warsaw Treaty secrecy on military matters already evident in more gradual moves in the late Brezhnev years. The Warsaw

Pact states remain far from being as open to both overt and covert collection of information on armed forces as the NATO countries. But the experience of the INF Treaty and of U.S.-Soviet negotiations on strategic nuclear forces, chemical and nuclear-testing negotiations, as well as the negotiation and first year's implementation of the Stockholm CDE Document, appear to place both alliances on a plane of equality as regards willingness to accept negotiated verification measures. In fact, it may leave the Pact somewhat ahead of European NATO members as regards acceptability of intrusive verification measures. Nonetheless, although the Soviet position has greatly changed, there remain practical limits on what military leaders of both alliances consider the other alliance should be permitted to see.

Two general problems of verifying an ATTU agreement should be mentioned at the outset. The first is that complete knowledge of the other side's forces is impossible. An ideal verification system would be able to make a "snapshot" of the status at any given time, i.e., obtain simultaneous accurate coverage of all military forces significant for compliance with the agreement. This would be possible for a limited number of military installations or activities. But, given the number of armaments, activities, and the large geographic area to be covered in an ATTU agreement, this degree of simultaneous coverage will not be feasible. As a result, limited portions of the forces to be verified will have to be covered by verification activities at different times. The difference between the ideal and the possible will inevitably create some uncertainty.

A second problem of verification is the complexity of verification activities and of the verification subject matter. Because verification strives for accuracy and precision, useful discussion of verification must also go beyond generalities into specific detail. A frequent reaction is that nothing so complex can be negotiated between East and West. One answer is that verification of similar levels of complexity has been negotiated in the INF Treaty and is being negotiated, although with real difficulty, in the U.S.-Soviet negotiations on the reduction of strategic arms. Yet this common reaction to discussion of verification points to the need to keep constantly in mind the principles of simplicity and economy of effort, and costs as well, in designing verification approaches.

But, here too, the ideal cannot be achieved: modern armed forces are highly complex organizations integrating a very wide range of human activities and equipment, including weapons of overlapping capability.

Efforts in the interests of simplicity of approach to identify a single key armament or activity to restrict and verify can usually be frustrated by increasing other armaments or activities. Costs of verification in personnel and equipment are considerable. When rigorous economy is practiced, there is an unavoidable tradeoff between cost and coverage. However, economic costs of verification are minor compared to the replacement costs of reduced armaments and the costs of reduced manpower.

Another point should be made before we proceed: this treatment of verification does not attempt a neutral approach to the issue or try to take into full account the interests of the Warsaw Pact as well as NATO. Instead, it emphasizes verification and compliance concerns which are characteristic for the West, as well as many common concerns. Readers will be able to obtain a corrective balance from the parallel essay in Part 2 by Andrzej Karkoszka.

In the West, it is generally agreed that the objectives of verification are to deter noncompliance or cheating, to detect militarily significant noncompliance in time to take counteraction, and to justify that counteraction. The ultimate objective of verification is, where feasible, to confirm compliance, leading to increased confidence by political leaders and publics on both sides that the agreement they have entered into has value. In this sense, successful verification between mutually suspicious participants is an important confidence-building measure, perhaps the most important of all.

The agreed objective of the Atlantic-to-the-Urals talks will be to make surprise attack or large-scale offensive action, including covert mobilization, more difficult through stabilizing measures and force reductions. Verification of an ATTU agreement—indeed, of any arms control agreement—should be deliberately configured to contribute to its main objective. However, a system to verify residual ceilings after force reductions should not be expected on its own to do the entire job of detecting possible moves toward attack. Verification will be a valuable supplement, but not a substitute, for a large ongoing information-collection effort directed toward that objective.

It is useful to keep in mind that the term verification covers a number of different activities. In American practice, the verification process is often divided into three components: (1) monitoring—collecting information on treaty compliance through satellites, sensors or inspectors, and technical analysis of this information to establish the facts; (2) verification as such—the political process of evaluating the information collected to assess whether there has been compliance or noncompliance; and (3) reaction to indications of violation. The present study deals mainly with monitoring an East-West force agreement in Europe rather than with verifying it in the broader sense. However, while drawing the reader's attention to the distinction between monitoring and verification, this study follows the popular use of the term "verification" where monitoring is often meant.

If the ATTU negotiations lead to conclusion of an East-West force reduction agreement, the central question which participating governments will be called on to answer will be, in essence, the same one asked in each of the bilateral U.S.-Soviet nuclear arms control agreements thus far concluded: will the agreed verification measures, taken in their totality, detect a degree of evasion or noncompliance which would be militarily significant in time to take counteraction, either to change the noncompliant behavior or to negate the military advantage it might have brought for the offending side?

This essay covers the following topics: (1) what is to be verified; (2) possible means of deliberate noncompliance; (3) verification assets at the disposal of both alliances; (4) the shortcomings of these assets and political and technical factors which will complicate verification; (5) the cooperative measures from both sides needed to facilitate verification; (6) organization, costs and personnel; and (7) a concluding assessment of the possible effectiveness of the verification measures suggested here.

What Is to Be Verified?

For illustrative purposes, we will examine here verification of a possible first-stage ATTU agreement, an agreement on the first of possible successive stages of force reduction by both alliances.

This first agreement might provide for reducing the tanks, armored personnel carriers, armed helicopters, artillery and fighter-bombers held by NATO active-duty units (i.e., not reserve units) to agreed lower levels in a Central European zone, as the area of greatest NATO-Pact force concentration. The same armaments held by active-duty Warsaw Pact forces in the Central European area (Category I divisions with over 75 percent of their wartime manning level and Category II units with over 50 percent of their wartime manning level) would be reduced to NATO's new levels in these armaments.

The Central European reduction area used here would include France,

Denmark, the Benelux countries and the FRG in the West; the GDR, Poland, Czechoslovakia, Hungary and the three western military districts of the USSR (Baltic, Byelorussian and Carpathian), in the East.

The main obligations entailed by such an agreement would be: (1) The primary obligation of both alliances would be to reduce a sufficient number of armaments of the types specified to come down to the new agreed level and not to exceed the resulting residual ceilings. Reductions could be by units holding the equipment to be reduced, in most cases by battalions, the smallest unit equipped with a single major armament, and by comparable air force units. U.S. units would be withdrawn to the United States, but their equipment could be stored in the reduction area with inspection rights for the Pact. Reduced Soviet units and the reduced units of participants whose entire territory is in the reduction area (see description of reduction area above) would be disbanded. (2) Thus, there would be a residual ceiling, i.e., a no-increase commitment, on the number of active-duty units of the type reduced both in Central Europe and in the remaining ATTU area. Units of other types, like infantry and anti-aircraft, would not be limited.

In this reduction model, both alliances would also commit themselves (3) not to increase the number of armaments of the type reduced held in individual reserve units inside the Central European reduction area (reserve units are comparable to Pact Category III units with under 25 percent of their wartime manning level) or to increase the number of those reserve units. (4) The overall numerical level of armaments of the type reduced in Central Europe which are held either by active-duty or reserve units in the remainder of the Atlantic-to-the-Urals area outside Central Europe would also be placed under a no-increase restriction.

Limits on Military Manpower?

Military manpower is the most mobile and concealable of all military resources and, consequently, the most difficult to verify; all soldiers have to do is to take off their uniforms and put on civilian clothing and they are virtually undetectable. Nonetheless, some manpower ceilings appear unavoidable in a first ATTU agreement. They might include: (5) an overall no-increase ceiling on active-duty military manpower of each alliance in the Atlantic-to-the-Urals area outside the Central European zone; and (6) an overall no-increase ceiling on the active-duty military manpower of each alliance in the Central European reduction zone. This ceiling would be lowered as active-duty units are disbanded by the amount of manpower of the disbanded units. (7) A third manpower ceiling, applied throughout the ATTU area, might limit the personnel of active-duty units of the type disbanded in the reduction program to their present strength and the active-duty personnel of reserve units of this type to no more than 25 percent of wartime strength.

The latter two provisions seem necessary to prevent expansion of the level of personnel of active-duty and reserve units outside the initial reduction area through assigning to them personnel of units reduced inside the area, and are also justified by the need to place agreed restrictions on reserve capability. In a reduction approach like this one, which emphasizes a shift from active-duty units to reserves with decreased readiness, it seems unavoidable to restrict the active-duty manning level of reserve units.

If holdings of designated armaments of both active-duty and reserve units in the entire Atlantic-to-the-Urals area were reduced from the outset, it might be possible to forgo limits on the active-duty manpower of reserve units. But we can predict that to the extent negotiations successfully deal with the capacity of the Warsaw Pact for surprise attack, the more NATO attention will turn to limiting the Pact's capacity to mobilize.

Requirements to verify manpower and armament levels in the ATTU area outside the Central European reduction area, as well as inside it, would greatly increase the difficulty and costs of verifying a first agreement. An alternative approach more closely meeting the criterion of simplicity and economy would be to focus initial reduction and verification efforts entirely on the key Central European area and to rely on intensive verification of that area to increase already existing warning of possible preparation for surprise attack. Since a successful first ATTU agreement is highly likely to lead to further reduction agreements covering the remainder of the ATTU area, this approach would not be unreasonable. But many in NATO would be concerned by the possibility of shifting manpower and armaments of units reduced in Central Europe to other units of Soviet forces in the absence of a restriction on buildup of these forces. Moreover, it may not be feasible to postpone negotiation on reduction programs covering the northern and southern flanks.

If considerations like these are considered primary, then it might be necessary to extend controls, including controls on manpower, to the entire Atlantic-to-the-Urals area in the way indicated. Nonetheless, the primary focus of verification would be on the level of reduced armaments and reduced units. Combat power results from combining trained soldiers with armaments in organized units; units and armaments are more verifiable than individual soldiers or airmen.

This reduction model could also include constraints, agreed restrictions on force deployment and activities, perhaps providing for pulling back certain specified specialized equipment—large ammunition depots, tank transporters, mine-clearing and petroleum, oils and lubricants (POL) equipment—and placing it in storage supervised by the opposing alliance.

The Breakout Problem

A necessary part of designing a verification system is dispassionate analysis of the main possibilities for evading the obligations of an agreement open to a determined adversary. Such analysis is value-free and says nothing about actual intentions. A pattern of repeated small-scale violations could indicate either a generally lax attitude toward compliance, a sloppy administrative system on the part of the inspected country, or a deliberate pattern of noncompliance. It is the task of verification analysts to imaginatively evaluate in advance of negotiating a verification system how residual ceilings might be violated in ways which would be successfully covert, would be military effective and would be reasonably economical, and to design verification measures to cope with these possibilities.

To attempt some objective standard of a scale at which deliberate noncompliance might become militarily significant, we might calculate as follows: the initial NATO Central Europe reductions under the proposed agreement might be 5 or 10 percent of NATO tanks, armored troop carriers and artillery. If the Warsaw Pact were able to establish a covert increase of forces exceeding NATO's own reductions, NATO's military position would have worsened.

Let's take tanks as an example. Measured against this standard, deliberate noncompliance on a small scale involving ten or even 100 tanks dispersed in concealed areas would not bring decisive military advantage (and far less advantage for concealment of conventional armaments than an equivalent effort to conceal nuclear armaments). Logically, deliberate violation would have to involve a large number of tanks to be militarily effective. It would theoretically be possible to deliberately disperse and conceal a large number of tanks in the large ATTU area. Many might not be detected. Yet the longer such equipment is stored without regular opportunities for training and maintenance, the less useful it would be. This would be a poor use of resources even for a policy of deliberate cheating. It is the combination of trained manpower, weapons and their organization into coherent units which creates combat power; one element alone is insufficient.

Systematic violation through large-scale non-reported training in the ATTU area of small illicit units using illicit tanks is another possibility. The combination of overflights, mobile ground inspection and the requirement to prenotify training exercises is a logical way to deal with this possibility, although it also indicates the desirability of a lower threshold of size for prenotification of military activities, especially for reserve exercises.

In a reduction approach which focuses on reducing active-duty units, another major possibility of violation would be illicit buildup of the manpower of reserve units. Assuring that reserve units remain reserve units can best be done by placing their equipment in secured storage and regulating withdrawal of these armaments for training. Indeed, some Soviet experts have urged that partially dismantling the equipment of reserve units and placing it in secured storage would, given the difficulty of verifying manpower levels, be preferable to manpower limits as a means of restricting reserve units. However, as discussed, some restriction on the number of active-duty personnel permitted to man reserve units seems necessary. If Soviet reserve units were permitted to have on hand their full wartime strength of active-duty personnel whenever they wished, coordinated ''breakout'' would be possible. Thus, the level of active-duty manpower of Pact reserve units, as well as their armaments, should be subject to restriction and inspection on the basis of continually updated data on specific units. There might also be limitations on the size of out-of-garrison activities by reserve units; such restrictions may create fewer difficulties than similar restraints on active-duty units, and it could be made obligatory to invite observers.

A further possibility of major evasion by the Soviet Union would be the sudden entry into the Atlantic-to-the-Urals area of large units normally stationed in the territory of the USSR beyond the Urals where the total number of Soviet forces would not be limited. This possibility can be lessened by use of exit/entry points along the Urals, by satellite overflights of Soviet territory inside and outside the reduction area, by low-flying overflights in the reduction area and by on-site inspection. It is improbable that organized units of battalion size or larger could be introduced into the reduction area, even if dispersed, without being identified in a relatively short period of time. A slow, covert buildup of restricted armaments might also take place through diverting restricted armaments produced in the reduction area from overseas shipment to accumulate an illicit increase in active-duty or reserve unit holdings of these armaments. Forces might also be built up through infiltration of platoon- or company-sized units into the ATTU area from outside it to pick up equipment concealed in the area at a time planned for attack.

We have pointed out that military power results from the combination of men and weapons organized and trained in units, and have also noted that military manpower is even more concealable than major armaments. Consequently, the most logical, effective method of systematic evasion of an ATTU agreement might be to use units permitted to have tanks or other limited armaments to train additional personnel beyond those of the units holding the equipment. Extra personnel could be attached to active-duty tank units in order to be trained on the tanks and other equipment authorized for the unit under a reduction agreement. In a breakout situation, these trained personnel would be suddenly equipped with concealed tanks. If there are no manpower limitations in an agreement, the training as such would not be a violation, and this possibility is an additional reason for manpower limitations in an agreement. The other methods of possible noncompliance described here would probably either be more visible, less effective, more costly or harder to organize. Consequently, efforts aimed at deterring the possibility of using permitted centers of military activity for organized noncompliance and detecting it if it occurred might be the most effective use of verification resources.

Verification Assets

To assess NATO's capability of dealing with deliberate noncompliance of these kinds, we will first turn to the verification assets or verification tools that both NATO and Pact governments would have available to help in monitoring compliance. At this point, we will limit ourselves to a brief descriptive listing, but it should be emphasized that all of these assets will be working together in a mutually reinforcing process. However, to avoid misleading impressions, later in the piece we will also describe some of the shortcomings of these assets.

From the outset, some early-warning and verification assets, especially those involving human inspectors and observers, could be deliberately combined. Doing so would have many benefits, among them, training and exercising both sides in verification at an early stage, and enabling NATO to follow the significant Soviet unilateral reductions announced by General Secretary Gorbachev in December 1988, as well as providing the West with assurance that withdrawn Soviet units do not return.

For example, exit and entry to the Phase I Central European reduction area could be through a limited number of checkpoints—airfields, ports, road and rail—permanently manned by personnel of the opposing alliance, and there could be fixed observer posts at a number of major ports, airfields, road and rail junctions inside the reduction area. Both types of observation posts would be designed with a double function in mind: both early warning and verification. For the same dual purpose, there could be provision in the initial agreement for at least one low-flying overflight inspection per year to each of the geographic sectors into which the entire Atlantic-to-the-Urals area would be divided, about 50 for the Pact and a smaller number for NATO.

Among verification assets, national technical means (NTM)—especially satellite photography and sensing, as well as electronic intelligence—will remain the most important single resource for verifying an ATTU agreement. In practice, verification assets will also include covert human intelligence collection efforts. These efforts, which will continue to be vigorously pursued by both alliances for their contribution to threat analysis and warning, will also develop some information of value for verification. For ground and air forces, high-resolution satellite photography can give specific information on types and numbers of equipment items stored in the open, precise dimensions of storage sheds and hangers, and, in part by showing the state of vegetation and grass cover, can provide useful information on the amount of activity going on in or near a given installation. However, because of the much greater number, smaller size and greater mobility of conventional armaments, and because of technical, cost and political shortcomings, these devices will probably not have the same salience they have in monitoring nuclear reductions.

On the other hand, sensor- and camera-equipped fixed-wing aircraft and helicopters will have greater importance. The range of aircraft with potential value for verification on the NATO side—the Warsaw Treaty has or will have equivalents for most of these—includes the AWACS aircraft now in service, equipped with radar to monitor flying aircraft of the opposing alliance; aircraft equipped with synthetic aperture radar, which can monitor stationery installations or objects on the ground; aircraft with equipment like the U.S. Joint Surveillance/Target Attack Radar System (JSTARS) which, when they enter service—perhaps within a decade—will have a capacity to monitor vehicle columns in motion; and low-flying fixed-wing aircraft and helicopters which have the capacity to photograph ground objects or to enable human observers to see what is going on on the ground.

Ground-based sensors (radar, infrared imaging devices, video monitors and X-rays), many equipped with cameras to record their images, can be used to provide information on movement of objects across a given line or out of an enclosed area. Tamper-resistant fiber-optic seals and tags, non-reproducible identifying devices which can be affixed to armaments with epoxy resin with a unique holographic signature making imitation difficult, have been developed to identify nuclear missiles and could be used to identify the "permitted" armaments still in use with active-duty forces in the field. Some devices of this type could also contain microchips capable of broadcasting a signal on interrogation or of sending continual telemetry signals with a tamper-resistant authentication code. Naturally, all active tags and seals would be removed in a situation of actual conflict.

A major potential application of sensors is for "secured storage," storage of armaments in a fenced area, in some cases, fiber-optic fencing, monitored by a selection of video and infrared sensors, and with a selection of sensors, including buried seismic weight sensors, dimension-measuring infrared imagers, and X-ray sensors at exits. The secured storage compound would be subject to short-notice inspection by the opposing alliance on the ground or from the air, as well as satellite observation. Large-scale breakout of stored equipment from several sites would provide wholly unambiguous indication of hostile intent.

Peripherally monitored secured sites similar to those described here have been established under the INF Treaty at Votkinsk, USSR, and Magna, Utah, in the United States. The main problem is cost. Full-scale manned sensor monitoring systems would require tamper-resistant mechanisms which are quite expensive, especially X-ray devices, which are both costly and difficult to maintain. The full range of possible equipment would probably not be needed for an ordinary equipment-storage site. In any event, there will always be a tradeoff between equipment cost and the assurance gained from using more sensors, one of the many tradeoff situations encountered in verification.

Short-notice inspection by teams from the opposing alliance to inspection sites of their own choice will be an extremely important verification asset for an ATTU agreement. Some interesting ways of relating the degree of concern over noncompliance to the intensity of verification effort, including inspections, are being developed by the Lawrence Livermore Laboratories and others through decision analysis which, among other things, requires assigning probability ratings to possible violation actions.

This work may in time produce greater precision, but in its present state, it can give a misleading impression of dependability. I do not believe it is yet possible accurately to quantify the degree of information obtained from each verification asset and then to combine them with quantified violation possibilities to form some quotient of certainty, or to measure accurately the subjective requirement for certainty and to achieve some dependable outcome. My own estimate of how many on-site inspections will be needed is based, on the one hand, on an estimated number of major centers of military activity, which I have identified as the most plausible sites of deliberate noncompliance and, second, on an informed estimate of what each alliance may consider acceptable for on-site inspection.

One major problem of monitoring ATTU reductions is the political acceptability to each alliance of intrusive aerial and ground inspection by the opposing alliance. Even where on-site inspection as such is acceptable, if inspections were unlimited, the sheer volume of inspections which would have to be considered may well pose political as well as major cost and organizational difficulties. Therefore, as also reflected in previous arms control experience, it is probable that neither NATO nor the Warsaw Pact alliance would wish to permit the other an unlimited number of on-site inspections. As a consequence, in the ATTU talks, participants may agree to limit inspection to an annual quota.

How big should the quota be? To verify the complex of Phase I obligations described here, an annual quota of about 350 short-notice inspections, ground or air, for each alliance may be necessary. This total is calculated on the basis of the seven obligations listed above, with coverage of the entire ATTU area: (1) one inspection per year to each active-duty division in the Warsaw Pact portion of the ATTU area.

Depending on what is counted and reduced and disbanded, there might be about 100 of these on the Pact side; (2) inspection of up to 100 reserve units including divisional secured storage sites and 30–50 separate storage sites, including those associated with production plants in the Atlantic-to-the-Urals area which produce armaments of the type reduced. If secured storage sites are monitored by permanent inspection teams instead of sensors—this possibility is discussed below—it would not be necessary to subject them to additional on-site inspection. If aircraft reductions are included in an agreement, an additional number of storage sites might be added, although observation of major airfields through fixed observation posts would also obviate or reduce the number of inspections needed here; and (3) provision for 100 anywhere, anytime, suspect site inspections of Pact territory at points other than designated sites in cases where there is suspicion that armaments whose level is restricted by agreement may be concealed.

Although the total annual quota of inspections is based primarily on the number of individual sites to be covered, there would be no requirement to visit each site. Some sites could be visited repeatedly. Moreover, there should be agreement to permit at least ten short-notice inspections simultaneously to sites of the inspecting side's own selection. The possibility of multiple simultaneous on-site inspections will intensify the deterrent effect of on-site inspection, although it also increases the number of inspecting teams each side must have available at one time.

As an alternative to a quota of suspect-site inspections carried out by outside inspectors flying or driving from outside the area to a designated site, each alliance could authorize a specified number of inspectors, say 20–30 for each country of the Warsaw Treaty in the reduction area, plus one team of the same size for each of the Soviet military districts. These teams would have the specific mission of carrying out suspect site inspections on a continuing basis throughout the territory of the opposing alliance using procedures somewhat similar to those used by the military liaison missions in Germany. In this approach, the number of inspectors is limited instead of the number of inspections.

The considerable amount of information available to both alliances by combining unilateral collection with agreed inspection and data exchange will be further amplified through the force-activity notifications, invited observers, and the small quota of on-site inspections which take place under the 1986 Stockholm Document. The NATO countries will seek in the CDE follow-up negotiations (CDE II) to obtain the information exchange they failed to obtain in CDE I. Prospects are good that they will succeed in doing so and also in expanding the scope of obligatory notifications of force activities, of observer invitations and of on-site inspections. Even the present level of agreements under the Stockholm Document presents each side with an authorized flow of information, especially on the field activities of the other alliance, which adds considerably to the information obtained by unilateral means.

Rationale and Value of Data Exchange

In my view—Andrzej Karkoszka takes a different view in Part 2 of this chapter—exchange of detailed data on the forces of each alliance at the outset of the new talks will be an essential verification asset for both sides. For years, the MBFR talks centered on NATO-Pact disagreement over the number of Warsaw Pact ground and air force personnel in Eastern Europe. NATO correctly insisted that the only way to resolve the discrepancy between the overall totals presented by each alliance was for each to present detailed data on its own forces, broken down into individual force components. But the Pact refused to present detailed figures, claiming that to do so in advance of mutual agreement to reduce forces would reveal sensitive security information. However, at the May 1988 Moscow summit with President Reagan, General Secretary Gorbachev authoritatively confirmed Warsaw Treaty willingness to engage in a detailed exchange of data, backed by on-site verification in cases of dispute. He also indicated that agreed data might be used as a basis for eliminating the numerical superiority in major armaments of whichever alliance had more of a given weapon.

The exchange of detailed data, with each alliance providing information on its own forces, including unit designation, location and subordination, with strength in men and weapons accounted down to the regimental/brigade level and comparable air force units, is, in fact, essential for the ATTU talks. However, before reductions proceed, it is not necessary, although desirable, that full correspondence result from this data exchange between NATO and Pact figures for total amounts of selected armaments held by Warsaw Pact forces—the prereduction data agreement which NATO sought in the earlier phases of MBFR is not required. Reduction obligations can instead be formulated through an obligation to reduce to the present NATO level minus some agreed number or, indeed, to some arbitrarily set numerical level for each reduced armament, without explicit reference to the data of either side. This concept was already reflected in NATO's proposal of December 1985 to reduce a small number of U.S. and Soviet personnel.

The real need for data exchange is for verification. NATO's verification agencies need to have a clear understanding of the holdings of individual Pact units in men and reducible weapons before reductions occur in order to provide a data base criterion, established in advance, for verification of unit holdings after reductions, through on-site inspection and other means of information collection. In on-site inspection, the inspected unit will be expected to provide an up-to-date report of its strength in men and controlled armaments and that report will be compared with initial Pact statements about the strength of the same unit, with NATO's own refined assessment of the unit's strength, and, of course, with what the inspectors see directly. Owing to Pact secrecy on military issues, NATO has up to now had to piece together its estimates of Pact forces from component fragments of information of varying quality. Consequently, its present figures may not be accurate for each individual Pact unit. In particular, NATO has to see from the data exchange how individual holdings in arms and men of specific Pact units combine into an overall total. It can compare Pact information with its own holdings on individual units and, in the event of major discrepancies, conduct on-site data validation inspections, which will at the same time provide valuable experience and training for personnel on both sides who will later verify reduction commitments. These inspections, equivalent to the baseline inspections in the INF Treaty, should take place over a two-to-three-year period from the beginning of the talks while negotiation on reductions is proceeding and be sufficiently numerous to cover each active-duty and reserve division and comparable air force units in the Eastern and Western portion of the reduction area.

The process of refining the data of both alliances is a time-consuming procedure and for that reason must begin at the outset of reduction negotiations. After adjustment through clarifying discussion of individual data items and the cumulative experience of periodic data updates and of on-site inspections, the overall data holdings of both alliances on Pact and NATO forces should ultimately move into closer correspondence.

General Secretary Gorbachev's December 1988 announcement of unilateral Soviet reductions, many of them in the area west of the Urals, is an important additional reason for detailed data exchange at the outset of the new talks. Unless NATO can have a detailed layout of Soviet forces valid for January 1, 1989, before the unilateral reductions begin and a second updated data presentation two years later covering the situation after completion of the withdrawals, it is likely not to be able to follow the course of the withdrawals and to be faced by confusing turbulence in its own picture of Soviet forces. For this purpose, neither the aggregate figures on Pact forces presented by NATO in November 1988 nor comparable figures which the Pact has presented, nor the presence of Western observers, official or unofficial, with withdrawn units, is likely to suffice.

Among the most important assets for verification is the increasing openness of the Soviet and other Warsaw Pact societies. Although it cannot be quantified, this factor could deter deliberate cheating and, with more certainty, would provide much extended political warning of major negative change in Soviet policy.

Factors Complicating Verification

The information sources, unilateral and mutually agreed, reviewed in the last section would produce a very large flow of information on forces of the opposing alliance to verify an ATTU agreement. Yet, despite the impressive array of verification assets described here, many factors make the problem of verifying force reductions extremely difficult. Some of these difficulties are generic and built into the problem of verifying partial reductions of very large amounts of equipment in an extensive area. Other difficulties are "man-made," like the desire to exempt sensitive installations from inspection, or resistance on political grounds to intrusive monitoring by the opposing alliance. A third category of difficulties stems from the short-comings of technical assets—NTMs and sensors.

Generic Difficulties

The Central European reduction area which would be verified in a first agreement will be large. Verification measures will verify the *partial* reduction of specified types of military equipment, leaving many thousands of armaments of the same type in active use, armaments whose production in the reduction area will also continue, rather than prohibiting either production or deployment of entire classes of armaments, as was done by the INF Treaty. In other words, each alliance will be monitoring high residual ceilings of reduced armaments, not their nonexistence.

These armaments are for the most part smaller than missiles, less dependent on visible ancillary equipment, and more mobile.

A START agreement will require provision for verification of warhead numbers and a solution for the difficult problem of how to verify agreed ceilings for sea-launched cruise missiles. But the main emphasis of verification will fall on large delivery systems visible to satellite imaging. Yet verification in even a first, limited Central European stage of an ATTU agreement, with reductions limited to tanks, artillery, armored personnel carriers, armed helicopters and ground-attack aircraft, would have to keep track of over 30,000 individual pieces of equipment deployed in field units and airfields in each alliance, roughly 20 times the amount in a strategic reduction agreement, mixed in with many items of unrestricted armaments, in hundreds of sites in the 11 countries which make up the suggested Central European reduction area.

Moreover, compliance with residual ceilings will have to be verified in the built-up environment of industrial, urbanized societies containing hundreds of thousands of buildings and shelters, as well as wooded areas where tanks or other armaments can be readily concealed. Much of the equipment to be monitored is already stored in shelters, and both alliances have large stocks of camouflage material and regularly practice its use. Divisional formations, a natural verification unit, are often widely dispersed and sometimes quartered in as many as ten separate garrison areas.

"Man-Made" Complications

Negotiated definitions of armaments to be reduced will be as precise as possible, but there are bound to be grey areas of possible dispute. For example, NATO wishes to focus on reduction of Warsaw Pact armor. But in modern armies, nearly all equipment intended for use in combat areas is armored: tanks, personnel carriers, artillery, anti-aircraft, combat bridging and reconnaissance vehicles. NATO itself has in service about 20 types of tanks and the Pact nine; and NATO has even more types of armored personnel carriers than it does of tanks. Although naval forces will be excluded by mutual agreement from reductions, they will provide additional scope for confusion—navies of both alliances in the suggested Central European area have aircraft, helicopters and other equipment used by ground forces. In all, there is a wide area here for confusion and dispute.

Among the man-made complications of verification, the issue of what is meant by a reduction may present even more difficulties. If reduction means agreement to destroy reduced equipment, as is clearly preferable from the viewpoint of building down the military potential of both alliances, that is one thing. Then, monitoring will focus on remaining equipment and be somewhat easier. Yet, rather than destroying reduced armaments, which are their most modern equipment, some NATO and Pact armies may prefer to hand them over to reserve units as insurance against future worsening of East-West relations, or to store them at designated locations. Reduction measures which involve complete withdrawal of reduced arms from the reduction area would also facilitate verification. But countries whose entire territory is inside the reduction area may not accept this approach, which would also preclude turning over reduced modern armaments to reserve units.

And, if we are discussing reduction of tanks, armored troop carriers, artillery, helicopters and ground-attack aircraft, what about continued production of these items in the reduction area? What will be done with new armaments produced, both those intended for forces in the area and for transfer or sale outside the area? A possible solution would be to place the output of these plants in secured storage adjacent to production facilities, subject to inspection by the opposing alliance, with notification of withdrawals for sale or military aid outside the reduction area or one-for-one replacement in units deployed in the reduction area.

Other requirements raised by one alliance or the other can cause serious difficulties for monitoring. For example, some NATO countries, like the United States and the FRG, have traditionally favored reduction of personnel or armament holdings through "thin-out," reducing the armament holdings of individual divisions, brigades or battalions by taking out individual items. The reduced units then continue to exist as active-duty units, as contrasted with reduction through disbanding or withdrawing complete units or converting them to reserve units by cutting their active-duty manpower below 25 percent. However, the task of verifying a reduction of tanks or other armaments by thin-out among all NATO or Pact units would be extremely difficult. In that event, all tank units would continue to exist, with much of their armament holdings and with a continual fluctuation for repair and replacement. Consequently, for verification reasons, it would appear nearly essential to reduce by units. Reduction by units is also by far the preferable way of reducing the combat potential of the two alliances.

For verification, ideally, too, the barracks or garrisons of reduced units should remain unoccupied or be turned over to civilian purposes. However, in the crowded, garrison-short Central European environment, this is likely to be impractical. More serious, even if reduction is by units, the NATO alliance, or perhaps both alliances, may insist on flexibility subsequently to establish new units of the type reduced with smaller armament holdings. If restructuring like this is permitted, it will complicate monitoring, even if it is accompanied by a requirement to notify the opposing alliance in advance of structural changes. Moreover, unless there is also a ceiling on military manpower, there could be an increase in the number and manpower of tank units following reductions, back to the earlier level or exceeding it, although with a smaller number of tanks per units.

Consequently, reduction by units of some specified size, plus an enduring residual ceiling on units of the type reduced, appears necessary. Even if residual ceilings are agreed concerning the number of active-duty units of the type reduced, e.g., tank or helicopter units, there remains the question of whether reduced active-duty units should be disbanded completely or themselves converted to reserve units using no more than 25 percent of their wartime manning level. Measures of this type will of course be reciprocal. To protect its own reserve structure, NATO could chose to permit the Soviet Union to establish additional reserve units with the equipment and a portion of the personnel of withdrawn units. However, on balance, given NATO concerns over existing Soviet reserve capabilities, it seems preferable to forgo this option. Complete disbandment of reduced units is a more effective means of reducing overall combat potential and also decreases the verification burden.

NATO will want to have collective, alliance-wide residual ceilings on armaments reduced in order to permit other allies to make up for unilateral reductions by one ally which might take place subsequent to negotiated reductions and in order to avoid any implication of individual national ceilings. This practice would greatly complicate effective monitoring if it meant, as it has in MBFR, that the alliances give collective data for the alliance as a whole rather than data for individual national contingents. One solution, if collective alliance-wide residual ceilings are still to be used, is to separate the obligation to maintain a ceiling from the obligation to supply data, so that national data can be provided by member-states of all alliances without any implied obligation of national ceilings—this point could be confirmed by explicit East-West agreement.

A further problem in this category of man-made difficulties for verification is the increasing use by both alliances of covered storage for equipment that can frustrate satellite and aircraft monitoring. This could especially be the case following reductions, when some storage facilities will no longer be used to full capacity, and assessment of equipment amounts can no longer be assisted by measuring storage capacity.

One of the most difficult of the man-made problems of verification is the desire of both alliances to exempt certain areas and installations from inspection by aircraft and ground inspectors carrying out suspect site inspections. (In practice, satellite observation cannot be prevented, although it can be made more difficult by use of shelters and natural and man-made camouflage.) Permanent and Temporary Restricted Areas are far more extensive in the Warsaw Pact than the NATO area and they will have to be drastically reduced by agreement, either in the ATTU negotiations or in CDE II. But there will remain a large number of installations which both alliances will wish to exempt from low-flying aircraft or ground inspection, such as nuclear storage sites. Yet many exempted sites could be used to conceal equipment of the type reduced.

In the INF negotiations, the United States drew back from "anywhere, anytime" inspections of all facilities in the United States. Agreement was reached at the December 1987 Washington summit to have suspect site inspections for strategic nuclear armaments. Yet, after a long effort in the START negotiations to reach U.S.-Soviet agreement on how to exempt many sensitive installations unrelated to strategic nuclear armaments from such inspection, in October 1988 the Reagan administration indicated that it had relinquished this objective. In the ATTU talks, the same problem will arise, complicated, at least in the NATO countries, by differing national views as to the sensitivity of specific installations.

As regards the general issue of exempted sites, here too, each alliance will have to work out some tradeoff between its desire to protect some of its own installations and its desire to have the right to inspect a maximum number of sites in the opposing alliance.

Shortcomings of Technical Assets

Technical assets for monitoring have a number of important shortcomings. Satellites are a limited resource. To have enough satellites in orbit to give continual close coverage of the Central European area or the whole ATTU area may never be feasible for economic reasons. Given limitations on resources and on interpretation facilities, priorities as to coverage become a problem. Moreover, Central Europe is estimated to be under cloud cover for 60 percent of the time during daylight hours and most present satellites cannot register under cloud or night conditions. New generations of satellites will probably possess infrared capability which can overcome some of these difficulties, but even they cannot deal readily with covered or forest storage. Ground-based sensors too are fallible. Seismic, radar, infrared and television sensors can be spoofed, and seals and identifying tags tampered with if sufficient effort and ingenuity are used. Mobility and camouflage can frustrate aerial inspection.

The major problems of secured-site inspection with peripheral fencing and storage is first, very high cost and second, that for sensor indications to be received and acted on, human inspectors must be on the site or the results must be beamed via a dedicated satellite. Either procedure adds greatly to costs. Consequently, until the problem of communicating sensor readings can be more cheaply solved, the cheapest and most effective way of establishing secured storage may be through ordinary wire fencing and manned patrols using vehicles on roads surrounding the fencing. I will present some details on this possibility in the section on personnel and costs.

There is, of course, no single answer to all of these verification complications. A careful combination and interaction of national technical means, human intelligence and the growing pool of information for each side from authorized observation under the Stockholm Document, and air and ground inspection and sensors, can significantly reduce their effects. NATO experts will have to give a great deal of thought to the most effective combination of their verification resources. It must be emphasized that an essential tool of verification at all times will be periodic detailed data exchange covering all active-duty and reserve ground and air force units in the reduction area, both manpower and equipment levels and locations down to battalion level, subject to repeated on-site inspection, and including data on production of reduced armaments, with production sites and amounts.

Cooperative Measures

Each alliance would commit itself to certain cooperative measures to facilitate inspection. On notice, tanks and other restricted armaments would be moved into the open out of shelter and storage facilities and ranged so that they could be photographed by satellite or low-flying aircraft. At the same time, ground inspection of unit shelters, roofed storage and repair facilities would take place; it would be made easier and more rapid by complete removal of the equipment from storage. Camouflage would be removed in units inspected and its use at the time of inspection forbidden. Where feasible, roofs would be removed from storage facilities. In cases of inspection of divisions and air units, as soon as a unit is designated for inspection, there would be an immediate prohibition of movement in or out of the garrison area and in a circle of, say, a 200-400-kilometer radius around it. Low-flying aircraft and satellite resources would check that this prohibition were maintained.

Participating countries would also be required to notify in advance production in the area of advanced models of restricted equipment, their introduction into the area, and their introduction into units in the area, at the same time notifying withdrawal of sufficient tanks to keep under the agreed limit. Withdrawal of tanks from secured storage for the purpose of training reserve units would be notified in advance, together with specification of the amount, period and area of use; observers would be invited and a numerical limit would be placed on this activity.

Inspections would, of course, cover holdings of all five types of reduced armaments. Inspectors would cover their tasks in low-flying aircraft or by ground transport. They would have the right to enter all shelters in garrisons capable of sheltering tanks except excluded areas, and could enter all storage, repair and production sites. They would test seals and sensors at secured storage sites.

To summarize points made elsewhere in the text, on the pattern of the INF Treaty, verification of an ATTU agreement would consist of: (1) baseline inspection of personnel and major equipment over a three-year period while reduction negotiations are continuing; (2) supervision of destruction, dismantling or conversion of reduced equipment; (3) close-out inspection of reduced arms and units and continuing on-site inspection of field units and storage sites; and (4) suspect site inspection. These measures would be supplemented by agreed early-warning overflight, and by NTM.

Verification of agreed restrictions on military activities or deployments will also be required in an ATTU agreement. Some such measures, like establishing Restricted Military Areas (disengagement areas) from which all heavy mobile armaments would be barred, will be far easier to verify than armament reduction; because, as in INF, what has to be verified is the complete absence of the banned equipment, not its numerical level. This feature alone, with the accompanying absence of the need to agree on data and to negotiate reduction terms, strongly commends Restricted Military Areas. Verifying other constraints mentioned, like the size of out-of-garrison activities or reserve unit training, will be more difficult, but aided if the limit is expressed in terms of combat formations as it is in the Stockholm Document.

Organization, Costs and Personnel

A verification task of this complexity will require carefully conceived organization both within the alliances and between them. Inside NATO (and presumably inside the Warsaw Pact), it will be necessary to set up a specific institution to plan the use of NATO's inspection quota for Pact forces, to implement inspections and to share and analyze inspection information. NATO inspection teams should be multilateral, although it will probably be sufficient to have only two to three allies represented on each team. The United States may well wish to be represented on many teams. It can also use the intra-NATO verification center as a place to share information obtained by NTMs with its allies. Other allies with NTMs and human intelligence sources can also use the center to present information for sharing. NATO's intra-alliance center would also receive information from observer and inspection teams and from agreed exchange of information under the Stockholm CDE agreement and any follow-up CDE agreement. The intra-alliance center would also have the function of notifying the NATO Council that compliance questions may exist. It should coordinate the 150 annual early-warning overflights and other observation and verification measures which each alliance might be authorized to make.

It would also be necessary to establish an East-West inter-alliance forum for discussion of compliance complaints. Serious compliance complaints could also be handled bilaterally, but the NATO requirement for multilateral information and cohesion also means a multilateral organization here—NATO will have to overcome its apprehensions over Soviet *droit de regard*, or right of surveillance over NATO forces, realizing that an East-West center will give it at least equal advantage with regard to Pact forces. This East-West forum should be given the additional task of functioning as a risk-reduction center to investigate and clarify low-level incidents like border-crossing by personnel and aircraft of the two alliances.

In this essay, I have proposed use of secured storage for certain types of reduction like aircraft reduction, for "reserve unit" equipment, like equipment of Soviet reserve divisions or United States POMCUS stocks and the equipment of withdrawn American units, large ammunition stocks, production sites in the ATTU area, or for armaments like tank transporters, on which special restrictions have been imposed. Earlier, I suggested that use of modular fiber-optic fencing and sensors to enclose such sites was impractical because sensor readings had to be communicated either to on-site human inspectors or via satellite.

Consequently, the most effective, cheapest form of secured storage may be by a small resident team of soldiers which patrol the perimeter of a fenced area. Equipment would be limited to a couple of all-terrain vehicles—perhaps some portable photoelectric sensors—and field radios. Communication with a single base in each participating state (a selected embassy) could be by telephone. The host state would be responsible for installing ordinary wire-mesh fencing and peripheral dirt roads; both would already exist in most cases. A complement of about 25 personnel might be needed for each site, ten on site at all times, a second rotating team of the same size, plus five spare people for sickness and leave. This approach would permit use of enlisted personnel drawn from already deployed military personnel at a cost, beyond normal pay and expenses, of U.S. $40,000 per man for language training and special instruction. Adding $10,000 per man for transport, $10,000 for rations, $100,000 for two trucks and prefabricated housing, there could be first-year costs of about $1.5 million per site.

At a cost of $1.5 million per site, 200 secured storage sites in the Pact portion of the ATTU area, plus personnel and equipment for perhaps 100 fixed observation posts at exit/entry points and other transport choke points inside the reduction area on the Pact side, would mean a total of perhaps $300–$500 million. In addition, personnel for this number of sites would be about 7,500 men, plus about 300 inspectors and 300 escort personnel, for a total of 8,000 military personnel drawn from a total pool of nearly 3 million per side. This is a maximal approach as regards the number of storage sites. Divisional storage sites for reserve units could be combined to cut the total number in half or even less. This is a fairly large sum, but only one-tenth of one percent of the $300 billion NATO spends each year for the European confrontation, and surely affordable.

Conclusions

The main question still to be evaluated is the effectiveness of the verification system roughed out here against a deliberate, carefully planned attempt to evade it. To recall our original question at the outset of the chapter, will the agreed verification measures in their totality, plus information from other sources described here, detect a militarily significant degree of evasion or noncompliance in time to take counteraction, either to change the noncompliant behavior or to negate the military advantage it might have brought from the offending side? In the verification approach described here, in addition to NATO's existing information-gathering assets (NTMs, which have good prospects of improving), and in addition to political warning, NATO would have available periodically repeated data exchange; information from up to 300 fixed inspection teams at exit/entry points, transport choke points, storage and production sites, and from approximately 200 annual inspections to units; plus up to 150 information early-warning overflights per year over the ATTU area; plus the flow of information from CDE measures.

The additional information gained from negotiated measures in an ATTU agreement would provide a great deal of assurance over the considerable amount of information already available that preparations for attack were not under way. Standing-start attack with minimal warning, now difficult, would become nearly impossible, and the warning time for short-preparation attack would be extended by several days, for full mobilization by a much longer period. However, even the exacting verification approach suggested here would find it considerably more difficult to completely eliminate the possibility of slow, covert buildup of forces over a longer time. The verification system described might not register a slow "thickening" of the armaments and manpower of Pact forces by as much as 20-30 percent but larger increases would be detectable in time.

Yet it is most unlikely, following initial stages of reduction, where NATO forces would reduce little and the Warsaw Pact would be reducing to parity with the new NATO levels by eliminating large numerical superiorities in most of the weapons systems suggested for reduction here, that the scale of such stealthy increases could be compared with the scale of Pact numerical superiorities before reductions: NATO would be better off militarily with an illicit Pact tank advantage of 20 percent over a common ceiling of 10,000 tanks per alliance in the Central European reduction area suggested here than with the current Pact superiority in the same area of 5,000–6,000 tanks.

Later in the reduction process, if the two alliances proceed to make deep cuts, and both reduce to a low level, the potential gains from covert buildup would become greater. Such an enterprise would take considerable skill and resources. It would also require a lot of luck—the risk that such a complex long-term scheme would be detected is considerable. It would, in addition, be very hard for Pact national leaders in a situation of increasing openness of their societies, to maintain an impenetrable distinction between outward amicability and a concealed determination to conquer Western Europe by force of arms. Even in a worst case, considerable political warning is likely to come out of the Soviet system. If the intent to attack follows an abrupt change of Soviet government, that change is likely to give political warning also. Moreover, even in such a case, the gain in warning of preparations for attack from both early warning and verification measures contained in the reduction agreement is likely to be enduring. In other words, although some degree of slow illicit increase might escape the meshes of the verification net, direct preparations for attack—mobilization of reserves, breakout of equipment from storage, forward movement of ammunition, load-up of munitions and fuel by ground-attack aircraft and helicopters—would be all the more observable because of the verification system. Even in this worst case, there would be an important net gain for NATO security.

Actions Needed

Several actions are needed to reduce the difficulty of reaching agreement on verification in the Atlantic-to-the-Urals talks:

–East-West negotiation on this subject should begin at the outset of the new talks and be combined with discussion of data and early-warning measures;
–NATO needs to carry out some field verification exercises complete with a "Red" Team doing its best to confuse and confound the inspectors;
–NATO needs to give more priority to developing and testing sensor and communications technology for secured storage—in coming decades, cheaper sensors and cheaper satellites should make it possible to monitor secured storage from a distance;

–As soon as is feasible, NATO and the Warsaw Pact should devise a small-scale cooperative test verification of a single unit in each alliance; and

–Finally, NATO should move now to establish the intra-NATO verification unit described in the organizational section of this report and charge it with the preparation of its verification position and the tasks described here.

VII

PART TWO

Verifying Conventional Force Reductions and Limitations

Andrzej Karkoszka,* Poland

As long as the contents of the prospective agreement on conventional arms limitation are unknown, the current debate over its future verification system is necessarily speculative. This study is therefore limited to some general considerations of the verification challenges posed by a future agreement, inasmuch as the scope of that agreement is discernable at this point in time. The essay is divided into three parts. The first describes in a general way the means and methods to be used in verification, with special attention paid to their applicability in the European context. The second addresses specific verification requirements for a range of general limitation measures. In the third part, the main problems for the effective application of verification will be considered, as far as they may be deduced from past experiences with verification of disarmament agreements and from the ongoing debates.

Means and Methods of Verification[1]

All means and methods of verification may be divided into technical and non-technical ones, and into national (governmental and non-governmental) and international (intra-alliance and inter-alliance) ones. In the category of technical means belong sensors on satellites and aircraft, and on the ground and in the water. Non-technical means and methods are the various forms of on-site inspections, permanent and temporary entry/

---

* The author is indebted to Dr. William C. Potter and General Hendrik van der Graaf for their valuable comments and suggestions.

exit observation posts, and mobile ground and air observation teams. The national (alliance) means and methods cover all kinds of technical means, the use of which does not necessitate the consent of the party observed (though their effectiveness may be dependent on the latter's cooperation), as well as diplomatic and intelligence services. Some authors, including Jonathan Dean in his companion piece, include covert intelligence-collection efforts in legitimate verification assets. In my opinion, covert intelligence activities, although practiced by states to obtain information which may be useful for verification purposes, have vastly different functions from those of treaty verification and cannot be included in the range of legitimate methods of verification. The international (cooperative) means and methods consist of various questionnaires (unified data exchange), various forms of inspections, exit/entry observation posts, international verification organizations, consultative processes, tagging and personal identification cards.

1. Satellites

Satellites and space stations carry various sensors: photographic and electro-optical cameras operating in the entire light spectrum (both visible light and infrared), synthetic aperture radars and radio and radar transmission interceptors.[2] In ideal conditions the satellite optical sensors provide very high resolution of detail—about ten centimeters in close-look operation and about one meter in wide-area observation. These ground resolutions permit observation and identification of all objects on the earth's surface, provided that there is daylight and no cloud cover. Europe, however, has rather extensive periods of cloud cover throughout the year which seriously inhibit the effectiveness of satellite photographic sensors. The infrared techniques permit sensors to see through clouds, darkness and camouflage, but their resolution is substantially worse; thus they can only establish the heat patterns of a given territory or location, indicating, for example, the intensity of operation at a production plant.

Imaging radars with resolution restricted to that of tens of meters, capable of observing only large structures and objects, have so far been used mainly to observe activities on the surface of the sea. With the use of nuclear power sources and with the advent of the most advanced computers, however, the United States is said to have begun operation of a new type of imaging radar, called Lacrosse, believed to be capable of creating detailed pictures with a resolution close to that of the best optical systems, irrespective of clouds and darkness. If the press reports are accurate, this powerful sensor will be focused on the territory of East European states and the western part of the USSR.[3]

The interception of radio and radar transmissions (signal and electronic intelligence) is carried out from satellites (and other platforms) on a vast scale, permitting the close monitoring of military activities, including ground, air and naval exercises, movements of forces, testing of new weapons systems and redeployment of formations.

In connection with the development of the Strategic Defense Initiative (SDI), a new type of sensor is being designed which will enable the observation from space of low-flying objects like aircraft and cruise missiles. If it materializes, this type of sensor will greatly enhance the capability of ground radars, used at present for this purpose, in observing air traffic far beyond their line of sight and currently obscured by the Earth's curvature.

Taken together, the capabilities of the present-day satellite sensors enable one to discover, locate and identify most military hardware and formations of personnel and associated equipment. They cannot, however, penetrate roofs and deep structures; they are still disturbed by bad weather conditions; and their coverage of a given territory is only temporary. They make a passage over a given location once in a predictable time-span—not a problem in the observation of a large construction or a stationary or slow-moving weapon, but a serious shortcoming in the observation of highly mobile conventional weapons and military personnel. The multiplication of satellites and/or increase of their maneuverability may be the right, albeit only partial and very costly, solution to this problem. In view of the prospective scope of European conventional arms limitations, it is obvious that no satellite system alone can guarantee data sufficient to ascertain full implementation of an agreement.

Quite apart from their technical shortcomings, the utility of satellites for European arms limitations is questionable from the *political* point of view. To be a useful instrument for ascertaining compliance or noncompliance by a given party, satellite-obtained data must be presented in a readable and authenticated form to an executive office, be it a state government or verification authority, empowered by an agreement to make a judgment. It is well known how difficult this process is inside the U.S. government.[4] It is unimaginable that sensitive satellite intelligence data could be shared among several governments, the allied and those from "the other side" alike.

The problem of utilizing satellite data possessed only by two states (or three, if one includes France in the near future) may be lessened to a certain degree if a verification system were to operate on an alliance-to-alliance basis, with both alliances having reciprocal rights to monitor each other. Each of the superpowers would provide data to its allies in a format it deemed appropriate to permit the assessment of the other side's compliance and to justify the demand for a particular form of verification. However, alliance-based data-sharing may be unacceptable to some states, the superpowers included: it would reveal national capabilities of the means of observation and it would be of little use to states lacking the necessary data-processing abilities. On the other hand, if only a final assessment were passed on to allied states, it would not satisfy national requirements for independent decisions concerning state security. Such a system could be seen as petrifying the existing division of the continent despite the ongoing political and military accommodation between East and West. Moreover, an intra-alliance assessment of compliance would exclude the neutral/nonaligned states of Europe. Wishing to tap the verification potential of satellite sensors and to avoid negative aspects of the superpowers' monopoly in this regard, a number of states promote the idea of international satellite observation systems, designed specifically for the tasks of disarmament verification and regional conflict resolution.[5] A proposal for an International Satellite Monitoring Agency has received strong support at the UN (with the exception of the two superpowers). However, it failed to materialize because of a wide range of political, organizational, technical and financial difficulties involved.[6] Recent interest on the part of the Soviet Union in the creation of the UN monitoring agency might signal an intensification of international efforts, although chances for a concrete result are still small. Even if successful, however, a UN monitoring agency would not be particularly useful for verifying specific European conventional arms limitations: the satellites' flight profile, their "tasking," the ground resolution required for their sensors—all this would have to be tailored to specific European needs.

Another often mentioned solution is to rely on the growing availability of pictures from civilian earth resources satellites.[7] Their ground resolution is said to range at present from 60 meters (Landsat) to 20 meters (SPOT, multi-spectral) or 10 meters (SPOT, black-and-white) and even 5 meters (commercially available Soviet images which may, however, originate from military reconnaissance satelites). The sensors they carry could provide far more detailed pictures if they were put in much lower orbits. Thus today's civilian space technology could already be useful for verification of arms limitation agreements. However, this technology is still in the hands of only a few states: the USSR, United States and France, with China, Japan, Canada and Israel trailing behind. The provision of surveillance images from earth resources satellites, especially if their ground resolution would be enhanced, would be tightly controlled by the respective governments. Thus, this type of satellite could not constitute the foundation of an international verification system in a highly sensitive military domain.

International developments in satellite technology indicate the increasing ability of several states to match the technological advances of the superpowers. Superpower monopoly of satellite-borne surveillance data is coming to the end. Although a number of non-European states have developed satellite surveillance technology (platforms, sensors, processing equipment, ground receiving stations), these capabilities are the most widely spread in Europe. France, Italy and Spain are already involved in the French Helios program (with the FRG possibly joining at a later stage). Several states cooperate in the European Space Agency on the ERS-1 satellite. Receiving stations and rudimentary processing equipment exist in socialist states cooperating in the Intercosmos program. Canada is in the final stage of preparations for its Paxsat A and B programs, with the latter offered as a means to verify multilateral arms control agreements in Europe. An interest in deploying observation satellites has been expressed by several European neutral and nonaligned states. Whether the three groups of states—Western, Eastern and the NNA—will go their separate ways or be able to coordinate their efforts aimed at the utilization of satellite surveillance technology depends on future political developments on the continent. With satellite observation technology more available internationally than ever before, the eventual agreement on arms reduction in Europe may provide an opportunity for an East-West breakthrough in the cooperative application of satellites in the international verification system. In a clearly cooperative atmosphere and stable East-West relations the rules for the dissemination of satellite-borne data could be established and a common satellite organization created. If this outcome proved to be too ambitious, the two or three groups of states in Europe would have to create their own, separate agencies. By doing nothing the European states would have to reckon with the shortcomings of the superpower monopoly on satellite surveillance which, in the European context, would be useful as a secondary means in the day-to-day operation of a verification system, serving as a trigger mechanism for activating other appropriate verification procedures, an ultimate backup for multilateral verification and an ultimate deterrent against violations.

2. *Aircraft*

Aircraft are routinely utilized in intelligence-gathering. They constitute one of the components of the national technical means (NTMs) of verification inasmuch as the data they provide helps to verify arms limitation agreements. These aircraft are highly specialized platforms, flying along states' borders and collecting data on the air-defense radar networks and their modes of operation, on missile tests, and on other radio traffic, from which the size of military activities may by and large be assumed.

More interesting from the point of view of their application to arms limitation verification are aircraft for early warning and air battle management of the AWACS or MOSS type. AWACS radar can survey and track air activity in the range of some 300 km (depending on the flight ceiling). At present its maritime version can also monitor ship movement at sea. With still further technical modifications it is possible to apply AWACS-type radar as a moving target indicator to monitor ground movements over vast ground areas. These potential applications of AWACS-type aircraft could have direct relevance for monitoring compliance with conventional arms agreements, either in the zones adjacent to the border line (200–300 km) if their flights are restricted as at present, or over broader areas if overflights in the other side's airspace is permitted.

This type of monitoring would be useful in checking certain military activities, but it would not provide the more detailed information needed to verify strict adherence to numerical limits on weapons and manpower. The ground-monitoring version of such aircraft, if designed, could fill the gap in observation between the exit/entry posts along a zonal border. The problem, however, is that only very limited number of such aircraft exist, and it is doubtful whether they could be diverted (and converted) from their present military missions to fulfill a verification role. Another possibility to "borrow" from military aircraft for verification purposes would be to utilize platforms and sensors developed in association with the long-range target and strike weapons systems, like NATO's FOFA concept, in which programs such as Pave-Mover or JSTARS are to detect the movement of ground vehicle formations at distances from 40 to 150 km.[8] Such "borrowing" may not be so fanciful an idea if one recalls that all existing technical means of verification (satellites included) were originally designed for purely military purposes.

In the case of military aircraft used for photographic aerial surveys two basic possibilities exist: first, using any of the numerous military reconnaissance aircraft with cameras mounted on them, and second, using any high-wing civilian or military transport aircraft or helicopter with the observation personnel equipped with hand-held cameras. In the first case it would be necessary for the parties concerned to agree on whether the aircraft's cameras and films were checked before and after the survey mission by both inspected and inspecting parties or operated freely by the inspecting party. Obviously, this issue does not exhaust the list of modalities (like, for example, flight paths, personnel composition and equipment used) to be agreed upon in the case of aerial surveys. The experience gained with the aerial surveying in the framework of the Stockholm CSBM agreement may be helpful in this regard.

Aerial surveying offers several advantages in comparison to other methods of surveillance:

–It is "democratic" (non-discriminating), since all European states possess aircraft or helicopters and equipment which can be used for this purpose;
–It is considerably cheaper than, for example, satellites or the extensive schemes of ground on-site inspections;
–It is flexible, because flights can be arranged faster and in immediate response to a perceived requirement. It can also be geared to coordinate with the work of other means and methods of verification, including inspection of exit/entry points. It can be focused on a specified area or perform a general, wide-area survey;
–It is less weather-dependent than photo-reconnaissance satellites and can provide detailed surveillance data with more real-time efficiency. It can cover large areas, several thousand square kilometers, say, in a few hours.

In order to be truly useful in arms limitation verification the aircraft would have to be equipped with a wider range of sensors than just the photographic equipment, including infrared scanners, side-looking and synthetic aperture radars, as well as with positioning equipment (taking advantage of, for example, the U.S. Global Positioning System). However, even with all this sophisticated equipment, aircraft, much as satellites, could not be used too often as a primary means of ascertaining the implementation of numerical limits on weapons and personnel. Their role should in most cases be seen as a backup system for all other forms of verification.

3. Ground Sensors

The existing networks of radars, like NATO's Air-Defense Ground Environment, although covering the entire length of the East-West borderline, have too short a range of observation to be considered useful in monitoring air activities deep in the other side's airspace. Furthermore, the existing ground-based signal-intercepting equipment may have only secondary utility for a verification regime, and this only in a zone adjacent to a borderline.

A variety of ground sensors, attended and unattended, have been developed for use in military operations (e.g., the McNamara Line in Vietnam), for surveillance of some interstate borders, for monitoring cease-fire and arms limitation agreements (like in an agreement between Israel and Egypt on the Sinai[9] or in the bilateral Soviet-American nuclear test threshold and INF treaties). Several technical devices are used with some success by the IAEA in safeguarding the peaceful use of nuclear materials.

These devices range from photographic and TV cameras to infrared cameras to acoustic, seismic, magnetic and chemical sensors. They operate in small ranges and, in the case of their application in verification systems, they must be implanted or installed by hand. Their use in practice depends on the character of the potential agreement. For a European conventional arms limitation agreement the unattended ground sensors may be very helpful in monitoring or signaling movement across a borderline; assisting in the accounting procedures at the checkpoints (factory portals or border entry/exit posts); controlling a perimeter around particular objects (magazines, factories); monitoring the closure of pro-duction facilities; and verifying the agreed production levels, guarding against the passage of very heavy vehicles.[10] Although their installation may require an on-site visit of foreign personnel, their operation and reporting of data may be executed with no or only periodic attendance. It is also possible to make them tamperproof, both in actual operation and in transmitting the data.

The more extensive the use of these sensors, however, the larger the load of data handling, film processing, tape readouts, etc., and the greater the number of potential false alarms to be cleared up, explained and checked. Moreover, not all states possess the required technology or the necessary production facilities for obtaining it. Thus their acceptance as a means of verification would depend on appropriate arrangements for sharing them between the parties to an agreement.

4. Tagging and Personal ID Cards

In view of the prospective agreement's stipulations on the numerical limits on personnel and weapons, interest is growing in designing tags which would facilitate the identication of each individual soldier and weapon.[11] A tag that is non-replicable or uniquely marked, easily observable and unremovable as a detection seal or label, would be attached to every tank, armored fighting vehicle, artillery piece or helicopter. The tags would be provided by the other side in accordance to a treaty-prescribed number of weapons in a given area. They would make it easier for an inspector to notice any weapon in excess of the agreed quantity both in operational units and in storage. However, it is not certain as yet whether all the aforementioned features of these tags really can be designed and their necessary quantity produced. Moreover, weapons often change location and their movement to and from the prescribed areas would necessitate constant tagging and untagging at entry/exit points by the inspecting personnel. Fixing and taking out tags would be particularly cumbersome, consuming time and personnel in the case of large-scale exercises involving large numbers of out-of-area forces, for example, of the "Reforger" type. Nevertheless, the basic advantage of tags, namely that they facilitate the identification and accounting of every major weapons system in a given area, may be significant enough to outweigh both the costs of their use and the probable unwillingness of the military to agree to so complete a disclosure of the deployment of each and every weapon.

The tagging of the individual soldier would be executed by means of a non-replicable personal card. Again, the number of such cards issued by the other side would be equal to the number of personnel permitted by the agreement in a given area, and each card would presumably indicate the unit or other specifics of the soldier's service assignment. Undoubtedly, such an identification system would in theory permit very precise monitoring of a numerically stable, fixed-location military force.

However, in reality the situation is quite the opposite: the nonindigenous forces are constantly rotated, the indigenous forces are fluctuating from one conscription period to another, and a number of soldiers may serve without uniform, thus being indistinguishable to inspectors. Insofar as the number of ID cards issued annually would have to be on the order of a million (depending on the area of application) and as the manpower levels have so dynamic a nature, the system of accounting based on them could become unmanageable. Thus the personal ID card does not seem to be a viable proposition; the high costs associated with it may well seem to be unjustified.

Exit/Entry Posts

In the original proposals on this matter, put forward in the mid-1950s and later during the MFR negotiations in Vienna, the fixed posts of observation were associated with the prevention of surprise attack,[12] whereas at present they are conceived primarily as a supplementary means of verification of the proper implementation of restrictions on number of personnel and weapons in well defined zones or subzones.[13] The observation of movement in and out of a zone is thus directly linked to the monitoring of the level of forces inside the zone. The entry/exit posts (EEPs) can be permanent (PEEPs) or temporary (TEEPs). The latter might be established in a case when large exercises or force movements to and from a zone would require opening additional points of entry/exit. The PEEPs would channel all movements of forces through a limited number of routes, making the observation and accounting of forces possible.

It is apparent that the concept of PEEPs would be valid as long as it is certain that no other entry/exit routes are used surreptitiously. Thus the system of PEEPs must be operationally connected with other verification means monitoring the routes existing in between the PEEPs and through the entry points (airports and seaports) inside the zone in question. This requirement may present difficulties when the zone or subzone is covered with extensive networks of roads and a large number of airfields. From this point of view it would be easier to monitor the shifts in force levels if the whole of Europe were treated as one zone (only nonindigenous forces would then be moving in and out and there would be a smaller number of routes used). The closer to the center of the continent, the larger the number of routes to check. It would also be impossible entirely to restrict travel of individual soldiers along civilian routes of transport. It should be observed that the number of rail, road and air routes into the Western part of Central Europe is greater than in the Eastern part. It seems that the 100 PEEPs envisaged by Jonathan Dean in Part 1 of this chapter to be established in the Eastern part of the reductions area is far too large a number, unjustified by the paucity of available air, ground and railroad connections between the probable zone of reductions and the adjacent territories to the East. Of all available routes of transportation (including airfields) only some, specified by an agreement, would be permitted to accommodate the military traffic to be controlled by PEEPs.

Because of the costs involved, it would be advisable to diminish as far as possible the number of zonal borders to be monitored (hence diminishing the number of PEEPs required). On the other hand, the more PEEPs, the more precise the overall assessment of forces inside the zone and the smaller the demand for inside-the-zone verification. The work of PEEPs could be greatly assisted if all movements through them would be pre-notified as to the timing, numbers and types of military formations involved. This information could be cross-checked with other information entering the verification system. The operation of PEEPs should not hamper too much the natural flow of transport across the borderline. Taking this requirement into account, the solution would seem to be the use of sampling methods to check the strength of the passing formations and, in addition, the remote accounting of weapons (possibly with the use of sensors).

6. On-Site Inspections

On-site inspections (OSI) in the framework of conventional arms limitations in Europe would probably be primarily oriented at those aspects of an agreement which would be most difficult to be monitored by other means and methods. This means first of all the residual manpower, weapons and the military equipment associated with the military units existing in the limitation zones. Weapons depots and magazines for logistics might also require on-site inspection. Less necessary, especially at the preliminary stages of the limitation process, would be the inspection of weapons production facilities. Finally, the process of weapons destruction and conversion into peaceful usage would certainly constitute a legitimate and acceptable focus of on-site inspection. As OSI is already taking place in arms limitation agreements, three basic categories appear to be relevant for conventional force limitations:

–permanent inspections covering the destruction/conversion processes, production of items under the agreement, and permanent entry/exit posts;
–routine inspections of the declared sites for military units and weapons and, possibly, logistics depots, organized according to specific rules, on a quota basis and at random; and
–challenge inspections of undeclared locations.

Inspection of Destruction/Conversion of Weapons

The function of this type of permanent inspection would be to ascertain that the destruction/conversion process proceeds according to the schedules established in an agreement both as far as numbers and types of weapons/equipment are concerned. The destruction sites would most probably be isolated from other military installations and the process itself would be agreed upon in detail. No serious difficulties for its verification are foreseen. In the conversion process the matter could be more complicated, since it would probably have to take place in a specialized production facility, civilian or military. Inspection of this process would have to avoid the disclosure of information not pertinent to the scope of an agreement on arms limitations.

Inspection of Weapons Production

It seems unavoidable that weapons production would have to be checked if the production facility were located in a zone of restricted ceilings on the particular type of weapon. Of the two possibilities for such inspections, namely inside and outside (perimeter) inspection, the latter would probably be preferred. The modalities for such an inspection were developed in the INF Treaty. However, the INF type of inspection seems applicable only to the production of large elements of a weapon or to its fully assembled form. In the case of smaller elements more stringent procedures for inspection would have to be designed. To check weapons production only by means of controlling the final assembly facilities may not be satisfactory, since ignorance as to the rate of production of various components of weapons raises the well-known and often overrated problem of "breakout," based on the assumption that clandestinely stocked parts can be quickly assembled into complete weapons systems.

Inspection of Units' Sites

It is assumed that the exchange of relevant data would take place before the inspection had begun. Once it arrived at the site of a military unit the perimeter would have to be closed and the verification team would have to check the correlation between the existing number of personnel and weapons/equipment and the data declared for the given unit and indicated in the books kept by the unit's administration in order to permit a proper explanation of absent or superfluous manpower and weapons. The unit's sleeping quarters and medical care facilities may be requested to be seen. The entire area occupied by the unit could be searched for undeclared weapons and equipment. The actual headcount for personnel could present a problem if the unit were large and its various elements widespread spatially and, moreover, if it employed a large number of civilian personnel. It could be assumed, therefore, that the accuracy of accounting for individual soldiers may not be foolproof. However, what order of discrepancy or uncertainty would be acceptable to the parties concerned can only be found at the negotiating table.

The accounting of the weapons stored or operated by a unit seems to be less open to discrepancies, as they are less mobile and more difficult to hide. Similarly, the specialized weapons depots of which inventories were declared and their documentation available to inspectors seem to present a fairly straightforward task. However, it might be that such a depot contains more than one type of weapon, some of which may not be covered by an agreement. The inspection team would not then have the right to gather any information on inventories of items not covered by an agreement, which may not be easily prevented.

No inspection should disturb for too long the normal activities of a unit being checked. Such a requirement sets a guideline for the planned size and composition of the inspecting team. Its work could be facilitated by the agreed upon questionnaires and the appropriate linguistic abilities of the inspecting team. A particular problem would ensue if a unit chosen for inspection would be out of garrison, taking part in exercises. An arms limitation agreement would have to foresee this eventuality, calling either for an exchange of information about such activities so that the inspection of this particular unit would not be planned at all in a given period, or for a provision permitting its inspection while in exercises, for example, in the form of area inspection, on the ground or from the air.

Challenge Inspections

The technical execution of challenge inspections of undeclared locations would not differ from that of routine inspections of declared sites. The difference between these two forms is in the political overtones associated with the demand for a prompt entry to a location which has not been declared by a state as falling under the scope of an agreement. It may be assumed that such a demand is based on strong distrust and suspicion of violation. Thus it is of utmost importance that the time limits for the execution of such inspections are carefully agreed upon and specific rules for their acceptance and, possibly, refusal established.

The Potential Tasks and Requirements of Verification

A range of limitation measures which might be agreed upon in Europe and their verification requirements is shown in Tables 1–4. The schematic construction of the tables is dictated by uncertainty concerning what might actually be agreed upon and also because the purpose of the tables is to indicate the possible objects, requirements and the most suitable means and methods of verification, and not to discuss the scope and modalities of various limitation measures. The tables envisage four kinds of limitations: (1) reductions by a certain amount of manpower, weapons, support equipment and logistics; (2) the establishment of stable, lower ceilings on these parameters; (3) the prohibition of some elements of military forces; and (4) thinning out of potentials in the form of zonal disengagement schemes. In reality these measures would not be clearly discernible from each other but rather would overlap in a comprehensive arms limitation regime. Accordingly, several means and methods applied to verify such separate undertakings would act in unity, mutually supporting each other.

1. The Relation Between the Type of Limitation Measures and Targets of Verification

Tables 1–4 enumerate various limitation measures according to the general method of their implementation. Thus reductions of manpower, weapons

Table 1 Reductions

Measure	General Method of Implementation	Implementation Procedures	Verification Target		Unit of Account	Verification Method	
			Primary	Secondary		Primary	Secondary
reduction of manpower	complete units disbanded	soldiers demobilized, commands dissolved, units' quarters destroyed or changing function or repossessed by other units	quarters of disbanded unit	quarters of other units	number of units, amount of personnel reduced	OSI	NTM, AS
	withdrawal of complete units beyond a zone	transfer through and beyond a zone	transfer across a borderline	quarters of withdrawn units, transfer through a zone	amount of personnel transferred, number of transport, number of units	PEEPs	NTM
	reduction of personnel on individual basis	soldiers demobilized on individual basis	number of personnel leaving the units	residual number of soldiers	individual soldier	OSI	
reduction of weapons inventories	reduction together with disbanded units by complete holdings	weapons destroyed or withdrawn beyond a zone or stored	unit's location, destruction site, or transfer across border or storage sites	other units' locations to check residuals	individual weapons, number of units	OSI, PEEPs	NTM
	withdrawal together with units beyond a zone	transfer through and beyond a zone	transfer across the border	transfer through a zone, quarters of withdrawn unit	individual weapons, means of transport, number of units	PEEPs	NTM, AS

	reduction of number of weapons of a given type in existing units	destruction, or withdrawal beyond a zone or storage	destruction site, transfer across the border, storage site	residuals in all units existing	individual weapons	OSI, tagging	NTM, AS
	reduction of number of a given type of weapon in a zone from depots	withdrawal beyond a zone or destruction	transfer across the border, destruction site	residuals in all units	individual weapons	OSI, tagging	NTM, AS
reduction of logistics	reduction together with disbanded units by complete holdings	equipment and other elements of logistical support destroyed or withdrawn beyond a zone or stored or converted	unit's location, destruction sites, conversion sites	other units' locations to check residuals	pieces of equipment, units of measurement for various elements of logistical support	OSI, PEEPs	NTM, AS, ground sensors
	reduction by withdrawal beyond a zone together with units	transfer through and beyond a zone	transfer across the border	transfer across the zone, unit's quarters	individual means of transport, pieces of equipment, etc. as above	OSI, PEEPs	NTM, AS
	reduction of stocks in a zone including logistics not associated with units	destruction or transfer beyond a zone or conversion	destruction sites, or transfer across the border, or conversion sites	check on all residual stocks	individual pieces of equipment, etc. as above	PEEPs, OSI	NTM

Table 2 Ceilings

Measure	General Method of Implementation	Implementation Procedures	Verification Target Primary	Verification Target Secondary	Unit of Account	Verification Method Primary	Verification Method Secondary
ceiling on overall manpower in a zone	reduction, or withdrawal of personnel (see Table 1)	units disbanded or transferred by units or on individual basis	overall number of personnel in a zone, units' quarters	number of personnel in reduced	individual soldier, number of units	OSI, PEEPs	NTM, AS
ceiling on certain category of military service (i.e. marines)	as above	as above	number of personnel of forces, certain category in a zone, locations of specified unit	all residual number of personnel reduced, training patterns	individual soldier, number of units	OSI, PEEPs	NTM, AS
ceiling on overall number of weapons in a zone	reduction by a given amount of weapons	transfer with units or on individual basis beyond a zone or destruction	number of weapons in units' locations and in storage sites	number of weapons transferred across the border or destroyed	individual weapon, number of units	OSI, PEEPs	NTM, AS
ceiling on logistics in a zone	reduction of existing stocks	withdrawal beyond a zone or destruction or conversion	amounts of logistic material or number of pieces of equipment in a zone, units' sites and storage sites	amounts of logistic material or equipment reduced, transferred destroyed, converted	individual pieces of equipment, or unit of measurement for other elements of logistic support	OSI, PEEPs	NTM

Table 3 Prohibitions

Measure	General Method of Implementation	Implementation Procedures	Verification Target		Unit of Account	Verification Method	
			Primary	Secondary		Primary	Secondary
prohibition of a certain military service in a zone	non-introduction, units disbanded or withdrawn from a zone or transformed into other type of service	soldiers demobilized, units dissolved, quarters destroyed or repossessed by other type of service	absence of a given type of military service, transfer of units across the border	all residual units, pattern of exercise	individual soldier, specified units	OSI, PEEPs, AS	NTM
prohibition of a certain weapons' category	non-introduction, withdrawal from a zone, destruction	transfer beyond a zone or destruction or conversion	absence of a given weapon in a zone, units' location	transfer across the border, storage, destruction process	individual weapon	OSI, PEEPs, AS	NTM
prohibition of certain logistic equipment	non-introduction, withdrawal, destruction, conversion	transfer beyond a zone, destruction or conversion	as above	as above	individual piece of equipment or unit of measurement	OSI, PEEPs, AS	

Table 4 Zonal Disengagement

Measure	General Method of Implementation	Implementation Procedures	Verification Target		Unit of Account	Verification Method	
			Primary	Secondary		Primary	Secondary
establishing layered zones of deployment of forces, weapons, and logistics	relocation of units with their weapons and logistics, relocation of logistics not associated with units, relocation of other structures	withdrawal of some units from their locations, establishment of new locations, same move for storage sites, withdrawal of some units and their holdings beyond a zone	units locations, storage sites, all supportive military structures, transfer across the borders dividing different layers		individual soldier, weapon, piece of equipment or unit of measurement, number of units	OSI, PEEPs, tagging	NTM, AS, ground sensors
establishment of a grid-pattern for deployment of forces, weapons, and logistics	as above	as above	as above but with the multiplication of intrazonal borders and crosspoints		as above	as above	as above

and logistics can be implemented either by complete disbandment of entire units, or their withdrawal beyond a zone's boundary, or by reducing the personnel or a given category of weapons system or logistic material from a unit on an individual basis. It is interesting to note that nearly all of the methods of reduction would use largely the same technical procedures: demobilization, destruction, conversion, storage or withdrawal beyond a zonal border. The primary objective of the verification system would be to ascertain whether the prescribed quantity of items under limitation had been reduced. Thus the primary goal for the verification of reductions would be "verification of changes." What is left after the reductions, that is, the residual forces, is not in this theoretical situation an object specified in a limitation measure. However, since the verification system most probably would be unable to check all the instances of the process of change, it would be helpful if the residuals were checked too. The actual assessment of the implementation of a limitation measure would then be much more complete. Thus, the monitoring of residuals is indicated in the tables as a secondary goal of verification. In the case of limitations specified as the establishment of ceilings on a given aspect of military forces, the situation is reversed. It is the outcome of the limitation process and not the process itself which is the object of an agreement. The primary object of verification is thus the existing level of particular elements of the forces, in other words, "verification of residuals," obtained in whatever way. However, because the verification would in the real world be unable to provide absolute certainty that the existing residual ceilings corresponded exactly to the prescribed limits, it would be helpful if the process leading to their establishment were checked too. Thus, the monitoring of the process of limitations is indicated in the tables as a secondary goal of verification in an agreement on ceilings.

It seems unquestionable that if the two respective limitation measures, on reductions and on ceilings, were to be verified only according to their primary goals, with the supportive, secondary targets left neglected, then the requirements for verification stringency—its technical and organizational abilities, and timeliness of reporting on all aspects of military activities—would have to be very demanding. Or, vice versa, if the states were able to agree on a very stringent, intrusive, buildup verification system to check the primary goals, then they could, in theory, forgo the secondary goals.

But what if one of the parties cheated in the process? With all other states fulfilling their obligations and reducing their forces, the transgressor would come out stronger. Whether the cheating and the ensuing surreptitious gain in power could be of any military importance depends, of course, on the scale of cheating, on the one hand, and on the scale of reductions of the other states, on the other. Since national technical means could always discover large-scale cheating, the violator would be forced to act cautiously, trespassing the agreed limits only by small percentages. This type of action could bring a significant result only over a longer period of time. Conventional weapons and forces differ from, say, strategic nuclear weapons inasmuch as a substantial numerical conventional superiority does not readily constitute any real military advantage. Moreover, the reductions which are debated in the European setting are to lead to the elimination of the existing asymmetries of military potentials, thus requiring much smaller reductions on the part of the numerically weaker side. This approach to reductions and ceilings, coupled with the impossibility of hiding the large-scale inventories of weapons and large formations of personnel, makes the threat of cheating being transformed into a substantial imbalance in the military situation between disarming states rather small. In the real world the purpose of arms limitation would be a new, well defined military situation, in which both the processes leading up to it and the final outcome (ceilings) would be specified in detail. The verification system would thus consist of both "verification of changes" (reductions as well as additions and modification) and "verification of residuals," mutually reinforcing the ability of states to rest assured that an agreement has been fully respected.

The above, somewhat simplified, analysis does not mention at all a problem of the so-called "initial verification" associated with an agreement on baseline data concerning respective military potentials. If an agreement were reachable on baseline data and the initial phase of verification were put in place just at the beginning of the actual process of limitation, the situation would be ideal from the point of view of comprehensiveness and effectiveness of verification. All three elements of the verification process—initial verification, monitoring of changes, and permanent scrutiny of residuals—would cross-check all elements of the complex military potentials of states, giving them very high levels of confidence. In this scenario the particular elements of the verification system may be less stringent and intrusive, the system less built-up and less costly. However, full-fledged initial verification, requiring in many instances intrusive means and methods, might be found politically difficult to accept. During the period when entire military systems would still be intact, the level of distrust and suspicion would be very high and thus the demand for verification would be the greatest. In contrast, at a later stage of limitations, with mutual confidence growing, the same means and methods might not be as difficult to accept—but they would also be less necessary. This observation describes in brief the dialectics of disarmament verification: when the demand is the highest, the execution of intrusive verification is the most difficult. However, as was said above, this controversy might not be so paralyzing if the ramifications of a limitation agreement, from initial steps through the entire process (divided, preferably, into stages) to the final outcome, are thoroughly considered. Even small discrepancies and transgressions would have to come to light in subsequent stages of this comprehensive and long-lasting process of verification. Knowing this, states would never enter an agreement if they intended to break it down by small-scale violations at the beginning of the process. Thus the initial verification does not need to be intrusive.

The demand for verification of baseline data *before* the actual agreement on limitations is concluded, that is, for what may be called "preliminary verification," is quite another matter. Once the data provided by one participant in the negotiations is contested by another, the only way to prove or disprove the figures is to verify them in place. However, at that moment the agreement would not yet exist and its verification system would not yet be agreed upon. If permitted on a temporary, one-time basis it could produce only a similarly temporary resolution of the controversies about the contested data. The figures describing military potential change constantly. And it is futile to consider the possibility that the verification system (not formally agreed upon) could operate during the course of the negotiations on the future limitations. For all these reasons it seems that a proposition to exchange the initial baseline data coupled with the demand that the data be mutually agreed upon and mutually verified before the actual agreement would be signed seems valid only as a kind of confidence-building measure (this differs from the position taken on this matter by Jonathan Dean in Part 1 of this chapter, and, incidentally, from the official pronouncements coming at the time of this writing from the Soviet Union).

2. The Problem of the Unit of Account

The tasks of verification are visibly easier the more sweeping the limitation measures. The prohibition of entire categories of weapons would be less demanding than their partial elimination; reductions carried out by entire units of known personnel would be more easily monitored than when manpower would be cut on an individual basis within the existing unit structures; the total elimination of logistical support systems from a given area would be less obscure than partial elimination. The basic reason is that these different limitations present different accounting tasks. Complete prohibitions present the easiest case—no counting at all. The elimination of entire units amounts to the elimination of all their manpower, weapons holdings, command centers, preferably also the barracks and associated structures. The monitoring and checking of the elimination of the entire depots is simpler than when their contents are diminished by a prescribed quantity of equipment and logistical material.

However, these observations do not mean that even if the larger units of account are the basis of verification their exact individual components, like individual soldiers or weapons or pieces of equipment, are never to be counted. This would permit too wide a margin of error to be acceptable. Once the exact numerical holdings and organizational structures of a given type of aggregate unit are known, it would seem sufficient to check these exact figures on a random basis to be assured that the overall limitations took place. However, it should be noted that the size and composition of various organizational components vary. Additionally, a variety of smaller military detachments are outside the normal organizational structures. These obstacles call for a detailed breakdown of the data provided by the parties to an agreement and may necessitate more frequent accounting of individual force elements. Moreover, the restrictions on weapons production and the process of weapons destruction necessitate individual accounting. Nevertheless, the fundamental method of accounting in a verification process cannot be solely or predominantly a unit of account such as each individual soldier or a weapon or "unit of measurement" in the case of some categories of logistical materials. These are too small, too mobile, too easy to disappear from the field of view of most means of observation used. To demand a full accounting of all of them at all times would be to demand an impossible task. The verified states would be too well aware of the possibility of random and exact checking on various locations and units to try to obfuscate their obligations. Thus the sampling method would greatly lessen the burden of verifying the quantitative aspects of the limitation process in case of small "units of account."

3. Verification Methods

The means and methods for verification were described in Part I. Here a point will be made on the differentiation between the "primary" and "secondary" means and methods. The division is based on a subjective assumption as to which would be more efficient and effective in fulfilling the tasks of verification. It is visible from Tables 1–4 that NTMs are depicted in the majority of cases as a secondary method and, conversely, OSIs of various kinds, including PEEPs, as a primary method. Technical capabilities are not the sole factor in this differentiation. After all, the most powerful NTMs may discern and identify even the smallest "units of account," if and when they are in the open. However, several things are not "in the open" and, moreover, the data from NTMs could not be a basis of permanent international assessment of the implementation of an agreement. For these reasons NTMs were relegated to a (crucial) role of permanent backup to all other verification means. Similarly, aerial surveying (AS), with all its potential for monitoring military activities and presence, is in most instances described as a secondary method of verification. However, different methods of verification are mutually supportive in a comprehensive system. Thus several secondary methods may actually have much larger verification abilities than a single "primary" one. They may also be less costly and less politically burdensome. Each case of a specific mixture of verification methods must be weighed against their cost-effectiveness, intrusiveness, timeliness and other parameters. Whatever the result of such assessment, it is clear that most of the probable conventional arms limitation measures would require on-site inspections as a basic tool of verification, working hand in hand with all other means.

4. Zonal Arrangements

Table 4 is concerned with two types of zonal disengagement schemes, one "layer" and the other one "grid-pattern." These two schemes would be implemented in similar procedures and necessitate the same methods of verification. The only difference between the two concepts is the multiplication of borderlines and cross-points to be checked in the case of the grid-pattern approach. Thus if the economy of verification is considered a priority, the layered concept seems advantageous. However, the grid-pattern zone, in which an area would be divided both horizontally and vertically into several subzones, with their borderlines monitored by PEEPs or other methods of verification, forecloses the possibility of clandestine concentrations of forces drawn from the wider zone. Whether such a result would warrant the substantial extension of the verification system, with all the costs involved, is open to question.

Some Premises for Effective Verification

The successful implementation of verification procedures depends on a number of political, organizational, financial and technical factors. Here only four general issues, linked to the effective implementation of verification, will be discussed: the exchange of data, organizational and financial matters, the level of acceptable intrusiveness and the influence of the political context.

1. Data Exchange

The availability of extensive data on military potentials before, during and after the process of implementation of the agreed limitations would have a fundamental influence on the effectiveness of the verification system. In the complex and fluid environment of the states' military systems, the prior knowledge of the manpower and weapons inventories, the deployment locations of units, the structural interconnections between them, their movement inside the area of limitation—all establish a pattern against which the findings of verification may be compared and assessed. The problem with data exchange is what should be the required level of detail at a given stage of negotiations and, later, at a given stage of limitations. In general, the details should be commensurate with the character and the stage of a limitation measure. However, this fairly straightforward rule can be interpreted in various ways. In order to avoid any possible contradictions and accusations, the format of data to be exchanged would always have to be precisely defined.

It seems that for political reasons the most difficult would be the preliminary exchange of data prior to an agreement. This is so because the degree of cooperation and trust between parties on security issues would still be limited. Moreover, at this stage discrepancies between each side's assessments of the other's military potentials would probably be greatest.

Notwithstanding the experiences of past negotiations on conventional arms limitations in Europe, it would seem that any small discrepancies in both sides' assessments of forces should not matter that much. After all, the preliminary exchange of data during the negotiations would have to be followed by much more detailed initial military blueprints at the moment an agreement entered into force, and subsequently by data exchanged during the process of limitations, these having been already scrupulously verified. It is both an advantageous and burdensome situation that the data always comes from two sources, that is, from the verified and the verifying state. This permits a cross-checking of figures and, in case they are uncontested, may be conducive to the smooth cooperation of the parties to an agreement: the provision of data would be a clear signal of good will, and its acceptance a signal of trust. Regrettably, in practice such a confluence of opinions on a complex set of military data between adversaries is difficult to expect.

In the context of the entire process of incremental data exchange and its prompt verification, it should be taken as a rule that the data provided by a state about itself and not the data provided by the outside sources should have considerable legitimacy. A state which would provide false figures about its military forces would find itself soon after an agreement entered into force in a very precarious situation, since the verification system could already at the preliminary stages of the limitation process alarm all other participating states about discrepancies between declared and existing potential. And it is quite a different matter to be doubted during the negotiations *before* signing an agreement and being caught red-handed *after* the agreement is in force.

It is a natural tendency on the part of states to demand from others maximum openness in the provision of data. Such a demand before the limitations are agreed upon could be objected to on political and military grounds. What level of knowledge about the other side is required in order to carry out purposeful and serious negotiations in which several technical matters are decided according to that knowledge, is always a contentious issue. Compromise thus has to be reached between, on the one hand, the minimum required level of data detail and the degree of its disaggregation for negotiations to proceed, and, on the other, the maximum level permitted by the state disclosing it.

The problem of data exchange looks quite different after an agreement is signed. From that moment on the states are under legal obligations to provide precise data on forces, their activities and their composition. Such data exchange would probably have an incremental nature commensurate with the process of limitation and would be constantly fed into the verification system for cross-checking.

Given the size of military potentials to be limited and verified, the amount of information passed between states and flowing from the verification system would be enormous. It seems that in order to be manageable and useful the data would have to be provided in a uniform way by all participants and gathered (processed, disseminated) in a central (one joint or two separate) data storage office by an appropriate institution, created by agreement.

2. Organizational and Financial Issues

The scope and the complexity of the future verification system safeguarding the implementation of a conventional arms limitation agreement in Europe surpass everything achieved so far in disarmament—NPT, SALT and INF agreements included. It is thus of utmost importance that the system is organized in a way which would secure its efficiency and impartiality, accepted as such by all participants even during political crisis, and that it would be financially sustainable. Although it may be taken as a rule of thumb that any verification system is less costly than the military force being reduced, it is nevertheless not entirely immaterial how much it would eventually cost. The bill for verification will probably be covered from quite different budgets than the weapons and forces under reductions. Thus the savings from these reductions may not be easily transferrable to cover verification costs but, most probably, will be used for other weapons and forces not under limitations. Most states see in conventional arms limitations an occasion to trim their budgets, and the competition from both the civilian and military sectors to grab the funds released by reductions may well impose modest budgets on a verification system.

Any method of verification agreed upon would entail similar elements: manpower (inspectors, interpreters, accompanying personnel, technicians), means of transport, means of communications, sensors and auxiliary equipment. Additionally it seems unavoidable that inspection teams will use helicopters and aircraft for aerial observation, thus their usage, fuel, pilots' salaries, servicing, and stationing quarters would add to the overall costs. Depending upon whether the information gathered by the verification system would be based entirely on national agencies or organized within the respective blocs or on an intra-bloc basis, the costs of the data collection, interpretation and storage would vary. Obviously, the wide internationalization of these activities would lessen the burdens incurred by an individual state. To the overall costs of verification the periodic review or consultative meetings would have to be added. It will not be an easy matter to agree on how these costs should be shared among participating states: whether they will be met from the common budget or covered by an individual state, each for its own verification effort. Most probably at the initial period of the verification process this first option will be recommended and later on a mixed system of financing could be adopted.

Among the general costs associated with the operation of a future verification system (though difficult to assess) would be those incurred by various production firms which would have to change their production procedures and rearrange their facilities in order to accommodate the verification requirements while keeping parts of their commercial production (not covered by the treaty) out of inspectors' eyes.

Permanent OSI. Permanent inspections would be located at the destruction, conversion, storage and production sites. It is hard to predict how many would be needed. The number of destruction sites could be limited if organized on a bloc basis. Taking into consideration that various weapons systems would be involved and that each probably would require a somewhat different destruction process, several destruction sites for either state-party would be needed. Each would require a number of inspectors plus the accompanying personnel. The destruction process may be connected with the establishment of the prescribed routes from the operational bases to the destruction sites. If so, this transfer may be put under observation—adding to the manpower needs and costs. The number of inspection teams to observe the production and conversion could vary from state to state, depending on what would have to be monitored (the entire production process or only some of its vital stages). The number of inspectors required for this task would depend on the character of the reductions and the scale of the production facility. Probably the permanent inspection teams would also have to be located at the various depots. Their number, again, is difficult to determine—it would depend on the agreement itself and on the availability of appropriate sensors which would assume the role of humans. A large part of the permanent inspectorate would be tasked to man all PEEPs and TEEPs, discussed below.

Routine OSI. As underlined in the preceding sections, it is assumed that the routine inspections would be carried out on a random basis, thus—in contrast to the assumption of Jonathan Dean in Part 1—not every unit would necessarily have to be visited and checked over a given period of reductions. It seems that it would suffice if only a small percentage of different locations, assumed here as some 5 percent of all existing sites, would be verified in detail by an OSI. Assuming at least ten sites per division and an additional number of non-divisional units, the overall number of sites to be potentially visited by routine inspection teams may be counted as 1,000–2,000 on each side.

Challenge OSI. In theory the personnel planned for challenge OSI could be drawn from the pool of those carrying out routine OSI. However, it might be necessary to carry out challenge OSI in locations different from the routine OSI in a moment when all manpower is "out in the field." Thus a certain number of inspectors would have to be on hand for this task at all times. Their number would depend on the permitted annual quota of challenge OSI for a single state.

Permanent Entry/Exit Points. The number of PEEPs (and TEEPs) would be specified in an agreement. It seems plausible that it would be smaller than the number of available border crossings. It might be that for political reasons the two sides would establish equal numbers of PEEPs, although various states' territorial configurations and differences in density of roads, ports and airfields call for more specific approaches, thus in reality entailing different numbers of PEEPs on both sides. The requirement for manpower at these points would greatly depend on the availability of reliable ground sensors.

Approximate Manpower and Costs of the Inspectorate. It is impossible at this stage to predict the actual size and operating costs of the inspectorate needed for verification of a future agreement on force reductions in Europe. As an illustration, and only as an illustration, a subjective guess on the personnel figures is given in Table 5.

As evident from Table 5 the future inspectorate would consist of some 1,000–4,000 persons on each side (in contrast to 2,000 envisaged by Jonathan Dean for PEEPs alone). This figure does not include the personnel required for running the verification bureaucracy, nor does it take into account the possibility of intra- or inter-bloc verification centers for collecting, processing and disseminating information on which the effective verification system would depend.

The cost of manpower differs in the East and in the West. Moreover, there are no data readily available about the cost of various sensors and technical facilities needed in the operation of verification. Thus

Table 5 Inspectorate

	Number of Sites	Number of Foreign Inspectors per Site	Number of Accompanying Personnel per Site	Overall Number of Foreign Inspectors	Overall Number of Accompanying Personnel	Overall Number of Inspectors
Permanent OSI						
Destruction	5–10	5–10	1–3	25–100	5–30	30–130
Production/conversion	20–40	4–10	4–8	80–400	80–320	160–720
PEEPs (including ports and airfields)	10	15–20	4–8	150–200	40–80	190–280
Routine OSI						
5 percent of units	100–200	5–10	1–2	500–2,000	100–400	600–2,400
Challenge OSI						
Unit locations	10	5–10	1–2	50–100	10–20	60–120
Overall	145–270	—	—	805–2,800	235–850	1,040–3,650
Total for both WTO and NATO	290–540	—	—	1,610–5,600	470–1,700	1,080–7,300

any estimate of the overall costs must be treated as purely hypothetical.

One way of approximating the potential costs involved would be to compare the size of the inspectorate envisaged for verification of an agreement in Europe with those of the INF Treaty and the 1975 Sinai agreement between Egypt and Israel. In both cases, this comparison has a number of qualifications because of obvious differences in tasks and scales. Moreover, in the case of the INF Treaty the known costs involved in its implementation also cover the destruction process which, naturally, should not be treated together with the costs of verification.

The verification (and destruction) costs for the United States under the INF Treaty were assumed to be some $200 million for the first years.[14] The costs of establishing the Sinai monitoring stations were counted in 1976 dollars as $19 million, and the operating costs were on average some $11 million a year.[15] The assumed size of an inspectorate for a conventional arms agreement in Europe is five to ten times larger than the tally of inspection personnel operating under the INF Treaty and about ten to twenty times larger that the one used in the Sinai monitoring. When multiplying the costs of these two cases of verification by factors of five and twenty we arrive at a figure of approximately $150 million to $2 billion for each side as the annual cost of the overall system of verification of a future agreement in Europe. Taking into account the possibility of a wider use of expensive forms of monitoring such as aircraft and helicopters (also used in the Sinai monitoring), costs of extensive communications and the need for sophisticated centers to gather all types of information, it seems that the larger figure may be closer to reality. However, the costs of verification tend to diminish once the system is in place and the burden of permanent OSI (for example, those linked to monitoring the destruction sites) declines.

The costs of NTM hardware are not taken into account here, as they would operate with or without a treaty on conventional arms reductions. There is, however, a need to mention the costs, however remote such a possibility might be, of an international satellite monitoring system. Its establishment in the form of two or three satellites would have to cost about $1 billion, and its operation something like $200 million per year. Since it is a rather hypothetical possibility it is not considered in detail here. It is worth mentioning at this point, however, that due to the expansion of hypothetical tasks of the NTMs (e.g., more extensive monitoring of the European landmass; the need for more detailed analysis of photographic and radar images of this landmass) the costs of analysis and interpretation of data gathered by NTMs would rise considerably after a future agreement in Europe.

Yet another method of verification mentioned above is the tags (and personal ID cards—if applicable at all) for major weapons. If designed and produced by the million, their individual costs would not be great— a few dollars a tag. What would be financially burdensome in this regard would be, as noted earlier, the increase in manpower needed to secure the appropriate operation of such verification and not so much the actual production of tags and IDs.

The total cost of the verification as extrapolated here, assumed to be on the order of above $1 billion annually for each side, seems large (several times larger than that assumed by Jonathan Dean). In view of the responsibilities incumbent upon the verification of conventional disarmament in Europe and the costs of maintaining the forces were they not limited, this magnitude of cost should be seen as fully justified and reasonable.

3. Level of Acceptable Intrusiveness

At a time when the inspectors called for by the INF Treaty are located deep in the interior of the USSR and the United States, penetrating once secret military bases in these and several other European states, when mutual monitoring of nuclear tests is carried out, and even further-reaching verification measures are debated in the START negotiations, it seems that intrusiveness is no longer an unacceptable feature of verification. However, as U.S. objections to some inspection schemes during the INF and START negotiations indicated, we have left only the stage of the propaganda game about verification. We have approached the stage of reality as to what is permissible and acceptable in verification. With the political difficulties of intrusive verification out of the way (at least on the part of the East), the governments entering into agreements on arms limitation confront the real problem: how to design the most effective verification for a given measure while protecting state and commercial secrets and properties.

In today's political atmosphere, characterized in part by the willingness to accept far-reaching verification obligations, the problem of intrusiveness applies only to a small part of the potential verification tasks. Nothing would be intrusive if it related to objects clearly covered by agreement, often declared in advance by the verified state and clearly distinguished from objects or activities that fall outside the scope of the agreement. This caveat may not always be fulfilled, and at those moments special precautions may have to be taken against the disclosure of state or commercial secrets.

Intrusiveness may, however, be a thorny issue in connection with challenge inspections of undeclared locations. This type of inspection may have an important deterrent function against different forms of possible violations. In some cases, by chance or by design, challenge inspections may be directed at places or activities which are outside the scope of agreement and at the same time are very sensitive from the point of a view of state security—like a nuclear weapons storage site, a command-and-control post serving primarily in the operation of nuclear weapons, an intelligence-gathering facility or a particular R&D laboratory. In such cases the inspection most probably could not take place and an agreement on conventional arms limitations would probably have to provide for a right of refusal, under extremely restrictive and well defined conditions. Additionally, to diminish the chance of a misguided demand for inspection and the occurrence of always troublesome refusals, the participating states could agree on a list of locations excluded in advance from any form of on-site inspection.

4. The Influence of the Political Context

The political context has a direct influence on the negotiation of verification provisions and their implementation and on the interpretation of information provided by verification.

An atmosphere of suspicion imposes a demand for a high level of confidence in the effectiveness of verification, measured by the probability of violations escaping detection. In such a situation the verification system may be a cumbersome, intrusive and costly one. It may even be counterproductive by overburdening the processing center with data, producing a higher rate of false alarms, and adding to the strain in inter-state relations.

It is the political context which determines whether demands for an exchange of preliminary data will be seen as excessive or acceptable.

During the implementation of verification provisions the participants may in a multitude of ways facilitate or obstruct the verification activities, while remaining in formal conformity with their obligations. The designers of an agreement can never foresee all contingencies in which verification may be carried out. In a good political climate small discrepancies of a bureaucratic nature may pass unnoticed or be neglected. During strained relations the same facts may lead to an overreaction.[16] The history of mutual accusations of minor and major transgressions of the SALT agreements provides many examples of such behavior.

It is imperative that the functioning of a verification system and the interpretation of its findings are insulated as much as possible from the fluctuations of the political relations between the parties to an agreement. Such insulation is difficult to achieve in bilateral agreements, which do not have this wider background of different national interests requiring moderation and accommodation. It seems more possible in a multilateral context, especially when the verification system, based on democratic principles, gives each participant equal access to information. In such a multilateral framework states can be kept from moving away from cooperation with the adversary and from the unilateral pursuit of security[17] because such individual action would precipitate a united negative response from the other participants in the system.

Notes

1 On various aspects of verification, see, for example, Seymour Melman, ed., *Inspection for Disarmament* (New York: Columbia University Press, 1958); Andrzej Karkoszka, *Strategic Disarmament, Verification and National Security* (London: Taylor and Francis for the Stockholm International Peace Research Institute [SIPRI], 1977); Allan Krass, *Verification—How Much Is Enough?* (London: Taylor and Francis for SIPRI, 1985); Roland M. Timerbayev, *Problems of Verification* (Moscow: Nauka Publishers, 1984); Ian Bellany and C.D. Blacker, eds., *The Verification of Arms Control Agreements* (London: Frank Cass and Co., Ltd., 1983); William C. Potter, ed., *Verification and Arms Control* (Lexington, MA: Lexington Books, 1985); William C. Potter, ed., *Verification and SALT: The Challenge of Strategic Deception* (Boulder, CO: Westview Press, 1980); Michael Krepon, *Arms Control Verification and Compliance*, Foreign Policy Association *Headline Series* No. 270 (September/October 1984).

2 Bhupendra Jasani, ed., *Outer Space—A New Dimension of the Arms Race* (London: Taylor and Francis for SIPRI, 1982); Richard A. Scribner, Theodore J. Ralston and William D. Metz, *The Verification Challenge. Problems and Promise of Strategic Nuclear Arms Control Verification* (Boston: Birkhauser, 1985); Scientific and Technical Aspects of Arms Control Verification by Satellite. Reply to the Thirty-third Annual Report of the Council. Assembly of Western European Union, 1988.

3 Craig Covault, "Atlantis' Radar Satellite Payload Opens New Reconnaissance Era," *Aviation Week and Space Technology*, December 12, 1988, pp. 26–28.

4 Michael Krepon and Sidney N. Graybeal, "Dealing with Future Treaty Implementation and Compliance Questions," in Elizabeth J. Kirk, ed., *Technology, Security, and Arms*

Control for the 1990s, 1988 Colloquium Reader (Washington, DC: AAAS Publication No. 88-21, 1988).

5 Johan Swahn, "International Surveillance Satellites—Open Skies for All," *Journal of Peace Research* 25, No. 3 (1988), pp. 229–244; "Verification: A Future European Satellite Agency," Assembly of Western European Union, Document 1159, November 3, 1988.

6 Study on the Implications of Establishing an International Satellite Monitoring Agency: Report of the Secretary General, UN General Assembly, New York, 1981; M. Abdel-Hady and A. Sadek, "Verification Using Satellites, Feasibility of an International or Multilateral Agency," in *Outer Space—A New Dimension of the Arms Race*, pp. 275–296; Craig Covault, "Soviets Endorse French Proposal for Space Reconnaissance Agency," *Aviation Week and Space Technology*, October 24, 1988.

7 Ann M. Florini, "The Opening Skies. Third Party Imaging Satellites and U.S. Security," *International Security* 13, No. 2 (Fall 1988), pp. 91–123.

8 "New Technology for NATO. Implementing Follow-On Forces Attack" (Washington, DC: Office of Technology Assessment, Congress of the United States, 1987).

9 US Sinai Support Mission, "Watch on Sinai," Department of State Publication No. 9131. General Foreign Policy Series 321; David Burton, "The Sinai Peacekeeping Experience: a Verification Paradigm for Europe," in *SIPRI Yearbook 1985* (London: Taylor and Francis, 1985), pp. 541–576.

10 Morton B. Berman, "Vehicle Detection in Emplaced Sensor Fields: A User's Guide to a Simulation Model and a Track-Identification Algorithm" (Santa Monica, CA: RAND Corporation, R-1186-PR, January 1973); Anthony P. Ciervo, "Automatic Identification: An Adaptive Pattern Recognition Algorithm" (Santa Monica, CA: the RAND Corporation R-1187-PR, January 1973).

11 A number of studies on using tags in verification were undertaken in connection with the strategic arms limitations. As far as application of tags in conventional arms limitations are considered, see, for example, "Requirements of a Tag for Conventional Arms Control," Western European Union, AG I (88) D/10, July 15, 1988.

12 Johan J. Holst, "Fixed Control Posts and European Stability," *Disarmament and Arms Control* 2, No. 3 (Summer 1964), pp. 262–297.

13 Clark C. Abt, "Progressive Zonal Inspection of Disarmament," *Disarmament and Arms Control* 2, No. 1 (Winter 1963–64), pp. 75–89.

14 Betty Lall and Eugenne Chollick, "The Intermediate Nuclear Forces Treaty: A Verification Breakthrough," *Journal of International Affairs* 4 (Spring 1988), pp. 23–26.

15 *International Herald Tribune*, January 16, 1979; U.S. Sinai Support Mission, *1976 Report to the Congress*; U.S. Sinai Support Mission, *1980 Report to the Congress*.

16 James K. Batten, *Arms Control and the Problem of Evasion* (Princeton, NJ: Center for International Studies, Woodrow Wilson School of Public and International Affairs, Princeton University, Research Monograph No. 4, June 30, 1962); Sidney N. Graybeal and Patricia Bliss McFate, "The Role of Verification in Arms Control," in *Technology, Security, and Arms Control for the 1990s*.

17 Gloria Duffy, "Conditions that Affect Arms Control Compliance," in Alexander L. George, Philip J. Farley and Alexander Dallin, eds., *U.S.-Soviet Security Cooperation. Achievements, Failures, Lessons* (New York: Oxford University Press, 1988).

VIII

PART ONE

Confidence- and Security-Building Measures

Timothy E. Wirth, United States

The Vienna negotiations represent a historic opportunity to restructure military relations in Europe to provide greater stability at less burden to our societies. Yet the challenge of reaching consensus on conventional arms reductions is formidable. Four decades of political mistrust and military confrontation will not likely yield to easy or quick solutions.

Confidence- and security-building measures (CSBMs) can play a unique role at this point in the history of arms control efforts in Europe by setting the pace for and building confidence in the search for a more cooperative European security order—one of improved stability, in which confrontation levels are reduced and, during the transition period from the current order, the risks of confrontation are minimized. A possible hierarchy of conventional arms control measures would suggest that conventional force reductions are the most onerous and difficult for states to accept; less so, perhaps, are constraints on how forces operate; and least demanding of all are measures aimed at achieving greater transparency and predictability of force structures or their activities. For this reason, confidence- and security-building measures should offer a distinct opportunity for relatively early progress towards greater stability and military *glasnost'* in the Vienna talks on Conventional Forces in Europe. They also have the advantage of building upon an edifice already constructed and tested to good effect: the Stockholm regime of CSBMs.

Over the last 30 years, CSBMs have figured in various strategic and conventional arms control deliberations, but none as ambitious as the Conference on Security and Cooperation in Europe (CSCE).[1] From Helsinki to Stockholm, an increasingly demanding set of confidence-building measures (CBMs) have evolved within the 35-nation CSCE process. The 1975 Helsinki Final Act contained a two-track set of non-binding CBMs: a notification regime calling for 21-days advance notice of maneuvers involving more than 25,000 troops; and an observation regime for notified military activities. The 1983 Madrid mandate for the follow-on CSCE Conference on Disarmament in Europe (CDE) stipulated that the participating states agreed to "undertake, in stages, new, effective and concrete action designed to make progress in strengthening confidence and security and in building disarmament."

Accordingly, a much more ambitious set of second-generation CSBMs was adopted at the Stockholm CDE meeting in 1986, measures that were to be "politically binding, militarily significant, adequately verifiable, and applicable to the whole of Europe." The Stockholm document included more rigorous notification and observation regimes, as well as new measures dealing with verification, constraints and annual military calendars. (A summary of the Stockholm provisions is included at Appendix A.) The CDE agreement represented a dramatic watershed in postwar arms control: the Soviet Union for the first time agreed to mandatory inspections on its territory. In spite of some early problems, implementation of the Stockholm accord has proven quite successful: during 1987 and 1988, over 80 military activities were notified and over 30 inspections took place in Europe.[2]

The CSCE and the Mutual and Balanced Force Reduction (MBFR) talks have constituted the two principal non-nuclear European security negotiations over the last 15 years. For various reasons, the CSCE was able to produce a successful record of modest achievement, while MBFR remained hopelessly stalemated (although the CDE profited by borrowing from many of the CSBM-like "associated measures" that were then current in MBFR). Following the conclusion of the CDE, and as interest in conventional arms control grew, a two-tier negotiating framework on European security emerged. One tier allowed the "disarmament" aspect of the CDE to be dealt with directly by the 23 members of the two military alliances in a new forum that would replace MBFR by focusing on conventional force reductions throughout a broader geographical area— i.e., all of Europe from the Atlantic to the Urals. The other tier effectively relegated the 35-member CDE to refinement and expansion of confidence- and security-building measures in the Atlantic-to-the-Urals (ATTU) zone.

The intent of this essay is to assess the prospects for this "other" negotiating framework and its potential development of a third-generation CSBM regime, and for that regime's relevance to the elaboration of a more cooperative European security system. Some consensus seems to be emerging about first steps in the area of data exchange. Soviet General Secretary Gorbachev proposed at the 1988 Moscow summit that data exchange constitute the first step in the Vienna process, while NATO's December 1988 communiqué[3] stressed data exchange and other transparency measures as a priority for the Stockholm follow-on effort. Beyond data, however, important differences exist in the Eastern and Western approaches to the Vienna talks, especially concerning the inclusion of independent air and naval activities (see Chapter 6 in this volume).

The Role of CSBMs

For the purposes of analysis, CSBMs can be divided into two categories: *transparency measures*, such as data exchange, exercise notification, and observers at military maneuvers; and *constraint measures*, such as limits on out-of-garrison activities or limits on forward-deployed equipment or other stationing of forces. It should be noted, however, that some transparency measures may constitute de facto constraints; the requirement to notify certain military activities implies that non-notified activities are prohibited. This chapter is limited to a discussion of transparency measures, leaving the discussion of constraints to Chapter 9.

Transparency measures may be further categorized in several ways: *information exchanges*, including exchange of data on military force structures, deployments and budgets; a *notification regime*, involving notification, well in advance of their occurrence whenever possible, of military exercises and maneuvers; *monitoring measures*, including inspection regimes for military exercises, permanent monitors at militarily critical facilities, unmanned sensors at key sites and joint overflight of monitoring aircraft; and *consultative mechanisms*, which could include exchange visits of military officers and discussion of operational military doctrine, as well as adjudication of problems arising over information exchanges, the notification regime or monitoring measures.

The intellectual underpinnings of CSBMs are drawn almost exclusively from the early analyses of the requirements of strategic nuclear stability and the reciprocal fear of surprise attack as a cause of war.[4] The risk of inadvertent conflict occurring as both sides mobilize out of fear that the other intends to strike first has been the subject of CSBM arms control efforts since the 1958 Surprise Attack Conference. Accordingly, the military utility of CSBMs has traditionally been judged on the basis of their contribution to stability expressed as reduced risk of surprise attack.

Existing national technical means of monitoring, however, make the prospect of true surprise (i.e., a "bolt from the blue," without any warning) attack increasingly unlikely. From a Western perspective, the two greatest military concerns are the threat of unreinforced, short-warning attack and mobilized large-scale offensive operations. Transparency measures can contribute to providing greater, more accurate and less ambiguous warning of offensive preparations in both cases. In a scenario involving a protracted military buildup, transparency measures could help complicate deception and degrade the readiness of forces subject to observation. CSBMs that provide greater actionable warning time inherently favor the defense and thereby contribute to stability.[5]

Although the military value of CSBMs should be judged on the basis of their contribution to warning, it is virtually impossible to provide a quantitative assessment of the additional warning which any particular measure or set of measures might generate (although it is possible to quantify the degree to which additional warning time might assist the defense). It is nonetheless clear that an ambitious set of third-generation CSBMs could help improve the quality and quantity of warning available to political decision-makers. Faced with the challenge of effective crisis decision-making among 16 nations, NATO's ability to respond cohesively to warning of war indicators could be enhanced through a multilateral transparency regime that helped reduce possibilities for ambiguous warning rather than simply providing more opportunities for it. Developing foolproof warning indicators with CSBMs represents a challenge, not a stumbling block, especially since dependable warning may become increasingly valuable to a defensive alliance faced with greater reliance on reserve forces as a result of demographic and resource constraints.

For several other reasons, confidence- and security-building measures should play a central role in the development of an integrated approach to a more cooperative European security order. By fostering greater transparency and predictability of military activities in general, CSBMs can contribute to military stability and help reduce the risk of war. Beyond that, they may also help pave the way for actual force reductions by providing early agreement on the composition and location of deployed forces, techniques to verify those deployments and other measures to facilitate reductions.[6] As Adam Rotfeld points out in his contribution to this chapter, many of the elements of the Jaruzelski proposal address these requirements.

There is also a great opportunity to put in place CSBM "transparency" measures that could help all interested parties monitor the unilateral Soviet force cuts outlined by Mikhail Gorbachev at the UN on December 7, 1988, or subsequent unilateral force reductions that any party may decide to undertake in Europe. Such further military *glasnost'* would help assure that the full benefit of Gorbachev's reductions will be realized; it would avoid a repetition of the uncertainty surrounding Brezhnev's 1979 withdrawal of the Sixth Guards Tank Division from East Germany. In short, CSBMs can help build confidence in unilateral as well as negotiated conventional arms cuts, while reducing the risk of war in their own right.

Building on Stockholm

An obvious starting point for negotiations on CSBMs is the Stockholm framework. Some of the proposals floated in Stockholm in 1984–1986 will undoubtedly be resurrected in Vienna. Other proposals will attempt to expand the measures previously agreed upon in Stockholm, while several proposals will seek to establish new measures altogether.

Information Measures

In spite of the frustrating and fruitless effort in MBFR to reach agreement on military data, it appears that there may now be an opportunity to make progress in this area. At the May 1988 U.S.-Soviet summit, General Secretary Gorbachev told President Reagan that Moscow was prepared to engage in a full exchange of military data as the first step in the conventional arms control process. As the contributions to this book by Richard Kugler and Alexei Arbatov, Nikolai Kishilov and Oleg Amirov make clear, there are significant differences between Eastern and Western views of the military balance. A much greater degree of data disaggregation, as well as explicit discussion of "counting rules," will be necessary if the forthcoming talks are to avoid the pitfalls of the MBFR experience. Generating an agreed data base will be a confidence-building measure in its own right, and a necessary precondition from which negotiated reduction targets may then proceed.

Pressing for an ambitious and early data exchange, however, carries with it the risk of bogging the talks down in technical disputes over counting rules and deployments. U.S. Representative Les Aspin, Chairman of the House Armed Services Committee, has recently argued that the data issue should be bypassed in the early phase precisely to avoid the data morass that doomed MBFR.[7] We should not expect full agreement on data at the outset, but instead we should view an agreed data base as a continuous process to be refined through inspections and other monitoring techniques.

Bruce George has proposed as a first step resurrecting the NATO Stockholm proposal for exchange of information on the normal peacetime deployment area and the designation of units participating in notifiable activities. Without such information, units may deploy to a notified activity, be observed so doing, and then redeploy to a third location following the exercise. By requiring unit designation and location disclosure, the potential for CDE-compliant use of military force for political intimidation would be diminished. Similarly, garrison-to-garrison movements should be subject to a notification requirement. The Stockholm document only requires that activities in the field involving various concentrations of forces be notified, thereby allowing for the possibility of CDE-compliant concentrations of forces in garrison.[8] Notification of out-of-garrison activity might also become a prerequisite for effective verification of a conventional force reduction agreement.

The Notification Regime

An unreinforced short-warning attack would require a high level of military readiness for an attacker to be confident of success. Readiness rests, in part, upon the training of troops in "alert exercises"—exercises which themselves can give cause for concern as precursors to war. Alert exercises, such as ammunition upload drills, are currently not subject to prenotification under the Stockholm regime because of concern that realistic training would be compromised by notification in advance of the exercise. A formula for including the aggregate number and time frames for allowable alert exercises could be considered in the Stockholm follow-on conference.

Another area not covered in the Stockholm regime is that of mobilization exercises. NATO proposed in 1984 that mobilization activities involving more than 25,000 troops or elements of three or more divisions should be notified at least 42 days in advance. Given the potential for large-scale mobilization exercises to cause concern on the part of potential adversaries, the inclusion of advance notification of such activities should be pressed in Vienna.

Monitoring Measures

The observer provisions of Stockholm could also be improved by increasing observer rights, e.g., to allow observers at notified exercises the same rights now accorded to challenge inspection teams (such as access to cameras and dictaphones). The lag time between notification and the beginning of an actual inspection could be decreased, perhaps in conjunction with a provision for roving monitors (addressed below). In addition, it might be useful to consider lowering the threshold of observable activities from the Stockholm limit of 17,000 troops in order to further contribute to military transparency in the ATTU zone.

Most important, we should press to increase the number of annual (passive) inspections that any given country is obliged to permit on its territory from the current level of three per year per country. These mandatory, short-notice inspections adopted in Stockholm have been successfully implemented to date. Verification of a conventional force reduction regime will certainly require a larger number of short-notice, on-site inspections—up to 350 per year, according to an estimate by Jonathan Dean in his contribution to this volume. Incremental increases in the CDE inspection regime would help improve the political acceptability and technical operation of a much more demanding future verification regime.

Beyond Stockholm

In addition to expanding the CDE measures, we should also seek in the next set of negotiations to pursue a new CSBM agenda beyond the parameters set at Stockholm. Such measures might include the following: a new inspection regime based on roving monitors; the use of unmanned sensors at fixed sites; a regime of overflight monitoring; notification of new systems deployment; the creation of an "information management center"; and an agenda for military exchanges and discussion of operational doctrine.

Monitoring Measures

A new monitoring regime involving permanent observers, roving inspectors and unmanned sensors could help narrow differences on data, while laying the foundation for a verification regime to accompany conventional force cuts. Increasing the Stockholm inspection quota, as noted above, would complement the more ambitious CSBMs addressed here.

Under the terms of the INF Treaty, permanent observers will be stationed at Votinsk in the Soviet Union and at Magna, Utah, in the U.S. in order to assure compliance with the production ban on INF-range missiles. A similar arrangement for permanent observers in Europe should be on the table at Vienna. Key entry/exit points, corps-level headquarters, airfields, marshalling areas, ports and other sites would be candidates for the cooperative placement of permanent observers. Such a regime would be able to determine the absence of major non-notified military activity. It would also serve as a precedent for monitoring arrangements for banned defense items or equipment held in agreed storage areas.

Whereas annual short-notice inspections have proved useful in reassuring all parties that non-notified exercises and activities were in fact non-notifiable under the terms of the CDE, the demands of greater transparency, the potential implementation of constraints and the need for force reductions that can be verified call for more robust on-site activities. This could be accomplished in the first instance by expanding the concept of the Military Liaison Missions which the four powers retain in Germany. Rather than relying exclusively on permanently stationed monitors at key military sites such as railyards and garrisons, a team of roving monitors would be able to inspect suspicious activities at short notice. Some "keep out" zones on both sides would most likely still apply, but the vast space to be covered in monitoring the Atlantic-to-the-Urals zone will require some more ambitious monitoring scheme if constraints and reduction measures are to be confidently implemented.

The enormous area of the ATTU zone also makes it difficult for all key facilities and military nodes to be fully covered by roving monitor teams. A broad range of unmanned sensors have been proposed for monitoring fixed points as a complement to permanent observers and inspections. Ivan Oerlich and Victor Utgoff have proposed the use of cooperatively placed, unmanned sensors to provide reassurance that preparations for a conventional attack are not under way.[9] They suggest placing seismic sensors in and around armored vehicle garrisons, along with a series of sensor lines composed of television cameras at major roads and railways and seismic sensors and passive sonars for riverine monitoring. Unmanned sensors could also play a useful role in monitoring compliance with a reduction accord, for example, by detecting the reintroduction of withdrawn assets via certain key transportation points.

An additional monitoring measure of potentially great significance— especially in cases demanding quick reaction information—is the use of low-altitude overflights. An overflight regime could enhance currently available information about force deployments, especially in rear areas. Low-level flights by fixed-wing aircraft, drones or helicopters could be limited to an annual quota, and could be conducted within specified geographic zones, including along the inter-German border. Such a regime would supplement information available from satellites and could be very useful in providing timely information on an alliance-wide basis. The use of sophisticated systems, such as AWACS and JSTARS, could also increase the level of information obtainable in this manner.

None of the measures described here alone could provide a full range of monitoring capabilities, but in conjunction with one another and with other measures they could play a useful role in enhancing transparency in the Atlantic-to-the-Urals zone and contributing to the development of an effective verification regime. They could also significantly assist in building a pattern of military predictability in Europe which would make deviations from routine peacetime activities more obvious—and therefore more politically, if not militarily, costly.

Consultative Mechanisms

Beyond the set of monitoring measures discussed above, there are other useful initiatives which should be explored. A new CSBM reporting requirement might be considered which would require all parties to report in advance the theater deployment of any new weapons system or force. Although the Western nations generally "warn" the world well in advance of any deployment through lengthy public debate, the East-bloc countries are not always as open. This reporting requirement would increase openness and predictability concerning force modernization. It would also provide an opportunity to assess the implications of new deployments before they occur with an eye towards stability criteria.

Many analysts have proposed the creation of a NATO-Warsaw Pact "risk reduction center" or "confidence-building center" or "crisis avoidance center." The Jaruzelski Plan envisions the establishment of procedures for resolving military disputes, as well as the creation of East-West "hot lines." Soviet General Secretary Gorbachev has proposed a "European center to reduce the threat to peace," and the Warsaw Treaty Organization formally proposed such a concept on October 28, 1988. The July 1988 joint communiqué of the West German Social Democratic Party (SPD) and the East German Socialist Unity Party (SED) called for establishing a "confidence-building center." Jonathan Dean of the Union of Concerned Scientists has called for the establishment of a NATO-Warsaw Pact "risk reduction center."[10]

It is suggested that such an entity could incorporate various elements—from a "hot-line" function to an arbitration board for compliance disputes. A distinction should be made, however, between a crisis prevention function and that of crisis management. In the classic sense of a CSBM, a crisis prevention center could seek to reduce the chance that ambiguity or misunderstanding might lead to conflict by clarifying— rather than resolving—the cause of a crisis. The task of crisis management would fall to national governments and mechanisms already in place, such as the North Atlantic Council.

An incremental approach to the creation of such a center would be prudent. Rather than attempting to create a comprehensive European security center, the initial focus should be on the pressing informational needs at hand. The success of such an enterprise might then justify more ambitious goals in the future. As a first step, such a center could assist in the implementation and monitoring of notification and, later, of potential constraint and reduction measures. The volume of information already exchanged under the CDE regime suggests that a single coordinating center makes good sense. The likely additional demands imposed by further transparency and constraint measures may make the creation of such a center a necessity. Additional functions might include publishing an annual report on military data, as well as attempting to define a standardized reporting scheme for national defense expenditures.

Finally, such a center might usefully serve as a forum for the professional military of the two blocs to discuss how to go about promoting greater military stability in Europe. Both sides profess to maintain purely defensive alliance structures at the most general level of doctrine. Yet, as always, the devil is in the detail, and in this case it is in the operational concepts and tactics applied by both sides in prosecuting their "defensive" campaigns. Such discussions could usefully address broad doctrinal issues, as well as more concrete definitional tasks of direct relevance to the search for military stability in Europe. Specifically, such an effort, as well as the work of a consultative center itself, could begin with an exchange of disaggregated data on forces and the "counting rules" used in arriving at such data. Defining the military meaning of "readiness" and criteria for establishing a readiness baseline might also constitute a useful initial focus.

The meeting between Admiral William Crowe, chairman of the U.S. Joint Chiefs of Staff, and Marshal Sergei Akhromeev, then head of the Soviet General Staff, in July 1988 opened the way for further meetings between military professionals of the two alliances. This process needs to be encouraged and a regime of some sort applied so that deliberations on doctrine may be put into a more disciplined framework, with possible implications for the negotiations themselves. This is all the more important in the case of conventional arms control, where the military have much more experience and influence than they do in the nuclear arena. General Secretary Gorbachev's promise to pursue "defensive restructuring" as part of the reductions package promised in his UN speech could serve as a starting point for such a dialogue.

The Inclusion of Naval Forces?

As Adam Rotfeld notes in his contribution to this chapter, the inclusion of independent air and naval activities in the CSCE negotiations remains a contentious issue.[11] While the mandate for the CDE does not explicitly identify independent air and naval activities for consideration, it does not rule them out either.

In a speech in Murmansk on October 1, 1987, General Secretary Gorbachev called for naval and air limits and CSBMs for the Baltic, North, Norwegian and Greenland seas. More specific suggestions were made by Soviet Foreign Minister Eduard Shevardnadze at the Third UN Special Session on Disarmament in June 1988 when he proposed: (1) advance notification of transfers and maneuvers of naval and associated air forces; (2) limitation of the number, scope and area of such exercises; (3) invitation of observers to air and naval exercises; and (4) information exchange on naval doctrine.

NATO has ample reason to be cautious about limits on its air and naval forces. Geography dictates that NATO must be, to a large degree, a maritime alliance, highly dependent upon the sea and air lines of communication to maintain the cohesiveness of its defense. This poses special Western requirements for maritime and air reinforcement capability across the Atlantic. As Dr. Rotfeld points out, measures that would "create distance" between allies do not contribute to building confidence.

Yet in spite of the understandable reluctance of Western navies to accept arms control limits on themselves, the logic of the developing dialogue on European security may well require that the West be prepared to engage in serious discussion on naval CSBMs. NATO has correctly, in my view, focused its initial efforts on the most destabilizing aspects of the conventional confrontation—the WTO's large superiority in offensive ground forces. If the Soviet Union were to successfully implement the promised unilateral reductions and if meaningful progress towards further stabilizing reductions in ground forces were to occur, NATO nations would be hard pressed to justify indefinitely their refusal to discuss areas of decided Western advantage.

Rather than seek to limit, reduce or otherwise constrain naval forces, the CDE talks might usefully focus on modest naval CSBMs. The historical precedents of the U.S.-Soviet and the U.K.-Soviet "Incidents-at-Sea" agreements represent successful first steps which might be refined and expanded multilaterally. In addition to this type of "rules of the road" measure, certain transparency measures in the naval arena—including notification of major fleet exercises and the exchange of observers—might be considered. In order to make clear that such measures relate to European security, initial focus on border seas, such as the Baltic, could be pursued.

Conclusion

The most serious progress to date in multilateral negotiations on European security has clearly been in the area of CSBMs in the CSCE. The less-ambitious nature of CSBMs (as compared to reduction proposals) and the mediating role played by the neutral and nonaligned (NNA) states has permitted the evolution—and successful implementation—of an increasingly demanding CSBM regime that is politically binding and applicable to all of Europe. As we work through the complexities of the Vienna negotiations, we should not lose sight of the incremental approach CSBMs offer in building a more cooperative European security system.

It will be a challenge for all participating states to make best use of the two-track set of negotiations. There will be a temptation on the part of NATO to focus most of its energies in the forum of 23, while the NNA quite naturally will want to concentrate on including ambitious measures in the 35. This procedural bifurcation offers the advantage of greater flexibility in pursuing negotiating strategies—it also contains the potential for stalemate. To a certain degree, CSBMs can figure in both sets of talks and could serve as a natural bridge between them. The challenge will be to assure that efforts in the two fora are complementary.

For several reasons, CSBMs should figure prominently in a coherent Western negotiating strategy on conventional forces in Europe. First, CSBMs have intrinsic merit: they can contribute to stability in Europe through greater openness, decreased capacity for short-warning attack and reduced likelihood of misunderstanding or miscalculation. Second, expanding the current regime of CSBMs offers a tangible, familiar and more attainable target for early achievement in the forthcoming talks than actual force reductions. Progress on CSBMs can help establish momentum which may well be needed to overcome the difficult obstacles to arms reductions, serving as the pacesetter rather than the backwater of conventional arms control. In short, CSBMs can help "improve stability" by increasing the transparency of military force structures and activities, and they can help "reduce confrontation" by maintaining progress and presenting a bridge toward more ambitious forms of arms control in Europe.

Most important, CSBMs will be a necessary component—indeed, a prerequisite in some cases, such as data exchange—of any conventional reductions and/or constraints package. It is difficult to foresee implementing any serious stabilizing measures in an arms reduction agreement without greater information about and monitoring of deployed forces. The promised unilateral withdrawal of six Soviet tank divisions from Eastern Europe offers a unique opportunity to demonstrate the utility of existing and new transparency measures in building confidence and monitoring military deployments.[12]

The Gorbachev UN initiative could serve as a catalyst for real progress in lowering the level of the East-West military confrontation in Europe. Specifically, we should seek to reach agreement on data through this process, perhaps by agreeing to figures for force levels after implementation of the promised Soviet unilateral reductions (similar in concept to the 1985 Western MBFR proposal). In order to monitor such reductions and residual levels, many of the more intrusive transparency measures addressed above should be considered for early implementation, including on-site inspections, permanent observers and overflights. Finally, the promise of "restructuring" made by General Secretary Gorbachev poses a distinct opportunity to begin a serious dialogue on military doctrine and force structure.

Agreement on CSBMs need not wait for prior agreement on constraints, reductions, redeployments or even further notification provisions. Instead, agreeing soon on an expanded set of CSBMs, particularly those in the information and monitoring area, would give both sides the opportunity to demonstrate that their intentions and preparations are truly defensive, and help pave the way towards other verifiable measures. The Vienna negotiations will be complex, time-consuming and frustrating. Yet there may now be a genuine opportunity to reverse the pattern of mistrust and confrontation which has divided Europe for more than four decades. Confidence- and security-building measures can play an important facilitating role early on at Vienna in the pursuit of a more cooperative European security system.

Appendix
Stockholm CSBMs Regime*

Notification

Type of Forces:	"Military activities in the field conducted as a single activity," national or multinational—i.e., ground forces (independent and combined); amphibious and airborne forces; transfers and concentrations; alert exercises
Threshold of Notification:	13,000 ground troops or 300 battle tanks if organized into a divisional structure or at least two brigades/regiments. Subthreshold for air forces: 200 sorties by aircraft, excluding helicopters.
Advance Warning:	3,000 amphibious or airborne troops 42 days—except for alert exercises, notifiable at once.

Observation

Threshold of Observation:	17,000 troops (ground) or 5,000 troops (amphibious airborne)
Exceptions:	No observation of restricted locations, installations or defense sites. No observation of alert activities having a duration of less than 72 hours

Annual Calendars

Exchange (each November 15 at the latest) of forecasts of notifiable military activities for the subsequent year, under a standardized form.

Constraints

Time and size constraints: two years of advance notice for any notifiable military activity beyond 40,000 troops; prohibition of military activities beyond 40,000 troops and under 75,000 troops unless notified one year in advance; prohibition of military activities beyond 75,000 troops unless notified two years in advance; unforecasted military activities should be "as few as possible."

Verification

Use of national technical means.
On-site, compulsory, short-notice (24 hours) and duration (48 hours) inspections; inspections on the ground, from the air by a maximum of four inspectors; passive quota (three inspections per year from different states other than members of the same military alliance); access, entry and unobstructed survey except for restricted areas the number and extent of which should be "as limited as possible."

---

* Excerpted from Victor-Yves Ghebali and Fred Tanner, "Confidence Building Measures in Arms Control: The Mouse that Roared?" *International Defense Review* (October 1988).

Notes

1 For general background on confidence-building measures, see John Borawski, *From the Atlantic to the Urals: Negotiating Arms Control at the Stockholm Conference* (Washington, DC: Pergamon-Brassey's, 1988); Bruce George, "Confidence Building Measures: Next Steps for Stability & Security" (Brussels: North Atlantic Assembly, 1988); Allen Lynch, ed., *Building Security in Europe: Confidence Building Measures and the CSCE* (New York: Institute for East-West Security Studies, 1986); and Jonathan Alford, ed., "The Future of Arms Control: Part III. Confidence Building Measures," *Adelphi Papers* 149 (London: International Institute for Strategic Studies, 1979). The emergence of CSBMs in European security deliberations is addressed in Victor-Yves Ghebali and Fred Tanner, "Confidence Building Measures in Arms Control: The Mouse That Roared?" *International Defense Review* 21, No. 10 (October, 1988).

2 U.S. Department of State, "24th Semiannual Report on the Implementation of the Helsinki Final Act, October 1, 1987–April 1, 1988" (Washington, DC: 1988). The report noted that "Warsaw Pact countries seem to have made a political decision in favor of effective implementation of the CSBMs regime that goes well beyond their efforts with regard to the [Helsinki CBMs]."

3 NATO's December 1988 Communiqué on Conventional Arms Control dedicated an entire section to transparency measures:

Greater transparency is an essential requirement for real stability. Therefore, within the framework of the CSCE process, the negotiations on confidence- and security-building measures form an essential complement to those on conventional stability. We are encouraged thus far by the successful implementation of the Stockholm Document and we consider that the momentum must be maintained.

In order to create transparency of military organization, we plan to introduce a proposal for a wide-ranging, comprehensive annual exchange of information concerning military organization, manpower and equipment as well as major weapon deployment programmes. To evaluate this information we will propose modalities for the establishment of a random evaluation system.

In addition, in order to build on the success of the Stockholm Document and to create greater transparency of military activities, we will propose measures in areas such as:
–more detailed information with regard to the notification of military exercises,
–improvements in the arrangements for observing military activities,
–greater openness and predictability about military activities,
–a strengthening of the regime for ensuring compliance and verification.

Finally, we shall propose additional measures designed to improve contacts and communications between participating states in the military field; to enhance access for military staffs and media representatives; and to increase mutual understanding of military capabilities, behavior and force postures. We will also propose modalities for an organized exchange of views on military doctrine tied to actual force structures, capabilities and dispositions in Europe.

(*Conventional Arms Control*, Statement Issued by the North Atlantic Council Meeting in Ministerial Session at NATO Headquarters, Brussels, 8–9 December 1988.)

4 Much of the early work is brought together in Thomas Schelling and Morton Halperin, *Strategy and Arms Control* (New York: Twentieth Century Fund, 1961).

5   The term "actionable warning" is defined as "warning that European publics will find convincing enough to allow their governments to take necessary mobilization steps" in *Soviet Readiness for War: Assessing One of the Major Sources of East-West Instability*, Report of the Defense Policy Panel, Committee on Armed Services, U.S. House of Representatives, December 5, 1988.

6   This basic theme is elaborated in Stanley R. Sloan and Mikaela Sawtelle, "Confidence Building Measures and Force Constraints for Stabilizing East-West Military Relations in Europe," Congressional Research Service, Report 88-591F, Library of Congress, 1988. Also see Stephen J. Flanagan and Andrew Hamilton, "Arms Control and Stability in Europe," *Survival* 30, No. 5 (September/October, 1988); and James Goodby, "Next Steps in Operational Arms Control," in Harry C. Blaney III, ed., *The Future of Conventional Arms Control in Europe* (Washington, DC: Foreign Service Institute, Department of State, 1988).

7   Les Aspin, "More on the Table: Expanding Arms Control Negotiations" (Washington, DC: House Armed Services Committee, 1988).

8   Bruce George, *Confidence Building Measures*.

9   Ivan Oelrich and Victor Utgoff, "Confidence Building with Unmanned Sensors in Central Europe," in Barry Blechman, ed., *Technology and the Limitation of International Conflict* (Lanham, MD: University Press of America, 1988). Also see Ivan Oelrich, "Cooperative Verification of Conventional Arms Limitations," in Blaney, *The Future of Conventional Arms Control in Europe*.

10 See his contribution to this volume.

11 For more on the Western debate on naval CSBMs, see Richard Haass, "Confidence Building and Naval Arms Control," in Alford, "The Future of Arms Control: Part III"; and Karsten Voigt, "General Report on Alliance Security: Towards Conventional Stability in Europe; The U.S. Maritime Strategy and Crisis Stability at Sea" (Brussels: North Atlantic Assembly, 1988).

12 This point is made by Phillip Karber, "Military Impact of the Gorbachev Reductions," paper presented in Brussels at a seminar for permanent ambassadors and military representatives to NATO, December 12, 1988.

VIII

PART TWO

CSBMs in Europe: A Future-Oriented Concept

Adam-Daniel Rotfeld, Poland

Introduction

Confidence- and security-building measures (CSBMs) occupy a special place in the various concepts of arms control and disarmament in Europe. Hopes pinned on a system of military confidence-building measures have increased particularly in periods when talks on the reduction and limitation of armaments produced little or no concrete results. The special treatment of CSBMs has sprung from a conviction that they would not only alleviate international tensions but also foster disarmament. Yet efforts to strengthen the confidence and security of states made by the Geneva Surprise Attack Conference (1958), or at the early stages of the Geneva Eighteen-Nation Disarmament Conference (1962), did not yield the desired results. During the same period of time the first serious theoretical studies highlighted the role and significance of direct lines of communication, early warning and notification, exchange of military missions, national technical means of verification and monitoring, satellite surveillance and establishment of observation posts and inspection zones.[1] Those measures have been designed to decrease the risk of an outbreak of war through accident, miscalculation or lack of communication.[2] The Soviet and American proposals made at that time spoke in unison about the need for advance notification of major troop movements and military maneuvers, and rapid and efficient communications between the respective heads of state and the UN secretary general. On June 20, 1963, the United States and the Soviet Union reached agreement on a direct line of communication between the Kremlin and the White House. Since then it has been technologically upgraded on the basis of a 1985 accord. Under subsequent Soviet-American treaties certain national means of verification have been set up, such as satellite surveillance and radioelectronic early-warning systems. In 1976, the right to on-site inspection was agreed in connection with the Soviet-American Peaceful Nuclear Explosions Treaty. These were the first modest attempts to establish international procedures. After a period of detailed analyses and studies they have been gradually integrated into the process of shaping a system of confidence and security between East and West.[3] An important step in this direction has been the incorporation into the CSCE Final Act of a section on confidence-building measures.

CSBMs and the CSCE Decisions

The aims of confidence-building measures, as stated in the CSCE Final Act, are:

–elimination of the causes of tension and the consolidation of peace and security in the world;
–reinforcement of mutual confidence and thereby promotion of greater stability and security in Europe;
–exclusion of the threat or use of force against the territorial integrity or political independence of any state; and
–reduction of the danger of armed conflict, and of a possible misunderstanding or mistaken calculation of military activity.

One of the basic objectives of CBMs is to reduce the possibility of surprise attack.[4] CBMs are designed to ensure the correct interpretation of an adversary's intentions in order to reduce the danger arising from unfounded suspicions and misperceptions which are often the result of prejudice or misjudgment.

One is struck by the contrast between the broadly conceived and somewhat anticipatory aims and the actual scope of the operative decisions of the relevant CSCE decisions. The Helsinki document provided in practice five confidence-building measures in the military sphere:

–prior notification of major military maneuvers (involving more than 25,000 troops);
–prior notification of other military maneuvers;
–prior notification of major military movements;
–exchange of observers; and

–other confidence-building measures (e.g., exchange by invitation of military personnel, visits by military delegations).

These were rather modest measures. Only in the case of prior notification of major military maneuvers was there any precise definition of parameters (ceilings, operative area and degree of obligation). It is fair to say that by and large the confidence-building measures envisaged in the CSCE Final Act were neither militarily significant nor of an obligatory nature. The zone of their application did not cover the whole of Europe nor was any provision made for verification and control procedures. Nonetheless, this was the first multilateral document testifying to a political will to initiate a process of reduction of the danger of armed conflict in Europe and the possibility of surprise attack. The recommended measures aimed at preventing misunderstanding, miscalculation or mis-interpretation of military activities.

The provisions on confidence-building measures included in the CSCE Final Act had more political and psychological than military significance. The next important step was the decisions of the CSCE Madrid meeting (September 6, 1983). The mandate eventually adopted at Madrid, which formed the basis of the Stockholm accord of September 19, 1986, was a compromise. An indication of the interest shown by other states is that a total of five proposals relating to military aspects of security were submitted by—in addition to Poland—France Romania, Sweden and Yugoslavia.

The Document finally adopted by the Stockholm Conference on Confidence- and Security-building Measures in Europe[5] is comprised of six chapters (104 provisions) and four annexes forming an integral part of the agreement reached.

The following brief recapitulation of the decisions of the Stockholm Conference shows that they incorporate a number of qualitatively new elements in one field of confidence- and security-building measures.

First, the decisions adopted at Stockholm are politically binding and thus, in contrast to the Final Act, obligatory.

Second, they are militarily significant in that they not only make it possible to form a picture of military activity in Europe (notifications and annual calendars) and observe its conduct, beginning at a relatively low quantitative ceiling (17,000 troops), but are also conducive to a certain limitation of its scale. This is of importance with regard to both major maneuvers and, to an even greater extent, troop transfers. Essentially, these are new aspects in relations between CSCE countries, let alone between states belonging to opposed alliances.

Third, the zone of application for military CSBMs is much wider than in the Final Act, and it is also worth noting that the extension has been effected entirely eastward. The formula from the Atlantic to the Urals encompasses the whole European continent without including even a part of either the United States or Canada. Furthermore, the measures agreed at Stockholm are not applicable to independent naval activities (unless they form an integral part of land operations on the European continent).

Fourth, there is no precedent in East-West relations for the verification measures agreed upon. Of particular significance are the decisions relating to on-site inspection, which will unquestionably contribute to the greater credibility of the entire system of confidence- and security-building measures. They are evidence of a fundamental change in the Warsaw Treaty states' position on this issue. Bearing in mind that verification has been a sticking-point in arms limitations, it will become evident that the new control and verification measures should serve as a kind of proving ground which could further agreement on reductions of conventional forces and armaments.

The controlling theme of the decisions contained in the Stockholm document is the desire that all CSCE states should feel more certain that surprise attack in Europe is impossible. The security of states in the contemporary world is founded on a triad of forces: land, sea and air. National security policies, based in effect on the concept of deterrence, depend on an equilibrium embracing all elements of the triad. Given an international system so organized, confidence- and security-building measures ought to correspond to the existing threats. Analysis of the decisions of the Stockholm conference indicates that the agreed measures apply chiefly, if not exclusively, to conventional land forces. Military activity on the sea or in the air comes within the scope of CSBMs only if it is an integral part of military activity on land. In other words, independent major naval exercises or large-scale deployment of air force units are excluded from the applicability of the Stockholm conference decisions. However, a policy of effective prevention of the possibility of surprise attack in the case of Poland, and still more the USSR, must make provision to an equal, if not greater, extent against threats from the sea and air as well as the land. In an analysis of the military problems of Polish security, experts from the Polish Army General Staff Academy have written that in the initial and most difficult phase of war Poland will not be faced with the necessity of confronting land forces or countering firepower of these forces. The chief threat will come from air strikes or airborne and amphibious operations. Nor can the possibility of operation by diversionary groups be ruled out.[6]

The Warsaw Treaty states' acceptance at Stockholm of measures offering greater insurance against land attack by conventional forces than from sea or air strikes involving nuclear weapons should effectively demolish the hoary old arguments about a threat from the East.

Looking back over the two years that have passed since the adoption of the Stockholm decisions a general picture is beginning to emerge of how effective they have been and what impact they have made on overall developments in Europe. It certainly has been a period of gathering experience and not infrequently also experimentation with new measures, the scope of which—it will be recalled—is without precedent in East-West relations.

Notifications received in 1987 and 1988 in accordance with the requirement to exchange annual calendars of military activities aroused no reservations. They conformed to the provisions adopted. A comparison of the 1987 calendar with the 1988 calendar shows decreasing numbers of military activities subject to prior notification. It is, however, hard to say just how much this has been determined by economic considerations such as the high cost of maneuvers, and how much it can be attributed to a more relaxed atmosphere and political will to restrain military activity. A certain weakness of the Stockholm decisions is that they do not provide for limitation of the frequency, number and ceilings for military exercises that are conducted during the same period of time. Another thing is that concentration of troops participating in maneuvers is much greater on the NATO side than on the side of the WTO. (For example, in September 1987, the NATO states conducted nine maneuvers with 394,000 troops, while the total number of WTO troops in simultaneous maneuvers did not exceed 90,000.) The provisions on notification, observation and control were in principle respected. There were some differences in the interpretation of the relevant provisions in this regard.

Strict and scrupulous implementation of the confidence- and security-building measures agreed at Stockholm will undoubtedly help to some extent to reinforce convictions that the intentions of states conducting military activities are peaceful and that the maneuvers carried out by them are not of a threatening or aggressive nature.

Nevertheless, it remains a fact that both present and future confidence-building measures have to do chiefly with the sphere of perception; they do not contribute to a reduction of military capabilities, of forces and armaments in Europe. Without a simultaneous decrease in military arsenals these measures can be an additional source of tensions, frictions and mutual suspicion. The Stockholm conference from the outset was treated as the beginning of a process of negotiation. Moreover, both France and Poland, the authors of the principal proposals submitted on this question in Madrid, assumed that in the next stage the Conference would, in accordance with its name, deal not only with confidence- and security-building but also with disarmament in Europe.

For this reason, in December 1986 Poland tabled at the Vienna meeting a proposal for supplementing the mandate agreed at Madrid so that it included consideration and adoption, on a basis of equality of rights, equilibrium and reciprocity, and equal respect for the security interests of all participating states, steps aimed at reductions of conventional forces and armaments in Europe. They were to be examined in parallel with confidence- and security-building measures which have been or will be submitted by any of the participating states. Particular consideration should be given to essentially new confidence-building and military-strategic stability-building measures directly connected with conventional force and armaments reductions and facilitating achievement of agreement in these matters.[7] The aim of the Polish proposal was to ensure the continuation of the Stockholm conference along lines seeking the broadest possible common denominator:

–in the substantive sphere, parallel discussion of confidence- and security-building measures, on the one hand, and force and armaments reductions, on the other;
–in the procedural sphere, the participation in the negotiations of the 35 states on an equal basis in accordance with the principle that the CSCE process cannot permit the introduction of different categories of states and different degrees of initiation.

During informal meeting of "the group of 23" (16 NATO and 7 WTO states) in Vienna the question of participation of neutral and nonaligned (NNA) states in the future conference turned into a major bone of contention between East and West. The NATO states—except for France—

demanded that arms reduction matters be excluded from the CSCE process. The diminution of military potentials in Europe was meant to be the exclusive subject of inter-bloc talks.[8]

A different approach was taken by the Soviet Union, Poland and other WTO states. They proposed that:

–a mandate agreed by the 23 NATO and WTO states form an integral part of the concluding document of the CSCE Vienna Meeting; and
–a mechanism be devised to ensure a two-way institutional link between talks within "the group of 23" on reductions and military stability in Europe, on the one hand, and the negotiations on CSBMs conducted by the 35 CSCE states, on the other.

A basis for a compromise solution was eventually provided by drafts submitted by Sweden,[9] Yugoslavia[10] and Cyprus.[11] The solution adopted at Vienna was initially included in the comprehensive proposal by the NNA states tabled on May 13, 1988. The document adopted in January 1989 articulated the accords reached after months of hard work in working bodies and drafting groups. On the question of future negotiations on CSBMs by 35 states, the document reads:

> The participating States have agreed that negotiation on confidence- and security-building measures will take place in order to build upon and expand the results already achieved at the Stockholm Conference with the aim of elaborating and adopting a new set of mutually complementary confidence- and security-building measures designed to reduce the risk of military confrontation in Europe. . . .

As regards negotiations by "the group of 23" concerning stability and conventional force reductions in Europe, the document reads: "These negotiations will be conducted within the framework of the CSCE process."

In this way a link has been established between the two planes of negotiations—within the framework of the CSCE process, yet without damaging the autonomous character of talks by the 23.

The future system of building confidence and security in Europe depends less on procedural arrangements or the relationship between the two negotiating planes than on the context and scope of future CSBMs. The Vienna document defined the aims of future negotiations as follows:

–to build upon and expand the results already achieved at the Stockholm conference;
–to elaborate and adopt a new set of mutually complementary CSBMs; and
–these CSBMs will be designed to reduce the risk of military confrontation in Europe.

It would be interesting to establish what kinds of measures could match these expectations and requirements.

The Stockholm Decisions and the New Measures

It stands to reason that the measures tabled and discussed at the Stockholm conference, but which did not win consensus, could again be put on the negotiating table during talks on new CSBMs. In view of such a possibility, one might expect, immediately after the closure of the Stockholm conference, that:

–WTO states will repeat postulates on supplementing the zone of application of CSBMs by the sea area and air space around Europe[12] (inclusion of independent naval and air force operations in areas surrounding Europe);[13] they will also seek decisions restraining military activity;
–The NATO states have signaled that their chief concern will be the expansion of military information ("greater openness and more predictability") as well as new measures to enhance stability and the scope of verification;[14]
–NNA states will again advance postulates which will be closer to WTO proposals on certain issues, for example, limitation of military activity, and on some other matters closer to the NATO position, like greater access to military information. They are also expected to present their proposals reflecting their specific position vis-à-vis East-West relations (e.g., with regard to a draft proposal to hold on demand ad hoc multilateral meetings on CSBMs to exchange views "on the routine implementation of the measures").[15]

Trying to reduce the whole problem of future measures to those postulates which had been tabled at Stockholm but were not included in the document of September 19, 1986, would be making things look more simple than they in fact are, specifically in light of the experience that has accumulated over the past two years since the Stockholm conference ended regarding the implementation of its decisions and the debates held at Vienna.

Recent changes of the political-military situation in Europe, and especially the Soviet-American INF Treaty on the elimination from Europe of two types of missiles and the opening of talks on conventional stability, have now created an atmosphere encouraging negotiations on a set of confidence-building measures much more ambitious than envisaged earlier. The questions remain of what these measures should actually be and whether they should lead mainly to reductions of military activity or perhaps to an expansion of military information (access to data) and greater scope of control and on-site inspection.

It now appears that the new-generation CSBMs cannot be seen in isolation from the processes going on along the East-West line. CSBMs have never been, are not and perhaps never will be the main determinant of the military-political situation. They can, however, considerably influence its shape within the framework of broader processes, including relations among the nuclear powers, relations between states from the two military blocs (talks within "the group of 23") and ultimately also relations between participants of the all-European process (talks among the 35 CSCE states). CSBMs could foster reductions of armed forces and conventional armaments in Europe. A new element that emerged after the Stockholm conference was a certain convergence of views of the three groups of countries (NATO, WTO and NNA) over the verifiability of the new measures. For example, Warsaw Treaty states, which in the past viewed with some reserve measures designed to facilitate openness and predictability, especially verification, inspection and exchange of information, have now included them into their recent proposals. In making their move the WTO states were falling back on their experience from the way the multilateral CSCE recommendations as well as the Stockholm decisions and the INF Treaty have been put into practice.

New Proposals

The Jaruzelski Plan.   Poland has proposed (paragraph 4 of the Jaruzelski Plan) that an agreement could be concluded "on appropriate far-reaching confidence- and security-building measures and the mechanisms for the strict verification of compliance with the undertaken commitments, including such which for various reasons it would be difficult to introduce to Europe as a whole."[16] Such measures might include, *inter alia*:

–an agreement on parameters to constrain the size and/or the intensity of the specified types of military activities;
–the exchange of military information; and
–procedures for the prompt clarification of situations arousing the concern of either side.

The Polish document devotes much space to national and international means of verification, including the possibility of establishing a control mechanism with the participation of the interested states and third parties. The control mechanism might include:

–an exchange of information indispensable for effective verification;
–notification of the commencement and completion of the withdrawal or reduction of armaments and their observation; and
–establishment of control points on the borders of the zone through which the arms would be withdrawn, as well as at large railway junctions, airfields and seaports.

The system could include a procedure of bilateral and multilateral consultations. For its part, the Polish government expressed its readiness to accept, on a reciprocal basis, any method of verification necessary to attain the purposes of the plan.

It is true that the Polish proposal is restricted only to the territory of Central Europe. That area—under the Jaruzelski Plan—embraces a zone that is wider than that mentioned in earlier Polish initiatives for an atom-free zone (the Rapacki Plan, 1957) or a nuclear freeze (the Gomulka Plan, 1963–1964) which covered only the territories of the two German states, Czechoslovakia and Poland. In the latest Polish proposal Central Europe is meant to include the territories of the FRG, the Benelux countries and Denmark on the NATO side, and the GDR, Czechoslovakia, Poland and Hungary on the WTO side.

The statement of the Polish government of June 14, 1988, contains a proposal to elaborate and accept new parameters constraining ground-force activities by applying, *inter alia*, "correspondingly further-reaching measures as the distance from the line of contact is decreased." The document explains that "such constraints could be applied to the movements of force, to the size, number, duration and frequency of military exercises including, for example, the possibility of simultaneous exercises, and also to bans on large exercises." That postulate is quite understandable in view of the fact that the Stockholm conference decisions have brought about a certain restriction of military activities. Even more important, these self-imposed limitations or constraints on military activity have been induced more by financial considerations and an improved East-West climate than by an obligation to respect concrete recommendations.[17]

The catalogue of new CSBMs proposed in the Polish statement covers the following:

–exchange of military information;
–procedures for the clarification of situations related to military activities and arousing the concern of either party;
–establishment of a system of "hot lines" between the highest state authorities and military high commands (such communication lines already exist between Washington and Moscow and between Paris and Moscow); and
–extension of contacts among representatives of armed forces (study visits and regular bilateral and multilateral working meetings).

The system of control envisaged in the Polish proposal would include observation and on-site inspection without the right of refusal. The system of mutual control could encompass:

–exchange of indispensable information, including lists of the types and kinds of armaments being withdrawn and their redeployment;
–notification of the commencement, progress and completion of the various measures; and
–establishment of permanent observation posts on the borders of the zone, at large railway junctions, air fields and sea ports through which the arms, equipment and specified military units would be transferred.

Also subject to control would be the weapons decommissioned from the armed forces as would be compliance with levels attained as the outcome of the reduction and/or withdrawal process. Poland expressed its readiness to establish an international consultative body with the possible inclusion of interested third parties. It would be primarily concerned with observation and inspection activities and would also investigate controversial issues. An important role in that organ could be played by representatives of the NNA states.

The Polish proposal refers first of all to Central Europe but it remains in strict relationship with the situation, security requirements and solutions on an all-European scale. During work on the document its authors have listened to opinions and suggestions of Western partners expressed both at official consultations with governmental officials and during meetings with experts on a non-governmental basis.

A Center for Prevention of Surprise Attack in Europe

On July 11, 1988, Mikhail Gorbachev announced in the Polish Parliament that "there is a need for a European center to temper the threat of war that could serve as a place for cooperation between NATO and the WTO. Such a center, which would be a permanent organization, could be transformed into a useful structure enhancing trust in the infallibility of peace in Europe." Speaking in support of that initiative, Wojciech Jaruzelski said that it corresponds to the Polish plan. He also expressed a readiness to actively contribute to the establishment of the center for the prevention of surprise attack in Europe. "Poland," said General Jaruzelski, "is ready to engage immediately in consultations on the Center, at the same time offering—should states interested consent—its territory as the center's seat."[18]

The idea to have such a center is not new. It is related to a broader concept of crisis-management mechanisms. In the United States it has been discussed chiefly in the context of providing reliable management of a mechanism that could track developments and remain in control, as was suggested by the experience of the Cuban missile crisis of 1962. In their report to the U.S. Arms Control and Disarmament Agency published in 1984, William Langer Ury and Richard Smoke of the Harvard Law School wrote: "Four key features of a crisis make it especially dangerous: little time to decide, high stakes, high uncertainty, and few usable options."[19]

The task of the European Center would be not so much the resolution of crisis situations but rather preventive activity, information and control. It would be a kind of clearinghouse for military-political matters in Europe.

The idea for a European center has been bruited about for quite some time at scientific symposia and conferences attended by representatives from West and East. Some experience in joint control and prevention of escalation of tensions and crisis situations has been gathered by institutions operating within the Allied Control Council for Germany.

Some of those bodies, such as, for example, the Committee for the Security of Flights in air corridors into Berlin, are still operative.

On March 22, 1988, acting on a bilateral basis, the U.S. and the USSR established nuclear risk control centers in Moscow and in Washington. That such solutions for the entire European continent are being looked at is best evidenced by various non-governmental documents and reports.[20]

In May 1987, a joint working group of the Polish United Workers' Party (PUWP) and the West German Social Democratic Party (SPD) issued a proposal for a European Council for Building Confidence, designed to serve as a forum for dialogue which would promote elaboration of political measures preventing tensions and crisis situations and encouraging the construction of peaceful structures in Europe. In July 1988, a similar working group of the East German Socialist Unity Party (SED) and the SPD submitted to the governments of the two German states a proposal to establish in Central Europe—along the line of contact of the two blocs—a zone of confidence and security. The regime of the zone was designed so as to convince both parties that, despite all their respective military capability, neither of them intended to launch a surprise attack. A qualitatively new element in the SED-SPD document is the idea of creating centers for confidence-building as permanent organs entrusted with the task of exchanging militarily important information and the results of observations. This would facilitate the governments involved in their efforts to forestall crisis situations in Central Europe and/or to resolve them through political means. The centers would use data from an agreed joint European satellite surveillance system. These data would also be supplied to every CSCE member-state.

The Committee of Foreign Ministers of Member-States of the Warsaw Treaty Organization in session in Budapest on October 28, 1988, incorporated a draft for the establishment in Europe of a center for diminishing the threat of war and prevention of surprise attack into its joint statement on confidence- and security-building measures and disarmament in Europe. The center would perform such tasks as information exchange, communications and consultations on operative clarification of situations arousing concern and suspicion. Matters concerning the center will be open for talks during a CSCE conference devoted to CSBMs. The outstanding issues include the scope and nature of information exchanged, organizational framework, mode of procedure and financing. It is nonetheless certain that such a center—even allowing for the fact that in its initial stages its functions would be limited to information exchange only—would contribute to stabilizing the military as well as political situation in Europe. The agreement to have a European center alone would be eloquent proof of serious change and progress in building confidence. It would set in motion a process of shaping lasting structures for preventing, controlling, applying and resolving crisis situations in Europe. So far the NATO states have responded with caution.

The United States for its part remains stubbornly negative on two other concepts: a gradual transformation of military doctrines toward a defensive character, and expansion of CSBMs to sea and ocean areas.

CSBMs on the Seas

The matter of expanding the zone of application of CSBMs to waters around Europe and making independent naval operations part of the regime of the agreed measures has been and still remains a major contentious issue.

In the official American assessment the extension of the CSBMs' zone of application to the Urals was correctly defined as "quite significant." However, the Soviet idea of extending the geographical area into the north Atlantic Ocean as compensation for its extension to the Ural Mountains cannot be rejected simply with the argument that the Soviet objective is "to negate the international principle recognizing free use of the high seas and thus possibly to interfere with movement of U.S. forces in contingencies involving areas of the world outside Europe."[21] This reasoning is not convincing for several reasons.

First, as a rule, international treaties and agreements limit the sovereign rights of states, including the freedom of naval activities; by conclusion of agreements the sovereignty of states is reflected with respect for their equal rights and the principle of reciprocity.

Second, free use of the high seas is reduced in many respects not only by the law of the sea, but sometimes even unilaterally (e.g., American and Soviet announcements about closed areas on the oceans for military testing).

Third, some limitations concerning the "adjoining sea and space area" included in the Final Act are not considered as a negation of the free use of the high seas.

Finally, the conferences in Helsinki, Madrid and Stockholm as well as in Vienna were and are concerned with the problems of security in

Europe. This can by no measure be reduced to military activities on the European continent. It would be hard, therefore, to accept the unilateral U.S. interpretation of the mandate as it would "clearly exclude independent air and naval activities from coverage."[22] For the time being, though, the problem of surprise military attack cannot be reduced to land activity only and should also encompass in agreed scope the surveillance and observation of naval forces, including submarines, aircraft and other instruments of surprise attack deployed on the sea and in the air, as stipulated by the Western experts at the Geneva Surprise Attack Conference.[23]

"The inclusion of naval and air exercises in CBMs could have both beneficial and detrimental effects on security," a Canadian researcher has written.[24] He has argued that many states, among them Norway, find Soviet naval maneuvers worrisome. But CBMs could also—as he has said—reduce military flexibility by depriving certain states of the minimal level of secrecy needed for an effective defense.

> Thus, while Norway, from a regional point of view, may favor notification of naval maneuvers, the United States, from a global naval perspective, may well find notification and exchanges of observers detrimental to coping with current and new military problems. Therefore, before such measures are introduced, regional and global strategic interests will have to be reconciled.[25]

In the Soviet view the climate of confidence can be enhanced "through the limitation of naval activities in some sea and ocean areas."[26] The Soviet initiatives are directed at limiting and lowering the level of military presence and activities in those areas where conflict is most probable. The Soviet Union is interested in withdrawing missile submarines, especially from the regions of combat patrolling, while limiting the mutually agreed areas of navigation. It aims at limiting deployments of new ballistic missile systems on submarines and prohibiting the deployment of long-range submarine-launched cruise missiles [LRSLCM] and ground-based cruise missiles.[27] In other words, from the Soviet viewpoint, the question of extending CSBMs to the seas and oceans is of vital importance for its security policy. This approach, supported by the other socialist states, did not find a sympathetic audience on the Western side during the Stockholm conference.

The idea of expanding CSBMs in the naval activity of states has recently gained greater currency. In October 1987 in Murmansk Mikhail

Gorbachev submitted a new proposal to convene a meeting of military experts from NATO and the WTO with the aim of discussing the reduction of naval activity and the extension of CSBMs to the seas. During his visit to Oslo in January 1988 Soviet Prime Minister Nikolai Ryzhkov developed this initiative and presented some specific new suggestions in this field. Also, Soviet Foreign Minister Eduard Shevardnadze made a statement in this respect during the general debate of the Third Special Session of the UN General Assembly on Disarmament (June 8, 1988). Shevardnadze suggested enhancing confidence through comparison of data on naval forces and discussion of the principles of their use and the aims of maneuvers and excercises at sea. He proposed the establishment of zones with lower density of armaments, and increasing confidence by with-drawing offensive naval forces and weapons systems from major inter-national ocean lanes. The goal on the seas should also be to preclude the possibility of surprise attack or large-scale offensive operations.

Naval CSBMs have been discussed by Pugwash experts[28] and directly between representatives of political parties from the Baltic region. A number of new solutions have been advanced. Particularly interesting are the postulates submitted by Norwegian Defense Minister Johan J. Holst in a paper he delivered at a Pugwash symposium. His examination of CSBMs at sea suggests the following tentative conclusions:[29]

–There is a need to develop such measures in a period of change in the operational pattern of the major naval powers in northern waters. The purpose is to prevent an unintended sharpening of tension and com-petition in sensitive waters.
–Particular emphasis should be attached to confidence- and security-building measures which could build upon traditional rules of behavior. Consistent with the principle of freedom of navigation, measures should be considered which promise to contribute to the prevention of incidents, inadvertent conflict and escalation. A basis for multilateral instruments exists in the Soviet-American and Anglo-Soviet agreements for the prevention of incidents at sea.
–Potential confidence- and security-building measures must be considered concretely. Measures which would contain and regulate the access of flag states to particular ocean areas could cast heavy shadows constrain-ing the political freedom of action of coastal states unless they take into account relevant geopolitical asymmetries. Norway depends on not being confined by the shadows cast by the Soviet naval forces which

are home-ported on the Kola peninsula. For this purpose allied "countershadows" are needed.

–Confidence must be constructed on a reciprocal basis. Reciprocity in northern waters must include the naval powers of particular importance for the defense of Norway. Measures which create distance between Norway and its allies do not contribute to Norwegian confidence. Consequently, confidence- and security-building measures for northern waters should be negotiated by the two alliances. Measures involving mutual notification and observation should include the major flag states as well as the coastal states affected because of their location.

Conclusions

The new third-generation CSBMs ought to be seen as an integral part of the process of diminishing military threat and consolidating military-political stability in Europe. From this point of view, of crucial importance will be the following:

–measures leading to restraining military activity, which would mean introduction of a regime of building down the scale and number of simultaneous exercises and their frequency, as well as putting limits on troop transfers and their equipment. Of serious importance would be an agreement to restrain military activity near state borders of other CSCE states;

–expansion of the zone of application of CSBMs to independent naval[30] and air activity and creation of zones of confidence and security, especially areas that are particularly sensitive in military terms in view of the accumulation of great arsenals of weapons and concentration of troops. One of the components of the Central European zone of confidence and security is the Baltic Sea area, where an agreed regime of application of specific CSBMs should be introduced. The Baltic coast states are interested in such a solution (it would not impair the security interests of any other state);

–the time is now ripe for initiating negotiations on the establishment of a center for prevention of surprise attack in Europe and lessening the threat of war;

–opening an East-West debate stimulating change in rendering military doctrines strictly defensive in character;

–setting up a special system of communications for clarification of certain situations arousing concern; and development of contacts between political leaders and military commanders from all states and establishment of contacts between alliances;

–refraining from steps in the sphere of arms buildup which would be incompatible with the goals of negotiations, and in particular non-enlargement of armed forces; and

–agreements on measures for elimination of negative stereotypes and "enemy images" and initiation of moves toward a better mutual understanding and strengthening confidence.

The search for a new generation of CSBMs must not be confined to certain types of measures which are of interest only for one group of states. This requires rejection of the dichotomous perspective in favor of a concept of an international system based on partnership. Experience teaches us that structures usually outlive the circumstances in which they have been established. The consecutive generations of CSBMs have reflected the need for stability and control of peacetime developments. Whether confidence and security structures created in peaceful circumstances could prove useful in the event of international tension and military confrontation is an open question. However, such structures could well serve the purposes of prevention and defuse tensions before they could degenerate into open conflict.

Notes

1 Thomas C. Schelling, "Arms Control: Proposal for a Special Surveillance Force," *World Politics* (October 1960); and Schelling, "The Role of Communication in Arms Control," in Evan Luard, ed., *First Steps in Disarmament* (London: Thames and Hudson, 1965), pp. 210–225. For a review of concepts see Charles R. Planck, *Sicherheit in Europa. Die Vorschlaege fuer Ruestungsbeschraenkung und Abruestung, 1955–1965* (Munich: R. Oldenbourg Verlag, 1968), pp. 29–96.

2 "Working Paper on Reduction of the Risk of War Through Accident, Miscalculation or Failure of Communication," END/70.

3 Jonathan Alford, ed., "The Future of Arms Control. Part III. Confidence-Building Measures," *Adelphi Papers* 149 (London: IISS, 1979); Comprehensive Study on Confidence-Building Measures (New York: UN Disarmament Study Series No. 7, 1982); Karl E. Birnbaum, ed., *Confidence-Building and East-West Relations, The Laxenbourg Papers*, No. 5 (Vienna: 1983); F. Stephen Larrabee and Dietrich Stobbe, eds., *Confidence-Building Measures in Europe* (New York: Institute for East-West Security Studies, 1983); Wolf Graf von Baudissin, ed., *From Distrust to Confidence. Concepts, Experiences and Dimensions of CBMs* Vol. II (Baden-Baden: 1983); Karl Kaiser, "Confidence-Building Measures," *Proceedings of an International Symposium* (May 24–27, 1983, Bonn); Adam D. Rotfeld,

ed., *From Confidence to Disarmament* (Warsaw: Polish Scientific Publishers, 1986); Rolf Berg and Adam D. Rotfeld, *Building Security in Europe. CBMs and the CSCE*, edited by Allen Lynch (New York: Institute for East-West Security Studies, 1986); R. B. Byers, F. Stephen Larrabee and Allen Lynch, eds., *Confidence-Building Measures and International Security* (New York: Institute for East-West Security Studies, 1987); Karl E. Birnbaum and Bo Huldt, eds., *From Stockholm to Vienna: Building Confidence and Security in Europe*, Conference Papers 9 (Stockholm: 1987); Ingo Peters, *Transatlantischer Konsens und Vertrauenbildung in Europa* (Baden-Baden: 1987).

4   On the prevention of surprise attack, see Andrzej Karkoszka, "Zapobieganie niespodziewanej napasci" [The Prevention of Surprise Attack], in Wojciech Multan, ed., *Negocjacje rozbrojeniowe po II wojnie swiatowej* [Disarmament Negotiation After the Second World War] (Warsaw: Polish Institute of International Affairs, 1985) pp. 277–312.

5   The full title of the document is as follows: Document of the Stockholm Conference on Confidence- and Security-Building Measures and Disarmament in Europe Convened in Accordance with the Relevant Provisions of the Concluding Document of the Madrid Meeting of the Conference on Security and Co-operation in Europe (Stockholm: 1986). The course of the negotiations has been outlined by John Borawski in *From the Atlantic to the Urals, Negotiating Arms Control at the Stockholm Conference* (Washington, DC: Pergamon-Brassey's, 1987).

6   Julian Kaczmarek, Wojciech Lepkowski and Zbigniew Paluch, "Wojskowe problemy bezpieczenstwa Polski" [The Military Aspects of Poland's Security], in Adam D. Rotfeld, ed., *Miedzynarodowe czynniki bezpieczenstwa Polski* [International Factors of the Security of Poland] (Warsaw: 1986), p. 66.

7   CSCE/WT. 1, Vienna, December 8, 1986.

8   CSCE/WT. 129 tabled by NATO states at Vienna on July 19, 1987.

9   CSCE/WT. 131, July 1987.

10 CSCE/WT. 133, September 22, 1987.

11 CSCE/WT. 134, September 22, 1987.

12 See "Contributions to a Seminar on the Stockholm Conference and CSCE Process organized by the Swedish Institute of International Affairs, June 4–5, 1987," in Birnbaum and Huldt, eds., *From Stockholm to Vienna: Building Confidence and Security in Europe*. Also Adam D. Rotfeld, "New CSBMs: A Polish View," in *PISM Occasional Papers* (Warsaw: Polish Institute of International Affairs, 1987), p. 24.

13 Concrete proposals were tabled at Stockholm on May 20, 1985, by the delegations of Bulgaria, Poland and the USSR (SC/WGB.3, naval exercises), and by the GDR, Hungary and USSR (SC/WGB.2, air force operations).

14 CSCE/WT.120, Vienna, July 10, 1987. For more on the NATO position, see Borawski, *From the Atlantic to the Urals*.

15 CSCE/SC.7, Stockholm, November 15, 1985.

16 Memorandum of the Government of the Polish People's Republic on Decreasing Armaments and Increasing Confidence in Central Europe (Warsaw: July 1987). Text in *Polish Plan to Decrease Armaments and Increase Confidence in Europe* (Warsaw: 1987), pp. 57–58.

17 In 1987, CSCE states exchanged a total of 47 notifications: 17 NATO, 25 WTO, 5 NNA. By comparison with 1987, the 1988 annual calendar shows a decrease in both the

number of exercises and the number of troops involved. It is, however, premature to assess to what extent it is the effect of budgetary constraints and how much responsibility could be laid at the door of an improved international situation.

18 For texts of the two speeches see *Trybuna Ludu*, July 12, 1988.

19 William Langer Ury and Richard Smoke, *Beyond the Hotline: Controlling a Nuclear Crisis. A Report to the U.S. Arms Control and Disarmament Agency* (Cambridge: Harvard University Press, 1984), p. iii.

20 The declaration on Security and Co-operation in Europe, adopted by the 10th Congress of the PUWP (Warsaw: July 3, 1986), reads as follows: ". . . we come out for the establishment of a European mechanism which would serve the purpose of reaching agreement on the means and methods of preventing and easing tensions and crises on our continent. This would help to reinforce the mutual CSBMs now being elaborated within the CSCE process." In Adam D. Rotfeld, ed., *Poland and the Implementation of the CSCE Decisions* (Warsaw: 1986), p. 147.

21 Max M. Kampelman, "An assessment of the Madrid CSCE Follow-up Meeting," *Department of State Bulletin* (September 1983), p. 64.

22 Ibid.

23 *Documents on Disarmament 1945–59*, Vol. II, doc. 319, 324, et al.

24 Aurel Braun, "CBMs, Security and Disarmament," in Robert Spencer, ed., *Canada and the CSCE* (Toronto: Center for International Studies, 1984), p. 223.

25 Ibid., pp. 223–234.

26 I. Khripunov, "Mery doveriia: problemy i perspektivy" [Confidence Measures: Problems and Perspectives], in *Diplomaticheskii Vestnik* (1984), p. 61.

27 Ibid.

28 Anders Boserup, "Maritime Defense Without Naval Threat. The Case of the Baltic," 5th Workshop of the Pugwash Study Group on Conventional Forces in Europe. Castiglioncello, Italy, October 9–12, 1986; Bjoern Moeller, "A Non-Offensive Maritime Strategy for the Nordic Area," Working Paper of the Center of Peace and Conflict Research, Copenhagen, No. 3 (1987).

29 Johan L. Holst, "Northern Europe and the High North. The Strategic Setting: Parameters for Confidence-Building and Arms Restraint," in *Naval Forces: Arms Restraint and Confidence-Building*. 52nd Pugwash Symposium, Oslo, June 23–26, 1988.

30 It is worth noting Resolution 200 on CBMs adopted by the North Atlantic Assembly, point 14 of which "Urges the North Atlantic's Alliance to explore naval confidence-building measures." AF 226, PC/88/6.

IX

PART ONE

Constraints in Europe

Richard E. Darilek and John K. Setear,* United States

Arms control can buy time and money, but not peace. That is the underlying thesis of this chapter as it moves from an introductory discussion of certain basic opportunities and limitations of arms control to a more specific focus on "constraints"—defined here as arms control measures that seek to prohibit or limit the current or future operational practices of conventional military forces—for both NATO and the Warsaw Treaty Organization in Europe. In this chapter we first place constraints within the broader context of conventional arms control measures. Next, we discuss the general contours of various possible constraint measures, suggesting the magnitudes of warning time and of money that can be gained from constraints. Finally, we develop (and illustrate with examples) several criteria for evaluating the potential utility of constraint measures.

Time, Money and Arms Control

Arms control is unlikely, by itself, to guarantee peace. Short of total disarmament, the means of war will continue to exist and, with them, the possibility of war. Irrationality and accident, for example, are likely to remain both possible and dangerous in a world of human beings and complex organizations. Indeed, even "coldly calculating" leaders may start wars. Evidence suggests that Japan attacked Pearl Harbor, despite a lack of confidence in the prospect of ultimate victory against the United States in World War II, because other options seemed to lead to even less desired outcomes and war presented at least some hope of success.

* The views expressed in this essay are solely those of the authors, and do not necessarily represent those of the RAND Corporation or any of its research sponsors.

National leaders do not base their decisions only on the calculations of diplomatic or military officials who make arms control agreements. Adolf Hitler's decision-making during the 1930s overturned various arms control agreements in the Nazis' march toward conquest and war in Europe. The major naval powers agreed to limit their construction of battleships at the Washington Naval Armaments Conference of 1921–1922; two decades later, the oceans were filled with the most powerful fleets the world had ever seen. Germany was almost completely disarmed and its Rhineland demilitarized after World War I, yet Germany conquered Europe from the Atlantic almost to the Urals by 1941.

Perhaps an even more important factor in the limited utility of arms control measures is that the treaties that codify them are written on paper, not in stone. A "breakout" from any arms control agreement is therefore always possible, even if the treaty as written creates a world in which war is an unattractive option for both sides. When one party to a treaty violates the agreement by simply returning its military forces to their pre-agreement state, there is little that the other party can then do—short of reactive responses in kind or preemptive military operations (which would hardly preserve peace). Hitler simply rearmed in the end, first quietly and then brazenly.

Arms control can, of course, buy something. It can buy time, because "breakouts" from a treaty take time and, once detected, such violations can serve as a warning to the side that adheres longer to the treaty. In the extra time provided by the alarm bells, the side being warned can take steps that may reduce the chances of war or that may improve its own chances if war should come. Great Britain might have rearmed after the remilitarization of the Rhineland or after the appearance of "pocket battleships," which violated the spirit, at least, of the Washington Conference. The United States might be able to fly its reinforcements to Europe after detecting highly suspicious Pact activity during a Western "challenge inspection" of Eastern territory, or the Soviet Union might step up its own strategic defense program after learning of the planned deployment of a U.S. SDI system that bypassed the ABM Treaty. Vigilance, or action induced by vigilance, cannot always dissuade aggressive behavior, but it may well be better than blissful ignorance.

Arms control can also save money. Prohibitions on theater nuclear missiles allow nations to forgo the procurement and deployment costs of planned and budgeted systems, as well as to forgo modernization of obsolescent models of such systems. A limit on the readiness of active-duty conventional military forces in Europe might allow savings in the numbers, and therefore the payrolls, of active-duty personnel, as well as in compensation paid to farmers for damage inflicted to fields by tanks and troops conducting exercises. Such fiscal considerations may not be as riveting as issues affecting the likelihood of war, but in a period of growing fiscal pressures for both East and West these savings, even if small, are likely to be welcomed.

Time, Money, Arms Control and Constraints

Where do constraints fit into the general arms control picture sketched above? We define "constraints" here as "measures directly limiting or prohibiting current or future operations by conventional military forces." Our focus is on non-nuclear military forces in Europe and, specifically, on the operations or deployments of those forces rather than on their numbers. Examples of constraints include weapons-free zones, regulation of the removal of ammunition from monitored central locations, limits on the size or frequency of military exercises, and controls on mobilization or training procedures.

We should emphasize the need under our definition of constraints for a direct link between individual measures and military operations. Although reductions in force structure obviously would have some effect on the ability to conduct military operations, that effect is indirect and not the result of a specific operational prohibition. Hence, we do not consider force-structure reductions themselves to be constraints, regardless of whether such measures involve reductions in existing levels of weapons and personnel or quantitative limits on future growth. In our view, constraints specifically and directly regulate such operational factors as where nations may deploy their existing military forces, how often and under what conditions these forces can exercise, and what changes can be made in their training status. Constraints, on the one hand, and force-structure measures, on the other, are not necessarily incompatible. Indeed, they may be complementary. But they are different.[1]

To see more readily where constraints fit into the overall arms control picture, one can construct a "breakout spectrum" that shows how long it would take a nation to violate a particular type of agreement and return its military forces to their pre-agreement state.[2] For example, a global arms control agreement that abolished all nuclear weapons as well as the capacity for generating weapons-grade nuclear materials would, once

Figure 1 The Breakout Spectrum

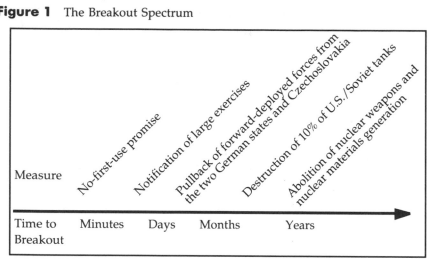

adhered to in its entirety, take a number of years to undo or reverse: a superpower that "broke out" of such an agreement would have to construct complicated nuclear-materials-generating plants from the ground up, as well as readapt or rebuild the complicated weapons that serve as nuclear delivery vehicles. Such a process might take decades.

Suppose instead that the United States and the Soviet Union were to agree to a declaratory measure stating that neither would be the first to use nuclear weapons, or to a confidence-building measure stipulating that neither would conduct an exercise of over 10,000 troops without first notifying the other. The "breakout time" for such measures would be essentially zero. The U.S. president or the Soviet general secretary could wake up one morning and decide to do what he had promised not to do. Although intentions can change overnight, the capabilities to pursue hostile (as well as peaceful) intentions would still remain.

Aligning these measures, and some other examples, along a timeline of breakout possibilities produces a "breakout spectrum" (see Figure 1). Constraints typically fall on the spectrum somewhere between "confidence- and security-building measures" (CSBMs) and what we call "force-structure" measures (see Figure 2). "Declaratory" measures, which occupy the far left end of the spectrum, involve declarations of intent by participants for which the breakout time can be almost instantaneous. CSBMs, of course, range from agreements to improve the flow of information among participants via notification of exercises and invitation of observers, as provided in the Helsinki Final Act of 1975, to provisions

Figure 2 The Breakout Spectrum (by category of measure)

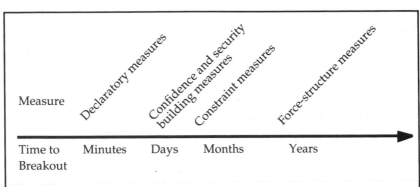

for on-site inspections and even to the rudimentary constraints on large-scale exercises in the Stockholm Document of 1986. The diverse requirements of these measures can be broken out of relatively quickly, simply by refusing to participate in an information exchange or by denying access to observers and inspectors.

"Force-structure" measures, which occupy the far right end of our breakout spectrum, involve such changes in the number or composition of military forces as the destruction of weapons systems, the elimination of units, or a prohibition on new types of equipment (e.g., precision-guided weapons). Breaking out of such agreements requires the construction or rebuilding of whole weapons systems or units, and building modern weapons systems generally takes years. Breaking out of a force-structure measure, therefore, can be expected to take years.

Constraints fall between CSBMs and force-structure measures on the breakout spectrum. To move troops back into a formerly demilitarized zone, for example, is likely to take more time than expelling (or refusing entrance to) a group of observers, but less time than reconstituting units that have been disbanded. Limitations on operations that improve readiness, such as a limit on training or exercising troops at the divisional level or above, would require as long to break out of as it takes to complete the relevant training—more than a few days, typically, but less than the years that may be required in the case of force-structure measures.

We can also use this breakout spectrum to identify with relative ease the margins of constraints. The CSBMs of the Stockholm Document come fairly close to the left edge of constraints on the breakout spectrum, primarily because of their inspection and so-called "constraining provisions."[3] These CSBMs relate to operations but do not place much of a constraint upon them. It is relatively easy to break out of notification requirements, for example, simply by failing to observe them. Although there is at least an implicit stricture in such measures against conducting stipulated exercises without the requisite notice, a violation cannot be completely confirmed unless and until a notifiable event occurs—i.e., after the breakout has happened.

To the right of CSBMs on our spectrum lie constraints. Any constraint has three basic components: *the object or activity being regulated* (e.g., tanks, or artillery and its ammunition, or divisional exercises); a *quantitative limit* on the deployment or activity of the regulated military units (e.g., zero tanks, or ten rounds withdrawn per storage site per day, or two field training exercises per year); and the *zone* in which the prohibition or limitation occurs (e.g, within 100 kilometers of any border between a NATO and a Pact member-state, or within the two German states and Czechoslovakia, or from the Atlantic to the Urals). Careful analysis must acknowledge all three aspects of constraints. A "thin-out" zone, for example, is an empty concept until one specifies that it comprises, say, a limit of five divisions for each alliance deployed in a zone of 50 kilometers on either side of the inter-German border (IGB).[4]

One significant subcategory of constraints are those measures that require redeployments of units or that separate crucial components of a unit (e.g., all tanks or ammunition stored some distance from the forces that would use them). Such redeployments and separations could take place either in relatively narrow or in very wide zones—a band of territory on both sides of the IGB, for example, or Central Europe as defined in the MBFR talks, or all of Europe from the Atlantic to the Urals. As a general rule, the larger the zone of application for deployment-oriented constraints, the longer it will take to break out of them. Breaking out of a tank-free zonal constraint that is 25-km wide on each side of the IGB should require about a day—some topping off of gas tanks, a short drive across the countryside, and some extra time for getting untangled from any traffic-control problems. In contrast, a tank or ammunition-free zonal constraint covering all of Europe would entail an amount of breakout time that, while substantially less than that required actually to rebuild units, could well stretch to months.

Some arms control possibilities include pulling forces out of the Atlantic-to-the-Urals zone but leaving them in the force structure of the relevant nation. Some analysts treat such measures as if they were reductions. In our view, such measures are not reductions. They are constraints, and the difference is more than merely one of terminology. A tank division removed from Germany and placed behind the Urals or across the Atlantic as the result of a constraint can return with the passage of several weeks' time and the expenditure of a few million dollars. A tank division removed by a reductions measure—its equipment destroyed and its personnel demobilized—cannot return until many months have elapsed and hundreds of millions of dollars have been expended.[5]

The other significant subcategory of constraints is the activity-oriented measure. Constraints focusing on the deployment of units, after all, are not intrinsically more worthwhile or effective than constraints focusing on the activities of units with unregulated deployments. Certain constraints in the latter category, such as a prohibition on training or exercising more than 100 men simultaneously, could well buy more time than certain deployment-oriented constraints, such as a 100-kilometer tank-free zone centered along the IGB. Training units to undertake battalion-level warfare, and then regimental/brigade and divisional warfare, is a time-consuming—and probably essential—task for any army that hopes to launch a successful offensive. Rolling 50 kilometers towards a border with well-trained units may not be a trivial task, but it is a far simpler one.

The *money* that arms control could save can be placed on a simple linear scale in roughly the same order as in the breakout spectrum—though in this case the scale is in budgetary rather than temporal units, and we must also place separately on the spectrum the two subcategories of constraints (see Figure 3). Declaratory measures and CSBMs are likely to provide minimal savings, since they have a minimal effect on the production or operation of military units or their equipment. Indeed, such measures probably involve a net financial *loss* given that the requisite observers or communications links involved in monitoring them require additional expenditures.

Force-structure measures, in contrast, can save huge sums of money—indeed, complete disarmament would theoretically save the entire defense budget of each participant. The purchase and fielding of complete weapons systems typically runs in the multiple billions; thus, force-structure limits that eliminate even a small number of as-yet-unpurchased systems can save significant amounts of procurement and deployment costs. Force-structure reductions that destroy existing systems obviously do not save the procurements costs of already-built weapons, but they

Figure 3 The Cost/Savings Spectrum

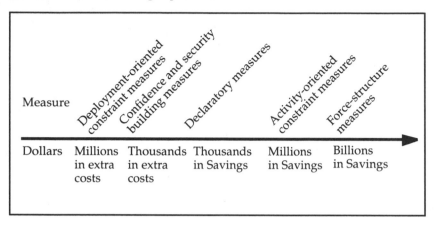

do eliminate the operations-and-maintenance (O&M) expenditures otherwise necessary to keep such systems in being. Agreements like the ABM
Treaty probably also saved sizable research and development costs,
among others, during the 1970s by prohibiting systems that would
otherwise have been tested, at least, and possibly even deployed.

As in the case of the breakout spectrum, activity-oriented constraints
seem likely to fall toward the middle of the cost/savings spectrum. O&M
expenditures can be significant—indeed, in the U.S. defense budget,
O&M outlays are roughly the same size as procurement outlays. We
cannot state with confidence, however, what proportion of O&M costs
are necessary simply to keep an active unit in being and what proportion
is necessary to keep the unit finely honed. Constraints would presumably
affect savings only on the latter portion of expenditures, while force-
structure measures can eliminate the need for O&M expenditures entirely
by eliminating the unit that would otherwise need to be operated and
maintained.

Deployment-oriented constraints, especially those involving permanent redeployments of large numbers of units, are likely to result in
cost increases, not cost savings. Such redeployments require the construction of new infrastructure—bases, parts stockpiles and ammunition
depots—for displaced units, and such construction is typically expensive.
In fact, large-scale redeployments would probably result in cost increases
greater than those involved in building and maintaining the communications links or teams of observers associated with declaratory measures
or CSBMs.

Figure 4 The Attack Options Spectrum (Pact Attacks)

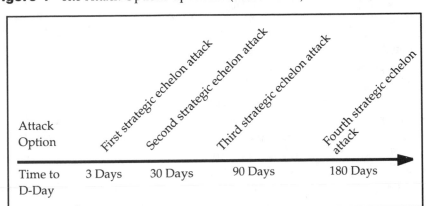

What Constraints Can and Cannot Do in Europe

If we switch from the general perspective of arms controllers to the specific perspective of military planners with responsibility for operations in Central Europe, we can redraw the "breakout spectrum" as an "attack-options" or "warning-time" spectrum (see Figure 4). We use potential attacks by the Warsaw Pact on NATO for our examples.[6]

Depending upon the amount of warning time that the Pact's planners and authorities are willing to risk providing to NATO, the Warsaw Pact can conceivably launch very different sorts of attacks upon NATO. At the left end of the options/warning spectrum lies an attack possibility that gives NATO very short warning of impending war. Such an attack might be launched by the forward-deployed units of the USSR in East Germany and Czechoslovakia, supplemented only by highly ready indigenous forces of the Warsaw Pact's northern tier (those of the German Democratic Republic, Czechoslovakia and Poland); the attack would probably be essentially unreinforced by other forces during the first few weeks of war. This scenario, which is often referred to as the "standing-start" or "unreinforced" attack, will for our purposes be denominated a "first-strategic-echelon" attack.

If the Pact is willing to risk providing NATO with a somewhat longer warning period,[7] then the opening stages of a war could see the forward movement of not only the ready forces in the GDR, Czechoslovakia and Poland but also those from the western military districts of the Soviet Union. These additional units would spend the extra days (or, possibly, weeks) of time available before the commencement of hostilities by bringing themselves up to full readiness and preparing for redeployment to areas much closer to the IGB. They might even commence such redeployment before the attack begins.[8] In any event, such forces would be available to serve as a "second strategic echelon" for conducting or reinforcing the initial attack.

Another scenario, which would potentially provide NATO with yet more warning time, would be to bring to full readiness essentially all existing military units of the Warsaw Treaty Organization. To transform even a small number of the many Pact cadre units—typically armed with outmoded or ill-maintained equipment and, by definition, under-manned—into full-fledged combat units would doubtless take a good deal of time, probably on the order of several months. Such an effort would provide the Soviets with what we might call a "third strategic echelon" that could be brought to bear against NATO. In exchange, NATO would gain—at least potentially—substantially longer warning of the impending conflict than it would receive of first- or second-strategic-echelon attacks.

Even further to the right on our options spectrum would lie attack possibilities in which the USSR and other members of the Pact were also able to raise completely new units from scratch before beginning any onslaught. If historical experience is any guide to estimating the lead time necessary for such an operation, the Pact would potentially provide NATO with at least six months' warning time before these new, "fourth-strategic-echelon" units were ready to attack across the West German border.

The additional warning time that *constraints* can provide to NATO defenders varies substantially depending upon which one of these various types of attack the Pact chooses to launch. We believe that constraints will buy relatively more useful warning time with respect to first- and second-strategic-echelon attacks than they will buy for third- and fourth-strategic-echelon attacks.

The reasons are fairly simple. The timelines for third- and fourth-strategic-echelon attacks include at their outset a large number of activities that only force-structure measures, not constraints, can effectively limit: the construction of brand-new units (in the case of fourth-strategic-echelon attacks) or the wholesale addition of personnel to existing but threadbare division flags (in the case of third-strategic-echelon attacks). In the case of first- and second-strategic-echelon attacks, by contrast, the attacker need only hone the men and equipment already in active military service and move them rapidly to the front line; these are the same areas of readiness and deployment on which constraints focus. Operational activities of the kind that constraints can potentially regulate are most directly associated with preparations for attacks by high-readiness forces; the third and fourth strategic echelons are low-readiness forces first brought to reasonable readiness by changes in force structure, not by a change in operations.

Constraints may have some utility in third- or fourth-strategic-echelon attacks, of course. The final preparations for a third- or fourth-strategic echelon attack are similar to the initial preparations for a first- or second-strategic-echelon attack—movement towards the border by forces far from the border, a burst of increased training by relatively ready units, and so forth. If the defending side had completely missed the warning signs unique to a third- or fourth-strategic-echelon buildup, then the defender might still obtain some benefit from seeing the attacker violate existing constraints.[9] The defender would also benefit if the attacker chose to launch a "constrained" attack—i.e., one that complied with the constraints up to the last minute and, thus, sacrificed optimal attack capabilities in hopes of minimizing warning time.[10]

Constraints can therefore buy hours, days or even weeks of useful warning, but not months. They can alleviate problems associated with short-warning attacks. They can reduce the desirability of first- and second-strategic-echelon attacks by depriving an attacker of the opportunity to make undetected preparations for such an attack. They cannot deter an attacker who believes that he can, *even if observed*, generate forces rapidly enough in comparison to the defender to launch a successful offensive. (Only force-structure measures would be effective in such cases.)

But if constraints can tip the balance so that what once would have been an unconstrained or surprise attack with a reasonable chance of success becomes a constrained or non-surprise attack with little chance of success, then constraints will obviously have made a very useful contribution—not a guarantee of peace in our time, but a very useful contribution. In such circumstances, the would-be attacker is driven towards adopting a third- or fourth-strategic-echelon-attack option. The additional warning time potentially available from constraints might prove sufficient for the defending side to construct a robust defense, or for political negotiations between the alliances to stop a crisis from becoming a war, or for the more cautious members of an alliance to prevail upon their less cautious members to put off the attack entirely.

Criteria for Evaluating Constraint Measures

Having explored the general position of constraints in the field of conventional arms control, and having specified the particular sorts of attacks against which they are potentially most useful, it remains for us to posit, develop and examine three criteria for evaluating any constraint that the preceding analysis suggests. We label these criteria "defensive asymmetry," "clarity" and "economy." Time and space limitations do not allow us to apply each criterion systematically to all constraint proposals made to date. Instead, we have concentrated here on creating a framework to assist those who must evaluate the desirability of actually negotiating and implementing the various constraint proposals.

A. Defensive Asymmetry

By "defensive asymmetry" we mean the degree to which a measure, if adhered to by both sides, results in an increase of the likelihood of successful defense. It is relatively easy to conceive of measures that hinder the operations of an attacker, but one must also ensure that the operations of the defender are not equally hindered. The ideal defensively asymmetrical measure would greatly hinder offensive operations by either alliance without hindering defensive operations at all.[11]

A defensively asymmetrical constraint should contribute to the stability of the military situation in Central Europe, much as a measure on strategic nuclear systems that encouraged the substitution of second-strike weapons for first-strike systems might contribute to military stability between the United States and the Soviet Union. By "stability," after all, we typically mean "a lack of incentives to begin a war." It is the attacker whom we can expect to decide whether to go to war. A measure that decreases the attacker's chances of succeeding on the offensive more than it decreases the defender's chance of successful defense should obviously lessen the attacker's incentives to go to war.

Although one might be tempted to lessen these incentives simply by hampering the attacker, our asymmetry criterion requires measures that hamper the attacker *more than the defender*. This requirement com-

plicates the evaluation of constraint measures. First, since the defender
will need to make use of virtually all of the same weapons systems as
the attacker, much more work needs to be done to determine which
current systems help the attacker more than they help the defender.[12]
NATO, for example, may decide to focus in its structural arms control
efforts upon tanks and artillery, among other things. A model of warfare
in which tanks and artillery are crucial weapons for the attacker accords
with one very important historical example: the offensives of the Red
Army against the German armies in 1944–1945. However, such a model
is inconsistent—or at least incomplete—with respect to several other
historical examples. The offensives of the Western allies against the
Germans in 1944–1945 employed tanks and aircraft as their crucial
components, as have the more recent examples of Israeli offensives in
the Middle East. The most recent engagements of the superpowers
themselves have established a crucial role for helicopters, though the
terrain and technological sophistication of their opponents in Vietnam
and Afghanistan were clearly quite different from those in Central Europe.
Just which weapons systems are disproportionately "offensive," therefore, is far from a simple matter.

Second, it is clear that tactical (and probably operational) offensives
are necessary for success by the side on the strategic defensive. A
complete inability to counterattack would mean that the front would
move only in one direction—the direction in which the attacker began
an offensive. And without a revolution in military doctrine, counteroffensives at the operational level are likely to be necessary if the defender
is ever to regain the initiative and restore its prewar borders.[13] Measures
designed to constrain "offensive" weapons systems, therefore, should
be examined for their effects at all levels—especially measures affecting
systems necessary for an effective strategic defense.[14]

Let us take one example of the difficulties involved in deciding which
measures are defensively asymmetrical: a relatively narrow "demilitarized" or "tank-free" zone straddling the IGB. In NATO's case, the
strategy of forward defense may be deeply entrenched politically, but
there are no deep entrenchments along the IGB. If the movement of
military units across equal distances (we discuss below the possibility of
asymmetrical zones involving unequal distances) is likely to take the
forces of each side a roughly equal amount of time, then NATO and Pact
forces that broke such a constraint simultaneously would arrive at the
unfortified border more or less simultaneously.[15] The defending forces,

however, would be without benefit of extensive defensive preparations on their own terrain. In addition, the attacker knows beforehand where he will attack and can therefore focus his efforts on moving troops forward into those crucial areas; the defender has no such advantage and may therefore be relatively less well prepared in the area of the attack's main thrust(s). Tank-free zones or zones of military disengagement in which military movements or maneuvers might be prohibited, as Manfred Mueller suggests in his contribution to this chapter, could therefore make matters worse for the defender, not better.

The search for defensively asymmetrical constraints is further complicated by the substantial numerical asymmetry that NATO suffers in at least some crucial weapons systems and unit deployments. If, as many believe, NATO currently walks a razor's edge in its ability simply to cover the front with a cohesive defense, then small changes in the overall balance could greatly affect the outcome of combat in Central Europe.[16] In these circumstances, it should not be surprising that the question of attacker-defender asymmetry can easily become entangled with measures seeking to reduce the overall Pact-NATO asymmetry. Issues of what we might call "alliance asymmetry," in fact, may be quite relevant to the intellectually purer "defensive asymmetry" criterion: if a particular constraint causes NATO to fall off its defensive razor's edge without significantly affecting the Pact's offensive capabilities, then small changes in the relative balance of NATO and the Pact can lead to large changes in the incentives for one side to go to war.

Finally, one should be careful about constraints that clearly have destabilizing aspects. If ammunition were located in centralized areas, for example, the side that struck first might be able to destroy huge quantities of enemy ammunition while expending very small quantities of its own weaponry. Constraints that encourage such preemptive action should be examined with special care before they are proposed.

Is there any hope for concocting a set of constraints that does meet the asymmetry criterion? In the absence of firm convictions about which weapons systems are disproportionately useful to the attacker, one is more or less limited to two approaches. One can implement constraints that prevent the *concentration of forces* that an attacker requires in the initial stages of an attack (but that a defender cannot risk, because of ignorance of enemy plans, until the attack has progressed significantly). Alternatively, one can wrest from the Pact an acknowledgment that its forces are *more offensive* than NATO's and then implement constraints that asymmetrically affect the Pact's forces.

Constraints that limit the concentration of forces by an attacker rest on two premises: 1) that the attacker will have to move substantial forces a significant distance forward before launching an attack across the border and 2) that the attacker will not be able to obtain a sufficient force ratio for success by evenly spreading his forces along that front line once they arrive. If these premises are correct, then the attacker must concentrate his forces for success.

One could implement a constraint on force concentration by agreeing upon peacetime deployments for each side's units and prohibiting their movement from those deployment areas by more than a certain amount.[17] If this "radius of free movement" is smaller than the distance that a particular unit must travel to reach the border, then the concentration of that unit near the border is effectively prohibited. Using current peacetime deployments for units between the Atlantic and the Urals but granting them only a very small radius of free movement, say 20 kilometers, would make an offensive difficult to launch without violating the constraint early on, given that most units of both sides are deployed significantly more than 20 kilometers from the IGB. As another example, one might prohibit any movement beyond current deployment areas that exceeded specified levels of activity (e.g., three or four divisions out of their garrisons at any one time).

One might also implement a constraint that focuses on prohibiting the concentration of forces near the border by setting up "crisis deployment zones" for units within a few dozen kilometers of the border (even for units with peacetime deployments far from the border), but setting very small radii of free movement. Both sides could then deploy their units for defense but could not move toward the border for an actual attack without violating the constraint. To the extent that measures taken by units in place—such as pre-plotting zones of fire, familiarization with terrain and emplacement of barriers—favor the defender and are available to these forward-deployed units, this arrangement would further improve the defender's prospects at the expense of the attacker's.

This latter constraint points out the importance of force-structure considerations even when one is considering constraints. If the above measure were to be implemented without any change in the existing force structure, and all units in the force structure were given crisis deployment zones near the border, NATO would not be at all happy with one possible result: the Warsaw Pact could deploy *all* of its units in Europe fairly near the border *and* point to its legal right to do so under the constraints measure. And if the Pact truly fears a NATO offensive, then the Pact would be equally unhappy with the movement forward of all NATO's forces. As we have said before, the existing force structure may remain a problem even in the presence of a rigorous set of constraint measures.[18]

One might note that constraints can even be pressed into service as partial substitutes for force-structure reductions. Suppose that the two sides could agree on a force structure, different from the current one, that made each side confident that its opponent could not launch a successful offensive. Even in the absence of an agreement to destroy all "offensive" units, one could give those units peacetime and crisis deployment zones far from the border. This would make both sides happier than they would be in the absence of such constraints. Unfortunately, the breakout time for such an agreement—the time that it took to redeploy the specified units to the border—would still remain discomfitingly short.

Another avenue of approach to obtaining constraints that meet the asymmetry criterion is to adopt constraints that asymmetrically affect the Warsaw Pact. The profitability of this approach depends upon two assumptions. The first is that the Warsaw Pact is the more offensively oriented alliance, as Richard Kugler argues in Chapter 2. If one accepts this argument, then constraints that asymmetrically affect the Pact will asymmetrically affect the most likely potential attacker, thus fulfilling the defensive asymmetry criterion. The second assumption necessary to justify much expenditure of effort on constraints with asymmetrical effects on the Pact versus NATO is that they are, or can become, "negotiable." For the sake of discussion, we shall assume here both that the Pact is more offensively oriented than NATO and that the Pact will accept constraints which asymmetrically affect it more than NATO.

A wide variety of constraints could then plausibly meet the defensive asymmetry criterion. Constraints could either asymmetrically affect the Pact on their face or be equally applicable to both parties but negotiated in such a way that their effect weighs much more heavily on the Pact. In the first case, constraints could include asymmetries in the weapons or units to which the constraint applies, or in the depth of the zones, or in the frequency of permissible exercises. Suppose, for example, that all

NATO forces were excluded from the 50 kilometers west of the IGB and the Pact's forces were excluded from the first 150 kilometers east of the IGB; or that all Pact units were excluded from the 50 kilometers east of the IGB but only NATO tanks were excluded from the 50 kilometers west of the IGB; or that the Pact could conduct no exercise of more than 15,000 troops (or approximately one division) and NATO could exercise no more than 90,000 troops (or approximately five divisions).

In the second case, one could implement constraints that on their face appear to apply evenhandedly to the two alliances but, because of asymmetries inherent in the current forces of the two alliances, affect the Pact's operational capabilities more than they affect NATO's. Suppose that each side could annually expend only 1,000 live rounds of tank ammunition in the area between the Atlantic and the Urals.[19] Since the Pact has so many more tanks, the proportion of its tank forces that would be trained and experienced in firing live tank rounds would be much smaller; thus the relative readiness of forces likely to engage in European tank combat would improve in NATO's favor. A similar argument might apply to relatively low, symmetrical ceilings on exercises: the Pact has many more weapons systems and troops to exercise, and a low, equal ceiling would therefore leave the Pact with a much smaller proportion of its forces trained and ready (or in place to attack, if an exercise were used to mask an actual attack) than NATO's.[20]

One might also simply freeze training and readiness at their current levels (if one could define and mutually agree on what was meant by "training" and "readiness"). At present, NATO's units may be better trained and more ready, on a unit-by-unit basis, than their counterparts in the Warsaw Pact. A freeze at current levels of training and readiness, therefore, would preserve a NATO advantage, if such a constraint were adhered to, or would provide warning if the Pact violated the constraint in order to bring its forces to a level of readiness comparable to NATO's.[21]

Some constraints, however, could apply evenhandedly to both alliances but hinder NATO more than the Pact because of existing asymmetries. Such measures might include, for example, the proposals by Manfred Mueller in his part of this chapter for banning maneuvers that exceed specified levels of troops or that take place in close proximity to one another. In deference to agricultural requirements in Western Europe, NATO can only conduct significant field exercises from late autumn to early spring. As a result, it tends to hold exercises that are larger, closer together in time and space, and fewer in number than those of the Warsaw Pact. While appearing to apply evenhandedly to both sides, therefore, Mueller's proposals could in fact affect NATO's defensive capabilities more adversely than they do the Warsaw Pact's.

Defensively asymmetrical measures ensure that an attacker who obeys such constraints suffers a significant penalty relative to the defender. As discussed above, however, arms control measures are not sacred, and even if they were an aggressor is frequently willing to be profane. A good constraint therefore would ensure that an attacker not only suffers a significant penalty for adhering to a constraint, but also for violating it. To impose that penalty, we turn to our second criterion: clarity.

B. Clarity

As employed here, the term "clarity" means the degree to which one alliance's breaking of a constraint inevitably provides meaningful warning to the other alliance. Clarity, as we use the word, goes beyond verifiability to include both the significance of the breach and the likelihood of a response to that breach. As discussed at some length above, an important yardstick by which to judge an arms control measure is what happens when it is broken, not simply what happens when it is adhered to scrupulously. This is especially true with constraints, since the forces themselves remain in being in the absence of force reductions.

There are both political and military aspects to clarity. What we call the "political" aspects of clarity include the precision with which legal and illegal actions are *identified* in an arms control agreement—the drafting skills of negotiators bent on reducing ambiguities, in essence—and the unanimity with which members *within* an alliance agree that violations of those measures should greatly increase the likelihood of concrete *responses*. A well-drafted agreement that clearly sets forth the regulated or prohibited activities, and into which the nations of both alliances solemnly enter, should contribute to both identification and response.

Suppose, for example, that the Soviet Union were to announce today that, in 1992, it would stage a field exercise involving all of the Group of Soviet Forces in Germany as a celebration of the seventy-fifth anniversary of Marxism-Leninism in the Soviet Union. Contrast this situation with one in which an agreed constraint exists that prohibits any field exercises involving over 50,000 troops within the two German states and Czechoslovakia. Although in both cases the military significance of the Soviet action would be the same—a very large number of highly ready troops

exercising within a relatively short march of the West German border—
the political significance is likely to be quite different. In both cases, to
be sure, there would be arguments about whether the Soviets were really
up to something sinister. But under an arms control regime in which
constraints clearly prohibit such large-scale exercises, the boundaries of
the discussion would be much narrower and the issues more clearly
presented. "Why are the Soviets doing this illegal thing?" is likely to be
a question with much more power to sharpen and focus the debate than
questions like "What is it that the Soviets are doing?" and "What are all
the reasons why they might do such a thing, even though, after all, they
are perfectly within their rights to do it?" The clear violation of a legally
agreed constraint speaks volumes about the intentions of the violating
party and for that reason, if nothing else, encourages a response from
the other party to the agreement.

One should therefore remember that an agreement between NATO
and the Warsaw Pact that simply ratifies the status quo can be useful,
especially in tandem with an agreement about which changes in that
status quo would violate the substance of an accord about constraints. A
clear, comprehensive agreement between the two alliances that sets forth
their force levels, deployments and exercise patterns would go a long
way towards clarifying future situations in which a violation is alleged.

The related topic of verifiability is another important aspect of political
clarity. If we pick constraints that are easy to verify regardless of the
verification regime employed, then we have improved verifiability, and
thus the clarity with which one side or the other can make its accusations
and decisions at the political level. Some types of constraints are likely
to be inherently easier to verify, regardless of the verification regime
employed. As Andrzej Karkoszka points out in Chapter 7, an absolute
prohibition on an activity is typically easier to verify than a numerical
limit on that activity. A small zone in which an activity is prohibited
permits the concentration of verification assets in or upon that zone,
other things being equal, and thus is easier to verify than a large zone,
regardless of the particular verification regime.

Some verification regimes are also likely to be better at verifying
constraints, regardless of the type of constraint. Extensive on-site observation, numerous on-demand inspections, and specified entry/exit "portals" into regulated zones are all likely to make a contribution to verification
beyond that made by national technical means, and to make that extra
contribution by helping to verify a host of different measures. In the

process, they should also improve the likelihood that the violation of a constraint measure will be detected and will prompt a concrete response.

There are military as well as political aspects to the clarity issue (in addition, of course, to the pointedly military aspects of the asymmetry criterion). Different military activities furnish different degrees of clarity in their indication of a decision to undertake offensive activity. Field exercises of offensive activities at the army or army group level, for example, are obviously clearer indications of military intent than small-unit training to repulse armored attacks. Activities that are crucial in the transformation of military forces from peacetime units to wartime attackers should be singled out—indeed, in the case of national and alliance-wide construction of intelligence-and-warning indicators, have presumably already been identified—and the most crucial of these activities should, all other things being equal, stand atop a basic checklist that could provide candidates for regulation with constraints.

C. Economy

Another aspect of the desirability of any constraint measure should be its effect on the military budgets of the nations in NATO and the Warsaw Pact. At a time of significant, though quite different, difficulties that the member nations of NATO, on the one hand, and of the Pact, on the other, are likely to have in maintaining current levels of military expenditures, budgetary savings are an important potential contribution of constraints. Moreover, in contrast to the defensive-asymmetry criterion— which requires one to estimate the outcome of a hypothetical war between forces that have not faced anyone in anger for decades and that use weapons systems rarely fired outside laboratories or test ranges—the two alliances have relatively firm data on how much their weapons systems, training programs and field exercises cost.

Constraints on training and on exercises are likely to result in some direct cost savings. Fewer exercises should result in lower expenditures on exercises. A similar situation may obtain with respect to any constraints on readiness at the unit-training level.[22] Constraints on deployments of particular units or weapons systems will have a more complicated effect. Redeployments of stationed forces from their current locations to their homelands are likely to result in significant capital expenditures for new basing facilities. Whether operating expenses for forces based at home are less than those for forces based abroad depends on a number of factors—exchange rates, offset payments, host-nation support, etc.—that we do not examine here. We hazard no guess, therefore, as to whether constraints requiring homeland redeployment of forces currently stationed abroad would result in significant savings.

Depending on the particular constraints adopted, there may also be some savings resulting from decreased maintenance or procurement costs. If, for example, tracked armored vehicles were prohibited within 100 kilometers of the IGB, scout units might eventually be converted to soft-skinned, wheeled vehicles at some savings.

One should also note that the expense of verifying constraints could be significant. A wide range of activities undertaken by a vast complex of forces are candidates for constraints. In many cases, the activities regulated have relatively unobtrusive signatures, especially in the case of widely dispersed support activities like the loading of ammunition or the storage of refined-petroleum products. The procedures adopted to verify constraints may thus need to be extensive and intrusive and, therefore, expensive.

Concluding Observations

Our three criteria for evaluating constraint measures are not new. Indeed, Thomas Schelling and Morton Halperin long ago set forth three criteria for arms control measures that have both continuing relevance and some correspondence to our criteria: a reduction in the probability of war occurring, a reduction in the destructiveness of wars that do occur, and a reduction in military expenditures.[23] Our economy criterion clearly corresponds to this last criterion, and rightly so. An awareness of the budgetary benefits of arms control has been low on many lists for many years. Current possibilities for reducing or otherwise limiting conventional forces, however, as well as the economic challenges facing the two alliances, provide an excellent opportunity to reintroduce the goal of frugality.

Our asymmetry and clarity criteria when considered together come close to corresponding to Schelling and Halperin's emphasis on arms control's potential contribution to reducing the *likelihood* and *destructiveness* of war. Taken together, the asymmetry and clarity objectives, if fulfilled, tend to force a would-be attacker to choose between one of two unattractive options: adhering to constraints and launching an attack under conditions that favor the defender, or breaking the constraints and launching an attack that provides the defender with much clearer or more timely warning. The likelihood of war in a world of asymmetrical and clear constraints presumably decreases as the attacker's chances of success diminish. And if an initially constrained attacker chooses to go to war, the resulting operational disadvantages of that attacker, or better preparedness by the defender, may well reduce the destructiveness that the attack can wreak.

What is new here is the application of such criteria to the particular · area of constraint measures. For some time, constraints have occupied the uncomfortable middle ground between Stockholm-type CSBMs and large-scale force-structure limits or reductions. Policy-makers and analysts have lacked a clear understanding of both the distinctive possibilities and the particular shortcomings that constraint measures, as a class, might entail. In addition, many in the military seem more vehemently opposed to constraints on their operations than they are opposed to measures regulating force structure: we will let you take away our instruments of war, they seem to say, but do not tell us how to use the ones we have left.

Caution in proceeding with constraints is in fact warranted. They are a relatively new phenomenon in the world of conventional arms control, and an especially complex one. What sorts of weapons, deployments or activities are actually offensive? How much training is sufficient for the defender, and how does one regulate training in any case? Can measures governing the operations or deployments of thousands of personnel and weapons be verified? What operations are most clearly "provocations" in the political sense? These are all difficult questions, and they are all being explored in the context of conventional arms control almost for the first time or, at least, for the first time in a long time. Moreover, the complex force structures and other machinery of each alliance—and the even greater complexity of NATO-Warsaw Pact interactions, whether in war or in peace—often seem to be at issue in their entirety as soon as one begins to push very hard in attempting to discover the effects of any specific constraint.

Finding constraints that satisfy all three of our criteria, therefore, is not an easy task. Limits on exercises or, more clearly put, on activities conducted by units beyond a certain radius of their normal peacetime locations (e.g., the radius of their garrisons, in the extreme case) look promising. So do constraints on where, when and how often such activities can take place. Such measures could pass the economy test with ease and the clarity test eventually, as experience with the Stockholm

CSBMs suggests. Whether they can ultimately satisfy the asymmetry criterion is the key question. Highly asymmetrical constraints on Warsaw Pact exercises, other training and readiness activities, and deployments are possible, as suggested above; whether all or even some of them are negotiable is another matter. Perhaps the time will come when such problems will be easier to solve because we have expanded our thinking beyond constraint measures by themselves and begun planning how best to incorporate them in wider-ranging arms control agreements. Such agreements could conceivably address the problem of defensive asymmetry more broadly, through force-structure measures as well as constraints.

Notes

1 We examine only briefly here ways of combining constraints with force-structure measures. However, we are aware that other contributors to this volume—including Manfred Mueller in part 2 of this chapter—tend to think and write about constraints as necessary or useful complements to force reductions. One reason for the difference in approaches may be that, while others keep an eye on the political negotiating framework for constraints, we focus more exclusively on the need to establish an analytic framework for them, one that is independent of any particular negotiating forum and that differentiates constraints from force-structure measures. See p. 394.

2 We should note that "breakout" in the sense we use it here—the time that it takes a nation to return its military forces to their pre-agreement state—is slightly different from some previous uses of the word, which focus on the time that it takes a nation to gain a militarily significant advantage from violating a particular measure. These two meanings are similar, but not identical. Our definition of breakout does not depend upon when or whether a violation imparts a militarily significant benefit, only upon when the violating side restores its preexisting military posture.

3 We do not consider the Stockholm document's "constraining provisions" to be full-fledged constraints, even though they call for notification two years in advance of exercises that exceed 40,000–75,000 troops. Without such notification, an exercise at those levels is prohibited by the Stockholm document; however, the document also provides exceptions for exercises, regardless of scale, conducted as "alerts." Despite this loophole, the close relationship of Stockholm's "constraining provisions" to constraints, both terminologically and substantively, is apparent.

4 We use "IGB" here and later to denote not only the border between the Federal Republic of Germany (FRG) and the German Democratic Republic (GDR) but also the border between Czechoslovakia and the FRG.

5 The distinction between reductions, on the one hand, and declaratory measures and CSBMs, on the other, is often expressed as a difference between "structural" and "operational" arms control. The understanding behind this distinction is that reductions directly affect military force "structure"—i.e., the elements (units, equipment, personnel) that comprise it, while declaratory measures and CSBMs involve the "operations"

of military forces—i.e., what the forces can do, regardless of how they are structured. Which of these two categories encompasses constraints is not always as clear as it might be. Activity-oriented constraints (e.g., limits on exercises) seem to fall squarely into the operational camp. However, deployment-oriented constraints—especially those involving wide-ranging zones from which specified elements of force structure are prohibited—tend to cause definitional problems. It is tempting to refer to such constraints as structural arms control measures or reductions, particularly since it seems that they are likely to be negotiated only in the context of a broader, reductions-oriented arms control agreement. In Chapter 8, for example, Edward Warner and David Ochmanek consider the removal of forces beyond the Atlantic or the Urals to be reductions.

6 Richard Kugler's contribution in Chapter 2 provides additional data on the forces and the force ratios involved in the attack options we discuss here. For three combat scenarios that appear to correspond to the first three attack options we discuss here, see also the contribution of Alexei Arbatov, Nikolai Kishilov and Oleg Amirov in that chapter.

7 We should note that, from the perspective of a conservative WTO military planner, the maximum possible warning time is always relevant. Even if NATO might not immediately detect a violation or respond to that violation, NATO *might* detect a violation and *might* immediately respond; hence, the conservative planner will treat such a possibility seriously to ensure that his plans are robust across a *variety* of hypotheses concerning the adversary's behavior.

8 Such a reinforced attack could also be accompanied by very short warning if the USSR were confident that it could conceal or delay preparations required to ready and position its rear-area units for reinforcement.

9 In light of the disparities in effective force ratios likely to exist if only one side has brought to full readiness its third or fourth strategic echelon, the role of constraints would serve roughly the same function as someone yelling "Look out!" to a person standing on the beach as a 50-foot tidal wave begins to break.

10 In the other half of this chapter, Manfred Mueller proposes limitations on peacetime force mobilization. Such mobilization may be necessary to conduct third- and fourth-strategic-echelon attacks. Whether limits on peacetime mobilization represent constraints or force-structure measures is not entirely clear (see fn. 5 above). Terminology aside, it may be desirable to introduce measures that restrict mobilization, especially if the two sides fail to reduce and limit their force levels substantially.

11 In *Toward a Conceptual Framework for Operational Arms Control in Europe's Central Region* (Santa Monica, CA: The RAND Corporation, R-3704-USDP, 1989), Paul K. Davis analyzes NATO's objectives and concludes that enabling the defender to defend successfully is or should be the primary Western goal. Eastern contributors to this volume, including our counterpart, Manfred Mueller, appear to agree on the need to accord primacy to measures that disproportionately favor the defender.

12 We are well aware that some future set of weapons systems might be readily distinguishable as more useful to the defender than to the attacker, or at least be an integral part of defense rather than of offense. Arms control agreements could even help bring clearly distinguishable defensive doctrines and weapons systems into existence. Such weapons are not on the drawing board, however, and such doctrines only exist in the pages of scholarly journals—not in the minds of most military officers.

Constraints that encourage the development of such systems are to be welcomed, but constraints negotiated in the next decade will at the very least need to account for the current configuration of forces and weapons systems.

13 Again, we are aware that such a revolution has been proposed under the rubric of "defensive defense." A revolution along these lines would require the destruction of vast numbers of current weapons systems, however, and probably also the reeducation of thousands of military minds. We focus in this piece on more immediately attainable possibilities.

14 On pp. 414–15, Manfred Mueller calls for the reduction of "offensive-strike" weapons systems and units, as well as for limitations on combat modernization or "the qualitative arms race." Many in the West, however, would either disagree with him strongly or couch similar proposals in more qualified terms. Such differing perspectives may result from the difficulties involved in determining whether a weapons system is disproportionately "offensive."

15 This is presumably the best that a defender could hope to do, *unless* the attacker were clumsy enough to reveal his intentions prematurely and the defender were confident enough to race preemptively to the border.

16 For an example of such an argument, see Richard Kugler's contribution in Chapter 2.

17 Such an agreement would need to allow for routine rotation of troops and for their movement to training areas.

18 In the other half of this chapter, Manfred Mueller addresses the problem by proposing that zones of military disengagement be supplemented by dissolution of indigenous units deemed particularly capable of attack (clearly a force-structure measure), as well as by withdrawal of foreign forces from such zones to their national territories (which we consider a constraint but others would call a reduction in force structure—see fn. 5 above).

19 Here as elsewhere in discussing potential constraint measures, we assume that they can be effectively verified. We discuss verification requirements below under the criterion of clarity.

20 One must qualify this statement with the acknowledgement that the attacker can choose not only the time and place of attack but also his attacking forces and, to some extent, the defending forces. The Pact could therefore attack with its most ready or best-trained forces against NATO forces that were trained poorly (or, if NATO distributed its training equally, trained exactly to the uniformly average level).

21 For an extended discussion of training and readiness issues in this context, see Davis, *Towards a Conceptual Framework for Operational Arms Control in Europe's Central Region.*

22 However, if expensive advanced computer simulators are employed extensively as substitutes for constrained activities, then the resulting situation could result in higher rather than lower training costs. Similarly, if a separation of weapons from their ammunition leads to more expenditures on ammunition transports, or a prohibition on bridging equipment leads to greater submersibility for new tanks, the costs of fielding a constrained force could be more, not less, than that of an unconstrained force.

The United States' POMCUS (Pre-positioned Overseas Material Configured in Unit Sets) units represent an extreme example of the potential costs of separating unit components: the personnel component of POMCUS units are so far from their equipment that *two* sets of equipment are needed, one for training in the United States and one for storage overseas for use in combat. Obviously there are factors other than cost at work in calculating the overall cost-effectiveness of POMCUS units.

23 Thomas C. Shelling and Morton H. Halperin, *Strategy and Arms Control* (New York: Twentieth Century Fund, 1961), p. 2. With the second criterion, Schelling and Halperin were interested in using arms control to limit intra-war escalation. We have no such hopes for constraints, but, as discussed below, we believe that constraints that fulfill our criteria can make a contribution to the more general principle of limiting destruction if a war starts.

IX
PART TWO

Constraints

Manfred Mueller, German Democratic Republic

In the special terminology which has developed in the field of arms control and security negotiations, constraints are understood as various measures directed at limiting the operational capability of military forces, as well as limiting the forces themselves. Such limitations can and should help to restrict the ability to carry out offensive actions, especially large-scale and/or surprise attack. Constraints should be introduced on a strictly balanced basis between the member-states of the Warsaw Treaty Organization (WTO) and NATO or between parts of the territory of the two alliances.

In terms of political-military measures likely to consolidate European security, constraints constitute a kind of link between confidence-building measures, on the one hand, and arms limitation agreements, on the other. Thus constraints can be a subject of negotiations in both areas. Only in recent years have constraints achieved a specific rank in international discussions corresponding to their potential role in the process of strengthening European security.

1. The European Situation and the Role of Constraints

The security situation in Europe, especially in Central Europe, is characterized by a fundamental contradiction. An analysis of the present social, industrial and ecological situation in Europe—particularly in Central Europe—shows that any war or military conflict in this region would be senseless and could not achieve rational aims. Military conflict in an area with hundreds of nuclear facilities, chemical plants and high-density modern cities would destroy what is intended to be conquered and at the same time put the existence of the aggressor at risk. The unavoidable breakdown of electric power systems alone would interrupt industry, water-supply, traffic and so on, with devastating and far-reaching consequences for societies and people, especially in urban areas. The unforeseeable effects of a large-scale attack on both the territory under seige and the attackers themselves leads one to the conclusion that the modern industrialized countries of Europe could not survive either a nuclear or a conventional war, regardless of which role—aggressor or defender—a state were to play. Thus, preventing any military conflict has become the *sine qua non* for the existence and development of the states of this region. This is particularly true for the two German states situated in the heart of Europe and sharing the longest border between any two states of the alliances. The principle agreed between their governments that never again should war be unleashed from German soil[2] is directed primarily at the policies of these two states themselves, but also at all other states with forces stationed on German territory. In recognition of this situation in Central Europe, in 1983 the GDR decided not to respond with a "political ice age" to the stationing of new U.S. missiles in Western Europe but rather with the more active pursuit of detente. This has been the driving force behind all subsequent GDR initiatives.

Central Europe has the world's highest concentration of nuclear and conventional forces structured for large-scale military operations. These forces do not have a rational role either in offensive or defensive terms. For this reason the WTO has changed its military doctrine and operational principles and has now started to reduce and restructure its armed forces through unilateral actions.

NATO, however, has reacted differently. During the last year, it has repeated its argument that deterrence with nuclear and conventional forces is the only rational policy, even if existing military asymmetries can be eliminated in negotiations.[3] At the same time, NATO seeks to further develop and modernize its nuclear and conventional systems. But even if European peace required deterrence, it could be achieved with only a fraction of the forces both sides currently possess.

There is also another problem. If we take into account the inadmiss-ability of war in Central Europe, the question arises as to what kind of military action can be regarded as possible and useful. To conquer a country is impossible. A surprise attack to seize limited territory may be conceivable, but there is no assurance that such an action would remain limited. A situation in which one side seeks to strike successfully against certain points on the other side, but the other side has neither the weapons nor the power to respond in kind, can lead to a new and dangerous threat. Therefore it is necessary not only to change and reduce existing force structures but also to limit, even prevent, the emergence of new weapons and new threats tailored to the European situation.

Thus the situation in Central Europe calls for a thorough and far-reaching reevaluation of the role of the military factor in European security. The reduction of both nuclear and conventional forces is possible and ought to be planned and executed in a sophisticated way. Obviously, difficulties in achieving negotiation results increase with the intricacy of the subject. Progress may be possible, but only if negotiations proceed step by step.

Given the complicated military-strategic situation on the continent today, and the fact that deep reductions are achievable only in a negotiation process, the role of military constraints in Europe is growing. If one or several elements of the European military confrontation are reduced, then constraints can help maintain a stable balance. They could be used previous to or as initial reduction steps and should accompany the entire reduction process in order to guarantee equal security for all participants during the transition period.

2. Categories of Constraints

Taking into account existing practice and proposals, it seems possible to categorize constraints in three ways. The first category is the *subject of limitations*, which includes:

–limitations on military movements, including maneuvers;
–limitations on concentrations;
–limitations on deployments;
–limitations on mobilization;
–limitations on military training;
–limitations on military equipment and modernization of weapons systems; and
–limitations on military depots and on specific logistic systems.

The second category is the *territorial dimension*. In this respect, the following possibilities have to be taken into account:

–global measures, especially those relevant to Europe;

–all-European measures, and agreements between the two alliances that refer to Europe from the Atlantic to the Urals;

–regional constraints related to parts of Europe, especially Central Europe, the Balkans and northern Europe; and

–subregional measures in limited areas on both sides of the border between the two military alliances.

The third category for constraints would be whether they are *unilateral or agreed upon*.

Unilateral measures have a long history in postwar Europe. For instance, the decision of a group of European states to be nonaligned or neutral has to be viewed as a decisive unilateral constraint. Some European states have formulated—sometimes even within their constitutions—limitations on or renunciations of particular weapons (e.g., nuclear and chemical) and limitations on their armed forces.[4] Unilateral constraints can play an even greater role in the future. For example, they could signal specific military behavior or intentions to neighboring states or the opposing alliance. That one-sided measures usually are not verified and can be terminated unilaterally of course must be taken into account but should not lead one to dismiss them out of hand.

Agreed and verified measures can play a significant role in strengthening European security, and therefore should constitute the standard form of constraints. In principle, such measures have to be constructed on a symmetrical and equal basis. But in some specific cases asymmetrical constraints also should be taken into consideration. In practice, constraints have to combine elements of all three categories.

Although the obstacles to real progress in security and disarmament in Europe seem immense, the prospects for progress are growing. But since success can only be achieved through a very complicated and long-term process, limited steps and measures—including military constraints—will play a great role. Constraints are restricted in scope, effect and security-building value. They are certainly not disarmament measures and they should not be seen as a substitute for disarmament. As isolated and self-contained measures, constraints are of only limited value, but if included in an arms reduction process their significance increases.

Although there are many types of constraints currently under discussion and other variants may come up in the future, this essay will concentrate on constraints important in the all-European context and the Central European region.

3. Limitations on Military Operational Movements

The Geographical Factor

In discussing the military situation of the two alliances, geography, it is often said, favors the WTO while placing NATO at a disadvantage. Thus the geographical factor prompts NATO to take certain compensatory measures, or at least to leave its options open.[5] In this view, limitations on movements and exercises are a real obstacle to training which involves the transfer of units from across the Atlantic and their cooperation with local troops.

But this is a very one-sided view of the geographical situation. It is true that the territory of the WTO in Europe is larger than that of NATO. Thus, stand-off operations can be carried out by WTO armed forces more easily than by NATO, which has only limited room for maneuver in Western Europe. But this situation does not produce a unilateral advantage for the Warsaw Treaty. Whereas the Warsaw Treaty has the advantage of the front line, NATO has the advantage of envelopment. By dint of its superior air and naval forces, NATO can carry out operations on all flanks of Warsaw Treaty territory.[6] From the perspective of military potential, control of the flanks is at least as important as control of the front line. Attention must also be paid to the fact that the territory of the WTO's major military power, the USSR, can be reached by both strategic and tactical nuclear weapons and even by conventional weapons, whereas the United States can be hit only by Soviet strategic weapons.

Moreover, one has to take a somewhat closer look at the lines of communication of the two military coalitions. Regarding the WTO, there are only four direct railroad lines between the USSR and Central Europe. All of them require a time-consuming change of rail gauge. They also cross a great number of bridges and other vulnerable points and their capacity is limited. Furthermore, there are no direct highways crossing Eastern Europe. For these reasons the GDR and the USSR have recently extended a system of ferries crossing the Baltic Sea in order to facilitate accelerated transport and trade. Modern sea transport systems across the Atlantic are likewise very fast and reliable and are difficult to disrupt by military means. Besides, the United States has considerable arms depots in Western Europe which allow it to bring up large numbers of troops by air.

These and other factors have to be taken into consideration when reevaluating geographical asymmetries in Europe in order to assess limitations of both sides' military forces and movements.[7]

Limitation of Maneuvers

Mutual monitoring of military activities by each side has been developed in Europe to such an extent that it is now possible to identify large, unannounced concentrations of troops and take appropriate counter-measures. But even prenotified and observed large-scale maneuvers (or series of maneuvers) could be used as a starting point for offensive actions or military threats. In September 1988, NATO's Reforger maneuvers involved more than 300,000 troops with modern combat equipment and exercises that advanced up to the GDR's frontier. Comprehensive logistical preparations were made for these maneuvers and accompanying meas-ures, including redeployment across the Atlantic. Such activities involve a high measure of concealment and consequently give rise to concern and distrust. The problem cannot be solved by long-term advance notification and observation of such maneuvers alone. One of the most urgently needed constraints is therefore a limitation on all maneuver activities.[8] In this regard, the following limitations could be considered:

–the limitation of troops and heavy equipment involved in a maneuver;
–limitations on the annual number of maneuvers; and
–prohibition of conducting several maneuvers at the same time or at short intervals.

On July 7, 1988, the GDR's Socialist Unity Party (SED) and the FRG's Social Democratic Party (SPD) put forward an initiative on the establish-ment of a zone of confidence and security in Central Europe. The initiative proposed an extension of the advance-notification period for maneuvers and a limitation on their scope. Maneuvers subject to notification should be banned from an area 50 kilometers wide along the line of contact between the WTO and NATO states.[9] This would further diminish the danger of surprise attack.

Further discussion seems necessary to influence the orientation of maneuvers. Maneuvers should correspond with the defense-oriented operational principles declared by both alliances. Observation of maneuvers and cooperative structures for their common evaluation may be a way to achieve this objective.

Limitations of Concentrations

Measures to limit the ability to concentrate troops or increase the time necessary for such concentration are of great importance to prevent surprise and large-scale attacks. The capability for rapid concentration grows as the mobility and number of the troops stationed in a limited area increases. Measures aimed against such concentrations must therefore seek to limit mobility and thin out peacetime deployments. Given the existing situation, both approaches are likely to be difficult. It might be useful, therefore, to develop a process that starts with simple measures that will gradually lead to a new security system. Specific measures for Central Europe and a zone of direct contact could certainly help (they are discussed further below). Steps to increase warning time through specific verification arrangements, especially for the Central European region, would also be useful. Such measures could include a division of the territories of both sides into different zones from east to west and also from north to south. Such a grid would establish a pattern of zones with each zone having four borders. Movements from one zone to another could be limited through verification, which would increase warning time and reduce the incentive for breakout. A general process of change in the deployment of troops could be aimed at achieving military structures which make concentrations for attack impossible.

Limitations on Mobilization

The potential and capability for mobilizing military reserves is still an element of military strength, albeit one of decreasing importance. Modern nuclear weapons, as well as conventional military means, have completely changed the picture of war. Mobilization measures could hardly be implemented in the area directly affected after conflict broke out. Consequently, provisions would have to be made mainly for areas that might not be turned into combat areas forthwith, and especially for mobilization measures prior to the outbreak of a conflict.

Yet peacetime mobilization cannot be considered from a purely theoretical and military point of view. *First*, such measures do not go unnoticed and would provoke quick political and military reactions from the other side. This is especially true when seen in connection with working agreements on extended confidence-building, verification of and reductions in conventional forces. *Second*, peacetime mobilization gives rise to questions about the purpose of arms control measures, since they indicate serious military intentions and most likely presage a violation of agreements. *Third*, present comprehensive mobilizations, though designed to be, at worst, merely threats, inflict considerable, and probably unbearable, damage on the state(s) resorting to these means. A general mobilization would bring to a standstill, *inter alia*, the main industry, traffic, food distribution and health services in the country mobilizing. Research shows that implementing large military operations following a period of mobilization seem rather questionable in Central Europe.

Nevertheless, limitations on the capability for mobilization should be a main element in the European arms limitation process. Should the alliances succeed in reaching agreements on substantial reductions of troops and armaments in Europe, limitations on mobilization would become an essential element in the maintenance of the agreement. It must be kept in mind, however, that reducing active forces tends to lead to a reduction in trained reservists. Since various demands on operating modern combat technology grow simultaneously, the size and value of mobilized forces become questionable. However, in order to ensure the observance of fixed ceilings by all parties involved, further considerations are required concerning the limitation of mobilization capacities. Such considerations could, in principle, begin with the following points:

–*First*, a system could be established that was safeguarded by continuous verification at sensitive points of mobilization. In this case, a complete ban rather than partial steps would surely be easier to verify. This approach, however, requires high expenditures, and a violation could not be completely ruled out, particularly by the larger countries.

–*Second*, limitations or a ban on the mobilization of reserves could also be achieved through stipulations concerning equipment. Where the amount of equipment and arms stored in depots is insufficient, mobilization is useless. Furthermore, once mobilization has begun, it is impossible to produce modern weapons in quantities necessary for comprehensive mobilization. Thus stipulations regarding limitations on stockpiles and their verification could be an effective means of restricting the potential for mobilization.[10] Large quantities of modern weapons are difficult to hide. If the commitment to general limitation of major weapons systems includes those stockpiled in designated depots, it is possible to limit the capacity for mobilization as well as to exercise relatively reliable verification. Expenditures on this would not be excessive. It would probably also be possible to establish a system for limiting mobilization that includes both troops and major weapons systems.

Although there are as yet no negotiations dealing with the problem of limiting mobilization, solutions should be sought within the context of agreements on reductions of troops and armaments.

4. Limitations of Major Weapons Systems

Since ideas about limitations on major weapons systems are dealt with in detail in Chapter 6, only certain aspects of the problem will be discussed here. In principle, one can hardly imagine troops being separated from the weapons for which they have been trained, or vice versa. In practice, a combination of measures have to be undertaken; that is clear in the wake of Mikhail Gorbachev's December 1988 reduction announcement.[11] On the one hand, whole units, especially those of an offensive nature, will be withdrawn from Central Europe and dissolved together with their weapons. On the other hand, specific weapons (tanks and artillery) will be taken out of units which will remain in existence. This will change the character and mission of these troops. It seems that this represents a realistic way to decrease and transform military forces into reasonable defensive structures.

Which Weapons Systems Should Be Reduced?

To answer this question one has to agree upon which weapons systems are seen as threatening by the two sides. Both NATO and the WTO declare that they do not intend to attack the other side. Nor does either side impute to the other the intention of direct attack.[12] But there are different assessments of the opponent's capability for attack. Whereas the Warsaw Treaty points to the existence of offensive elements on both sides that have to be eliminated, NATO perceives such capacities exclusively on the side of its counterpart and denies its own capabilities for attack.[13] For this reason NATO demands that the WTO take measures to eliminate asymmetries in tanks, armored vehicles and artillery without taking into account existing qualitative differences in these systems. At the same time, NATO resists including the modern elements of offensive-strike systems in the process of strengthening stability. These elements include, *inter alia*, modern fighter-bombers, combat helicopters, airborne and seaborne troops and tactical missiles. But, as stated above, these are the military forces which are specifically tailored to the present situation in Central Europe. They are able to attack, destroy and even occupy the other side's lifelines and territories. Under these circumstances, one could hope to gain territory worth conquering. But advancing large numbers of tanks and engaging thousands of artillery systems in the face of retaliatory measures by the other side would only result in the total destruction of both sides. Thus, besides eliminating asymmetries and generally lowering the level of armed forces, both the old and the modern offensive-strike systems must be subject to limitations.

The special characteristics of these units are their modern means of attack, their offense-oriented training and their capability for rapid concentration and deep and surprise strikes. In contrast, maintaining a specified number of tanks or artillery as part of or in connection with infantry units can hardly be regarded as a threat. If fixed quantities of such units exist on both sides in specified areas, a surprise offensive of any size is rather unlikely.

Limiting Modern Strike Aircraft

There is an ongoing discussion in both East and West of the offensive role of strike aircraft and possibilities for verifying their limitation.[14] Aircraft designed for ground missions are a decisive element in an offensive capability,[15] and thus reduction of offensive capabilities requires the reduction of strike aircraft as an essential item in eliminating asymmetries and in all phases of a reduction process. Since most military aircraft have multiple roles, differentiation and verification should cover not only the type of aircraft but also secondary elements such as installations for carrying both weapons and ground-tracking search sensors. One very effective measure would be the verification of airports. Strike aircraft have a limited range. They need airfields and depots stocked with the specific weapons they carry. Limitations on the depots for such weapons would limit the capacity of strike aircraft and also their rapid redeployment from far away to the front line. A combination of all these measures makes it possible to control with a relatively high degree of certainty limitations on strike aircraft and other modern offensive means.

Limitations on Modernization

The modernization of conventional and nuclear weapons is one of the main problems in preserving military stability in Europe. The experience of past decades has shown that modernization can wreck agreements on limitations and reductions of weapons. At the time SALT I was negotiated, one side was capable of equipping its missiles with multiple independently targeted reentry vehicles (MIRVs) and resisted including them in the limitations. The desired advantage was soon reversed, however, when the other side also attained this capability more quickly than expected and was able to equip its heavier missiles with even more warheads. Today the inventors of MIRVs argue that it would be better to return to missiles carrying only one warhead.

If the problem of modernization cannot be solved, the following is a likely scenario: as part of conventional arms reductions in Europe, the heavy tank will be defined and its number limited on both sides. But probably at some future point a combat machine not included in the definition will be developed and, consequently, will not be covered by the limitations, although it may possess the same or even better combat capabilities. Perhaps this example is not quite to the point. But it cannot be ruled out, and it can be reinforced by many other examples. Under such conditions there is hardly a chance for lasting stability, confidence and security to flourish.

It has been declared that technological progress cannot be stopped and, therefore, its military uses cannot be prevented. The first statement is correct, the second is not. What is decisive is the political viewpoint from which states approach these problems. As long as the two alliances consider each other enemies and military rivals this problem can hardly be resolved. But if a process is started which gradually eliminates military as well as non-military forms of confrontation and brings about increasing cooperation in important spheres between states with different social systems, it can also include agreements on the limitation of the qualitative arms race.

Unlike other constraints—the content of which is already under discussion—limitations on the qualitative arms race in Europe should first of all be dealt with through deliberating certain mechanisms. In view of the diversity and pace of the qualitative arms race, there can hardly be any efficient prophylactic ban. Probably the establishment of a consultative system similar to the one existing between the USSR and the United States regarding the ABM Treaty would be more promising. Provided that, as a result of agreements, there were stipulations on major weapons systems in Europe, a consultative system could be established to discuss new developments. Since weapons systems might emerge in many forms, it would be advisable to establish a permanent center involving experts from all participating countries. This center could function as follows:

–*First*, all states concerned would undertake to present to the center new weapons systems which, according to their effects, are banned or limited prior to their introduction in Europe. In this way it would be possible to discover whether the new systems would be subject to limitations or whether a ban or a new limitation would be required to maintain the agreed situation.

–*Second*, each participant would be entitled to express to the center its concerns about new weapons systems in other states and to request the possessor to answer its questions and to demonstrate the new weapon.

–*Third*, the center's experts could carry out analyses and give recommendations to the member-states.

Such a consultative mechanism would not, of course, offer an absolutely foolproof barrier against the continued qualitative arms race in Europe. Nevertheless this mechanism could reduce incentives for modernization and strengthen the cooperative elements of European security and mutual trust.

5. Zonal Limitations in Central Europe

In Central Europe great parts of NATO and WTO military forces face each other along the border between the GDR and Czechoslovakia, on one side, and the FRG, on the other—a stretch of some 1,000 kilometers. This is the longest continuous border between states of the two alliances. Furthermore, a number of sensitive political problems exist in this area with a certain crisis potential. Thus it is understandable that steps are being considered to prevent conflicts which would threaten the existence of the states in this area. Limitations on military forces are of heightened importance in this region.

A set of proposals on this theme made by individual socialist countries have found support at the last two sessions of the WTO Political Consultative Committee held in Berlin in 1987 and in Warsaw in 1988.[16] Taken together, they propose a new security situation in Central Europe. While the Polish Jaruzelski Plan[17] covers a wider Central European area, the proposals of the GDR and Czechoslovakia concentrate mainly on the zone of direct contact between the two alliances. These proposals therefore complement one another.

The basic idea of these proposals is to reduce the armed forces of both sides to agreed equal levels, to limit their offensive capability through restructuring and to install a specific regime of verification and confidence-building. The reduction and limitation of conventional forces is combined with measures in the nuclear and chemical fields.

Nuclear- and Chemical-Weapons-Free Zones

The proposal for the establishment of a 150-kilometer nuclear-weapons-free corridor on each side of the border in Central Europe made by the GDR's SED and the FRG's SPD includes the possibility of extension to a Central European nuclear-weapons-free zone. By demanding the withdrawal of all dual-capable systems (nuclear and conventional), it offers an important starting point for conventional limitations.[18]

The idea of establishing a chemical-weapons-free zone in Central Europe is also regaining credibility.[19] The slow progress of and renewed delays in the Geneva negotiations for a global ban on chemical weapons have increased interest in such a zone. The detailed verification and monitoring mechanisms proposed for the zone would strengthen mutual trust. At the same time, the zone could serve as a testing ground for the measures of verification associated with a global ban.

The main aim of nuclear- and chemical-weapons-free zones in Central Europe is to prevent a process of escalation. This is a limited but decisive goal. The zones are ascribed unattainable aims, and then such objectives are declared impossible or even dangerous. This is especially true of the assertion that nuclear-weapons-free zones in Europe aim at the denuclearization of the continent, which is declared impossible because of the necessity of continued nuclear deterrence.[20] But a realistic assessment shows that limited areas free of nuclear weapons do not signify a general denuclearization. If the corridor were to come into existence, U.S. nuclear weapons would be stationed deeper in Europe and even in Central

Europe. The small corridor, it is said, would create regions of diminished security, and would be meaningless since nuclear weapons can be launched into it.[21] These arguments offset each other. If, under certain circumstances, nuclear weapons can be fired into the nuclear-weapons-free corridor, how is nuclear deterrence diminished? If one speaks of diminished security, one must, first of all, think of the present situation in Central Europe where forward-based nuclear and chemical weapons are dangerous and entail a high risk of escalation. Moreover, their existence is inconsistent with the official NATO theory of intra-war deterrence, which is based on the possibility of ending a conflict immediately after it has broken out.[22]

It seems that the resistance to such zones is not based on rational security thinking, but mainly on distrust and the fear that behind these proposals may be far-reaching anti-American intentions. But this is not the case, and such distrust limits the process of strengthening European security.

Conventional Disengagement in Central Europe

Besides ideas concerning the establishment of zones in Central Europe free from chemical and nuclear weapons, recent proposals for areas of military disengagement have once again become topical. These ideas were considered important as early as the 1950s, when initiatives came mainly from Poland and the UK and were taken up by other countries. Today, such concepts are being developed by various European countries, primarily in Central Europe. Both the Warsaw Treaty and NATO have included in their arms reduction approaches special measures for Central Europe, but the specific proposals differ greatly. The main questions to be resolved are: (1) which region should be subject to special measures; (2) what kind of measures should be proposed; and (3) should such special measures for Central Europe be part of all-European agreements, or is it possible to undertake them (or part of them) before an agreement on all-European measures is reached.

Regarding the territory subject to special Central European regulations, the Warsaw Treaty member-states maintain the following position: Central Europe is seen as a zone, similar to that defined in the MBFR talks, but with the possibility of certain extensions.[23] At the same time, within the Central European region, a special zone of direct contact of the two alliances (with specific limitations) should be agreed upon. In principle, the depth of this zone should be equal on both sides.[24] For the nuclear-weapons-free corridor a depth of 150 kilometers on each side is proposed. This also could be a starting point for a discussion on zones for conventional limitations. But the concrete depth depends on the measures, and smaller territories also have to be taken into account.

Measures worth considering for the Central European region could include the withdrawal or dissolution of units deemed particularly capable of attack. Common ceilings could be fixed for the number of troops. Their structures could be changed so that after several stages the following principles would regulate the situation: the nearer to the border of the other side, the less mobile, less armored, less grouped and trained for offensive actions existing forces should be. Instead they should be structured and trained for holding territory, with high firepower for limited distances. Means of tactical counteroffensive should then be stationed further back in similar agreed upon distances. Because a general reduction of troops is proposed, such measures would not result in a new massing of forces behind the limitation zone. At the same time, Central Europe should be subject to a special regime of control and monitoring. This should include the installation of cooperative mechanisms; the establishment of hotlines between the states in the region; national and international centers jointly assessing the verification results; and discussion of potential developments and events which could lead to crisis situations.

While the need for a special regime for *Central Europe* per se is increasingly recognized in NATO, the measures proposed are rather limited. Central Europe is often defined as a larger territory (even from the Atlantic to the Urals). Some analysts propose special zones of direct contact, but often with asymmetrical areas and limited constraints. At the same time, however, there is growing interest among the publics of the West European countries in measures that lower the threat of military confrontation in the region. Far-reaching but unofficial concepts have been worked out.[25] Such expressions of growing public involvement will undoubtedly influence future developments in Central Europe.

Whether Central European constraints have to wait for all-European solutions is open to question. The more flexible both sides can be, the better. A general shift in the Central European situation toward structural defensiveness is only possible within the framework of all-European agreements. Despite the extremely complicated problems to be solved in the Atlantic-to-the-Urals negotiations, it should be possible to agree upon certain constraint measures in Central Europe as a starting point. These constraints could provide experience for future broader measures and strengthen confidence and security in this sensitive part of the continent.

Notes

1 The consequences of any war in Europe, especially in Central Europe, have become the subject of intensive research only recently. An in-depth study on this subject was presented to the First Congress of GDR Scientists for Peace in November 1988. Findings will soon being published. See also: Hylke Tromp, ed., *Non-nuclear War in Europe* (Groningen: 1986); and Manfred Mueller and Hermann Scheer, "Ist atomare Abschreckung zeitgemaess?" *Horizont* (1988), pp. 10–11.

2 *Neues Deutschland*, March 13, 1985.

3 This position was stated by the NATO summit of March 1988, in *Bulletin des Presse- und Informationsamtes der Bundesregierung* 34 (1988), p. 287.

4 This was a consequence of obligations under the postwar treaties, but also follows from the membership of European states in international arms limitation treaties such as the NPT and the chemical weapons convention.

5 See fn. 3.

6 The offensive strategy of the U.S. Navy against the WTO's flanks is analyzed in "Nordatlantische Versammlung, Militaerausschuss, Entwurf eines Gesamtberichtes ueber die Sicherheit des Buendnisses," Document AF 216, MC(88) 6, pp. 40–55.

7 The role of the geographical factor was also discussed in Andre Brie, Andrzej Karkoszka, Manfred Mueller and Helga Schirmeister, *Conventional Disarmament in Europe*, UN Publication UNIDIR/88/15, pp. 17–20.

8 Concrete proposals for the limitation of maneuvers are part of the comprehensive paper of the members of the Warsaw Treaty on confidence- and security-building measures of October 28, 1988. *Neues Deutschland*, October 29–30, 1988.

9 "Vorschlag fuer eine Zone des Vertrauens und der Sicherheit in Zentraleuropa," *Neues Deutschland*, July 8, 1988.

10 Some concepts for reductions of weapons in Europe prefer not to destroy the weapons but put them in depots under control (see Jonathan Dean's essay in this book). But the rationale for maintaining such great depots seems questionable. It is expensive, and leads to a greater breakout possibility. Depots should, therefore, also be limited to a reasonable degree.

11 Speech of Mikhail Gorbachev at the United Nations, *Neues Deutschland*, December 8, 1988.

12 These different positions were expressed at the last summit meetings of the two alliances. See *Session of the Political Consultative Committee of the Warsaw Treaty States, Berlin, 28–29 May 1987* (Dresden: 1987); and fn. 3.

13 Operational plans of the U.S. and NATO, such as AirLand Battle and FOFA, are not only the basis for demands for weapons systems with an offensive character, but they also include training and principles for their use.

14 Problems of strike aircraft or ground-attack aircraft are discussed in some of the previous chapters of this book.

15 The military literature of East and West, in analyzing modern experiences and the

European situation, comes to the conclusion that strike aircraft are decisive for air superiority. Only with air superiority can offensive actions be executed. This fact, however, makes forward-based airfields an early or even preemptive target of a conflict. The massive stationing of strike aircraft on forward-based airfields has to be seen as a signal for an attack. For discussion of the problem see Horst Afheldt, *Defensive Verteidigung* (Hamburg: Rowohlt, 1983).

16 See *Berlin and Warsaw Meeting of the Political Consultative Committee of Member States of the Warsaw Treaty*. See fn. 2 and *Neues Deutschland*, July 18, 1988.

17 *Memorandum of the Government of the Polish People's Republic on Decreasing Armaments and Increasing Confidence in Central Europe* (Warsaw: 1987). See also Daniel Rotfeld's contribution in this book.

18 Text of the initiative in Carl Lanius and Manfred Uschner, *Weg mit dem Teufelszeug* (Berlin: Dietz-Verlag, 1988), pp. 235–241.

19 Text of the initiative, in Karlheinz Lohs and Manfred Uschner, *Fuer ein chemiewaffenfreies Europa* (Berlin: Dietz-Verlag, 1986), pp. 171–178.

20 Such arguments were often used in Western publications. See, *inter alia*, Karl Lamers, "Konventionelle Abruestung in Europa," *Aus Politik und Zeitgeschichte. Beilage zu Das Parlament* B 18/88, pp.18–19.

21 These arguments were used by the government of the FRG. See, "Antwort der Bundesregierung auf den Vorschlag der DDR zur Errichtung eines kernwaffenfreien Korridors," *Bulletin des Presse- und Informationsamtes der Bundesregierung* 21 (1983), p. 191.

22 An explanation of this element of NATO strategy is given by Robert Osgood and Henning Wegener, *Study on Deterrence*, UN Publication A/41/432, pp. 39–41.

23 The Jaruzelski Plan includes Hungary and Denmark.

24 Jonathan Dean proposes a zone of 50 km in the West and 100–150 km in the East. In light of the discussion in this chapter of the geographical factor, such a proposal cannot be seen as a realistic basis for agreement. (Jonathan Dean, "The NATO-Warsaw Pact Confrontation in the Twenty-first Century," paper for the American Committee for U.S.-Soviet Relations, pp. 13–15. Most of the other elements of this paper are very useful for further discussion of an improved security situation in Central Europe.)

25 Projects for alternative defense structures have been worked out primarily within the FRG during the last ten years. They now govern the official security policy of the Social democrats in the FRG and they influence the security thinking of most of the members of the Socialist International. In recent years, non-offensive defense thinking and the search for alternatives to nuclear deterrence strategy have spread in all member countries of NATO. See also, Bjoern Moeller, ed., "NOD: Non-Offensive Defence," Bibliography, *International Research Newsletter*, Center of Peace and Conflict Research, University of Copenhagen.

PART ONE

Nuclear Weapons and Conventional Arms Control

Arnold Kanter,* United States

Introduction

The INF Treaty will eliminate an entire class of nuclear weapons that have figured prominently in assessments of European security. General Secretary Gorbachev's December 7, 1988, announcement of unilateral reductions in Soviet conventional capabilities and the opening of the talks on Conventional Forces in Europe (CFE) between the two alliances hold the promise of stabilizing the conventional balance in Europe at lower levels. The Strategic Arms Reductions Talks (START) between the two superpowers likewise hold the promise of stabilizing the strategic nuclear balance at lower levels. In brief, the landscape of European security is undergoing change and, while analysts differ about the odds and the timetable, there is at least some prospect of it being fundamentally transformed.

These developments provide the backdrop against which the debate about the future of the remaining nuclear weapons in Europe is being played out. This debate is framed by the recently reiterated official NATO view that "nuclear weapons will continue to make an essential contribution to NATO's strategy of deterrence for the foreseeable future" and its determination to keep them "up-to-date where necessary,"[1] on the one hand, and by General Secretary Gorbachev's recently reiterated call "to work toward the complete elimination of tactical nuclear weapons on the continent,"[2] on the other. Thus the debate raises three questions.

* The views expressed in this essay are solely those of the author, and do not necessarily represent those of the U.S. Government or any of its agencies, the RAND Corporation or any of its research sponsors.

First, what is the role of, and requirement for, nuclear weapons in NATO's strategy of deterrence? Second, what conditions would or should lead to their reduction and, perhaps, their complete elimination? In particular, how would a negotiated agreement to redress the present imbalance in conventional forces that exists between NATO and the Warsaw Treaty Organization (WTO) affect NATO's perceived requirements for continued dependence on nuclear weapons? Third, during the time when a perceived NATO requirement for nuclear weapons remains, under what conditions will it be necessary to modernize these weapons, and under what conditions can modernization be forgone? This chapter explores these three questions in an effort to shed light on the relationship between the conventional balance and theater nuclear weapons, and on the implications of conventional arms control for NATO's strategy of flexible response.

The Debate about Nuclear Weapons in Europe

The nominal premises underpinning the respective sides of the debate might be summarized as follows. As suggested by Alexei Vasiliev's analysis in his companion piece, those who would like to see theater nuclear weapons reduced or eliminated probably would argue that they are no better—and more likely worse—than a necessary evil. This view holds that theater nuclear weapons are inherently destabilizing, and that their elimination would reduce the risks of war—or at least of nuclear escalation—in Europe as well as facilitate improved East-West relations that would, in turn, lead to enhanced mutual security. As a corollary, the NATO strategy of flexible response, which includes the option of nuclear first use in response to conventional attacks, is seen as unrealistic and dangerous.

This side of the debate also might argue that even the logic of NATO's own rationale for its nuclear requirements—to compensate for conventional imbalances and to deter nuclear attack—should lead one to conclude that there is no basis for the alliance's pessimistic assumption that "nuclear weapons will continue to make an essential contribution to NATO's strategy of deterrence for the foreseeable future." That is, negotiations to achieve a stable balance of conventional forces at lower levels undercuts one of the rationales for NATO's nuclear weapons, while negotiations to eliminate theater nuclear weapons on both sides would eliminate the other. In the interim, according to this view, nuclear modernization is both unnecessary and undesirable. It is unnecessary because there is no reason to waste money modernizing systems that are planned for reduction and elimination. More important, it is undesirable because modernization—which would fuel the arms race and undercut political trust—would become an additional obstacle to reaching future agreements to limit conventional and nuclear arms.

On the other side of the debate are those who see a continuing need for NATO's strategy of flexible response and for the nuclear capabilities that underpin it. They would point out that both the security of the NATO allies and the stability of East-West relations have been well served by NATO's strategy for a generation. They would argue—as NATO Secretary General Manfred Woerner did at the December 1988 NATO Ministerial—that there is no connection between the unilateral reductions announced by General Secretary Gorbachev and NATO's nuclear posture due in part to the fact that, even after they are implemented, they would leave a substantial imbalance of conventional forces and a continuing requirement for tactical nuclear weapons to offset the imbalance.[3] Those who hold this view would likewise note that the fifteen-year history of MBFR suggests both that the CFE talks may go on for a very long time, and that there is no guarantee that they will ultimately culminate in a mutually satisfactory agreement. In any event, the implications of CFE for future NATO nuclear requirements would depend importantly on the details of any agreement that emerged.

Given these uncertainties about timetables and outcomes, this side of the debate holds that any discussion about the impact of an improved conventional balance on NATO's nuclear requirements, much less about new negotiations to reduce further nuclear weapons in Europe, would be somewhere between very premature and entirely hypothetical. Meanwhile, the issue of the need to modernize NATO's nuclear capabilities can be largely determined on the technical and military merits, that is, on what improvements may be required in light of the obsolescence of current systems and changes in WTO capabilities that would degrade their effectiveness.

If the foregoing is a reasonable characterization of the debate, then it is clear that not only are the two sides talking past each other, but also that several important issues are not being addressed. For example, it simply is not realistic to assume that it will be possible to keep theater nuclear weapons off the political agenda for the indefinite future. Eastern proposals for further nuclear reductions are likely to find growing resonance among Western publics, especially in the FRG, where 68 percent of the population in a recent poll said it opposed nuclear modernization and an even larger percentage said it wanted all nuclear weapons off German soil.[4] In addition, not only is NATO likely to make further unilateral reductions in its nuclear weapons (beyond the 2,400 removed since 1979), but certain dual-capable delivery systems—most likely artillery but possibly also aircraft—will be included in the CFE Talks. Consequently, NATO will find itself in de facto negotiations about some of its nuclear capabilities, and the results of CFE (if any) inevitably will affect *both* the conventional balance and the respective nuclear capabilities of the two alliances. Considerations such as these suggest that questions about the basis for NATO's nuclear requirements, the desirability and prospects for new nuclear talks, and the impact of changes in the conventional balance on those requirements are neither hypothetical nor premature.

On the other side, a focus that is confined to the military balance in Europe omits consideration of the nuclear forces and threats that would remain even after a START agreement and even if all of the nuclear weapons now deployed in Europe were eliminated. In addition, it is far from self-evident that reductions in conventional forces per se would lead to a *stable* balance or, if it did, that such a balance would be *robust* rather than fragile. It is not even clear that, given a persisting nuclear backdrop, "conventional deterrence" is a meaningful concept, or that the elimination of options short of strategic nuclear exchanges would reduce either the risks of nuclear war or the devastation it would cause. Put simply, the case remains to be made that a reduction in, or even the elimination of, nuclear weapons in Europe would achieve the goals that its advocates define as the objective. More on this below.

Moreover, a narrow focus on the strictly military functions and purely military rationales for NATO's nuclear weapons overlooks the important political functions that these capabilities perform.[5] It is true that NATO's nuclear deterrent is intended in part to offset Warsaw Pact *conventional* superiority. Arms control agreements or unilateral Warsaw Pact reductions that substantially reduced these large conventional asymmetries could help ease NATO nuclear requirements. (Implementation of the unilateral reductions announced by General Secretary Gorbachev on December 7, 1988, would be a step in the right direction, but by itself would not substantially affect the Warsaw Pact's current conventional superiority.) NATO's nuclear capabilities also are designed in part to deter *nuclear* first use by the Pact. Arms control agreements (or unilateral reductions) that—building on the INF Treaty—reduced or eliminated the Warsaw Pact's short-range nuclear forces (SNF) could reduce NATO's own nuclear requirements.

In fact, however, the role of nuclear weapons in NATO is broader and more fundamental than simply offsetting Warsaw Pact conventional superiority and deterring Soviet nuclear strikes. It is concerned as much with *assuring the allies* that the United States is committed—militarily as well as politically—to their security as with directly *deterring the Soviets*. Consequently, even if the WTO were to agree to reductions that left both sides with equal conventional capabilities, NATO could still have a strong interest in maintaining and qualitatively modernizing its nuclear forces. Conversely, proposals aimed at the complete elimination of nuclear weapons in Europe could be seen as threatening—whether or not intending—to overturn NATO's strategy of flexible response and to undermine the alliance. Substantial changes in NATO's strategy or nuclear capabilities, in turn, could have profound consequences, not only for the cohesion of the NATO alliance, but also for the stability of East-West relations.

In brief, an evaluation of NATO's nuclear requirements—and of their relationship to the conventional balance and conventional arms control—depends on an appreciation of the strategic and political, as well as strictly military, functions of NATO's nuclear capabilities. That is the subject to which we now turn.

The Evolution of NATO Strategy

The origins of the role nuclear weapons play in NATO strategy can be traced to the early postwar period. During the 1950s, NATO believed that it confronted a hostile Soviet Union that had overwhelming conventional superiority.[6] It looked to its superiority in nuclear weapons to compensate for its conventional inferiority. Many Western officials and analysts during this period also argued that nuclear weapons were inexpensive relative to conventional weapons, that they were an excellent substitute for shortages in NATO's military manpower, and that they inherently favored the defense.

These perspectives were at the heart of the NATO strategy promulgated in 1957 (MC-14/2), which was premised on the early and massive use of theater and strategic nuclear weapons in response to conventional aggression. This strategy held that NATO's across-the-board nuclear superiority gave it "escalation dominance": confronted with conventional aggression, it could escalate to the nuclear level at which the WTO could not effectively respond. Consequently, the threat to escalate was seen to be highly credible. The U.S. assurance that its strategic forces were "coupled" to the defense of its European allies was likewise seen to be credible because, during this period, the United States itself was substantially immune from large-scale Soviet nuclear attacks. In brief, Western leaders during the 1950s tended to believe that NATO's nuclear superiority either compensated for the substantial imbalance in conventional forces it faced, or simply rendered that imbalance irrelevant.

NATO's early reliance on nuclear weapons and the threat of nuclear escalation was accompanied by the deployment of U.S. nuclear weapons in Europe. In large part, this was due to the substantially greater military and economic strength of the United States compared to its allies during the early postwar period, as well as to its preponderant control of the West's nuclear capabilities. It also was due to technical considerations, notably the range limitations of the delivery systems of the day such as B-47 bombers, which required that they largely be based in or staged through Western Europe. The political consequence, however, was to reinforce the coupling of U.S. nuclear forces to NATO security. When tactical nuclear weapons were introduced into the NATO force structure beginning around 1954, they were integrated into forces already in existence rather than organized into separate units. That is, the delivery systems used to support NATO's tactical nuclear capabilities have been "dual-capable" from the beginning.

Beginning in the 1960s, several developments occurred which combined to change NATO strategy and the role of theater nuclear weapons in support of that strategy. Because of superficial similarities to the earlier strategy and forces, however, these changes and their significance are not always fully appreciated.

First, the WTO's conventional forces, although still clearly superior, no longer appeared so overwhelming that there seemed to be no alternative to early resort to nuclear weapons by NATO. It now appeared as though substantial, but feasible, NATO investments in conventional capabilities would allow more time before escalation to the nuclear level would be necessary. NATO's efforts to raise the nuclear threshold by strengthening its conventional capabilities have continued, but have been countered by a renewed growth of Soviet non-nuclear forces beginning in the mid-1960s, and by steady but cumulatively impressive qualitative improvements in WTO—especially Soviet—conventional capabilities.[7] Indeed, most Western analyses indicate that the WTO now exceeds NATO in virtually every category of conventional weapons.

Second, the nuclear superiority the West had previously enjoyed first diminished and then disappeared. The acquisition of substantial strategic and theater nuclear capabilities by the Soviet Union has meant that, if NATO's nuclear weapons had ever been the "great equalizer"— much less an instrument of "nuclear intimidation"—they no longer are. (During the same period, NATO's views on the distinctive attributes of nuclear weapons also evolved, and it no longer seemed as clear that either they could be used to offset shortfalls in manpower, or they intrinsically favored the defense.) The general consensus is that there now is rough parity between the United States and the Soviet Union at the strategic nuclear level. A START agreement would preserve this relationship at somewhat lower levels, but would still permit each superpower to maintain and modernize a substantial force somewhere in the neighborhood of 8,000–9,000 weapons. The WTO also has achieved nuclear superiority in the theater, especially with the introduction of the SS-20. Although the INF Treaty will eliminate the intermediate-range ground-launched missiles on both sides, each alliance will continue to deploy substantial nuclear capabilities in Europe, and the East will continue to have superiority in certain categories, notably short-range nuclear missiles.

These changes in the nuclear balance and in the West's analysis of the conventional balance had profound implications for NATO strategy and for the role of NATO nuclear weapons. Central among these was the loss of "escalation dominance," i.e., it no longer was necessarily to NATO's advantage to escalate the conflict because WTO capabilities could be equal to or greater than those of NATO at the next level of violence, up to and including strategic nuclear exchanges. Consequently, the threat to use nuclear weapons in response to conventional aggression no longer seemed as credible. The growing vulnerability of the United States to Soviet nuclear weapons likewise cast increasing doubts on the credibility of "extended deterrence," i.e., the U.S. commitment to employ its nuclear arsenal, if necessary, in defense of its NATO allies in Europe.

The NATO Strategy of "Flexible Response"

NATO adapted its strategy in light of these developments. The new strategy of "flexible response" (MC-14/3), adopted in 1967, reflected an increased emphasis on conventional capabilities for direct defense of NATO territory, and a reduced but still central role for theater nuclear weapons, including the option of nuclear first use. The enhancement of conventional capabilities was intended to raise the nuclear threshold by permitting NATO to fight at the conventional level before having to cross it, and thereby to enhance the credibility of its threat to escalate to the nuclear level if necessary. The multiplication of conventional and nuclear options was designed to increase the prospects for (but by no means ensuring) escalation control by permitting NATO to respond to aggression at the lowest possible level, rather than be forced to escalate simply because it lacked less risky or destructive alternatives, as well as increasing the credibility of NATO's escalatory threats. The modernization of theater-based nuclear capabilities that could reach targets on Soviet territory was aimed at undercutting any presumption that a war could be confined to Eastern and Western Europe or that an attacker's homeland could remain immune from retaliation. Although it has undergone some evolution and adaptation, flexible response continues to be NATO strategy today.

In implementation of the flexible response strategy, NATO's conventional capabilities have been steadily modernized. NATO also has reduced its nuclear weapons. The 1979 "dual-track" decision to deploy ground-launched cruise missiles (GLCMs) and Pershing 2 missiles also entailed a unilateral reduction of 1,000 nuclear weapons deployed in Europe. NATO decided at its 1983 Montebello meeting to make further unilateral cuts of 1,400 weapons. The missiles that will be destroyed under the terms of the INF Treaty will result in additional reductions.

One would, however, be hard put to find in official NATO documents over the last 20 years a simple, clear statement of the role nuclear weapons are intended to play in the strategy of flexible response. This is due in part to the fact that nuclear weapons are seen as filling several roles, including offsetting the conventional imbalance and deterring nuclear attack. It also arises from the fact that NATO's nuclear weapons perform strategic and political as well as military functions. Finally, it is because different NATO allies assign differing priorities to these various roles and functions. As a consequence, formal articulations of the strategy reflect the results of officially unacknowledged compromises and artfully drafted ambiguities.

The authors of the recent report on *Discriminate Deterrence* nicely captured the problems one encounters in trying to pin down how exactly NATO views nuclear weapons:

> Sometimes it has seemed as though NATO plans to use battlefield or even theater-wide nuclear weapons for their direct effect in repelling the Soviet invasion. At other times, NATO officials posit a different strategy—that what NATO really intends in threatening to use nuclear weapons is to point up the perils of escalation and, in effect, concentrate the minds of Soviet leaders on the apocalypse at the end of that road.[8]

The answer to this apparent paradox is that NATO's nuclear weapons are intended to perform both military and political functions, and that there is no need to specify the relative emphasis that should be placed on each role or, more precisely, that contrasting the political and military functions of nuclear weapons is a false dichotomy. Indeed, the credibility of the threat to use nuclear weapons is thought by many to rest importantly on their military utility.

The *military* functions of nuclear weapons in NATO strategy include deterring or breaking up concentrations of conventional forces near the battlefront as well as in the second and third echelons, attacking key fixed targets such as airbases and logistic choke points, and deterring first use of nuclear (and perhaps also chemical) weapons by the adversary.[9] The introduction of improved target-acquisition capabilities into the NATO force structure should increase the technical feasibility and military effectiveness of such nuclear strikes, especially at longer ranges. The availability of flexible nuclear capabilities and employment options to perform these functions provide at least some possibility of controlling escalation while protecting paramount security interests.

The *political* and *strategic* functions of nuclear weapons are, crudely put, to open Pandora's box. As was argued above, when the United States had nuclear superiority, the credibility of extended deterrence rested on the belief that the United States and NATO enjoyed escalation dominance at virtually any level of nuclear conflict. Now, the credibility of that policy rests on the willingness of the United States and NATO to embark on a course that runs some *risk* of eventually involving widespread use of strategic nuclear weapons, even though that outcome is one that no one intended or desired.

This threat, in essence, to risk "losing control" is the opposite side of the coin from escalation control. NATO strategy cannot and does not assume that escalation could be readily and easily controlled. Indeed, if that were the case, then the credibility of extended deterrence would be undermined. The problem, of course, is not too much but too little control. Because of these irreducible uncertainties and the potentially catastrophic consequences of failure, however, NATO can both make every effort to avoid unwanted escalation and still base its security policy on the chance that it will fail.

The threat to risk losing control also is different—and inherently more credible—than a threat "to provoke our own annihilation," as some critics have characterized current NATO strategy and the U.S. nuclear commitment. It differs in its quality and its credibility from a threat deriving from escalation dominance. These differences have two direct consequences.

First, the fact that, once begun, the escalation process could eventually result in the widespread nuclear destruction of the United States leaves an irreducible doubt—especially on the part of the European NATO allies who feel their security to be most directly at stake—about whether the United States would in fact embark on such a course if deterrence failed. That doubt is at the core of their concerns about the depth and durability of the U.S. commitment to NATO.

Perhaps more to the point, it is a doubt that substantially defines the political and strategic requirements that NATO's nuclear capabilities must satisfy. As noted above, the United States will continue to have substantial strategic nuclear capabilities, even under a START agreement. British and French nuclear forces, which are not covered by either START or the INF Treaty, are undergoing significant expansion as a concomitant of modernization and will soon comprise approximately 1,200 warheads that are capable of reaching Soviet territory. Arguably, U.S. strategic nuclear forces and/or the independent British and French nuclear forces ought to be sufficient by themselves to *deter* WTO aggression in the sense of being able to attack a vast number of targets in Eastern Europe and the Soviet Union.

They cannot by themselves, however, *assure* the NATO allies that the United States strategic deterrent is coupled to their security, and that the United States can and will risk its own nuclear devastation in order to defend them. As a corollary, they cannot ensure that the WTO would be persuaded in all cases that, if NATO's conventional defenses were threatened with collapse, it would cross the nuclear threshold. Paradoxically, therefore, more—or at least more specialized—nuclear capabilities may be required to fulfill the assurance than the deterrence function. But unless the NATO allies have that confidence and the WTO is thoroughly persuaded, extended deterrence would be undermined and with it, NATO cohesion. The implications of such developments for not only West-West, but also East-West, relations could be profound, and it is not self-evident that they would be largely or entirely beneficial.

Second and related, the credibility of the threat to risk "losing control" depends importantly on the absence of any clear stopping points on the nuclear side of the firebreak, i.e., on an unbroken "powder trail" of nuclear options and risks leading to strategic nuclear exchanges between the Soviet Union and the United States. [10] This (rather than the deployment of SS-20s per se) was a major motivation behind the 1979 NATO decision to deploy the GLCMs and Pershing 2 missiles, especially on the part of the European allies. [11] Likewise, much of the discussion and debate about the need to modernize NATO's nuclear forces and to meet its theater nuclear requirements—notwithstanding INF Treaty constraints—stem from a belief that the failure to do so will open gaps in the powder trail. This is the essential connection between the details of nuclear force modernization and the credibility of the policy of extended deterrence.

It follows that *U.S.* nuclear weapons in the theater perform several distinctive functions apart from whatever strictly military capabilities they provide, and however well third-country nuclear forces or improved conventional forces can substitute *militarily* for these capabilities. First, they couple the U.S. strategic deterrent to the defense of NATO and form the core of the policy of extended deterrence. Second, they couple the United States politically to Europe by complementing the American conventional presence that underscores the U.S. security commitment to NATO. Finally, U.S. nuclear weapons are the distinctive basis for its claim to leadership of the alliance. With the waning of American economic preponderance and the modernization of allied military capabilities, U.S. nuclear weapons are increasingly *the* basis for its claims to leadership simply because there is no substitute for them. Consequently, if and as the role of nuclear weapons in NATO is diminished, so too will be the role of the United States in the alliance. It is worth emphasizing, moreover, that far from challenging the United States for the mantle of leadership, none of the allies either wants to assume it or wants any of its European partners to wear it. Even if the United States desired to play a lesser role, there is no obvious candidate on the horizon to fill the void and perform the functions that are indispensable to alliance cohesion. Lacking confidence about the shape of successor security arrangements, it also is not clear that the East would want either the United States to abdicate its leadership role in NATO or a much more fragmented alliance which could lead to an increased number of independent nuclear deterrents.

This survey of the functions of nuclear weapons in NATO strategy and of the distinctive functions of U.S. nuclear weapons leads to three conclusions that are crucial to evaluating various options for meeting NATO's nuclear requirements:

–*Nuclear weapons* perform important functions in NATO for which conventional weapons of equal military capability and effectiveness cannot substitute.

–Nuclear weapons *based in the theater* perform important functions in NATO for which nuclear weapons of equal military capability and effectiveness based elsewhere (either in the United States or at sea) cannot substitute.

–U.S. nuclear weapons perform important functions in NATO for which the nuclear weapons of other NATO allies (i.e., France and the U.K.) having equal military capability and efffectiveness cannot substitute.

These conclusions imply that NATO's qualitative nuclear requirements are, within limits, somewhat independent of changes in the strategic nuclear and conventional balances, and are likely to remain so until there are—or NATO chooses to precipitate—fundamental changes in the broader strategic environment. They also indicate that, in the interim, there are no ready or fully adequate substitutes for U.S. nuclear weapons based in the theater. Finally, they suggest a continuing need to modernize NATO's nuclear capabilities so long as they play their current key role in European security and stability. All this said, there still appear to be opportunities to reduce the numbers of nuclear weapons deployed in Europe.

The Future of NATO Nuclear Weapons

The United States already plans to modernize its nuclear artillery. It is in the process of replacing its current inventory of nuclear rounds for its 203-mm artillery with new shells that will have greater range, accuracy and safety features. There also are plans to undertake a similar modernization of the 155-mm artillery, but implementation depends, in part, on Congress lifting its ceiling of 925 new nuclear rounds. The obsolescent Lance missiles are under consideration for replacement during the 1990s with a follow-on system that is intended to have improved survivability, greater accuracy and longer range. Finally, a new air-to-surface nuclear missile may be deployed.[12]

Nuclear Artillery. There is a growing consensus among Western officials and defense analysts that, within the context of modernization, NATO can tolerate substantial cuts in its nuclear artillery (perhaps on the order of 50 percent or more) while preserving the essential political and strategic—if not necessarily all of the military—functions performed by these systems. As suggested by SACEUR General John Galvin and others,[13] one way to accomplish this would be an application of the "build-down" approach. That is, reductions in nuclear artillery could be explicitly tied to modernization of the remaining force, perhaps in something like a 2-to-1 ratio: two "old" nuclear rounds would be removed as one "new" round was deployed. Just as it has done previously over the past decade, NATO can undertake these cuts unilaterally rather than risk long delays by insisting on reciprocal unilateral reductions by the WTO or proposing a new round of time-consuming negotiations. Similarly, although the CFE talks almost certainly will address limitations on artillery, the nuclear implications of reductions in these dual-capable systems should not become a formal topic—and another potential stumbling block—in CFE.

Longer-range Systems. As noted above, the strategy of flexible response emphasizes the need for a broad range of options, both to strengthen the coupling of the U.S. strategic deterrent to the defense of NATO and to enhance the prospects for escalation control. Just as NATO's decision to deploy GLCMs and Pershing 2 missiles was not directly the result of the Soviet deployment of SS-20s, so too the INF Treaty has not obviated NATO's perceived need for options between short-range nuclear artillery and missiles and U.S. central strategic systems. This requirement was recently reiterated by NATO's Nuclear Planning Group which stated that ". . . [F]or the foreseeable future NATO requires diversified, survivable, and operationally flexible nuclear forces in Europe across the entire spectrum of ranges. . . ."[14] Modernization of NATO's longer-range nuclear capabilities in the future probably will be based primarily on nuclear-capable aircraft based in the theater, notwithstanding the associated opportunity costs for NATO conventional capabilities, and the potential inclusion of these dual-capable platforms in CFE.

Such modernization is likely to entail the deployment of an air-to-surface missile (ASM) to increase confidence in the ability to penetrate and, in doing so, to reduce the number of aircraft that need to be allocated exclusively to nuclear missions.[15] Unless it is economically advantageous as well as politically realistic to plan on equipping U.S. aircraft with a European ASM, such a missile (and surely the warhead it carries) should be American, rather than French (the ASMP) or Franco-British (the proposed ASLP).[16] It could be carried on U.S. F-15Es based in the U.K. (and, perhaps, the FRG); on U.S. F-111E/Fs now based in the U.K.; or on F-111Gs (formerly FB-111s) that may be moved to Britain. To reinforce the alliance's principle of "shared risk," it also should be made available for deployment on British, West German and Italian Tornadoes under "programs of cooperation" at the same time it is deployed on U.S. aircraft (rather than after all the designated U.S. aircraft have been equipped). To respond further to West German concerns about "singularity," nuclear ASM-equipped F-15Es could be deployed at co-located operating bases in the Netherlands and Belgium as well as in the U.K. If reports that the new U.S. ASM will be based on the SRAM II are correct,[17] then it also could be carried by F-16s based in several allied countries, including Belgium and the Netherlands, as well as Italy and Turkey. In brief, it is logistically feasible and may be politically desirable to base NATO's modernized longer-range nuclear capabilities in the same countries in which the INF missiles were deployed.[18] Such a distribution of nuclear-capable aircraft should improve their survivability by dispersing them among a larger number of admittedly vulnerable airbases, but need not lead to an increase in overall numbers.

As in the case of nuclear artillery, while the qualitative requirements for this longer-range capability flow from NATO's political and strategic requirements, the quantitative requirements ought to be sensitive to changes in the conventional and nuclear balance. Likewise, deployment of these modernized capabilities could be made part of the "build-down" approach, described above, in order to promote an overall reduction in NATO's nuclear arsenal. Like the modernization of nuclear artillery, however, these initiatives should be undertaken unilaterally by NATO rather than becoming entangled either in new nuclear negotiations or in CFE.

Short-range Missiles. How NATO should respond to the growing obsolescence of its Lance surface-to-surface missiles is more complicated and controversial. On the one hand, the Lance missiles perform a valuable role in the strategy of flexible response, due in part to their twin virtues of high survivability and good penetration capabilities, and in part to their capacity to relieve some of the burden on dual-capable aircraft. These characteristics also contribute to stability by enhancing the prospects for escalation control. The Follow-on-to-Lance (FOTL) presumably would be even better on all counts. In brief, these missiles provide valuable capabilities that should not be lightly forgone. On the other hand, modernization of Lance is a controversial issue both within NATO and between East and West. Its military utility needs to be weighed against the risks that it will impose excessive strains on NATO cohesion or poison the atmosphere for East-West negotiations on other issues, including CFE.

A decision on Lance modernization probably need not be made soon, despite the fact that the current system will reach the end of its useful service life within a few years. This is because deployment of a conventional version of what is the leading candidate for FOTL, the U.S. Army Tactical Missile System (ATACMS), already is planned for the early 1990s; a study to make ATACMS dual-capable has been authorized by Congress; and the launcher for ATACMS—the Multiple Launch Rocket System (MLRS)—already is in the force.[19] Moreover, the life of the existing Lance almost certainly can be extended several years, albeit at some non-trivial cost.

It is even clearer, however, that the vast WTO superiority in short-range missiles (perhaps on the order of 10-to-1 in launchers) precludes *unilateral* NATO reductions or phasing out of these systems.[20] Mutual negotiated cuts in short-range missiles *might* contribute to mutual security, not only by reducing the number of nuclear weapons deployed in Europe, but also by constraining the conventional and chemical threats that tactical ballistic missiles can pose. At the same time, such negotiations would pose difficulties and risks for both sides. Assuming the goal would be reductions to equal levels, the East's substantial superiority in short-range missiles means that the WTO would have to be willing to contemplate an agreement that required it to make much larger reductions than NATO. The West, meanwhile, could be justifiably concerned that the East would exploit the talks to pursue its goal of denuclearization, either by pressing for a "third zero" on short-range missiles, and/or by trying to expand the talks to include other theater nuclear capabilities. For the reasons explained above, NATO probably would find the former and almost certainly the latter outcome unacceptable.

In view of the delicacy of the issue and the pitfalls that surround it, it is hard to argue that negotiations about short-range nuclear missiles are a matter requiring urgent action. The probable NATO timetable for Lance modernization permits the issue to be deferred, at least for a time. In the interim, the CFE talks will have had an opportunity to get off to a good start and acquire momentum before the complication of possible new nuclear talks is introduced.

Theater Nuclear Weapons and Stability

Although the foregoing discussion has emphasized the military, strategic and political roles of theater nuclear weapons in strengthening NATO security, it would be a mistake to conclude that the stability of the military balance in Europe suffers the consequences. On the contrary, there does not appear to be anything intrinsic to nuclear weapons deployed in Europe that makes them a greater threat to stability than the nuclear weapons deployed on the homelands of the two superpowers or in their ballistic-missile submarines.

The case that theater nuclear weapons pose a distinctive threat to stability largely rests on two related assumptions, both of which appear to be mistaken, or at least in need of substantial qualification. The first is that, by their very existence, theater nuclear weapons constitute an escalatory risk. The second is that, once a stable balance of conventional forces is achieved, both alliances can depend on "conventional deterrence" instead of deterrence based on theater nuclear weapons for security.

The problem with the first assumption is that the risks of escalation stem from nuclear weapons per se, not just those in the theater. As noted above, even if all of the nuclear weapons now deployed in Europe were eliminated, both superpowers, as well as the U.K. and France among the aliies, would retain substantial nuclear arsenals. There is no technical reason why nominally "strategic" weapons such as SS-25s could not be used to attack targets now covered by theater nuclear weapons such as SS-20s. Indeed, a number of warheads on U.S. submarine-launched ballistic missiles have been assigned to SACEUR for some years. Until these strategic and third-country nuclear arsenals are sharply reduced or eliminated, the risks of escalation will remain, whatever the future status of theater nuclear weapons. Moreover, while it surely is true that it is more credible to respond to conventional and nuclear attacks on NATO with nuclear forces deployed in Europe, likewise it is true that the availability of these less-than-strategic options hold out some hope for stopping escalation short of central strategic exchanges. The question of the net impact that these two, somewhat contradictory, characteristics of theater nuclear weapons have on escalation probably is unanswerable.

The problem with the second assumption is with the concept of "conventional deterrence" itself. First, as other chapters in this volume make clear, there is no assurance that conventional reductions per se will lead to a stable balance of forces. Second, there can be no assurance that even a stable balance of conventional forces will yield robust "conventional deterrence" in the sense that both sides will be confident that the attacker always would lose much more than he would gain if he initiated a conflict. Not only are there far more imponderables that can significantly affect the outcome of a conventional war than a nuclear war, but pre-nuclear history is replete with examples in which the side with lesser military forces in fact prevailed. Put simply, conventional forces alone are inadequate for confident deterrence of conventional aggression. Finally and most important, the existence of nuclear weapons renders the concept of "conventional deterrence" all but meaningless. Whatever the balance of conventional forces, the losing side in a conventional war in Europe always retains the option of threatening to escalate to the nuclear level. The absence of theater nuclear weapons might render the threat less credible, but not necessarily less likely to be implemented, and surely no less destructive if it were.

In brief, there is no necessary conflict between NATO's perceived security requirements and a mutual East-West interest in a stable military balance. Not only is it difficult to imagine robust stability in the absence of conditions that satisfy the legitimate security requirements of both alliances, but theater nuclear weapons need not detract and may contribute to those conditions and to the stability of the balance.

Conclusion

This chapter has argued that NATO will have a requirement for nuclear weapons for the foreseeable future. The requirement stems in part from the present imbalance in conventional forces. At best, it will take some years before a stable conventional balance is achieved. NATO's nuclear requirements also are a reflection of the strategic and political, as well as military, roles that NATO nuclear weapons perform. These roles, which are important to East-West stability as well as to NATO security, are substantially independent of the details of the conventional balance. They might well be less important in a different security regime, but the changes required to move into a different regime would be far-reaching and could entail the transformation of East-East and West-West as well as East-West relations. In the meantime, NATO's nuclear capabilities should be modernized as necessary in response to obsolescence, improved capabilities, etc., so that they can continue to perform these roles, as well as to incorporate improvement in security and safety. Finally, NATO's nuclear requirements derive from a recognition that, even once achieved, a stable balance of conventional forces is not equivalent to "conventional deterrence." A necessary (but not sufficient) condition for conventional deterrence is the elimination of all, not just theater, nuclear weapons.

This analysis should not be regarded as a counsel of despair. On the one hand, it rejects the proposition that nuclear weapons in Europe, per se, are either destabilizing or dangerous. On the other hand, it has outlined a series of *qualitative* requirements for NATO's nuclear weapons, but also suggested a variety of factors that can influence the *quantitative* requirements. In doing so, it has identified the potential for further unilateral reductions in NATO's nuclear inventory and raised the possibility of future negotiations to achieve other reductions. The prospects for both negotiated and unilateral reductions in theater nuclear weapons will increase further as progress is made toward achieving a stable conventional balance of forces at lower levels. These trends may not foreshadow the millennium of a nuclear-free Europe, but do point to a range of opportunities for strengthening mutual security and stability while steadily shrinking the nuclear inventories of the two alliances.

Notes

1 NATO Press Service, "NATO Nuclear Planning Group: Final Communiqué," Press Release M-NPG-2(88)63, October 28, 1988.
2 General Secretary Gorbachev renewed his proposal in his meeting with Chancellor Helmut Kohl, as reported in *Pravda*, October 26, 1988.
3 See the comments by Woerner and other NATO officials at the December 1988 NATO Ministerial reported in Robert Pear, "NATO Praises Soviet Arms Cuts but Doesn't Offer Any of its Own," *The New York Times*, December 10, 1988.
4 Cited in Ronald D. Asmus, "West Germany Faces Nuclear Modernization," *Survival* 30, No. 6 (November/December 1988), p. 513. There is a widespread expectation that

General Secretary Gorbachev's announcement of unilateral conventional force reductions will further erode popular support for NATO nuclear modernization. See Pear, "NATO Praises Soviet Arms Cuts"; and Steve Holand, "Ploy Threatens Missile Upgrade," *Washington Times*, December 12, 1988.

5 It should be emphasized that Alexei Vasiliev's companion piece explicitly recognizes and discusses, albeit critically, some of these political functions.

6 With the benefit of hindsight, it now seems likely that the West overestimated the Soviet Union's conventional capabilities during this period, failing to take account of the fact that many of the oft-cited "175 Soviet divisions" existed only on paper or at very low manning and readiness levels. Ironically, at about the same time that Western analyses were coming to appreciate that earlier estimates of Soviet conventional capabilities probably had been exaggerated, those capabilities began to undergo significant improvements.

7 John M. Collins, *U.S.-Soviet Military Balance: 1960–1980. Conflicts and Capabilities* (New York: McGraw-Hill, 1980), pp. 306–307. See also International Institute of Strategic Studies, *The Military Balance: 1983–1984* (London: IISS, 1983), p. 137: "The numerical balance over the last 20 years has slowly but steadily moved in favor of the East. At the same time the West has largely lost the technological edge which allowed NATO to believe that quality could substitute for numbers."

8 *Discriminate Deterrence: Report of the Commission on Integrated Long-Term Strategy* (Washington, DC: U.S. Government Printing Office, January 1988), p. 27. Ironically, the same report came in for widespread criticism, particularly in Europe, precisely because it chose to reduce the ambiguity by giving emphasis to one function—the military—over the other. After declaring that "we cannot rely on threats to provoke our own annihilation if carried out" (p. 2), it argued that "The Alliance should threaten to use nuclear weapons not as a link to a wider and more devastating war—although the risk of further escalation would still be there—but mainly as an instrument for denying success to the invading Soviet forces" (p. 30).

9 See Walter B. Slocombe, "Extended Deterrence," *Washington Quarterly* 7, No. 4 (Fall 1984), p. 98.

10 Like most metaphors, both "firebreak" and "powder trail" are imperfect. To some, the former term mistakenly connotes plans to confine any conflict to Europe. To others, the latter term mistakenly confers an automaticity on the escalation process that, if true, would undermine NATO's strategy of flexible response.

11 James A. Thomson, "The LRTNF Decision: Evolution of U.S. Theater Nuclear Policy, 1975–9," *International Affairs* 60, No. 4 (Fall 1984), p. 606. As with most NATO nuclear decisions, the 1979 one stemmed from multiple sources. As noted above, another, and somewhat contradictory, motivation was to enhance the flexibility of NATO's nuclear options in order to permit it to respond at the lowest appropriate level and, concomitantly, enhance the prospects for escalation control.

12 See Jesse James, "Tactical Nuclear Modernization—The NATO Decision That Won't Go Away," *Arms Control Today* 18, No. 10 (December 1988), p. 213; and "After the INF Treaty: U.S. Nuclear Buildup in Europe," *Defense Monitor* 17, No. 2 (1988), pp. 6–7.

13 See, for example, *Baltimore Sun*, August 11, 1988, p. 2. It should be noted that General Galvin tied such unilateral reductions to specific initiatives in addition to modernization of nuclear artillery, such as, for example, an improved surface-to-surface missile and a new air-to-surface missile.

14 NATO Press Service, "NATO Nuclear Planning Group: Final Communiqué," Press Release M-NPG-2(88)63, October 28, 1988.

15 It should be noted that there already are modern, long-range, air-to-surface missiles in the Soviet inventory, including the AS-15 (up to 3,000 kilometers) and the AS-13 (approximately 800 kilometers), as well as the AGM-86B (approximately 3,000 kilometers) in the U.S. inventory.

16 There have been reports that the odds against a joint French-British air-to-surface missile are large and growing. See, for example, Duncan Lennox, "Will the UK Decide on SRAM 2?" *Jane's Defence Weekly*, December 10, 1988, p. 1473.

17 *Economist*, November 5–11, 1988, p. 5. RAND colleague Peter Wilson has offered the intriguing suggestion that AV-8B Harriers be modified to carry SRAM II. Exploiting Harrier's V/STOL capabilities would reduce the dependence of aircraft carrying ASMs on a small number of vulnerable airbases. Enhanced survivability for ASMs could be especially important if there is no successor to Lance.

18 Whether those same countries, notably Belgium and the Netherlands, would be politically willing and able to face a renewed domestic controversy about NATO nuclear modernization is a different—and difficult—matter.

19 Whether it is desirable to field a nuclear version of ATACMS is a separate question which is beyond the scope of the present discussion. Suffice it to say that, given the problems of reliably distinguishing between conventional and nuclear variants of a given weapons system—highlighted by the START debate about SLCM limits— verification of some future arms control constraints on short-range nuclear missiles could jeopardize the conventional capabilities provided by ATACMS.

20 The Warsaw Treaty Organization deploys approximately 1,400–1,500 launchers for its FROG, SCUD and SS-21 short-range missiles compared to 88 launchers in NATO for the Lance missile. Both alliances, of course, have more than one missile per launcher available. See International Institute of Strategic Studies, *The Military Balance: 1988– 1989* (London: IISS, 1988), Tables 1–2; and U.S. Department of Defense, *Soviet Military Power: An Assessment of the Threat, 1988* (Washington, DC: U.S. Government Printing Office, 1988), p. 109.

PART TWO

Nuclear Weapons and the Reduction of Conventional Weapons

Alexei A. Vasiliev, USSR

The exchange of ratified documents in Moscow in May 1988 put into operation the treaty on the elimination of Soviet and American intermediate- and shorter-range missiles signed in December 1987. This is the first treaty in history that has stipulated the destruction of two classes of U.S. and Soviet nuclear weapons. Its ratification signifies the practical beginning of the construction of a world without nuclear weapons, and establishes new standards and approaches for limiting and reducing arms.

The ratification of the INF Treaty sharply frames the question of moving to the next stage, an integral part of which is the reduction of non-nuclear weapons in a world oversaturated with nuclear weapons. The Soviet position on this issue is well known: the USSR has proposed the complete elimination of nuclear weapons. No less well known is the position of the West. It is based on the view that nuclear weapons are the main guarantee of security. An objective assessment of this problem is complicated by the East-West confrontation that has persisted for many years, the complex political and military structure of the opposing military alliances, mountains of accumulated weapons, and the existence in the West of entrenched groups that have a significant interest in continuing the confrontation.

The starting points for developing approaches to analyzing these problems are those principles with which, perhaps, everyone may agree today. In the first place, in modern conditions any war, whether nuclear or conventional, between the United States and the USSR or between

NATO and the WTO, would lead to a catastrophe and is therefore impermissible. In a joint statement at the Moscow summit, the Soviet and U.S. leaders again solemnly reaffirmed "our conviction that a nuclear war cannot be won and must never be unleashed, and our resolve to prevent any war between the Soviet Union and the United States, whether nuclear or conventional."[1]

Second, the elimination of entire classes of nuclear arms, such as, for example, intermediate- and shorter-range missiles, increases the role of conventional weapons both in the political and military sense.

To this we must add that nuclear weapons have already long ago become an integral part of conventional forces. However, the development of conventional weapons is proceeding in such a direction that their destructive and combat characteristics are increasingly approaching those of nuclear weapons.

The issue of the interaction of nuclear arms with the reduction of conventional weapons has numerous aspects. I will dwell here on the three which appear to be the most important ones for this subject:

–The political role of nuclear weapons in European security;
–The role of nuclear weapons at the initial stage of a conflict, before it has moved beyond the "nuclear threshold." (It is quite obvious that such a stage, if a conflict arises, may never be. However, it should be worthwhile to examine such a hypothetical instance, since this may help illuminate those problems connected with the Western notions of the possibility of its "escalation control" and the role established in these concepts for nuclear weapons); and
–The position of nuclear weapons in the European arms control process.

Nuclear Deterrence, Threat Perceptions and European Security: Reducing the Uncertainties

The functions of nuclear weapons in the pre-conflict stage have repeatedly been examined by both Soviet and Western specialists. It would be simplest of all to state that in reality nuclear weapons, particularly European nuclear weapons, fulfill no real function in deterring an attack. This is undoubtedly the case if we analyze the consequences of their use. Proceeding from this fact, in the course of the negotiations between Soviet General Secretary Mikhail S. Gorbachev and West German Chancellor Helmut Kohl, the Soviet Union again proposed "to work toward the complete elimination of tactical nuclear weapons on the continent."[2] However, this proposal has still not found the required response among Western political and military leaders. Therefore it is necessary to consider the fact that, in the framework of the strategy of "deterrence," nuclear weapons are part of the political environment in which we live, and in this respect fulfill certain political functions. As to how they do this, however, East and West fundamentally disagree with each other.

In the first place, it is worthwhile to observe that nuclear weapons in NATO are a symbol and an indicator of the unity of the alliance.[3] This symbol is made manifest through the deployment of U.S. weapons on the territory of the FRG. NATO's official documents work in the same direction as well. In the documents of the WTO, and in official Soviet statements, not once has the readiness to use force for protecting against aggression aimed at the USSR or its allies been emphasized.[4] The radical difference is that NATO does not exclude first use of nuclear weapons (including at the very outset of a conflict), whereas the USSR has unilaterally rejected this option.[5]

As is known, the argument of WTO superiority in non-nuclear weapons serves as the basis for the West's refusal to adhere to the no-first-use principle proposed by the USSR. The fact that the WTO call to eliminate imbalances and asymmetries does not readily appeal to NATO's willingness to renounce nuclear weapons in Europe reveals the deeper roots of NATO's adherence to nuclear deterrence, and emphasizes the perception of this strategy as primarily a political factor that links the NATO member-states into a unified military alliance. The primacy of the political functions of nuclear weapons in NATO renders them irrational for their military function, which also explains (if this can be considered an explanation) many well-known contradictions, some of which will be examined below.

Theoretically, the question of nuclear weapons as an indicator of the monolithic nature of NATO seems quite simple: in the event that a conflict were to move to the nuclear level, for example on the territory of the FRG, the nuclear forces deployed there would be brought to bear. Since these are American forces, the United States would automatically become a participant in the conflict. In such a way the path to "vertical" nuclear escalation would be opened, which would extend to general nuclear war and the use of strategic arms.

In the event that the "aggressor" would somehow avoid escalation along this route, the threat of "horizontal" nuclear escalation would await him. The nuclear forces of the United Kingdom and France at some stage (although which one is not clear) would enter into the conflict. It is obvious that the United States would serve the role of the main guarantor while the forces of the U.K. and France would assume an auxiliary role.

Neither the USSR nor the WTO as a whole plans to attack NATO or any of its members. But it is possible, even necessary, to discuss the flaws in this scheme that hinder the reduction of conventional arms, since they directly affect the theme of this chapter.

The main political defect coincides with the central flaw of the deterrence concept. Peace that is based upon threat cannot last. And the threat that spurs on the arms race has, to some extent, been devalued. The arms race has been transformed into an independent political factor which has acquired its own laws and inertia, destabilized the situation and hindered disarmament.[6]

In discussing "deterrence" as U.S. and NATO doctrine, General Secretary Gorbachev has justifiably observed that

> Each model of behavior has its own internal logic: when a threat is used as a means of policy, it is natural to wish that such a threat in each instance will be perceived in all seriousness. There may be only one conclusion: the policy of deterrence, examined in a historical perspective, not only does not decrease but may even increase the possibility of military conflicts.[7]

This is one of the basic contradictions of the deterrence doctrine of which many Western specialists are aware. Along with other contradictions, it also provokes criticism within NATO itself. However, the problem is not limited to this. In addition, the question of the "price" of the nuclear symbol of alliance unity also arises. The problem is obvious: the symbol of unity simultaneously stands for both the totality of the alliance and the inevitability of the destruction of its member-states. There appears to be a seemingly unresolvable tangle of contradictions. At its basis lies the hope that reality will never force it to be resolved in practice.

It must be said that in the USSR the irrational character of "security" guaranteed by nuclear arms is also well understood. We have critically examined our own policies of the recent past, when, responding to challenges from the United States, "we have not always used the capability to guarantee the security of the state through political means, and as a result we became drawn into an arms race."[8]

The enormous mistrust between the United States and the USSR, between NATO and the WTO, that has accumulated over the decades has engendered a tendency to study carefully the other side's "intentions" as they flow through the prism of ideological disagreements and political differences. We ourselves had to pass through the difficult stage of cognition before we could come to the conclusion that the philosophy of peaceful coexistence is a universal principle of international relations, which must be examined "in the context of the realities of the nuclear age,"[9] rather than as a special form of the class struggle.

The exaggerated role given to ideological differences in assessing the threat to security facilitates the negative perception of the prospects for the future and strongly complicates the realistic assessment of the true state of affairs. This concerns particularly the perception of the strength of the political alliance, the readiness of its participants to fulfill the obligations they have assumed in whatever conditions may arise. It is not difficult to see that the perception of NATO unity based on its readiness to take a suicidal step by using nuclear weapons does not create a feeling of security but one of doom. There are only two ways out: refuse to use nuclear weapons, or, to the contrary, strengthen the emphasis on their use. The first option is not compatible with existing Western concepts of the political role of nuclear weapons. The ability of the United States to guarantee the security of its European allies against the "WTO threat" lies mainly in the nuclear sphere, and therefore a rejection of nuclear weapons would be viewed as splitting NATO. Thus, NATO chooses the second option.

The paradox is that in reality the WTO and the USSR also require a high level of security for the NATO countries as well as for themselves, since "the fears and anxieties of the nuclear age engender unpredictability in politics and in specific actions."[10] The vital necessity of stability in the military-political realm inevitably leads to the thought that security can only be mutual.

Undoubtedly it is possible to imagine a stable situation in Europe without nuclear weapons and at lower levels of conventional arms. The logic of the doctrine of deterrence pushes us on to another path, forcing us to cling to these weapons, to worry about their buildup and modernization. In this way nuclear weapons form a material obstacle to the shift from confrontation to cooperation, and hinder the process of improving relations.

Politically, the direct consequence of the increased attention given to the durability of alliance obligations in NATO was the formation of a peculiar "rule of inertia" of relations in the framework of a United States-Western Europe-WTO triangle. Accordingly, the improvement of U.S.-Soviet relations is watched closely in Western Europe, which is fearful of manifestations of American isolationism in this area, especially through the weakening of the U.S. nuclear guarantee. At the same time a worsening of U.S.-Soviet relations leads, as a rule, to attempts to smooth over the sharp corners as fears of the possibility of a real test of the strength of these guarantees are intensified in Europe.

The stabilizing role of this kind of inertia is clear. But it stabilizes the situation at a sufficiently low level. In connection with the potential warming of Soviet-American relations the question arises of measures in the military-political area which would permit using selected positive tendencies to raise the level of trust and move to higher levels of stability. There is only one way to this end: through a parallel improvement of relations between all members of the triangle, between NATO and the WTO. However, it is obvious that a radical improvement of relations in a region where countries hold each other nuclear hostages is extremely difficult. Nuclear weapons are becoming a clear obstacle to moving to a higher level of political stability.

A special issue is the question of the nuclear forces of France and the U.K. Today, one cannot pretend that these forces simply do not exist, or that they are "targeted on all azimuths." In fact, these two countries possess hundreds of nuclear weapons, each of which can inflict immense damage on the countries of the WTO in particular. However, counter-arguments also exist, including, for example, the notion that there are only hundreds of these warheads, not thousands, like the United States and the USSR have. Another argument is based on the perception of France's and the U.K.'s own security, and that the destruction of their nuclear weapons in conditions of a Soviet-American nuclear hegemony would mean a departure from the principle of general security.

Owing to these considerations, the reduction of these forces in the framework of the Soviet program for the elimination of nuclear weapons has been set aside until the United States and the USSR by their own example open the road to nuclear disarmament.[11]

Decisive changes in the understanding of national interests have taken place in the course of *perestroika* in the USSR. From positions of a new understanding of the country's national interests "the contention in the minds and deeds of various strategists that the Soviet Union could be just as strong as any possible coalition of opposing states" has been condemned.[12] Recognizing this position as an open road to nuclear disarmament, it is impossible not to acknowledge that to a significant degree it is the consequence of NATO's strategy of intimidation and, more to the point, of the function that nuclear weapons carry out as an "indicator of unity" among the allies.

Uncertainty in assessing the level of threat by both sides is one of the most complex and contradictory factors of military policy. On the one hand, uncertainty hinders an aggressor's strategic calculations and deters him from attack. On the other hand, it can completely distort the political picture in the region. Yet the problem is incredibly more complex. Uncertainty facilitates seeing the other side as a potential aggressor, forcing his actions to be predicted precisely on such a worst-case basis. By virtue of this, uncertainty is a politically destabilizing factor which restrains the growth of trust between the sides—i.e., it creates an obstacle to the main objective function of new political thinking while emphasizing the necessity of permanently preparing for a military confrontation.

The fact that the Soviet Union's political obligations have hardly been fully examined in the West is closely tied to a number of factors of uncertainty. It seems that the three-stage plan for reducing the level of confrontation in Europe proposed at the Warsaw session of the WTO Political Consultative Committee has not yet received the necessary attention and assessment on the part of NATO.

It is known that at the basis of NATO's notions of Soviet strategy for using nuclear weapons in the European theater in conjunction with conventional weapons lie thoughts of the possibility of the combined use of conventional, nuclear and chemical arms, the use of the factor of surprise, and the concentration of nuclear and conventional arms as key elements for preparing for high-speed breakthrough operations in the theater. It must be said that Soviet proposals in recent years starkly contradict such notions. They propose, as a first stage, the elimination of the existing asymmetries and imbalances in Europe and reducing the arms deployed there.[13] This proposal, in conjunction with the scope of the disarmament process, encompasses the entire European continent from the Atlantic to the Urals, and considering the proposed level of verification, renders impossible the premeditated preparation of any deep offensive operations. The USSR's recognition of its significant (20,000) superiority[14] in tanks and, in turn, its readiness to eliminate it in the framework of the first stage of the reductions, attests to the absence of considerations to use this superiority for conducting deep offensive tank operations. The unilateral Soviet initiative advanced by Gorbachev in his December 1988 UN speech is a convincing demonstration of the USSR's serious attitude toward this issue.

A radical reduction of uncertainty on both sides would above all reveal the excessive and destabilizing character of the functions given to nuclear weapons in Europe by NATO. In this respect, confidence-building measures, joint NATO and WTO organs for clarifying vague situations and the continuation of meetings and consultations between American and Soviet and NATO and WTO military leaders would play a positive role.

It seems that the time has passed when secrecy played an important role in guaranteeing security. On the one hand, advances in the development of means for gathering information in recent years have hindered the planning of a surprise attack. The improvement of satellites with multi-channel observation systems, over-the-horizon radars, and other means for gathering and processing information assures a sufficiently complete picture of the state of the other side's armed forces practically in real time, ruling out the capability for implementing any kind of large-scale, secretly prepared operations. On the other hand, the negative influence of the increased level of secrecy is quite obvious. It influences the perception of real goals and intentions, as well as the assessment of the seriousness of steps in the area of disarmament and guaranteeing security through collective means.

An important negative role is played by uncertainty connected with the lack of information on the state and composition of both sides' armed forces, on mobilization measures, and on the intensity with which these measures are being undertaken. In this respect, people usually have in mind the USSR and the WTO. In fact, it is impossible to deny the lack of official data on the basic parameters and structure of the Soviet armed forces and the forces of the WTO. However, important changes have recently taken place in this direction. In particular, the USSR has proposed to exchange initial data on the composition of both sides' armed forces and assure the corresponding verification of this data.[15] At the same time, we cannot help but observe the lack of corresponding official data from NATO. This is especially striking now, on the threshold of the negotiations, since frequently unofficial data carry quite large discrepancies, and often contradict each other.[16]

The picture illustrated here of the contradictions between the emphasis on nuclear intimidation flowing from the existing doctrine of deterrence and the necessity for reducing the level of tension, a key part of which is the reduction of conventional arms, clearly points to the necessity of revising the bases on which U.S. and NATO policy is built in this area and of renouncing concepts that include the use of nuclear weapons as an integral part of threat.

The only escape lies in the realization of a set of joint and unilateral measures (and not only in the military-political realm) directed at increasing mutual trust. The reduction of conventional arms will facilitate this, while the preservation of the emphasis on nuclear deterrence will obstruct it.

Experience has shown that the military-political situation in Europe is quite stable. But it is stable at a low level of mutual trust, which hinders cooperation in the interests of mutual security. Moreover, such a level of stability is insufficient to be able to face with confidence an unpredictable future with its political vagaries. In such conditions, time becomes a factor that works against both sides.

Certainly, I am not speaking about instantaneous radical transformations. The political basis of the policy of restructuring Soviet-American relations and NATO-WTO relations in the military-political sphere is still too narrow to be able to realistically expect quick and easy successes in this area. However, certain steps are quite possible.

The Role of Nuclear Weapons in a European Conflict

The foregoing has underscored the dubious assumption that in the event of a military conflict in Europe the use of nuclear weapons would follow a certain time lag. Still more doubtful is the assumption that, at the stage preceding movement across the nuclear threshold, the threat of using nuclear weapons may facilitate the cessation of the conflict on conditions favorable to one of the sides (usually thought to be NATO), i.e., the achievement of victory.

It may be said that tactical nuclear forces are limited to two purposes: to compensate for imbalances in the event of a surprise attack by conventional forces, and to be used as a transitional element for escalating the conflict to the strategic level. The main divergences between the NATO and WTO positions on this issue relate to the ability to control conflict escalation.

Soviet military thought does not consider it possible to build strategy upon such an assumption. To this must be added that the presence in

Table 1 Targets on the Territory of European NATO Countries and within Range of WTO Conventional Weapons

Target	Southern Flank	Center	Northern Flank
Hydroelectric stations (dams)	44	73/56[1,2]	60/2
Fossil-fuel power plants	35	63/46	4/1
Nuclear power plants	0/3	26/20	1
Nuclear energy enterprises	−/5[3]	26/16	3
Chemical enterprises	14/19	49/45	5/1
Oil			
Petrochemical enterprises	−	29/−	−
Port terminals	−	10/−	−
Depots	−	9/−	−
Refineries	−	53/−	−
Gas			
Compressor stations	−/6	7/6	−
Underground depots	−	20/1	−
Locks (dams)	−	140(7)/−	−
Reservoirs (3 cubic km)	1	1/1	0

[1] [2] [3] See footnotes, p. 452.

Europe of a great number of nuclear power plants, reserves of fuel and dangerous chemicals, dams and so on force us to think that any conflict, as a result of its devastating consequences, would be as bad as a full-scale nuclear war (see Tables 1 and 2). A tragic "life-sized experiment," the disaster at the Chernobyl atomic energy station in the USSR, proved that even at the initial stage of a conflict, independent of political and military decisions, damage inevitably oversteps the "acceptable limits," regardless of the standards by which these limits are measured. In such a way the very idea of escalation loses its purely "vertical" component, the increase of the degree of destruction in the area where the conflict broke out, while preserving only its "horizontal" aspect, the spasmodic growth of the conflict to the level of total nuclear war.

It is possible to some degree to explain the differences in views on the role of nuclear weapons in a military conflict in the European theater by the fact that humanity, fortunately, has not yet had the opportunity

Table 2 Targets on the Territory of WTO Countries and within Range of NATO Conventional Weapons

Target	Southern Flank	Center	Northern Flank
Hydroelectric stations (dams)	28/9	33/8[1,2]	5
Fossil-fuel power plants	41/8	42/9	3
Nuclear power plants	4	9	2
Nuclear energy enterprises	−[3]	−	−
Chemical enterprises	41/4	51/4	3/1
Oil			
Petrochemical enterprises	−	−	−
Port terminals	8	1	1
Depots	−	−	−
Refineries	23	19	1
Gas			
Compressor stations	−	−	−
Underground depots	−	3	−
Locks (dams)	−	−	−
Reservoirs (3 cubic km)	1	0/8	0

1. Located at a distance of less than 800 kilometers/located at a distance of more than 800 kilometers, but within the combat radius of the Su-24, Tu-22M, Tu-16, F-111, Mirage-IV and Buccaneer.
2. An 800-km combat radius is the range of fire in accordance with the NATO Follow-on Forces Attack (FOFA) concept. See *Razoruzhenie i bezopasnost'*, *1987* [Disarmament and Security, 1987] (Moscow: Novosti Press Agency, 1988).
3. (−) denotes an absence of corresponding data.

Sources for Tables 1 and 2:

B. E. Byzov, *Atlas ofitsera* [The Officer's Atlas] (Moscow: Voenno-topograficheskoe upravlenie, 1984).

Laender der Erde (Berlin: Wirtschaft, 1985).

An Atlas of Nuclear Energy (Atlanta: Georgia State University, 1984).

Karte der Wasserstrassen in West- und Mitteldeutschland und den Beneluxlaendern (Beratung: K. Nusbaum; Dueren: Peterson, 1980).

Erdoelraffinerien. Leitungen. Petrochemie in der BRD, in Belgien, den Niederlanden und Ostfrankenreich (Essen: Glueckauf, 1977).

Das europaeische Erdgas-Verbundsystem (Essen: Glueckauf, 1977).

to test the hypotheses advanced in this respect. However, the Soviet point of view seems to be more realistic. The essence of the doubts about how realistic Western views are concerns not only the character of the premises of escalation control from the military point of view but also the internal contradiction of the political functions of nuclear weapons.

In reality, if nuclear weapons compensate for imbalances in the number and structure of arms and for an aggressor's ability to undertake a surprise attack, then in this way the conflict is allegedly "confined" to the European region, remaining within its boundaries. If tactical nuclear weapons are considered only a link in the chain of escalation, however, then one is in fact talking about shifting the conflict to the global level. This contradiction cannot be resolved by simply "combining" both of these factors, since:

–In each of these scenarios there are various victims of the conflict. In the first case, it would be Europe, especially Central Europe; in the second case, primarily the USSR and the United States.

–The "choice" of the option hardly depends on a unilateral decision by one of the sides. The diversity of factors that determine this "choice" generally forces one to consider it completely unpredictable.

To this one may also add an argument of a general character. Despite what the proponents of strengthening deterrence say, one must recognize that a significant emphasis on nuclear weapons in Europe will weaken deterrence, because the presence of nuclear weapons in the structure of the armed forces of both sides will force the sides to be oriented toward their use (for example, by virtue of their relatively low cost). Hence the problem arises that under any scheme for reducing conventional arms, even the most far-reaching, the role of nuclear weapons is strengthened, and thus the significance of measures for reducing conventional arms will be lost. Nuclear weapons will decrease the political significance of limiting conventional arms, once again acting in a direction that hinders the strengthening of stability and trust on the continent.

At the same time, the conflict of interests between the sides that influences the formation of the structure of NATO's armaments in Europe dictates the necessity of the presence there of large conventional arsenals. For the West Europeans it is the reassurance of survival, and for the United States it is a forced concession to NATO's European members— another indicator of the strength of the alliance. The notion, familiar to many specialists, of the necessity to have deployed and correspondingly concentrated, even in peacetime, large (even larger than in a non-nuclear scenario) conventional forces in a potential nuclear battlefield operates in the same direction. This is explained by the breach of communications and mobilization systems for reserves after the first use of weapons of mass destruction, and the inevitable resulting difficulties of replacing losses.[17]

It follows from here that nuclear deterrence by its essence cannot exist outside the expanding arsenals of conventional weapons and their continual qualitative improvement. The mutual linkage of nuclear and conventional arms arises, creating insurmountable difficulties in the path of the radical reduction of both conventional and nuclear arms.

The concept of deterrence has always devoted significant attention to predicting the development of events should deterrence "fail": such a number of nuclear forces and such a level of their combat-readiness was (and continues to be) foreseen that each side would have no doubts that in any conflict scenario a retaliatory strike would be no less destructive than a first strike. These threats in turn must force the other side to refrain from launching a first strike. As for the first use of nuclear weapons, this inevitably implies that such a strike must be strong enough to force the enemy to cease all offensive actions and request a truce on conditions favorable to the Western side, the side that used nuclear weapons first. At the same time "compensation" for a nuclear strike is not necessarily sought against the place where the attack was implemented. In fact, the only question in the matter is the infliction of equal or greater damage upon the aggressor. One must observe that a conflict's "horizontal escalation" is hardly the only step in the linkage between conventional and nuclear weapons in NATO's official plans. It is obvious that this concept, in all its vagueness, restricts the area for the use of conventional weapons, deliberately giving them a secondary role.

To be sure, such flaws of deterrence have not gone unnoticed. As a positive step we may consider, for example, the attempt to mitigate the concept's aggressive aspects manifested in advancing the idea of a "gain/denial" type concept. Much is still unclear in it. However, in my opinion, its main ideas—localizing the conflict and counteracting its escalation to higher levels—appear as steps in the right direction.[18] It seems that a more stable situation in Europe could be constructed on this basis.[19] And, no less important, it could serve as the foundation for the radical improvement of the military-political situation in Europe on the basis of a radical reduction of arms and a movement to levels of reasonable sufficiency. It is regrettable that the ideas of the concept still have not penetrated into NATO's official documents and have not affected NATO's military plans.

It is obvious that, in the event of the realization of such a scheme, stability would be sharply increased through reducing (even to the point of complete elimination) the material capabilities for conducting offensive and counteroffensive operations and the means for conducting surprise actions (e.g., strike aviation and reconnaissance-strike complexes). It is also clear that the logic of the concept contradicts the preservation of tactical nuclear weapons, since it is directed against the escalation of the conflict (at a minimum, against "horizontal escalation") and stipulates a balance of forces at decreased levels. Moreover, the ability of nuclear weapons to tip any balance of non-nuclear forces makes it incompatible with this concept.

Regarding the concept's military aspect, it must be said that an assessment of any potential, whether conventional armed forces alone or in combination with nuclear forces, demands highly complex analytical research, including an analysis of numerous models for the action of ground, naval and air forces. On the whole, a military assessment of this strategy has a number of uncertain features, although as studies show, there are many configurations for the armed forces of both sides which could guarantee a situation under which the capability for a surprise attack would be sharply reduced, as would be the capability for obtaining unilateral advantages through the use of force under any scenario.

As the analysis shows, arguments that justified the deployment and modernization of nuclear weapons in Europe and the necessity of their use in the event that "deterrence fails" are directed at preserving the strategy of deterrence and not at guaranteeing security on the continent. Doubts about the ability to implement "escalation control" cannot be refuted by the supporters of this theory on the basis of experience. The fact that even the massive use of conventional weapons in Europe will lead to unthinkable destruction implies the senselessness of the existence of nuclear weapons as an additional means of deterrence for both sides.

At the same time the damage to stability inflicted by the perception on both sides of the ability to use nuclear weapons in the course of a European conflict is obvious. Specialists have observed the unpredictable and surprise character of a shift to combat actions with the massive use of any kinds of weapons. This orients the sides toward the maintenance of a high level of combat-readiness of their nuclear forces[20] and toward the increased accumulation of conventional forces and arms. The desta-bilizing character of these measures, manifested through the mechanisms of distrust and uncertainty examined above, is obvious. To this may be added the possiblity of accidental or unauthorized use of weapons.

A way out of these contradictions can be found in the realization of a set of measures that guarantee the defensive structure of opposing forces at decreased levels of conventional arms. Movement toward this state of "absolute defense"[21] is incompatible with the preservation of nuclear weapons, which guarantee "absolute destruction."

Conventional Reductions and Nuclear Weapons

The link between nuclear forces and conventional arms becomes quite apparent upon comparison of the problems of the radical reduction of strategic nuclear weapons and conventional forces. There can be no doubt that an agreement to reduce strategic offensive weapons would exert a positive influence on the course of negotiations on conventional weapons. It is no less obvious that a reduction of conventional arms will change the correlation between conventional and tactical nuclear weapons which influences the state of stability and security. This places on the agenda the question of the relationship of reductions of conventional and tactical nuclear weapons.

We often hear that there is a surplus of weapons in the world, and that the accumulated arsenals can destroy all life on Earth several times over. This principle also applies to the European continent. However, even the logic of the advocates of retaining nuclear weapons in Europe must then, at a minimum, consider the *correlation* of nuclear and non-nuclear components in the reduction of conventional weapons—i.e., the reduction of nuclear weapons as well. Moreover, the destructive power of nuclear weapons in comparison to conventional weapons demands faster rates of their reduction.

Any thought about the complete elimination of nuclear weapons provokes a sharply negative reaction in the West. The Soviet Union, as is known, already proposed in January 1986 a program for the complete elimination of nuclear weapons by the year 2000. In this proposal it is observed that "along with removing weapons of mass destruction from states' arsenals, the Soviet Union proposes to make conventional arms and armed forces a subject of the agreed reductions."[22]

The whole world should have welcomed these proposals. Their realization would have been in the common interest, providing no one with any advantages, and would have been a deliverance from the nuclear threat. But few influential public officials, scientists or governments in the West supported them. The most diverse arguments have been advanced against them. It has been said, for example, that it is impossible to eliminate nuclear weapons, because it is impossible to eliminate the knowledge and the technology for their creation. It has been stated that their elimination would unilaterally favor the Soviet Union because it has a preponderance in conventional forces. And it has also been observed that nuclear weapons are the only guarantee of security and that they have prevented and will continue to prevent war. But these arguments fail to take into account the negotiations to ban and destroy chemical weapons currently being conducted (the state of knowledge and technology for their production is not a hindrance); the fact that the Soviet Union does not propose the elimination of nuclear weapons immediately, but over a 15-year period; and the fact that simultaneously the WTO has proposed a program for reducing conventional arms, which is directed at establishing parity at lower levels.

On the whole, Western arguments reflect a psychological and political unpreparedness to renounce nuclear weapons and to move toward their complete elimination. In fact, the problem here is quite the same: the inertia of deterrence and reluctance to replace it with new approaches to ensure security.

With what can the concept of deterrent be replaced, what kind of connection must there be between nuclear and conventional weapons in solving problems of security in the future, and is it possible in general to establish a reliable security guarantee by non-nuclear means without reducing the degree of one's own or common security?

In his summary statement at the scientific conference of the USSR Ministry of Foreign Affairs, Foreign Minister Eduard Shevardnadze said that "a non-offensive doctrine, the principle of reasonable sufficiency, the implementation of formulas on forces sufficient for defense but insufficient for attack, must bring the idea of comprehensive security to the practical level."[23] The way to security passes through the replacement of the existing nuclear strategy by a purely defensive, non-nuclear strategy. This implies progress towards agreements on forces sufficient only for guaranteeing security, but insufficient for conducting offensive actions. For this, they must have a structure, arms and deployment that would exclude the military-technical capability for a surprise attack or for the implementation of offensive actions.

Clear notions about doctrines and guarantees of their fulfillment are extremely important for assessing these aspects of using military force. The member-states of the Warsaw Pact have announced a shift to a purely defensive military doctrine directed at preventing war. They have appealed to the member-states of NATO to conduct a comparison and joint discussion of doctrines with the purpose of bringing military theory and practice into accord with the demands of defensive strategy and the principles of sufficiency for defense. It is known that NATO doctrine also does not proceed from the assumption of first use of force. However, the issue is not the declaratory side of doctrines, but the concrete practical measures directed at fulfilling it. In this connection, the question of the material indicators and practical guarantees of non-offensiveness becomes extremely important.

Regardless of how the CFE negotiations proceed, their objective, as it follows from the mandate, is to increase stability along with decreasing weapons. The destructive consequences of using just conventional arms on the continent in and of themselves are able to exert a deterring influence. However, as long as nuclear weapons are preserved in Europe, they will slow the pace of movement toward a higher level of stability. Perhaps the main task that must be resolved in the near future is the creation of practical international mechanisms that block the use of nuclear weapons, localize the potential opportunities for their use (including unauthorized use) and hinder nuclear escalation. "Armed conflict, and even more so, war, is the failure of diplomacy," stated Shevardnadze. "But even in such a turn of affairs, it is obliged to secure the maximal reduction of damage, the most rapid conclusion of the conflict and the elimination of its negative consequences."[24] It would seem that the adoption of a set of international measures to prevent such a possibility would facilitate the improvement of stability in the region. In the framework of these same measures it would also be possible to develop guarantees that localize the use (including unauthorized use) of nuclear weapons.

It is necessary to observe that the problem of localizing armed conflict if tactical nuclear weapons were being used is extremely complex. Here, the above-mentioned mechanism of escalation would exert a strong destabilizing influence. Therefore the problem of creating a corresponding international mechanism acquires an important and urgent character.[25]

Nevertheless, it would be worthwhile to think about whether the preservation of the nuclear component in spite of the initial WTO proposals would not threaten extreme destabilization in Europe. For this, the configuration and structure of nuclear forces in conjunction with conventional forces should not threaten the territory of the other side with a surprise attack, and, moreover, should emphasize their purely defensive character and be oriented toward the impossibility of being used as an element of implementing large-scale, surprise offensive operations.

The structure of nuclear forces in combination with measures for verifying their status, concentration and movement must promote both sides' confidence in the existence of real boundaries to escalation, which must be maximally limited and rule out the use of nuclear weapons at the initial stage of an armed conflict.

The Soviet program is oriented toward eliminating nuclear weapons by the end of the century. We would like to greet the year 2000 in a non-nuclear world, "or at least in a world that has seriously begun to rid itself of nuclear weapons."[26] In moving toward this objective, a special role falls to the political means of guaranteeing security, in particular to efforts at broadening and implementing a wide spectrum of confidence-building measures between states. It is precisely the increase of trust that may serve as the key that opens the doors to implementing new approaches and new solutions that respond to contemporary demands.

At the same time it seems that the complexity of the subject under discussion calls for a high level of analytic efforts and scientific expertise which must precede a solution to the problem. The necessity of decreasing the potential for a surprise attack, creating war risk-reduction centers in Europe with corresponding mechanisms that permit strengthening control over the development of events in time of a crisis seems obvious even today. The problem lies in developing concrete programs that facilitate the resolution of these tasks. It is necessary to observe that the presence in Europe of a great number of nuclear weapons hinders their resolution. The task is further complicated by the fact that nuclear weapons are still insufficiently covered by confidence-building measures. It is clear that genuine trust in the military-political area can be achieved only through non-offensive non-nuclear structures of both sides' forces. An understanding of this principle would permit the planning of a system of measures that would facilitate progress from the current situation toward the final objective.

The nuclear component of strategy is the strongest catalyst of the arms race, and therefore its role inevitably must be reduced in order, ultimately, to remove it forever. The new situation demands new approaches, based on the main assumption that any arguments, disagreements or problems must take place in conditions of peaceful coexistence and be resolved by political means.

Notes

1 *Sovetsko-amerikanskaia vstrecha na vysshem urovne. Moskva, 29 maia–2 iiunia 1988 g. Dokumenty i materialy* [Soviet-American Summit Meeting. Moscow, 29 May–2 June 1988. Documents and Materials] (Moscow: Politizdat, 1988), pp. 186–187.

2 *Pravda*, October 26, 1988.

3 Since WTO military theory does not recognize the ability to control a conflict's escalation, this function for the WTO is expressed as a reaction to the NATO position through the declaration of the USSR's readiness to defend itself and its allies. In NATO this declaration is significantly broader.

4 *Pravda*, May 30, 1987.

5 *Pravda*, July 16, 1982.

6 A. Kokoshin and A. Vassiliev, "Die Abschrechungsdoktrin der USA und der Sowjetische Standpunkt zur Verhinderung eines Nuklearkrieges," *IPW Berichte* No. 10 (1984).

7 Mikhail S. Gorbachev, *Za bez'iadernyi mir, za gumanizm mezhdunarodnykh otnoshenii. Rech' na vstreche s uchastnikami mezhdunarodnogo foruma "Za bez'iadernyi mir, za vyzhivanue chelovechestva" 16 fevralia 1987 g.* [For a Nuclear-free World, for Humanism in International Relations. Speech at a Meeting with Participants in the International Forum, "For a Nuclear-free World, for the Survival of Humanity," 16 February 1987] (Moscow: Politizdat, 1987), pp. 15–16.

8 *Pravda*, May 22, 1988.

9 "XIX Vsesoiuznaia konferentsiia KPSS: vneshniaia politika i diplomatiia. Doklad chlena Politbiuro TsK KPSS, ministra inostrannykh del SSSR E. A. Shevardnadze na nauchno-prakticheskoi Konferentsii MID SSSR" [19th All-Union Conference of the CPSU: Foreign Policy and Diplomacy. Report of Member of the Politburo of the Central Committee of the CPSU and USSR Minister of Foreign Affairs E. A. Shevardnadze on the Scientific-Practical Conference of the USSR Ministry of Foreign Affairs], *Mezhdunarodnaia zhizn'* No. 9 (September 1988), p. 15.

10 Mikhail S. Gorbachev, *Politicheskii doklad TsK KPSS XXVII s'ezda KPSS* [Political Report of the Central Committee of the CPSU of the 27th Congress of the CPSU] (Moscow: Politizdat, 1986), p. 82.

11 *Zaiavlenie General'nogo sekretaria TsK KPSS M. S. Gorbacheva 15 ianvaria 1986 g.* [Declaration of General Secretary of the Central Committee of the CPSU M. S. Gorbachev, 15 January 1986] (Moscow: Politizdat, 1986), p. 5.

12 This statement was made by Mikhail S. Gorbachev at a conference of officials of the USSR Foreign Ministry in May 1986. See *Mezhdunarodnaia zhizn'* No. 9 (September 1988), p. 18.

13 "Statement of WTO States. Warsaw, July 15–16, 1988," *Vestnik Ministerstva inostrannykh del SSSR*, No. 15 (August 15, 1988), pp. 11–20.

14 Dmitrii T. Iazov, "O voennom balanse sil i raketno-iadernom paritete" [On the Military Balance of Forces and Nuclear Missile Parity], *Pravda*, February 8, 1988, p. 5.

15 *Vestnik MID SSSR* No. 15, p. 12.

16 *Razoruzhenie i bezopasnost', 1986 g.* [Disarmament and Security, 1986], Vol. 1 (Moscow: Novosti Press Agency, 1987), p. 220. Recent publications of the WTO and NATO have to some extent solved this problem.

17 Andrei A. Kokoshin, "Razvitie voennogo dela i sokrashchenie vooruzhennykh sil i obychnykh vooruzhenii" [The Development of Military Operations and the Reduction of Armed Forces and Conventional Arms], *MEMO* No. 1 (January 1988), pp. 25–26.

18 Similar ideas are being examined by Soviet scientists as well. See, for example, Andrei A. Kokoshin and Valentin V. Larionov, "Protivostoianie sil obshchego naznacheniia v kontekste obespecheniia strategicheskoi stabil'nosti" [The Confrontation of General-purpose Forces in the Context of Preserving Strategic Stability], *MEMO* No. 6 (June 1988), pp. 26–28.

19 Judging by the attention that this concept has attracted and the modest number of available publications, it appears to approach the ideas of nonoffensive defense.

20 V. Shabanov, " 'Obychnaia' voina: novye opasnosti" ["Conventional War": New Dangers], *Novoe vremia*, November 14, 1986, p. 8.

21 "Absolute defense" is Clausewitz's expression: "Absolute defense is found in complete contradiction with the state of war." See Karl von Clausewitz, *O voine* [On War], vol. 2 (Moscow: 1937), p. 5.

22 *Zaiavlenie General'nogo sekretaria TsK KPSS M. S. Gorbacheva. 15 ianvaria 1986 g.* (Moscow: Politizdat, 1986), pp. 11.

23 "XIX Vsesoiuznaia konferentsiia KPSS: vneshniaia politika i diplomatiia. Zakliuchitel'noe slovo E.A. Shevardnadze" [19th All-Union Conference of the CPSU: Foreign Policy and Diplomacy. Closing Remarks of E.A. Shevardnadze], *Mezhdunarodnaia zhizn'* No. 9 (September 1988), p. 64.

24 "XIX Vsesoiuznaia konferentsiia KPSS: vneshniaia politika i diplomatiia. Doklad chlena Politbiuro TsK KPSS, ministra inostrannykh del SSSR E. A. Shevardnadze na nauchno-prakticheskoi konferentsii MID SSSR," *Mezhdunarodnaia zhizn'* No. 9 (September 1988), p. 12.

25 This issue is examined by Kokoshin and Larionov, "Protivostoianie sil obshchego naznacheniia," p. 30.

26 "Interv'iu M. S. Gorbacheva zhurnalu *Shpigel'* (FRG)" [Inter'iu of M. S. Gorbachev to the Journal *Spiegel* (FRG)], *Pravda*, October 24, 1988.

CONCLUSION

What Next for Conventional Forces in Europe?

Robert D. Blackwill and F. Stephen Larrabee

The essays in this book demonstrate vividly the extraordinary transformation since Gorbachev has come to power in the nature and quality of East-West exchanges on these fundamental issues of European security. At least in these pages, the rhetorical tide is receding. At the same time the essays underscore the abiding impediments to achieving greater stability in Europe at lower levels of armaments.

The key issue from the Western point of view is the degree to which Gorbachev's championship of "new thinking" will be implemented at the operational military level. Gorbachev's speech to the UN in December 1988 gives some hope that this may be the case. His announcement of his intention to, *inter alia*, withdraw by 1991 half of the 10,000 Soviet tanks in Eastern Europe and to destroy in all 18,000 combat vehicles of the Red Army went far beyond what most Western experts—including the editors of this volume—expected.[1] While the capacity for surprise attack can, of course, never be entirely "eliminated," the announced Soviet unilateral withdrawal from Eastern Europe, if implemented as promised, would significantly reduce the danger of unreinforced attack by the WTO. According to some estimates, it could give NATO seven days of additional warning as the 5,000 Soviet tanks and related manpower are moved back to forward positions in advance of an invasion. While neither of us has regarded a standing-start attack by the Warsaw Pact (either out of the blue or during a crisis) as a contingency the West was likely to face, nevertheless Gorbachev's initiative when completed should greatly diminish that worst-case scenario.[2] In and of itself, the Soviet unilateral move will therefore be an important contribution to enhancing conventional stability in Europe.

While an important first step, Gorbachev's UN initiative has by no means wiped away the many long-standing disputes between the alliances concerning conventional forces and arms control in Europe. With that in mind, in the following pages we examine briefly traditional NATO/WTO perspectives on the subject; try to judge which of these boulders are likely to remain on the road; and identify the most promising avenues for progress in promoting increased stability in conventional forces.

As Gorbachev's speech in New York underscores, this is a risky enterprise. What appeared close to impossible only a short time ago—that the USSR would withdraw 50 percent of its tanks from Eastern Europe—will soon begin to occur. And while such dramatic moves are not likely to be reciprocated by the West, it is possible that a combination of the weight of Soviet diplomacy and cooperative conduct, NATO's formidable budgetary constraints, and U.S. complaints about burden-sharing will also produce unforeseen actions concerning conventional forces on the part of Western governments. Nevertheless, no matter how many surprises await us, there will probably remain nuts in this area too tough to crack. We will begin with those.

The opening essays of this book are an acute indication of how difficult it will be for East and West in the next decade to develop together a set of agreed political goals for the continent. One obstacle is the uncertainty surrounding developments in Eastern Europe. Gorbachev has begun the most intense dialogue ever between Moscow and its allies on restructuring the relations between the socialist countries within the WTO, but this process at best will take many years to accomplish. Along the way, instability and perhaps turmoil in Eastern Europe could test Soviet willingness to allow real political diversity in Eastern Europe, and also challenge Gorbachev's standing at home. In short, there is a danger that the architecture of the Eastern half of the "European house" may prove too fragile and uncertain to foster combined efforts with the West to redesign radically the political context of postwar Europe in the period ahead.

The West also has its Gordian knots. Despite the incremental and positive growth of Franco-German cooperation, the Federal Republic's long-term goal of breaking down, and eventually removing, the barriers to closer relations with the GDR is incompatible with France's historic perception of its own role and interests on the continent. And Paris is not the only capital in Western Europe that would worry about large-scale reductions that led to a redrawn geostrategic map of Europe in which the two German states working together would be increasingly intertwined and influential. This fact of European life, which cannot be discussed formally within NATO and certainly not with the other side, will place serious constraints on the West's capacity to organize itself to engage in a fruitful dialogue with the East on Europe's future shape. Moreover, until the removal of the European Community's internal tariff barriers in 1992, and probably thereafter, much of Western Europe's attention will be devoted to this profound internal change, and therefore less to questions pertaining to East-West economic cooperation. Indeed, the 1992 EC arrangements may actually impede the development of economic ties with Eastern Europe.

Despite these complicating factors, one can expect much generalized talk in the years ahead about the future evolution of European political systems and about the obvious requirement to begin to conceive of a Europe safely settled into a post-Cold War phase. For the reasons indicated above, we do not expect such ephemeralities to get very far for quite some time, if then. Instead, the attempt to limit and reduce conventional forces in Europe will most likely take place within a geopolitical context that looks much like that of today.

Another blind alley to avoid is attempting to reach a mutual understanding between the two sides in Europe with regard to the state of the conventional military balance. NATO argues strenuously, as it has for more than 30 years, that the Warsaw Pact enjoys clear conventional superiority. Gorbachev's December 1988 UN initiative has softened but not shaken that conviction. The nations of the Eastern bloc assert that a rough conventional balance exists in Europe. As if these fundamentally differing perspectives were not wide enough apart, the entire subject of measuring Europe's conventional balance is so enormously complicated that it occasionally confounds even the most dedicated analyst of the subject.

Above and beyond these more technical factors, the politics of this issue also will exert a prevailing influence on the positions of the two alliances. To put it bluntly, neither side is likely for years to change its basic public description of the conventional balance and thus be obligated to explain why, including to publics and parliaments, it had been so misguided in the past.

Yet enumerating these many impediments to official exchanges that would attempt to narrow the great East-West divide on the nature of the conventional balance still does not nearly capture the intractability of this problem. Measuring military power in Europe, of course, goes far beyond the simple bean count of the sides' static forces. What all useful methodologies on this matter are after is some rendition of how combat between NATO and the Warsaw Pact, under differing assumptions, might actually turn out.

Making such calculations involves the most sensitive possible assumptions concerning the political and military integrity of each alliance; judgments of how well the armies of individual nations would fight; the speed and quality of crisis decision-making; the capabilities of engaged units and their weapons systems; the speed and efficiency with which reinforcements would arrive at the front; the impact of logistics, intelligence, command and control and geography on the battlefield; and so forth. With this sort of highly classified information at issue and at risk, that the 23 members of the two alliances could engage in a productive discussion seems to us unlikely.

A similar, if more manageable task, concerns military doctrine. There is no doubt that a major debate is under way in Moscow regarding the future direction and operational manifestations of Soviet military doctrine.[3] Soviet journals, both military and civilian, are filled with analyses regarding the historical antecedents of current Soviet doctrine and assertions of its abiding defensive nature. As Alexei Arbatov suggests in Chapter 6, some elements of Soviet force posture and deployments might in the past have led Western governments to misinterpret the solely defensive purpose of Soviet force posture. At the same time, many Eastern analysts inside and outside government continue to regard NATO's posture as offensive. Thus, we have simultaneously an evolving and lively debate in the USSR on the relationship between Soviet and Warsaw Pact pronouncements on military doctrine and the East's actual force posture; and continuing suspicion on each side with respect to the other alliance's military organization and probable intentions in a crisis and/or conflict.

In these circumstances, the question naturally arises whether official exchanges among the 23 members of the two blocs on military doctrine are likely to reduce suspicions and clarify intentions in a helpful way. The obstacles here are considerable because, as Peer Lange and Andrei Kokoshin illustrate in Chapter 5, the two sides mean quite different things by doctrine. Thus there is a danger that such discussions could bog down in fruitless semantic bickering. To avoid such a debate discussions on doctrine must be linked directly to force postures. In particular the success of such discussions will depend in large measure on how much real transparency each alliance is willing to allow concerning its forces, deployments and military operations. Whatever other value they may have, general political dicta will be insufficient to persuade serious security specialists that defensive rhetoric necessarily means defensive war plans. Thus, the best and most reassuring way to begin such an East-West dialogue on military doctrine would be to institute a thorough and deeply disaggregated exchange of data on the conventional forces of the two alliances in Europe. This exchange of information should be keyed to the battalion level and should include unit location, subordination, manning levels and major conventional weapons holdings by type and model.

Not wishing to arouse the ghosts of MBFR, let us stress that the purpose here is not an early agreement among the 23 on data. We believe that such an accord would be too complex to negotiate. Nor do we think the sides would, through such information exchanges and discussions, quickly wash away their postwar perspectives. But a detailed enumeration of data of the kind we propose would form a solid basis for talks among the 23 on military doctrine. With this degree of disaggregation in hand, East and West would be in a far better position than at present to question intensively the relationship between defensively expressed intentions in summit statements and the like, and the actual force posture and capability on each side of the dividing line in Europe. Disagreements and differing interpretations would certainly ensue as operational modes of military behavior were slowly exposed. But over the long term such talks among military officers, unlike ministerial communiqués, could begin to strip away gradually some of the distrust which has accumulated on the continent during the past 40-plus years.

There is, of course, a close relationship between data exchange and reduction schemes. The more information on conventional forces available to the two sides, the more profitable official discussions will be about how best to cut these forces. Nevertheless, for our purposes, we wish now to put the data question aside and concentrate instead on the primary issues of drawing down conventional arms.

At first glance, and second too, the respective differences of view and emphases on the part of the two blocs are daunting. Moscow denies that it wishes to increase Soviet influence over the security affairs of all of Europe. Some Western leaders remain unconvinced. This is hardly a trivial point. Under Gorbachev, Soviet European security policy has been geared in public to Moscow's desire that all nations on the continent be free from military or political intimidation. Yet many Western governments remain profoundly skeptical.

Eastern suspicions about NATO's objectives in the new talks are equally vivid. As Alexander Konovalov's contribution in particular underscores, the Warsaw Pact worries especially about NATO's deep-strike capability, manifested through its Follow-on Forces Attack (FOFA) and AirLand Battle concepts. Moreover, the East frequently repeats the charge that the United States and its allies could launch a preemptive first nuclear strike against Pact forces and then mop up with their newly acquired conventional superiority. A somewhat more subterranean anxiety sometimes mentioned by the East is that NATO wishes to use the CFE talks to begin to redraw the political map of Europe and loosen Moscow's ties with its East European allies. Through this design, some Soviet officials worry, the FRG may hope a conventional arms control agreement might further its ultimate objective of reunifying Germany.

With these mutual doubts about the other side's real intentions so widespread, we see no utility in arguments about what broad political objectives the two alliances are actually trying to accomplish through their conventional arms control proposals. In such exchanges, candor is likely to be the victim of negotiating and intra-alliance exigencies. Rather, we would suggest at the outset a more analytical approach.

Through this practical method, the sides would have something to build upon. All 23 nations participating in the CFE talks say they wish to "eliminate" the capability for surprise attack and for large-scale offensive action. Each proposal put forward on this subject should therefore be rigorously judged by whether it promotes those two shared objectives, and by its verifiability.

As noted earlier, Gorbachev's UN initiative, when implemented, will lessen the danger of unreinforced invasion by heavily armored units. It does not, however, address the East's persistent assertion—highlighted in particular in Alexei Arbatov's contribution—that NATO air forces, both in conventional and nuclear modes and including U.S. naval aviation, represent a corresponding short-warning threat to the Warsaw Pact. Taking into account the projected Soviet unilateral cuts in Eastern Europe, we may see the alliances concentrating through their conventional arms control proposals on two quite different military contingencies.

The West will probably now work to codify through a treaty with the Pact the 5,000 Soviet tank reduction in Eastern Europe. At the same time, NATO is likely in the future to be even more mindful of the remaining WTO capability to mount a mobilized, large-scale offensive against Western Europe. We can anticipate that the West's proposals and public presentation will stress this massive residual threat from the East somewhat more than the surprise-attack option, and seek to reduce it through further very large reductions in Soviet tanks, artillery and combat fighting vehicles in the European portion of the USSR.

Moscow will retain, if not intensify after the Gorbachev initiative, its view that a conventional arms control agreement must carry with it limitations on Western ground-attack aircraft which, the East argues, would be the spearhead of a NATO surprise attack eastward. So with one side emphasizing large-scale offensives and their armored component and the other surprise attack and aircraft, the military implications of Soviet unilateral withdrawals from Eastern Europe may further entangle negotiations among the 23.

In the absence of Western willingness to put aircraft into the mix of an initial agreement to reduce conventional forces in Europe, it is doubtful whether Gorbachev will go on unilaterally reducing the size of the Soviet military establishment deployed forward, especially since such a course on his part would almost certainly run into strong opposition from the General Staff.

Thus, early progress in the CFE talks appears to hinge on two central questions:

–Will the East be willing to accept much deeper reductions to parity or something close to it in its armored forces?
–Will the West agree that reductions and limitations on combat aircraft based in Europe can be part of a first conventional arms control agreement?

Putting aside the many definitional problems of limiting aircraft, this question also raises in stark terms the future of nuclear weapons in Europe and their delivery systems. No other European security issue so divides the two sides as the advisability of maintaining nuclear deterrence on the continent. NATO's hesitancy to include aircraft in an arms control agreement partially derives from its anxiety, in the aftermath of the INF Treaty and Gorbachev's many initiatives, that continuing modernization of U.S. nuclear weapons in Europe will become increasingly difficult, if not in some cases impossible. In that event, NATO's nuclear deterrence could gradually fade away. The intense Soviet campaign against nuclear weapons in Europe only further excites Western governments.

The West's willingness, then, to include aircraft in the new talks would seem to rest on one or more of three changes in the current situation: (1) either governments will take power in the FRG, U.K., France and/or the United States that share Moscow's stated nuclear neuralgia; (2) these and other NATO governments will achieve sufficient U.S. nuclear modernization in Europe to feel secure in limiting nuclear-capable aircraft in order to try to close a conventional force deal with the Warsaw Pact (this could include a decision by Moscow to reduce the intensity of its anti-nuclear effort); and/or (3) the force of budgetary constraints, Gorbachev's peace offensive and public opinion will lead NATO in time to acquiesce on the aircraft issue, despite its misgivings on the nuclear side.

In any event, the key conceptual question facing the CFE talks appears to be whether the two sides should or can find an early intersection between armor and aircraft. That issue, more than any other, will tell the tale in the first years of the new negotiations.

With this degree of uncertainty relating to cutting conventional forces in Europe through a treaty, it is no wonder that possible further confidence- and security-building measures (CSBMs) beyond the Stockholm CDE regime are now a subject of increased attention in both East and West. Here, too, Gorbachev's unilateral withdrawals from Eastern Europe will probably alter to some degree the central objectives of CSBMs on the continent. With the danger of unreinforced attack materially reduced, the long-standing Western preoccupation with increased transparency in the forward area through mutual confidence-building will also probably decrease to some extent, although not disappear altogether. One can expect more interest in CSBMs that would address large-scale offensive operations.

These measures would not be meant in the first instance to provide early warning since the movement of many divisions, and the mobilization which would probably go along with such major activity, would be evident. This is not to say that specific information through CSBMs on the direction, speed and makeup of such divisions on the move would not be valuable or that both alliances would not profit from detailed knowledge regarding the pace and magnitude of mobilization efforts. In addition, the presence of on-site observers from the other alliance or the NNA states would tend to certify threatening behavior in a more politically powerful way. But such additional transparency would supplement a great deal of information already available to the superpowers, because of the sheer size of the other side's preparations, through national technical means.

This being the case, we would guess that proposals calling for constraints on the activities of military forces in Europe will assume more prominence. These concepts range from thin-out or exclusion zones for various conventional weapons systems; to limits on exercise size, national makeup, location, duration and operational purpose; to restrictions of various sorts on mobilization activities. In our view, much more analytical work needs to be done on the advantages and disadvantages of these various kinds of constraint possibilities and their effect on both offensive operations and defensive capability.

This brings us, finally, to the political dimension of the search for a conventional arms control agreement in Europe. MBFR remains a sharp reminder of how hard it is to maintain the interest of politicians from either side in a negotiation that seems to be going nowhere. After a burst of involvement in the Vienna talks in the 1971–1973 period, political leaders in both alliances concluded that their arms control energy should be channeled elsewhere. This was not unwarranted.

Given the current differences between the two sides' opening positions in the CFE negotiations, an initial deadlock in the talks is not to be excluded. In view of the slow pace of East-West arms control negotiations in the past 25 years, this need not send off alarm bells if it happens. It is far better to negotiate steadily and carefully, with attention to detail, than to try to sprint recklessly ahead to the finish without a clear conception of objectives.

But having said that, one wonders how much patience political leaderships in each alliance will have if CFE gets off to a halting start. Gorbachev has already demonstrated his capacity to overcome bureaucratic obstacles and, as in the INF Treaty and his UN speech, be responsive to the expressed security concerns of NATO. At the same time, there is an obvious limit to his ability and willingness to make intermittent unilateral concessions, both because such Soviet moves at some point would no longer serve the long-term security interests of the USSR and because Gorbachev in such circumstances would likely face resistance from his military colleagues. Yet if the West does not give in on the aircraft issue, the Soviet leader will be confronted with the choice of making further concessions or risking an extended stalemate in the talks.

Not a happy alternative, particularly for a man as much in a hurry to reform the domestic economy of the Soviet Union as Gorbachev appears to be.

There is a corresponding set of dilemmas for the West. With 16 sovereign nations more or less jointly forging the NATO position, changes in the Western conventional arms control position will probably be slow in coming. This intra-alliance sluggishness is quite apart from the present majority view in NATO that parity in selected ground-force equipment should precede any compromise on the aircraft question. Nevertheless, there are likely to be strong domestic political pressures within NATO countries, including on the Bush administration, to push the CFE effort quickly ahead because of budgetary realities and the desire to match Gorbachev's initiatives. And if these new negotiations replicate the paralyzed features of MBFR, it is far from certain that Western governments will be able to resist pressures for unilateral cuts in NATO forces, or fallbacks in the West's conventional arms control position, to make a treaty virtue out of a domestic budget necessity.

In short, each side appears to have less capacity to wait the other out than in the many long years of the MBFR talks. However, this may not necessarily produce a solution to the present differences between the two alliances. Rather, it could simply increase the intensity and the rancor of East-West exchanges and the temptation to play to the public galleries.

All the same, it is crucial for the political level from Moscow to Washington to stay closely involved with this revitalized effort to reduce fairly conventional forces on the continent. If Eastern and Western leaders lose interest in this endeavor, it is improbable that experts, no matter how well intentioned, will produce an accord. The problems are too knotty for that. The precedents are too entrenched and discouraging for that.

It is equally important to keep in mind that revived attempts to negotiate a conventional arms control agreement in Europe will occur in the context of a European security environment that has been remarkably stable since the last East-West crisis on the continent with any military overtones, in the early 1960s over Berlin. We should remember that ambitious though our appetites might be to reduce conventional forces, East and West could, if not careful, negotiate treaties or take unilateral military steps in the period ahead that would introduce uncertainty into a security situation between NATO and the Warsaw Pact that is currently relatively stable. In short, there is no guarantee that fewer conventional forces in Europe would make a conflict less likely. As we hope this volume demonstrates, the net effect of such reductions would depend on a variety of factors, particularly the effect of such reductions on actual military capabilities for launching a surprise attack or carrying out large-scale offensive actions.

Notes

1 It is revealing to note that Gorbachev's announced unilateral cuts in Eastern Europe are much more far-reaching than the most ambitious NATO proposal at MBFR which called for the withdrawal from the GDR of the five divisions of a Soviet tank army, 68,000 men and 1,900 tanks.

2 This assumes that Soviet forces in Eastern Europe are not reorganized and reequipped to compensate for the withdrawal and that NATO does not recreate this threat by overly weakening its own forces forward.

3 For a good discussion of this debate see in particular Edward L. Warner III, "New Thinking and Old Realities in Soviet Defense Policy," *Survival* 31, No. 1 (January/February 1989), pp 13–33; also Raymond L. Garthoff, "New Thinking in Soviet Military Doctrine," *The Washington Quarterly* 11, No. 3 (Summer 1988), pp. 131–158; and F. Stephen Larrabee, "Gorbachev and the Soviet Military," *Foreign Affairs* 66, No. 5 (Summer 1988), pp. 1002–1026.

INDEX